NATURAL RIGHTS INDIVIDUALISM AND PROGRESSIVISM IN AMERICAN POLITICAL PHILOSOPHY

Edited by

Ellen Frankel Paul, Fred D. Miller, Jr., and Jeffrey Paul

CAMBRIDGE UNIVERSITY PRESS

PUBLISHED BY THE PRESS SYNDICATE OF THE UNIVERSITY OF CAMBRIDGE
The Pitt Building, Trumpington Street, Cambridge, United Kingdom

CAMBRIDGE UNIVERSITY PRESS
The Edinburgh Building, Cambridge CB2 8RU, UK
32 Avenue of the Americas, New York, NY 10013-2473, USA
477 Williamstown Road, Port Melbourne, VIC 3207, Australia
Ruiz de Alarcón 13, 28014 Madrid, Spain
Dock House, The Waterfront, Cape Town 8001, South Africa

http://www.cambridge.org

First published 2012

Printed in the United States of America

Typeface Palatino 10/12 pt.

A catalog record for this book is available from the British Library

Library of Congress Cataloging-in-Publication Data
Natural Rights Individualism and Progressivism in American Political Philosophy /
edited by Ellen Frankel Paul, Fred D. Miller, Jr., and Jeffrey Paul.
p. cm.
ISBN 978-1-107-64194-5 (pbk.)

1. Political science--United States--Philosophy. 2. Natural law--Philosophy.
3. Individualism--United States. 4. Progressivism (United States politics).
I. Paul, Ellen Frankel. II. Miller, Fred Dycus, 1944- III. Paul, Jeffrey.

JA84.U5N275 2012
323.01--dc23

The essays in this book have also been published,
without introduction and index, in the semiannual journal
Social Philosophy & Policy, Volume 29, Number 2,
which is available by subscription.

CONTENTS

INTRODUCTION

In 1776, the American Declaration of Independence appealed to "the Laws of Nature and of Nature's God" and affirmed "these Truths to be self-evident, that all Men are created equal, that they are endowed by their Creator with certain unalienable Rights, that among these are Life, Liberty, and the Pursuit of Happiness . . . ." In 1935, John Dewey, professor emeritus of philosophy at Columbia University, declared, "Natural rights and natural liberties exist only in the kingdom of mythological social zoology."[1] These opposing pronouncements on natural rights represent two separate and antithetical American political traditions: natural rights individualism, the original Lockean tradition of the Founding; and Progressivism, the collectivist reaction to individualism which arose initially in the newly established universities in the decades following the Civil War. The tensions between these two manifestly disparate traditions in the country's political and legal philosophy have set the stage for most of the principal disputes in its political, constitutional, and economic history over the past century and a quarter.

The essays in this collection investigate in turn these two political traditions and their critical interactions. The first series of essays deals with the development of natural rights individualism, some examining its origins in the thought of the seminal political theorist, John Locke, and the influential constitutional theorist, Montesquieu, others the impact of their theories on intellectual leaders during the American Revolution and the Founding era, and still others the culmination of this tradition in the writings of nineteenth-century individualists such as Lysander Spooner. The second series of essays focuses on the Progressive repudiation of natural rights individualism and its far-reaching effect on American politics and public policy. Two essays explain why theorists such as Dewey objected to natural rights and consider how Progressivism led to a new view of the nature and role of government. Other essays consider the import of Progressivism for policy issues such as race relations and property rights. The concluding two essays offer contrasting assessments of the relationship of Progressivism to the Lockean tradition of the Founding in the course of exploring the pivotal role of Theodore Roosevelt and Woodrow Wilson—who were Progressive theorists as well as United States Presidents—in the transformation of American politics and jurisprudence during the twentieth century.

The collection opens with Thomas G. West's essay "The Ground of Locke's Law of Nature." According to West, while it is clear that the

---

[1] John Dewey, *Liberalism and Social Action* (New York: G. P. Putnam's Sons, 1935), 15.

natural law political philosophy of John Locke was the original basis of America's constitutional democracy, it is unclear what the precise character of that foundation is; furthermore, it is widely thought that whatever the nature of the foundation, it is in any event inadequate. West responds to the prevalent critical stance toward Locke among scholars by arguing that, when properly understood in the context of multiple Lockean written works and with an appreciation of Locke's unique methodology, Locke's foundation is more plausible than is commonly believed. As a matter of methodology, Locke weaves different strands of argument on the law of nature through his different books to create a complex and complete argument; also, West contends, Locke deploys implausible arguments intentionally in order to capture the minds of readers who might be disposed toward such arguments. One important element in the larger argument of Locke's political philosophy concerns the equality of human beings. A correct understanding of Locke's position on the equality of individuals does not take him to claim that all individuals are equal in the sense that they have equal talents or equal ability in the state of nature to comprehend the law of nature that they are under, but rather affirms the more limited interpretation that individuals are equally able to access the law of nature and act in accordance with it when they are in civil society where the rule of law provides for the promulgation and enforcement of such law. West concludes that Locke's views on the law of nature are not based on divine revelation, a juridical doctrine of individual rights, self-ownership, or self-preservation, or on reasoning from premises that are not rooted in the empirical world. He argues that the true ground of Locke's view resides in his understanding of the conditions of human happiness.

In "Montesquieu's Natural Rights Constitutionalism," Paul A. Rahe considers the role of the political thought of Montesquieu in the Founding principles and documents of the United States. Rahe suggests ways in which Montesquieu's philosophy of natural law compares with the natural law philosophies of John Locke and Thomas Hobbes and explores Montesquieu's criteria of good government. Laws are to be assessed in part, Montesquieu argues, in terms of their goodness of fit with the dispositions and nature of the people subject to them as well as the nature of the world such people live in and their reasons for establishing government in the first place. Furthermore, those governments which offend natural rights, for example by failing to allow for the exercise of self-defense or by allowing slavery—both of which Montesquieu condemns as an affront to principles of equality and self-preservation—are assessed negatively by Montesquieu. Rahe describes Montesquieu as a thinker whose views of natural right are motivated by an aversion to despotism and a love of liberty akin to the thought of John Locke and embraced by the American Founders.

The third essay in the volume, "The Idea of Rights in the Imperial Crisis" by Craig Yirush, examines the idea of rights advanced by the American colonists in the imperial crisis from 1763–1776. Yirush argues that the colonists viewed all English subjects as having the same fundamental rights as individuals everywhere in the British empire. These individual rights to life, liberty, and property were in turn guaranteed by the colonists' right to consent to their taxation. The American colonists insisted that these rights could only be protected by colonial legislatures because they were not represented in the British Parliament. This in turn meant that the colonists required the ability to govern themselves in all internal matters, a claim which ultimately led to the idea that each colony should be a "free state," independent of king and parliament. While the colonists began by defending these rights on the basis of their legal inheritance as Englishmen, they gradually moved toward a more radical claim: that these rights were theirs based on the law of nature, and thus open to all men in principle. This move to natural rights was based in part on the colonists' claim that they had migrated to America, a place inhabited by indigenous peoples whom they viewed as "savages" and thus outside of the jurisdiction of the English common law. Yirush further explains, however, that the radical move to natural rights was in tension with the loose confederation which emerged in the years after 1776 in which each colony was a quasi-independent republican state and in which the rights of minorities—Native Americans, African Americans, religious dissenters, and Loyalists—could not be effectively protected by the federal government.

The nature of the moral theory of the American Revolutionary and Founding periods is also the theme of C. Bradley Thompson's contribution to the collection. "On Declaring the Moral Laws and Rights of Nature" examines this moral theory by focusing on two key concepts: moral laws and moral rights of nature. In order to illuminate these concepts, Thompson considers a series of questions important from the perspective of America's Revolutionary generation: What are the moral laws and rights of nature? What is the difference between a law and a right of nature? Are nature's moral laws and rights descriptive, prescriptive, or both? What are the attributes and sanctions of nature's laws and rights? And finally, how did America's Founding Fathers use the laws and rights of nature to establish their political institutions? In order to answer these questions, Thompson focuses on the American Declaration of Independence, the core text universally recognized as a symbol of America's revolutionary mind and moral theory.

In the fifth essay in the volume, "Lysander Spooner: Nineteenth-Century America's Last Natural Rights Theorist," Eric Mack articulates the ideas of Lysander Spooner, a thinker he identifies as the last powerful advocate of rights in nineteenth-century America. According to Mack, in addition to Spooner's compelling antebellum attacks on slavery, he developed forceful arguments on behalf of a strongly individualistic conception of natural law and private property rights and against coercive moralism, coercive paternalism, and state authority and legislation. The essay focuses on the theoretical core of Spooner's position which is his doctrine of natural rights. Mack situates Spooner within the libertarian tradition in political thought by examining the theories of Thomas Hodgskin and the early Herbert Spencer. Mack offers support for the contention that Spooner's views are robustly Lockean by showing that they are significantly more Lockean than the views of either Hodgskin or the early Spencer.

Natural rights had been attacked before the Progressive era by the racial science of ethnology, advocates of philosophy of history, and followers of Charles Darwin, but the Progressives launched the most thoroughgoing and systematic critique in American history. In the sixth essay of the volume, "Progressivism and the Doctrine of Natural Rights," James W. Ceaser discusses the Progressives' critique of the Founders' doctrine of natural right. The leading thinker conducting the critique of natural rights was American philosopher John Dewey. Dewey deployed five primary criticisms. Ceaser examines these criticisms in turn. First, he explains, Dewey argued that America had entered an entirely new age of social and economic organization requiring a political theory different from what may have been required at the time of the American Founding. This fact provided reason to abandon thinking in terms of natural rights in favor of more progressive thinking. According to Dewey's second argument, all theoretical claims of truth, such as claims about natural rights, are merely relative to the age in which they emerge and thrive. Third, Dewey, in a Marxian move, argued that theoretical ideas serve the aims of different classes, with different rights, problematically representing the political and economic interests of the emerging bourgeoisie. Dewey also, in his fourth primary argument, criticized the natural rights tradition on the grounds that natural rights encouraged diminished goals for human beings, emphasizing the fulfillment of individual self-interest rather than a higher ideal of human development and social cooperation. Lastly, Dewey charged that any metaphysical claim in politics, such as those made in the natural rights tradition, is undemocratic by virtue of ascribing a standard of right that is prior to and that overrules a decision of a democratic majority. Ceaser concludes his essay by considering the influence of Dewey's Progressive critique on the modern liberal heirs of the Progressives.

The collection continues with an essay by Eldon J. Eisenach, titled "Some Second Thoughts on Progressivism and Rights." Eisenach describes the ways in which Progressive intellectuals attacked individualist understandings of rights and mechanistic understandings of constitutional government during the Progressive movement. He examines the ways in which Progressivism differed from New Deal liberalism, especially regarding "big government." Progressive understandings of politics rest both on a distinction between "governments" and "states," derived from Alexis de Tocqueville, and on Abraham Lincoln's understandings of popular sovereignty. The distinction between governments and states is reinforced by Progressives' stress on an articulate and coherent public opinion that would provide democratic legitimacy to all forms of governing institutions, both public and private, that serve the common good. The civil war experience was the Progressives' model, one which they first thought would be reincarnated in the preparation for World War I. Eisenach explains that given both public and private assaults on free speech, Progressives in the 1920s often led the movement for protections of civil liberties and for new respect paid to the First Amendment. The essay concludes by examining the continuities and discontinuities of Progressive political thought in contemporary political discourse.

In her contribution to the collection, Tiffany Jones Miller explains that scholarly discussions of the turn-of-the-century Progressive movement frequently ignore or give only cursory attention to the Progressives' racial views and policies. In "Freedom, History, and Race in Progressive Thought," Miller suggests that those scholars who do pay greater attention to these features of Progressive thought nonetheless tend to dismiss them as being somehow paradoxical or inconsistent with what they regard as the movement's core, "democratic" principles. Miller, consequently, aims to explain the origin and nature of the movement's core principles, and to show that the reformers' racial views and policies, far from being inconsistent with these principles, were in fact their natural outgrowth. The Progressives' support for the colonial subjugation of the Filipinos, Miller argues, as well as the disfranchisement and segregation of American blacks, reflects a critical transformation in the character or content of public policy. This transformation was necessitated by the Progressives' rejection of the individualism of the American Founding in favor of a new conception of "individualism" chiefly inspired by early-nineteenth-century German idealism.

The collection continues with "The Progressive Era Assault on Individualism and Property Rights," by James W. Ely, Jr. Ely's essay takes up the examination, also undertaken in the previous three essays, of the far-reaching attack on individualism and property rights which characterized the Progressive era of the early twentieth century. Scholars and political figures associated with Progressivism, Ely explains, not only criticized the individualist values of classical liberalism, but also rejected the traditional notion of limited government espoused by the Framers of the Constitution. They expressed great confidence in regulatory agencies, staffed by experts, to effectuate policy. Such Progressives paved the way for the later triumph of statist ideology with the New Deal in the 1930s. Ely traces the source of the Progressives antipathy to individual rights and explains that leading Progressive intellectuals stressed the perceived need for increased governmental power and governance by an educated elite. Furthermore, Ely argues, Progressivism had an impact on constitutional law giving rise to "sociological jurisprudence" and its concomitant skepticism about courts and emphasis on judicial deference to legislative judgments. According to Ely, the Progressives looked with disfavor on any constitutional doctrine which curtailed government authority. Ely concludes that the Progressive movement left a lasting legacy of diminished regard for individualism and a jurisprudence which stripped property of strong constitutional protection.

In his essay, "Saving Locke from Marx: The Labor Theory of Value in Intellectual Property Theory," Adam Mossoff notes that while the labor theory of value is fundamental to John Locke's justification of property rights, critics have charged that it fails to justify intellectual property rights. The source of the difficulty, these critics contend, is that the labor theory of value cannot justify a right to the full economic value in an invention or book because the creator's physical labor contributes only partly to the market value of these products since market value is, at least in part, socially created. Mossoff charges that philosophers Robert Nozick and G. A. Cohen, among others, illicitly dismiss the labor theory of value as illogical or incoherent because these philosophers redefine Locke's concepts of labor and value in strictly physical and economic terms—terms which are more akin to Karl Marx's labor theory of economic value. Yet the principle of interpretive charity, Mossoff argues, demands reconsideration of Locke's theory in its own terms and in the full context of his natural law ethical theory, especially in considering how Locke himself justifies intellectual property rights. Mossoff thus examines Locke's theory of property, adopting an approach that integrates Locke's arguments about labor and natural law from throughout his various works. Locke's concept of labor, in this context, means "production," which has intellectual as well as physical characteristics, Mossoff contends, and his concept of value denotes that which is useful in the flourishing life of a rational being, which is a conception of the good that is more robust than mere physical status or economic wealth. This interpretation, Mossoff concludes, explains why he says that inventions exemplify his labor-based property theory and why he argues for property rights in written work.

In "Roosevelt, Wilson, and the Democratic Theory of National Progressivism," Ronald J. Pestritto explains that the American Progressive movement argued both for a democratization of the political process and for deference to expert administrators. Relying on the work of Theodore Roosevelt and Woodrow Wilson, Pestritto explores the evident tension in simultaneously advocating democratization and deference to expertise, and makes some preliminary suggestions regarding how the tension might be reconciled—at least in the eyes of the adherents of Progressivism—into a single democratic theory. Pestritto notes that both Roosevelt and Wilson criticize the principles of the original Constitution for being insufficiently democratic and overly suspicious of the popular will and both want to make public opinion a more direct force in national politics. At the same time, however, both are also suspicious of politics and its potential for corruption by "special interests," and thus both look for ways of empowering expert administrative agencies and insulating them from political influence. Pestritto argues that Wilson seems to understand the potential conflict between these two aims more than Roosevelt does, but both Roosevelt and Wilson, Pestritto relates, look to a popularized presidency as a means of attempting to reconcile consent and expertise.

The collection concludes with "On the Separation of Powers: Liberal and Progressive Constitutionalism," by Michael Zuckert. In this essay, Zuckert identifies one of the primary targets of Progressive constitutional criticism as the system of separation of powers. The American Founders, motivated by a concern to avoid the concentration of political power and abuses that might ensue from such concentration, advocated separation of legislative, executive, and judicial functions and accompanying powers. Woodrow Wilson, Zuckert notes, was especially critical of this feature of American constitutionalism, and wanted to replace the separation of powers with the conceptual and institutional distinction, informed by foreign administrative techniques, between politics and administration. Wilson argued that the separation of powers failed, in fact, truly to disperse power and claimed that there would always be a center of power, and in the American case this center was Congress. While Wilson rejected the notion of the separation of powers and disagreed otherwise with the Founding principles, he did hold some principles in common with the Founding philosophy, notably a commitment to individualism. Zuckert argues that an examination of the doctrine of separation of powers in the work of John Locke demonstrates that Wilson had an extremely truncated and generally inaccurate view of the point and intended operation of the separation of powers, and that it was this fact, not principled rejection of the philosophy of the American Founding, that motivated his criticisms of the separation of powers.

Natural rights individualism and Progressivism represent a fundamental dichotomy in American political ideology. The essays in this volume offer valuable insights concerning the leading advocates of these two traditions and concerning the profound and far-reaching impact of their ideas on political theory and practice.

ACKNOWLEDGMENTS

The editors wish to acknowledge several individuals at the Social Philosophy and Policy Center, Bowling Green State University, who provided invaluable assistance in the preparation of this volume. They include Mary Dilsaver, Terrie Weaver, and Brandon Byrd.

The editors also extend special thanks to Administrative Editor Tamara Sharp for attending to innumerable day-to-day details of the book's preparation, and to Managing Editor Pamela Phillips for providing dedicated assistance throughout the editorial and production process.

CONTRIBUTORS

Thomas G. West is Paul Ermine Potter and Dawn Tibbetts Potter Professor of Politics at Hillsdale College, and Senior Fellow of the Claremont Institute. He is the author of *Plato's Apology of Socrates: An Interpretation* (1979) and *Vindicating the Founders: Race, Sex, Class, and Justice in the Origins of America* (1997). He is co-translator of the best-selling *Four Texts on Socrates: Plato's Euthyphro, Apology, and Crito, and Aristophanes' Clouds* (1984, rev. ed. 1998). Recent publications include "Freedom of Speech in the Founding and in Modern Liberalism," "The Transformation of Protestant Theology as a Condition of the American Revolution," "Progressivism and the Transformation of American Government," and "The Economic Theory of the American Founding."

Paul A. Rahe is Professor of History at Hillsdale College, holds the Charles O. Lee and Louise K. Lee Chair in the Western Heritage, and is the author of *Republics Ancient and Modern: Classical Republicanism and the American Revolution* (1992), *Against Throne and Altar: Machiavelli and Political Theory under the English Republic* (2008), *Montesquieu and the Logic of Liberty: War, Religion, Commerce, Climate, Terrain, Technology, Uneasiness of Mind, the Spirit of Political Vigilance, and the Foundations of the Modern Republic* (2009), and *Soft Despotism, Democracy's Drift: Montesquieu, Rousseau, Tocqueville, and the Modern Prospect* (2009). Professor Rahe has been awarded research fellowships by the Center for Hellenic Study, the National Humanities Center, the Institute of Current World Affairs, the Olin Foundation, Washington University's Center for the History of Freedom, the National Endowment for the Humanities, the Woodrow Wilson International Center for Scholars in Washington, D. C., Clare Hall at Cambridge University, All Souls College at Oxford, the American Academy in Berlin, and the Social Philosophy and Policy Center at Bowling Green State University.

Craig Yirush is Associate Professor of History at the University of California, Los Angeles where he teaches early American history. He received his doctorate in history from Johns Hopkins in 2004, and has held fellowships at the John Carter Brown Library and the Charles Warren Center at Harvard. His research is in early modern political theory, with a particular interest in empire and the problem of indigenous rights. His first book, *Settlers, Liberty, and Empire: The Roots of Early American Political Theory, 1675–1775*, was published by Cambridge University Press in 2011.

C. Bradley Thompson is Professor of Political Science at Clemson University, where he teaches political philosophy, and is also Executive Director of the Clemson Institute for the Study of Capitalism. He is the author of five books, including *Neoconservatism: An Obituary for an Idea* (2010) and the award-winning *John Adams and the Spirit of Liberty* (1998). He is also the editor of *Freedom and School Choice in American Education* (2011, with Greg Forster), *Antislavery Political Writings, 1833–1860: A Reader* (2004), and *The Revolutionary Writings of John Adams* (2000). Currently he is completing a book tentatively entitled *The Ideological Origins of American Constitutionalism*.

Eric Mack is Professor of Philosophy at Tulane University, where he is also a faculty member of the Murphy Institute of Political Economy. He specializes in social and political philosophy, ethics, and the philosophy of law. He is the editor of Auberon Herbert's *The Right and Wrong of Compulsion by the State and Other Essays* (1978) and Herbert Spencer's *Man versus the State: With Six Essays on Government, Society, and Freedom* (1981), and the author of *John Locke* (2009). Among his more recent essays are: "Individualism and Libertarian Rights" in *Contemporary Debates in Political Philosophy*, "What is Left in Left-Libertarianism?" in *Hillel Steiner and the Anatomy of Justice*, "The Natural Right of Property" in *Social Philosophy and Policy*, "Nozickan Arguments for the More-Than-Minimal State," forthcoming in *Cambridge Companion to Anarchy, State, and Utopia*, and "Friedrich Hayek on the Nature of Social Order and Law," forthcoming in *Twentieth Century Political Philosophy*.

James W. Ceaser is Harry F. Byrd Professor of Politics at the University of Virginia, where he has taught since 1976, and a Visiting Fellow at the Hoover Institution. He is the author of several books on American politics and political thought, including *Presidential Selection* (1979), *Liberal Democracy and Political Science* (1990), *Reconstructing America* (1996), *Nature and History in American Political Development* (2006), and *Designing a Polity* (2010). He has also coauthored a series on American national elections since 1992. Professor Ceaser currently serves as a presidential appointee to the National Historical Publications and Records Commission and is a frequent contributor to the popular press.

Eldon J. Eisenach is Professor Emeritus of Political Science at the University of Tulsa, and taught previously at Penn State University and Cornell University. He is the author of numerous books, including *The Lost Promise of Progressivism* (1994), *The Next Religious Establishment: National Identity and Political Theology in Post-Protestant America* (2000), and *Narrative Power and Liberal Truth: Hobbes, Locke, Bentham, and Mill* (2002), and the editor of *Mill and the Moral Character of Liberalism* (1999) and *The Social and Political Thought of American Progressivism* (2006). He serves on editorial boards for *History of Political Thought*, *Studies in American Political Development*, and *Politics and Religion*.

Tiffany Jones Miller is Associate Professor of Politics at the University of Dallas. She is especially interested in the intersection of political philosophy and American political thought and practice. She has published on various aspects of the theory and practice of the American Founding and Progressivism, and is currently writing a book on the turn-of-the-twentieth-century Progressive movement's impact on the domestic policy reforms of the Progressive era, New Deal, and Great Society.

James W. Ely, Jr. is Milton R. Underwood Professor Emeritus of Law, and Professor Emeritus of History at Vanderbilt University. He is the author or editor of numerous books, including *The Chief Justiceship of Melville W. Fuller, 1888–1910* (1995); *Railroads and American Law* (2001); *The Bill of Rights in Modern America*, rev. ed. (2008) (with David J. Bodenhamer); *The Guardian of Every Other Right: A Constitutional History of Property Rights*, 3rd ed. (2008); and *American Legal History: Cases and Materials*, 4th ed. (2011) (with Kermit L. Hall and Paul Finkelman). He is also a former associate editor of the *American Journal of Legal History*. Professor Ely has authored a wide range of articles dealing with the rights of property owners in American constitutional history. In 2006, he received the Brigham-Kanner Property Rights Prize. He is presently at work on a book dealing with the history of the contract clause.

Adam Mossoff is Professor of Law at George Mason University School of Law, where he teaches and writes in the areas of intellectual property and property law. His scholarship explores the intersection of intellectual property law and property theory, addressing how natural rights philosophy and the jurisprudential theory known as legal realism affected the creation and subsequent evolution of American patent law. His publications include "Patents as Constitutional Private Property: The Historical Protection of Patents under the Takings Clause," "What is Property? Putting the Pieces Back Together," and "Rethinking the Development of Patents: An Intellectual History, 1550–1800."

Ronald J. Pestritto is Graduate Dean and Associate Professor of Politics at Hillsdale College, where he teaches political philosophy, American political thought, and American politics, and holds the Charles and Lucia Shipley Chair in the American Constitution. He is also Senior Fellow of the College's Kirby Center for Constitutional Studies and Citizenship, Senior Fellow of the Claremont Institute for the Study of Statesmanship and Political Philosophy and Academic Fellow of the Foundation for Defense of Democracies. He is the author of *American Progressivism* (2008), *Woodrow Wilson and the Roots of Modern Liberalism* (2005), and *Founding the Criminal Law: Punishment and Political Thought in the Origins of America* (2000). He is the editor of *Woodrow Wilson: The Essential Political Writings* (2005) and co-editor with Thomas G. West of a three-book series on American political thought (2003, 2004, 2006). Professor Pestritto has also served as a Visiting Scholar at the Social Philosophy and Policy Center at Bowling Green State University, and has written widely on Progressivism and the administrative state for publications such as the *Wall Street Journal* and the *Claremont Review of Books*.

Michael Zuckert is Nancy R. Dreux Professor of Political Science at the University of Notre Dame. He has written extensively on the liberal tradition in political philosophy and American constitutionalism. He is the author of several books, including *The Natural Rights Republic* (1996), *Launching Liberalism: John Locke and the Liberal Tradition* (2002), and, most recently, *Natural Rights and American Constitutionalism* (2011).

ACKNOWLEDGMENT

The editors gratefully acknowledge Liberty Fund, Inc., for holding the conference at which the original versions of these essays were presented and discussed.

THE GROUND OF LOCKE'S LAW OF NATURE

By Thomas G. West

I. Introduction

What is the foundation of John Locke's political philosophy? This question is controversial among scholars, to be sure, but it is also relevant for political life today. America's constitutional democracy was originally based on Locke's political teaching, but few would say that his teaching is sufficient to sustain a sound constitutional democracy. Conservatives such as Daniel Mahoney argue that the "principle" of American democracy is "the [Lockean] liberty and equality of human beings," a principle that has become in our time "an unreflective dogma eroding the traditions, authoritative institutions, and spiritual presuppositions that allow human beings to live free, civilized, and decent lives."[1] Liberals follow the claim of Progressive-Era intellectuals such as Herbert Croly, who asserts that the "Jeffersonian principle" of individual rights has caused "the inequalities of power generated in the American economic and political system."[2] Scholars and public intellectuals of all persuasions are therefore constantly on the lookout for some non-Lockean doctrine as an adequate ground for political life in the twenty-first century. My essay is meant to revive a willingness to examine Locke as if he might be right. I do not commit the absurdity of claiming to have demonstrated the truth of Locke's teaching. But I will show that his theory is much more plausible than we have been led to believe.

My contention here is that the foundation of Locke's moral and political theory has long been misunderstood. It provides a far more satisfactory basis for political and moral life than has been acknowledged. Before we can consider the question of whether Lockean political thought is worthy of being revived, however, we need to understand what his view is. The present essay is meant to show that Locke's teaching on the law of nature is not based on divine revelation,[3] or a juridical doctrine of individual

[1] Daniel J. Mahoney, *The Conservative Foundations of the Liberal Order: Defending Democracy against Its Modern Enemies and Immoderate Friends* (Wilmington, DE: ISI Books, 2010), xiii, 36.
[2] Herbert Croly, *The Promise of American Life* (1909) (Boston: Northeastern University Press, 1989), 190.
[3] This is the position of Jeremy Waldron, *God, Locke, and Equality: Christian Foundations in Locke's Political Thought* (Cambridge: Cambridge University Press, 2002), 13. Waldron doubts that "one can even make sense of a position like Locke's . . . [on] basic equality . . . apart from the specifically biblical and Christian teaching that he associated with it." Later in the chapter I will show that Waldron is partly correct, although not because of Locke's Christian commitments.

doi:10.1017/S0265052511000392
© 2012 Social Philosophy & Policy Foundation. Printed in the USA.

rights,[4] or self-ownership,[5] or self-preservation,[6] or reasoning from premises that are not rooted in the empirical world.[7] I will argue, on the contrary, that the real ground of Locke's teaching is found in his understanding of the conditions of human happiness.

This conclusion, however, is far from evident on the surface of Locke's writings. Locke draws his reader into an amazingly complex line of reasoning, scattered up and down in several of his books, leading finally to the real basis of his teaching on the law of nature. Locke engages the reader in a dialogue, in which initially plausible arguments are put forward, then implicitly questioned, leading to new arguments, which again are questioned, and so on. Along the way, one's understanding of the subject constantly deepens as one follows what Locke calls the "long and sometimes intricate deductions of reason"[8] which are necessary to reach the ultimate ground of the law of nature. Locke writes treatises, not Platonic dialogues. But his treatises are written in such a way that the reader will have a hard time penetrating them if he does not follow Locke's *logos* wherever it leads. Locke says that understanding the epistles of St. Paul requires "sober inquisitive readers" who bring "stubborn attention, and more than common application" to the task.[9] The same goes for reading Locke himself. As we will see, a dialogical thread will take us from one of Locke's books to another, until we put together all the relevant passages to show the complete picture of his argument.

Most scholars agree that Locke's arguments for a law of nature are insufficient. It is a "fact," writes John Dunn, "that such a demonstration is not in principle possible and that the development of Locke's ideas had drawn the difficulties of such an effort sharply to his attention." Dunn also remarks, "There is, however, little agreement among interpreters of

[4] A. John Simmons, *The Lockean Theory of Rights* (Princeton: Princeton University Press, 1992), 3, speaks of "the theory of rights on which his philosophy rests."

[5] Michael P. Zuckert, *Natural Rights and the New Republicanism* (Princeton: Princeton University Press, 1994), 285–86, argues that the foundation of Locke's doctrine of rights, which is more fundamental than his doctrine of natural law, lies in the right of self-ownership. I will show that the law of nature is more fundamental than the self-ownership doctrine, although I agree with Zuckert that its origin is not "transcendent."

[6] Thomas L. Pangle, *The Spirit of Modern Republicanism: The Moral Vision of the American Founders and the Philosophy of Locke* (Chicago: University of Chicago Press, 1988), esp. 198–209.

[7] Peter C. Myers, *Our Only Star and Compass: Locke and the Struggle for Political Rationality* (Lanham, MD: Rowman & Littlefield, 1998), calls this the "conventionalist" position. See Eugene Miller, "Locke on the Meaning of Political Language: The Teaching of the *Essay Concerning Human Understanding*," *Political Science Reviewer* 9 (Fall 1979): 163–93; cf. Leo Strauss, *Natural Right and History* (Chicago: University of Chicago Press, 1953), 250–51.

[8] John Locke, *The Reasonableness of Christianity, As Delivered in the Scriptures* (1695), ed. John C. Higgins-Biddle (Oxford: Clarendon Press, 1999), chap. 14, 266 (pagination of the first edition, printed in the margin). The same pagination is found in the margin of the reprint of Higgins-Biddle's *Reasonableness* in John Locke, *Writings on Religion*, ed. Victor Nuovo (Oxford: Clarendon Press, 2002).

[9] Locke, "The Preface: An Essay for the Understanding of St. Paul's Epistles by Consulting St. Paul Himself," in *A Paraphrase and Notes on the Epistles of St. Paul* (1707), ed. Arthur W. Wainwright (Oxford: Clarendon Press, 1987), 1:107, 111.

Locke's thought on the significance that should be attached to these facts."[10] This is my point of departure.

I begin with the *Second Treatise*, because that is where most readers begin.[11] Hardly anyone reads the *First Treatise* today, and, as far as I can tell, ever did. The *Second Treatise* is where Locke lays out most of the political doctrines that he is famous for. At the beginning of chapter 2, Locke gives us two arguments that profess to explain how we know that we are governed by the law of nature, and part of what that law requires of us.

First, "creatures of the same species and rank, . . . born to all the same advantages of nature, and use of the same faculties, should also be equal one amongst another without subordination."[12] Second, "being all equal and independent, no one ought to harm another in his life, health, liberty, or possessions: for men being all the workmanship of one omnipotent and infinitely wise maker, all the servants of one sovereign master, . . . they are his property, whose workmanship they are, made to last during his, not one another's pleasure."[13] In a word, Locke's first argument appears to be that all human beings possess "the same advantages of nature," and the second is that we are all God's property and therefore we may not harm each other.

II. The *Second Treatise* Argument from Equal Talents

The first argument claims that creatures "promiscuously born to all the same advantages of nature, and the use of the same faculties" have no natural right to rule each other. How do we know that human beings do in fact share the "same advantages of nature"? Locke adds this explanatory remark: "unless the lord and master of them all should, by any manifest declaration of his will, set one above another, and confer on him by an evident and clear appointment an undoubted right to dominion and sovereignty."[14] But this addition does not prove that all human beings share "the same advantages of nature." It says only that there is no "undoubted right" to rule, a claim that is obviously true, since there are many who will doubt any purported claim to "dominion and sover-

---

[10] John Dunn, *The Political Thought of John Locke: An Historical Account of the Argument of the Two Treatises of Government* (Cambridge: Cambridge University Press, 1987), 187. Leo Strauss agrees in "Locke's Doctrine of Natural Law, chap. 8 of *What Is Political Philosophy? And Other Studies* (Glencoe, IL: Free Press, 1959).

[11] John Locke, *Two Treatises of Government* (1690), 2d ed., ed. Peter Laslett (Cambridge: Cambridge University Press, 1970). In my quotations from Locke, I have modernized capitalization, punctuation, spelling, and italics. Books I and II of the *Two Treatises* are commonly called (as I will call them) the *First Treatise* and *Second Treatise*, although those are not Locke's titles.

[12] Locke, *Second Treatise*, chap. 2, sec. 4.

[13] Ibid., chap. 2, sec. 6.

[14] Ibid., chap. 2, sec. 4.

eignty." But what is the evidence that people actually share the same natural advantages? Locke provides none in the *Second Treatise*.

The same argument from equality also appears in the *First Treatise*: "man has a natural freedom, . . . since all that share in the same common nature, faculties, and powers are in nature equal, and ought to partake in the same common rights and privileges." [15] But in the *First Treatise* Locke provides no more evidence that all share "the same . . . faculties, and powers" than he does in the *Second*. In the *First Treatise*, this statement occurs in a summary of the whole argument of the *Treatise* up to that point. Strangely, however, this particular explanation of a right to "natural freedom" is brought up in the *First Treatise* for the first and only time in this single statement, unprepared by what precedes it, and unsupported by what follows.

I emphasize the absence of evidence in the *Two Treatises* because the most obvious difficulty with these extreme statements of human equality of talents is that according to Locke himself, in many other passages, human beings are emphatically not "creatures" sharing "promiscuously" in "all the same advantages of nature." In fact, in the *Second Treatise* passage in question, Locke does not quite say that human beings *are* "born to all the same advantages of nature." He says only that "creatures [assuming any such creatures exist] of the same . . . rank promiscuously born to all the same advantages of nature" should be "equal one amongst another." Locke seems to use this coy formulation as a way of quietly distancing himself from the absurd view that human beings naturally possess equal talents ("advantages of nature").

Locke tells us forthrightly at the beginning of chapter 6 of the *Second Treatise* that human beings are *not* in fact "born to all the same advantages," for "excellency of parts . . . may place [some people] above the common level." [16] In other words, some have more of the "advantages of nature" than others. What Locke means by "excellency of parts" may be seen in the section entitled "Parts" in his book *Conduct of the Understanding*:

> There is, it is visible, great variety in men's understandings, and their natural constitutions put so wide a difference between some men in this respect that art and industry would never be able to master, and their very natures seem to want a foundation to raise on it, that which other men easily attain unto. Amongst men of equal education there is great inequality of parts. [17]

---

[15] Locke, *First Treatise*, chap. 6, sec. 67.
[16] Locke, *Second Treatise*, chap. 6, sections 6 and 54.
[17] Locke, *Of the Conduct of the Understanding* (1706), in *Some Thoughts Concerning Education and Of the Conduct of the Understanding*, ed. Ruth W. Grant and Nathan Tarcov (Indianapolis: Hackett, 1996), sec. 2. *Conduct* was originally intended to be the longest chapter in an expanded edition of his *Essay Concerning Human Understanding*. Locke never found time to complete it. He left instructions for his literary executor that *Conduct* was to be dealt with

If this "great inequality" lies in "their *natural* constitutions," "their very *natures*," then obviously human beings are born very unequal in regard to the "advantages of nature" that they enjoy.

In the *Essay Concerning Human Understanding*, Locke states bluntly how huge this inequality is: "There are some men of one, some but of two syllogisms, and no more. . . . [T]here is a greater distance between some men and others [in regard to their understandings] . . . than between some men and some beasts." In this passage of the *Essay* Locke refuses to say whether this "distance" is due to "the dullness or untractableness of those faculties, for want of use; or, as some think, in the natural differences of men's souls."[18] But in the passage of *Conduct* just quoted, Locke leaves no doubt that nature is a source of substantial inequality in intellectual capacity.[19]

Even when people have sufficient natural talent to develop their reason, they frequently fail to do so. "[M]en of low and mean education, who have never elevated their thoughts above the spade and the plow," Locke writes, are "no more capable of reasoning than almost a perfect natural." Yet this is the condition of most people in regard to "matters of concernment, especially those of religion." So Locke asks whether human beings are "rational animals." He answers: not necessarily, and not usually: "though we all call ourselves so, because we are born to it if we please, yet we may truly say nature gives us but the seeds of it; . . . it is use and exercise only that makes us so, and we are indeed so no further than industry and application has carried us."[20]

III. The *Second Treatise* Argument from Equal Capacity of Knowing the Law

In chapter 6 of the *Second Treatise*, we find that Locke's awareness of inequality of "parts" leads him to revise the ground of the teaching of the law of nature regarding "the equality, which all men are in, in respect of

---

"as you think fit." It was published shortly after his death. See Roger Woolhouse, *Locke: A Biography* (Cambridge: Cambridge University Press, 2007), 386, 458.

[18] Locke, *An Essay Concerning Human Understanding* (4th ed., 1700), ed. Peter H. Nidditch (Oxford: Clarendon Press, 1975), bk. 4, chap. 20, sec. 5. Also sec. 3: "[A] great part of mankind are, by the natural and unalterable state of things in this world, and the constitution of human affairs, unavoidably given over to invincible ignorance" of the most important matters of their lives.

[19] Waldron, *God, Locke, and Equality*, 72, acknowledges that Locke discerns "enormous differences in reason and rational ability among those we are accustomed to call human." This leads Waldron to the conclusion that Locke's human beings do not clearly constitute a single species, and that there can therefore be no fundamental human equality, unless God is brought into the argument to guarantee the oneness of humanity (81 and elsewhere). Beginning with this same observation ("enormous differences in . . . rational ability"), my argument goes in a different direction.

[20] Locke, *Conduct of the Understanding*, sec. 6. A "natural," in Locke's sense, is an idiot, someone grossly deficient in the usual intellectual powers.

jurisdiction or dominion one over another." Now he says that people are equal insofar as each possesses "such a degree of reason, wherein he might be supposed capable of knowing the law, and so living within the rules of it." Children "are not born in this full state of equality, though they are born to it." When they reach the age of reason, when they can be presumed to know the law they are under, they are set free from the authority of their parents. Locke remarks that in England, a "capacity of knowing that law ... is supposed by that law, at the age of one and twenty years, and in some cases sooner." Only those who are rational should be free. Otherwise, they will harm themselves. Others who have reason need to will for them. "To turn [a child] loose to an unrestrained liberty, before he has reason to guide him, is not the allowing him the privilege of his nature, to be free; but to thrust him out amongst brutes, and abandon him to a state as wretched, and as much beneath that of a man, as theirs."[21]

This limited argument for equality in regard to jurisdiction or dominion—that people are equal in regard to their presumed ability to know the law they are under—seems plausible with respect to people living in civil society. In that case, the law is easy to know at the age of twenty-one because it is published by the government. The difficult question is whether most adults can also be presumed to know the law *in the state of nature*, when they are "only ... under the law of nature."[22]

Locke sometimes gives the impression, as in chapter 2, that it is easy to know the law of nature in the state of nature, "so plain was it writ in the hearts of all mankind." Locke also says there that the law of nature is as "intelligible and plain to a rational creature, and a studier of that law, as the positive laws of commonwealths, nay possibly plainer; as much as reason is easier to be understood, than the ... municipal laws of countries."[23] But the impression left by these words is belied by the words themselves. The law of nature is *only* known to "a rational creature, and a studier of that law." How many people in the state of nature are "studiers"? In chapter 9, Locke gives an unequivocal answer: "though the law of nature be plain and intelligible to all rational creatures; yet men ... [are] *ignorant for want of study of it*."[24] Few if any know the law of nature in the state of nature.

If we read the passage in chapter 2 in light of the statement just quoted from chapter 9, we understand that Locke is only saying that the law of nature is "as intelligible and plain" as the municipal law *only* "as much as reason is easier to be understood" than that law. But the later passage makes clear that reason is *not* "easier to be understood" than the municipal law. Therefore, since reason is less easily

---

[21] Locke, *Second Treatise*, chap. 6, sections 54–55, 59, 60, 63.
[22] Ibid., chap. 6, sec. 59.
[23] Ibid., chap. 2, sections 11, 12.
[24] Ibid., chap. 9, sec. 124, my emphasis.

understood (because of "want of study"), the municipal law of the country is more easily understood.[25]

Leo Strauss explains how some people could know the law of nature in the state of nature in this way:

> But only such men could know the law of nature while living in a state of nature who have already lived in civil society, or rather in a civil society in which reason has been properly cultivated. An example of men who are in the state of nature under the law of nature would therefore be an elite among the English colonists in America rather than the wild Indians. A better example would be that of any highly civilized men after the breakdown of their society [e.g., after the collapse of British authority in 1774 but before the formation of new constitutions in 1776] .[26]

The civilized survivors of a plane crash living on an uninhabited island in the South Pacific would also "know" the law of nature in the sense that they would remember, and habitually continue to follow (at least for a time), the basic rules of conduct established by the civil law they previously lived under. If they had come from a well-governed society, the civil laws would have been to a significant degree the same as the law of nature (e.g., do not use coercion to dominate others). But this would not be knowledge of the law of nature, since it would merely be *belief* about what should and should not be done. Only a highly educated elite few—if any—would have actual knowledge of the law of nature. One is reminded of Rousseau's complaint against "the moderns" such as Locke: "it is impossible to understand the law of nature and consequently to obey it without being a great reasoner and a profound metaphysician." [27] It seems that Rousseau was right.

We are compelled to conclude, first, that according to Locke himself, human beings are not born equal in regard to talents (this is the argument for equality in the *Second Treatise,* chapter 2), and second, that in a state of nature, they are not naturally equal in regard to knowledge of the law they are under (the argument for equality in chapter 6). The unavoidable conclusion, on the basis of Locke's own arguments, is that unless adults are living in political society, where they are "capable of

---

[25] Quite a few scholars have noted that Locke's law of nature is unknown in the rude state of nature, e.g., Zuckert, *Natural Rights and the New Republicanism,* 274: "in the state of nature . . . human beings are 'ignorant' of the law of nature (II 124)." Fewer scholars have noticed the shockingly anti-egalitarian implications of that ignorance in light of the argument in chapter 6 for "equality . . . in respect of jurisdiction or dominion."

[26] Strauss, *Natural Right and History,* 230.

[27] Jean-Jacques Rousseau, *Discourse on the Origin and Foundations of Inequality among Men* (1755), Preface, in *The First and Second Discourses,* ed. Roger D. Masters (New York: Bedford/ St. Martin's, 1964), 94.

knowing the law, and so living within the rules of it," they are not in the "full state of equality" that they are supposedly "born to." [28] Being ignorant of the law, they have no more right to liberty than "lunatics or idiots." [29]

This, of course, is a version of the classic argument for rule by the rational and wise over the irrational and unwise, without the consent of the governed. Locke states explicitly that "he that is not come to the use of his reason, cannot be said to be under this law [of nature]; and Adam's children, being not presently as soon as born under this law of reason, were not presently free." [30] Children are governed without their consent because their parents, having reason, know the law they are under. Children do not. But in a rude state of nature, the adults are in the same irrational condition as the children. Since "where there is no law, there is no freedom" [31] no one in that state has a right to liberty except those rare persons, if any can be found, who know the law of nature. Locke's teaching on equality in chapter 6, it seems, paradoxically legitimates the rule of a minority of wise men (who know the law of nature) over the multitude (who are ignorant of the law of nature). Only in political society, where most adults know the law they are under, can a general right of freedom be established on the basis of the present argument.

This line of argument makes us attentive to the "aristocratic" implications of this remark of Locke in chapter 5:

> God gave the world to men in common; but since he gave it them for their benefit, and the greatest conveniences of life they were capable to draw from it, it cannot be supposed he meant it should always remain common and uncultivated. He gave it to the use of the industrious and rational (and labour was to be his title to it), not to the fancy or covetousness of the quarrelsome and contentious.[32]

Locke implies that in a state of nature, only the rational and industrious have property rights in land. How "rational" does one have to be to qualify? Is it enough merely to mix one's labor with something outside of oneself? Or must one also be "rational" in the sense of chapter 6, "knowing the law, and so living within the rules of it"? [33] Even the beasts have the ability to mix their labor with their environment. Birds seize worms and build nests. It would seem that a more robust rationality is required. But that would lead us back to the difficulty just discussed.

[28] Locke, *Second Treatise*, chap. 6, sec. 55.
[29] Ibid., chap. 6, sec. 60.
[30] Ibid., chap. 6, sec. 57.
[31] Ibid.
[32] Ibid., chap. 5, sec. 34.
[33] Ibid., chap. 6, sec. 60.

Locke's acknowledgment of what Strauss calls "the special right of the more reasonable men" [34] is especially noticeable in his discussion of prerogative later in the *Second Treatise*. For what is prerogative but the rule of the wise over the unwise without their consent? "Prerogative is nothing but the power of doing public good without a rule." [35] By violating the written law and instead following "the fundamental law of nature and government, [that] . . . all the members of the society are to be preserved," [36] he who exercises prerogative elevates his own rational insight above the law established by the legislative to which the people have consented. Locke argues that the purpose of civil society is to enable men to escape the state of nature by creating a society, ruled by general laws, grounded in the consent of the governed. When government officials operate outside the law, when they "rule by extemporary arbitrary decrees," [37] it puts men back into the state of nature—ordinarily, an undesirable condition. Yet we learn in the chapter on prerogative that "a good prince, who is mindful of the trust put into his hands, and careful of the good of his people, cannot have too much prerogative, that is, power to do good." [38] In other words, when faced with a choice between the rule of law based on the consent of the governed, and the rule of the wise man exercising prerogative based on his own judgment of the public good, Locke unhesitatingly sides with the rule of the wise against the rule of the majority. "Such God-like princes indeed had some title to arbitrary power, by that argument that would prove absolute monarchy the best government, as that which God himself governs the universe by: because such kings partake of his wisdom and goodness." [39]

Could this really be Locke's opinion about human inequality? Locke tells us that "one may destroy a man who makes war upon him . . . for the same reason, that he may kill a wolf or a lion; because such men are not under the ties of the common law of reason, . . . and so may be treated as beasts of prey." [40] People who "quit the principles of human nature," [41] i.e., the "common law of reason," are in this decisive respect no different than wild beasts. If they are not actually subhuman, they act as if they were.

In his own subdued way, Locke is as much of an "elitist" as Plato or Aristotle before him. But unlike these men, and in spite of everything I have written in this paper so far, Locke wants to promote a society that is based on the conviction that all human beings really are by nature equal. Locke knows that the lawless rule of the wise by prerogative is danger-

---

[34] Strauss, *Natural Right and History,* 233.
[35] Locke, *Second Treatise,* chap. 14, sec. 166.
[36] Ibid., chap. 14, sec. 159.
[37] Ibid., chap. 11, sec. 136.
[38] Ibid., chap. 14, sec. 164.
[39] Ibid., chap. 14, sec. 166.
[40] Ibid., chap. 3, sec. 16.
[41] Ibid., chap. 2, sec. 10.

ous. Right after the "God-like prince" statement just quoted, Locke mentions the popular saying "that the reigns of good princes have been always most dangerous to the liberties of their people" because they create a "precedent" that enables bad princes to assert a fictitious "right in them to do, for the harm of the people, if they so pleased." [42] For Locke, the rule of law, based on consent of the governed and the equality of all members of the society, should prevail most of the time.

We will consider later additional reasons why Locke, being fully conscious of the huge differences among human beings, would not want to ground the good society on aristocratic or monarchical rule—even though he concedes in theory, and to some extent in practice, that the rule of the wise is best.

IV. THE SECOND TREATISE ARGUMENT FROM DIVINE OWNERSHIP

We must now consider Locke's second argument for the law of nature at the beginning of the *Second Treatise:* that human beings are God's property, being produced by God's "workmanship," and therefore may not harm each other.

In the *Second Treatise,* Locke provides as little evidence for his divine workmanship argument as he does for his argument from equal talents.[43] The claim that men are forbidden from harming God's property, which he repeats in chapter 6 in regard to parental duties to children (children also being God's workmanship), is a bare unsupported assertion. One can perhaps grant that reason is able to say that all human beings are God's workmanship (as is everything in the world), if we understand by the word "God" a supreme being or principle, whatever it may be, that orders the natural world. In the *First Treatise,* Locke shows that fathers cannot claim the right to rule their children as their "workmanship," since God or nature does almost all of the "work." Fathers (and mothers) supply merely the material seeds, not the design and shaping of the matter into a human form.[44] Even an atheist might be willing to grant the existence of divine workmanship in this sense, which would equate God with nature or the principle of nature. In Locke's *Essay on Human Understanding,* this is the only kind of God that reason can even pretend to prove the existence of. Locke argues there that human reason can discover the existence of "a God" who is "the most powerful" being (not necessarily omnipotent) and who is a "knowing intelligent being" (not necessarily omniscient).[45] I leave aside the question of whether Locke's proof of God's existence in the *Essay* is alto-

---

[42] Ibid., chap. 14, sec. 166.

[43] Again, the point is well known to scholars, e.g., Simmons, *Lockean Theory,* 17: "The law [of nature] binds us, we are told, because we are all God's 'workmanship', although no real explanation of that claim is offered."

[44] Locke, *First Treatise,* chap. 6, sections 52–54.

[45] Locke, *Essay,* bk. 4, chap. 10, sections 1, 4, and 5.

gether cogent.[46] I merely note that his proof, such as it is, has no moral dimension at all. A most powerful and knowing God is one thing. A God who issues commands and prohibitions to human beings is another. Obviously the Biblical God, known by divine revelation, does issue such commands. But the question here is whether reason unaided by faith can demonstrate that the mere idea of divine workmanship implies the existence of divine commandments. Let us posit that a God created or made the world. Let us add that it follows that God owns everything in the world. How, then, would we know that we may not make use of any of his property without his permission? Perhaps God made the world and set its creatures free to act as they think best. God might be like the gods of Lucretius, uncaring about what human beings do.

There is another weakness in Locke's workmanship argument. Assuming we have the right to use inferior creatures as we wish, why should not human beings who know the law of nature use ignorant human beings as they wish? In chapter 2 of the *Second Treatise,* Locke repeats the claim he had made (or rather vaguely suggested) two sections earlier, saying that men possess "like faculties, sharing all in one community of nature." [47] But here we meet the same problem we met with Locke's argument from equality. Some men are greatly inferior to other men. Nature may be "one community," but that community includes beings of many different ranks. Again, if Locke is not confused, he must have another argument in mind for the equal right to life and liberty.

To complicate things further, Locke applies the workmanship argument to parents in chapter 6 of the *Second Treatise:* "by the law of nature, [parents have always been] under an obligation to preserve, nourish, and educate the children they had begotten, not as their own workmanship, but the workmanship of their own maker, the Almighty." [48] This assertion is even more puzzling than the one in chapter 2, which spoke of our obligation to all mankind indiscriminately (everyone is "bound to preserve himself, and . . . as much as he can, to preserve the rest of mankind").[49] In chapter 6 we are told that beyond this general obligation to preserve all others, parents have a particular obligation to their own children as God's workmanship, an obligation that includes not only their mere preservation, but also their nourishment and education. Here too no argument is supplied to link the fact that their children (like all men) are products of divine workmanship, and the special parental duty to this particular tiny group.[50]

[46] William T. Bluhm, Neil Wintfeld, and Stuart H. Teger, "Locke's Idea of God: Rational Truth or Political Myth?" *Journal of Politics* 42, no. 2 (1980): 414–38.

[47] Locke, *Second Treatise,* chap. 2, sections 4, 6.

[48] Ibid., chap. 6, sec. 56.

[49] Ibid., chap. 2, sec. 6.

[50] Scholars sometimes neglect or underemphasize the passages in the *Second Treatise* where Locke speaks of positive duties to other men and of parents to children. For example, Steven Forde, "Natural Law, Theology, and Morality in Locke," *American Journal of Political Science* 45, no. 2 (April 2001): 401–2, 408 ("Locke's rights . . . entail duties on the part of others. . . .

I conclude that the argument in the *Second Treatise* for the law of nature on the basis of the claim that men are God's property or workmanship—an argument, by the way, which seems to have resonated hardly at all with later admirers of Locke such as the American Founders—is an assertion unsupported by reason.

V. Why Locke Uses Bad Arguments

We have seen that Locke uses defective arguments in the *Second Treatise*. This raises three questions. Was Locke aware that he was using bad arguments? If so, why did he use them? Third, how could the *Second Treatise*, one of the most influential books ever written, have been so persuasive to its readers, if it is really built on such a flimsy foundation? For almost the whole edifice of the *Second Treatise*—the social compact origin of government, the purpose of government (securing the equal right to life, liberty, and estate), the need for representation of the public in the legislative, the right to revolution—is built on the initial foundation of liberty and equality established by the law of nature.

There is evidence that Locke was fully aware of the weakness of the arguments for the law of nature in the *Second Treatise*. As many scholars have observed, Locke is the kind of writer who is willing to allow his less attentive readers to rest satisfied with inadequate arguments if they find such arguments persuasive.[51] In Harvey Mansfield's memorable formulation, Locke "leaves one trail for the sceptical and another for the pious, the latter more plainly marked but leading in circles, so that eventually the pious will have to follow the sceptics' trail if they wish to get anywhere."[52] In a letter to one of his critics, Locke admits that he made deliberate use of a weak argument in the *Essay on Human Understanding* in his proof of the existence of God:

[T]hese are purely negative, duties to do no harm. . . . The *Second Treatise* appeals to very little beyond immediate self-interest.") In his long discussion of Lockean natural law in *Natural Rights and the New Republicanism*, 187–288, Zuckert similarly focuses almost exclusively on Locke's doctrine of natural rights as opposed to the duty of everyone to preserve others and of parents to care for their children. If the objection is raised that Locke's duty to others is conditional—only "when his own preservation comes not in competition, ought he, as much as he can, to preserve the rest of mankind" (*Second Treatise*, chap. 2, sec. 6)—one may respond that no major classical or medieval philosopher teaches, as a natural right or natural law duty, that one is obliged to sacrifice one's own life to preserve another's.

[51] Locke's use of the technique of esoteric writing—concealing things from inattentive readers through the use of various literary devices such as the use of deliberately inadequate arguments, and indicating his real meaning "between the lines"—has been well documented by Strauss, *Natural Right and History*, 206–9; Pangle, *Spirit of Modern Republicanism*, 137–38; Michael P. Zuckert, *Launching Liberalism: On Lockean Political Philosophy* (Lawrence, KS: University Press of Kansas, 2002), 82–106.

[52] Harvey C. Mansfield, "On the Political Character of Property in Locke," in Alkis Kontos, ed., *Powers, Possessions, and Freedom: Essays in Honor of C.B. Macpherson* (Toronto: University of Toronto Press, 1979), 29.

I look upon the argument there spoken of [in *Essay*, bk. 4, chap. 10], as not conclusive. . . . And since not all, nor the most of those that believe a God, are at the pains, or have the skill, to examine and clearly comprehend the demonstrations of his being, *I was unwilling to show the weakness of the argument there spoken of*; since possibly by it some men might be confirmed in the belief of a God, which is enough to preserve in them true sentiments of religion and morality.[53]

Having willingly made use of a defective argument in the *Essay*, Locke would obviously be willing to do the same in the *Two Treatises*, if he thought it would promote "true sentiments of . . . morality" in his readers. It is reasonable to conclude that Locke may have done just that, for the law of nature is Locke's basic moral law. The "fundamental law of nature [is that] man [is] to be preserved as much as possible," and "the preservation of all mankind, as much as in him lies, . . . is *everyone's duty*, and the true principle to regulate our religion, politics, *and morality* by." [54]

Locke explains his view of the problem of communication of one's thoughts at the beginning of his *Essay on Human Understanding*. He addresses himself there to two kinds of readers. One he calls the "hunter." The mind's "searches after truth, he explains, are a sort of hawking and hunting," and the hunter is someone "who has raised himself above the alms-basket, and, not content to live lazily on scraps of begged opinions, sets his own thoughts on work, to find and follow truth." The other kind of reader is the one who takes his thoughts "upon trust from others." This reader is "not following truth, but some meaner consideration; and it is not worth while to be concerned, what he says or thinks, who says or thinks only as he is directed by another." [55]

Locke explains that he started writing the *Essay* "for my own information, and the satisfaction of a few friends, who acknowledged themselves not to have sufficiently considered it [namely, the human understanding]." Two pages later, he continues: "I plainly tell all my readers, except half a dozen, this treatise was not at first intended for them." In other words, his initial audience was that "half a dozen" who, like Socrates, "acknowledge themselves not to have sufficiently considered," i.e., who know that they do not know. These are the hunters. But Locke eventually decided to "let it go abroad" to the general public.[56] That creates a problem, because most people "live lazily on scraps of begged opinions," as

---

[53] Locke, A Letter to the Right Rev. Edward Lord Bishop of Worcester, in *The Works of John Locke in Ten Volumes* (1801) (Elibron Classics, 1991), 4: 53–54, my emphasis.

[54] Locke, *Second Treatise*, chap. 3, sec. 16; Locke, *Some Thoughts Concerning Education* (5th ed., 1705, but corrected on the basis of earlier editions), ed. John W. and Jean S. Yolton (Oxford: Clarendon Press, 1989), sec. 116, emphasis added.

[55] Locke, *Essay Concerning Human Understanding*, "Epistle to the Reader," 6–7.

[56] Ibid., 7, 9.

Locke explains at length in the second-last chapter of the *Essay*.[57] He therefore had to write his book in a way that would reach both the hunters and the lazy. "I desire it should be understood by whoever gives himself the pains to read it," he writes. Wishing to be "as useful as I may, I think it necessary to make what I have to say, as easy and intelligible to all sorts of readers, as I can."[58]

But it is not easy to make a book intelligible to "all sorts of readers":

> We have our understandings no less different than our palates; and he that thinks the same truth shall be equally relished by everyone in the same dress, may as well hope to feast everyone with the same sort of cookery: the meat may be the same, and the nourishment good, yet everyone not be able to receive it with that seasoning: and it must be dressed another way, if you will have it go down with some, even of strong constitutions.[59]

How then does one "dress" the truth differently for different readers, so that it will "go down" without aversion? Locke discusses that topic, using the same swallowing metaphor, at the beginning of the *First Treatise*.

Locke speaks explicitly there of the need to conceal one's real opinions in order to be persuasive to all readers. He does so by discussing the manner of writing of Robert Filmer, the advocate of absolute monarchy who is Locke's target in the *First Treatise*. Locke observes that Filmer "commits the fault that he himself . . . objects to" in another writer, a certain Hunton, who, as Filmer complains, fails to define monarchy. Locke notes that just as Hunton fails to define monarchy, so also Filmer fails to define fatherly authority, which is the foundation of his whole argument for absolute monarchy. Locke concludes that Filmer made an intentional blunder, because he, Filmer, is aware that his real view of fatherly and kingly authority

> would make a very odd and frightful figure, and very disagreeing with what either children imagine of their parents, or subjects of their kings, if he should have given us the whole draft together, in that gigantic form he had painted it in his own fancy; and therefore, like a wary physician, when he would have his patient swallow some harsh or corrosive liquor, he mingles it with a large quantity of that which may dilute it, that the scattered parts may *go down* with less feeling, and cause less aversion.[60]

---

[57] Locke, *Essay*, bk. 4, chap. 20.
[58] Locke, *Essay*, "Epistle to the Reader," 9.
[59] Ibid., 8.
[60] Locke, *First Treatise*, chap. 2, sec. 7, my emphasis.

Let us apply Locke's observation about Filmer to Locke himself. As we have seen, he fails to provide the real foundation of his doctrine of the law of nature in the *Second Treatise*—at least in the passages we have discussed so far. Perhaps there is something "odd and frightful" in Locke's true understanding of the law of nature. Locke compares Filmer to a "wary physician," who presents his "harsh" argument in a way that conceals its real import, so that it will "go down with less feeling, and cause less aversion." Locke was a practicing physician, and he was certainly "wary." He follows Filmer's example himself, as we see in the quotation from the *Essay*, where he admits that he too uses arguments that have been "dressed" to make them "go down" more easily. Later in the *Essay*, Locke writes, "'Tis evident how much men love to deceive, and be deceived." People live in delusion—Plato's cave—and they like it that way. "And 'tis in vain to find fault with those arts of deceiving, wherein men find pleasure to be deceived."[61]

I conclude that Locke was aware of the limitations of the arguments for the law of nature in the *Second Treatise*. He seems to have thought them "useful" as long as they were persuasive, thereby confirming his readers in "true sentiments of religion and morality." The law of nature is a moral doctrine and, so far as God is the author of nature, it is also a religious doctrine. We will consider presently additional reasons why Locke did not wish to state explicitly the true ground of his argument for the law of nature, especially in the *Second Treatise*, probably the one book of his that would most likely be read by those who are content with opinions lazily acquired from the "alms basket."

Locke's arguments for a natural law right to liberty from equality of talents and equal knowledge of the law are likely to appeal to people who are not born into the ruling elite of a society, and whose spirited pride inclines them against the view that some people are born to rule and others born to submit. And the divine workmanship argument is likely to be attractive to religious believers among Locke's readers. Here, perhaps, we get a glimpse of part of Locke's strategy: to persuade Christians that their faith supports the idea of the law of nature, and to persuade non-Christians that reason, in this respect, does not conflict with the teachings of faith.

VI. The *First Treatise* Argument from Strong Natural Passions

Given the absence of a rational foundation for the law of nature in the *Second Treatise*, Locke drives us back to the *First Treatise*. At first glance, the *First Treatise* is both boring and irrelevant, so one is tempted to ignore it. It is *boring* because much of it consists of long-winded arguments

---

[61] Locke, *Essay*, bk. 3, chap. 10, sec. 34.

against a position (divine-right absolute monarchy) that no one takes seriously anymore. It seems *irrelevant* because the question of the law of nature, supposedly discovered by reason, seems to be unrelated to the faith-based claims discussed in the *First Treatise*.

However, Locke does address the law of nature in chapter 9. The chapter begins with a tedious discussion of whether, according to the Bible, Adam's supposed right to absolute monarchy does or does not pass on to his heirs. To explain his own understanding of children's right of inheritance, Locke suddenly turns to an argument from reason alone:

> God, I say, having made man and the world thus, spoke to him, (that is) directed him by his senses and reason ... to the use of those things, which were serviceable for his subsistence, and given him as the means of his preservation. And therefore ... man had a right to a use of the creatures, by the will and grant of God. For the desire, strong desire, of preserving his life and being, having been planted in him as a principle of action by God himself, reason, which was the voice of God in him, could not but teach him and assure him, that pursuing that natural inclination he had to preserve his being, he followed the will of his maker.[62]

In this passage, the term "God" is used as an equivalent to "nature," for God "spoke" to man through his nature, his senses and reason.[63] God planted in human nature a strong desire for self-preservation, from which reason concludes "that pursuing that natural inclination ... he followed the will of his maker, and therefore had a right" to make use of the things in the world to preserve himself. This strong desire of self-preservation, Locke continues, "is the foundation of a right to the creatures for the particular support and use of each individual person himself."[64]

The argument here promises to be the explanation of Locke's divine workmanship argument that we looked for in vain in the *Second Treatise*. Locke's claim ("I say") is that if our "maker" planted in us a "strong desire," it must be permissible to act on that desire and to appropriate the things we need ("food and raiment"[65]) to achieve the object of that strong desire for self-preservation.

Applying the argument to the question at hand, Locke then asks on what ground children have a right to inherit their parents' property. He answers that it must be something "natural": "God planted in men, and wrought into the very principles of their nature," a second "strong desire," namely, "propagating their kind, and continuing themselves in their posterity, and

[62] Locke, *First Treatise*, chap. 9, sec. 86.
[63] Accordingly, Locke uses the phrase "God and nature" twice in the pages immediately following the passage quoted here (ibid., chap. 9, sections 90 and 93).
[64] Ibid., chap. 9, sec. 86.
[65] Ibid.

this gives children a title to share in the property of their parents, and a right to inherit." He adds this explanation: "men being by a like obligation bound to preserve what they have begotten, as to preserve themselves, their issue come to have a right in the goods they are possessed of."[66]

The sentence just quoted is obscure. Locke is saying that there is a "like obligation" to preserve oneself and to preserve one's offspring. What makes the obligation "like"? In the case of self-preservation, we were told in section 86 that the obligation follows from the "natural inclination he [man] had to preserve his being." In the case of preserving one's offspring, the obligation is "like" because it too follows from a natural inclination, namely, of "continuing themselves in their posterity." From the point of view of the parent, the child is another self. A few pages later, Locke mentions that parents are "taught by natural love and tenderness to provide for them [their children], *as a part of themselves*" (my emphasis).[67]

In both cases—self-preservation and procreation—Locke repeats the phrase "strong desire." Considering the "strong desire" for self-preservation, reason concludes that there is a right to "property in the creatures," for example in animals that we kill and eat. Locke implies that reason's similar assessment of the "strong desire" for self-perpetuation leads to the conclusion that parents have a right to generate and provide for their offspring, whom they regard "as a part of themselves." In both cases, what is a right from one point of view— that of the person who wants to preserve or to perpetuate himself—is an obligation from another. If life is good, we have an obligation to acquire "things fit for food and raiment" to avoid the evil of death.[68] By parallel reasoning, the parents' right to provide for their offspring is also an obligation. From the child's point of view, the parents' obligation is a right to be cared for, including a right to inherit. "[T]his right of being nourished and maintained by their parents, ... God and nature has given to children, and obliged parents to as a duty."[69] In a nearby passage, Locke links this discussion of rights and duties explicitly to the law of nature: children "have, by the law of nature, and right of inheritance," a title in their parents' goods after they die.[70]

In one case Locke derives a self-interested right (to eat meat) from a self-interested passion (to survive). In the other case Locke derives an apparently unselfish duty (to care for one's child) from a selfish passion (to perpetuate oneself through one's offspring). Both are equally grounded in strong passions of the individual, ultimately rooted in the desire for self-preservation.

[66] Ibid., chap. 9, sec. 88.
[67] Ibid., chap. 9, sections 88, 97
[68] Ibid., chap. 9, sections 86, 88, 92.
[69] Ibid., chap. 9, sec. 90.
[70] Ibid., chap. 9, sec. 91.

Locke's treatment of the parental desire to have children—"propagating their kind, and continuing themselves in their posterity"[71]—is similar to Aristotle's. He too argues that the desire to produce offspring arises "from a natural striving to leave behind another that is like oneself."[72] Aristotle also anticipates Locke's description of parental love of their children in terms of self-love. Aristotle writes that poets love their poems for the same reason that benefactors love to benefit people and parents love their children: "we exist by means of activity (for this consists in living and acting). And in his activity, the maker of something somehow *is* the work; he therefore feels affection for the work because he feels affection also for his own existence."[73] For Locke, "natural love and tenderness" leads parents to provide for children "as a part of themselves."[74] Locke and Aristotle both know well that parents sometimes sacrifice themselves for their offspring, but for both men, that apparent selflessness is animated by a more fundamental self-love.

To return to Locke's argument, it seems that the *strength* of the two strong passions (self-preservation and self-perpetuation) is the sole ground of the natural *right* (permission) to eat meat and to procreate, and therefore also of the obligation (duty) requiring us to preserve ourselves and our children. But if that is Locke's position, what about other strong passions that are given to us by nature, such as the love of domination? Later in the *First Treatise*, Locke speaks of "man's *natural* ambition, which of its self is but too keen" (my emphasis).[75] He also stresses both the strength and naturalness of this passion in *Some Thoughts Concerning Education*: "children love liberty. . . . I now tell you they love something more: and that is dominion. . . . This love of power and dominion shows itself very early. . . ."[76] Does Locke's argument legitimize tyrannical ambition?

The answer is no. Locke's argument is that *reason* infers the right to eat meat from the passion for self-preservation. Locke evidently means that if the desire is to be the foundation of a right and an obligation, reason must evaluate the desire and pronounce it to be good. It must lead toward things "necessary or useful to [one's] being."[77] Locke is speaking here not merely of things "necessary" for mere existence, but also things "useful to his being," "for the subsistence *and comfort* of his life," that is, for his well-being, his good.[78]

[71] Ibid., chap. 9, sec. 88.
[72] Aristotle, *The Politics*, trans. Carnes Lord (Chicago: University of Chicago Press, 1984), bk. 1, chap. 2.
[73] Aristotle, *Nicomachean Ethics*, trans. Robert C. Bartlett and Susan D. Collins (Chicago: University of Chicago Press, 2011), bk. 9, chap. 7, 1168a7–9.
[74] Locke, *First Treatise*, chap. 9, sec. 97.
[75] Ibid., chap. 11, sec. 106.
[76] Locke, *Some Thoughts Concerning Education*, sec. 104.
[77] Locke, *First Treatise*, chap. 9, sec. 86.
[78] Ibid., chap. 9, sec. 92, my emphasis.

If reason must first evaluate a desire before it can be rightly followed, it follows that there may be some "strong desire[s]" that reason will pronounce to be *not* good. Two such desires condemned by Locke are "vain ambition, and *amor sceleratus habendi,* evil concupiscence," which "corrupt . . . men's minds into a mistake of true power and honour." "[E]vil concupiscence" leads men to appropriate goods by fighting instead of labor, while "man's natural ambition," if unchecked, is "but too keen [and] lay[s] a sure and lasting foundation of endless contention and disorder." Both passions lead to the "state of war," which is "a state of enmity and destruction." Those who are "rational" are not "quarrelsome and contentious." [79]

But we need to consider more precisely Locke's understanding of how reason should evaluate the passions. How do we know that war and violence are bad? Perhaps Achilles was right in rejecting obscure longevity and choosing instead a glorious life in the state of war, ending in violent death.

VII. WHY NATURE IS TOO AMBIGUOUS TO BE THE STANDARD

One plausible answer to the question—how does reason know what is right?—is that there is a standard established by nature that reason discovers. The very expressions "law of *nature*" and "*natural* right" seem to confirm that suggestion. But in fact, Locke shows that nature by itself is too ambiguous to guide human life.

Locke takes up the question whether nature can be a standard in chapter 6 of the *First Treatise.* This chapter is a critique of Filmer's assertion that fathers rightfully have unlimited power over their children. In the course of his discussion, Locke remarks that even wolves "obey God and *nature* in being tender and careful of their offspring," but that human fathers sometimes murder their own children. Locke calls this the "most *unnatural* murder, human nature is capable of" (my emphasis). [80] Locke then offers the reader a lurid account of Peruvian Indians who "made their captives [taken in war] their mistresses, and choicely nourished the children they had by them, till about thirteen years old they butchered and ate them; and they served the mothers after the same fashion, when they grew past child bearing, and ceased to bring them any more roasters." [81] Quoting Psalm 106, Locke recalls that even in the Bible the Israelites "shed innocent blood, even the blood of their sons and of their daughters, when they sacrificed unto the idols of Canaan." [82]

---

[79] Locke, *Second Treatise,* chap. 8, sec. 111; *First Treatise,* chap. 11, sec. 106; *Second Treatise,* chap. 3, sec. 16;

[80] Locke, *First Treatise,* chap. 6, sec. 57.

[81] Ibid., chap. 6, sec. 56.

[82] Ibid., chap. 6, sec. 58, quoting Psalm 106:38.

Considering such terrible practices, Locke remarks that one might "have reason to think, that the woods and forests, where the irrational untaught inhabitants *keep right by following nature,* are fitter to give us rules, than cities and palaces, where those that call themselves civil and rational, go out of their way, by the authority of example" (my emphasis).[83] He implies that human beings could avoid such savage cruelty if only they would "follow ... nature." In the next paragraph, Locke continues with his argument that nature can guide reason: "adultery, incest, and sodomy" are "sins," he says, because "they *cross the main intention of nature,* which willeth the increase of mankind, and the continuation of the species in the highest perfection, and the distinction of families, with the security of the marriage bed, as necessary thereunto" (my emphasis).[84]

These passages suggest that reason should be guided by nature in its judgment of the several human passions. The desire for self-preservation and parental love of offspring would be right because these desires follow "the main intention of nature." Murder of children and cannibalism would be wrong because they are "unnatural."

Locke himself indicates the problem with this suggestion by raising this question: "Is it the privilege of man alone to act more *contrary to nature* than the wild and most untamed part of the creation?" (my emphasis).[85] If "man alone," acts "contrary to nature," it seems that nature itself, human nature, is the source of this "unnatural" conduct. The problem, as Locke describes it, is that the imagination, together with the passions, lead human beings to make up and believe in "fashion" and "custom" (what the Greeks called *nomos*) that lead them astray. Man is

> a creature whose thoughts are more than the sands, and wider than the ocean, where fancy and passion must needs run him into strange courses, if reason, which is his only star and compass, be not that he steers by. The imagination is always restless, and suggests variety of thoughts, and the will, reason being laid aside, is ready for every extravagant project; and in this state, he that goes farthest out of the way, is thought fittest to lead, and is sure of most followers: and when fashion hath once established what folly or craft began, custom makes it sacred, and it will be thought impudence, or madness, to contradict or question it.[86]

Human beings are creatures of "fancy and passion," with restless imaginations. That is their nature. True, they have the capacity for reason, but,

---

[83] Ibid.
[84] Ibid., chap. 6, sec. 59.
[85] Ibid., chap. 6, sec. 56.
[86] Ibid., chap. 6, sec. 58. This aspect of Locke's analysis of human nature is well analyzed by Myers, *Our Only Star and Compass,* chap. 4.

as we saw earlier, in the discussion of human inequality, most make little use of it. By nature, reason is weak and passions are strong. Reason is generally "laid aside." Most people blindly follow supposedly "sacred" customs whose real origins lie in "folly or craft." One such custom is the Peruvian Indian cannibalism of one's own offspring. Another is the "fashionable" child sacrifice practiced by the ancient Israelites. Man cannot be guided by nature alone because human nature itself leads human beings into actions that Locke calls "unnatural" and "cross the main intention of nature." The root of the problem lies in human nature itself, as Locke states with perfect clarity in his *Education:* "the most shameful nakedness" in children is "their natural wrong inclinations and ignorance."[87]

Locke says that *reason*—not nature—is our "only star and compass."[88] Reason cannot follow nature because nature—meaning human nature— points in two directions. First, nature itself is the source of "fancy and passion," which lead to the bizarre or destructive customs that "it will be thought impudence, or madness, to contradict or question."[89] But nature points in a more civilized direction when it teaches parents "by natural love and tenderness, to provide for [their children], as a part of themselves."[90] Nature leads parents to love and defend their children to the death; but because of the weakness of reason, nature also leads parents to kill or eat their own children.

One sees the same tension inherent in nature in regard to despotic government. Locke argues that is it not good for people to be ruled by governors with unlimited power over them. Yet human nature itself leads people to submit without complaint to governors of that kind. Locke admits, in fact, that people are not *naturally* inclined toward political liberty and living according to the law of *nature.* Instead, "in the beginning of things," they experienced as children "the father's government of the childhood of those sprung from him . . . , [which] accustomed them to the rule of one man. It was no wonder," Locke continues, "that they should pitch upon, and *naturally* run into, that form of government, which from their infancy they had been all accustomed to" (my emphasis).[91] The law of nature, discovered by reason, must counteract the tendency of human beings to "*naturally* run into" absolute monarchy.

Locke's famously ambiguous presentation of the state of nature in the *Second Treatise* is another example of the difficulty under discussion. Near the beginning of that *Treatise,* Locke tells us that the state of nature is "a state of perfect freedom" and "also of equality," and that state "has a law of nature to govern it."[92] At the beginning of chapter 3, he leaves the

---

[87] Locke, *Some Thoughts Concerning Education,* sec. 90.
[88] Locke, *First Treatise,* chap. 6, sec. 58.
[89] Ibid.
[90] Ibid., chap. 9, sec. 97.
[91] Locke, *Second Treatise,* chap. 8, sec. 107.
[92] Ibid., chap. 2, sections 4, 6, 7.

reader with the strong impression that the state of nature is "a state of peace, good will, mutual assistance, and preservation."[93] As a matter of fact, "properly" or strictly speaking, Locke does define the state of nature that way: "Men living together according to reason, without a common superior on earth with authority to judge between them, is *properly* the state of nature" (my emphasis).[94] The state of nature would surely be a state of peace if people really did live together "according to reason," refraining from harming each other, respecting each other's property, helping each other in time of need, and conscientiously nurturing and educating their children.

However, as we saw earlier, in chapter 9 Locke states explicitly that the law of nature is mostly unknown and unenforced in the state of nature. The consequence is that each person is "constantly exposed to the invasion of others." Since most people are "no strict observers of equity and justice, . . . this state is very unsafe, very insecure." The state of nature is "full of fears and continual dangers."[95] "Properly" or by strict definition, then, the state of nature is a condition of peace governed by reason and law (the law of nature). But if the state of nature is understood as people living together without a government to enforce rules against mutual injury, then that state is likely to be violent and lawless.

Both accounts of the state of nature are true, but the term *nature* is used differently in each case. Carl Becker has a plausible suggestion:

> The eighteenth century had to appeal, as it were, from nature drunk to nature sober. Now the test or standard by which this appeal could be validly made was found in nature itself—in reason and conscience; for reason and conscience were parts of man's nature too. . . . Natural law, as a basis for good government, could never be found in the undifferentiated nature of man, but only in human reason applying the test of good and bad to human conduct.[96]

Locke's twofold account of the state of nature—what Becker calls "nature drunk" and "nature sober"—corresponds to what we have observed about the dual face of nature in the *First Treatise*.

Becker's suggestion is tempting, but there is a big problem with it, if he means to say that this is Locke's view.[97] Man is emphatically *not* by nature rational, according to Locke. Only one man—Adam—was rational from the start. The rest of us begin life as irrational babies, and we acquire

---

[93] Ibid., chap. 3, sec. 19.

[94] Ibid.

[95] Ibid., chap. 9, sec. 123.

[96] Carl L. Becker, *The Declaration of Independence: A Study in the History of Political Ideas* (New York: Knopf, 1948), 60–61.

[97] In ibid., 62–73, Becker argues that Locke is in substantial agreement with the "eighteenth century."

reason only through education and effort. "Adam was created a perfect man, . . . and so was capable from the first instant of his being to . . . govern his actions according to the dictates of the law of reason. . . . [But other human beings] are all born infants, weak and helpless, without knowledge or understanding."[98] They are in need of parental care and education, without which they cannot become rational. Further, most human beings acquire at best only the rudiments of reason, as we saw earlier in the paper. Therefore, Becker cannot be correct, at least not with regard to Locke, when he says that "reason . . . [was] part of man's nature too."

VIII. Is Nature Worthless?

Although nature as such cannot be a guide to life for Locke, one should not make the mistake of concluding that nature is altogether worthless. Some scholars attribute that view to Locke. Leo Strauss initiated this approach in *Natural Right and History*. In his presentation of Locke in that work, nature is all bad: "the negation of nature is the way toward happiness." Nature gives man almost nothing of value. "According to Locke, man and not nature, the work of man and not the gift of nature, is the origin of almost everything valuable." Mis-paraphrasing Locke, Strauss says, "nature and the earth furnished only the worthless materials, as in themselves." Locke actually writes "almost worthless"; Strauss thereby overstates Locke's negative stance toward nature.[99]

It is unlikely that Strauss himself believed this caricature of Locke. Strauss's other major published statements on Locke—chapter 8 of *What is Political Philosophy?* and chapter 2 of *Liberalism*—are much more respectful.[100] Neither chapter includes the implausible assimilation of Locke to Hegel ("freedom is negativity") found in *Natural Right and History*, or the absurd claim in the first chapter of *What Is Political Philosophy?* that Locke believed that he had found "an immoral or amoral substitute for morality" in "acquisitiveness[,] . . . an utterly selfish passion."[101] If acquisitiveness really were an adequate substitute for morality, Locke would have seen no need for a law of nature imposing on parents the duty to nourish and educate their children. Nor would Locke have written that "No doctrines adverse and contrary to human society, *or to the good morals that are*

---

[98] Locke, *Second Treatise*, chap. 6, sec. 56.

[99] Strauss, *Natural Right and History*, 248–51. The mis-paraphrase is from Locke, *Second Treatise*, chap. 5, sec. 43.

[100] Strauss, *What Is Political Philosophy?*, chap. 8, and Strauss, *Liberalism: Ancient and Modern* (New York: Free Press, 1968), chap. 2.

[101] Strauss, *Natural Right and History*, 251; *What Is Political Philosophy?*, 49. Strauss treats Locke and Hegel as if they are in agreement in *Natural Right and History*, 250–51: "labor is, in the words of Hegel, a negative attitude toward nature. . . . [F]reedom is negativity."

necessary to the preservation of civil society, are to be tolerated by the magistrate" (my emphasis).[102]

Why would Strauss deliberately misrepresent Locke? I cannot prove here what I am about to say, but I will offer a suggestion. His motive seems to have been pedagogical. Strauss's lifelong agenda was to restore philosophy in the modern world. Since recent versions of modern philosophy had led to the reigning positivism and historicism, both of which deny the possibility of philosophy (in the sense of ascending from opinion to knowledge), Strauss seems to have decided that the philosophers most likely to appeal to modern readers were the Greek classics. Plato's Socratic dialogues in particular could be presented as non-dogmatic and therefore as less vulnerable to the critique of those who dismiss philosophy as such because it is dogmatic. Strauss therefore wanted to instill in his readers, as their first reaction to his work, a moral revulsion against modernity, so that they would be more open to the attractions of classical political philosophy. But Strauss clearly wanted his more attentive readers, on mature consideration, to give Locke his due, as one may see especially in chapter 8 of *What Is Political Philosophy?*

By deliberately exaggerating Locke's hostility to nature, it was rhetorically easier for Strauss to situate him on the slippery slope leading from Machiavelli, who abandoned virtue as the end of politics, to Heidegger, who embraced radical historicism and Hitler. In order to give his readers an incentive to return to the classics, Strauss had to exaggerate the continuity within the history of modern philosophy in order to show, or rather to suggest, how the entire modern philosophic enterprise led to historicism and political irresponsibility. In Strauss's narrative, modernity did so in two ways. First, the early moderns supposedly rejected the idea that human nature is naturally oriented toward the good. To promote that view, Strauss found it useful to overstate the early modern opposition to the Socratic idea of philosophy and the permanence and goodness of nature. Second, by making the early moderns seem unconcerned with human excellence and preoccupied with what is low but solid, he made Rousseau's revolt against the Enlightenment in the name of virtue seem more plausible. Strauss's first point overstates the affinity between the "first wave" of modernity (which includes Locke) and the "second wave" (Kant, Hegel, Marx), thus giving the superficial reader the impression that modernity is a straight-line descent from Machiavelli to Heidegger and Hitler. The second point gives a somewhat moralistic account of why the "second wave" (starting with Rousseau) broke with the first without abandoning the ground it shared with the first.

In reality, however, the "first wave" did not abandon nature altogether as a source of good things and, properly understood, as a guide

---

[102] Locke, *Epistola de Tolerantia* ("Letter on Toleration") (Gouda, Netherlands: Justum ab Hoeve, 1689), 73, my translation.

to life; the "second wave" did. For example, in Kant, happiness is no longer the end of human life (as it still is for Hobbes and Locke); morality and freedom are. For Marx, nature is simply to be conquered in the course of the historical process, but nature remains a source of good for Locke.[103]

In spite of these and other difficulties with Strauss's public or popular doctrine, it has been taken to heart by quite a few of his readers. Pierre Manent, for example, argues that modern politics (in part established by Locke) "is founded on the emancipation of the will." Manent attributes to modern philosophy the view that human beings have every right to liberate themselves from the tyranny of any limitation, orientation, or seeming necessity imposed by God or nature.[104] This claim contradicts Locke's explicit denunciation of the doctrine of *pro ratione voluntas*, "putting will in the place of reason." [105] Peter Lawler argues that Locke would have had no objection to same-sex marriage,[106] although Locke says the "chief end" of marriage is "procreation," which is impossible for same-sex "spouses." Besides, Locke explicitly criticizes "sodomy" (it "cross[es] the main intention of nature, which willeth the increase of mankind") and opposes divorce when the children are too young to shift for themselves (marriage "ought to last, even after procreation, so long as is necessary to the nourishment and support of the young ones").[107]

These scholars are correct, of course, when they say that according to Locke, God and nature do not spontaneously provide for the needs of human life, and that human beings therefore have much to do on their own. Has any philosopher ever said otherwise? Human labor does have to transform the materials given by nature, many of which are, as Locke rightly says, "almost worthless, as in themselves" because they stand in need of cultivation and improvement before they can become useful for human life. But Locke distinguishes between the value of materials "as in themselves" and their value in regard to potency. Nature provides us with the crucial capacity for reason. In a passage quoted earlier, Locke writes, "we all call ourselves [rational], . . . yet we may truly say nature gives us but the seeds of it; . . . it is use and exercise only that makes us so, and we are indeed so no further than industry and application has

---

[103] Strauss presents the deliberately exaggerated teaching sketched in the last two paragraphs in *What Is Political Philosophy?* chap. 1, part III. It is no accident that this chapter of that book, because of its title, is one of the first things that Strauss's readers are likely to encounter. It was in my case.

[104] Pierre Manent, *Modern Liberty and Its Discontents*, ed. Daniel J. Mahoney and Paul Seaton (Lanham, MD: Rowman & Littlefield, 1998), 105, 99.

[105] Locke, *First Treatise*, chap. 6, sec. 51. The entire *First Treatise* is a refutation of the doctrine that will should take the place of reason. See especially chap. 6, sec. 58 ("reason, his only star and compass").

[106] Peter Augustine Lawler, "Natural Law, Our Constitution, and Our Democracy," in Ronald J. Pestritto and Thomas G. West, ed., *Modern America and the Legacy of the Founding* (Lanham, MD: Lexington Books, 2006), 213.

[107] Locke, *First Treatise*, chap. 6, sec. 59; *Second Treatise*, chap. 7, sec. 78.

carried us." [108] These indispensable "seeds" of reason are "the gift of nature," not "the work of man" (to use Strauss's expressions quoted in the first paragraph of this section of the essay). Locke would therefore agree with a remark that Strauss makes in a different context: "Man's creative abilities, which are more admirable than any of his products, are not themselves produced by man: the genius of Shakespeare was not the work of Shakespeare." [109]

Locke calls reason the "candle of the Lord," [110] a metaphor that captures perfectly the ambiguity of his conception of nature. God and nature give us the candle, but the means to light the candle—the matches—have to be found out by human art and effort. It is not the "negation of nature," as Strauss maintains, but the cultivation, *cultura,* of nature's "seeds," that makes us rational. Nature also beneficently provides human beings with the experience of pleasure and pain, without which, says Locke, "we should have no reason to prefer one thought or action to another; . . . And so we should neither stir our bodies nor employ our minds. . . . In which state man, however furnished with the faculties of understanding and will, would be a very idle unactive creature, and pass his time only in a lazy, lethargic dream." [111] This means that nature would not be beneficent if it provided us with everything we need, if we were not forced to respond to the absence of pleasure or the presence of pain. Paradoxically, scarcity and want are the condition of human virtue and excellence. Franklin Roosevelt was fond of saying, "Necessitous men are not free men." [112] Locke held the opposite view: were it not for necessity, we would be unfree. The "penury of his condition" in the state of nature "forced [man] to labour." [113] Without that spur, the seeds of his reason would have lain fallow, and he would never have cultivated it or his other talents. He would have been "idle," "unactive," "lazy," and "lethargic," like a pig wallowing contentedly in the muck. He would have been unfree, "enslaved in that which should be the freest part of man, the . . . understanding." [114]

Locke is not a Platonist. But Plato anticipates Locke's assessment of what human life would be like in the absence of appropriate cultivation of the natural materials of human nature and the external world. In book 3 of the *Laws,* the Athenian stranger describes the barely rational

---

[108] Locke, *Conduct of the Understanding,* sec. 6.

[109] Strauss, *Natural Right and History,* 92.

[110] Locke, *Reasonableness of Christianity,* chap. 14, p. 253.

[111] Locke, *Essay,* bk. 2, chap. 7, sec. 3.

[112] Franklin D. Roosevelt, Acceptance Speech for the Renomination for the Presidency, June 27, 1936, in Public Papers and Addresses of Franklin D. Roosevelt, American Presidency Project, www.presidency.ucsb.edu; repeated in State of the Union Message to Congress, January 11, 1944, ibid.

[113] Locke, *Second Treatise,* chap. 5, sec. 32, 35.

[114] Locke, *Essay,* bk. 4, chap. 20, sec. 4. Compare the philosophic poet Virgil: God "willed that our way be hard," but the harshness of nature had the beneficial effect of compelling us to undertake "pitiless hard labor," leading to the invention of "the various arts one by one." *Georgics,* bk. 1, lines 119-67, trans. Karl Maurer, in an email from the translator.

primitive condition of man. He is full of "naive simplicity" and "inexperienced in the many beautiful things that go with urban life" prior to the development of the productive arts and education.[115]

In the context where Locke speaks of the "almost worthless materials, as in themselves," he does not say or imply that all of nature is worthless or hostile to human life. He is speaking very specifically of breadmaking. It requires the "plowman's pains, the reaper's and thresher's toil, and the baker's sweat," along with many other things which he lists. From the point of view of what it takes to get a loaf of bread ready for the customer, it is simply a fact, and not a break with the premodern philosophic tradition, that the unimproved materials supplied by nature are "almost worthless."

Locke gives a judicious assessment of the value of nature's gifts in *Conduct of the Understanding*:

> even most of those excellences which are looked on as natural endowments will be found, when examined into more narrowly, to be the product of exercise, and to be raised to that pitch only by repeated actions. . . . I do not deny that natural disposition may often give the first rise to it; but that never carries a man far without use and exercise, and it is practice alone that brings the powers of the mind as well as those of the body to their perfection.[116]

"[U]se and exercise" would have no effect without the original "natural endowments." As noted earlier, Locke holds that deficiencies in "their natural constitutions," "their very natures," [117] makes it impossible for some people to become rational in any significant degree.

Locke himself seems to have been partly responsible for some readers' misunderstanding of the important ways in which nature is both good and bad for man, and not wholly bad or indifferent. In the *Second Treatise*, Locke lists three things that "labor makes the far greatest part of the value of," namely, bread, wine, and cloth.[118] But although "bread" and "clothing" are "more useful commodities . . . than acorns . . . [and] leaves, skins, or moss," wine is different. Putting wine in the middle of this list of three quietly draws attention to Locke's deliberate exaggeration, in the chapter on property, of the value of labor and the worthlessness of nature.[119] Wine is cer-

---

[115] *The Laws of Plato*, trans. Thomas L. Pangle (New York: Basic Books, 1980), bk. 3, 677a–678b, 679c.

[116] Locke, *Conduct of the Understanding*, sec. 4.

[117] Ibid., sec. 6.

[118] Locke, *Second Treatise*, chap. 5, sec. 42.

[119] Locke, *Reasonableness of Christianity*, 247–48: a writer sometimes puts something in the center of a list in order to indicate its importance. Locke's example is the Biblical letter of Paul to the Hebrews: "This description of faith (that we might not mistake what he means by that faith, without which we cannot please God, and which recommended the saints of old) St. Paul places in the middle of the list of those who were eminent for the faith."

tainly more valuable than water in the sense that it is more expensive. But wine is less useful to human life than water. If we had only wine to drink, we would live short lives as drunkards and die young. True, wine adds pleasure to life, but only by making us more imaginative and less rational. That is appropriate for recreation, but not for the important business of life. That requires reason, and water is more supportive of that than wine.

In an article on interest rates, Locke states explicitly that water is more valuable than wine:

> What more useful or necessary things are there to the being, or well being, of men, than air and water? And yet these have generally no price at all, nor yield any money: because their quantity is immensely greater than their vent, in most places of the world. But, as soon as ever water (for air still offers itself everywhere, without restraint, or inclosure, and therefore is nowhere of any price) comes any where to be reduced into any proportion to its consumption, it begins presently to have a price, and is sometimes sold dearer than wine.[120]

Locke adds that "the bounty of providence has made their production large." In regard to air and water, and in many other cases, "providence" or nature really is bountiful. So much for Locke's supposed view that nature is "almost worthless."

Why would Locke have deliberately understated the worth of nature in the *Two Treatises?* Perhaps he exaggerated nature's hostility to man "because he had to wean us . . . from millennia-old pampering (softening) due to belief in creation and providence." (Strauss applied this expression to Nietzsche,[121] but I believe it describes part of Locke's intention precisely.) Like Machiavelli and Shakespeare before him, Locke wanted us to man up, showing that we can solve at least some of the problems of human life if we adopt a more assertive posture toward nature and make better use of our talents. Providence made woman "bring forth her children in sorrow and pain," but it would not be "sinful" to invent "a remedy for it."[122] Locke anticipates modern anesthetics. Machiavelli laments that many "still have the opinion that the things of the world are in a mode governed by Fortuna and God, that men with their prudence are unable to correct them . . . and . . . that it does not do to sweat much over things but to let them go to be governed by chance." But although

> it could be true that Fortuna is the arbiter of half our actions, . . . she lets the other half, or nearly that, be governed by us. And I liken her

---

[120] Locke, *Some Considerations of the Lowering of Interest and Raising the Value of Money* (1691), in *Works of John Locke,* 5: 41.

[121] Strauss to Karl Löwith, June 23, 1935, in Strauss and Löwith, "Correspondence Concerning Modernity," *Independent Journal of Philosophy* vol. 5/6 (1988): 183.

[122] Locke, *First Treatise,* chap. 5, sec. 47.

to one of those violent rivers which, when they become angry, . . . destroy trees and buildings. . . . [I]t does not follow that men, when there are quiet times, cannot therefore make provisions with defenses and embankments.[123]

Shakespeare's comic heroes likewise show how prudent management of affairs can thwart the incipient tragedies that are always at hand to wreck our aspiration for happiness.[124]

IX. HAPPINESS AS REASON'S STANDARD

But if human nature cannot guide reason, where does reason find its guide? Locke gives us an important or rather decisive clue to his reasoning on the ground of the law of nature in an apparently casual remark in the *Second Treatise*, chapter 6. "Law, in its true notion," he writes, "is not so much the limitation as the direction of a free and intelligent agent to his proper interest, and prescribes no farther than is for the general good of those under that law. Could they be happier without it, the law, as an useless thing would of itself vanish." [125] True law—and this would obviously include the law of nature—directs those under it to their "proper interest," their "general good," that is, to what makes them "happier." Happiness is the standard, not nature, and certainly not the strength of the passions of self-preservation and self-perpetuation through offspring. Since Locke also says that "reason . . . is that law," [126] i.e., the law of nature, we may infer that the law of nature is a set of rules or rather guidelines, discovered by reason, "for the general good of those under that law." If those under it "could be happier without it," it would "of itself vanish," because reason would declare it harmful. A reasonable assessment of what promotes happiness, then, is, in this passage, Locke's sole standard for law "in its true notion." The self-interest of all, understood not as immediate self-interest or mere self-preservation, but rather as the good or happiness of all, is Locke's ultimate standard for reason, and it is the real basis of the law of nature. This is confirmed explicitly in a parallel passage in the *First Treatise:* "the positive laws of the society [should be] made conformable to the laws of nature for the public good, i.e. the good of every particular member of that society, as far as by common rules, it can be provided for." [127]

We will have to consider later the reasons why Locke thought it best to conceal or rather to de-emphasize happiness as the basis of the law of

---

[123] Niccolo Machiavelli, *The Prince* (1513), trans. Leo Paul S. de Alvarez, 2d ed. (Long Grove, IL: Waveland Press, 1989), chap. 25, 146–47.

[124] Two such comedies are *Measure for Measure* and *The Merchant of Venice.*

[125] Locke, *Second Treatise,* chap. 6, sec. 57.

[126] Ibid., chap. 2, sec. 6.

[127] Locke, *First Treatise,* chap. 9, sec. 92.

nature and the end that reason should look to. The most obvious point is that a merely consequentialist argument for morality—do it because you will be happier—is not likely to be a sufficient incentive to perform one's obligations when they conflict with one's apparent self-interest.

Locke leaves unanswered the question of the relation between the passions for self-preservation and procreation, on the one hand, and happiness on the other. Why would Locke suggest (in the passages in the *First Treatise* discussed earlier) that the law of nature is grounded in such common passions, if its real standard is something higher and seemingly nobler, happiness and our *"proper* interest," as opposed to something low, mere preservation and production of offspring? And how does reason know that human beings are better off if they follow these commonplace desires, as opposed to the rare ambition of those who aspire to do great things, even if at the expense of their less able fellow men?

To answer these questions, we must turn to Locke's only extended consideration of human happiness, in book 2, chapter 21, of his *Essay on Human Understanding*. Happiness is the goal of human life. It is that "which we all aim at in *all* our actions" [128] (my emphasis). In other words, the pursuit of happiness is the fundamental natural inclination—not self-preservation, as is often said of Locke.[129] "Nature, I confess, has put into man a desire of happiness, and an aversion to misery: these . . . influence all our actions without ceasing: these may be observed in all persons and all ages, steady and universal." [130] Locke defines happiness as "the utmost pleasure we are capable of." [131] In *Some Thoughts Concerning Education*, Locke repeats the thought: "The happiness that all men so steadily pursue consist[s] in pleasure." [132] That is because the good for human beings is pleasure. "Things then are good or evil, only in reference to pleasure or pain. That we call good, which is apt to cause or increase pleasure, or diminish pain in us." [133]

Locke seems to be (but is not) advocating a doctrine of crude hedonism. Anything that happens to give us pleasure, it might appear, is without further ado to be called good. The more we have of any random pleasures, it would seem, the happier we will be. Locke's argument seems to

---

[128] Locke, *Essay*, bk. 2, chap. 21, sec. 36.

[129] Pangle, *Spirit of Modern Republicanism*, 206, argues that the *Essay's* "emphasis on the pursuit of happiness" and not self-preservation is to be contrasted with the emphasis in the *Two Treatises* on "self-preservation and property" and corresponding de-emphasis on the pursuit of happiness. So far I agree. But Pangle draws a conclusion that the evidence does not support: that there is "a clear ascent from the former [*Essay*] to the latter [*Two Treatises*]." In the end, Pangle maintains, "preservation is the regulatory principle for happiness" in Locke's argument. My argument is the opposite: happiness is the regulatory principle for preservation, because happiness is the end of human life, and preservation is only part of the means.

[130] Locke, *Essay*, bk. 1, chap. 3, sec. 3.

[131] Ibid., bk. 2, chap. 21, sec. 43.

[132] Locke, *Some Thoughts Concerning Education*, sec. 143.

[133] Locke, *Essay*, bk. 2, chap. 20, sec. 2.

equate the ways of life of the noblest and the most despicable human types—the statesman, the philosopher, the poet, the lowly bourgeois, the thief, the drug addict, and the mass murdering tyrant—as long as the life in question is pleasant.

But that is not what Locke means. He rejects the equation of happiness with the enjoyment of any and every pleasure. He does so because our present choices for pleasure (or for the relief of pain) will lead to future pain if we choose wrongly. "[A]s to present pleasure and pain," Locke writes, "the mind ... never mistakes that which is really good or evil; that which is the greater pleasure, or the greater pain, is really just as it appears." The problem is that "when we compare present pleasure or pain with future (which is usually the case in the most important determinations of the will), we often make wrong judgments."[134] We fail to anticipate, and therefore to be moved by, the future pain that will follow our present wrong indulgences: "Were the pleasure of drinking accompanied, the very moment a man takes off his glass, with that sick stomach and aching head, which, in some men, are sure to follow not many hours after; I think nobody, whatever pleasure he had in his cups, would, on these conditions, ever let wine touch his lips; which yet he daily swallows."[135]

Locke explains this paradox by arguing that what "determines the will in regard to our actions" is not any remote consideration of happiness and misery, but rather the unease of present desire. "For desire being nothing but an uneasiness in the want of an absent good, in reference to any pain felt, ease is that absent good" (sec. 31). We feel the present pain (desire), and we are stirred to be rid of it (ease), not noticing or considering the more remote consequences of achieving that short-term "ease." "Nothing, as we passionately think, can exceed, or almost equal, the uneasiness that sits so heavily upon us" (sec. 64). And so "that absent [long term] good ... seldom is able to counterbalance any uneasiness ... which is present" (sec. 65). Consequently, people are foolishly "apt to take up with any pleasure at hand, or that custom has endeared to them" (sec. 68):

> [L]et a drunkard see that his health decays, his estate wastes; discredit and diseases, and the want of all things, even of his beloved drink, attends him in the course he follows; yet the returns of uneasiness to miss his companions, the habitual thirst after his cups, at the usual time, drives him to the tavern, though he has in his view the loss of health and plenty, and perhaps of the joys of another life. (sec. 35)

---

[134] Locke, *Essay*, bk. 2, chap. 21, sec. 63.
[135] Ibid. In the rest of this section, I will put all references to *Essay*, bk. 2, chap. 21, in the text, where I will provide only the section number.

This leads Locke to lament the "weak and narrow constitution of our minds" and "our narrow souls" (sec. 64) as the cause of this fundamental human problem: although happiness is our deepest and constant longing, we constantly do things that make us miserable.

But this gloomy state of affairs has a remedy, and that is reason. Reason *can* change the mistaken bias of our passions and direct them to "true happiness." "[T]he forbearance of a too hasty compliance with our desires, . . . so that our understandings may be free to examine, and reason unbiased give its judgment" is "that whereon a right direction of our conduct to true happiness depends." Consequently,

> it is in this we should employ our chief care and endeavours. In this we should take pains to suit the relish of our minds to the true intrinsic good or ill that is in things, and not permit an allowed or supposed possible great and weighty good to slip out of our thoughts . . . till, by a due consideration of its true worth, we have formed appetites in our minds suitable to it, and made ourselves uneasy in the want of it, or in the fear of losing it. (sec. 53)

The use of reason in our choices is consequently of the greatest importance for our happiness or misery. This is above all why reason should be our "only star and compass."[136] For "the highest perfection of intellectual nature lies in a careful and constant pursuit of true and solid happiness." We must take care "that we mistake not imaginary for real happiness" (sec. 51). A man who by a "too hasty choice" does something that will likely lead to misery "has imposed on himself wrong measures of good and evil. . . . He has vitiated his own palate, and must be answerable to himself. . . . The eternal law and nature of things must not be altered to comply with his ill-ordered choice" (sec. 56). Everything depends on the competent use of reason to enable us to assess the probable consequences of our actions and so to make the right choices.

This conclusion brings us back to the question of the status of nature. If happiness is Locke's standard, then nature is vindicated. Although man constantly mistakes his true interest and pursues happiness incompetently — because of the inadequacy of nature to guide him rightly — nevertheless it is the same nature that "has put into man a desire of happiness, and an aversion to misery," a desire that Locke admits to be man's defining "innate practical principle." If all goes well, reason, for which nature provides the seeds, working together with that fundamental natural desire, determines a man's choices in life. In this sense Locke continues to follow the standard of living according to nature.

---

[136] Locke, *First Treatise*, sec. 58.

X. Locke's Denial of a Single Highest Good

We seem finally to have reached the desired explanation for Locke's claim, in the *First Treatise*, that reason approves of the passions of self-preservation and procreation. We would only have to fill in the details of how the choices following from these passions produce happiness. Locke's hedonism properly understood would then lead human beings, by consequentialist reasoning, to a moral law that promotes parental care of offspring and mutual respect for each other's life, liberty, and estate.

But a major obstacle stands in the way of that conclusion. In one of the most famous passages of the *Essay*, Locke denies the existence of a highest good for human beings: "the philosophers of old did in vain inquire, whether *summum bonum* consisted in riches, or bodily delights, or virtue, or contemplation: and they might have as reasonably disputed, whether the best relish were to be found in apples, plums, or nuts, and have divided themselves into sects upon it." Since different people have different palates, what is pleasant to the taste of one may be repulsive to another. "Cheese or lobsters, . . . though very agreeable and delicious fare to some, are to others extremely nauseous and offensive."[137]

Locke appears to endorse a simplistic relativism in this almost shocking statement. He seems to be contradicting everything we have just discussed. If people are so different from one another, it would seem that there can be no intelligible account of the human good. Yet in the passages quoted on the past few pages, we have seen that Locke emphatically asserts that "the highest perfection of our intellectual nature" is something that really exists, and that it "lies in a careful and constant pursuit of true and solid happiness."[138] How can we reconcile Locke's apparent relativism with his insistence that happiness is something "true and solid" that reason is able to discover? In spite of his assurances to the contrary, is Locke preparing the way for that well-known pronouncement of the U.S. Supreme Court, that there is a fundamental right to "define one's own concept of existence, of meaning, of the universe, and of the mystery of human life"?[139]

Locke clarifies his argument against a *summum bonum* with a revealing image: "Men may choose different things, and yet all choose right; supposing them only like a company of poor insects; whereof some are bees, delighted with flowers and their sweetness; others beetles, delighted with other kinds of viands. . . ."[140] In Locke's metaphor, human beings are like two categories of insects: bees seeking the sweetness of flowers, and bee-

---

[137] Locke, *Essay*, bk. 2, ch. 21, sec. 55.

[138] Ibid., bk. 2, ch. 21, sec. 51.

[139] *Lawrence v. Texas*, 539 U.S. 558, 574 (2003) (majority opinion of Justice Anthony Kennedy).

[140] Locke, *Essay*, bk. 2, chap. 21, sec. 55. The context of Locke's remark is the assumption, which he verbally denies in the passage in question, that there is no pleasure or pain in a life after death. My argument in the text does not depend on the existence or nonexistence of an afterlife, because Locke's contrast holds good either way.

tles living on other kinds of food, unnamed by Locke. (Beetles often feed on decaying organic matter such as feces.) At the beginning of the *Essay,* in the "Epistle to the Reader," Locke describes himself as a "hunter" after truth. The hunter's delight is said to be "greater and more constant" than any other: "the UNDERSTANDING . . . as it is the most elevated faculty of the soul, so it is employed with a greater and more constant delight than any of the other[s]. . . . [E]very moment of . . . [the hunter's] pursuit will reward his pains with some delight."[141] In the dedicatory epistle to the *Essay,* Locke compares his book to a "basket of flowers,"[142] thereby connecting the hunter's way of life with that of the flower-seeking bees.

Locke's simile suggests that there are two human types: "bees" and "beetles." A few pages earlier, Locke had mentioned as examples two human types: the "studious man" and the "epicure." The "studious man" aims at "the delight of knowledge," like the hunter of the "Epistle to the Reader." But the epicure places "his satisfaction in sensual pleasures."[143] In his discussion of the epicure and the studious man, Locke remarks that, as "for the pleasures of sense, they have too many followers" for anyone to doubt their existence.[144] Is this the human equivalent of dung-eating beetles? Could Locke be suggesting that most people are "beetles," who, if they were free to indulge their hearts' desire, would seek out nothing but degraded sensual pleasures? Locke makes no explicit judgment on whether bees make a better dietary choice than beetles. Both eat the food that is suitable for them. But the difference between sweet-smelling flowers and foul excrement suggests that the bees have the better of it. One is reminded of Machiavelli's famous letter to Vettori: "On the coming of evening, I return to my house and enter my study. . . . I enter the ancient courts of ancient men, where, received by them with affection, I feed on that food which only is mine, and which I was born for, where I am not ashamed to speak with them . . . ; and they in their kindness answer me."[145] Few are born for the food of the greatest minds.

But is it really true that in Locke's writings, mankind faces the stark choice between the heights of intellectual insight ("bees") and the depths of degraded sensuality ("beetles")? If we look at the works in which Locke treats education, we find not just two but three major human types, corresponding to his three kinds of education. For the vulgar, Locke advocates a religious education, discussed in *The Reasonableness of Christianity.* Locke explains there that the "bulk of mankind" needs religious instruction because using reason to determine how to live requires "long, and sometimes intricate deductions. . . . Such trains of reasonings the

[141] Locke, *Essay,* "Epistle to the Reader," 6.
[142] Locke, *Essay,* "Epistle Dedicatory," 3.
[143] Locke, *Essay,* bk. 2, chap. 21, sec. 43.
[144] Ibid.
[145] Machiavelli, letter to Vettori, Dec. 10, 1513, in *Machiavelli: The Chief Works and Others,* trans. Allan Gilbert (Durham: Duke University Press, 1965), 2: 929.

greatest part of mankind have neither leisure to weigh; nor, for want of education and use, skill to judge of." [146] He continues,

> The greatest part of mankind want leisure or capacity for demonstration; nor can they carry a train of proofs. . . . And you may as soon hope to have all the day-labourers and tradesmen, the spinsters and dairy maids perfect mathematicians, as to have them perfect in ethics this way. Hearing plain commands, is the sure and only course to bring them to obedience and practice. The greatest part cannot know, and therefore they must believe. . . . [G]iving plain and direct rules of morality and obedience . . . [is] likelier to enlighten the bulk of mankind, and set them right in their duties, and bring them to do them, than by reasoning with them from general notions and principles of human reason." [147]

The second kind of education is that of gentlemen, described in *Some Thoughts Concerning Education*. Their pleasure lies especially in living in accord with that which is honorable, or, as the Greeks called it, *to kalon*. The gentlemen are to be taught by appealing to their love of honor and abhorrence of disgrace, by habituation through praise and blame:

> [C]hildren [should] . . . be brought to conceive, that those that are commended and in esteem for doing well, will necessarily be beloved and cherished by everybody, and have all other good things as a consequence of it. . . . In this way the objects of their desires are made assisting to virtue. . . . If by these means you can come once to shame them out of their faults, . . . and make them in love with the pleasure of being well thought on, you may turn them as you please, and they will be in love with all the ways of virtue.[148]

Love of pleasure ("the pleasure of being well thought on") is gradually transformed into love of "all the ways of virtue." The goal of this education is an internalized sense of the noble and base that can never thenceforth be erased:

> It is virtue then, direct virtue, which is the hard and valuable part to be aimed at in education. . . . This is the solid and substantial good, which . . . the labour and art of education should furnish the mind with, and fasten there, and never cease till the young man had a true relish of it, and placed his strength, his glory, and his pleasure in it.[149]

[146] Locke, *Reasonableness*, chap. 14, 266.
[147] Ibid., chap. 14, 279–80.
[148] Locke, *Some Thoughts Concerning Education*, sec. 58.
[149] Ibid., sec. 70.

Locke's third education is the "conduct of the understanding," that is, the education of the human mind toward philosophic reason and insight, discussed in his book of the same name.

These three kinds of education correspond to the three kinds of human beings discussed by Aristotle in his *Nicomachean Ethics*. First are "the many and crudest," who "appear altogether slavish," "choosing a life of fatted cattle." These are Locke's "epicures" or "beetles." Next are those who "pursue honor, so that they may be convinced that they themselves are good; at any rate, they seek to be honored by the prudent, . . . and for their virtue." These correspond to Locke's gentlemen, whose dominant principle is love of honor and the honorable. Finally, there is the "contemplative (*theoretikos*) life," that of the philosopher.[150] This is Locke's "studious man" or "hunter," who, "not content to live lazily on scraps of begged opinions, sets his own thoughts on work, to find and follow truth."[151]

Locke's teaching on the *summum bonum* might be acceptable to an Aristotle or a Plato, if explained in the following way. Each person has his or her own "palate," talents, and disposition, and is therefore fundamentally limited in life choices likely to be beneficial to himself. For that reason, the philosophic life cannot be the *summum bonum*, the highest good, for everyone. Only by considering a person's nature, the range of its passions and its tastes, its intellectual strengths and weaknesses, can a rational path to happiness for each person be found. No classical philosopher would advocate the philosophic life for someone whose inclinations lead him to the life of a farmer or businessman. Locke's book on education describes how parents should cope differently with children of different temperaments. "Some men by the unalterable frame of their constitutions, are . . . tractable or obstinate, curious or careless, quick or slow. . . . These native propensies, these prevalencies of constitution, are not to be cured by rules, or a direct contest; . . . though with art they may be much mended. . . ." And in another place he writes, "If it be any father's misfortune to have a son . . . [who is uneducably] perverse and untractable, I know not what more he can do but pray for him."[152] If a person does not have the talent and inclination for it, trying to live the philosophic life, or even the life of a gentleman, will be a waste of time, a painful labor that produces frustration, anxiety, and boredom. It will not be pleasant. It will lead to misery, not to happiness. We have already quoted Locke's sober observation that "their natural constitutions put so wide a difference between some men in this respect [namely, in their understandings] that . . . their very natures seem to want a foundation to raise on it that which other men easily attain unto."[153]

---

[150] Aristotle, *Nicomachean Ethics*, bk. 1, chap. 5, 1095b14–1096a5.
[151] Locke, *Essay*, "Epistle to the Reader," 6.
[152] Locke, *Some Thoughts Concerning Education*, sec. 101–2, 87.
[153] Locke, *Conduct*, sec. 2.

Plato is no less aware of this obstacle to the philosophic life. In the *Republic,* Socrates remarks: "those steady, not easily changeable dispositions, which one would be inclined to count on as trustworthy and which in war are hard to move in the face of fears, act the same way in the face of studies. They are hard to move and hard to teach, as if they had become numb, and they are filled with sleep and yawning when they must work through anything of the sort."[154]

If one adopts the idea of a single highest good for all human beings, one is more or less compelled to accept the harsh conclusion of Leo Strauss: "If striving for knowledge of the eternal truth is the ultimate end of man, ... the man who is merely just or moral without being a philosopher appears as a mutilated human being."[155] Strauss tentatively attributes that view to the classics in the passage from which this line is quoted. Locke resists this conclusion. He implies that belittling the nonphilosopher in this way is like criticizing a beetle for not being a bee. It is not in the nature of a beetle to be a bee. Aristotle says that "nature is an end: what each thing is—for example, a human being, a horse, or a household— when its coming into being is complete, is, we assert, the nature of that thing."[156] Are we then to conclude that everything in the world that falls short of perfection is mutilated or unnatural? As Strauss's remark implies, that would lead to the absurd or repellent conclusion that almost the whole human race—everyone that we would call "normal" in daily life—is "mutilated."

Locke's passage mocking the classical search for the *summum bonum* is famous and often quoted. But later in the *Essay,* in a passage that is noticed far less often, Locke writes that human beings "are both concerned and fitted to search out their *summum bonum.*"[157] In this passage Locke admits that there *is* a *summum bonum*—not one single good for everyone, to be sure, but a genuine highest good for each person. We quoted earlier Locke's remark that "the highest perfection of intellectual nature lies in a careful and constant pursuit of true and solid happiness."[158] The way of life that leads to happiness is indeed relative to each person, but there is also a highest good, a "true intrinsic good,"[159] that is unique to each person. Each of us must "search out" that good by the use of reason and observation.

Locke is certainly a relativist in the sense that the path to happiness is not the same for everyone. But he is not a relativist in the usual meaning of that term. Far from agreeing with the U.S. Supreme Court that each person may "define [his] own concept of existence, of meaning, of the

---

[154] *The Republic of Plato,* trans Allan Bloom (New York: Basic Books, 1968), bk. 6, 503c–d.
[155] Strauss, *Natural Right and History,* 151.
[156] Aristotle, *Politics,* bk. 1, chap. 2.
[157] Locke, *Essay,* bk. 4, chap. 12, sec. 11.
[158] Ibid., bk. 2, chap. 21, sec. 52.
[159] Ibid., bk. 2, chap. 21, sec. 53.

universe, and of the mystery of human life,"[160] Locke is reaffirming an insight that we find in the classics: that the philosophic life is best for those few who have the talent and inclination for it. To be sure, unlike the classics, Locke practices the virtue of civility ("a gentle, courteous, affable carriage towards the lower ranks of men")[161] by his reticence concerning his opinion that he enjoys a life superior to that of others. Locke does not trumpet his conclusion that he lives with the sweetness of flowers while most others are content to eat dung. Does it really make sense to crow that the life of the mind is best, when most have no capacity or desire for it? Locke refuses to insult those whose natures or conditions make them incapable of such a life. Besides, if they are not capable of it, that life really is not the highest good *for them.*

XI. CAN THERE BE A COMMON GOOD?

The upshot of Locke's chapter on happiness in the *Essay* seems to be that there cannot be a common good for society, for the same reason that there cannot be a single highest good (*summum bonum*) for everyone. People are different, and reason must search out the individual good for each. However, we recall the earlier quotations from the *Two Treatises* affirming the existence of a common or public good.[162] In the *First Treatise,* when the law of nature is enforced by "the positive laws of the society," it promotes "the good of every particular member of that society, as far as by common rules, it can be provided for."[163] In the *Second Treatise,* Locke ties the common or "general good" to individual happiness ("his proper interest," "happier"): all law, "in its true notion, is . . . the direction of a free and intelligent agent to his proper interest, and . . . is for the general good of those under that law. Could they be happier without it, the law, as an useless thing, would of itself vanish."[164]

One might wonder whether the law of nature truly promotes the happiness of every single person at all times and in all conditions. Locke alludes to this difficulty when he notes that there are times when death may be preferable to life, such as a condition in which "the hardship of his slavery outweigh[s] the value of his life."[165] Homer's Achilles had no doubt that a brief, violent life of war is far preferable to a long, uneventful existence at peace. Locke perhaps acknowledges the point when he says

---

[160] *Lawrence v. Texas,* 574.

[161] Locke, *Some Thoughts Concerning Education,* sec. 117.

[162] Locke uses the expression "common good" in *Second Treatise,* chap. 9, sec. 131; the equivalent phrase "public good" appears more frequently, e.g., chap. 1, sec. 3; chap. 7, sec. 89.

[163] Locke, *First Treatise,* chap. 9, sec. 92.

[164] Locke, *Second Treatise,* chap. 6, sec. 57.

[165] Locke, *Second Treatise,* chap. 4, sec. 23.

that civil laws made in conformity with the laws of nature only promote the good of everyone "as far as by common rules, it can be provided for." If Locke was thinking of the "palate" of the "great butchers of mankind"[166] such as Alexander the Great, he is perhaps tacitly proposing an alliance between the philosophers and the people who are not thirsting with ambition to be conquerors. For the members of this alliance—which would include the vast majority of mankind—the laws of nature would be unambiguously good. The happiness of the Achilles-Alexander-Caesar types must be sacrificed to that of the philosophers and the people. There is no perfect solution to the human problem.

There are many passages, in the *Two Treatises* and elsewhere, in which Locke goes beyond these abstract formulations and names specific things that are good for everyone, for example, life and property,[167] generating and raising children,[168] liberty,[169] and friendship.[170] Virtue is spoken of throughout the *Education* as something without which we cannot be happy, in part because it is an indispensable condition of love and friendship. Virtue makes a person "valued and beloved by others, acceptable or tolerable to himself. Without that, I think, he will be happy neither in this nor the other world."[171] (The parallel passage in Aristotle's *Ethics:* "The base person, therefore, does not appear to be disposed in a friendly way even toward himself, because he possesses nothing lovable. If, therefore, to be thus disposed is to be extremely miserable, a person must . . . attempt to be decent, since in this way he would both be disposed toward himself in a friendly way and become a friend to another.")[172]

How do we reconcile this seeming contradiction between the denial of a highest good in the name of idiosyncratic hedonism and the affirmation of a common good that sounds strongly moralistic? Locke's answer is not explicit, but it can be easily inferred. His argument about human diversity is only part of the truth. Human beings are also alike in important respects. To that extent they share a common nature and therefore belong to the same species. To that extent there *can* be a common good beneficial to each. The chapter on happiness in the *Essay* highlights the ways in which human beings are different, leading to the conclusion that happiness is relative to the individual. In the *Two Treatises*, in contrast, the focus is on those elements of human nature that are common to all. This is the real basis of the difference noted by Pangle that was quoted earlier[173]: happiness is an explicit theme of the *Essay*, while preservation and property come to the fore in the *Two Treatises*. The fact that human beings share

---

[166] Locke, *Some Thoughts Concerning Education*, sec. 116.
[167] Locke, *First Treatise*, chap. 9, sec. 86.
[168] Ibid., chap. 9, sec. 88.
[169] Locke, *Second Treatise*, chap. 3, sec. 17.
[170] Locke, *Some Thoughts Concerning Education*, end of "Epistle Dedicatory" and sec. 96.
[171] Ibid., sec. 135.
[172] Aristotle, *Nicomachean Ethics*, bk. 9, chap. 4, 1166b25–29.
[173] Pangle, *Spirit of Modern Republicanism*, 206, quoted in note 129 above.

some important common qualities makes possible a general agreement about some (but not all) of what contributes to human happiness.

In a well known passage of the *Essay*, Locke appears to raise doubts about the existence of species because of the difficulty of finding a definition that includes all whom we call (for example) "human beings." "[O]ur boundaries of species are not exactly conformable to those in nature." How then can Locke consistently speak of a common human nature? But Locke also admits that although the boundaries of species "whereby men sort them" are artificially made by us and therefore somewhat arbitrary, nevertheless nature does produce things with persistent common characteristics.[174] Locke's analysis of the imperfect rationality of human nature, discussed earlier in this paper, is part of his effort to classify the human species more accurately than has been customary. In spite of differences in regard to rationality, human beings do share enough common characteristics to make it possible to speak of a partial common good.

Reason is the link between the two complementary treatments of happiness in the two books. In the *Essay*, reason makes possible choices particular to each person that are more likely to lead to happiness and away from misery. In the *Two Treatises*, reason is equated with the law of nature, which is a collection of rules or principles that enable human beings in general to be "happier" when they follow it. In both cases, reason enables people to make choices that serve their "proper interest."[175]

The human nature that is common to all includes the body along with the passions that seek preservation of life and species. Providing for the body's needs, and restraining and directing the destructive passions, is therefore good for everyone and belongs to the law of nature. One should try to preserve oneself and, if it is not dangerous to oneself, also to preserve others,[176] for we benefit from the existence of others who are willing to live peacefully with us. Quarreling with them unnecessarily leads to war, violence, and death. Further, procreating and raising children belongs to the law of nature, for every society needs to produce and raise future citizens, and parents generally take pleasure in perpetuating themselves. Locke mentions children and friends as an example of things that are the source of pleasure not only once but all the time: "Thus the being and welfare of a man's children or friends, producing constant delight in him, he is said constantly to love them."[177] That can only happen if people have children and raise them sufficiently well to shift for themselves. Therefore, the law of nature includes the institution of marriage as a compact that exists for the procreation and nourishing of children, in which no-fault divorce is ruled out as long as there are children

---

[174] Locke, *Essay*, bk. 3, chap. 6, sections 30, 37.
[175] Locke, *Second Treatise*, chap. 6, sec. 57.
[176] Ibid., chap. 2, sec. 6.
[177] Locke, *Essay*, bk. 2, chap. 20, sec. 5.

who need their parents' care.[178] Adultery, homosexuality, and incest are to be discouraged, because they "cross the main intention of nature" by interfering with procreation or the integrity of "the marriage bed."[179]

Supplementing these fundamental rules in the *Two Treatises*, Locke's *Education* adds others, following the same principle—preservation of oneself and all mankind—that we find in the *Treatises*: "And truly, if the preservation of all mankind, as much as in him lies, were everyone's persuasion, as indeed it is everyone's duty, and the true principle to regulate our religion, politics, and morality by, the world would be much quieter and better natured than it is."[180] In that book, some of the rules or rather virtues promoting that end are honesty, industriousness, justice, moderation, generosity, courage, and civility. Preservation and self-perpetuation, along with friendship and the other blessings that follow those things, are goods that everyone can enjoy—as opposed to the austere delights of the studious man investigating the nature of the human mind. It is not the strength of the passions for life and offspring, but their actual contribution to the happiness of everyone, that makes them part of the law of nature.

If we follow these rules of reason, we will generally live longer. We will be more likely to live in peace with our fellow human beings. We will have a kind of bodily access to eternity through our children. Marriage and property will enable us to enjoy the sensual pleasures in due measure, i.e., in such a way that we can continue to enjoy them in the future. We will have a greater abundance of material goods, thus escaping the penury and pains of the primitive state of nature. And finally, we will possess the kind of character that will enable us to enjoy the pleasures of love and friendship, especially with our children.

In the *Letter on Toleration*, Locke offers a "consequentialist" presentation of his political teaching, in which the ultimate end of human life, happiness, is explicitly named as its basis:

> Besides the immortal soul, the life of a human being is also in this world, precarious, in fact, and of uncertain duration. To sustain it he must work for earthly conveniences, which he will acquire, or has already acquired, by labor and industry. For the things necessary for *living well and happily* [my emphasis] are not born spontaneously. Hence a human being, because of these matters, has another care. The wickedness of human beings is such that most prefer to enjoy the fruits of other men's labor rather than work to provide for themselves. Therefore, to protect a human being's acquisitions, such as riches and talents, or the things that furnish them, such as liberty of

[178] Locke, *Second Treatise*, chap. 7, sections 77–81.
[179] Locke, *First Treatise*, chap. 6, sec. 59.
[180] Locke, *Some Thoughts Concerning Education*, sec. 116.

body and strength, one must enter into society with others, so that by mutual help and combined forces, each may have private and secure possession of these things useful for life. . . . But human beings entering into civil society, by a mutual compact of assistance for the defense of the things of this life, may nevertheless be deprived of their own things, either by the robbery and fraud of citizens, or by the hostile attack of outsiders. For the latter evil, the remedy to be sought is in arms, riches, and multitude of citizens; for the former, in laws. And the care over all these matters, and the power, are entrusted by society to the magistrates. The legislative, which is the supreme power in every commonwealth, has this origin, is constituted for these uses, and is circumscribed by these bounds, namely, that it look out for the private possessions of the individuals, as well as the whole people and its public interests, and that it prosper and increase in peace and wealth, so that by its own strength it may be safe against the invasion of foreigners as far as possible.[181]

I quote the entire passage to show that in this overview of the teaching of the *Second Treatise,* Locke altogether avoids the language of the law of nature or natural rights. The explanation is wholly in terms of what is useful for human happiness ("living well and happily"). In the *Second Treatise* he defends the same political order in juridical or natural-law terms, keeping the consequentialist reasoning of the passage just quoted in the background. What the law of nature adds to the quoted overview from the *Letter on Toleration* is the language of moral obligation. In the next section I will explain why this rights-and-duties language is indispensable for Locke's project.

The fact that human beings share a common nature in part, but also differ in important ways, points to one of the characteristic features of the Lockean political order: limited government. If government seeks to provide the complete happiness of the citizens, as opposed to the conditions of happiness, it is trying to do more than it can do well. Government should aim at preserving each person's life and promoting its continuation through marriage and family. But the individual's own pursuit of happiness, which is largely left to private choice, will necessarily go beyond those minimal conditions.

XII. The Limits of Reason and the Need for Moral Law

If, as Locke argues, the choice of the best way of life for oneself depends on accurately evaluating and shaping one's desires, then it is up to each person to find out what choices are best for him or her. This is the task of reason. However, as we have already seen, Locke believes that the bulk of

---

[181] Locke, *Epistola de Tolerantia* ("Letter on Toleration"), 68–69, my translation.

mankind is irredeemably ignorant. Reason should be, but mostly is not, our "only star and compass." [182]

In the second last chapter of the *Essay on Human Understanding,* Locke explains more fully why it is impossible for most people to use reason to guide their lives. First, they lack the opportunity for the necessary study and meditation, because "the greatest part of mankind . . . are given up to labor. . . . [A]ll their whole time and pains is laid out to still the croaking of their own bellies and the cries of their children." Second, many people are simply too dull to be able to think capably: "there is a difference of degrees in men's understandings . . . to so great a latitude, that one may . . . affirm that there is a greater distance between some men and others in this respect, than between some men and some beasts." [183] Third, those who have the time and talent to cultivate their reason are often unwilling to do so:

> Their hot pursuit of pleasure, or constant drudgery in business, engages some men's thoughts elsewhere, [as does] laziness . . . or a particular aversion for books. . . . [Others,] out of fear that an impartial inquiry would not favour those opinions which best suit their prejudices, . . . content themselves . . . to take upon trust what they find convenient and in fashion." [184]

Fourth, those who do cultivate their reason often refuse to listen to its conclusions. Some of our opinions, going back to childhood, we revere as sacred. Sometimes rational insights conflict with our pride or other passions: "a learned professor, [will hardly allow] his authority of forty years standing, wrought out of hard rock, Greek and Latin, with no small expence of time and candle, and confirmed by general tradition and a reverend beard, [to be] in an instant overturned" by the arguments of a young "upstart." But what "keeps in ignorance or error more people than all the other [causes] together" is blind deference to "common received opinions, either of our friends, or party; neighborhood, or country." [185]

Perhaps most surprising of all, Locke concludes his chapter on error by noting that most people are not even in error about "those doctrines they keep such a stir about" because they have no opinions at all about them. Few of "the partisans of most of the sects in the world" have any clear idea of what it is they supposedly believe in, and for which they are perhaps ready to fight and die. Most "are resolved to stick to a party that education or interest has engaged them in; and there, like the common soldiers of an army, show their courage and warmth as their leaders

---

[182] Locke, *First Treatise,* sec. 58.
[183] Locke, *Essay,* bk. 4, chap. 20, sections 2, 5.
[184] Ibid., sec. 6.
[185] Ibid., sections 9, 11, 17.

direct, without ever examining, or even so much as knowing, the cause they contend for." [186]

In *The Reasonableness of Christianity*, Locke applies the lesson of this penultimate chapter of the *Essay* to the specific problem of the law of nature. He argues there that it is "too hard a task for unassisted reason to establish morality in all its parts upon a true foundation, with a clear and convincing light." It takes "long and sometimes intricate deductions of reason to be made out to them. Such trains of reasoning the greatest part of mankind have neither leisure to weigh; nor, for want of education and use, skill to judge it." [187]

But the problem does not lie merely in the difficulty of discovering the precepts of the law of nature. Locke admits that some of the ancient philosophers did more or less discover the law of nature: "there were up and down scattered sayings of wise men, conformable to right reason. The law of nature, was the law of convenience too: and 'tis no wonder that those men of parts, and studious of virtue, . . . should by meditation light on the right, even from the observable convenience and beauty of it." But the usefulness or beauty of rules for the ordering of society does not make them morally binding. The classical moral teaching "could never rise up to the force of a law." Why not? Because "a morality, whereof the world could be convinced . . . must have its authority either from reason or revelation. 'Tis not every writer of morals, or compiler of it from others, that can thereby be erected into a lawgiver to mankind." [188]

Locke is saying that philosophers (like himself) have long known the basics of the law of nature. The content of that law—refraining from mutual injury, the requirements of the family, the cultivation of the conditions of civic and personal love and friendship—has long been understood. Precisely because human beings are so unreasonable, Locke is saying, it was unreasonable for the philosophers to have expected their reasonable moral teachings to be accepted without backing them up with a doctrine of a lawgiver who rewards and punishes. Locke suggests that philosophers such as Aristotle were deficient in this important respect: "[T]he philosophers who spoke from reason made not much mention of the deity in their ethics. They depended on reason and her oracles, which contain nothing but truth. But yet some parts of that truth lie too deep for our natural powers easily to reach, and make plain and visible to mankind, without some light from above to direct them." In *Reasonableness*, where Locke modestly if only temporarily submits himself unquestioningly to the authority of Scripture, the "lawgiver to mankind" who rewards and punishes, the "deity" providing "light from above," is God, speaking

---

[186] Ibid., sec. 18.
[187] Locke, *Reasonableness of Christianity*, chap. 14, 265–66.
[188] Ibid., chap. 14, 270–71.

through Jesus Christ. Among other things, what makes Christianity reasonable, in Locke's argument, is its acknowledgment, as it were, of the irrationality of the "illiterate bulk of mankind." This acknowledgment can be seen in its blunt and simple teaching that human beings must submit to God's commandments, backed up with "something solid and powerful to move them," namely, a "view of heaven and hell." "Hearing plain commands, is the sure and only course to bring them to obedience and practice. The greatest part cannot know, and therefore they must believe." [189]

Another thing that makes Christianity "reasonable" is its content: "under the [Christian] law of works is comprehended also the law of nature, knowable by reason. . . . [T]he eternal law of right is of eternal obligation, and therefore remains in force still under the gospel." [190]

XIII. THREE KINDS OF MORAL LAW

Happiness depends on following reason. But since most people are incapable of understanding their own interest through their own reason, nothing is left but to appeal to their irrational passions, their fear of punishment and hope of reward. A parent governs his young child because "[h]e that understands for him, must will for him too." [191] Most adults, like children, also need commands issued by someone, divine or human, who is reasonable. The conclusion is inevitable. They may not be able to foresee the long term consequences of their foolish choices, but they can certainly be made to listen to a lawgiver offering rewards or threatening punishments.

From the argument of *Reasonableness*, one might expect Locke to conclude that all that is needed is Christianity. This impression seems to be confirmed in the *Essay*: "the true ground of morality . . . can only be the will and law of a God who sees men in the dark, [and] has in his hand rewards and punishments." [192] Insofar as the law of nature is merely a compendium of what is generally useful or convenient for human life, it is not a law in the proper sense. By adding rewards and punishments, Christianity takes the content of the mere "law" of nature and turns it into a real moral law.[193]

---

[189] Ibid., chap. 14, 276, 269; chap. 1, 2; chap. 14, 288, 279.

[190] Ibid., chap. 3, 18–19.

[191] Locke, *Second Treatise,* chap. 6, sec. 58.

[192] Locke, *Essay,* bk. 1, chap. 3, sec. 6, my emphasis.

[193] I leave aside the question of whether there are significant conflicts between the commandments of Jesus in the New Testament and the law of nature. Locke's general procedure, following the example of Thomas Aquinas, is to write as if there is a complete agreement, while occasionally allowing the attentive reader to notice that this is not always the case. Locke indicates several such conflicts in *Reasonableness,* chap. 12, most obviously on 218–19. See Pangle, *Spirit of Modern Republicanism,* 151–58. To the extent that there is a conflict, it seems that Christianity stands in need of being understood in light of reason.

However, later in the *Essay*, Locke deepens or modifies his apparent view that divine law, backed with heaven and hell, is the only effective kind of moral law. In book 2, chapter 28, we learn that there are three kinds of moral law. First, the divine law, in Locke's presentation there, is made known to us "by the light of nature, or the voice of revelation." It is "the only true touchstone of moral rectitude."[194] Whether we learn it from revelation or reason, it requires us to obey the law of nature.

But the divine law, even when backed by divine rewards and punishments, is not sufficient. "The penalties that attend the breach of God's laws, some, nay, perhaps most men, seldom seriously reflect on; and amongst those that do, many, whilst they break the law, entertain thoughts of future reconciliation."[195] There is the additional problem of unbelief, since the threatened punishments do not take place in this life. There is a need for more immediate enforcement than the promise of a remote prospect of heaven or hell.

Civil law, therefore, is a second and more effective kind of moral law. "This law nobody overlooks, the rewards and punishments that enforce it being ready at hand." But there are two problems with civil law. One is that its content is determined not by reason, but by the will of the lawgiver, who, in most times and places, is not very rational. In the *Second Treatise*, Locke shows how a government *can* be established whose civil law enforces the law of nature. But he cannot show that such a government is very likely to be established. In fact, most governments that currently exist, or existed in the past, fail to measure up to the high standard of Locke's civil society, which requires explicit consent to join, a strict rule of law, and periodic elections of part of the lawmaking body.[196] The second defect of civil law is that although its penalties are certainly impressive and "ready at hand," they are not always effective. "[A]s to the punishments due from the laws of the commonwealth, . . . [people] frequently flatter themselves with the hopes of impunity," as we see in the long list of crimes committed daily.[197]

That brings Locke to the third kind of moral law, the "law of opinion, or reputation." This is the most powerful moral law of all: "no man escapes the punishment of their censure and dislike, who offends against the fashion and opinion of the company he keeps. . . . [T]he greatest part [of mankind]," he continues, "govern themselves chiefly, if not solely, by this law of fashion; and so they do that which keeps them in reputation with their company, [and pay] little regard [to] the

---

[194] Locke, *Essay*, bk. 2, chap. 28, sec. 8.
[195] Ibid., sec. 12.
[196] Locke, *Second Treatise*, chap. 8, sec. 122; chap. 11, sections 136–37; chap. 11, sec. 138 (government cannot take "property," i.e., life, liberty, or estate, without the consent of the people in person or through elected representatives: Locke implies that laws imprisoning or fining criminals—depriving them of "estate" or life—must receive this consent).
[197] Locke, *Essay*, bk. 2, chap. 28, sections 10, 12.

laws of God, or the magistrate."[198] This "law of fashion" is so effective because everyone needs friends or at least associates. No one wants to live alone. The approval or disapproval of others will determine invitations to parties, decisions to hire and fire, the possibility of love or marriage, and the ability to make friends. Affectionate smiles, hugs, praise, and terms like "cool" and "nice guy," and on the negative side, smiles of contempt, insults, pretending not to see someone, refusal to shake hands, terms like "jerk," and simply treating a person as a "nobody"—these are among the rewards and weapons with which the law of fashion is enforced. Fashion, of course, is as arbitrary as the civil law, because both depend on mere will, and will may or may not be informed by reason. The law of fashion, even more than divine or civil law, must conform to the law of nature, if enforcing obedience to that law is to be achieved.

Locke's book on education teaches parents to make use of the law of fashion to instill into children a sense of honor and shame as the most effective means of getting them to acquire moral virtue. If the parents' law of fashion prevails, the children will be more likely as adults to resist the peer pressure that might lead them into self-destructive courses. But it is not only parents who can shape the law of fashion. Writers too can also have a big effect, as Locke laments in the case of Filmer in the *Two Treatises*.[199] All of Locke's books are devoted to changing the "law of fashion" among his readers. He aims to create a climate of moral opinion that will shame the immoral, the quarrelsome, and the contentious, and honor the decent, the rational, and the industrious. In particular, Locke's books are designed to change elite opinion, which in turn shapes common opinion: "if those of that rank [the gentlemen] are by their education once set right, they will quickly bring all the rest into order."[200] The leading men will form a consensus promoting sensible opinions about divine law (as sketched in Locke's *Reasonableness, Toleration,* and *St. Paul*), sound politics for promoting a civil law based on the law of nature (*Two Treatises, Toleration*), and the kind of moral fashion in society that will make people "better natured" (*Some Thoughts Concerning Education*). Locke succeeded to a remarkable degree, as one can see over the course of the eighteenth century, especially in the English colonies in America.

The conclusions of reason concerning rules promoting the public good—the law of nature—can become real moral laws if they come to be commanded by government and by one's family, friends, and associates, and if they are believed to be commanded by God. In regard to its content or precepts, the law of nature has its ground in an argu-

---

[198] Ibid., sec. 12.
[199] Locke, *Two Treatises of Government*, Preface.
[200] Locke, *Some Thoughts Concerning Education*, "Epistle Dedicatory."

ment from common convenience or interest. To the extent to which the law of nature is enforced and obeyed, the happiness of the members of society is promoted. But that law would remain undiscovered if the reason of mankind in general were to be relied upon. And when the philosophers do discover the precepts of the law of nature, these precepts remain ineffectual. The law of nature, founded in reason's judgment of what is useful for human life, has force only when it takes on a juridical or legal character. So although the mere law of nature is not a moral law in the strict sense (because "that which is ... necessary and essential to a law [is] a power to enforce it"),[201] it can become a moral law when its content is incorporated into divine revelation, civil law, or the law of fashion.

People who live in a society that has a sound religious doctrine, with the right kinds of political laws, and a sensible social consensus about right and wrong, have a good chance to attain personal happiness, within the limits of their own nature, because they will be compelled by these three kinds of moral law to do at least part of what their reason would have told them to do, if only they had been able or willing to use it.

XIV. CONCLUSION

I sum up the path we have followed in this essay. In the *Second Treatise,* Locke argues that we know what is commanded by the law of nature (that no one should take away another's liberty or harm him in his person or property) by considering the implication of the equality of human faculties, or by seeing that it is reasonable to allow people their freedom if they have equal knowledge of the law that they are under. But this argument fails because according to Locke himself, the disparity among human beings, in regard to the capacity to reason, is too great.

Locke also uses an argument from divine ownership—that God owns everything because he created it; that God forbids human beings from harming each other, although he permits them to harm animals and plants. But in the *Second Treatise,* at any rate, this argument is asserted with hardly any evidence.

I suggested that Locke's explanation for writing differently for attentive and non-attentive readers—the "hunters" and the "lazy"—can help to account for the deficiencies of these arguments of the *Second Treatise.*

Going a little deeper, we find in the *First Treatise* that Locke justifies the right to use the things of the world for life, and the obligation to care for one's offspring, by reason's approval of the strong passions for self-preservation and for self-perpetuation through children. But he cannot mean that the strength of the passions gives them their legitimacy, because he frequently condemns the strong passion for domination.

[201] Locke, *Essay,* bk. 2, chap. 28, sec. 12.

At first it appears that Locke's standard in the *First Treatise* for judging the rightness of these two passions is that they are "according to nature." But nature, as Locke understands it, cannot provide a standard for reason, because the same human nature that causes parents to love their children also leads parents, through their irrational but natural imaginations, to think it is right to cannibalize or sacrifice their own children.

Locke's real standard for reason's judgment of human conduct is happiness, as is briefly indicated in the *Two Treatises,* but is argued for at length in the *Essay on Human Understanding.* When reason is doing its proper job, it suspends the immediate indulgence of our desires, and stops to evaluate possible objects of desire with a view to long term pleasure and pain. Locke denies that there is a single common good for all human beings. But he insists that for each person, there are better and worse choices, depending on the particular qualities of the individual in question.

This notion of an idiosyncratic path to happiness for everyone would seem to exclude the possibility of a common good for each. But Locke says that the law of nature benefits all who are under it. There must, then, be something that human beings have in common, in spite of all their differences, that makes it possible for a set of common rules to promote the individual good of all. These common goods—such as life and procreation of offspring—are elements or conditions of happiness, but cannot constitute complete happiness, because of the reality of human differences in other respects.

Locke acknowledges, however, that rules promoting a common good are not necessarily moral commandments. That is a problem because most people do not reason well enough to discover the law of nature on their own. Nor, even if they did know the content of the law of nature, would they obey it consistently. In order for the law of nature to be known, and to be understood as morally binding, there is a need for a lawgiver who first promulgates it and then provides for rewards and punishments. Locke's analysis of the three kinds of moral laws shows us how the provisions of the law of nature can become popularly accepted as well as properly enforced: as a law of God, as required by government, and as sustained by the moral consensus of society in private life. If all three moral laws can sustain the conclusions of reason in this way, the bulk of mankind will be more likely to attain the happiness they long for.

Locke's several books contribute, each in its own way, to his complete argument on the law of nature. I know of no philosopher except Plato who directs his readers so pointedly from one book to another as they follow the thread of a complex argument that appears to be merely "scattered up and down in his writings"[202] but is in fact carefully arranged from start to finish.

[202] Locke, *First Treatise,* chap. 2, sec. 9.

Locke's reasoning on the law of nature leads us to conclude that he has a far richer understanding of the limits of reason, and the importance of nonrational features of society such as religion and customs, than he is generally credited with. Locke's critics sometimes reproach him for his failure to understand these things. Locke was far ahead of them.

Politics, Hillsdale College

MONTESQUIEU'S NATURAL RIGHTS CONSTITUTIONALISM

By Paul A. Rahe

I. Introduction

In 1900, on the eve of the twentieth century, E. L. Godkin—founder and longtime editor of *The Nation* and for sixteen years editor-in-chief of *The New York Evening Post*—surveyed the American political landscape, as he had so often done in the four decades preceding, and registered profound dismay. "The Declaration of Independence," he wrote, "no longer arouses enthusiasm; it is an embarrassing instrument which requires to be explained away. The Constitution is said to be 'outgrown.'" Those who once "boasted that it had secured for the negro the rights of humanity and of citizenship" now listen "in silence to the proclamation of white supremacy" and make "no protest against the nullifications of the Fifteenth Amendment."[1]

Godkin's observations were both accurate and prescient. They reflected the impact of Progressivism and forecast its consequences. He did not live to witness the 1912 presidential campaign. Had he done so, he might have been inconsolable. For the victor in that contest went all out in his campaign in an attempt to educate the American people in the principles underpinning the species of thinking that regarded the Declaration as an embarrassment, the Constitution as an anachronism, and white supremacy as a consummation devoutly to be wished. "We are in the presence of a new organization of society," Woodrow Wilson told prospective voters. This generation is witness to "a new social stage, a new era of human relationships, a new stage-setting for the drama of life," in which "the old political formulas" do not apply. "They read now like documents taken out of a forgotten age." Above all, he insisted, what Thomas Jefferson once taught is now out of date. It is "what we used to think in the old-fashioned days when life was very simple."[2]

Wilson's tone was patronizing. As president of Princeton University, persuaded that the older generation was "out of sympathy with the cre-

---

[1] Edwin Lawrence Godkin, "The Eclipse of Liberalism," *The Nation* 71, no. 1832 (9 August 1900): 105–6.

[2] Consider Woodrow Wilson, *The New Freedom: A Call for the Emancipation of the Generous Energies of a People* (New York: Doubleday, Page, and Company, 1913), esp. 3–7, 19–22, in light of Robert Eden, "Opinion Leadership and the Problem of Executive Power: Woodrow Wilson's Original Position," *Review of Politics* 57, no. 3 (1995): 483–503, and "The Rhetorical Presidency and the Eclipse of Executive Power: Woodrow Wilson's *Constitutional Government in the United States*," *Polity* 28, no. 3 (1996): 357–78, and see Ronald J. Pestritto, *Woodrow Wilson and the Roots of American Liberalism* (Lanham, MD: Rowman and Littlefield, 2005).

doi:10.1017/S0265052512000027

ative, formative and progressive forces of society," he had tried "to make
the young gentlemen of the rising generation as unlike their fathers as
possible." Now, if his listeners voted for him, he intimated that he would
do something similar as the President of the United States. To begin with,
he would convince his compatriots to get "beyond the Declaration of
Independence." That document "did not mention the questions of our
day," he observed. "It is of no consequence to us"—not, in any case,
"unless we can translate its general terms into examples of the present
day and substitute them in some vital way for the examples it itself gives,
so concrete, so intimately involved in the circumstances of the day in
which it was conceived and written." And, strikingly, Wilson made no
attempt to produce such a translation himself, for he thought the Declaration "an eminently practical document, meant for the use of practical
men; not a thesis for philosophers, but a whip for tyrants; not a theory of
government, but a program of action"—once apt, now no more than a
memory.[3]

Wilson would also attempt to persuade his compatriots to dispense
with the Constitution. For Charles-Louis de Secondat, baron de La Brède
et de Montesquieu, whom he mentioned by name, he displayed even less
respect than he reserved for Jefferson, and he had little use for the frame
of government established in the fledgling United States under the French
philosopher's influence. The separation of powers embodied therein, the
system of balances and checks, and the division of authority between
nation and state were, he thought, regrettable. "Government," he told his
listeners,

> is not a machine; but a living thing. It falls, not under the theory of the
> universe, but under the theory of organic life. It is accountable to Dar-
> win, not to Newton. It is modified by its environment, necessitated by
> its tasks, shaped to its functions by the sheer pressure of life. No liv-
> ing things can have its organs offset against each other, as checks, and
> live. On the contrary, its life is dependent upon their quick co-operation,
> their ready response to the commands of instinct or intelligence, their
> amicable community of purpose. . . . There can be no successful gov-
> ernment without the intimate, instinctive co-ordination of the organs
> of life and action. . . . Living political constitutions must be Darwinian
> in structure and in practice.

All that he and his fellow Progressives wished or desired was
permission—in an era in which "development" and "evolution" were
the scientific words—to interpret the Constitution according to Darwinian principle.[4]

---

[3] Wilson, *The New Freedom,* 41–54.
[4] Ibid.

Had E. L. Godkin lived to hear or read the speeches Wilson delivered in the course of the 1912 campaign, he would not have been surprised to learn thereafter that one of the latter's very first acts as President was to make white supremacy the rule within the federal government by segregating the civil service and requiring that future applicants betray their race and open themselves up for rejection by supplying a photograph.[5] Godkin was no less cognizant than Wilson of the connection between the Declaration of Independence, American constitutionalism, and the presumption that individuals by nature equal and free deserve equal protection and equal treatment under the law.

Whether Godkin would have mentioned Jefferson and Montesquieu in the same breath, as Wilson did, we do not know. The connection between the two is by no means self-evident. Jefferson is most famous for his statement of first principles, Montesquieu, for his contribution to the study of political psychology and political architecture—and it is by no means obvious that the latter was, like the former, an exponent of modern natural right. After all, Jean-Jacques Rousseau charged that Montesquieu limited himself to the sphere of positive right,[6] and David Hume thought him a rationalist on the model of René Descartes's great Augustinian admirer Nicolas Malebranche.[7] Some scholars argue that the French *philosophe* operated within the peculiarly modern natural-right understanding first laid out by Thomas Hobbes in the seventeenth century and subsequently taken up and refined by John Locke,[8] but it is by no means obvious that they are right.

[5] See Kathleen Long Wohlgemuth, "Wilson's Appointment Policy and the Negro," *Journal of Southern History* 24, no. 4 (1958): 457–71, and "Woodrow Wilson and Federal Segregation," *Journal of Negro History* 44, no. 2 (1959): 158–73; Arthur S. Link, *Wilson: The New Freedom* (Princeton, NJ: Princeton University Press, 1956), 243–52; Henry Blumenthal, "Woodrow Wilson and the Race Question," *Journal of Negro History* 48, no. 1 (1963): 1–21; Nicholas Patler, *Jim Crow and the Wilson Administration: Protesting Federal Segregation in the Early Twentieth Century* (Boulder: University Press of Colorado, 2004); and Bruce Barlett, *Wrong on Race: The Democratic Party's Buried Past* (New York: Palgrave Macmillan, 2008), 95–110. Compare Ray Stannard Baker, *Woodrow Wilson, Life and Letters Vol. IV: President, 1913–1914* (Garden City, NY: Doubleday, Doran, 1931), 220–25.

[6] See Jean-Jacques Rousseau, *Émile, ou De l'Éducation* (1762), ed. Charles Wirz, bk. 5, in Bernard Gagnebin and Marcel Raymond, eds., *Œuvres complètes de Jean-Jacques Rousseau* (Paris: Bibliothèque de la Pléiade, 1959–1995), vol. 4: 836–37. In more recent times, Montesquieu has even been described as a sociologist of sorts: see Émile Durkheim, "Montesquieu's Contribution to the Rise of Social Science," *Montesquieu and Rousseau: Forerunners of Sociology*, trans. Ralph Mannheim (Ann Arbor: University of Michigan Press, 1965), 1–64, and Pierre Manent, *The City of Man*, trans. Marc A. LePain (Princeton, NJ: Princeton University Press, 1998), 11–85 (esp. 50–85).

[7] See David Hume, *An Enquiry Concerning the Principles of Morals*, sec. 3, pt. 2, in Hume, *Enquiries Concerning the Human Understanding and Concerning the Principles of Morals*, 2d ed., L. A. Selby-Bigge, ed. (Oxford, UK: Clarendon Press, 1902), 197n. See also George Klosko, "Montesquieu's Science of Politics: Absolute Values and Ethical Relativism in *L'Esprit des lois*," *Studies on Voltaire and the Eighteenth Century* 189 (1980): 153–77.

[8] See Thomas L. Pangle, *Montesquieu's Philosophy of Liberalism: A Commentary on The Spirit of the Laws* (Chicago: University of Chicago Press, 1973), 20–47, and Michael Zuckert, "Natural Law, Natural Rights, and Classical Liberalism: On Montesquieu's Critique of Hobbes," in Ellen Frankel Paul, Fred D. Miller, Jr., and Jeffrey Paul, eds., *Natural Law and Modern Moral*

II. Natural Right

It is easy to see why some of Montesquieu's most discerning readers should be at odds in their understanding of the foundations of his thinking.[9] *The Spirit of Laws* (1748) is a work immense in size and scope, and its argument and structure are exceedingly complex. Like Montesquieu's epistolary novel, *Persian Letters* (1721), moreover, it is a literary work— playful, elliptical, subtle, and sometimes seemingly self-contradictory— designed, as its author once hinted, first and foremost to make his readers think, and not simply and solely to make them read.[10] When charged with obscurity,[11] Montesquieu at first expressed annoyance;[12] then, he intimated that his book was "a great machine made to produce an effect." There might, he observed, be "wheels" within the machine visibly turning "in directions opposed," but the "assemblage" does not "get in its own way" and the machine does not "bring itself to a halt." Instead, its "separate parts, which appear at first to destroy themselves, unite together for the object proposed." [13]

Playfulness and subtlety were not the only sources of confusion. Montesquieu also had to write with the censor in mind.[14] Indirection was sometimes on his part required. In some measure he had to conceal his design.[15]

Philosophy (New York: Cambridge University Press 2001), 227–51, and Zuckert, "Natural Rights and Modern Constitutionalism," *Northwestern Journal of International Human Rights* 2 (2004): secs. 2–26. For a partial affirmation and helpful qualification of this view, see Neil G. Robertson, "Rousseau, Montesquieu and the Origins of Inequality," *Animus* 12 (2008): 60–69.

[9] What immediately follows is an abbreviated restatement of the argument advanced in Paul A. Rahe, "Montesquieu, Natural Law, and Natural Right," Website on Natural Law, Natural Rights, and American Constitutionalism, The Witherspoon Institute, Princeton, New Jersey: http://www.nlnrac.org/earlymodern/montesquieu.

[10] See Charles-Louis de Secondat, baron de La Brède et de Montesquieu, *De l'Esprit des lois*, pt. 2, bk. 11, chap. 20, which I cite from Roger Caillois, ed. *Œuvres complètes de Montesquieu* (Paris: Bibliothèque de la Pléiade, 1949–1951), vol. 2: 225–995. All translations are my own.

[11] See Joseph de La Porte, *Observations sur l'Esprit des lois, ou L'Art de lire ce livre, et de l'entendre et d'en juger* (Amsterdam: Pierre Mortier, 1751).

[12] Charles de Secondat, baron de La Brède et de Montesquieu, *Mes pensées*, No. 2057, which I cite from Montesquieu, *Pensées, Le Spicilège*, ed. Louis Desgraves (Paris: Laffont, 1991), 185–658.

[13] Ibid., no. 2092.

[14] See Robert Shackleton, "Censure and Censorship: Impediments to Free Publication in the Age of Enlightenment," *The Library Chronicle of the University of Texas at Austin* n. s. 6 (1973): 25–41, which is reprinted in Shackleton, *Essays on Montesquieu and on the Enlightenment*, ed. David Gilson and Martin Smith (Oxford, UK: The Voltaire Foundation, 1988), 405–20, and William Hanley, "The Policing of Thought: Censorship in Eighteenth-Century France," *Studies on Voltaire and the Eighteenth Century* 183 (1980): 265–95. Montesquieu had considerable experience with the censorship apparatus: see Edgar Mass, *Literatur und Zensur in der frühen Aufklärung: Produktion, Distribution und Rezeption der Lettres persanes* (Frankfurt am Main: Vittorio Klostermann, 1981), 5–68, 139–205, and Paul A. Rahe, "The Book That Never Was: Montesquieu's *Considerations on the Romans* in Historical Context," *History of Political Thought* 26, no. 1 (2005): 43–89.

[15] On Montesquieu's mode of composition, see Pangle, *Montesquieu's Philosophy of Liberalism*, 11–19, and Bertrand Binoche, *Introduction à De l'Esprit des lois de Montesquieu* (Paris: Presses Universitaires de France, 1998), 8–27.

Given the influence exercised by the Roman Catholic Church, he had to be especially careful to remain in the vicinity (if not within the confines) of orthodoxy in his treatment of matters metaphysical, and, of course, he could not say anything overtly hostile to the French monarchy.

When Rousseau remarked that Montesquieu had deliberately side-stepped articulating "principles of political right," when he asserted that his predecessor had "contented himself with treating positive right under established governments,"[16] he was giving too much weight to Montesquieu's politic denial that he had composed his *Spirit of Laws* "to censure that which is established in any country at all"; he was accepting as true the latter's no less politic assertion that "each nation will find here the reasons for its maxims";[17] and he was understating the significance of Montesquieu's unrelenting campaign against prejudice, his open condemnation of despotism, and his readiness to criticize not only particular institutions and practices but forms of government as well.[18] When Hume mocked the metaphysical claims articulated in the initial chapter of the first book of *The Spirit of Laws*,[19] he failed to consider whether these were consistent with their author's account of the state of nature and of the emergence of political society in the two chapters immediately thereafter.[20] Neither of Montesquieu's two greatest contemporaries read him with sufficient sympathy, close attention, and care.

When, in his first chapter, Montesquieu contends that "to say that there is nothing just or unjust but what positive laws ordain or prohibit is to say

[16] Rousseau, *Émile, ou De l'Éducation*, bk. 5, in *Œuvres complètes de Jean-Jacques Rousseau*, vol. 4: 836–37.

[17] Montesquieu, *De l'Esprit des lois*, Pref.

[18] Cf., however, Robertson, "Rousseau, Montesquieu and the Origins of Inequality," 60–69.

[19] See Hume, *An Enquiry Concerning the Principles of Morals*, sec. 3, pt. 2, in Hume, *Enquiries Concerning the Human Understanding and Concerning the Principles of Morals*, 197n.

[20] These chapters have received considerable attention. In addition to the secondary literature cited in notes 7–8, above, see David Lowenthal, "Book I of Montesquieu's *Spirit of the Laws*," *American Political Science Review* 53, no. 2 (1959): 485–98; Mark H. Waddicor, *Montesquieu and the Philosophy of Natural Law* (The Hague: Martinus Nijhoff, 1970), 65–99; Jean Goldzinck, "Sur le Chapitre 1, du livre 1, de *l'Esprit des lois* de Montesquieu," in *Analyses and réflexions sur Montesquieu, De l'Esprit des lois: La Nature et la loi* (Paris: Ellipses, 1987), 107–19; Pierre Rétat, "Les Ambiguïtés de la notion de loi chez Montesquieu: Analyse du livre I de *L'Esprit des lois*," in *De la Tyrannie au totalitarisme: Recherche sur les ambiguïtés de la philosophie politique* (Lyon: L'Hermès, 1986), 125–35; Stanley Rosen, "Politics and Nature in Montesquieu," in Rosen, *The Elusiveness of the Ordinary: Studies in the Possibility of Philosophy* (New Haven, CT: Yale University Press, 2002), 14–53; Yoshie Kawade, "La Liberté civile contre la théorie réformiste de l'État souverain: Le Combat de Montesquieu," in Caroline Jacot Grapa, Nicole Jacques-Lefèvre, Yannick Séité, and Carine Trevisan, eds., *Le Travail des lumières: Pour Georges Benrekassa* (Paris: Honoré Champion, 2002), 203–23; and Stuart D. Warner, "Montesquieu's Prelude: An Interpretation of Book I of *The Spirit of Laws*," in Svetozar Minkov and Stephane Douard, eds., *Enlightening Revolutions: Essays in Honor of Ralph Lerner* (Lanham, MD: Lexington Books, 2006), 159–87. Also pertinent are Sharon R. Krause, "History and the Human Soul in Montesquieu," *History of Political Thought* 24, no. 2 (2003): 235–61 (at 235–52), and Krause, "Laws, Passion, and the Attractions of Right Action in Montesquieu," *Philosophy and Social Criticism* 32, no. 2 (2006): 211–30.

that, before a circle was drawn, all its radii were not equal," he appears to
be asserting that natural law is a deductive science. When, however, in the
two chapters immediately subsequent, he describes the stages by which a
solitary being is drawn by his passions first into association with other
human beings, then (and only then) into intestine war, and thereafter into
the institution of a state equipped with a system of political and civil right,
into wars between states, and into the development of a *ius gentium*, he is
sketching a hypothetical history meant to illuminate the logic underlying
human experience and to clarify the ends which the various types of law
are meant to serve.[21]

In the first of these three chapters, Montesquieu accommodates the
censor. In the second and third, where he might have alluded to the
Garden of Eden and the Fall in the manner of a political theologian,
he opts, instead, to recast Thomas Hobbes' alternative account of man's
original condition.[22] But, although he appropriates the Englishman's
premises, he turns them against his conclusions, offering an account of
natural right intended as a partial corrective to Locke as well. If Montesquieu was, as some suppose, a natural law theorist of a traditional sort,
there is little sign of it after the first chapter of *The Spirit of Laws*. The
evaluative stance that he adopts throughout the remainder of that work
dovetails nicely with the variation on the Hobbesian and Lockean positions that he outlines in its second and third chapters. It is, he inti-
mates, a dictate of what we would call objective natural right that one
respect the subjective rights that men retain when they depart of their
own volition from their natural state.

Montesquieu distinguishes himself from Hobbes in a manner that was
destined to become commonplace in the course of the eighteenth century.[23] Like the author of *Leviathan* (1651), he took man to be a passionate
animal endowed with, but not in a straightforward fashion governed by,
reason; and, like him, he had a healthy respect for the role that came to be
played in human affairs by fear. But he did not regard fear as the only
passion to be reckoned on. Nor did he think it primordial. There are "laws
of nature" rooted in "the constitution of our being," he asserted, and he
agreed with Hobbes that "to know them well, one must consider" the
situation of the individual "before the establishment of societies," for he,
too, was persuaded that "the laws of nature are those which he would
receive in such a state." Montesquieu insists, however, that such a man

---

[21] Cf. Montesquieu, *De l'Esprit des lois*, pt. 1, bk. 1, chap. 1 with ibid., pt. 1, bk. 1, chaps.
2–3.

[22] What Montesquieu does should be considered in light of the puckish remarks of Jean-
Jacques Rousseau, *Discours sur l'origine et les fondemens de l'inégalité parmis les hommes*, in
Œuvres complètes de Jean-Jacques Rousseau, vol. 3: 132–33.

[23] Among others, Jean-Jacques Rousseau followed Montesquieu's example: see Paul A.
Rahe, *Soft Despotism, Democracy's Drift: Montesquieu, Rousseau, Tocqueville, and the Modern
Prospect* (New Haven: Yale University Press, 2009), 61–140 (esp. 96–115), and Robertson,
"Rousseau, Montesquieu and the Origins of Inequality," 60–69.

would not be instinctively aggressive, as Hobbes had contended. In the beginning, he would not be sufficiently knowledgeable and speculative to be able to imagine establishing his own dominion. Instead, he would be acutely sensitive to his own weakness, timid, and instinctively inclined to keep the peace and seek nourishment, which would be for him natural laws. He would also be sociable—drawn to his own kind initially by an awareness of reciprocal fear, by "the pleasure that an animal feels at the approach of an animal of its own kind," and by "the charm that the two sexes inspire in one another by their difference"—and "the natural appeal" that human beings make to one another would constitute for him a third law. The knowledge attained in the course of human interaction would constitute yet another bond, "and the desire to live in society" would be for primitive man "a fourth natural law." [24]

Of course, Montesquieu was perfectly prepared to acknowledge that, in time, men would contract a desire "to subjugate one another," but he insisted that this would not happen until societies had been established and men had begun to speculate, and this desire would initially be restrained by mores of the sort that constitute political and civil right among hunter-gatherers and nomads, which would quickly develop in response to the danger posed. As Montesquieu subsequently makes clear, organized political society—and despotism—come much later in time and tend to be coeval with the discovery of agriculture, the institution of property in land, and the invention of coinage. [25]

The overall point that Montesquieu seeks to make by way of this hypothetical history is that nature does, indeed, have a teaching for man, but that this teaching is as complex as the skein of human passions, that its practical dictates differ from one situation to another, and that, in politics, there is no one passion to be reckoned on; no single, all-encompassing imperative to be fulfilled; and no form of government that is always and everywhere superior. In this regard, his outlook was not unlike that evidenced in *The Statesman* by Plato, who acknowledged the existence of a multiplicity of disparate goods, who compared statesmanship with weaving, and who believed that, in lawgiving and in the formulation of public policy, there is no substitute for prudence. [26]

In his *Persian Letters*, Montesquieu floated the notion that the government "most in conformity with Reason" and "most perfect" is "a Government gentle," free from unnecessary "severity," which "moves towards its end with minimal expense" by conducting "men in the manner that

---

[24] Cf. Montesquieu, *De l'Esprit des lois*, pt. 1, bk. 1, chaps. 2–3, with Thomas Hobbes, *Leviathan*, ed. C. B. Macpherson (Harmondsworth, UK: Penguin, 1968), pt. 1, chaps. 1–15 (esp. chaps. 11–15).

[25] See Montesquieu, *De l'Esprit des lois*, pt. 1, bk. 1, chaps. 2–3; bk 8, chap. 3; pt. 3, bk. 18, chaps. 1–2, 8–18, 26, and 30.

[26] See Plato, *Politicus*, 279a1–283b5, cited from John Burnet, ed., *Platonis opera* (Oxford: Clarendon Press, 1900–1907).

accords best with their propensities and inclinations." In his *magnum opus,* he refined this argument, contending that "the government most in conformity with nature is that government whose particular disposition best relates to the disposition of the people for whom it is established." Montesquieu may have endorsed a species of universalism when he defined "law, in general," as "human reason, insofar as it governs all the peoples of the earth," but he insisted at that same time on qualifying this claim. To "the political and civil laws of each nation," he attributed a measure of rationality. Despite their disparity, he said, these laws are "nothing other than the particular cases to which this human reason applies itself." [27]

The author of *The Spirit of Laws* was trained in the law, and he had once been a judge. His outlook resembled in certain respects that of the English jurist Sir Edward Coke. Neither was inclined to embrace abstract schemes, but both believed that, by way of the artificial reasoning of jurists, natural right could and should inform the evolution of the law.[28] In explaining what he had in mind, Montesquieu argued that "reason has a natural" and even "a tyrannical empire" over man. If, he observed, "one resists" reason, "this resistance" itself will nonetheless prove to be the foundation of reason's "triumph." Circumstances will force a reconsideration. "Just a little time," he writes, "and one is forced to return to her side." To reasoning as a process, to trial and error, and to piecemeal reform, especially when carried out gradually and unobtrusively by judges in the ordinary course of their duties, he was, in consequence, the greatest of friends; and this is why he thought it possible, on the basis of the "principles" that he had with great effort articulated in his book, to specify the logic or *esprit* evident in laws produced in the course of time by the repeated application of "human reasoning" to "particular cases." But, by the same token, to rationalism left in politics unchecked, unbridled, and unobstructed he was firmly—even fiercely— opposed. It was his aim "to prove" that "the spirit of moderation ought to be that of the legislator." [29]

There was, however, an obstacle to the sway of what Montesquieu had in mind when he spoke of moderation, and it was exemplified in different

[27] Cf. Charles de Secondat, baron de La Bréde et de Montesquieu, *Lettres persanes* (1721), ed. Edgar Mass, no. 78, cited from Jean Ehrard, Catherine Volpilhac-Auger, et al., eds., *Œuvres complètes de Montesquieu* (Oxford, UK: The Voltaire Foundation, 1998) vol. 1: 137–566, with Montesquieu, *De l'Esprit des lois,* pt. 1, bk. 1, chap. 3.
[28] After reading Stephen A. Siegel, "The Aristotelian Basis of English Law, 1450–1800," *New York University Law Review* 56 (1981): 18–59, and James R. Stoner, "Common Law and Natural Law," *Benchmark* 5 (1993): 93–102, see Georges Benrekassa, "Philosophie du droit et histoire dans les livres XXVII et XXVIII de *L'Esprit des lois,*" in Benrekassa, *Le Concentrique et l'excentrique: Marges des lumières* (Paris: Payot, 1980), 155–82, and consider Paul O. Carrese, *The Cloaking of Power: Montesquieu, Blackstone, and the Rise of Judicial Activism* (Chicago: University of Chicago Press, 2003), 1–104.
[29] Consider Montesquieu, *De l'Esprit des lois,* Pref., pt. 1, bk. 1, chap. 3; pt. 6, bk. 28, chaps. 6 and 38; and bk. 29, chap. 1, in light of Michael Oakeshott, "Rationalism in Politics," in Oakeshott, *Rationalism in Politics and Other Essays* (London: Methuen, 1962), 1–36.

ways by Hobbes and Locke. It is "a misfortune attached to the human condition," Montesquieu observes, but one cannot deny the fact:

> Great men who are moderate are rare; and as it is always easier to follow one's strength [*force*] than to arrest it, within the class of superior people, one may perhaps with greater facility find people extremely virtuous than men extremely wise.
>
> The soul takes so much delight in dominating other souls; even those who love the good love themselves so strongly that there is no one who is not so unfortunate as to still have reason to doubt his own good intentions: and, in truth, our actions depend on so many things that it is a thousand times easier to do good than to do it well.[30]

In this passage, Montesquieu draws attention to the fact that there is something inherently immoderate and perhaps even tyrannical at the heart of all forms of political idealism and public spiritedness. There is another passage in which he spells out the consequences.

"There are," he observed, "certain ideas of uniformity, which sometimes lay hold of men of great spirit," such as Charlemagne, "and which infallibly strike small spirits, who find in it a species of perfection that they recognize because it is impossible that they not discover it: in public administration the same weights, in commerce the same measures, in the State the same laws, in all parts the same religion." Montesquieu himself doubted whether uniformity was "always without exception à *propos*"; and, by way of posing a rhetorical question, he insisted that "greatness of genius consists more in knowing in what case uniformity is needed and in what case differences are required." [31] In contrast with Hobbes and the champions of enlightened despotism, in opposition to Locke and those who flatly denied the legitimacy of absolute monarchy, he thought the political and social diversity produced in different lands by the process of trial and error apt to be consistent with the dictates of reason. When he suggested that governments need to be tailored to the dispositions of the peoples for whom they are framed, he added that it would be "a very great accident if the laws of one nation" were "able to suit another." [32]

To explain why this should be so, Montesquieu outlined the overall argument of his work. First, and most important, he contended, one must consider the laws in relation "to the nature and to the principle of the government which is established, or which one wishes to establish," for that there be some such *rapport* is a matter of necessity: "either the laws form this government, as do the political laws, or they maintain it, as do the civil laws." Then, he added that one can also expect the laws to be related

---

[30] Montesquieu, *De l'Esprit des lois*, pt. 6, bk. 28, chap. 41.
[31] Ibid., pt. 6, bk. 29, chap. 18.
[32] Ibid., pt. 1, bk. 1, chap. 3.

to the country in its *physical aspect*; to the climate, whether it be icy, broiling, or temperate; to the quality of the terrain, to the country's situation, to its size; to the species of life adopted by the peoples, whether they be husbandmen, hunters, or herdsmen; it should be related to the degree of liberty that the constitution is able to tolerate, to the religion of the inhabitants, to their inclinations, to the riches they possess, to their number, their commerce, their mores, their manners. Finally, the laws have relations with one another; they have relations with their origin, with the object of the legislator, with the order of things on which they are established.

"It is," he concluded, "from all of these perspectives that one must consider the laws";[33] and, of course, this is precisely what he did in his massive tome.

Montesquieu did this, and he did more. After taking all of these *rapports* into consideration, he sat in judgment on the governments established and on their laws, assessing the latter not only in terms of their situational propriety but also with an eye to natural right. In the preface to his *Spirit of Laws*, Montesquieu asserts,

It is not a matter indifferent that the people be enlightened [*éclairé*]. The prejudices of the magistrates had their beginning as the prejudices of the nation. . . . I would believe myself the happiest of mortals if I could act in such a manner as to make it possible for human beings to cure themselves of their prejudices.

When Montesquieu speaks of "prejudices," he has in mind "not that which causes one to be unaware of [*ce qui fait qu'on ignore de*] certain things but that which causes one to be unaware of oneself [*ce qui fait qu'on s'ignore soi-même*]." "Man" he describes as "that flexible being who accommodates himself in society to the thoughts and impressions of others." As such, he "is equally capable of knowing his own nature when one shows it to him and of losing even the sentiment of it when one conceals it from him."[34]

In Montesquieu's judgment, the task of the philosopher is to dispel human self-forgetfulness by bringing home to man just who and what he really is: a being born in the state of nature equal to his fellows who loses that equality when he enters society and has it restored to him "again through the laws."[35] From enlightenment in this regard, the French philosophe believed, a profound moral progress will ensue—for the "knowledge" produced by enlightenment will not only "enable human

---

[33] Ibid. In this connection, see Alberto Postigliola, "Forme di razionalità e livelli di legalità in Montesquieu," *Rivista di storia della filosofia* 49, no. 1 (January 1994): 73–109.
[34] Montesquieu, *De l'Esprit des lois*, Pref.
[35] See ibid., pt. 1, bk. 1, chaps. 1–3; bk. 8, chap. 3; and pt. 3, bk. 15, chap. 8.

beings to cure themselves of their prejudices" but make them "gentle [*doux*]"—since "reason leads" men "to humanity," and "only prejudices cause them to renounce it."[36]

Although Montesquieu was profoundly sensitive to the tyrannical potential inherent in the speculative spirit—although he was inclined initially to withhold judgment, to respect diversity, to be suspicious of rationalism in politics, to reject the taste for uniformity, and to trust in the process of trial, error, and reconsideration, especially as this process was reflected in the common-law traditions of Europe—he was not apt simply to acquiesce in the drift of things. He may have been reluctant much of the time to specify the dictates of natural right in particular circumstances, but he insisted that there are "laws of nature" distinct from "local laws,"[37] and he sometimes bluntly addressed grievous breaches of nature's dictates which were commonplace in his own time.

Woodrow Wilson was right to link Montesquieu and Jefferson. For on the rare occasions when Montesquieu did assert himself in this fashion, what he had to say tended not only to be consistent with the logical implications of the argument presented by Locke in his *Two Treatises of Government* (1690) but also to anticipate the principles subsequently espoused by Jefferson. Thus, for example, Montesquieu is no less committed to the notion of human self-ownership than was Locke, and he is no less sensitive than were Locke and Jefferson to the fact that, when human beings enter into civil society, they retain *in extremis* a natural right to self-defense. In consequence, he regards statutes that fail to allow for its exercise as contrary to natural law.[38] In similar fashion, he condemns the monarchical propensity for making war out of a longing for glory and asserts that, given the ends for which government has been established among men, it is contrary to right for a polity to initiate war in circumstances in which the political community's self-preservation is not at stake.[39] Montesquieu is no less blunt in his categorical rejection of slavery—which is inconsistent, he points out, with what we learn concerning the natural equality of men and the ends of political order from tracing the path which human beings take from the state of nature to civil society, and which can be justified only insofar as holding others in servitude is temporarily required for one's own self-preservation.[40] It was with an eye to the ends of political order that he also intimated that the persecution visited on the Jews by

---

[36] See ibid., Préf.; pt. 1, bk. 1, chap. 1; and pt. 3, bk. 15, chap. 3.

[37] Ibid., pt. 5, bk. 26, chap. 14.

[38] See ibid., pt. 2, bk. 10, chap. 2, and pt. 5, bk. 26, chaps. 3 and 7. Zuckert, "Natural Rights and Modern Constitutionalism," sec. 15, rightly emphasizes Montesquieu's adherence to the Lockean position on self-ownership.

[39] See Montesquieu, *De l'Esprit des lois*, pt. 2, bk. 10, chaps. 2–4, and pt. 5, bk. 24, chap. 3.

[40] Consider ibid., pt. 3, bk. 15, chaps. 1–2, 5, and 7–10, in light of ibid., pt. 1, bk. 1, chaps. 1–3, and bk. 8, chap. 3; and see ibid., pt. 2, bk.10, chap. 3.

the Inquisition is contrary to "the feeble lights of justice that nature gives us."[41]

Where, in appealing to the dictates of nature, Montesquieu not only works out the unstated implications of Locke's argument but goes beyond it entirely, his commitments reflect the manner in which his account of man's natural condition and his departure from it deviates from the story told in *The Two Treatises of Government*. Thus, for example, when Montesquieu contends that "the laws of modesty [*la pudicité*]," as these apply to women, "are a part of natural right and ought to be felt by all the nations of the world" and, again, when he insists that civil law respect the natural obligations pertaining within the family,[42] he has in mind what can be inferred from his own analysis of the pre-political sociability of man.

One could even argue that Montesquieu's general posture regarding forms of government and particular laws follows from his understanding of nature and nature's laws. It is by no means an accident that he first alludes to "natural right" in the very chapter in which he first draws a distinction between moderate and despotic governments. One could sum up his case against the latter by noting—as Montesquieu does, in fact, note—that a despot may be restrained by "the laws of religion," which apply to him as they apply to his subjects, but that he cannot be restrained by objective "natural right" and forced to respect the subjective natural rights adhering to individuals as such because, when a man becomes a prince within such a form of government, he is "no longer assumed to be a man" subject—as he would be were he a mere man—to the terms of the tacit agreement that gives rise to civil society among men.[43]

III. The Constitution of Liberty

It is this general posture with regard to natural right that explains Montesquieu's interest in what he calls "political liberty." When he first makes the latter subject thematic, he draws attention to the ambiguities inherent in the popular usage of the term. Then, for the purpose of clarity, he draws a sharp distinction between "the power of the people" and "the liberty of the people." To clarify further, he distinguishes liberty also from the "independence" possessed by those in the state of nature, denying emphatically that "political liberty . . . consists in doing what one wants." In a political order, he explains, "in a state, in a society where there are laws, liberty can consist only in being able to do what one ought to want and in not being constrained to do what one ought not to want." Put less cryptically, "liberty is the right to do everything the laws permit; and if

---

[41] Ibid., pt. 5, bk. 25, chap. 13. Note also ibid., pt. 2, bk. 12, chap. 5, and pt. 5, bk. 26, chaps. 11–12.

[42] See ibid., pt. 3, bk. 15, chap. 12, and pt. 5, bk. 26, chaps. 3–6, 8, and 14.

[43] Ibid., pt. 1, bk. 3, chap. 10.

one citizen were able to do what they forbid, he would no longer have liberty because the others would likewise possess this same capacity." That which Montesquieu calls "political liberty in its relation with the constitution" is the unfettered freedom to act within the protected space opened up by the rule of law.[44]

Montesquieu was not, as the emphasis he placed on political liberty in these passages might be taken to suggest, a doctrinaire republican persuaded that no government but a republic can be legitimate. Indeed, he was not, strictly speaking, a republican at all. After distinguishing between "the liberty of the people" and "the power of the people," he went on to advance the startling claim that "democracy and aristocracy are not in their nature free States," then to add that "political liberty is not to be found except in moderate governments" and "not always" there. Political liberty, he explains, "is not present except where there is no abuse of power, and it is an eternal experience that every man who has power is drawn to abuse it; he proceeds until he finds the limits." It is in alluding to the human propensity for the abuse of power that he pointedly criticizes the passion for the public good, the instinct for self-sacrifice, and the love of equality that he elsewhere identifies as the psychological principle underpinning republican government and setting it in motion. "Who would say it!" he exclaims. "Even virtue has a need for limits."[45]

It is in this context that Montesquieu brings up the system of deeply embedded institutional constraints and restraints, balances, and checks that we would now call constitutionalism. To prevent those most likely to strive for what he calls "independence" from being "able to abuse power," he observes, "it is necessary that in the disposition of things power check power." It is his claim that "a constitution can be such that no one will be constrained to do things that the law does not require or prevented from doing those which the law permits him to do."[46] But he evidently thinks it unnatural for there to be checks on power in a republic. Those who constitute the ruling order in such a polity are not inclined to distrust their own capacity; they do not tend to suppose that they are themselves apt to do wrong. The public-spiritedness which they do possess is at odds with the spirit of moderation, and it leads them to prefer what they take to be the public interest to the freedom accorded their fellow citizens by the silence of the law.

To grasp more fully what Montesquieu has in mind when he speaks of political liberty, one must attend to the distinction he draws between

[44] Ibid., pt. 2, bk. 11, chaps. 1–3. Cf. ibid., pt. 1, bk. 5, chap. 12; pt. 5, bk. 24, chap. 2; and bk. 26, chap. 15, and see John Locke, *Two Treatises of Government: A Critical Edition with an Introduction and Apparatus Criticus*, 2d ed., ed. Peter Laslett (Cambridge, UK: Cambridge University Press, 1970), *Second Treatise*, chap. 4, sec. 22; chap. 6, sec. 57; and chap. 9, sec. 123.

[45] Consider Montesquieu, *De l'Esprit des lois*, pt. 2, bk. 11, chaps. 2 and 4, in light of ibid., pt. 1, bk. 2, chap. 1; bk. 3, chap. 3; bk. 4, chaps. 5–8; and pt. 2, bk. 11, chap. 6, pp. 397–98.

[46] Ibid., pt. 2, bk. 11, chap. 4.

"political liberty in its relation with the constitution" and "political liberty in its relation with the citizen." In one passage, he tells us that the latter is "that tranquility of mind [*esprit*] which comes from the opinion that each has of his security," adding that, if he is to possess "this liberty, it is necessary that the government be such that one citizen be unable to fear [*craindre*] another citizen." In another, he defines it as "security, or, at least, the opinion that one has of one's security," adding that "it can happen that the constitution will be free and the citizen not" and that "the citizen will be free and the constitution not"; that while "only the disposition of the laws, and even the fundamental laws," can "form liberty in its relation with the constitution," liberty "in its relation with the citizen" can be made to arise "from the mores, from the manners, and from the received examples" prevalent within a political community and that it is less effectively promoted by political arrangements than by "certain civil laws."[47]

In the latter passage, Montesquieu goes on to assert that "the knowledge which one has acquired in some countries and which one will acquire in others with regard to the surest regulations that one can hold to in criminal judgments interests human kind more than anything else that there is in the world," and thereafter he devotes chapter after chapter to examining these regulations. Then, he turns to taxation, emphasizing its psychological impact on those taxed, and linking "duties," such as those "on commodities," that "the people least feel" with both "moderate government" and "the spirit of liberty."[48] Political liberty in its relation with the citizen, which appears to be the chief focus of his investigation, is evidently a state of mind. When human beings enter into civil society, what they seek is not just the substance of personal security but the tranquility of mind attendant on it.

Political psychology looms large in Montesquieu's overall argument. At the outset, he tells us, each form of government is set in motion by a particular passion or set of passions—despotism, by fear; democratic republicanism, by virtue and the love of equality; civic aristocracy, by an enforced moderation; and monarchy, by the longing for honor.[49] That political liberty is not to be found in a despotism goes without saying. That it is difficult to sustain within republics of virtue may at first seem odd to us, but Montesquieu suggests that the idealism required is intimidating and hard to confine within the rule of law.[50] Given the peculiar fashion in which Montesquieu articulates his argument, one might then be tempted to suppose that, in his judgment, monarchy on the traditional European model is the natural home of political liberty. The French *philosophe* was certainly prepared to assert that a well-regulated monarchy of the sort

---

[47] Ibid., pt. 2, bk. 11, chaps. 1 and 6, p. 397, and pt. 2, bk. 12, chaps. 1–2.
[48] See ibid., pt. 2, bk. 12, chaps. 2–30, and bk. 13, chaps. 1–20 (esp. chaps. 7–8 and 14).
[49] See ibid., pt. 1, bk. 1, chap. 3, and bk. 3, chaps. 1–9.
[50] See ibid. pt. 2, bk. 11, chap. 4.

once prevalent throughout western Christendom—in which there is a landed nobility governed by a code of honor and the king exercises the legislative and executive powers while leaving judgment in court to a caste of men trained in jurisprudence and honor-bound to uphold the law—is a moderate form of government conducive to the rule of law and apt to safeguard "the security of individuals" and even give rise to "a spirit of liberty."[51]

As I have tried to demonstrate in detail elsewhere, however, Montesquieu held an adverse opinion regarding monarchy that he could not openly espouse in *ancien régime* France. Put simply, he was persuaded that traditional European monarchy's day was done; and, although he feared that it might collapse into despotism, he did not otherwise lament its prospective demise. As a young man, he had witnessed France's defeat in the War of the Spanish Succession (1701–1714), and he understood what it portended. He recognized that it was in the nature of this species of one-man rule to pursue conquest and glory. He was aware that its ethos of honor rendered it less able to engage in commerce than polities straightforwardly devoted to trade. He realized that in an age of commerce—in which money was to an ever-increasing degree the sinews of war—monarchies of this sort were unlikely to be able to project power as effectively as polities based on commerce, and he knew that repeated defeats on the field of the sword would shake such a regime to its foundations. He was, moreover, sensitive to the manner in which commerce, which presupposes a species of contractual equality between seller and buyer, threatened to erode the aristocratic spirit essential to monarchy, and he was aware that, in an age of enlightenment, monarchy on this model could not sustain the ethos of false honor that served as its psychological principle and uphold the artificial distinctions and ranks central to its very nature. Indeed, as a proponent of enlightenment persuaded that human beings are by nature equal, he thought that ethos incoherent and those distinctions and ranks morally reprehensible.[52]

The author of *The Spirit of Laws* appears to have thought the well-regulated, law-abiding monarchies of medieval and early modern Europe an improvement on the republics of classical antiquity, but he was also no less sensitive than Locke and Jefferson to the manner in which their core institutions were based on harmful prejudices at odds with what nature has to teach us concerning the natural equality of man, and he judged

[51] Consider ibid. pt. 1, bk. 2, chaps. 1 and 4; bk. 3, chaps. 5–10; bk. 4, chap. 2; bk. 5, chaps. 9–19; bk. 6, chaps. 1–10 and 21; bk. 7, chaps. 4–5, 8–9, and 15; bk. 8, chaps. 6–9 and 17–18; and pt. 2, bk. 11, chap. 7, in light of Paul A. Rahe, *Montesquieu and the Logic of Liberty: War, Religion, Commerce, Climate, Terrain, Technology, Uneasiness of Mind, the Spirit of Political Vigilance, and the Foundations of the Modern Republic* (New Haven, CT: Yale University Press, 2009), 74–76, 78–84.

[52] See Rahe, *Montesquieu and the Logic of Liberty*, 186–211, and Paul A. Rahe, "Montesquieu's Critique of Monarchy: A Self-Destructive Anachronism," in *Montesquieu et la civilité, Annuaire de l'Institut Michel Villey* 2010, no. 2 (Paris: Dalloz, 2011), 209–28.

them, in any case, no longer viable. Fortunately, there was an alternative. In England, the old monarchy had undergone a profound transformation, and the result—which had forced itself on the attention of Europe when, in the wake of the Glorious Revolution (1688–1689), the duke of Marlborough had repeatedly annihilated the legions of Louis XIV's France— was, Montesquieu implied, "a popular state," which had to be understood as "a republic" of sorts.[53] Once, with greater precision, he even alluded obliquely to the English form of government as "a republic concealed under the form of a monarchy."[54]

This species of republic differed from the republics of virtue dominant in antiquity in four particulars. First, it was in its nature "a free State."[55] In fact, it had "political liberty" as its "direct object."[56] Second, the structure or nature of its government was defined by an elaborate and complex distribution and separation of the legislative, executive, and judicial powers that distinguished it from all existing monarchies and from other republics both ancient and modern.[57] One could not say of it what Montesquieu said of despotism with its pervasive ethos of fear—that it "jumps up, so to speak, before our eyes; it is uniform throughout: as the passions alone are necessary for its establishment, the whole world is good enough for that." Instead, one had to repeat what he said concerning the formation of "a moderate government" more generally—that to form such a government, "it is necessary to combine powers, to regulate them, to temper them, to make them act, to give, so to speak, a ballast to one in order to put it in a condition to resist another; this is a masterpiece of legislation, which chance rarely produces and prudence is rarely allowed to produce."[58]

Third, the English polity resembled a type of republican government not unknown in antiquity but at that time marginal—which, unlike virtuous republicanism,[59] had survived into Christian times, and which Montesquieu termed variously "a democracy" or "republic based [fondée] on commerce."[60] And, fourth, it had, at best, a tenuous relationship with

[53] Montesquieu, De l'Esprit des lois, pt. 1, bk. 2, chap. 4, and bk. 6, chap. 3; and pt. 2, bk. 12, chap. 19.
[54] Montesquieu, De l'Esprit des lois, pt. 1, bk. 5, chap. 19, p. 304. In seventeenth- and eighteenth-century Britain, this understanding of the English constitution was the common sense of the matter: see the evidence collected in Rahe, Montesquieu and the Logic of Liberty, 270, n. 52. That, in deploying this phrase, Montesquieu had England and nowhere else in mind was perfectly evident to readers at the time: see Letter from David Hume to Montesquieu on 10 April 1749, in J. Y. T. Greig, ed., Letters of David Hume (Oxford: Clarendon Press, 1932), vol. 1: 133–38 (at 134, with n. 5).
[55] Ibid., pt. 2, bk. 11, chap. 6, pp. 399, 403, and pt. 3, bk. 19, chap. 27, p. 583.
[56] Ibid., pt. 2, bk. 11, chap. 5.
[57] See ibid., pt. 2, bk. 11, chap. 6. Cf. ibid., pt. 2, bk. 11, chaps. 7–20. In this connection, note Zuckert, "Natural Rights and Modern Constitutionalism," secs. 27–46.
[58] Montesquieu, De l'Esprit des lois, pt. 1, bk. 5, chap. 14, p. 297.
[59] See ibid., pt. 1, bk. 4, chap. 4.
[60] Note ibid., pt. 1, bk. 5, chap. 6, and pt. 4, bk. 20, chap. 17; and consider ibid., pt. 3, bk. 19, chap. 27, pp. 577–80; pt. 4, bk. 20, chaps. 7 and 12–14; and bk. 21, chap. 7, in light of ibid.,

religion, for the English had divested themselves of what Montesquieu called "harmful prejudices" and were as Christians lukewarm to the point of indifference.[61] As Montesquieu put it, the English were "the people in the world who best understood how to exploit at the same time three great things: religion, commerce, and liberty."[62]

In this mix, commerce played a crucial role. Montesquieu saw it as an adjunct to enlightenment apt to produce comparable consequences. "Commerce," he wrote, "cures destructive prejudices" and promotes "gentle mores [*moeurs douces*]"—first by causing a "knowledge of the mores of all the nations to penetrate everywhere," and then by encouraging men to "compare" their own ways with those adopted elsewhere.[63] Its "natural effect" is also "to promote peace," for "two nations who do business together render themselves reciprocally dependent: if it is to the interest of one to buy, the other has an interest in selling; all such unions are based on mutual needs."[64] The republics of antiquity were oriented to conquest and war;[65] their modern, commercial counterparts have as their *esprit* "peace and moderation."[66] When forced into war, Montesquieu's England, thanks to its commercial wealth, could command vast resources with which to project power, but its focus on trade meant that it had no particular interest in territorial acquisition and that it was inclined to subordinate its political to its commercial interests. It was an enemy, Montesquieu intimated, that one had no need to acquire and very good reason to avoid.[67]

In similar fashion, Montesquieu believed, commerce intensifies earthly temptations and subverts religious zeal and the fanaticism that so often accompanies it. "As a general rule," he observes, "invitations contribute more forcefully to changing religion than do penalties," and prudence dictates that one

> attack religion by favor, by the conveniences [*commodités*] of life, by the hope of fortune; not by that which warns one of one's mortality but by that which makes one forget it; not by that which provokes indignation but by that which casts one into a disposition lukewarm

---

pt. 4, bk. 20, chaps. 4–6, 17, and 21. In this connection, see Rahe, *Montesquieu and the Logic of Liberty*, 224–38.

[61] Montesquieu, *De l'Esprit des lois*, pt. 3, bk. 19, chap. 27, pp. 578, 580–81. The phrase "harmful" or "destructive prejudices" recurs throughout the book: note ibid., pt. 2, bk. 10, chap. 4; pt. 4, bk. 20, chap. 1; and pt. 5, bk. 25, chaps. 12–13.

[62] Ibid., pt. 4, bk. 20, chap. 7.

[63] Ibid., pt. 4, bk. 20, chap. 1.

[64] Ibid., pt. 4, bk. 20, chap. 2.

[65] See ibid., pt. 1, bk. 3, chap. 3; bk. 4, chap. 8; bk. 5, chap. 6; bk. 7, chap. 2; and pt. 2, bk. 11, chap. 5. Note also Montesquieu, *Considérations sur les causes de la grandeur des Romains et de leur décadence* (1734), ed. Françoise Weil and Cecil Courtney, which I cite from Ehrard, Volpilhac-Auger, et al., eds., *Œuvres complètes de Montesquieu*, vol. 2: 87–285.

[66] Montesquieu, *De l'Esprit des lois*, pt. 2, bk. 9, chap. 2.

[67] See ibid., pt. 3, bk. 19, chap. 27, pp. 577–80, and pt. 4, bk. 20, chap. 7.

[*quit jette dans la tiédeur*] so that other passions act on our souls and those which religion inspires fall silent.[68]

Such are predictably the effects of the "solid luxury" produced by trade among a commercial people, such as the English, who are "always occupied with their own interests."[69]

For the most part, in his *Spirit of Laws*, Montesquieu emphasizes the role played by climate, terrain, territorial size, technology, commerce, religion, and the setting for war in determining the range of available political choices. In general, moreover, he gives priority to mores and manners. Forms of government are sometimes made to seem almost epiphenomenal. England is, however, an exception. In its case—and, insofar as we can tell, only in its case—"the mores follow the laws." In its case, the laws contribute mightily to the formation of "the manners and the character" of the nation as well.[70]

The laws that Montesquieu has in mind when he makes this monumental claim are those which form what he calls "the constitution of England" by distributing and separating the three powers. If monarchies on the European model are "moderate," if they foster what Montesquieu calls "a spirit of liberty" able perhaps to "contribute as much to happiness as liberty itself," if those who live under monarchical rule have no reason to "fear" anyone in particular, it is largely because Europe's kings do not themselves exercise "the power of judging" but delegate it to a particular order capable of resisting their blandishments and honor-bound to do so if what the monarchs seek is contrary to the law.[71] This is doubly true in England where there is trial by jury and "the power of judging, so terrible among men" is "attached neither to a certain condition nor to a certain profession" and "becomes, so to speak, invisible and null." In consequence, in England, "one does not continually have one's judges before one's eyes; and one fears the magistracy and not the magistrates." Moreover, the fact that the jury in England is made up of the peers of the accused means that "he cannot be of the mind that he has fallen into the hands of those inclined to do him violence,"[72] and later, when Montesquieu singles out for praise particular laws concerning crimes and taxation which he thinks most apt to foster "political liberty in its relation with the citizen," the examples he has in mind are more often than not English in origin.[73]

England differs also from the ordinary European monarchy in that it distinguishes the legislative from the executive power and distributes the

---

[68] Ibid., pt. 5, bk. 25, chap. 12.

[69] Ibid., pt. 3, bk. 19, chap. 27, p. 581.

[70] Ibid., pt. 3, bk. 19, chaps. 26–27.

[71] See ibid., pt. 2, bk. 11, chap. 6, pp. 396–98.

[72] Ibid., pt. 2, bk. 11, chap. 6, pp. 398–99.

[73] Survey ibid., pt. 2, bks. 12–13; then, consider ibid., pt. 1, bk. 6, chaps. 3 and 16–17, and pt. 2, bk. 13, chaps. 12–13 and 19–20. Note, however, ibid., pt. 2, bk. 12, chap. 19.

two functions to separate bodies, conferring on the monarch a responsibility for defending the realm and executing the laws and on the House of Commons, checked by the House of Lords, a responsibility for making laws. This distribution and separation of these two powers has any number of good effects. To begin with, it means that one does not fear that laws tyrannically made will be tyrannically enforced. In fact, the body that makes the laws faces the sobering prospect that those same laws will be executed against its members—which is an encouragement to be fair-minded in legislating. Although the actual execution of the laws is in other hands, the legislative power is accorded a role in oversight after the fact, and the division between Lords and Commons not only encourages careful, repeated deliberation. It also provides the well-to-do with a safeguard against oppression. Montesquieu also places emphasis on the representative principle, arguing that a relatively small, elected body can deliberate in a more intelligent manner than the people as a whole, and stressing that the prospect of the next election serves to keep those in the House of Commons faithful to their constituents.[74]

Long before the publication of his *Spirit of Laws*, in a work entitled *Considerations on the Causes of the Greatness of the Romans and their Decline* (1733), Montesquieu had identified "the Government of England" as "one of the wisest in Europe," explaining that there is within it "a Body [*Corps*]" which

> examines this government continually and continually examines itself; and such are this body's errors that they never last long, and are useful in giving the Nation a spirit of attentiveness [*l'esprit d'attention*].
>
> In a word, a free Government, which is to say, a government always agitated, knows no way in which to sustain itself if it is not by its own Laws capable of self-correction.[75]

From this opinion, Montesquieu never deviated. He had studied English history with some care. He was aware that, from the time of James I in the first two decades of the seventeenth century on, its politics had been characterized by a tension between what the English called "the Court" and what they dubbed "the Country." Time and again, the latter had risen up in high dudgeon to denounce through its representatives in Parliament what was perceived as favoritism, corruption, arbitrary rule, conspiracy, and Papist predilections on the part of a Court thought to be intent on encroaching on the rights of ordinary Englishmen and the prerogatives possessed by Parliament.

---

[74] See ibid., pt. 2, bk. 11, chap. 6.
[75] Montesquieu, *Considérations sur les causes de la grandeur des Romains et de leur décadence*, chap. 8, ll. 101–6.

As Montesquieu knew, these tensions had produced the English civil war of the 1640s, the execution of Charles I in 1649, the rule of the Rump Parliament and the Protectorate of Oliver Cromwell in the 1650s, followed by the Restoration of the monarchy in 1660 and, in time, the Glorious Revolution of 1688–1689. By the time Montesquieu arrived in England in the late 1720s, political pressures that had given rise to turbulence and bloodshed time and again were now being settled peacefully through electioneering and balloting, and monarchs found themselves forced to appoint as ministers those who had the confidence of Parliament. In England's historians, he had had Rica observe in his *Persian Letters*, "one sees liberty constantly spring forth from the fires of discord and of sedition," and one finds "the Prince always tottering on a throne" which is itself "unshakable." If the "Nation" is "impatient," this character remarks, it is nonetheless "wise in its very fury." [76]

Montesquieu found the dynamics of English politics both instructive and amusing. "The hatred" that had long existed between Court and Country he regarded as a permanent feature. This hatred "would endure," he observed, "because it would always be powerless," and it would be powerless because "the parties" inspired by the separation of powers would be "composed of free men" who would be inclined to switch sides if either the executive power or the legislative power appeared to have "secured too much." [77]

The English were a commercial people who lived in what Montesquieu called "a republic concealed under the form of a monarchy." The regime under which they were reared, being neither republican in the classical sense nor genuinely monarchical, did little to inculcate in them a spirit of self-sacrifice and even less to inspire in them a love of honor and glory. Instead, it left Englishmen to their own devices; and, in the absence of direction from above, they tended to succumb to the restlessness and anxiety that Montesquieu called *inquiétude.* In such a nation, he remarked, the charges lodged by the party in opposition to the executive branch "would augment even more" than usual "the terrors" to which a people so disposed were naturally prone, for they "would never know really whether they were in danger or not." [78]

Ordinarily, of course, the legislature, which enjoyed the confidence of the people, would be in a position to moderate their fears. "In this fashion," Montesquieu noted, when "the terrors impressed" on the populace lacked "a certain object, they would produce nothing but vain clamors and name-calling; and they would have this good effect: that they would stretch all the springs of government and render the citizens attentive." If, however, the terrors fanned by the party opposed to the English executive

---

[76] Montesquieu, *Lettres persanes*, no. 130.
[77] Montesquieu, *De l'Esprit des lois*, pt. 3, bk. 19, chap. 27.
[78] Ibid.

were ever "to appear on the occasion of an overturning of the fundamental laws," he observed, "they would be muted, lethal, excruciating and produce catastrophes: before long, one would see a frightful calm, during which the whole would unite itself against the power violating the laws." Moreover, he added, if such "disputes took shape on the occasion of a violation of the fundamental laws, and if a foreign power appeared," as happened with the arrival of the Dutch Stadholder William of Orange in 1688, "there would be a revolution, which would change neither the form of the government nor its constitution: for the revolutions to which liberty gives shape are nothing but a confirmation of liberty."[79]

IV. Geographical Imperatives

There is one other dimension of this arrangement that deserves attention. Montesquieu was acutely aware that, in ancient Greece, all of the republics were exceedingly small; and—as he makes evident in the first part of his *Spirit of Laws*—he knew perfectly well why this was the case. He knew that they could not instill in the citizens the requisite public-spiritedness if they ceased to be face-to-face communities in which the citizens could easily pay "a singular attention to one another."[80] He was also aware, however, that classical Rome—although it began as a small *civitas* no larger than an ordinary Greek *pólis*—came in time to rule not only Italy, but Spain, North Africa, the entire Mediterranean basin, and Gaul, and he recognized that, in the process of doing so, its citizen body became larger and larger and larger until the Roman *respublica* bore hardly any resemblance to a Greek *pólis*.

Republican Rome's expansion, its aggrandizement, its achievement of grandeur is the subject of the first half of his *Considerations on the Romans*, and the main point that Montesquieu seeks to drive home by way of his narrative is that Rome's expansion destroyed the republic. It did so, he makes clear, in the way that the Greeks had in mind when they refused to do what the Romans would later do—naturalize freedmen and other foreigners. In other words, it paved the way for its own ruin by eliminating the cohesion of the citizen body, by destroying its solidarity, and by making it impossible for it to elicit from the citizens public-spiritedness and civic virtue, as it once had done, through a civic *paideía*. But it also laid itself low in another fashion—for Rome's expansion required it to confer arbitrary power for extended periods on magistrates called proconsuls who were sent out with legions of soldiers to govern its provinces, suppress rebellions, and defend the borders of the empire, and these proconsuls, leading long-service armies increasingly made up of propertyless soldiers who were only

---

[79] Ibid.

[80] See ibid., pt. 1, bk. 3, chap. 3; bk. 4, chaps. 5–8; bk. 5, chaps. 2–7; bk. 7, chaps. 1–2 and 8–9; and bk. 8, chaps. 1–3 and 11–16.

notionally citizens, proved republican Rome's undoing. Rome was, in sum, the exception that proved the rule. It put the strictures laid down by the Greeks to the test, and eventually—as the Greeks predicted would happen—the republic collapsed.[81]

Montesquieu returned to this question in his *Spirit of Laws*. This work is a gigantic book, and it is difficult to know which elements within it are the most salient. There is, however, one passage in which Montesquieu tells us outright that what he is about to say is fundamental to everything else that he says. "I," he writes near the end of the first of the work's six parts, "shall be able to be understood only when the next four chapters have been read."[82] Then, in those four chapters, he argues that forms of government are closely related to the size of the territory that must be governed. Republics are well-suited to territories small in extent; monarchies, to territories of intermediate size; and despotisms to territories great in size.[83]

"It is in the nature of a republic," Montesquieu writes, "to possess only a small territory." In a large republic, "interests become particular; a man senses then that he can be happy, great, glorious without his fatherland; and soon that he can be great solely on the ruins of his fatherland." One consequence of such a republic's size is that "the common good is sacrificed to a thousand considerations; it is subordinated to the exceptions; it depends on accidents." The situation "in a small" republic is more favorable: there, "the public good is more fully felt, better known, closer to each citizen; abuses are less extensive there and as a consequence less well protected."[84]

By way of contrast, Montesquieu adds, "A large empire presupposes a despotic authority in the one who governs." One cannot deny that "promptness in decision-making is required to compensate for the distance of the places to which orders are sent"; that "fear is required to prevent negligence on the part of the governor or magistrate operating at a great distance"; that, in such circumstances, "law must be lodged in a single head" and that "it must change unceasingly," for "accidents" really do "multiply in a state in proportion to its magnitude."[85] This, he does not have to say, was the experience of Rome.

Montesquieu stops at this point to let the force of the geographical imperative sink in. Later, he will return to the question and suggest federalism as an expedient. In war, individual republics are at a disadvantage when confronted by a monarchy or despotism: they lack the

---

[81] See Montesquieu, *Considérations sur les causes de la grandeur des Romains et de leur décadence*, chaps. 1–13, and Montesquieu, *De l'Esprit des lois*, pt. 2, bk. 11, chap. 6, pp. 403–7; and chaps. 12–19.

[82] Ibid., pt. 1, bk. 8, chap. 15.

[83] See ibid., pt. 1, bk. 8, chaps. 16–19.

[84] Ibid., pt. 1, bk. 8, chap. 16.

[85] Ibid., pt. 1, bk. 8, chap. 19.

resources and the manpower necessary for an effective defense. If joined together in a confederation, however, they can have it both ways. Each republic can benefit from the advantage associated with diminutive size and sustain itself as such. In wartime, as a united body, they can pool resources and manpower and thereby become formidable to their adversaries. Moreover, these republics can support one another in yet another fashion. A would-be usurper would not possess equal credit in all of the federated states. "If he rendered himself excessively powerful in one, he would alarm all the others; if he subjugated a part, the part which remained free would still be able to mount resistance to him with forces independent of those he had usurped and overcome him before he had fully established himself." In similar fashion, if a sedition or some species of abuse were to take place in one member of the confederation, the other members could step in and suppress it.[86]

When he turns to England, Montesquieu is strangely—one might even say, ostentatiously—silent concerning the geographical imperative that he had hitherto so strongly emphasized. This was arguably one of the matters that the author of *The Spirit of Laws* had in mind when he wrote, "Silence sometimes expresses more than any discourse."[87] For it is at the very end of the book in which he discussed the constitution of England that he remarked, "It is not necessary always to so exhaust a subject that one leaves nothing for the reader to do. The task is not to make him read but to make him think."[88] One need only pause and reflect to realize that the territory governed under the English constitution is far too large to be encompassed by a republic of virtue. It is not, in fact, clear that Montesquieu thought that there were any limits to the territory that could be governed by the "republic concealed under the form of a monarchy" that he discovered when he visited Great Britain in the 1720s. Montesquieu makes no mention of such limits, and it is easy to see that the principle of representation expands in one way the geographical boundaries that such a polity can comprehend while the separation of powers does so in another way—for England's unitary executive can act in an emergency with as much vigor and dispatch as a despot; and, though he cannot be held personally accountable for abuses attendant on what he has done in this regard, his counsellors can.[89]

Montesquieu is also ostentatiously silent in another particular. He never specifies what the psychological principle that sets the English form of government in motion might be. It cannot be fear, the principle animating despotism—for the English clearly possess "political liberty in its relation with the constitution," if not also "political liberty in its relation with the citizen." No one in England has reason to fear anyone

---

[86] See ibid., pt. 2, bk. 9, chaps. 1–3.
[87] Ibid., pt. 2, bk. 12, chap. 12.
[88] Ibid., pt. 2, bk. 11, chap. 20.
[89] See ibid., pt. 2, bk. 11, chap. 6, pp. 399–407.

else in particular. Nor can it be virtue—for Montesquieu attributes the failure of England's republican experiment during the interregnum to a lack of virtue on the part of the English people,[90] and he never once uses the term in referring to the English of his own day. Moreover, it is hard to see how virtue could be instilled in a people so numerous who are situated on so extended a territory. It would, in fact, appear to be the case that one could say of England what Montesquieu says concerning monarchy: that, in it, "policy makes great things happen with as little of virtue as it can" and that, "just as in the most beautiful machines, art also employs as little of movement, of forces, of wheels as is possible. The state subsists independently of love of the fatherland, of desire for true glory, of self-renunciation, of the sacrifice of one's dearest interests, and of all those heroic virtues which we find in the ancients and know only from hearing them spoken of."[91] But if there is a psychological principle that substitutes for virtue and animates the English polity, it cannot be monarchical honor, which Montesquieu never once mentions in England's regard.

In a sense, there is no such principle. In England, Montesquieu tells us, all of the passions are left free. When this happens, to judge by Montesquieu's description of the national character of the English, *inquiétude* becomes the dominant psychological disposition. But this is not his final word on the question, for he also allows us to see that the uneasiness that has Englishmen in its grip is in turn given a focus and rendered less inchoate by the never-ending conflict that takes place in England between the legislative and executive powers. In effect, *inquiétude* is transformed thereby into a salutary, if irrational, species of partisan jealousy that does, in fact, animate the polity and that safeguards it as well by encouraging attentiveness on the part of the public and by causing Parliament to cast a beady eye on the Crown and vice versa as well.[92]

V. AMERICAN CONSTITUTIONALISM

Montesquieu's attempt to articulate a species of modern natural right consistent with a restoration of prudential statesmanship to its rightful place was widely appreciated at the time. Overnight, *The Spirit of Laws* became the political Bible of learned men and would-be statesmen everywhere in Europe, and beyond. In Britain, it shaped the thinking of Edmund Burke, Edward Gibbon, William Blackstone, Adam Smith, Adam Ferguson, John Robertson, John Millar, Lord Kames, and Dugald Stew-

---

[90] See ibid., pt. 1, bk. 3, chap. 3.
[91] Ibid., pt. 1, bk. 3, chap. 5.
[92] Consider ibid., pt. 3, bk. 19, chap. 27, pp. 574–77, in light of Rahe, *Montesquieu and the Logic of Liberty*, 65–143.

art among others,[93] and in America, it inspired the Framers of the Constitution and their opponents, the Antifederalists, as well.[94] In Italy, it had a profound effect on Cesare Beccaria,[95] and in Germany, it was fundamental for Georg Wilhelm Friedrich Hegel.[96] In France, it was the starting point for all subsequent political thought.[97] Its impact can hardly be overestimated.[98] In the course of the eighteenth century, Montesquieu's *magnum opus* was translated into English, Italian, German, Latin,

[93] Note Frank T. H. Fletcher, *Montesquieu and English Politics, 1750–1800* (London: E. Arnold and Co., 1939), and William Stewart, "Montesquieu vu par les Anglais depuis deux siècles," in *Actes du congrès Montesquieu réuni à Bordeaux du 23 au 26 mai 1955* (Bordeaux: Imприméries Delmas, 1956), 339–48; then, see Cecil Patrick Courtney, *Montesquieu and Burke* (Oxford, UK: Blackwell, 1963); Carrese, *The Cloaking of Power*, 1–177; David Carrithers, "The Enlightenment Science of Society," in Christopher Fox, Roy Porter, and Robert Wokler, eds., *Inventing Human Science: Eighteenth-Century Domains* (Berkeley: University of California Press, 1995), 232–70; Sheila M. Mason, "Les Héritiers écossais de Montesquieu: Continuité d'inspiration et métamorophose de valeurs," in *La Fortune de Montesquieu: Montesquieu écrivain* (Bordeaux: Bibliothèque Municipale, 1995), 143–54; and James Moore, "Montesquieu and the Scottish Enlightenment," in Rebecca E. Kingston, ed., *Montesquieu and his Legacy* (Albany: State University of New York Press, 2008), 179–98.

[94] Note Paul Merrill Spurlin, *Montesquieu in America, 1760–1801* (University: Louisiana State University Press, 1940), and see James W. Muller, "The American Framers' Debt to Montesquieu," in James W. Muller, ed., *The Revival of Constitutionalism* (Lincoln: University of Nebraska Press, 1988), 87–102; Anne M. Cohler, *Montesquieu's Comparative Politics and the Spirit of American Constitutionalism* (Lawrence: University Press of Kansas, 1988); Matthew P. Bergman, "Montesquieu's Theory of Government and the Framing of the American Constitution," *Pepperdine Law Review* 18, no. 1 (1990): 1–42; Paul A. Rahe, *Republics Ancient and Modern: Classical Republicanism and the American Revolution* (Chapel Hill: University of North Carolina Press, 1992), bk. 2, chap. 3, sec. 4; bk. 3, prol.; chap. 1, secs. 3–7; chap. 2, sec. 2; chap. 3, secs. 4–5; chap. 4, secs. 3–5, 7, and 9; and chap. 5, secs. 3 and 6; Bernard Manin, "Checks, Balances and Boundaries: The Separation of Powers in the Constitutional Debate of 1787," in Biancamaria Fontana, ed., *The Invention of the Modern Republic* (Cambridge, UK: Cambridge University Press, 1994), 27–62; Zuckert, "Natural Rights and Modern Constitutionalism," secs. 47–79; Lee Ward, "Montesquieu on Federalism and Anglo-Gothic Constitutionalism," *Publius* 37, no. 4 (2007): 551–77; and Jacob Levy, "Montesquieu's Constitutional Legacies," in Kingston, ed., *Montesquieu and his Legacy*, 115–38.

[95] See Catherine Larrère, "Droit de punir et qualification des crimes de Montesquieu à Beccaria," in Michel Porret, ed., *Beccaria et la culture juridique des lumières* (Geneva: Droz, 1997), 89–108, and David W. Carrithers, "Montesquieu's Philosophy of Punishment," *History of Political Thought* 19, no. 2 (1998): 213–40.

[96] See Michael A. Mosher, "The Particulars of a Universal Politics: Hegel's Adaptation of Montesquieu's Typology," *American Political Science Review* 78, no. 1 (1984): 179–88, and Kawade, "La Liberté civile contre la théorie réformiste de l'État souverain," 203–23.

[97] See Roberto Romani, "All Montesquieu's Sons: The Place of *Esprit Général, Caractère National,* and *Mœurs* in French Political Philosophy, 1748–1789," *Studies on Voltaire and the Eighteenth Century* 362 (1998): 189–235, whose reading of Montesquieu and of his critics and heirs nonetheless leaves something to be desired. The case of Denis Diderot is of special interest: see Arthur M. Wilson, "The Concept of *Mœurs* in Diderot's Social and Political Thought," in W. H. Barber et al., eds., *The Age of the Enlightenment: Studies Presented to Theodore Besterman* (Edinburgh: Oliver and Boyd, 1967), 188–99.

[98] In this connection, see the essays collected in the two-volume study: Domenico Felice, ed., *Montesquieu e i suoi interpreti* (Pisa: Edizioni ETS, 2005). Note also Catherine Volpilhac-Auger, "*L'Esprit des lois,* une lecture *ad usum Delphini*?" in Grapa, Jacques-Lefèvre, Séité, and Trevisan, eds., *Le Travail des lumières,* 137–71.

Danish, Dutch, Polish, and Russian and appeared in more than one hundred sixty editions.[99]

Nowhere was the book more important than in the fledgling United States. In *The Federalist*, James Madison called the author of *The Spirit of Laws* an "oracle," and both Madison and Alexander Hamilton spoke of him as "the celebrated Montesquieu."[100] They sensed what subsequent scholarship has shown to be true: that no political writer was more often cited and none was thought to be of greater authority in the era of American constitution-making.[101] They knew, moreover, that in England and on the continent of Europe Montesquieu was thought to be of similar stature. Indeed, having carefully read his *Spirit of Laws* themselves, they knew why, throughout the Christian West, he was held in such regard; and, though they took issue with him on particular matters, it was within the framework of his understanding of the relationship between natural right and constitutionalism that they sought to articulate a constitutional scheme appropriate to the particular dispositions of the American people for whom it was framed.

There were five passages in Montesquieu that caught the American eye. In his discussion of the national character of the English, Montesquieu alluded to their colonists in North America, noting England's indifference to territorial acquisition, suggesting that, when it did send out colonies, it did so, in the manner of ancient Carthage and medieval Venice, "more to extend the reach of its commerce than its sphere of domination," and adding that it was apt to confer on its colonists "its own form of government"—which would bring "with it prosperity" so that "one would see great peoples take shape in the forests which they were sent to inhabit."[102] This encouraged Americans, such as Benjamin Franklin and Hamilton, to think of the new republic in North America as a successor to England—like it in situation, character, commercial focus, and ability to project power.[103]

The second of these was the passage in which Montesquieu denied that it is possible to sustain a republic on an extended territory, which

[99] See Cecil Patrick Courtney, "*L'Esprit des lois* dans la perspective d l'histoire du livre (1748–1800)," in Michel Porret and Catherine Volpilhac-Auger, eds., *Le Temps de Montesquieu: Actes du colloque international de Genève (28–31 October 1998)* (Geneva: Droz, 2002), 66–96.

[100] See *Federalist Nos.* 47 (Madison) and 78 (Hamilton), which I cite from Jacob E. Cooke, ed., *The Federalist* (Middletown, CT: Wesleyan University Press, 1961).

[101] See Donald S. Lutz, "The Relative Influence of European Writers on Late Eighteenth-Century American Political Thought," *The American Political Science Review* 78, no. 1 (1984): 189–97.

[102] Consider Montesquieu, *De l'Esprit des lois*, pt. 3, bk. 19, chap. 27, p. 578, in light of ibid., pt. 4, bk. 21, chap. 21.

[103] Both Franklin and Hamilton were especially sensitive to the new republic's potential to become a great power on the English model: see Gerald Stourzh, *Benjamin Franklin and American Foreign Policy*, 2d ed. (Chicago: University of Chicago Press, 1969), and Karl-Friedrich Walling, *Republican Empire: Alexander Hamilton on War and Free Government* (Lawrence: University Press of Kansas, 1999).

posed a challenge to the aspirations that animated the nascent republic. This passage was frequently cited by the Antifederalists,[104] and Federalists responded in three ways. One could observe, as Hamilton did, that states such as Massachusetts, New York, Pennsylvania, Virginia, North Carolina, and Georgia were themselves too large to meet Montesquieu's criterion, and one could point, as he also did, to the third of the passages that drew attention in America—Montesquieu's suggestion that a group of republics could overcome the geographical imperative by forming a federation.[105] One could also deploy the fourth and fifth of these passages—in which Montesquieu discusses the principle of representation, the separation of powers, and the ongoing struggle between Court and Country to which it gives rise—against his geographical claim, as Madison did, by arguing in a manner reminiscent of David Hume that territorial extension can be of advantage to a republic based on representation and that the diversity of opinions, passions, and interests resulting from geographical extension can render it difficult, if not impossible, for a majority faction to form.[106]

In effect, the Americans hedged their bets by adopting both of Montesquieu's expedients. Faced with the task of establishing a republic on an extended territory, they established a hybrid regime—"partly federal, and partly national"—made up of comparatively small republics,[107] and they adopted the principle of representation and a separation of powers both within the federal government and within the state governments, fortifying themselves in this fashion against the prospect that the sheer size of the territory encompassed by the United States of America would occasion frequent emergencies that would eventuate in a massive concentra-

[104] Consider Herbert J. Storing, ed., *The Complete Anti-Federalist* (Chicago: University of Chicago Press, 1981), vol. 2, no. 3, para. 7 (Robert Yates and John Lansing, "Reasons of Dissent"); no. 4, para. 44 (Luther Martin, "The Genuine Information Delivered to the Legislature of the State of Maryland"); no. 6, paras. 10–21 (Letters of Cato III); no. 7, paras. 17–19 (Letters of Centinel I); no. 8, paras. 15–19 (Letters from the Federal Farmer II); vol. 3, no. 3, para. 20 (Essays of an Old Whig IV); no. 11, paras. 16–17 (The Address and Reasons of Dissent of the Minority of the Convention of Pennsylvania To Their Constituents); no. 14, para. 7 (The Fallacies of the Freeman Detected by A Farmer); vol. 4, no. 6, paras. 16–17 (Letters of Agrippa IV); no. 28, para. 4 (Observations on the New Constitution, and on the Federal and State Conventions By A Columbian Patriot); vol. 5, no. 5, paras. 5–6 (Address by John Francis Mercer); no. 7, paras. 6–9 (Address by Cato Uticensis); no. 16, para. 11 (Speeches of Patrick Henry in the Virginia State Ratifying Convention); no. 17, para. 1 (Speech of George Mason in the Virginia Ratifying Convention); no. 21, paras. 12–13 (James Monroe, *Some Observations on the Constitution*); vol. 6, no. 12, para. 9 (Speeches by Melancton Smith [in the New York Ratifying Convention]); no. 13, paras. 14–18 (Notes of Speeches Given by George Clinton before the New York State Ratifying Convention) in light of Montesquieu, *De l'Esprit des lois*, pt. 1, bk. 8, chaps. 15–20.

[105] Consider *Federalist No. 9* (Hamilton), in light of Montesquieu, *De l'Esprit des lois*, pt. 2, bk. 9, chaps. 1–3.

[106] Consider *Federalist No. 10* (Madison), in light of Montesquieu, *De l'Esprit des lois*, pt. 2, bk. 11, chap. 6, and pt. 3, bk. 19, chap. 27; and see David Hume, "Idea of a Perfect Commonwealth," in Hume, *Essays Moral, Political, and Literary*, rev. ed., ed. Eugene F. Miller (Indianapolis, IN: Liberty Fund, 1985), 512–29 (esp. 525, 527–28).

[107] See *Federalist No. 39* (Madison).

tion of power in the central government and a massive expansion of the executive power.

In the process, of course, the Americans had to make certain adjustments. The separation of powers in Montesquieu's England was buttressed by the existence of a monarch and a nobility entrenched in the executive and in part of the legislative power. The Americans did not possess resources of this sort, and so, in the absence of juridically distinct orders, they had to construct their system of separated powers at both the federal and state levels on a purely republican foundation. The Americans faced one additional difficulty. Their constitutional order was not a product of the ages. It did not have its foundation in mores and manners. It was a rational construct, and it took the form of a written document. Moreover, the order spelled out in that document was hybrid in form, and it was inevitable that there be conflicts between the laws passed by the national government and those adopted in the states. It was essential that there be a superintending power to adjudicate disputes between the two and to prevent Congress and the state legislatures from acting in a manner contrary to the terms of the Constitution. To meet this need the Framers of the Constitution, after considerable deliberation, opted to establish a system of federal courts headed by a Supreme Court graced with the power of judicial review.[108] Here, too, the Americans owed something to Montesquieu—for, in his account of monarchy, he celebrated the fact that, in France, the monarch did not himself exercise the power of judging but left it to the *Parlement* of Paris and the provincial *parlements*, which were not only charged with interpreting and applying the law but expected to refuse to register new legislation if their members found it inconsistent with the existing body of law—a responsibility closely akin to judicial review.[109]

The deliberations of the Framers and their ruminations on the themes announced by Montesquieu did not end with the Constitution's ratification. In the early 1790s, when Madison began thinking about the political consequences inherent in the ambitious program of economic development charted by Hamilton in his capacity as George Washington's Secretary of the Treasury, he had occasion to reconsider Montesquieu's analysis of the relationship between forms of government and the size of the territory they were suited to govern.[110] He believed that "a consolidation

---

[108] See Paul A. Rahe, "Background to *Marbury v. Madison:* The Debate Concerning Judicial Review at the Federal Convention and during the Ratification Period," in Élisabeth Zoller, ed., *Marbury v. Madison: 1803-2003: Un dialogue franco-américain/A French-American Dialogue* (Paris: Dalloz, 2003), 19–36.

[109] See Montesquieu, *De l'Esprit des lois*, pt. 1, bk. 2, chap. 4; bk. 3, chaps. 5–7 and 10; bk. 4, chap. 2; bk. 5, chaps. 9–12; and bk. 8, chaps. 6–9. On the role played by the courts in the evolution of the French monarchy, see ibid., pt. 6, bks. 28, 30–31. For a discussion of Montesquieu's influence on William Blackstone and, through him, on the American understanding of jurisprudence, see Carrese, *The Cloaking of Power*, 1–230.

[110] See Rahe, *Republics Ancient and Modern*, bk. 3, chap. 3, sec. 1–chap. 4, sec. 9 (esp. bk. 3, chap. 4, sec. 9), and Colleen A. Sheehan, *James Madison and the Spirit of Republican Self-Government* (New York: Cambridge University Press, 2009).

of the States into one government" was implicit in Hamilton's assertion of federal prerogatives, and he feared that such a consolidation would neutralize the expedients suggested by Montesquieu and instituted by the Framers and leave "the whole government to that *self directed course,* which, it must be owned, is the natural propensity of every government." [111]

First, he thought, the separation of powers would give way to centralized administration of the sort that typified despotism. If there was such a consolidation, Madison contended, if federalism was subverted and the national government by one means or another took over the prerogatives of the states and the localities, the legislature situated in the new nation's capital would quickly prove to be incompetent "to regulate all the various objects belonging to the local governments," and this "would evidently force a transfer of many of" those objects "to the executive department." [112]

Second, he contended, because the state and local governments are close to the people—in sight and mind, within reach and control—they are the natural instruments of civic agency. If, however, they were to be made dependent on and subject to a national government out of sight and mind and beyond reach and control, the sheer size of the country would stand in the way of concerted popular political action, preventing "that control" on the national legislature "which is essential to a faithful discharge of its trust, [since] neither the voice nor the sense of ten or twenty millions of people, spread through so many latitudes as are comprehended within the United States, could ever be combined or called into effect, if deprived of those local organs, through which both can now be conveyed." In such circumstances, he warned, "the impossibility of acting together, might be succeeded by the inefficacy of partial expressions of the public mind, and this at length, by a universal silence and insensibility." It was the absence of effective popular checks that would leave the national government to a *"self directed course."* [113]

In short, Madison revisited Montesquieu's argument concerning republics and the extent of territory suitable to them. And, at a time when the territory was much smaller than it is now, and the population was not even one-fifteenth of what it is now, he began to worry that the extent of territory encompassed by the United States and the size of its population might be too great. He was, moreover, virtually certain that, if the federal government were allowed to encroach on the prerogatives of the states and the localities, as he believed Hamilton intended, despotism of one sort or another would be the result.

---

[111] James Madison, "Consolidation," for *The National Gazette,* 3 December 1791, in William T. Hutchinson, William M. E. Rachal, et al., eds., *The Papers of James Madison* (Chicago: University of Chicago Press, 1962–1977. Charlottesville, VA: University Press of Virginia, 1977), vol. 14: 137–39.

[112] Ibid.

[113] Ibid.

VI. Conclusion

As should be clear by now, it is by no means fortuitous that, in the speeches which he delivered in the course of the 1912 American presidential election, Woodrow Wilson chose to discuss Thomas Jefferson in tandem with the baron de Montesquieu. As Wilson recognized, there is a close kinship between the Declaration of Independence and *The Spirit of Laws*. One cannot fully adopt the prudential teaching embedded in the latter without embracing something very much like the political doctrine outlined in the opening paragraphs of the former. Nor is it an accident that the Framers of the American Constitution and their critics among the Antifederalists paid such close attention to *The Spirit of Laws*. One cannot attempt to put into practice the principles outlined in the opening paragraphs of Jefferson's masterpiece without giving consideration, in much the same fashion as Montesquieu did, to the circumstances, constitutional provisions, and legal practices most conducive to sustaining liberty in modern circumstances.

For all of this, as I have tried to demonstrate here, there is a reason. As is well known, John Locke's *Two Treatises of Government* was the principal inspiration for Jefferson's great effort to explain to a candid world why so many of Britain's colonists had opted for independence and why they were right to do so.[114] In similar fashion, as I have attempted to demonstrate here, the way of thinking about constitutionalism that Montesquieu bequeathed to the American Founding Fathers was based on an understanding of the state of nature, of objective natural right, and of subjective natural rights fundamentally similar to but not identical with that found in Locke's book.

It stands to reason, then, that, if we want to understand the present discontents, we should take note of Wilson's argument and begin by reflecting on the significance of Progressivism's repudiation of the political principles of the Declaration of Independence and of its rejection of the prudential teaching of *The Spirit of Laws*. James Madison may well have been wrong about the dangers implicit in Alexander Hamilton's program. Something of the sort was instituted by Abraham Lincoln and the Republican Party in the immediate aftermath of the election of 1860,[115] and it did not have in the decades following anything like the consequences that Madison feared. But this does not mean that the anxiety inspired by his ruminations on the geographical imperatives explored by Montesquieu was entirely unjustified. In the twentieth century—when, as E. L. Godkin pointed out, Lincoln's beloved Declaration of Independence had come to seem an embarrassment and the Constitution he defended, an anachronism; when a victorious presidential candidate in his cam-

---

[114] See Rahe, *Republics Ancient and Modern*, bk. 3, Prologue.
[115] See James M. McPherson, *Abraham Lincoln and the Second American Revolution* (New York: Oxford University Press, 1991).

paign rhetoric insisted on dismissing both Jefferson and Montesquieu with disdain as out of date—a gradual and deliberate consolidation of power in the hands of the central government really did begin to take place, and it had precisely the consequences that Madison feared and so abhorred.

In the century that has passed since all of this began, the legislative power lodged within the federal government has proved to be inadequate to the task of managing in fine detail so large and diverse a country. It has transferred to administrative agencies lodged within the executive the power to make rules and regulations that have the force of law, and in the course of a series of administrations that advertised their radical break with America's past by calling themselves The New Freedom, The New Deal, The New Frontier, The Great Society, and, perhaps most tellingly, The New Foundation, the size and scope of the administrative state has become gargantuan. In the process, the state and local governments have become dependent on federal largess, which always comes with strings attached in the form of funded or unfunded "mandates" designed to make these governments fall in line with federal policy. Civic agency, rooted as it normally is in locality, has withered as the localities have lost their leverage, and the civic associations so admired by Alexis de Tocqueville have for the most part become lobbying operations with offices in Washington focused on influencing federal policy, and many of them have also become recipients of government grants and reliable instruments not only for the implementation of federal policy but also for its defense. Moreover, as Madison predicted, to a degree hitherto hardly imaginable, the federal government has assumed a self-directed course in defiance of the popular will.

What we are witnessing not only in the United States but abroad as well is democracy's drift in the direction of what Tocqueville called "soft despotism." [116] That Americans still retain at least a remnant of the salutary spirit of jealousy that animated the old struggle between Country and Court was made clear on the first Tuesday in November, 2010.[117] If, however, they are to succeed in reversing democracy's soft despotic drift, they will have to take the advice implicit in Godkin's lament, recover the understanding of natural right articulated in the Declaration of Independence, and attend to the institutional logic inherent in the species of constitutionalism pioneered by Montesquieu and refined and applied to American circumstances by the Framers of the Constitution of the United States.

History, Hillsdale College

---

[116] See Rahe, *Soft Despotism, Democracy's Drift*, 141–280.

[117] See Paul A. Rahe, "How Should Elites Think About the Tea Party?" *Commentary* 131, no. 2 (2011): 13–18.

THE IDEA OF RIGHTS IN THE IMPERIAL CRISIS

By Craig Yirush

I. Introduction

Rights were at the heart of the American Revolutionaries' case against Crown and Parliament. Yet there have been few scholarly accounts of the idea of rights in the American Founding. Even in the heated debate which dominated the last generation of revolutionary historiography between those who advanced a classical republican or communitarian interpretation of the Founding and those who defended a liberal or individualistic one, participants eschewed any close examination of what rights meant to the Founding generation. Instead, both sides defined liberalism as a political philosophy which rejected a classical idea of the public good, and defended instead the legitimacy of competing economic and political interests, leaving little room for a less reductive, more rights-based account of the formation of the American republic.[1] Nor have early Americanists engaged with scholars of medieval and early modern European political thought who have been conducting a complicated debate on the origins and meaning of rights—in particular on when the modern idea of an individual natural right was first articulated.[2] To the extent that the idea of rights in the American Founding has been studied, it has been largely as a byproduct of these European debates, with a number of prominent scholars concluding that natural law duties trumped rights in revolutionary discourse, thereby challenging an understanding of the revolution as primarily about individual liberty.[3] Other scholars see the Americans as

---

[1] For example, Gordon Wood's influential argument that the revolution saw a transformation from a republican politics of virtue to a liberal politics of interests. See Wood, *The Creation of the American Republic, 1776–1787* (Chapel Hill: University of North Carolina Press, 1969). For one of the few exceptions, see Michael Zuckert's superb account of the idea of rights available to the colonists in Michael Zuckert, *Natural Rights and the New Republicanism* (Princeton: Princeton University Press, 1994). On the classical republicanism versus liberalism debate, see Daniel T. Rodgers, "Republicanism: The Career of a Concept," *Journal of American History* 79 (1992): 11–38.

[2] For an overview of these debates, see Francis Oakley's *Natural Laws, Laws of Nature, Natural Rights: Continuity and Discontinuity in the History of Ideas* (New York: Continuum Publishing, 2006). James Hutson is one of the few Americanists who takes seriously these European debates, arguing that the Americans (though confused on some level about what rights meant) gradually adopted an individualistic or "subjective" understanding of the concept. See Hutson, "The Emergence of a Modern Concept of a Right in America: The Contribution of Michael Villey," in Barry Shain, ed., *The Nature of Rights at the American Founding and Beyond* (Charlottesville: University of Virginia Press, 2007), 25–63.

[3] For an argument about the centrality of duties, see Knud Haakonssen, "From Natural Law to the Rights of Man: a European Perspective on American Debates," in his *Natural Law*

doi:10.1017/S026505251100032X

simply confused about what rights meant. As Jack Rakove, one of the leading scholars of early American constitutionalism puts it, early Americans used the concepts of rights with "a flabby imprecision."[4]

In order to explore what early Americans meant when they claimed certain rights, this essay will examine the arguments they made against Crown and Parliament in the imperial crisis (1763-1776), a period often slighted in the scholarship on the American Founding in favor of the seminal events of the 1780s which culminated in the federal constitution. The imperial crisis, however, was crucial to the development of early American rights theory since it was the time in which rights were asserted most forcefully during the Founding. Once independence had been achieved, political debate (at least within the Euro-American settler community) centered mainly on how to design a viable constitution for a republican federation rather than on the more theoretical question of the nature and origin of rights. In its account of the imperial crisis, this essay will focus on two interrelated but conceptually distinct kinds of rights the colonists claimed—the rights of Englishmen which, they insisted, were an integral part of their common law legal heritage, and which have been largely overlooked by political theorists who study the Founding[5]; and natural rights, which in principle applied to all people everywhere, and which become increasingly central to the colonial case against Britain. To get at their understanding of rights, the essay will canvas a representative sample of colonial opinion, discussing the protests of official bodies—the assemblies, the Stamp Act Congress, the Continental Congresses—alongside some of the more influential colonial pamphlets.[6]

II. Imperial Reforms and Colonial Resistance, 1764-1766

In the aftermath of the Seven Years' War (1756-1763), the king's ministers in Parliament, burdened by the debt Britain had incurred to defeat the French and disillusioned by the colonists' unwillingness to pay their share of the costs of the war, decided to reform the empire by centralizing

---

and Moral Philosophy: from Grotius to the Scottish Enlightenment (Cambridge: Cambridge University Press, 1996), 310-42; as well as Barry Shain, "Rights Natural and Civil in the Declaration of Independence," in Shain, ed., *The Nature of Rights at the American Founding and Beyond*, 116-62.

[4] Rakove, *Original Meanings: Politics and Ideas in the Making of the Constitution* (New York: Vintage Books, 1999), 290.

[5] For example Alan Gibson's sophisticated account of the historiography of the founding contains no index entry for the common law or English rights. See Gibson, *Understanding the Founding: The Crucial Questions* (Lawrence: University Press of Kansas, 2007). For the centrality of the common law to the American Revolution, see Jack P. Greene, *The Constitutional Origins of the American Revolution* (New York: Cambridge University Press, 2011).

[6] I am indebted to conversations with Barry Shain on the need to study a more representative sample of colonial opinion, including the official or state papers of the revolution.

power in London.[7] Beginning in 1763, they strengthened the empire's system of trade regulation (the Navigation Acts), making it easier for customs officials to prosecute colonial smugglers, and attempting (in the Sugar Act of 1764) to raise a revenue from import duties on goods imported into the colonies. Concerned that the colonial desire to settle in the territory newly conquered from the French (in particularly the fertile lands of the Ohio Valley) would exacerbate already tense relations with the Native Americans, they made the momentous decision to keep an army in America after the peace had been signed. They also decided to limit westward settlement, reserving valuable land west of the Appalachians for the Native Americans in the Royal Proclamation of 1763. And in order to pay for the cost of colonial defense, Parliament passed a stamp tax in the spring of 1765 which affected a wide range of goods and services in the colonies, from playing cards to newspapers to court documents, the use of which required the purchase of special stamped paper.[8]

With the exception of the Royal Proclamation, these initiatives all emanated from the king's ministers in the House of Commons and the House of Lords. This was crucial as it made the long-standing question of what rights the colonist could claim in the empire rest on the authority of Parliament, an authority which the leading jurists of England were coming to see as in principle unlimited. According to William Blackstone, author of a widely influential legal treatise, Parliament could "do every thing that is not naturally impossible; and therefore some have scrupled to call it's power, by a figure rather too bold, the omnipotence of Parliament. True it is, that what they do, no authority on earth can undo."[9]

The first responses to the ministry's reforms came in the fall of 1764, as the colonial assemblies protested both the Sugar Act and the pending Stamp Act. In a series of petitions to the king and both houses of Parliament, the colonial assemblies resisted these imperial reforms with a powerful and widely shared account of their right to be free from nonconsensual taxation, as well as to enjoy a degree of internal autonomy or self-government in the empire, which they in turn argued was necessary if their individual rights as Britons outside the realm were to be secure.[10] As the New York assembly's petition to the House of Commons put it: "an Exemption from the Burthen of ungranted, involuntary Taxes, must be

[7] On which, see Fred Anderson's *Crucible of War: The Seven Years' War and the Fate of Empire in British America, 1754–1766* (New York: Vintage Books, 2001), 557–651.

[8] For details on the scope and the rates of tax, see Edmund S. Morgan, *The Stamp Act Crisis: Prologue to Revolution* (1953; Chapel Hill: University of North Carolina Press, 1995), 73–74.

[9] William Blackstone, *Commentaries on the Laws of England*, Vol. 1. Stanley N. Katz, ed. (1765; Chicago: University of Chicago Press, 1979), 156.

[10] For an argument that the colonies always maintained an exclusive right to tax themselves, and thus were not, contrary to the claims of the Progressive historians in the early twentieth century, inconsistent or opportunistic in their opposition to British policy, first objecting only to internal taxes, and then external, see Edmund S. Morgan, "Colonial Ideas of Parliamentary Power, 1764–1766," *The William and Mary Quarterly*, 5 (1948): 311–41.

the grand Principle of every free State." Without such a right "vested in themselves, exclusive of all others," the assembly argued, "there can be no Happiness, no Liberty," and "no Security," "for who can call that his own, which may be taken away at the Pleasure of another." The principle of consensual taxation was, the assembly insisted, "the natural Right of Mankind."[11]

The New York assembly also grounded their case for colonial rights on a series of claims about the conditions of settlement in America. As the assembly informed the Commons, in settling America they had "submitted to Poverty, Barbarian Wars, Loss of Blood ... and ten Thousand unutterable Hardships, to enlarge the Trade, Wealth, and Dominion of the Nation." As such, they claimed an "Exemption" from Parliamentary taxation not as a "Privilege" but "as their Right."[12] In other words, because they had created an empire for the Crown by their own efforts, defending themselves against a "barbarian Enemy," they had a right to "a civil Constitution" which was "permanent" and could be "transmitted to their latest Posterity."[13]

Although the New York assembly conceded that Parliament had the right to levy duties for the sole purpose of regulating the empire's trade, it resisted any further extension of Parliament's authority. Indeed, it argued that "History" cannot "furnish an Instance of a Constitution" which permits "one Part of a Dominion to be taxed by another, and that too in Effect, but by a Branch of the other Part." Having reduced Parliament to merely a "Branch" of the government of one part of the empire, the New York assembly added that it had a financial interest in making Britons "on one Side of the Atlantic" "submit to the most unsupportable Oppression and Tyranny."[14] And it warned that the imposition of such a tyranny would "turn a vast fertile, prosperous Region, into a dreary Wilderness; impoverish Great-Britain, and shake the Power and Independency of the most opulent and flourishing Empire in the World."[15]

In December 1764, the Virginia House of Burgesses sent a petition to the king with a remarkably similar account of the rights of the colonists in the empire. According to the burgesses, it was "a fundamental Principle of the British Constitution" that "the People are not subject to any Taxes but such as are laid on them by their own Consent."[16] The burgesses also insisted that they had this "Right" as *both* "Men" and as "Descendents of Britons"—that is, they grounded their rights on both the common law (and its historical legacy) as well as the more universal basis of the law of

---

[11] The New York Petition to the House of Commons, October 18th, 1764, in Morgan, *Prologue to Revolution*, 9–10.

[12] Ibid., 10.

[13] Ibid., 9, 11.

[14] Ibid., 10. The New York assembly even claimed to prefer absolute monarchy to rule by Parliament on the grounds that it tended to treat its subjects more equally.

[15] Ibid., 13–14.

[16] Ibid., 14.

nature. As the assembly's memorial to the House of Lords put it: these
new taxes would be "subversive" of "that Freedom which all Men, especially those who derive their Constitution from Britain, have a Right to
enjoy."[17] The burgesses also insisted that their migration across the Atlantic (and thus outside the realm) had not in any way diminished their
rights. As they informed the Lords, because "their Ancestors brought
with them every Right and Privilege they could with Justice claim in their
Mother Kingdom, their Descendants ... cannot be deprived of those
rights without injustice." As the burgesses told the Commons, the "Privilege" of consensual taxation was "inherent in the Persons who discovered and settled" Virginia, and was not "renounced or forfeited by their
Removal hither." Moreover, they and their ancestors had extended the
territory and dominion of Britain, and in return for their efforts the king
had guaranteed them all the "Rights and Immunities of British Subjects"
in a royal charter (and later in the commissions to royal governors), along
with the "Power" to pass laws for the general welfare (with the consent
of the governor and council). In this manner, the king had expressed his
"tender" regard for "the Rights of his American Subjects," rights which
the burgesses insisted were a "sacred Birthright and most valuable
Inheritance."[18]

The initial protests by New York and Virginia in 1764 were echoed in
the protests against the Stamp Act in 1765. In all, eight colonies sent
some form of official protest to London. Rhode Island's Resolves claimed
that the "People of this Colony" had "the Right of being governed by
their own Assembly in the Articles of Taxes and internal Police."[19]
Pennsylvania's assembly resolved "That the inhabitants of this Province are entitled to all the Liberties, Rights and Privileges of his Majesty's Subjects in Great-Britain or elsewhere," adding that "the
Constitution of Government in this Province is founded on the natural
Rights of Mankind, and the noble Principles of English Liberty." The
Pennsylvania assembly went on to claim that it is "the inherent Birthright and indubitable Privilege, of every British Subject, to be taxed
only by his own Consent, or that of his legal Representatives, in Con-
junction with his Majesty, or his Substitutes."[20] According to the Maryland assembly, "the first Adventurers and Settlers of this Province"
"brought with them and transmitted to their Posterity and all other his
Majestys (sic) Subjects since Inhabiting in this Province all the Liberties
privileges Franchise and Immunities that any time have been held
enjoyed and possessed by the People of Great Britain." And while the
assemblymen in Maryland also rested their claim to be exempt from
Parliamentary taxes on their charter, they were careful to insist that the

[17] Ibid., 15.
[18] Ibid., 16.
[19] Ibid., 50–51.
[20] Ibid., 51–52.

"said Charter is Declaratory of the Constitutional Rights and Privileges of the Freemen of this Province"—that is, it did not create the rights but merely declared them.[21] The South Carolina assembly insisted that the king's subjects in America were "intitled to all the inherent Rights and Liberties of His natural born Subjects within the Kingdom of Great Britain." And they insisted that the right to consent to taxation by their chosen representatives (or "given personally") is "inseparably essential to the Freedom of a People, and the undoubted Right of Englishmen." Indeed, the colony's representatives insisted, their "Happiness" depends on the "full and free enjoyment of their Rights and Liberties."[22] The Massachusetts General Court maintained that the security of property from arbitrary seizure is one of the "essential Rights of the British Constitution of Government, which are founded in the Law of God and Nature, and are the common Rights of Mankind." Only by exercising the "Powers of Government" granted in the royal charter, the General Court insisted, could they secure their "constitutional Rights."[23]

The Stamp Act Congress met in the fall of 1765 with twenty seven delegates from nine colonies in attendance. Virginia, Georgia and North Carolina were not able to elect any delegates because their governors refused to convene assemblies (and New Hampshire declined to attend). In its petitions to the king, the Commons and the Lords, the Congress echoed the earlier arguments of the colonial assemblies, claiming that the colonists were entitled to "all the inherent Rights and Liberties of the Natives of Great Britain." Most importantly, this meant that they had a right to be exempt from all taxation not imposed by their "several Legislatures."[24] Moreover, their "remote situation" made it impossible for them to be represented anywhere but in their "respective subordinate Legislature." As such, the colonies had a "full power of Legislation, agreeable to the English Constitution," but at the same time the Congress acknowledged a constitutionally vague "Subordination to Parliament."[25] This tension between the rights of the colonists organized in self-governing colonies and the sovereign claims of Parliament was to be central to the ensuing imperial crisis.

In addition to the official protests, numerous Britons on both sides of the Atlantic picked up their pens and wrote pamphlets and newspaper essays both for and against the Sugar Act and the Stamp Act. In order to get a sense of what kind of case was made for colonial rights in this large literature, I will focus on two prominent British American pamphlets, one by Stephen Hopkins (1701–1785), the governor of Rhode Island, and the other by Richard Bland (1710–1776), a prominent member of the Virginia House of Burgesses.

[21] Ibid., 52–53.
[22] Ibid., 58.
[23] Ibid., 56–57.
[24] Ibid., 66.
[25] Ibid., 64–65.

In *The Rights of Colonies Examined*, Hopkins opposed the new imperial policies because "British subjects in America have equal rights with those in Britain." Moreover, he argued, "they do not hold these rights as a privilege granted them, nor enjoy them as a grace and favor bestowed, but possess them as an inherent, indefeasible right, as they and their ancestors were freeborn subjects, justly and naturally entitled to all the rights and advantages of the British constitution."[26] Given this, Parliament's attempt to tax the colonies was a violation of their "just and long enjoyed rights," for to be taxed at the "mere will" of another is to be placed in a state of "abject slavery." Hopkins also invoked the colonial charters in his case against Parliament, arguing that all of the New England colonies had made a compact with the king "before their departure" which "fully settled" "the terms of their freedom and the relation they should stand in to the mother country in their emigrant state." According to its terms, they would be "subject to the King and dependent on the kingdom of Great Britain"; and "in return they were to receive protection and enjoy all the rights and freedoms of freeborn Englishmen."[27] Finally, Hopkins defended the colonists' rights by claiming that "at their own expense" they had "transported themselves to America," and "with great risk and difficulty settled among savages, and in a very surprising manner formed new colonies in the wilderness."[28] For this reason, Hopkins included in his list of grievances the Royal Proclamation's prohibition on western settlement. As he pointed out, the colonists had "exulted" in the defeat of the French, yet they "reaped no sort of advantage by these conquests," gaining "not . . . a single acre of land," and having "no part in the Indian or interior trade."[29]

Despite this strong assertion of colonial rights, Hopkins did not deny that there were some areas in which Parliament had jurisdiction over them. The colonies, he noted, have their own legislatures which provide for their "peace and internal government, yet there are many things of a more general nature, quite out of reach of these particular legislatures, which it is necessary should be regulated, ordered and governed." For example, the "commerce of the whole" and indeed "everything that concerns the proper interest and fit government of the whole commonwealth." In these areas, he conceded, it is "absolutely necessary" to have "some supreme and overruling authority with power to make laws and form regulations for the good of all, and to compel their execution and observation."[30] Nevertheless, Hopkins denied that Parliament was sovereign over America, for, he argued, its members only represent the people of Great Britain and thus their power cannot "exceed that of their

[26] Stephen Hopkins, *The Rights of the Colonies Examined* (Providence, 1764), 9.
[27] Ibid., 16.
[28] Ibid., 4–5.
[29] Ibid., 21.
[30] Ibid., 10.

constituents." Rather, in an "imperial state" consisting of "many separate governments each of which hath peculiar privileges" and in which no one part is superior to and able to "make laws for or to tax" the "lesser part," "all laws and all taxes which bind the whole must be made by the whole."[31] Here Hopkins gave the example of Germany in which no one state (or even the emperor) could bind the rest of the states; only the imperial diet in which they were all represented could. But, Hopkins rejected the idea of colonial representation in Parliament as unworkable. In its place, he offered the idea of voluntary gifts to the Crown, which the colonists had "cheerfully" granted in the past, and which were preferable to compelling them by an "unconstitutional method."[32]

Unlike Hopkins, Richard Bland's *An Inquiry into the Rights of the British Colonies* defended colonial rights solely on the basis of the law of nature.[33] Indeed, unlike previous colonial spokesmen, he made a sharp distinction between the constitution of Great Britain (in which, Parliamentary spokesmen argued, there were unrepresented subjects who were still bound by Parliamentary laws) and that of the empire. In Bland's view, the constitution of the realm was not a guide to the relationship between the colonies and the metropole, for "the colonies in North America" were "founded by Englishmen" in "this uncultivated and almost uninhabited country," and "without any expence to the nation."[34] Because we "can receive no Light from the Laws of the Kingdom, or from ancient History, to direct us in our Inquiry," Bland argued, "we must have recourse to the Law of Nature, and those Rights of Mankind which flow from it."[35] According to Bland, "Men in a State of Nature are absolutely free and independent of one another as to sovereign jurisdiction, but when they enter into a Society, and by their own Consent become Members of it, they must submit to the Laws of the Society according to which they agree to be governed." According to Bland, this right existed because "their Submission to the publick authority of the State, do not oblige them to continue in it longer than they find it will conduce to their Happiness, which they have a natural Right to promote. This natural Right remains with every Man, and he cannot justly be deprived of it by any civil Authority."[36] For Bland, then, when

> Men exercise this Right, and withdraw themselves from their Country, they recover their natural Freedom and Independence: The Jurisdiction and Sovereignty of the State they quitted ceases; and if they

[31] Ibid., 19–20.
[32] Ibid., 22.
[33] Richard Bland, *An Inquiry into the Rights of the British Colonies* (Williamsburg: Alexander Purdie, & Co., 1766).
[34] Ibid., 12.
[35] Ibid., 14.
[36] Ibid., 10.

unite, and by common Consent take Possession of a new Country, and form themselves into a political Society, they become a sovereign State, independent of the State from which they separated.[37]

Bland applied these normative claims to the settlement of America, arguing that the English colonists had exercised their natural right to exit the realm and establish new polities on the far side of the Atlantic. Bland then claimed that they had chosen to make a compact with the English king, who granted them a royal charter with all "the rights and privileges of Englishmen," in return for which they had expanded his empire. According to Bland, under the terms of the charter, they "were respected as a distinct State, independent, as to their *internal* Government, of the original Kingdom, but united with her, as to their *external* Polity, in the closest League and Amity, under the same Allegiance, and enjoying the Benefits of a reciprocal Intercourse."[38] Moreover, Bland noted, when the first colonists had ventured across the Atlantic, America "was possessed by a savage People, scattered through the Country, who were not subject to the *English* Dominion, nor owed Obedience to its Laws."[39] Given that America was unoccupied save for the "savage" and therefore stateless Native Americans, the original colonists faced no barriers to the exercise of their natural right to choose the form of government they wanted to live under.

Bland however equivocated about the central issue of Parliamentary sovereignty, conceding that the "Colonies are subordinate to the Authority of Parliament," which was "without doubt, supreme within the body of the kingdom," and "cannot be abridged by any other power." But he did not think that Parliament could violate the colonists' right of "directing their internal government by laws made with their own consent"[40] For Bland, "Great" as "the Power of Parliament . . . is" "it cannot constitutionally deprive the People of their *natural* Rights; nor, in Virtue of the same Principle, can it deprive them of their *civil* Rights, which are founded in Compact, without their own Consent."[41] And indeed, he came close to sanctioning a right of resistance to Parliament, claiming that it would be in a state of war with the colonists if it violated their rights. However, Bland then backed away from this radical stance, conceding Parliament's authority (based on precedent going back to the Restoration) to regulate the trade of the empire, and counseling more petitions as a mean of redressing colonial grievances.

The pamphlets of Hopkins and Bland, along with the resolves of the colonial assemblies and a specially constituted pan-colonial congress, contain strong evidence for the existence of a coherent and widely shared

[37] Ibid., 14.
[38] Ibid., 20.
[39] Ibid., 20–21.
[40] Ibid., 16–17.
[41] Ibid., 26.

understanding of rights in British North America in the first phase of the imperial crisis. All of the colonies insisted that Parliament had no right to tax them for revenue of any sort, maintaining that if this right were violated it would lead to the undermining of other important rights, most centrally of individual colonists to property and, more broadly, to liberty. These rights were also seen as *inherent* in each English subject—they were a "birthright" and not a "privilege" that could be revoked by Crown or Parliament. Some colonial spokesmen also held that the rights of English-men were equivalent to (or were an expression of) the rights of mankind.

The colonists also argued that their individual rights as Englishmen (or as men) entailed a right to an "internal" governing authority in which they could pass laws for themselves immune from the jurisdiction of the king and Parliament. On this view each of the colonies constituted a "free state" as the New York assembly put it in 1764. This internal autonomy, though subordinate to Parliament's authority to regulate imperial rela-tions, was seen as crucial to the protection of the colonists' individual rights to liberty and property, for only by having a say in the taxes imposed on them and, crucially, the laws that bound them could they be truly free. And finally, the colonies grounded their rights in the risk-taking and labor required to settle America, which, they claimed, was "wilderness" inhabited by "savages" before they arrived. This depiction of America as an alien place outside the realm of England, and thus outside the jurisdiction of the common law at the time of first settlement, would become an increasingly important argument in the imperial crisis as it enabled the colonists to base their case against the king and Parlia-ment on the natural rights of men in a state of nature rather than on the rights of Englishmen.

III. The Townshend Duties Crisis, 1767–1770

The repeal of the Stamp Act in early 1766 was followed by the passage of the Declaratory Act which underlined the emerging Blackstonian con-sensus that Parliament had "full power and authority to make laws and statutes of sufficient force and validity to bind the colonies and people of *America* ... in all cases whatsoever."[42] And the new ministry, led by Charles Townshend, levied a new round of duties in the spring of 1767 on the mistaken belief that the colonists only objected to internal taxes like those levied in the Stamp Act but not to external taxes such as the customs duties that they had long been paying as part of the Navigation Acts. Townshend planned to use the money raised by his new import duties to pay for the salaries of the colonial governors and other royal officials. By doing so, he intended to make the executive power of the Crown inde-

---

[42] The Declaratory Act (March 18th, 1766), in Greene, ed., *Colonies to Nation: A Documen-tary History of the American Revolution, 1763–1789* (New York: McGraw-Hill, 1967), 85.

pendent of the legislative power of the colonial assemblies.[43] Moreover, these new duties would be collected in America by an American Board of Customs Commissioners headquartered in Boston whose salaries would be paid out of the monies they collected.[44] The following year, four new vice-admiralty courts were established in the major ports.[45] The ministry also decided to move the troops who had been guarding the Proclamation line in the west into the cities in order to better assert Parliament's authority.[46] And finally, in the summer of 1767, the ministry passed an act suspending the New York assembly, which, in contravention of the Quartering Act, had refused to provide the troops in the colony with sufficient shelter and supplies.[47]

Although no pan-colonial congress met to protest Townshend's policies, there was a widespread campaign to boycott British goods, which culminated in nonimportation and nonconsumption agreements enforced by local committees throughout America.[48] In Massachusetts in early 1768, the assembly, at the instigation of Samuel Adams, sent a circular letter to the other colonies protesting the new duties on the grounds that "it is an essential, unalterable right in nature, engrafted into the British constitution, as a fundamental law . . . that what a man had honestly acquired is absolutely his own" and "cannot be taken from him without his consent." The circular letter also expressed concern that Townshend's plan to pay the salaries of the governors, judges and "other civil officers" would "endanger the happiness and security of the subject." And it went on to state that "American subjects" had these rights "exclusive of any consideration of charter rights"; rather, they had "natural and constitutional" rights as "free men and subjects." The circular letter also insisted that the constitution of "free states" was "fixed."[49]

[43] On which, see Lawrence H. Gipson, *The Coming of the Revolution, 1763–1775* (New York: Harper Brothers, 1954), 174–75.

[44] See Olive M. Dickerson, *The Navigation Acts and the American Revolution* (Philadelphia, 1951); and Thomas C. Barrow, *Trade and Empire: The British Customs Service in Colonial America, 1660–1775* (Cambridge, MA: Harvard University Press, 1967).

[45] James Munro and Sir Almeric Fizroy, eds., *Acts of the Privy Council Colonial Series.* Volume V (1766–1783) (London: His Majesty's Stationery Office, 1912), 151–53.

[46] In April 1768, following the Treaty of Stanwix, a new boundary was drawn, opening more land for settlement in the Ohio Valley than the Proclamation line decreed in 1763. This in turn facilitated the movement of troops into the colonial cities as the protests over the new Revenue Act gathered pace. See John Alden, *A History of the American Revolution* (New York: Alfred A. Knopf, 1969), 93–94.

[47] On these measures, see Robert Middlekauff, *The Glorious Cause: The American Revolution, 1763–1789* (1982; expanded edition, New York: Oxford University Press, 2005), 149–58. On the suspension of the New York legislature, see Nicholas Varga, "The New York Restraining Act: Its Passage and Some Effects, 1766–1768," *New York History* 37 (1956): 233–58.

[48] For the nonimportation agreements adopted in Boston (in August, 1768, after earlier attempts had fallen through), and in Charleston (July, 1769), see Merrill Jensen, ed., *American Colonial Documents to 1776.* Volume IX of David Douglas, ed., *English Historical Documents* (London: Eyre & Spottiswoode, 1955), 724–26. By the end of 1769, every colony had adopted some form of nonimportation.

[49] Jensen, ed., *American Colonial Documents*, 714–16.

The most widely read colonial attack on the Townshend Act came from the pen of John Dickinson, who had played an important role in the Stamp Act Congress. In a series of *Letters from a Farmer in Pennsylvania* published in colonial newspapers in 1767 and 1768 (and then reprinted as a pamphlet), Dickinson insisted that the Townshend duties were in fact taxes (despite their name) because they were enacted "for the sole purpose of levying money," rather than to regulate trade within the empire. And, like the opponents of the Stamp Act, he responded to the ministry with "a total denial of the power of Parliament to lay upon these colonies any 'tax' whatsoever." Dickinson also laid out the larger threat to liberty posed by taxation without consent, arguing that the monies Parliament would collect could be used for the creation of a pliant judiciary (which served at pleasure), the payment of the salaries of royal governors (freeing the executive from the control of the colonial legislatures), and the funding of a "standing" (that is, permanent) army in the colonies, all of which, he argued, would be fatal to the survival of a "free state."[50]

Other opponents of the Townshend Act pursued the more radical natural rights arguments that Bland had laid out in his opposition to the Stamp Act. One of the most sophisticated was the pamphlet of Dickinson's fellow Pennsylvanian, William Hicks, *The Nature and Extent of Parliamentary Power Considered,* originally written just before the repeal of the Stamp Act, but updated in 1768 to include a consideration of the measures passed by Townshend.[51] Hicks based his opposition to the Townshend Acts on "that equality which we have received from nature, and which we find so firmly supported by the laws of our mother country."[52] Moreover, Hicks argued, when the settlers "crossed the Atlantic to settle the deserts of America, they bro't with them the spirit of the English government."[53] Once in America and thus unable to be represented in Parliament, they had applied to "their Prince for such protection and assistance as might raise them to an equality with their brethren of England."[54] As a consequence, the colonists were only subject to laws made "by regular agreement with the deputy of the Crown." And it followed from this that "the Lords and Commons of England" cannot "covenant with the Crown for the limiting and restraining our natural liberty."[55]

By arguing that the colonists had a natural right of equality, which they had exercised by making a contract with the Crown, Hicks was able to deny Parliamentary authority in the empire *tout court*. In its place, he offered an explicitly federal vision of the empire—the colonies were, for

[50] Dickinson, *Letters from a Farmer in Pennsylvania*, in Forrest McDonald, ed., *Empire and Nation* (1962; Indianapolis: Liberty Fund, 1999), Letter IV, Letter IX, Letter XI, passim.
[51] William Hicks, *The Nature and Extent of Parliamentary Power Considered* (John Holt: New York, 1768).
[52] Ibid., 25.
[53] Ibid., 22.
[54] Ibid., 23.
[55] Ibid., 20.

Hicks, "so many different counties of the same kingdom," which, because they were unable to be represented in the "general council," were governed by their own assemblies with the concurrence of the king. In such an arrangement, "the restraining power lodged in the Crown" will "insure" that this "policy" was conducive to the general good. After all, Hicks claimed, "we cannot suppose that a wise and just Prince would ever consent to sacrifice the interest and happiness of any one part to the selfish views of another."[56]

IV. From Tea Party to Revolution

Due to widespread opposition in the colonies, the new ministry under Lord North repealed all of the Townshend duties in the spring of 1770, save the one on tea, which North intended to use to pay the salaries of royal officials in the colonies.[57] Three years of commercial prosperity and relative calm ensued. During this time, the colonists imported tea and paid the duty that Townshend had levied in 1767. The Board of Customs Commissioners, however, remained in place; the Royal Navy continued to patrol the coasts looking for smugglers; and British troops stayed in Boston.

But when the North ministry, in a bid to help the financially troubled East India Company, passed the Tea Act in 1773, opposition in New York and Philadelphia was so strong that the tea was never brought ashore. In Boston, however, the governor refused to allow the ships to leave the harbor. In response, a mob dumped the tea in the harbor, ensuring that the tax would not be paid.

In response to Boston's Tea Party, Parliament passed legislation known collectively as the Coercive Acts (March–June, 1774). The first closed the port of Boston to all commerce until the East India Company was compensated for the loss of tea. The second altered the Massachusetts charter for the first time since 1691, giving the king the power to appoint the upper house of the colony's legislature. It also allowed the governor to appoint all provincial judges and sheriffs, and limited the number of town meetings to one a year without the permission of the governor. A third act provided for the removal out of the colony of any magistrate, soldier, or customs official indicted for a capitol offence and unlikely to receive an impartial trial in a colonial court. A fourth act provided for the quartering of troops in the colonies. At the same time, General Thomas Gage, who was the commander-in-chief of British forces, also became the civil governor of the colony.[58]

[56] Ibid., 25.
[57] Oliver M. Dickerson, "Use Made of the Revenue from the Tax on Tea," *The New England Quarterly* 31 (1958), 232–43.
[58] For the Coercive Acts, see Jensen, ed., *American Colonial Documents*, 779–85.

Although the Coercive Acts were directed solely at Massachusetts, they radicalized the opposition to Britain in all of the mainland colonies. In response, James Wilson (1742–1798), a recent émigré from Scotland, and Thomas Jefferson (1743–1826), a young Virginia lawyer, denied Parliamentary authority over the colonies altogether. In doing so, they crystallized the vision of the empire based on natural rights and internal autonomy that had been developing since the early 1760s, adding to it the claim that the colonies were independent states.

In his 1774 pamphlet *Considerations on the Nature and Extent of the Legislative Authority of the British Parliament*, Wilson rejected the Coercive Acts on the grounds that "All men are, by nature, equal and free." In particular, he insisted that all men have "rights" to which they are "entitled by the supreme and controulable laws of nature," as well as "the fundamental principles of the British constitution."[59] Chief among these was the right to consent to all laws that bound them. As Wilson put it: "No one has a right to any authority over another without his consent: All lawful government is founded on the consent of those, who are subject to it." In Wilson's view, "Such consent was given with a view to ensure and to encrease the happiness of the governed above what they could enjoy in an independent and unconnected state of nature." And because "This rule is founded on the law of nature," Wilson argued, "It must control every political maxim: it must regulate the Legislature itself. The people have a right to insist that this rule be served; and are entitled to demand a moral security that the Legislature will observe it."[60]

Given this, Wilson denied that Parliament had a "supreme irresistible uncontrolled authority over" the colonies.[61] Indeed, since all just authority derived from the people's natural rights, Parliament could have no authority over Britons who had not consented to its laws. To argue otherwise, Wilson insisted, implied that one group of subjects could bind another without their consent, even though both had equal natural rights.

Jefferson's 1774 *Summary View of the Rights of British America* made the same argument. According to Jefferson:

> our ancestors, before their emigration to America, were the free inhabitants of the British dominions in Europe, and possessed a right which nature has given to all men, of departing from the country in which chance, not choice, has placed them, of going in quest of new habitations, and of there establishing new societies, under such laws as to them shall seem most likely to promote public happiness.[62]

[59] James Wilson, *Considerations on the Nature and Extent of the Legislative Authority of the British Parliament* (Philadelphia, 1774), 2.
[60] Ibid., 3.
[61] Ibid., 3–4.
[62] Thomas Jefferson, *Summary View of the Rights of British America* (Williamsburg, 1774), 6.

Indeed, Jefferson argued, "America was conquered" and "her settlements made, and firmly established, at the expence of individuals, and not of the British public."[63] It was "for themselves they fought, for themselves they conquered, and for themselves alone they have a right to hold." Britain, Jefferson argued, did not expend a "shilling" to assist the American colonies until after they were firmly established, and had become commercially valuable.[64]

After these "settlements" had been made "in the wilds of America," Jefferson contended that the "emigrants" chose "to adopt that system of laws under which they had hitherto lived in the mother country, and to continue their union with her by submitting themselves to the same common sovereign, who was thereby made" the sole link connecting "the several American states."[65] In place of Parliamentary sovereignty, then, Jefferson envisioned a federal empire, an association of "states" wherein the Crown held the executive power. But if the Crown acted arbitrarily, Jefferson argued, "the power reverts to the people, who may exercise it to unlimited extent, either assembling together in person, sending deputies, or in any other way they may think proper."[66]

Jefferson's *Summary View* was written for the Virginia delegates to a new pan-colonial Continental Congress, the first such body to meet since the Stamp Act Congress in 1765. After convening, the delegates rejected the Pennsylvanian Joseph Galloway's (1731–1803) plan of union, which would have created a legislature with representation from all of the colonies, overseen by a president appointed by the Crown.[67] The Congress also constituted a committee to draft a statement of rights, which led to a wide-ranging debate about the basis of colonial rights.[68] Richard Henry Lee (1733–1794) of Virginia, argued that Congress should make its claim "upon the broadest bottom, the ground of nature," for, according to Lee, when "our ancestors" arrived in America, they "found ... no government." Lee was also adamant that rights to "Life and liberty" cannot "be given up when we enter society." However, Lee did not see these natural rights as inconsistent with those based on the common law, and he argued that the Congress should rest its claims on a "fourfold foundation: on

[63] Jefferson compared the migration to America with that of the Saxons to Britain. For the role that this historical understanding played in Jefferson's political thought, see H. Trevor Colbourn, *The Lamp of Experience: Whig History and the Intellectual Origins of the American Revolution* (Chapel Hill: University of North Carolina Press, 1965), 158–84.

[64] Jefferson, *Summary View*, 6.

[65] Ibid., 7, 16.

[66] Ibid., 19.

[67] For a copy of the plan, see Julian P. Boyd, ed., *Anglo-American Union: Joseph Galloway's Plans to Preserve the British Empire, 1774–1778* (Philadelphia: University of Pennsylvania Press, 1941), 112–14; and for a discussion of why it failed to win approval, see Jon E. Ferling, *The Loyalist Mind: Joseph Galloway and the American Revolution* (University Park: The Pennsylvania State University Press, 1977), 26–31.

[68] On these debates, see Neil York, "The First Continental Congress and the Problem of American Rights," *The Pennsylvania Magazine of History and Biography* CXXII (1998): 353–83.

nature, on the British constitution, on charters, and on immemorial usage."
John Jay (1745–1829) of New York agreed that it was "necessary to recur
to the law of nature" as well as "the British constitution to ascertain our
rights," adding that the colonists originally had "a right to emigrate" and
"erect what government they please." As for whether the settlers could
eschew their allegiance, Jay argued that "there is no allegiance without
protection."[69]

However, several prominent members of the committee wanted Congress to make its case solely on the basis of the English rights. John
Rutledge of South Carolina held that subjects could not "alienate" their
"allegiance," and thus the original emigrants to America did not have the
right to establish "what constitution they please." For Rutledge, colonial
claims were "well founded on the British constitution, and not on the law
of nature." James Duane (1733–1797) of New York concurred, holding
that "the law of nature" was but "a feeble support," and that the Congress
should rest its case on "the laws and constitutions of the country from
whence we sprung." The future Loyalist, Joseph Galloway, insisted that
he could not find "the rights of Americans" in the "state of nature," but
only in "political society"; that is, in "the constitution of the English
government."[70]

Like many of the earlier colonial petitions and resolves, the Congressional Declaration of Rights which this committee produced put these
two kinds of rights alongside each other, seeing no necessary incom-
patibility between them. It held that "the inhabitants of the English
colonies in North America, by the immutable laws of nature, the principles of the English constitution, and the several charters or compacts"
had rights to "life, liberty and property," which they "have never ceded
to any sovereign power." Moreover, their ancestors, "who first settled
these colonies, were at the time of their emigration from the mother
country, entitled to all the rights, liberties, and immunities of free and
natural-born subjects within the realm of England." Since the "foundation of English liberty, and of all free government, is a right in the
people to participate in their legislative council," and since they "cannot properly be represented in British Parliament," Congress claimed
that the colonists "are entitled to a free and exclusive power of legislation in their several provincial legislatures," subject only to the "negative" of the "sovereign, in such manner as has been heretofore used
and accustomed."[71] The Declaration denounced the presence of a standing army in the colonies, and reiterated the colonists' right to jury
trials, and to the benefit of such Parliamentary statutes as they found
"by experience" to be suitable to local circumstances. The Congress did

[69] Jensen, ed., *American Colonial Documents*, 803–5.
[70] Ibid., 803–5.
[71] Ibid., 805–8.

concede that Parliament had the authority to regulate colonial trade, but made it clear that this was only with the colonists' "consent," and only when its acts were truly for the "commercial advantage" of the "whole empire."[72]

In the winter of 1775, after the Congress had adjourned, John Adams (1735–1826) penned the most comprehensive defense of colonial rights in the entire imperial crisis.[73] Writing as *Novanglus*, Adams argued that the great "defect" in the imperial constitution was that "*colonization*" was "*casus omissus* at common law." That is, "no provision" had been "made in this law for governing colonies beyond the Atlantic, or beyond the four seas, by authority of parliament; no, nor for the king to grant charters to subjects to settle in foreign countries."[74] As a result, instead of invoking principles of "law, or justice, or reason," Britain was asserting its sovereignty on the basis of "mere power," and was preparing to "resort to war and conquest" in a vain attempt to subdue the colonies.[75] If this was the case, Adams asked, how then "do we New Englandmen derive our laws"? His answer was unequivocal: "not from Parliament, not from common law, but from the law of nature, and the compact made with the king in our charters." Furthermore, Adams argued, the King had no legitimate authority in America that was not derived from that of the colonists. This was because America was "not a conquered, but a discovered country." That is, it "came not to the king by descent, but was explored by the colonists. It came not by marriage to the king, but was purchased by the colonists of the savages. It was not granted of the king by his grace, but was dearly, very dearly earned by the planters, in the labor, blood, and treasure which they expended to subdue it by cultivation." As a result, the rights of the colonists stood "upon no grounds, then, of law or policy, but what are found in the law of nature, and their express contracts in their charters, and their implied contracts in the commissions to governors and terms of settlement."[76]

For Adams, then, the legal foundation of the empire was based on the law of nature and not common law—indeed, in his view, "English liberties" were "but certain rights of nature, reserved to the citizen by the English constitution," rights which "cleaved to our ancestors when they

[72] Ibid., 805–8.

[73] *Novanglus; Or, A History of the Dispute with America*, reprinted in C. Bradley Thompson, ed., *The Revolutionary Writings of John Adams* (Indianapolis: Liberty Fund, 2000), 148–284. Adams' essays were written between January and April, 1775. The citations to *Novanglus* that follow refer to Thompson's edition. On Adams's political ideas, see C. Bradley Thompson, *John Adams and the Spirit of Liberty* (Lawrence: University Press of Kansas, 1998). See also, James Muldoon, "Discovery, Grant, Charter, Conquest, or Purchase: John Adams on the Legal Basis for English Possession of North America," in Christopher L. Tomlins, ed., *The Many Legalities of Early America* (Chapel Hill: The University of North Carolina Press, 2001), 25–46.

[74] *Novanglus, Letter VII*, 221; *Letter VIII*, 237.

[75] Ibid., *Letter VII*, 227.

[76] Ibid., *Letter XII*, 278.

crossed the Atlantic." And, Adams argued, these rights would "have inhered in them if, instead of coming to New England, they had gone to Otaheite or Patagonia, even although they had taken no patent or charter from the king at all." Adams even went so far as to claim that the original colonists "had a clear right to have erected in this wilderness a British constitution, or a perfect democracy, or any other form of government they saw fit."[77]

Following the clashes between the colonial militiamen and the British soldiers at Lexington and Concord in the spring of 1775, the Continental Congress prepared for war, putting George Washington (1732–1799) in charge of an army, and issuing a declaration, written by both Thomas Jefferson and John Dickinson, justifying the taking up of arms.[78] At the same time, however, the Congressional moderates led by John Dickinson, insisted on sending one last petition to the King seeking reconciliation. But in August, two days after he received this Olive Branch petition, George III issued a royal proclamation declaring the colonies in open rebellion.[79] And in December, the king assented to the Prohibitory Act which ended all trade with the colonies and sanctioned the seizure of their ships on the high seas as if they were "open enemies."[80]

The king's intransigence emboldened those in Congress who wanted to secede from the empire.[81] In May 1776, Congress passed a resolution which accused the king and Parliament of excluding "the inhabitants of these united colonies from the protection of his Crown." It then instructed the colonies to suppress all royal authority, and to "adopt such government as shall, in the opinion of the representatives of the people, best conduce to the happiness and safety of their constituents . . ."[82] And on June 7th, responding to instructions from the Virginia House of Burgesses, its senior delegate, Richard Henry Lee, moved "that these United Colonies are, and of right ought to be, free and independent States . . ."[83] This claim was echoed in the Declaration of Independence the following month which based the case for independence on the "Laws of Nature and of

---

[77] Ibid., *Letter VIII*, 238.

[78] Jensen, ed., *American Colonial Documents*, 842–47.

[79] Both the Olive Branch Petition and the King's proclamation are in Jensen, ed., *American Colonial Documents*, 847–51.

[80] Ibid., 853.

[81] For the argument that in the final years of the imperial crisis George III was "actively committed to a policy of coercion in America," see Andrew Jackson O'Shaughnessy, "'If Others Will Not Be Active I Must Drive': George III and the American Revolution," *Early American Studies* I (2004): 9, and passim. On the "abrupt transformations in popular attitudes" to the king between 1774 and 1776, see William D. Liddle, "'A Patriot King or None': Lord Bolingbroke and the American Renunciation of George III," *The Journal of American History* 65 (1979): 968, and *passim*. On the attachment to monarchy in British America, see Brendan McConville, *The King's Three Faces: The Rise and Fall of Royal America, 1688–1776* (Chapel Hill: The University of North Carolina Press, 2006).

[82] Jensen, ed., *American Colonial Documents*, 854.

[83] Ibid., 867–68.

Nature's God," and on the unalienable natural rights to life, liberty, and property which flowed from them.[84]

The Declaration was an eloquent summation of the colonial case against British authority, its concern for the protection of individual rights to life, liberty, and property—with the right of all individuals to consent to any tax or law which bound them being important corollaries of these more fundamental rights—echoing the arguments in the many petitions, resolves and declarations issued by the colonists in the fraught years between 1764 and 1776. From the beginning of the imperial crisis, these rights were understood by colonial spokesmen to be "inherent" in individuals, something which was a "birthright" of all "freeborn" Englishmen, the product of a long historical inheritance (hence the frequent use of the adjective "ancient") and thus sanctified by time. But as we have seen, the idea of individual natural rights appeared in the early protests against the Stamp Act and gradually became more central to the colonial case against the king and Parliament. Both ways of thinking about rights were concerned with the individual and with his right to be free in person and property from arbitrary authority, and both understood rights as grounded in something more fundamental than mere positive law (whether it be "nature," or "custom," or "history"). The widespread claim that English rights were the subject's "birthright" was also compatible with the law of nature, as both saw rights as inhering in the individual rather than being the grant of a sovereign authority. As well, both natural law and common law placed a premium on consent as the foundation of all legitimate political authority; and they were as one in rejecting the idea that law was the mere will or command of the sovereign. Contrary to the claims of some recent scholarship, none of the colonial writings in the imperial crisis spoke of these rights as subordinate to a set of overarching or binding natural law duties.[85] Nor does a close reading of the colonial position suggest that they were arguing (in the Declaration and elsewhere) primarily for corporate or group rights (the rights of "states") as against the rights of individuals; rather, the colonists saw the autonomy which they claimed for their colonies as necessary for the protection of the individual rights of the inhabitants of those jurisdictions.[86]

While the product of European and English political and legal theory, the idea of rights articulated in the imperial crisis was also shaped by peculiarly American circumstances. As we have seen, the colonists argued

[84] "The Declaration of Independence," in Cynthia A. Kierner, ed., *Revolutionary America, 1750–1815: Source and Interpretation* (New Jersey: Pearson Education, 2003), 137–39.

[85] As Barry Shain argues in his essay on the idea of rights in the Declaration of Independence. See Shain, "Rights Natural and Civil in the Declaration of Independence," in Shain, ed., *The Nature of Rights at the American Founding and Beyond,* 120 and passim.

[86] As both Shain (see Ibid.) and David Armitage argue. See Armitage, *The Declaration of Independence: A Global History* (Cambridge: Harvard University Press, 2007), 17. For a discussion of this question, see the contributions to the "Critical Forum: David Armitage, *The Declaration of Independence: A Global History,*" *William and Mary Quarterly* 65 (2008): 347–69.

that in the extra-European world, which they viewed as a "wilderness" surrounded by hostile "savages," the law of nature (and the natural rights that flowed from it) were the normative standard for judging political conduct.[87] Moreover, the claim that the colonists had taken their individual rights across the Atlantic (and thus out of the realm and the ambit of the common law) also reinforced the idea that they had these rights independent of any system of domestic or municipal law. On this reading of the imperial crisis, the shift to natural law and natural rights was not the product of a last minute "leap out of history" (and thus away from the customary confines of English constitutionalism) on the eve of the Revolution.[88] Rather, the adoption of natural rights by British American elites was integral to the jurisdictionally contested imperial world they inhabited. On this view, the ultimate source of political and legal authority in the empire was the natural right of all men to leave the state they inhabited and establish a new one elsewhere.[89]

This adoption of natural rights was, of course, radical in the sense that it supplied a justification for a total renunciation of royal authority, which the English constitution could not do.[90] But it was also perfectly compatible with the voluntary adoption of English rights by subjects situated in this state of nature, as many colonists began to argue in the crucial years

[87] I develop this argument at greater length in *Settlers, Liberty and Empire: The Roots of Early American Political Theory, 1675–1775* (New York: Cambridge University Press, 2011), where I draw on a large body of recent scholarship which suggests that the revival of natural law thinking in early modern Europe was driven by the need to find transnational legal norms to justify European expansion into the New World. For examples of this large literature, see Richard Tuck, *The Rights of War and Peace: Political Thought and the International Order from Grotius to Kant* (New York: Oxford University Press, 1999). On Grotius's imperial thought, see Edward Keene, *Beyond the Anarchical Society: Grotius, Colonialism and Order in World Politics* (Cambridge: Cambridge University Press, 2002). On Locke and empire, see Barbara Arneil, *John Locke and America: The Defence of English Colonialism* (Oxford: The Clarendon Press, 1996); James Tully "Rediscovering America: The *Two Treatises* and Aboriginal Rights," in Tully, *An Approach to Political Philosophy: Locke in Contexts* (Cambridge: Cambridge University Press, 1993), 137–76; "Aboriginal Property and Western Theory: Recovering a Middle Ground," *Social Philosophy and Policy* 11 (1994): 153–80; and "Placing the 'Two Treatises'," in Phillipson and Skinner, eds., *Political Discourse in Early Modern Britain* (Cambridge: Cambridge University Press, 1993), 253–80. For more recent work on Locke and empire, see Duncan Ivison, "Locke, Liberalism and Empire," in Peter Anstey, ed., *The Philosophy of John Locke: New Perspectives* (London: Routledge, 2003), 86–105; and David Armitage, "John Locke, Carolina, and the *Two Treatises of Government*," *Political Theory* 32 (2004): 602–27.

[88] A claim made in T. H. Breen's Harmsworth lecture, *The Lockean Moment: The Language of Rights on the Eve of the American Revolution* (Oxford University Press, 2001), 12; as well as in Breen's "Ideology and Nationalism on the Eve of the American Revolution: Revisions Once More in Need of Revising," *The Journal of American History* 84 (1997): 13–39.

[89] It is for this reason (among others) that I reject John Phillip Reid's account of the constitutional case for the colonists in which he denies that they were at all influenced by the idea of natural rights, even as he correctly notes that they made arguments based on what he calls the "migration purchase" argument. See Reid, *Constitutional History of the American Revolution*, abr. ed. (Madison: University of Wisconsin Press, 1995).

[90] On which, see J. G. A. Pocock, *The Ancient Constitution and the Feudal Law: A Study of English Historical Thought in the Seventeenth Century* (1957; revised edition: Cambridge: Cambridge University Press, 1987), 354.

before independence. Moreover, the new republican state constitutions formed in the crucial years between 1776 and 1780 contained preambles with stirring declarations of natural rights, while the body of these documents was largely composed of claims to English legal rights.[91]

V. CONCLUSION

What I want to suggest by way of conclusion is that the political settlement of the revolution was to some extent in tension with the concern for individual rights expressed so forcefully in the years before 1776. For the culmination of the long struggle against king and Parliament was not the independence of one sovereign nation but of thirteen republican states, each of which (the Declaration stated) had the "full Power to levy War, conclude Peace, contract Alliances, establish Commerce, and to do all other Acts and things which INDEPENDENT STATES may of right do."[92] That this was the political outcome of the Revolution should not surprise us given the way in which colonists argued for internal autonomy in the imperial crisis, an argument which was itself the product of a long history of self-government in the empire. In their view, individual rights were best protected by having ultimate political authority close to the people, and then if necessary to join these local polities together in a loose federation (much as the empire had been before the 1760s). And this is exactly what happened in the years immediately after 1776 as the former colonies of the empire became republican states and drafted written constitutions (the first in modern history) guaranteeing many of the rights which the colonists had felt were threatened in the old empire. Yet as James Madison (1751–1836) and others began to realize in the 1780s, these new republican states, unchecked by the very weak central authority of the Articles of Confederation (1781), were often as coercive as the unbounded power of Parliament had been. This was true, most obviously, in the case of the Loyalists who found their claims for compensation blocked by states claiming to be immune from the terms of the Treaty of Paris (1783). African Americans, too, found their legal status little changed, especially in the southern states, and no doubt wished that there existed a strong central authority to protect their rights. And when one came in 1787–1788, with the drafting and ratification of a new federal constitution, it failed to improve their lot much (and may have worsened it

[91] On the attempt by post-revolutionary American jurists to incorporate republican ideals of natural rights and equality into the common law, see Ellen Holmes Pearson, "Revising Custom, Embracing Choice: Early American Legal Scholars and the Republicanization of the Common Law," in Eliga H. Gould and Peter Onuf, eds., *Empire and Nation: The American Revolution in the Atlantic World* (Baltimore: The Johns Hopkins University Press, 2005), 93–111.
[92] "The Declaration of Independence," Kierner, 137–39.

considerably).[93] Despite the movement for disestablishment after the revolution, religious minorities in New England found that the Bill of Rights protected the states from the federal government rather than shielding individuals from the coercive power of local majorities.[94] And finally, as a close reading of the arguments the colonists made in the imperial crisis suggests, Native Americans suffered the most in the aftermath of revolution. For one outcome of the removal of Crown authority after 1776 was the freeing up of individual colonists, organized in newly sovereign states, to move westward, claiming Native territory as their own based on conquest and labor, and largely ignoring (most famously in the case of Georgia) federal authority. None of this is to say that the revolutionary legacy of individual rights and constitutional government was not an emancipatory force; rather, it is to point out that the particular relationship between individual rights and local government which came out of the revolution was not necessarily conducive to liberty. More broadly, the legacy of the revolution should remind us that individual rights are not always secure in decentralized federations; and that if we are concerned to protect them we should be open to the idea that a strong central authority is just as likely to do so as the kind of local autonomy cherished by so many of the revolutionaries.[95]

History, U.C.L.A.

---

[93] On which, see David Waldstreicher, *Slavery's Constitution: From Revolution to Ratification* (New York: Hill and Wang, 2009).

[94] For the limited nature of the First Amendment, see James Hutson, *Church and State in America: The First Two Centuries* (New York: Cambridge University Press, 2008), 159.

[95] A point made by the political theorist Jacob Levy in "Federalism and the Old and New Liberalisms," *Social Philosophy and Policy* 24 (2007): 306–26.

ON DECLARING THE LAWS AND RIGHTS OF NATURE

By C. Bradley Thompson

I. Introduction

In 1776, American Revolutionaries dissolved the political bands connecting them to king and country, and they established a new nation based on certain philosophic principles. In contrast to the monarchical and aristocratic societies of Europe, the Founding Fathers established governments, according to John Taylor of Caroline (1753–1824), "rooted in moral or intellectual principles" rather than in "orders, clans or [castes]."[1] John Adams (1735–1826) captured the deepest meaning of the American Revolution when he asked and answered a simple but crucial question:

> What do we mean by the Revolution? The War? That was no part of the Revolution; it was only an *effect* and *consequence* of it. The Revolution was in the minds of the people, and this was effected, from 1760 to 1775, in the course of fifteen years before a drop of blood was shed at Lexington.[2]

Adams was suggesting that the deepest *cause* of the American Revolution was to be found in a radical transformation of the colonists' most basic values and principles. Put more precisely, the question inspired by Adams was this: how was the American mind revolutionized in the years between 1760 and 1775 and what new ideas shaped America's revolutionary consciousness?

This much is clear: American Revolutionaries appealed to moral principles they considered to be absolute, permanent, and true in order to justify the extraordinary course of action they were about to embark upon. Tom Paine (1737–1809) identified the philosophic essence of the Revolution when he declared in the *Rights of Man* (1791) "the Indepen-

---

[1] John Taylor of Caroline, *An Inquiry into the Principles and Policy of the Government of the United States* (Fredricksburg, 1814), 6–7; quoted in Yehoshua Arieli, *Individualism and Nationalism in American Ideology* (Baltimore, MD: Penguin Books, 1964), 167. John Taylor of Caroline was a writer and a politician from Virginia associated with the Jeffersonian Democrats. In addition to *An Inquiry into the Principles and Policy of Government*, Taylor's best known works include *Construction Construed and Constitutions Vindicated* (1820), and *Tyranny Unmasked* (1822).

[2] John Adams to Thomas Jefferson, August 24, 1815, in *The Works of John Adams*, 10 vols. ed. Charles Francis Adams (Boston: Little, Brown and Co., 1856), X: 172.

doi:10.1017/S0265052511000318

dence of America was accompanied by a Revolution in the principles and practice of Governments . . . Government founded on a *moral theory . . . on the indefeasible hereditary Rights of Man.*"[3] Identifying the meaning of that "moral theory" is the principal theme of this essay.

Our goal then in what follows is to reconstruct and elucidate the Founders' moral theory by focusing on two key concepts of that doctrine: the moral *laws* and the moral *rights* of nature. In particular, we shall examine several important questions from the perspective of America's Revolutionary Founders. For instance: What are the moral laws and rights of nature? What is the difference between a law and a right of nature, and how are the laws and rights of nature related to each other? Are nature's moral laws and rights descriptive, prescriptive, or both? What are the attributes and sanctions of nature's laws and rights, and how are they promulgated? What is the source of nature's laws and rights? And finally, how did America's Founding Fathers use the moral laws and rights of nature to establish their political institutions?

To answer these questions, we shall focus on the core text generally recognized as the symbol of America's revolutionary mind and moral theory: the Declaration of Independence. In using the Declaration as our philosophical scaffolding, we are confronted at the outset with a methodological dilemma: the Declaration was written by one man, edited by a committee, approved by a congress, and was said by Thomas Jefferson, the document's principal author, to be an "expression of the American mind."[4] In order to tease out the full meaning of the Declaration as an "expression of the American mind," our first challenge therefore is to go beyond the text and examine the larger intellectual and political context of the time. That extended climate of opinion includes the official public petitions of the 1760s and 1770s, the writings of various Enlightenment thinkers in Europe and America both before and just after 1776, and the writings and speeches of American Revolutionaries such as James Otis, Samuel Adams, John Adams, James Wilson, George Mason, and Thomas Paine, not to mention Jefferson's extended corpus. By broadening the scope of our study beyond the text of the Declaration, we are, however, confronted with a second methodological challenge: the Founding generation did not always agree with each other on all philosophical questions. For example, the Founding generation was not simply of one mind with regard to the ultimate sources of nature's laws and rights. This essay therefore seeks to elucidate the common understanding held by most Americans about concepts such as the laws and rights of nature, while also recognizing those areas where they disagreed. Our ultimate task, then, is to reveal

---

[3] Tom Paine, *Rights of Man* in *Rights of Man, Common Sense and Other Political Writings,* ed. Mark Philp (Oxford: Oxford University Press, 1995), 210, 213.

[4] Thomas Jefferson to Henry Lee, May 8, 1825 in *The Life and Writings of Thomas Jefferson,* ed. Adrienne Koch and William Peden (New York: The Modern Library, 1944), 719.

the Declaration's deepest meaning by examining its moral philosophy within a broader historical context.[5]

II. On Declaring the Laws of Nature

By dissolving the political bands that had formerly connected them to Great Britain, American colonists were reclaiming the right of self government to which the "Laws of Nature and of Nature's God" entitled them. But what exactly did Jefferson and the other Founders mean when they spoke of the "Laws of Nature and of Nature's God"? The Revolutionary generation's understanding and use of this concept is one of the most important but least understood principles of the American Founding period, despite the fact that much has been written on the subject. Scholars of the Revolutionary period—both of the skeptical and fileopietistic variety— have for too long treated the Declaration's most interesting philosophic concepts as little more than "glittering generalities"—as either historically contingent or as unquestionably true.[6] The result in either case has been the same: a lack of serious thinking about the Declaration's deepest meaning.

What students of the American Founding most need is an understanding—from the perspective of Revolutionary-era Americans—of what a moral law of nature *is* (including its attributes and sanctions), how it is promulgated, what its source is, how it differs from a right of nature, and how eighteenth-century American statesmen used it in a political, legal, and constitutional context. We are less concerned here with enumerating different instances of nature's moral laws than we are in understanding how Americans of the Revolutionary period defined and used the concept. The central question is this: What *is* a moral law of nature?

---

[5] In using the Declaration of Independence as an "expression of the American mind," I do not mean to suggest, however, that the members of America's Founding generation were in full agreement with each other on all philosophical issues in 1776. The fact is, as I will demonstrate, they were not, although there was broad agreement on most moral issues. Strictly speaking, the Declaration may not even represent entirely Thomas Jefferson's deepest philosophic views. The document was intended to represent the views of all Americans, most of whom were devoutly Christian and some of whom were slaveowners. This is important to remember because it helps us to understand why, for instance, Jefferson may have spoken of rights coming from a "Creator" and why he excluded property from his list of unalienable rights.

[6] Over the course of the last century a good deal of the scholarship on the American Revolutionary and Founding periods, and on the Declaration of Independence in particular, has been of either the "skeptical" or "fileopietistic" variety. Scholars in the "skeptical" camp tend to view the principles of the Declaration through the lens of historicism, that is, as true or relevant for the period in which they were first invoked and used but outdated and inapplicable to the changed conditions of the modern world. The classic interpretation of the Declaration from the "skeptical" camp is Carl L. Becker's *The Declaration of Independence: A Study in the History of Political Ideas* (New York: Vintage Books, 1922), 277. Scholars in the "fileopietistic" camp tend to view the principles of the Declaration through the lens of intrinsicism, that is, as unquestioningly and eternally true and worthy of a reverence bordering on the quasi-religious. A recent effort of this sort is Matthew Spalding's *We Still Hold These Truths: Rediscovering Our Principles, Reclaiming Our Future* (Wilmington, DE: ISI Books, 2009), 36–44, 58–60, 215–39.

Throughout much of the eighteenth century, and certainly in the period between 1765 and 1800, American thinkers and statesmen invoked regularly the "law of nature" idea as a guiding principle of their moral and political thought. Indeed, it was the starting point and foundation for their reflections on serious political matters. In reaction to the British Parliament's passage of the Stamp Act in 1765, John Adams encouraged his fellow colonial Americans to "study the law of nature" and to search for the foundation of all just government "in the frame of human nature, in the constitution of the intellectual and moral world."[7] Such laws are not created by human will, but are rather discovered, defined, formulated, recognized, and enforced by man. The laws of nature transcend the commands made by legislatures, and they operate regardless of whether they are recognized and enforced by any political institution.

Many eighteenth-century Anglo-American statesmen and jurists understood that the purpose of statutory law was to embody and reflect the law of nature. In fact, many Revolutionary statesmen of the Founding era believed that any positive law which violated the laws of nature was necessarily null and void.[8] In 1772, Samuel Adams (1722–1803) writing for the Committee of Correspondence of the Boston Town Meeting declared "All positive and civil laws should conform, as far as possible, to the law of natural reason and equity." Two years later, James Wilson (1742–1798) — one of the Revolutionary generation's best thinkers, a signer of the Declaration of Independence, a framer of the Constitution, and later a justice of the Supreme Court—announced, quoting the Swiss legal and political theorist, Jean-Jacques Burlamaqui (1694–1748), that "happiness" is the "*first* law of every government," which is a rule, he wrote, "founded on the law of nature" and which "must regulate the legislature itself." That same year, the First Continental Congress in its "Declaration and Resolves" invoked "the immutable laws of nature" against Parliament's recently passed Coercive Acts. A year later, in 1775, Alexander Hamilton followed Wilson's lead and defended the actions of the Continental Congress with a direct appeal to the laws of nature:

> When the first principles of civil society are violated, and the rights of a whole people are invaded, the common forms of municipal law are not to be regarded. Men may then betake themselves to the law of nature; and, if they but conform their actions to that standard, all

[7] John Adams, "A Dissertation on the Canon and Feudal Law (1765)," in *The Revolutionary Writings of John Adams*, selected and with a Foreword by C. Bradley Thompson (Indianapolis, IN: Liberty Fund, 2000), 33. The Stamp Act of 1765 imposed a direct tax on Britain's American colonies by requiring the colonists to purchase stamped paper for various legal documents, magazines, newspapers, and many other types of paper used by the colonists. The purpose of the tax was to help offset British war expenses in the American colonies during the recently concluded Seven Years' War.

[8] See, for instance, the view of James Otis, "The Rights of the British Colonies Asserted and Proved [1764]," in *Colonies to Nation, 1763–1789: A Documentary History of the American Revolution,* ed. Jack P. Greene (New York: W. W. Norton & Company, 1975), 28–33.

cavils against them betray either ignorance or dishonesty. There are some events in society, to which human laws cannot extend, but when applied to them, lose all their force and efficacy. In short, when human laws contradict or discountenance the means which are necessary to preserve the essential rights of any society, they defeat the proper end of all laws, and so become null and void.[9]

Generally speaking, then, the standard Enlightenment view of the "law of nature" doctrine said that nature and man's nature are knowable by reason, and that from nature and man's nature can be induced certain natural moral and political laws that should guide man's individual ethical and social behavior.

Let us turn now to a fuller examination of how eighteenth-century Americans understood and used the moral concept "law of nature." Following John Locke (1632–1704) and later Enlightenment philosophers, colonial Americans typically defined the law of nature as a dictate of "right reason." Revolutionary-era pamphlets, sermons, and official declarations and petitions are replete with similar attempts to associate the moral laws of nature with "right reason." They most often said that the laws of nature were promulgated through a *discovery* process—that is, by the application of right or proper reasoning to the study of nature and human nature.[10] Still, we are left wondering what exactly the Founding generation meant when they declared the laws of nature as synonymous with reason.

Consider the case of John Adams. As early as 1756, a twenty-one-year-old Adams was writing in his *Diary* that reason is man's only tool for

[9] Samuel Adams, "The Rights of the Colonists, The Report of the Committee of Correspondence to the Boston Town Meeting, November 20, 1772; James Wilson, "Considerations on the Nature and Extent of the Legislative Authority of the British Parliament [1774]" in *The Works of James Wilson*, 2 vols., ed. Robert Green McCloskey (Cambridge, MA: Harvard University Press, 1967), II: 723; "Declaration and Resolves of the First Continental Congress [1774]," in *Colonies to Nation, 1763–1789*, 244; Alexander Hamilton, "The Farmer Refuted [1775]" in *The Revolutionary Writings of Alexander Hamilton*, ed. Richard B. Vernier (Indianapolis, IN: Liberty Fund, 2008), 105.

[10] The proposition that the laws of nature were known through inductive reasoning was not uniform, however, amongst the Founding generation. In the years after the Revolution, some Founders such as James Wilson argued that certain moral laws of nature were known to man through an innate moral sense. In his *Lectures on Law* [1790–1791], Wilson advanced a very different view of how the moral laws of nature are known than the one presented here: "If I am asked ... how do you know that you ought to do that, of which your conscience enjoins the performance? I can only say, I *feel* that such is my duty. Here investigation must stop; reasoning can go no farther. The science of morals, as well as other sciences, is founded on truths, that cannot be discovered or proved by reasoning. ... We cannot, therefore, begin to reason, till we are furnished, otherwise than by reason, with some truths, on which we can found our arguments. Even in mathematicks, we must be provided with axioms perceived intuitively to be true, before our demonstrations can commence. Morality, like mathematicks, has its intuitive truths, without which we cannot make a single step in our reasonings upon the subject." James Wilson, "Lectures on Law," in *The Works of James Wilson*, I: 133.

determining what is morally right. Man has been given "reason," he argued, "to find out the Truth, and the real Design and true End of our Existence." For Adams and virtually all of the Founding generation, the moral law of nature was synonymous with reason: "Law is human Reason," he asserted; it governs "all the Inhabitants of the Earth; the political and civil laws of each Nation should be only the particular Cases, in which human Reason is applied." In fact, "Nature and Truth or rather Truth and right are invariably the same in all Times and in all Places. And Reason, pure unbiassed Reason perceives them alike in all Times and in all Places."[11]

As a young man, John Adams took seriously the possibility that there are laws of nature and principles of natural justice grounded in an objective moral order that can be known through the use of reason. Reason itself, however, cannot be in the strict sense a law of nature. It is simply a means or a method by which to discover the laws of nature. Put differently, the moral laws of nature denote a relationship between existence broadly speaking and man's consciousness, that is, between nature and human nature. In other words, moral principles are *necessary* and must be discovered because man, given his particular nature as a volitional and rational being, bears a certain relationship to the world in which he lives, including his relationship to other men. As Adams put it in 1765,

> Tis impossible to judge with much Præcision of the true Motives and Qualities of human Actions, or of the Propriety of Rules contrived to govern them, without considering with like Attention, all the Passions, Appetites, Affections in Nature from which they flow. *An intimate Knowledge therefore of the intellectual and moral World is the sole foundation on which a stable structure of Knowledge can be erected.*[12]

Untutored reason was not, however, enough for Adams and his fellow Americans. "Right" reason was a method—the proper method—for thinking and acquiring knowledge. And it was principally that "method," Adams mused, that allowed Isaac Newton (1642–1727) to discover and demonstrate "the true system of the World." Newton rose above other English scientists of the time because he had "employed Experiment and [Geometry?]"—that is, induction and deduction—in scientific inquiry. "It [is] the Method then," concluded Adams, that discovers nature's secrets and potentially reveals the moral laws of nature.[13]

---

[11] John Adams, *Diary and Autobiography of John Adams,* 4 vols., ed. L. H. Butterfield (Cambridge, MA: Harvard University Press 1962), I: 43–44, 117, 26.

[12] "Draft of a letter to Jonathan Sewell," *Diary and Autobiography of John Adams,* I: 123 (emphasis added). Compare with John Locke, *An Essay Concerning Human Understanding,* I: 1, 5–9.

[13] "Draft of a Letter to an Unidentified Correspondent [1758]," *The Earliest Diary of John Adams,* ed. L. H. Butterfield (Cambridge, MA: Harvard University Press, 1966), 71–72.

Advocating something like the "historical plain method" advanced by Locke in his *Essay Concerning Human Understanding* (1690), Adams defined "Natural Phylosophy" as "the Art of deducing the generall laws and properties of material substances, from a series of *analogous* observations."

> The manner of reasoning in this art is not strictly demonstrative, and by Consequence the knowledge hence acquired, not absolutely Scientifical, because the facts that we reason upon, are perceived by Sence and not by the internal Action of the mind Contemplating its Ideas. But these Facts being presumed true in the form of Axioms, subsequent reasonings about them may be in the strictest sence, scientifical. This Art informs us, in what manner bodies will influence us and each other in given Circumstances, and so teaches us, to avoid the noxious and imbrace the beneficial qualities of matter.[14]

The Lockean method of "right reason" applied as much to the study of man and society as to the study of nature. Adams and the thinking Revolutionaries who joined him assumed that moral and political philosophers must devote themselves to observing and experiencing the world around them, to examining their own ideas and passions introspectively, and to studying the history of mankind. The primary mode of reasoning applied by Revolutionary Americans to discovering the moral laws of nature was therefore inductive. The very same method they would have used to investigate the physical laws of nature—i.e., an empirical-a posteriori-inductive mode of reasoning—was also used to uncover and reveal the moral laws of nature.

No Founding Father *before* the Revolution thought longer and harder about the philosophic method by which to reveal the moral laws of nature than John Adams. By observing empirically the nature of "terrestrial enjoyments" and sufferings—i.e., the rewards and punishments consonant with the moral law of nature—Adams thought it possible to reason backward from effects to causes and then forward again to the principles that might guide human action. The most important and fruitful field of study for Adams was that of human nature, or what he often referred to as the "Constitution of our Minds and Bodies."[15] From a very early age, he drove himself to understand and give an account of his own mental operations and those of others. "Let me search for the Clue, which Led great Shakespeare into the Labyrinth of mental Nature! Let me examine how men think," he demanded of himself. Adams always began with himself, turning inward and observing his passions and the operation of his own mental processes: "Here I should moderate my Passions, regulate my Desires, increase my Veneration of Virtue, and Resolution to pursue it,

---

[14] *Diary and Autobiography of John Adams* (March 3, 1756), I: 11.
[15] Ibid., 42.

here I should range the whole material and Intellectual World, as far as human Powers can comprehend it, in silent Contemplation."[16]

In the years *after* the Revolution, Ethan Allen (1738–1789) was one of America's leading thinkers in search of the moral laws of nature. In *Reason: the Only Oracle of Man* (1785), Allen identified the process by which the laws of nature are known. Nature is like a book and the Book of Nature can be read, he reasoned analogously, but it must be opened first before it can be read. And how is the Book of Nature opened? Allen insisted that it must be opened and then read inductively. Nature's laws are discovered through our experience of cause-and-effect relationships. He argued that experience teaches man that all consequences have causes, that the events of the world that we experience are causally dependent on preceding ones. The Book of Nature says that all entities in nature are interconnected and that nature's order and harmony are not the result of "blind chance." To change the metaphor, the universe—that vast system of cause and effect—is run like a perfectly calibrated watch by God the Watchmaker and its promulgation "is co-extensive and co-existent with, and binding on all intelligent beings in the universe."[17]

Not surprisingly, Enlightenment-era Americans saw a direct relationship between the scientific laws of nature and the moral laws of nature as they apply to man. Many Americans would echo Montesquieu's description of the laws of nature in the *Persian Letters* (1721), wherein he defines them as the relations between things. "Justice" or the moral law, he wrote, "is a relation of suitability, which actually exists between two things." The laws of nature describe the *forces, regular actions* and *relations* between entities of various kinds, both in nature and in society. They describe the way nature and human nature are related, and they prescribe moral rules of behavior. As early as 1725, Benjamin Franklin (1706–1790), one of the editors of the Declaration of Independence and the quintessentially enlightened thinker, identified how eighteenth-century Americans typically saw the relationship between the scientific and moral laws of nature: "How exact and regular is every Thing in the *natural* world! How wisely in every Part contriv'd! . . . All the heavenly Bodies, the Stars and Planets, are regulated with the utmost wisdom! And can we suppose less care to be taken in the order of the *Moral* than in the *Natural* System."[18]

In 1766, in the wake of the Stamp Act crisis, Richard Bland (1710–1776), an American statesman, writer, and planter, mocked the common British viewpoint that the Britannic empire was a vast physical system revolving

---

[16] Ibid., 61; *Earliest Diary*, 77; *Diary and Autobiography of John Adams*, I: 65. This paragraph is drawn from Thompson, *John Adams and the Spirit of Liberty*, 19–20.

[17] Ethan Allen, "Reason: the Only Oracle of Man [1785]," in *The American Deists: Voices of Reason and Dissent in the Early Republic*, ed. Kerry S. Walters (Lawrence, KS: University Press of Kansas, 1992), 149, 164.

[18] Montesquieu, *Persian Letters*, translated and with an Introduction by C. J. Betts (New York: Penguin Books, 1973), 162–63; Benjamin Franklin, "A Dissertation on Liberty and Necessity, Pleasure and Pain" in *The American Deists: Voices of Reason and Dissent in the Early Republic*, 59.

around the dictates of Whitehall. Bland noted that there were Newtonian "laws of attraction in natural as well as political philosophy," and "that Bodies in Contact, and cemented by mutual Interests, cohere more strongly than those which are at a Distance, and have no common Interests to preserve." Bland charged the British with violating this law of nature in order to destroy the colonies "whose real Interests are the same, and therefore ought to be united in the closest Communication, are to be disjoined, and all intercommunication between them prevented." A generation later, Elihu Palmer (1764–1806), one of America's leading advocates of Deism in the quarter century after the end of the War for Independence, presented the Enlightenment view quite clearly in his treatise on the *Principles of Nature* (1801), stating that there are laws of nature that define man's "physical relation . . . to all existence" (i.e., descriptive scientific laws) and there are laws of nature that define man's moral relationship "to his own species and to all other inferior animals" (i.e., prescriptive moral laws).[19] Both forms of the law of nature are an instance of, and are necessitated by, the law of causality as they apply to man and his relationship to nature and human nature. The careful, painstaking observation of nature, sometimes enhanced through social experimentation and trial and error, leads man from the facts of nature or human nature to a mechanical law or a moral principle, from change or indeterminacy to a fixed, lawlike pattern in nature or a certain moral principle for man.

We can better understand how the Founding generation understood the idea of a moral law of nature by seeing it in the form of an *"if-given-then"* conditional imperative. Their reasoning about the moral laws of nature went something like this: *If* you want to achieve the following outcome ____(x)____, *given* certain facts of nature and human nature ____(y)____, *then* you must recognize and respect the following ____(z)____ principles or rules.[20] These principles or rules are the moral laws of nature. A simple example will illustrate the Founders' moral reasoning. Assume for the moment that you are a liberty-loving American colonist and the year is 1776. *If* you want to continue living in a free and just society (e.g., one that respects the rights of individuals), *given* the legislation passed by the British Parliament and supported by the Crown during the preceding eleven years (e.g., the Sugar, Stamp, Declaratory,

---

[19] Richard Bland, "An Inquiry into the Rights of the British Colonies [1766]," in *American Political Writing during the Founding Era, 1760–1805,* 2 vols., eds. Charles S. Hyneman and Donald S. Lutz (Indianapolis, IN: LibertyPress, 1983), I: 85; Elihu Palmer, "Principles of Nature; or, A Development of the Moral Causes of Happiness and Misery among the Human Species [1801]," in *The American Deists: Voices of Reason and Dissent in the Early Republic,* 266.

[20] For a philosophic explication of this conditional imperative, see Ayn Rand, "Causality Versus Duty," in *Philosophy: Who Needs It* (New York: Signet Books, 1982), 99. Also see Leonard Peikoff, *Objectivism: The Philosophy of Ayn Rand* (New York: Dutton Books, 1991), 241–49, and Randy E. Barnett, *The Structure of Liberty: Justice and the Rule of Law* (Oxford: Oxford University Press, 1998), 4–12.

Townshend, Tea, and Coercive Acts, which not only taxed the colonists without their consent, but also denied them long established common law rights), *then* you must take the appropriate actions necessary to secure your freedom (e.g., to declare your independence from Great Britain and to defend your freedom with arms if required). The moral laws of nature are those rules that can be induced and deduced from man's metaphysical condition as it applies both to his relationship with nature and to other men.

In 1787, Pastor Elizur Goodrich delivered an election day sermon on "The Principles of Civil Union and Happiness Considered and Recommended" to the governor and general assembly of Connecticut in which he described some of the principal characteristics of the moral laws of nature as understood by the Founding generation:

> The principles of society are the laws, which Almighty God has established in the moral world, and made *necessary* to be observed by mankind; in order to promote their true happiness, in their transactions and intercourse. These laws may be considered as principles, in respect of their fixedness and operation; and as maxims, since by the knowledge of them, we discover those rules of conduct, which direct mankind to the highest perfection, and supreme happiness of their nature. They are as fixed and unchangeable as the laws which operate in the natural world. Human art in order to produce certain effects, must conform to the principles and laws, which the Almighty Creator has established in the natural world.[21]

In other words, reality is the standard from which man must make certain choices and take certain actions that will result in consequences that either diminish or further his life and happiness. The laws of nature provide men with principles of action by which to guide their conduct in the pursuit of certain ends (e.g., their "true happiness").

The law of nature as it applies to man and his relations with others was understood by the Revolutionary generation to be a code of moral principles defining and regulating man's relationship to nature and/or his relationship to other men. In 1762, during that period when the American mind was in the process of being revolutionized, the Reverend Abraham Williams (1727–1784) described the laws of nature as "those Rules of Behaviour . . . [describing] the Relation [men] bear to one another."[22] The ultimate goal of the moral laws of nature was to expand man's freedom and to protect and promote his well-being and happiness in a social context.

[21] Elizur Goodrich, "The Principles of Civil Union and Happiness Considered and Recommended [1787]," in *Political Sermons of the American Founding: 1730–1805,* ed. Ellis Sandoz (Indianapolis: Liberty Press, 1991), 914 (emphasis added).
[22] Abraham Williams, "An Election Sermon [1762]," in *American Political Writing during the Founding Era, 1760–1805,* I: 7.

Generally speaking, the Founding generation considered the moral laws of nature to have the following attributes: they must be necessary (i.e., governed by the law of cause and effect), absolute, fixed, universal, eternal, uniform, orderly, harmonious, rationally demonstrable, and unalienable. James Otis characterized the qualities of the moral laws of nature in this pithy statement: "The laws of nature are uniform and invariable. The same causes will produce the same effects from generation to generation."[23]

The Declaration of Independence speaks of the "Laws of Nature and of Nature's God," a phrase that captures rather nicely the Revolutionary generation's ambiguity or split-mind about the nature, source, and sanctions associated with the laws of nature. In his 1775 pamphlet *The Farmer Refuted*, Alexander Hamilton summed up what was probably the common sense of the subject amongst Americans (and doing it while quoting, ironically enough, Blackstone). "Good and wise men, in all ages," according to Hamilton, have

> supposed that the Deity, from the relations we stand in to Himself and to each other, has constituted an eternal and immutable law, which is indispensably obligatory upon all mankind, prior to any human institution whatever.
>
> This is what is called the law of nature, "which, being coeval with mankind, and dictated by God himself, is, of course, superior in obligations to any other. It is binding over all the globe, in all countries, and at all times. No human laws are of any validity, if contrary to this; and such of them as are valid derive all their authority, mediately or immediately, from this original."

Jefferson's equivocation in the Declaration of Independence, however, leaves open the question whether nature simply, or nature's God, is the source of these laws. Are there, or can there be, moral laws of nature without the existence of a divine creator? This much can be said with confidence: when Jefferson wrote of "Nature's God" he almost certainly meant the impersonal, far removed deist god that set the world in motion according to laws that were meant to govern in his absence. The Declaration's God is not the God of the Old Testament (nor is it even the God of the New Testament) but is Nature's God. And Jefferson's God is posited but not known. Indeed, he need not be known. What can be known, however, and what is immediately relevant to the Declaration, is nature and its laws.[24] Thus, Jefferson could tell his nephew, Peter Carr, that

---

[23] James Otis, "A Vindication of the British Colonies . . . ," in *Pamphlets of the American Revolution, 1750–1765*, ed. Bernard Bailyn (Cambridge, MA: Harvard University Press, 1965), 554.
[24] Michael Zuckert draws a similar conclusion in *The Natural Rights Republic*, 57–66.

"those facts in the Bible which contradict the laws of nature, must be examined with more care, and under a variety of faces."[25]

The Founding generation almost to a man considered God to be the source or first cause of nature's laws, but it is also true that a few attempted to pick up where John Locke failed—that is, to establish a demonstrative science of ethics that did not necessarily rely on the existence of God to be operational. In this latter category, we might include Thomas Jefferson, John Adams, Ethan Allen, and Elihu Palmer. It is important to note that all four were believers, but they also attempted to ground the laws of nature on what we might call metaphysical law or what Thomas Jefferson variously referred to as the "laws of our being," the "order of nature," the "moral law of our nature," and "universal law."[26] In this way, they followed a tradition extending from Grotius, Locke, and Montesquieu down to the Founders, which said that the moral law of nature would still be valid and operational even if, in the words of Grotius, "there is no God, or that he has no Care of human affairs."[27]

Several Revolutionary-era thinkers came very close to adopting a similar position. Ethan Allen, for instance, echoing Montesquieu in the *Persian Letters,* wrote that the moral laws of nature are derived not from books of philosophy but from the Book of Nature—that is, from "the fitness of things."[28] Moral science, according to Allen, is known by reason and derived from experience. In other words, we can know the laws of nature without proving either the existence of God or the immortality of souls. Likewise, Elihu Palmer, seemingly combining Grotius and Montesquieu, stated the fundamental issue in unmistakable terms:

> If a thousand Gods existed, *or if nature existed independent of any;* the *moral relation* between man and man would remain exactly the same in either case. *Moral principle is the result of this relation,* it is founded in the properties of our nature and it is as indestructible as the basis on which it rests. If we could abandon for a moment every theistical idea, it would nevertheless remain substantially true, that the happiness of society must depend upon the exercise of equal and reciprocal justice.

[25] Thomas Jefferson to Peter Carr, August 10, 1787, *The Portable Thomas Jefferson,* 425–26.

[26] Thomas Jefferson to Georgetown Republicans, 1809, *Writings,* XVI: 349; Thomas Jefferson to M. Correa de Serra, April 19, 1814, *Writings,* XIX: 210; Thomas Jefferson, "Opinion on the French Treaties," April 28, 1793, *Writings,* III: 228; Thomas Jefferson, "A Summary View of the Rights of British-America [1774]" in *Colonies to Nation, 1763–1789,* 228. Michael Zuckert has referred to what I am calling metaphysical law as the "ultimate realities." (See Zuckert, *The Natural Rights Republic,* 57–58, 61.)

[27] Hugo Grotius, *De jure belli ac pacis libri tres* [1625], Prolegomena, II, trans. by Francis W. Kelsey and others for The Classics of International Law series, ed. J. B. Scott (Oxford, London: 1925).

[28] Ethan Allen, "Reason the Only Oracle of Man," in *The American Deists: Voices of Reason and Dissent in the Early Republic,* 177.

This is the revolution toward which the American mind was slowly moving—toward a view of natural justice grounded in a potentially god-less metaphysical law. The challenge of this law was to discover the naturally proper "moral relation between man and man" that would promote a flourishing human life and serve as the basis for a new legal and political order. Such a law would exist, to repeat Palmer's felicitous expression, whether "a thousand Gods existed, or if nature existed independent of any."[29]

America's Revolutionary thinkers typically identified the particular content of the laws of nature and their sanctions based on where they located the source of those laws. Not surprisingly, they viewed the substance of the laws of nature in one of two ways: as either God centered and duty based on the one hand, or as man centered and rights based on the other. Those who saw God as the first cause of the laws of nature (e.g., James Wilson, John Witherspoon, and the colonies' religious leaders) typically established two laws as fundamental: first, the law to obey God's commands; and second, the Golden Rule to "Do unto others as you would have them do unto you." The sanctions associated with God's laws of nature were dependent upon the immortality of souls and the promise of eternal bliss or suffering in the afterlife.[30] Contrariwise, those who turned to nature and to what John Adams referred to as the "constitution of the human mind" as the first cause of the laws of nature (e.g., John Adams, Thomas Jefferson, Ethan Allen, Elihu Palmer, and various colonial deists) typically established two laws as fundamental: first, the law of self-preservation; and second, the law to respect the rights of others. The punishments associated with violating the secular first law of nature were penury, misery, and death, and the rewards for obeying it were life, health, and happiness. The punishments for violating the secular second law of nature were social neglect and contempt, and the rewards for obeying it were social esteem and admiration.[31]

In sum, there was a consensus across a broad spectrum of American opinion in 1776 that the political laws of a free and just society should reflect the fundamental moral laws of nature. When Jefferson wrote in the Declaration of Independence that the Americans were now prepared to break their familial ties with Great Britain and to establish new political

[29] Elihu Palmer, "Principles of Nature; or, A Development of the Moral Causes of Happiness and Misery among the Human Species," in *The American Deists: Voices of Reason and Dissent in the Early Republic*, 264 (emphasis added).

[30] See John Wise, "A Vindication of the Government of New England [1717]," in *Puritan Political Ideas: 1558–1794*, ed. Edmund S. Morgan (Indianapolis, IN: Bobbs-Merrill Company, Inc., 1965), 251–67; Abraham Williams, "An Election Sermon [1762]," in *American Political Writing during the Founding Era, 1760–1805*, I: 3–18; Elizur Goodrich, "The Principles of Civil Union and Happiness Considered and Recommended [1787]," in *Political Sermons of the American Founding: 1730–1805*, 909–40.

[31] See John Adams, "Discourses on Davila [1791]," in *The Political Writings of John Adams*, ed. George W. Carey (Washington, DC: Regnery Publishing, Inc., 2000), 310–15.

societies on the basis of the "Laws of Nature and of Nature's God," he was expressing what he referred to as the common sentiments of the "American mind." Virtually all Americans during the Revolutionary period believed that there are moral laws of nature, that such laws must be discovered, that they transcended the laws of men, that they were discovered through reason and by studying the Book of Nature, that they described cause-and-effect relationships between man and nature and between man and man, that they prescribed principles of action and moral rules of behavior, and that such laws are fixed, absolute, universal, and eternal. Not all Americans agreed on the exact content of those laws or whether their ultimate source was to be found in "Nature" or in "Nature's God," but Jefferson's felicitous ambiguity was also an expression of the "American mind."

III. On Declaring the Rights of Nature

Let us turn now to an examination of the Revolutionary generation's understanding and use of the concept "unalienable" or "natural" rights. Among the Declaration's self-evident truths is the claim that all men "are endowed by their Creator with certain unalienable Rights, that among these are Life, Liberty, and the Pursuit of Happiness." The principle of "natural rights" was the moral heart and soul of the American Revolution. In 1809, Jefferson told the Georgetown Republicans that the principles fought for in 1776

> of which the charter of our independence is the record, were sanctioned by the *laws of our being,* and we but obeyed them in pursuing undeviatingly the course they called for. It issued finally in that inestimable state of freedom which alone can ensure to man the enjoyment of his equal rights.[32]

American Revolutionaries studied and used the doctrine of "unalienable rights" for two related purposes in the years between 1765 and 1790: first, as the standard by which to measure and judge the actions of king and Parliament during the years of the imperial crisis[33] (i.e., 1765–1776), and second, as the moral foundation on which to build their constitutional structures and political institutions (i.e., 1776–1790). In other words, the Declaration of Independence and its natural-rights philosophy were

---

[32] Thomas Jefferson to the Republicans of Georgetown, March 8, 1809, *Writings,* XIV: 349 (emphasis added).

[33] The "imperial crisis" is that period in American colonial history dating approximately between the passage of the Sugar Act in 1764 and the outbreak of armed hostilities between Great Britain and her American colonies in 1775.

used to mark the end of an old regime and to found a new revolutionary order.[34]

American Revolutionaries did not discover the concept "natural rights," but they did present to the world the first public proclamation and practical application of that philosophy. They were the first people in history to openly and explicitly ground their political institutions on this relatively new philosophic principle. The Revolution presented the American people, Jefferson noted, with "an album on which we were free to write what we pleased. We had no occasion to search into musty records, to hunt up royal parchments, or to investigate the laws and institutions of a semi-barbarous ancestry. We appealed to those of nature, and found them engraved on our hearts."[35]

At the most fundamental level, the American Revolution was about rights—the inalienable and natural rights of the individual. It was the failure of George III to protect their rights from the repeated usurpations of Parliament and then his own acts of violence against the colonists that ultimately justified Revolution. From the passage of the Stamp Act in 1765 to the final battle at Yorktown in 1781, the American colonists conceptualized their conflict with Great Britain in the language of *natural* rights.[36] Indeed, it provided the philosophic grammar of the Revolution.[37] As early as 1764 James Otis in his "The Rights of the British Colonies Asserted and Proved" announced that the American colonists were "entitled to all the natural, essential, inherent and inseparable rights of our fellow subjects in Great-Britain." Such rights, he claimed, "no man or body of men, not excepting the parliament, justly, equitably and consistently with their own rights and the constitution, can take away." Two years later, Richard Bland spoke for most Americans in his "An Enquiry into the Rights of the British Colonies" when he proclaimed that his

---

[34] The dual nature of the Founders' use of the natural rights philosophy is nicely captured in Pauline Maier, *American Scripture: Making the Declaration of Independence* (New York: Random House, 1997). Also see Robert Webking, *The American Revolution and the Politics of Liberty* (Baton Rouge, LA: Louisiana State University Press, 1988).

[35] Thomas Jefferson to Major John Cartwright, June 5, 1824 in *The Writings of Thomas Jefferson*, 20 vols., ed. Andrew A. Lipscomb and Albert Ellery Bergh (Washington D.C.: Thomas Jefferson Memorial Association, 1903), XVI: 51 (hereafter cited as *Writings*), XVI: 48.

[36] For a very different interpretation of the role of rights in the American Revolution, see John Phillip Reid, *Constitutional History of the American Revolution: The Authority of Rights* (Madison, WI: The University of Wisconsin Press, 1986), and Reid, "The Irrelevance of the Declaration," in *Law in the American Revolution and the Revolution in the Law: A Collection of Review Essays on American Legal History*, ed. Hendrik Hartog (New York: New York University Press, 1981): 46–89. Reid wants to downplay the influence of natural-rights theory in the American Revolution and instead sees American Revolutionaries as being more influenced by the English common law tradition.

[37] American rights talk is not, as Mary Ann Glendon has argued, a dialect. It is, instead, metaphorically speaking, a grammar. Rights are the way in which we organize and order our social relations. It is the traditional civil or common law rights of different places and times (e.g., the rights of Englishmen) that provides the dialect of rights. See Mary Ann Glendon, *Rights Talk: The Impoverishment of Political Discourse* (New York: The Free Press, 1991), 109.

countrymen "must have recourse to the law of nature, and those rights of mankind which flow from it." Man has rights, Thomas Jefferson claimed in his 1774 "A Summary View of the Rights of British-America," that "nature has given to all men" and which no man-made law can take away or abridge. Such rights, he continued, are "derived from the laws of nature" and "human nature" and are not the "gift of their chief magistrate." From the beginning of the imperial crisis to the end, the Revolution was about rights—the natural, unalienable rights of man. Thus, the Declaration of Independence was, as Jefferson put it, the "declaratory charter of our rights, and of the rights of man."[38]

America's Revolutionary Founders also used the doctrine of natural, unalienable rights in the decade after 1776 as the immovable foundation on which to anchor and permanently fix their constitutional structures. America's constitutions, Jefferson wrote, were defined by and built on "the immovable basis of equal right and reason," and such rights of nature are "the objects for the protection of which society is formed and municipal laws established." Man's natural rights, James Wilson declared, are the "great pillars on which chiefly rest the criminal and civil codes of the municipal law."[39] Many of the state constitutions adopted during the Revolutionary period began with, included, or were accompanied by a formal declaration of rights, including most importantly man's natural rights.[40] In their attempt to "fix" their constitutions as fundamental law, America's Revolutionary constitution-makers searched for and found in the natural rights philosophy that permanent, granite-like moral foundation on which to build their governments. This was possible, Jefferson insisted, because "Nothing is unchangeable but the inherent and unalienable rights of man."[41]

Our task now is to elucidate—from the Founders' perspective—what rights are and the ground on which they stand. As with the concept "law of nature," the principle of "unalienable rights" (also variously characterized as "natural rights," the "rights of man" and the "rights of nature") has been the subject of much scholarly attention over the past few decades

[38] James Otis, "The Rights of the British Colonies Asserted and Proved," in *Colonies to Nation, 1763–1789*, 28–29; Richard Bland, "An Enquiry into the Rights of the British Colonies," in *Colonies to Nation*, 89; Thomas Jefferson, "A Summary View of the Rights of British-America," in *Colonies to Nation*, 228–29, 237; Thomas Jefferson to Samuel Adams Wells, May 12, 1819, *Writings*, XV: 200.

[39] Thomas Jefferson to James Sullivan, February 9, 1797, *Writings*, IX: 379; Thomas Jefferson to James Monroe, September 7, 1797, *Writings*, IX: 422; James Wilson, *Lectures on Law*, in *The Works of James Wilson*, II: 609.

[40] See Bernard Schwartz, "Revolutionary Declarations and Constitutions," chap. in *The Great Rights of Mankind: A History of the American Bill of Rights* (Madison, WI: Madison House, 1992), 53–91.

[41] The Virginia Bill of Rights can be downloaded from the internet at: http://www.constitution.org/bor/vir_bor.htm; The Massachusetts Constitution of 1780 can be downloaded off the internet at: http://www.nhinet.org/ccs/docs/ma-1780.htm. Thomas Jefferson to Major John Cartwright, June 5, 1824, *Writings*, XVI: 48.

that has depicted the concept as either an absurdity or a trite common-place.[42] What we lack and most need is an understanding of *how* the Revolutionary generation answered or might have answered the simplest but most important question: What *is* a natural right or a right of nature? More to the point, what function does it serve, how does it differ from a law of nature, what is its source, and how is it validated? Important corollary questions include: What does it mean to say that men have been *"endowed* by their Creator" with unalienable rights, and why are such rights said to be "unalienable" as opposed to conventional or historical? What did Jefferson and the other Revolutionaries mean by the rights to life, liberty, and the pursuit of happiness? How do these natural rights stand in relation to each other?

Our greatest challenge in answering these questions is the simple fact that the Founding generation never really addressed them in any mean-ingful way. The idea of rights was mostly just asserted as a self-evident truth rather than validated philosophically. The truth of the matter, how-ever, is that they are anything but self-evident. Our task then in what follows is to reconstruct the view of rights held by American Revolution-aries from a broad survey of the extant literature from the period.

Eighteenth-century Anglo-Americans were obsessed with their rights. When the Stamp Act was passed in 1765, Britain's American colonists responded immediately with an arsenal of rights-based arguments. The debate was kicked off with a bitter and sometimes abusive polemical exchange between Judge Martin Howard (d. 1781) of Rhode Island and James Otis (1725–1783). Howard staked out the traditional view of rights held by many Anglo-American Tories. In order to determine the rights of the colonies and the mother country, he declared that right-thinking men must "shun the walk of metaphysics." Instead of beginning with an abstract individual who possesses abstract rights in a hypothetical state of nature, Howard began with natural political communities and man's "true nat-ural relation[s]" as the primary unit of moral and political value. The judge did not think man is an isolated individual but is born and lives his life entwined in a variety of different social relationships. Such relations are ordered, according to Howard, not by man's natural rights but by his natural, "reciprocal duties." To the extent that man has rights, they are born not of nature but of history, of man's conventional social and polit-ical relations that have developed over the course of many centuries. Thus, Howard eschewed the idea of natural rights for what he and most Englishmen spoke of as "the rights of Englishmen." Howard did recog-

---

[42] Alasdair MacIntyre has summed up with admirable clarity the typical academic phi-losopher's view of natural rights, when he declared that no such rights exist and that a belief in them is akin to a belief in "witches and unicorns." (See *After Virtue: A Study in Moral Theory*, [Notre Dame, IN: University of Notre Dame Press, 1980], pp. 68–70.) Many conser-vatives, by contrast, assume the existence and the meaning of natural rights without ever explaining what they are and the function they serve.

nize what he called "personal" rights"—i.e., "those of life, liberty, and estate"—that are "every subject's birthright," but such rights are not, he argued, "self-existent." Instead, they are grounded in and defined by English common law. In the end, however, Howard and most Anglo-American Tories believed that the common law was synonymous with the "sense and virtue of the British parliament," which meant that the "rights of Englishmen" were ultimately human creations subject to the vicissitudes of parliamentary whim.

James Otis's utter contempt for what he called Howard's "Filmerian" performance demonstrates just how far American Whigs had come by the 1760s in their understanding of rights.[43] Howard and his Tory friends in England saw no difference, according to Otis, between "power and right," which means that they did not and could not understand the concept "*natural* rights." For colonial Americans, this represented an unbridgeable intellectual and moral gulf and was the deepest source of their conflict with Great Britain. Nature's rights, according to Otis, are "inherent" and "indefeasible," and they are derived, not from history and the actions of kings and parliaments, but from the "laws of God and nature." Otis rejected Howard's characterization of the rights to life, liberty, and estate as "personal" rights, which suggested to him that they are derived from the relationship that Englishmen have with their king and with each other through the common law. Furthermore, man's natural rights, Otis claimed, provide the fixed, unchanging foundation of man's civil rights, particularly the civil rights of Englishmen. Indeed, the "natural absolute personal rights of individuals are so far from being opposed to political or civil rights that they are the very basis of all municipal laws." In other words, Otis and many of his Whig compatriots saw the common law as representing the instantiation and application of man's natural rights to the particular circumstances of life in Old and New England.[44] At the deepest philosophical and jurisprudential level, the imperial crisis was about where to locate the source of man's rights to life, liberty, and property: Anglo-American Tories located the fundamental rights in history, while Anglo-American Whigs located man's rights in nature.

In 1805, forty years after the Howard-Otis exchange, James Otis's sister, Mercy Otis Warren (1728–1814), felt the need to refight the intellectual battles of the 1760s and 1770s as though they were still living issues, particularly those that involved the question of rights. In her *History of the*

---

[43] Otis's accusation that Howard was advancing a "Filmerian" position was meant as a term of abuse to suggest that Howard was promoting the views of Sir Robert Filmer, the seventeenth-century English political theorist who advocated absolute monarchy grounded in a theory of divine rights.

[44] Martin Howard, Jr., "A Letter From a Gentleman of Halifax" [1765], in *Pamphlets of the American Revolution, 1750–1765*, 534–36, 538; James Otis, "A Vindication of the British Colonies . . . [1765]," in *Pamphlets of the American Revolution, 1750–1765*, 554, 558–63. See James Stoner, *Common Law and Liberal Theory: Coke, Hobbes, and the Origins of American Constitutionalism* (Lawrence, KS: University Press of Kansas, 1992).

Rise, Progress, and Termination of the American Revolution [1805], Warren
lashed out at the estimable English jurist and arch-Tory, William Murray,
1st Earl of Mansfield (1705–1793), for what she took to be his corrupt view
of the relationship between politics and principle. More to the point, she
exploded with righteous indignation when she recalled that Mansfield, a
man of "superior talents, profound erudition, law knowledge, and philosophical abilities," had claimed in the House of Commons in 1775 "'that
the original question of *right* ought no longer be considered" as Parliament considered what to do with the colonies. Instead, he continued, "the
justice of the cause must give way to the present situation.'" Warren
rejected Mansfield's pragmatic relativism and "sophistical reasoning,"
insisting instead that questions of truth and right should only be resolved
by the "dictates of justice" and by appeals to "the immutable laws of
justice" and to the "principles of rectitude." [45] The "original question of
right" was for Warren and the American Whigs the single most important
question.

In the end, however, it may very well have been the Loyalist Chief
Justice, Thomas Hutchinson (1711–1780) of Massachusetts, who best captured the importance of rights to colonial Americans when he told the
1769 session of the Suffolk County (Boston) grand jury "The bare Mention
of the Word *Rights* always strikes an Englishman in a peculiar Manner."
Hutchinson went on to define what would become the central theoretical
and practical problem of the American Revolution: "[I]n Order to support
and defend the Rights, of which we are so fond," he continued, "we ought
to have a just Apprehension of what they are, and whereon they stand." [46]
Just so. Hutchinson's question is still ours.

Let us turn now more directly to examining how Jefferson and his
fellow Revolutionaries understood what a natural right *is*. Their view of
rights began with several basic assumptions. First, America's Revolutionaries assumed that there is an intimate relationship between what man *is*
and how he *ought* to act. They were serious students of man's natural
constitution, and they viewed man's metaphysical nature as defined by
two primary qualities: rationality and free will. Their view of human
nature was probably best summed up in the pre-Revolutionary period by
the Reverend Elisha Williams (1694–1755), who wrote in 1744 that man's
nature is such that he has been given "an understanding to direct his
actions" and a "freedom of will and liberty" in acting. Man's freedom and
"liberty of acting according to his will (without being subject to the will
of another) is," Williams continued, "grounded on his having reason,
which is able to instruct him in that law he is to govern himself by, and

---

[45] Mercy Otis Warren, *History of the Rise, Progress, and Termination of the American Revolution* [1805], in Two Volumes, Foreword by Lester H. Cohen (Indianapolis: Liberty Fund,
1994): I: 154.
[46] Quoted in Reid, *Constitutional History of the American Revolution: The Authority of
Rights*, 3.

make him know how far he is left to the freedom of his own will. So that we are born free as we are born rational." [47] Virtually every leading member of America's Revolutionary generation would have agreed with the Reverend Daniel Shute of Hingham, Massachusetts (1722–1802), when he explained to his congregation in 1768 that man is a "rational moral agent." They believed that freedom—the freedom to think, choose, and act—is a metaphysical requirement and a necessary condition of human flourishing. They assumed that reason is man's only means for living and living well, and so he must be free to think. According to John Perkins (1698–1781) of Boston, "moral freedom" is the "exclusive property of the rational nature." That man is endowed "with reason and understanding, instead of more instinctive powers," Perkins wrote in 1771, "shows that we were ordain'd for self-direction." [48] Freedom is that state or condition in which men have the power and authority to act on their own judgment without the coercion of other men or of government. More particularly, freedom is that state or condition in which an individual has the liberty to choose from an array of alternative actions. In other words, individuals must be free to pursue their own rational self-interest unhindered by the force or coercion of others. This is precisely why "[n]o one," Jefferson opined, "has a right to obstruct another exercising his faculties innocently for the relief of sensibilities made a part of his nature." Thus, the great achievement of the American Revolution, Jefferson noted, was to issue "finally in that inestimable state of freedom which alone can ensure to man the enjoyment of his equal rights." [49]

Second, American Revolutionaries assumed that the individual is the primary unit of moral and political value. Given their view of man as a rational and volitional being and given their view of human equality, they assumed that each man is a morally autonomous and sovereign entity, which means that each man is an end in himself and not the means to someone else's end. Hence, as Connecticut minister, Moses Mather (1719–1806) argued in 1775, "man hath an absolute property in, and right of dominion over himself, his powers and faculties; with self-love to stimulate, and reason to guide him, in the free use and exercise of them, independent of, and uncontrollable by any." Every

---

[47] Elisha Williams, "The Essential Rights and Liberties of Protestants," in *Political Sermons of the American Founding Era, 1730–1805*, 56. Williams was a Congregational minister, legislator, jurist, and rector of Yale College during the early to middle decades of the eighteenth century.

[48] Daniel Shute, "An Election Sermon," in *American Political Writing during the Founding Era, 1760–1805*, Charles Hyneman and Donald S. Lutz, 2 vols. (Indianapolis, IN: LibertyPress, 1983): I: 111; A Well-Wisher to Mankind [John Perkins], "Theory of Agency: Or, An Essay on the Nature, Source and Extent of Moral Freedom," in *American Political Writing during the Founding Era, 1760–1805*, I: 139, 148. Perkins was a physician from Lynn, Massachusetts, who was best known in New England for having authored various pamphlets on earthquakes, comets, and various other natural phenomena.

[49] Thomas Jefferson to Pierre Samuel Dupont de Nemours, April 24, 1816, *Writings*, XIV: 490; Thomas Jefferson to Georgetown Republicans, 1809, *Writings*, XVI: 349.

man is, by nature, according to Mather, "his own legislator, judge, and avenger, and absolute lord of his property."[50] Because individual men are naturally equal and free, because they are not by nature subordinate to others, because they are naturally autonomous and independent from others, they must—as a metaphysical necessity—take those actions necessary to preserve and promote their own lives. They must, in other words, be self-sustaining. The Founding generation assumed that individuals are morally self-owning and self-governing, which means that they must be the beneficiaries of their own ideas and actions.[51] "Every man, and every body of men on earth," Jefferson wrote, "possesses the right of self-government. They receive it with their being from the hand of nature." In fact, he thought it would be "ridiculous to suppose that a man has less rights in himself than one of his neighbors, or all of them put together." *That*, he continued, "would be slavery."[52] This is why no person is legitimately the master or the slave of another; this is why Jefferson would not grant even Sir Isaac Newton the authority to declare himself "lord of the person or property of others."[53]

Third, the Revolutionary generation also assumed (at least by implication) that the only thing that can restrain or destroy a man's freedom is the initiation (or the threat) of physical force against him, either by other individuals or by governments. Force is that state or condition where physical coercion is used or threatened against individuals to prevent them from thinking and acting on their judgment. "No man has a natural right to commit aggression on the equal rights of another," Jefferson asserted, "and this is all from which the laws ought to restrain him."[54] Ultimately, force represents the denial of judgment and choice. Such was the meaning of the Stamp, Townshend, Tea and Coercive Acts for the Americans. Even worse, the Declaratory Act (1766) hung over the Americans like the "Sword of Damocles."[55] It represented the ever-impending threat of force. At the deepest philosophical level, then, the ultimate goal

[50] Moses Mather, "America's Appeal to the Impartial World," in *Political Sermons of the American Founding Era, 1730–1805*, ed. Ellis Sandoz (Indianapolis, IN: LibertyPress, 1990), 444, 446. Mather, born into a famous New England family of divines, was the congregational minister for Darien, Connecticut, for sixty-four years between 1742 and 1806. Mather was one of America's most vocal religious leaders in support of liberty and independence.

[51] This is not to say, as Karl Marx suggested in "On the Jewish Question," that the eighteenth-century natural rights philosophy turns men into "an isolated monad, withdrawn into himself." (Cf. Karl Marx, "On the Jewish Questions," in *The Marx-Engels Reader*, ed. Robert C. Tucker [New York: Norton, 1972], 40.) The purpose of rights is to serve as a bridge between individuals and civil society. They are the mechanism by which men can live together peacefully and form voluntary associations.

[52] Thomas Jefferson, "Opinion on the Residence Bill," 1790, *Writings*, III: 60; Thomas Jefferson to Colonel James Monroe, May 20, 1782, *Writings*, IV: 196.

[53] Thomas Jefferson to Henri Gregoire, February 25, 1809, in *The Portable Thomas Jefferson*, ed. Merrill D. Peterson, (New York: Penguin Books, 1975), 517.

[54] Thomas Jefferson to Francis W. Gilmer, June 7, 1816, *Writings*, XV: 24.

[55] The Declaratory Act was passed by the British parliament in 1766. Its purpose was to assert the authority of parliament over the colonies "in all cases whatsoever" despite its face-saving repeal of the Stamp Act.

of the Revolution was, as Jefferson put it, to banish "all arbitrary and unnecessary restraint on individual action," thereby leaving men "free to do whatever does not violate the equal rights of another."[56]

Based on the foregoing three assumptions, we can now reconstruct the way in which American Revolutionaries defined the nature of nature's rights. To that end, we must understand why the Founders thought rights necessary, the context in which they thought such rights arose, and what they saw as the purpose of rights. Eighteenth-century Americans took for granted that men—all men everywhere—have *natural* rights that are inalienable, indefeasible, inherent, universal, eternal, and absolute and that such rights are not the creation of human will. Colonial Whigs rejected the view that kings and legislatures create man's natural rights. Such rights were not and could never be, according to James Otis, matters of "favor and grace." Man's rights, John Adams wrote in his "A Dissertation on the Canon and Feudal Law," are "undoubtedly, antecedent to all earthly government," and they "cannot be repealed or restrained by human laws." Certainly the rights claimed by the colonists, Adams insisted, were "not the grants of princes or parliaments." Indeed, they are "original rights," "inherent and essential," and "established as preliminaries, even before a parliament existed." Man's rights were therefore understood by America's Founders to be pre-political and synonymous in some way with nature and human nature.[57]

From the middle of the eighteenth century through to the early decades of the nineteenth century, American statesmen and political writers thoroughly embraced the doctrine of natural rights. Just as the Stamp Act crisis was beginning in 1765, for instance, John Dickinson (1732–1808), one of most respected lawyers and writers in the American colonies, claimed that the liberties of men are "founded on the acknowledged rights of human nature." The following year, John Adams located the source of man's natural rights "in the frame of human nature," and "in the constitution of the intellectual and moral world." Likewise, Thomas Jefferson identified man's rights with the "hand of nature," and elsewhere he said they were "founded in our natural wants" and "sanctioned by the laws of our being." James Wilson, a signer of the Declaration of Independence and a principal architect of the federal Constitution, delivered a series of lectures starting in 1790 attended by George Washington, John Adams, Thomas Jefferson, and Alexander Hamilton in which he sought to demonstrate how the rights of man are "laid deeply in the human frame" and on the "immovable basis of nature."[58]

---

[56] Report of the Commissioners for the University of Virginia," August 4, 1818, in *The Portable Thomas Jefferson*, 334.

[57] James Otis, "A Vindication of the British Colonies ..." in *Pamphlets of the American Revolution, 1750–1765*, 559; John Adams, "A Dissertation on the Canon and Feudal Law," in *The Revolutionary Writings of John Adams*, 22.

[58] John Dickinson, "Speech on a Petition for a Change of Government of the Colony of Pennsylvania ... 1764," in Paul L. Ford, ed., *Writings of John Dickinson* (Philadelphia: The

But how exactly are the rights of nature natural? In other words, what makes a natural right natural?

The rights of nature were understood by America's Revolutionary generation to be a *necessary*, that is, an objective requirement of human life. That's why they were willing to fight and die for them. The rights of nature recognize what man is (i.e., a rational and a volitional being who must act on his judgment), and they define his moral requirements (i.e., freedom) in the context of living in society with other men. "Man," Jefferson wrote, "[is] a rational animal," which is why he is and must be "endowed by nature with rights." [59] In other words, by virtue of the fact that the free exercise of his rational faculty is man's fundamental mode of survival, he must therefore discover and recognize certain moral principles that sanction and protect the use of his rational faculty in the context of civil association. In his lecture "Of the Natural Rights of Individuals" delivered in 1791, James Wilson captured the essence of what a right is: "that life, and whatever is *necessary* for the safety of life, are the natural rights of man." [60] To wit: Because man is a being with a certain nature, the concept "rights" recognizes that it is both necessary and *right* that he be free to choose and pursue those actions that are required to support his life; that it is necessary and *right* that he freely exercise his rational faculty in order to gain knowledge, choose values, and act in accordance with his own judgment; that it is necessary and *right* that he act in order to acquire, keep, use, and dispose of the property he has created to support his life; and that it is necessary and *right* that he live for, benefit from, and enjoy the achievement of his highest values. In his *Lectures on Moral Philosophy* developed and delivered many times at Princeton in the years between 1768 and 1794 and almost certainly attended by his most famous student, James Madison, John Witherspoon professed that the rights of nature "are essential to man." A man has a "natural right," Dickinson continued, "to act for his own preservation, and to defend himself from injury." Rights are a moral requirement of human well-being. [61] It is in this sense that it is proper to speak of man's rights as "natural."

A right of nature was understood by the Revolutionary generation to be a rationally discovered moral principle used to establish, preserve, and

---

Historical Society of Pennsylvania, 1895), 34; John Adams, "A Dissertation on the Canon and Feudal Law," in *The Revolutionary Writings of John Adams,* 33; Thomas Jefferson, "Opinion on the Residence Bill," 1790, *Writings,* III: 60; Thomas Jefferson to Pierre Samuel Dupont de Nemours, April 24, 1816, *Writings,* XIV: 490; Thomas Jefferson to the Republicans of Georgetown, March 8, 1809, *Writings,* XIV: 349; James Wilson, *Lectures on Law* [1790–1792], in *The Works of James Wilson,* ed. Robert Green McCloskey, 2 vols. (Cambridge, MA: Harvard University Press, 1967), II: 609.

[59] Thomas Jefferson to William Johnson, June 12, 1823, *Writings,* XV: 441.

[60] James Wilson, *Lectures on Law,* in *The Works of James Wilson,* ed. Robert Green McCloskey, 2 vols. (Cambridge, MA: Harvard University Press, 1967), II: 596.

[61] John Witherspoon, *Lectures on Moral Philosophy,*" in *The Selected Writings of John Witherspoon,* ed. Thomas Miller (Carbondale, Ill: Southern Illinois University Press, 1990), 181. Witherspoon's Princeton lectures were not published until after his death in 1794. The lectures were first published in 1802.

protect the conditions necessary for human flourishing within the context of civil association. In this sense, rights are morally unalienable precisely because they are necessary. Put differently, a man's life, liberty, and property are his by natural right. They are his as a selfish possession. Rights as such, the Founders held, are owned by each and every individual as a form of moral property, i.e., as a title, which means that their violation by individuals, groups, or governments should be treated as a crime. As James Madison wrote in a 1792 essay on "Property": "In a word, as a man is said to have a right to his property, he may be equally said to have a property in his rights."[62] To have property in one's rights is to say that each and every individual has sovereignty over and controls his freedom to act in civil society.

Strictly speaking, a right, as understood by the Revolutionary generation, is necessarily associated with or complementary to freedom—the freedom to think and act—a freedom that is necessary to preserve and promote one's own life. Rights define spheres of freedom and human action in a social setting. The Founders treated rights and freedom as one, as necessarily and logically connected, as a unity. In other words, without freedom there can be no rights, and vice versa. Man's right (i.e., that which is the right course of action necessary to sustain his life and achieve his values) necessitates freedom (i.e., the power to act free from the physical compulsion of other men). At the core of Jefferson's philosophy was the belief that there is a "right independent of force," and that "right" is connected to freedom of action.[63] This is what the Founding generation called justice, which "consists in giving or permitting others to enjoy whatever they have a perfect right to—and making such a use of our own rights as not to encroach upon the rights of others."[64]

The Founders' use of the concept "rights" can be viewed as having a dual character: it served as both a *license* and a *fence*. As a license, rights provide a moral and legal sanction recognizing the freedom of individuals to act in a social context in the pursuit of life-enhancing values. As Jefferson put it: "Under the law of nature, all men are born free, every one comes into the world with a right to his own person, which includes the liberty of moving and using it at his own will. This is what is called personal liberty, and is given him by the Author of nature, because *necessary* for his own sustenance." As a fence, rights define and erect for each and every individual defensive boundaries against the initiation of physical force by others. They are, as Jefferson once said, "fences which experience has proved peculiarly efficacious against wrong." Rights recognized and protected shield men, according to James Wilson, from "different

---

[62] James Madison, "Property," in *The Mind of the Founder: Sources of the Political Thought of James Madison* (Indianapolis: Bobbs-Merrill, 1973), 244.

[63] Thomas Jefferson to Pierre Samuel Dupont de Nemours, April 24, 1816, *Writings*, XIV: 490.

[64] John Witherspoon, "Lectures on Moral Philosophy," in *The Selected Writings of John Witherspoon*, 183.

degrees of aggression," including "threatening, assault, battery, wounding, mayhem, homicide."[65] In this sense, rights establish barriers of human action between individuals in their relations with each other and between individuals in their relations with the State.[66] In sum, the concept "rights" means a morally and legally recognized license to act freely in order to produce, acquire, possess, use, and trade property for the purpose of attaining happiness, and it means a morally and legally recognized barrier against the arbitrary initiation of physical force against oneself or anyone else.

In order for a rights-based society to be operative and to function according to its basic moral rules, the rights of nature must be recognized universally as *reciprocal*. A truly civilized society, Jefferson claimed in his *Notes on the State of Virginia*, is one that respects "those rights in others which we value in ourselves." Rights provide the moral boundary lines by which society marks out and prevents one man from "violating the similar rights of other sensible beings." Witherspoon professed in his *Lectures on Moral Philosophy* that "as our own happiness is a lawful object or end, we are supposed to have each a right to prosecute this; but as our prosecutions may interfere, we limit each other's rights, and a man is said to have a right or power to promote his own happiness only by those means which are not in themselves criminal or injurious to others."[67] Indeed, the discovery, recognition, and protection of man's natural rights is the necessary precondition for a civilized society. The rights of nature provide men with an absolute standard of justice, right, and political action, which in turn permits and encourages men to pursue the values (e.g., trade, voluntary associations, wealth) necessary for their well-being. The concept "natural rights" therefore provides the fundamental principle by which individuals in civil society can be simultaneously set free and ordered morally.

And how are such rights known and promulgated? The rights of nature are not created by kings or parliaments but are, rather, *discovered* — discovered as rational principles the purpose of which is to promote human flourishing. According to John Dickinson, American colonists through their various charters prior to 1776 considered their rights to be *"declarations* but not *gifts* of liberties." In his "Address to the Committee

[65] Thomas Jefferson, "Argument in the Case of Howell vs. Netherland", April, 1770 in *The Works of Thomas Jefferson*, 10 vols. ed. Paul Leicester Ford (New York and London, G. P. Putnam's Sons, 1904-5), I: 376 (emphasis added); Thomas Jefferson to Noah Webster, December 4, 1790, *Writings*, VIII: 112-13; James Wilson, *Lectures on Law*, in *The Works of James Wilson*, II: 597, 609.

[66] On the idea of rights as licenses and fences, see Thomas Jefferson to Isaac H. Tiffany, April 4, 1819, *Writings*, in *Jefferson: Political Writings*, eds. Joyce Appleby and Terrence Ball (Cambridge: Cambridge University Press, 1999), 224; Thomas Jefferson to Noah Webster, December 4, 1790, *Writings*, VIII: 112-13.

[67] Thomas Jefferson, "Notes on the State of Virginia," in *The Portable Thomas Jefferson*, ed. Merrill D. Peterson (New York: Penguin Books, 1975), 96-97; Thomas Jefferson to Samuel Dupont de Nemours, April 24, 1816, *Writings*, XIV: 490; John Witherspoon, "Lectures on Moral Philosophy," in *The Selected Writings of John Witherspoon*, 181.

of Correspondence in Barbados," Dickinson summed up the American Revolutionary position on rights, what and where their source is, and how they are promulgated. Kings and parliaments, he announced, could never *"give* the *rights essential to happiness."* Instead, the Americans

> claim them from a higher source—from the King of kings, and Lord of all the earth. They are not annexed to us by parchments and seals. They are created in us by the decrees of Providence, which establish the laws of our nature. They are born with us; exist with us; and cannot be taken from us by any human power, without taking our lives. In short, they are founded on the immutable maxims of reason and justice.

In other words, men do not legislate natural rights. They are not a subjective creation. And if man's natural rights were not given to him as the favors or gifts of kings and parliaments, there was then just one way in which they could be made real or brought to life: they must be first *discovered* through reason and then publicly *recognized,* which means defined, declared, and protected. Thus, the "Business of *Legislation,*" Abraham Williams announced in 1762, is to "investigate," "discover," and "publish the Rules of Equity . . . and to annex such Sanctions as Reason directs, to secure the Rights and Properties of the Society, and of every Individual." Similarly, the primary purpose of a bill of rights, according to William Whiting (1730-1792) of Berkshire County in Massachusetts, was to *"ascertain* and clearly describe the rights of nature, including the rights of conscience, and that security of person and property." Even the best-written laws—including Magna Carta, the English Bill of Rights and the Declaration of Independence—authored by the wisest and most virtuous men do not create rights. Instead, such laws "must be considered as only *declaratory* of our rights," announced Silas Downer (1729–1785) of Providence, Rhode Island in 1768, "and in affirmance of them." Thomas Jefferson, discussing the "rightful limits" of legislators' power in 1816, pronounced "their true office is to *declare* and enforce only natural rights and duties, and to take none of them from us."[68] Rights discovered and declared are rights that exist *in* nature independent of human will.

---

[68] John Dickinson, "An Address to the Committee of Correspondence in Barbados" (Philadelphia, 1766), in Ford, ed., *Writings of John Dickinson,* 261–62; Abraham Williams, "An Election Sermon," in *American Political Writing during the Founding Era, 1760–1805,* I: 11, 15; William Whiting, "An Address to the Inhabitants of Berkshire County, Mass.," in *American Political Writing during the Founding Era, 1760–1805,* I: 474 (emphasis added); [Silas Downer], "A Discourse at the Dedication of the Tree of Liberty," in *American Political Writing during the Founding Era, 1760–1805,* I: 100 (emphasis added); Thomas Jefferson to Francis W. Gilmer, June 7, 1816, *Writings,* XV: 24 (emphasis added). Though his treatment is brief, Bernard Bailyn glimpsed the transition in American Revolutionary thought from the "rights of Englishmen" to the "rights of man." See *The Ideological Origins of the American Revolution,* enlarged ed., (Cambridge, MA: The Belknap Press of Harvard University Press, 1992), 184–98.

The actual content of man's natural rights was familiar to all of the Founding generation. "Among" those rights listed as "unalienable" in the Declaration of Independence are "Life, Liberty, and the Pursuit of Happiness." These are the most fundamental of man's natural rights (we shall include property as well), although the American Revolutionaries did think there were subsidiary natural rights as well (e.g., the rights to free emigration, free trade, free exercise of religion, freedom of conscience, speech, press and assembly, to bear arms, and to one's reputation).[69] The Declaration and the Founding generation viewed the rights of nature as fulfilling certain functions: the right to life is the standard; the rights to liberty and property are the means; and the right of the pursuit of happiness is the motive and the end.

The Founders' theory of individual rights said that man, given his nature, has a *right to life* (the fundamental right from which all others derive), which means that each individual is fully sovereign over his own life, that his life is sacrosanct and cannot be harmed or taken away by another, and that he has the moral right to pursue life-promoting values. The Declaration of Independence, every state bill or declaration of rights, and every discussion of natural rights in Revolutionary America understood the right to life to be the standard, the mother right from which all other rights are born. "Self-preservation" is "a great and primary law of nature," Jonathan Mayhew declared in 1766, "and to be considered as antecedent to all civil laws and institutions, which are subordinate and subservient to the other." And in 1793, in his "Opinion on the French Treaties," Jefferson made clear that the "moral law" of man's nature dictated that if and when performance of an obligation "becomes *self-destructive* to the party, the law of self-preservation overrules the laws of obligation in others." [70] Self-preservation is the first law of nature because life is the standard of that which is right by nature.

The Founders' theory of individual rights said that man, given his nature, has a *right to liberty*, which means the unobstructed freedom to think, choose, act, produce, and acquire values material and spiritual. Liberty is the first and necessary corollary of the right to life. In fact, life and liberty are inseparable. The Founding generation used the concept "liberty" in two different but necessarily related senses. They understood liberty as both an existential fact of human nature (i.e., man is a volitional

---

[69] For a helpful discussion of the subsidiary natural rights, see Philip A. Hamburger, "Natural Rights, Natural Law, and American Constitutions," *The Yale Law Journal* 102 (Jan., 1993): 907–60.

[70] Jonathan Mayhew, "The Snare Broken," in *Political Sermons of the American Founding Era, 1730–1805*, ed. Ellis Sandoz (Indianapolis, IN: LibertyPress, 1990), 263. Thomas Jefferson, "Opinion on the French Treaties," April 28, 1793, *Writings*, III: 228–29. Also see Simeon Howard, "A Sermon Preached to the Ancient and Honorable Artillery Company in Boston," in *American Political Writing during the Founding Era, 1760–1805*, I: 191; Gad Hitchcock, "An Election Sermon," "A Sermon Preached to the Ancient and Honorable Artillery Company in Boston," in *American Political Writing during the Founding Era, 1760–1805*, I: 294.

being by nature), but also as a moral requirement of human flourishing (i.e., man must have and must use his liberty in order to flourish). As an existential fact, liberty is, as John Adams defined it, "a self-determining power in an intellectual agent. It implies thought and choice and power; it can elect between objects, indifferent in point of morality, neither morally good nor morally evil." [71] In other words, man has the ability, the free will, the liberty to choose good or evil. Such liberty or free will is not, however, automatic. It must be consciously activated. Thus, liberty is also a moral requirement of human flourishing. The "is" of liberty implies the "ought" of liberty. Not only does man have liberty as a fact of his nature, but he must also have liberty as a moral requirement of his life. He must be free in order to think and take those actions necessary to promote his life, which means that he must be free from the coercion of others. Thus, liberty is opposed, as Simeon Howard of Boston put it in 1773, "to external force and constraint, and to such force and constraint only, as we may suffer from men." [72] Ironically, if man is to live in a free society he must choose to do so and he must act to keep and preserve his freedom. Political liberty is a choice. Given that man is a rational and a volitional being, to deny him the freedom to think, choose, and act is to deny him his nature and his means of survival. Thus, liberty is to moral action what oxygen is to breathing.

Liberty does not mean, however, simply doing what one wants or desires. Liberty for Adams, Jefferson, and the rest of the Founding generation did not mean the Hobbesean liberty to do as one lists. The natural right to liberty means the freedom of choice and action in a social setting. Ironically enough, the natural right to liberty means limits and boundaries. Thomas Jefferson captured the twofold nature of liberty: "Of liberty I would say that, in the whole plenitude of its extent, it is unobstructed action according to our will. But *rightful liberty* is unobstructed action according to our will within limits drawn around us by the equal rights of others. I do not add 'within the limits of the law,' because law is often but the tyrant's will, and always so when it violates the right of an individual." [73] Liberty is a right, which means that it is defined by boundaries.

The Founders' theory of individual rights also said that man, given his nature, has a *right to property*, which means the freedom to keep, use, and dispose of the product of one's physical and mental labor. The absence of

[71] John Adams to John Taylor of Caroline, April 15, 1814 in *The Political Writings of John Adams*, ed. George W. Carey, 369.

[72] Simeon Howard, "A Sermon Preached to the Ancient and Honorable Artillery Company in Boston," in *American Political Writing during the Founding Era, 1760–1805*, I: 187.

[73] Thomas Jefferson to Isaac Tiffany, April 4, 1819, in *Jefferson: Political Writings*, 224 (emphasis added). For one of the most philosophically sophisticated treatments of liberty written during the Revolutionary period, see John Perkins, "Theory of Agency: Or, An Essay on the Nature, Source and Extent of Moral Freedom [1771]," in *American Political Writing during the Founding Era, 1760–1805*, I: 137–57.

an explicit right to private property in the Declaration should in no way lead us to conclude, however, as do some historians, that Jefferson and the rest of the Revolutionary generation did not support such a right. Nothing could be further from the truth.[74] A brief digression is necessarily in order. The natural right to property, Jefferson wrote in 1816, is founded in human nature, "in our natural wants, in the means by which we are endowed to satisfy those wants, and the right to what we acquire by those means without violating the similar rights" of others. Discovering, recognizing, and protecting the right to property is a necessary condition of human flourishing. The American people above all others, Jefferson noted, have a "due sense of our equal right to . . . the acquisitions of our own industry."[75] Arthur Lee (1740–1792), an American diplomat and statesman during the War for Independence, summed up in 1775 the importance the Revolutionary generation placed on property as a natural right when he declared, "The Right of property is the guardian of every other Right, and to deprive the people of this, is in fact to deprive them of their Liberty." Twelve years later, James Madison reinforced Lee's claim in *Federalist No. Ten* by suggesting that the "first object of government" is to protect the "diversity in the faculties of men, from which the rights of property originate."[76] Madison understood man's natural right to property as an extension of his need to think and to think rationally.

Justice and the very idea of republican government were, according to John Adams, synonymous with the protection of private property and the liberty to pursue it. In his *A Defence of the Constitutions of Government of the United State of America* (1787–1788), Adams argued forcefully that constitutions, the rule of law, and properly constructed republican governments exist primarily to protect man's natural right to property:

> *Res populi* . . . signified a government, in which the property of the public, or people, and of every one of them, was secured and protected by law. This idea, indeed, implies liberty; because property cannot be secure unless the man be at liberty to acquire, use, or part with it, at his discretion, and unless he have his personal liberty of life and limb, motion and rest, for that purpose. It implies, moreover, that the property and liberty of all men, not merely of a majority, should be safe; for the people, or public, comprehends more than a majority, it comprehends all and every individual; and the property

---

[74] For the claim that Jefferson does not regard property to be a natural right, see Richard Matthews, *The Radical Politics of Thomas Jefferson* (Lawrence, KS: University Press of Kansas, 1985), 27.

[75] Thomas Jefferson to Samuel Dupont de Nemours, April 24, 1816, *Writings*, XIV: 490; Thomas Jefferson, "First Inaugural," 1801, *Writings*, III: 320.

[76] Quoted in James W. Ely, Jr., *The Guardian of Every Other Right: A Constitutional History of Property Rights*, 2d ed., (Oxford: Oxford University Press, 1998), 26; James Madison, *The Federalist*, Edited, with Introduction and Notes, by Jacob E. Cooke (Hanover, NH: University Press of New England, 1961), 58.

of every citizen is a part of the public property, as each citizen is a part of the public, people, or community. The property, therefore, of every man has a share in government, and is more powerful than any citizen, or party of citizens; it is governed only by the law.

No nation, Adams wrote, could be considered civilized or free until it had institutionalized and made inviolable the "precepts" "'THOU SHALT NOT Covet,' and 'THOU SHALT NOT STEAL.'"[77] Adams, Jefferson, and the rest of the Founders could not and would not have recognized an intrinsic and positive rights-claim to some *thing*, to the means of existence—to food, shelter, daycare, health care, a job, an education, and so on. In other words, they would not have recognized the right to life to mean that one man has a rights-claim on the liberty and property of another.[78] Jefferson argued, for instance, that extra taxes on the wealthy would violate natural right:

> To take from one, because it is thought that his industry and that of his fathers has acquired too much, in order to spare to others, who, or whose fathers have not exercised equal industry or skill, is to violate arbitrarily the first principle of association, the guarantee to every one of a free exercise of his industry, and the fruits acquired by it.[79]

The Founding generation universally considered property to be a fundamental, natural right. They would spend the next eighty years, however, debating the nature and content of property—a debate that ended with Abraham Lincoln's Emancipation Proclamation (1863).

Lastly, the Founders' theory of individual rights said that man, given his nature, has a *right to the pursuit of happiness*, which means the freedom to choose and pursue those values that lead to one's own personal happiness. It is a law of man's nature, Jefferson wrote, for each and every man "to pursue his own happiness." Individuals, rather than governments or seminaries of wise men, are the best judges of their own road to happiness. Man has been left free, Jefferson opined, "in the choice of place as well as mode, and we may safely call on the whole body of English jurists to produce the map on which nature has traced for each individual the geographical line which she forbids him to cross in pursuit of happiness." This means that each person has the right to live his life and to pursue values in any way he chooses so long as he respects the reciprocal rights of others. The individual right to the pursuit of happiness did not, how-

---

[77] Adams, *The Works of John Adams*, 10 vols., edited by Charles Francis Adams (Boston, 1850–1856): V, 453–54; VI, 8–9.

[78] Chattel slavery is of course the anomaly to the Founding generation's view of rights.

[79] Thomas Jefferson to Joseph Milligan, April 6, 1816, *Writing*, XIV: 466.

ever, imply subjectivism for Jefferson. Each and every man could and should pursue happiness as he defined it, but Jefferson did not think that various pursuits and forms of happiness were equal. True happiness, Jefferson insisted, was connected to virtue: "The order of nature" is "that individual happiness shall be inseparable from the practice of virtue." Happiness was not possible to man, he told a preceptor at Fryeburg Academy in Maine, "without virtue." Exactly how or what Jefferson defined as virtue is not entirely known, but this much we can say with confidence: he believed that the "first elements of morality" combined with wisdom were the necessary preconditions for individuals to "work out their own greatest happiness." Indeed, he equated the "wise" man with the "happy man." Virtue and the "greatest happiness," Jefferson believed, were attainable by all men rich or poor independent of the "condition of life in which chance has placed them, but is always the result of a good conscience, good health, occupation, and freedom in all just pursuits."[80]

Having thus far examined how the Revolutionary generation understood the nature and content of man's rights, let us now briefly examine how they viewed the relationship between the different rights of nature. America's Revolutionary Founders viewed nature's rights as a logically ordered and unified whole that serves the fundamental right, i.e., the right to life. Man's natural rights are, as Samuel Adams put it in 1772, "evident branches of, rather than deductions from, the duty of self-preservation, commonly called the first law of nature."[81] In other words, the right to life cannot be separated from the right to liberty, property, or the pursuit of happiness and vice versa. The right to life requires liberty—the *right* to liberty—the liberty necessary to think and act on one's own judgment in order to promote one's life. The right to liberty necessitates property—the *right* to keep and/or to trade the fruits of one's labor—the property necessary to sustain one's life and liberty. The right to property culminates in the right to the pursuit of one's happiness—the *right* to pursue one's own material and spiritual values—the happiness necessary to live a satisfying, self-fulfilling life. Or, as John Dickinson put it in the context of the imperial crisis:

> It would be an insult on the divine Majesty to say, that he has given or allowed any man or body of men *a right to make me miserable*. If no man or body of men has *such a right*, I have a *right to be happy*. If there

---

[80] Thomas Jefferson to John Manners, June 12, 1817, *Writings*, XV: 124; Thomas Jefferson to J. Correa de Serra, April 19, 1814, *Writings*, XIX: 210; Thomas Jefferson to Amos J. Cook, January 21, 1816, *Writings*, IV: 405; Thomas Jefferson, *Notes on the State of Virginia* in *The Portable Thomas Jefferson*, 196–97; Thomas Jefferson to Amos J. Cook, January 21, 1816, *Writings*, IV: 405; Thomas Jefferson, *Notes on the State of Virginia* in *The Portable Thomas Jefferson*, 196–97.

[81] [Samuel Adams], "A State of the Rights of the Colonists," *Tracts of the American Revolution*, 235. For a contemporary analysis of rights as a logical unity, see Leonard Peikoff, *Objectivism: The Philosophy of Ayn Rand*, 352.

can be no happiness without freedom, I have a *right to be free*. If I cannot enjoy freedom without security of property, I have a *right to be thus secured*. If my property cannot be secure, in case others over whom I have no kind of influence may take it from me by taxes, under pretence of the public good, and for enforcing their demands, may subject me to arbitrary, expensive, and remote jurisdictions, I have an *exclusive right* to lay taxes on my property, either by myself or those I can trust; of necessity to judge in such instances of the public good; and to be exempt from such jurisdictions. But no man can be secure in his property, who is "liable to impositions, that have NOTHING BUT THE WILL OF THE IMPOSERS to direct them in the measure;" and that make "JUSTICE TO CROUCH UNDER THEIR LOAD."[82]

We come now to our final two questions: Where did the Revolutionary generation think man's "unalienable rights" come from, and how did they distinguish between the laws and rights of nature?

What did Jefferson and the Revolutionary generation think was the source of man's rights? Here, as with their understanding and use of the concept "laws of nature," the Founders were somewhat ambiguous. This much we know with certainty: they did not think that man's *natural* rights come from history, culture, parliaments, or the Bible. We also know with certainty that most of America's Revolutionary Founders assumed that God or the Creator was the ultimate source of man's rights just as he was the source of nature's laws. The first obvious thing to note is that man's rights are said in the Declaration of Independence to be *endowed* or given to man by his "Creator"—by God, even though we do not find them listed anywhere in scripture.[83] Jefferson's "Creator" is the source of man's rights but his "Creator" is also "Nature's God" and "Nature's God" is, as we have already seen, virtually synonymous for Jefferson with nature pure and simple.[84] Jefferson's God is obviously not the stern, omnipres-

---

[82] John Dickinson, "An Address to the Committee of Correspondence in Barbados" (Philadelphia, 1766), in Ford, ed., *Writings of John Dickinson*, 262.

[83] From a philosophic perspective, what could it possibly mean to say that God endows man with rights? Consider the following analogy. The Declaration seems to be suggesting that one, rights are a metaphysical *thing*, comparable to, say, a seed; and two, that God has somehow planted the *seed* of rights *in* man at birth. The suggestion here is that the Creator's "rights seed" is inalienable because it is a gift from God, which means that it is wrought in man's natural constitution, that it cannot be taken away by other men or governments, and that all men everywhere have these rights. This "rights seed" must be, however, watered, nourished, and protected in order to grow and flourish, which is why it has not been universally recognized. There are, of course, two obvious problems with this view: first, the existence of God is arbitrarily asserted rather than proved, and second, even if there were a God, unaided reason could not demonstrate that God had planted *in* man the seed of rights. The "rights seed" will not show up on an MRI.

[84] For the view that Jefferson's God is "Nature's God, see Daniel Boorstin, *The Lost World of Thomas Jefferson* (Chicago: University of Chicago Press, 1948), 29ff.; also Jean Yarbrough, *American Virtues: Thomas Jefferson on the Character of a Free People* (Lawrence, KS: University Press of Kansas, 1998), 7; and Michael Zuckert, *The Natural Rights Republic*, 25, 59–60.

ent and vengeful God of the Old Testament. Rather, his Creator is "Nature's God" and Nature's god is the Deist's God of the Enlightenment. In other words, Jefferson's God acts through and is known to man by the scientific laws of nature and man's rights are a gift of nature or nature's God. The metaphysical law to which the Declaration appeals and on which it grounds its moral principles is thus nature. Whereas English Whigs deduced their view of rights from an "Anglo-Saxon source" and English Tories deduced their view of rights from a "Norman" source, American Revolutionaries grounded their rights by appealing to "nature," or what Jefferson referred to as the "laws of our being," the "order of nature," the "moral law of our nature," and "universal law." The rights of nature are validated in and by "reality," according to Jefferson, by appealing "to the true fountains of evidence," the head and heart of every rational and honest man. It is there nature has written her moral laws, and where every man may read them for himself."[85] Notice that in this last iteration of man's rights, Jefferson has cut God out of the picture entirely. The rights of nature can be known without God's intervention or assistance.

Lastly, how did the Founders understand the differences and the relationship between a "law of nature" and a "right of nature"? This is a complicated subject and a difficult question to answer because none of the Founding Fathers addressed it directly or in any meaningful way. To the degree that even a few mentioned the relationship in passing, they did seem to suggest that the rights of nature issue from the laws of nature. In his "Summary View," Thomas Jefferson claimed that the rights of nature are "derived from the laws of nature," and the Continental Congress in its "Declaration and Resolves" asserted that the colonists' rights were grounded in the "immutable laws of nature." The Founders' view on this matter is, however, open to a decisive criticism. Natural rights or the rights of nature represent, as we have seen, a recognition of certain facts of human nature. They are moral principles, grounded in man's metaphysical nature, that sanction and protect his freedom of action. The laws of nature are, by contrast, moral-legal principles the purpose of which is to recognize and protect man's rights. In other words, the laws of nature are a consequence of, or follow from, the rights of nature. The laws of nature are deductions from the rights of nature.

To sum up: The Founders' use of the concept "rights" consisted of four interconnected, constituent elements: first, they served as principles

---

[85] Thomas Jefferson to Major John Cartwright, June 5, 1824, *Writings*, XVI: 43–44; Thomas Jefferson to Georgetown Republicans, 1809, *Writings*, XVI: 349; Thomas Jefferson to M. Correa de Serra, April 19, 1814, *Writings*, XIX: 210; Thomas Jefferson, "Opinion on the French Treaties," April 28, 1793, *Writings*, III: 228; Thomas Jefferson, "A Summary View of the Rights of British-America" in *Colonies to Nation, 1763–1789*, 228; Thomas Jefferson, "Opinion on the French Treaties," April 28, 1793, *Writings*, III: 228–29. In fact, the existence and necessity of rights can be validated by simply studying reality—by comparing the general levels of wealth and happiness that exist between those nations that respect property rights and those which do not.

grounded in a recognition of what man is—i.e., of his metaphysical nature (e.g., what he requires and must use for his survival and well-being); second, they defined the conditions necessary for man to act in association with other individuals; third, they sanctioned his freedom to act so that he might pursue those values necessary to live and live well; and fourth, they established boundaries around each and every individual that defined action in a social context. Thus, when the Americans declared their independence from Great Britain, they were creating a sphere of freedom not only relative to king and parliament, but also in which each man could declare his independence from his fellow citizens. Even more radically, the long-term consequence and meaning of the Revolution was to liberate men from unchosen obligations to each other as they were freed from the arbitrary commands of government. This revolution in thought and practice would have enormous implications for the development of a new American society in the nineteenth century.[86]

IV. Conclusion

The Declaration of Independence tells us a good deal about the men who signed it and led the Revolution. American Revolutionaries announced to the world their right to self-government, and they backed up their words with their lives, their fortunes, and their sacred honor. They did not evade, rationalize, turn the other cheek, or shirk their commitment or responsibility to their highest values. Instead, they responded by organizing boycotts, protesting and resisting usurpations, writing letters, petitions and remonstrances, liberating boxes of tea, and eventually going to war. They held their moral principles as absolutes and they practiced them consistently, without compromise or contradiction. They chose to act in ways that they thought right and just, regardless of the immediate consequences, precisely because they understood the value and importance of acting according to their moral principles. The Declaration of Independence and the war that followed represent a heroic integration of mind and body. Thus, the linchpin that united theory and practice in the Founders' moral universe was the virtue of integrity—the principle of being principled.

When Patrick Henry proclaimed "Give me liberty, or give me death," it was no idle pledge. And at the fateful moment when fifty-six men formally signed their declaration of independence, they heroically assumed full responsibility for the war that was sure to come. On July 3, 1776, the day after he had delivered one of the greatest speeches in American history, a speech which moved the Continental Congress to vote for Independence and for which he was later called the "Atlas of Independence,"

---

[86] For an examination of the new society created by the American Revolution, see Gordon S. Wood, *The Radicalism of the American Revolution* (New York: Vintage, 1993).

John Adams summed up to his beloved wife, Abigail, the meaning of their declaration of independence. I know of no statement that better captures the American sense of life.

> You will think me transported with enthusiasm, but I am not. I am well aware of the toil, and blood, and treasure, that it will cost us to maintain this declaration, and support and defend these States. Yet, through all the gloom, I can see the rays of lavishing light and glory. I can see that the end is more than worth all the means, and that posterity will triumph in that day's transaction.[87]

Despite the vicissitudes that befell them—the hardships of war, the blood and toil, the starvation, the imprisonment and torture, the destruction of home and property, the loss of family and loved ones, and finally death itself—the American Revolutionaries refused to compromise, and they refused to surrender. The American Revolution represents one of the rare and great moments in history when theory and practice were one.

Political Science, Clemson University

---

[87] John Adams to Abigail Adams, July 3, 1776, *Adams Family Papers: An Electronic Archive.* Massachusetts Historical Society, Butterfield, L. H., ed. *Adams Family Correspondence.* Vol. 2. (Cambridge, MA: Belknap Press of Harvard University Press, 1963).

LYSANDER SPOONER: NINETEENTH-CENTURY AMERICA'S LAST NATURAL RIGHTS THEORIST*

By Eric Mack

I. Introduction

The main purpose of this essay is to articulate the ideas of the last powerful advocate of natural rights in nineteenth century America. That last powerful advocate was the Massachusetts born radical libertarian Lysander Spooner (1808–1887). Spooner produced an impressive body of anti-slavery and anti-statist writings that included *The Unconstitutionality of Slavery* (1845 and 1846), *A Defense Fugitive Slaves* (1850), *An Essay on Trial by Jury* (1852) *The Law of Intellectual Property* (1855), *No Treason No. 6: The Constitution of No Authority* (1870), "Vices are not Crimes" (1875), *Natural Law* (1882), and *A Letter to Grover Cleveland* (1886).[1] Robert Nozick strongly commended the study of Spooner and his ideological colleague, the author and publisher Benjamin Tucker, saying that "It cannot be over-emphasized how lively, stimulating, and interesting are the writings and arguments of Spooner and Tucker . . ."[2] Unfortunately, despite its force and conceptual rigor, there has been little scholarly examination of Spooner's thought. This is especially the case with regard to Spooner's account of natural rights.[3] This essay seeks to fill that scholarly gap by examining Spooner's case for affirming strongly individualistic natural rights and by arguing that there is considerably more to Spooner's case

* I thank the editors of *Social Philosophy and Policy* for their extremely helpful comments on an earlier draft of this essay.

[1] For all of these works except the essay "Vices are not Crimes," see *The Collected Works of Lysander Spooner,* ed. Charles Shivley (Weston, MA: M&S Press, 1971). The wonderful full title of the open letter to Cleveland is *A Letter to Grover Cleveland, on His False Inaugural Address, The Usurpations and Crimes of Lawmakers and Judges, and the Consequent Poverty, Ignorance, and Servitude of the People.* "For Vices are not Crimes" see *The Lysander Spooner Reader,* ed. George Smith (San Francisco: Fox & Wilkes, 1992). The best general survey of Spooner's life and work is still the chapter on Spooner (entitled "Dissident Among Dissidents") in James Martin, *Men against the State* (Colorado Springs: Ralph Myles Publisher, 1970).

[2] Robert Nozick, *Anarchy, State, and Utopia* (New York: Basic Books, 1974), 335. The best general survey of Tucker's life and work remains the two chapters on Tucker in Martin's *Men against the State.*

[3] On Spooner's constitutional thought, see Randy Barnett, "Was Slavery Unconstitutional Before the Thirteenth Amendment?: Lysander Spooner's Theory of Interpretation" *Pacific Law Journal* 28 (1997): 977, and Helen Knowles, "Securing 'The Blessings of Liberty' for All," *NYU Journal of Law and Liberty* 34 (June 2010). Also see Roderick Long, "Inside and Outside Spooner's Natural Law Jurisprudence"—available at: http://praxeology.net/Spooner-OB.doc and discussed below.

doi:10.1017/S0265052511000264
© 2012 Social Philosophy & Policy Foundation. Printed in the USA.

for the authority of such rights than may first meet the eye. I maintain that Spooner's doctrine of rights is strikingly Lockean. For, like John Locke, his position rests on the ideas that: (1) rational individuals seek their own happiness; (2) the recognition of others as rational seekers of happiness on a moral par with oneself requires one to acknowledge everyone's equal right to seek happiness; (3) a significant component of this right to seek happiness is the right of discretionary control over one's own person; and (4) the right each has over his own person includes a right of each to his own labor and this right is the basis for property rights in extra-personal objects.[4]

To provide some context for Spooner's natural rights doctrine, I will describe briefly some of the views of two other radical libertarian advocates who were writing in England around the time that Spooner began to address questions of political and legal theory in the late 1830s—Thomas Hodgskin (1787–1869) and the early Herbert Spencer (1820–1903). The discussions of Hodgskin and the early Spencer will help fill in the picture of an ongoing radical libertarian tradition in which Spooner belongs; and these discussions should help us appreciate the special features of Spooner's Lockean radicalism.[5] In particular, I will contrast what I call a "supervenient" conception of natural rights that is found in Hodgskin with a "beneficial norm" conception of rights that is found in Spencer. According to the former, an individual's basic rights arise from certain more fundamental properties of that individual while, according to the latter, an individual's basic rights are claims to be treated in accord with those rules general compliance with which is advantageous to all individuals. I shall maintain that despite initial appearances to the contrary, Spooner joins Locke in subscribing to the supervenient conception. I should emphasize that I will be focusing on the basic doctrines about rights that Hodgskin, the early Spencer, and Spooner offer and not their further conclusions about what political and legal institutions are acceptable or unacceptable.

During the latter decades of the nineteenth century—at the time that Spooner was authoring his most forceful statements of rights-oriented radical libertarianism—belief in natural rights and in the anti-statist conclusions associated with natural rights doctrine were attacked on a variety of fronts—especially by the quasi-Hegelian advocates of the "new"

---

[4] John Locke, *Two Treatises of Government*, ed. Peter Laslett (Cambridge: Cambridge University Press, 1960), especially chapters 2–5 of the *Second Treatise*.

[5] Despite many striking similarities between Hodgskin and Spooner, Hodgskin is never mentioned by Spooner. Spencer is also never mentioned although Spooner certainly had some acquaintance with Spencer's views. Indeed, Locke is mentioned—fairly incidentally—only three times in *The Collected Works of Lysander Spooner*. Locke is not mentioned at all in Spooner's *The Law of Intellectual Property* despite passages that closely track arguments from *The Two Treatises of Government* (see notes 127 and 128) or in Spooner's "Vices are not Crimes" even though this essay reads like an updating of Locke's *A Letter Concerning Toleration*, ed. James Tully (Indianapolis: Hackett Publishing, 1983). One cannot seek out influences on Spooner's thought through an examination of his citations.

liberalism in Britain and by advocates of Progressivism in the United States. Invocation of natural rights or similarly fundamental and restrictive principles of justice—like Herbert Spencer's "law of equal freedom"—and the incorporation of such rights or restrictive norms into the United States Constitution were generally depicted as intellectually antiquated resistance to a hardheaded and scientific willingness to pursue social progress through experimentation with expanded state power. Of course, the best known instance of this dismissal of natural rights thinking and its constitutional analogues was Oliver Wendell Holmes's (utterly confused) quip in his dissent in *Lochner v. New York*. "The Fourteenth Amendment does not enact Mr. Herbert Spencer's *Social Statics*."[6]

It is often thought that the United States Supreme Court decisions of the late nineteenth and early twentieth centuries that so agitated Progressives like Holmes reflected constitutional theorizing that embodied natural rights thinking. For instance, in his recent illuminating book on the constitutional and political context of the *Lochner* decision, David Bernstein refers to this constitutional theorizing as "natural rights jurisprudence."[7] The suggestion is that the authors of this constitutional theorizing—in particular, Thomas M. Cooley (1824–1898) and Christopher G. Tiedeman (1857–1903)—must themselves have been natural rights theorists; hence, they stand as counterexamples to my claim that Spooner was nineteenth-century America's last natural rights theorist. But this suggestion is mistaken.

Cooley's 1868 *A Treatise on Constitutional Limitations*[8] did propose fundamental constitutional limits on the authority of government; but within it there is no attempt whatsoever to ground these limitations on any theory of natural rights. It is even more striking that Tiedeman's 1890 treatise, *The Unwritten Constitution of the United States*,[9] is in reality much closer to a historicist repudiation of the natural rights tradition than to an endorsement of that tradition. Tiedeman diverges from (what he takes to be) the legal positivism of Jeremy Bentham and John Austin *only* by insisting that there is an evolving positive morality that continually influences the character of current positive law.[10] (Neither Bentham nor Austin would in fact have denied this.) Tiedeman holds that the evolved positive morality of late-nineteenth-century America includes "so-called"[11] natural rights of life, liberty, and property. However, belief in these "so-called"

---

[6] *Lochner v. New York*, 198 U.S. 75 (1905). Part of the confusion is that Holmes goes on to refer to Spencer's moral-philosophical doctrine as "a particular economic theory."

[7] David Bernstein, *Rehabilitating Lochner* (Chicago: University of Chicago Press, 2011). Randy Barnett also describes Cooley and Tiedeman as Lockeans and strongly suggests that they advanced a Lockean conception of natural rights. See *Barnett's Restoring the Lost Constitution* (Princeton: Princeton University Press, 2004), 323–31.

[8] Thomas M. Cooley, *A Treatise on Constitutional Limitations* (Boston: Little Brown, 1868).

[9] Christopher G. Tiedeman, *The Unwritten Constitution of the United States* (New York: G.P. Putnam's Sons, 1890).

[10] Ibid., 73.

[11] Ibid., 71.

natural rights is simply a social fact that helps to explain the tendency of jurists in the late nineteenth century "to seize hold of these general declarations of rights as an authority for them to lay their interdict upon all legislative acts which interfere with the individual's natural rights even though these acts do not violate any specific or special provision of the Constitution." [12] However, belief in these rights has no objective validity. Some have held that "all men are possessed of certain natural rights, rights enjoyed by them in a state of nature, and which no government can rightfully infringe or take away." [13] According to Tiedeman, in a phrase that Holmes himself might have uttered, such belief "reaches the extreme limits of absurdity." [14]

II. Hodgskin on Natural Rights, Natural Property, and the Condemnation of Law

Thomas Hodgskin was a cashiered British naval officer, a popular writer on economics and politics, and an early editor of *The Economist* (1846–1855).[15] His major works included *An Essay on Naval Discipline* (1813), *Labour Defended against the Claims of Capital* (1825), *Popular Political Economy* (1827), and *The Natural and Artificial Right of Property Contrasted* (1832). Hodgskin sought to combine Lockean principles of self-ownership and rights to the fruits of one's labor, a labor theory of value that implied the unnaturalness and illegitimacy of income based on returns to capital, and a Smithian belief that harmonious and mutually beneficial economic order arises insofar and only insofar as natural rights are recognized and respected. Hodgskin broke with utilitarianism in the early 1820s at least in part because leading utilitarians—e.g., James Mill—supported a ban on labor organizing. More fundamentally, Hodgskin rejected Bentham's dismissal of natural rights and Bentham's insistence that all rights are created by the command of the sovereign. Due to his defense of the rights of

[12] Ibid., 81.
[13] Ibid., 70-1.
[14] Ibid., 70. The last *judicial* manifestations of nineteenth-century natural rights thinking were the early-twentieth-century U.S. Supreme Court decisions that struck down state government prohibitions of foreign language education and even of all private education. These decisions invoked the natural rights of parents to determine the character of their children's education. Thus, it is very notable that in 1890 Tiedeman had already *rejected* this approach. Tiedeman took this "supposed natural right" of parents to be disappearing from our evolving morality. "We are . . . on the eve of witnessing the abrogation of the supposed natural right of the parent to control the actions of his minor child, and to educate it spiritually and intellectually as he should see fit." (75) Instead, morality and judicial opinion are coming to treat "this control of the child as a trust, reposed by the State in the parent for the benefit of the child, and that whenever the State should determine that the trust is not being properly executed, or that the public interests or the interests of the child require the execution of the trust by the State itself, there is no limit to the power of that State to interfere with the parental control." (75)
[15] See David Stack, *Nature and Artifice: The Life and Thought of Thomas Hodgskin* (London: Royal Historical Society, 1997).

labor and his condemnation of interest, rent, and profits, Hodgskin is often misdescribed as a socialist. In fact, he was a defender of private property rights and voluntary market interactions who held—perhaps mistakenly—that illicit governmental intervention on behalf of owners of capital had diverted a great deal of economic interaction from its natural and beneficial course.

As the title of Hodgskin's best known work, *The Natural and Artificial Right of Property Contrasted*,[16] indicates, Hodgskin contrasts natural rights of property with artificial rights of property. Hodgskin begins the first substantive chapter of this work with extensive passages from Locke's *Second Treatise* in which, in well-known fashion, Locke grounds each individual's rights over his own labor on that individual's self-proprietorship and grounds that individual's rights over particular external objects on that individual's mixing of his labor with the raw natural ingredients of those objects. Hodgskin is eager to appropriate this Lockean doctrine in order to argue against "Mr. Bentham's impious theory" that legislation, rather than nature or God, establishes rights.[17] However, Hodgskin offers his own reformulation of these Lockean themes. It is a reformulation that seems to reveal that Hodgskin had some trouble with the distinction between descriptive regularities and prescriptive rules and, hence, had difficulty assigning a distinct necessary role to each in his account of desirable natural social order.

Hodgskin begins with suggestive claims about a deep connection between one's apprehension of one's "personal identity" or one's "individuality" and one's apprehension of one's ownership of or authority over the elements that make up one's personal identity or individuality.

> Each individual learns his own shape and form, and even the existence of his limbs and body, from seeing and feeling them. These constitute his notion of *personal* identity, both for himself and others; and it is impossible to conceive—it is in fact a contradiction to say— that a man's limbs and body do not belong to himself: for the words, him, self, and his body, signify the same material thing.[18]

The idea seems to be that seeing these elements as one's own in the sense of one's rightful holdings is implicated or entailed in one's seeing these

---

[16] Thomas Hodgskin, *The Natural and Artificial Right of Property Contrasted* (London: B. Steil, 1832). Citations by chapter and page are to the online version of this work available at the Online Library of Liberty, http://oll.libertyfund.org/.

[17] Hodgskin offers no citation to Bentham. Bentham's vehement rejection of natural rights and insistence that all rights are creatures of state legislation appears in his "A Fragment on Government" and his "Anarchical Fallacies." See respectively vol. 1 and vol. 2 of *The Works of Jeremy Bentham*, ed. John Bowring (Edinburgh: William Tait, 1838–1843), available online at http://oll.libertyfund.org.

[18] *The Natural and Artificial Right of Property Contrasted*, chaps. 2, 4.

elements as constituting one's person (and not some other object or person). To see oneself as a person is to see the elements that constitute oneself as one's own (in the sense of rightful possessions). In whatever manner we read these passages concerning self-ownership, we can see that Hodgskin takes an individual's rights to rest on some bedrock natural feature of the rightholder, some morally fertile feature of each individual rightholder in virtue of which that rightholder possesses a certain set of natural rights. So Hodgskin's doctrine seems to embody what I have called the supervenient conception of rights.

A crucial indication of this supervenient conception is that any person's normal workaday observation of another individual is taken to be sufficient to reveal that individual's natural rights to the observor. It is at least a near implication of a supervenient conception of rights that the recognition of rights should be a fairly easy and straightforward process. Simple, uncorrupted people and, perhaps, especially children should readily recognize the rights of those around them. And Hodgskin does affirm that the simple smith or carpenter has this awareness of natural rights as do "children long before they ever hear of law," i.e., of legislation.[19]

We have seen that Hodgskin offers a reformulation of Locke's affirmation of self-ownership. Here is Hodgskin's reformulation of the Lockean move from the "mine-ness" of one's labor to the "mine-ness" of that to which one has extended one's labor:

> The ideas expressed by the words mine and thine, as applied to the produce of labour, are simply then an extended form of the ideas of personal identity and individuality We readily spread them from our hands and other limbs, to the things the hands seize, or fashion, or create, or the legs hunt down and overtake... As nature gives to labour whatever it produces—as we extend the idea of personal individuality to what is produced by every individual—not merely is a right of property established by nature, we see also that she takes means to make known the existence of that right. It is as impossible for men not to have a notion of a right of property, as it is for them to want the idea of personal identity.[20]

According to Hodgskin, each person may dispose of his property for his "own separate and selfish use and enjoyment."[21] Indeed, the whole order of natural rights exists to serve [t]he great and immediate object of all man's exertions [which] is man's own happiness."[22] Justice is to be admin-

---

[19] Ibid., chaps. 2, 8.
[20] Ibid., chaps. 2, 5.
[21] Ibid., chap. 2.
[22] Thomas Hodgskin, "Peace, Law, and Order," a lecture delivered in the Hall of the National Association, London, September 29, 1842 available at http://praxeology.net/TH-PLO.htm, 8.

istered so that "each man may be secured in the possession of what he produces, and producing it, what he owns, and thus be enabled to feed and clothe himself."[23] Along with Locke, Hodgskin holds that persons' moral rights over themselves, their labor, and their legitimately acquired possessions serve and somehow have their rationale in the propriety of each man's pursuit of his own happiness.[24]

As with Hodgskin's remarks on behalf of self-ownership, there is a reading of Hodgskin's doctrine of property rights in external objects that reduces those rights to claims about how the world is—i.e., how nature or God has arranged the world to be.

> The power to labour is a gift of nature to each individual; and the power which belongs to each, cannot be confounded with that which belongs to another... Nature ... creates man with wants, and conjoins with them the power to gratify them. . .[25]

Through their individual powers nature also gives to each individual "her separate gifts—as, for example, the fish she bestows on him who baits a hook and watches the line" and none of these gifts can be "confounded with those she gives to another." Thus, nature or God "gives to labour, *if violence and wrong interfere not*, whatever it can make."

> [A]ntecedently to the use of force or fraud, and antecedently to all legislation, nature bestows on every individual what his labour produces, just as she gives him his own body, she bestows the wish and the power to produce, she couples them with the expectation of enjoying that which is produced, and she confirms in the labourer's possession, *if no wrong be practiced*, as long as he wishes to possess, whatever he makes or produces.[26]

The obvious question is, why is the violence that transfers some product from its producer to another *wrong*? Why isn't an object that is transferred by force or fraud as much a gift of nature or God to its recipient as an object held by its initial appropriator or producer is a gift of nature or God to that producer (until someone else takes it by force)?

It is striking that Hodgskin's answer is that forced transfers are wrong in virtue of not being natural, i.e., in virtue of not being in accord with the way the world actual is. We are told that such forced transfers are wrong because "it must be at all times more difficult for one man to take, by

---

[23] Ibid., 8.

[24] For this aspect of Locke's thought, see Eric Mack, *John Locke* (London: Continuum Publishing, 2009), chap. 2.

[25] *The Natural and Artificial Right of Property Contrasted*, chaps. 2, 3.

[26] Ibid., chaps. 2, 4, emphasis added.

force, from another what the latter has already made, than to make something similar for himself."[27] Nature condemns forced transfers by "making it generally more difficult and dangerous to take from another, than for each, by his labour, to provide for himself." Forced transfers are unnatural and wrong simply because they run contrary to the actual course of human existence.

> To desire or enforce any other species of appropriation [than appropriation through production or voluntary exchange] is a presumptuous interference with the laws of nature or of the Deity, not less absurd, or wicked in principle, than to decree a new course to the winds, or a different return of the seasons.[28]

Of course, Hodgskin recognizes that the world is full of forced transfers; indeed, he is all about complaining about those transfers. To condemn these forced transfers Hodgskin has to hold that somehow they are unnatural and, hence, are contrary to nature's or God's arrangements for human life. Hodgskin must be thinking that such transfers are, at least characteristically, the product of legislation; they are the product of the legislative creation of "artificial" property. For this reason, these forced transfers are artificial, unnatural, and, hence, wrongful. Unfortunately, if the "natural" is that which actually and regularly occurs, legislatively induced transfers are as natural as producers retaining the fruits of their labors. Hodgskin cannot mark off forced transfers as wrongful by showing that they are less a fact of human life than producers retaining possession of their creations. In order successfully to mark off the forced transfers as wrongful, he would have to show that they violate the rights of the producers—rights which are not themselves established by the (alleged) factual regularity that producers retain their products.

So, we see in Hodgskin an unfortunate tendency to identify or ground the *propriety* of a certain pattern within human life with or on the *factual occurrence* of that pattern. This tendency explains a feature of Hodgskin's position that we shall come to shortly, namely, that Hodgskin does not seem to include a distinct normative element—the compliance of individuals with *norms of conduct*—among the conditions that explain the "admirable harmony"[29] of natural market orders. Thus, Hodgskin seems to see this admirable harmony as being entirely the product of factual regularities of human action.

Two other aspects of Hodgkin's views about natural rights need to be mentioned before turning to his notion of admirable harmony. First, Hodgskin holds that an individual's natural right to any parcel of land depends upon that individual's current occupancy and cultivation of that

---

[27] Ibid., chaps. 2, 6.
[28] "Peace, Law, and Order," 13.
[29] Ibid., 11.

parcel.[30] Hence, rental income from land is illicit. In virtue of his absence the putative lessor loses his property right, and in virtue of his presence and engagement with the land the putative lessee acquires a natural right to it.[31] This is as it should be for Hodgskin because the payment of rent transfers the fruits of the current cultivator's labor to the nonlaboring prior owner and thereby violates the principle that *all* remuneration should track labor performed.[32]

Hodgskin does not mention a comparable occupancy and use condition for made objects, e.g., chiseled stone hatchets. And one would expect that he would allow the producer of such a hatchet to let it lie around for a week or two without thereby losing his right to it. (Yet, if there can be absentee ownership of hatchets, why can't those owners lease their hatchets to willing leaseholders and thereby receive *licit* rental income?) Hodgskin does, however, suggest a basis for differentiating between chiseled stone hatchets and parcels of cultivated land. Unlike chiseled hatchets land that is left alone quickly reverts to its natural state.[33] In Lockean terms—which Hodgskin does not employ here—Hodgskin's dubious claim is that labor invested in stone hatchets (and *also* less clunky and more finely-tuned artifacts) persists, but the labor invested in cultivated parcels dissipates (very rapidly) and, hence, the rights to the (formerly) cultivated parcels withers away. Only a very strong premise about the dissipation of labor invested in land would allow Hodgskin to endorse a labor-mixing account of property rights in cultivated parcels while rejecting all absentee ownership of land.

Another and perhaps somewhat conflicting aspect of Hodgskin's natural rights view is that individuals may readily acquire rights to very unequal holdings.

> Men are born with different capacities and powers, and with different means, therefore, of self-aggrandisement and self-instruction. One man is more industrious and skillful than another, and he acquires more wealth: he may be parsimonious, and keep together what he acquires; he may add heap to heap till he abound in riches. . . That some men should be richer than others is a part of the natural order of society.[34]

---

[30] *The Natural and Artificial Right of Property Contrasted,* chaps. 3, 6. Hodgskin twice quotes Locke's limitation of rightfully held land to that which that man "tills, plants, and improves, cultivates, and can use, the product of . . ." However, Hodgskin ignores Locke's explanation of how the introduction of money circumvents this limitation.

[31] Would occupancy and cultivation by one's *hired* labor suffice to sustain one's right to the land?

[32] From this premise, a narrow understanding of "labor," and some primitive economics Hodgskin derives his "socialist" conclusion that all rental income, interest, and profit is illicit. Since the illicit is unnatural, all these forms of income must derive from that which is supremely artificial, viz., legislation.

[33] *The Natural and Artificial Right of Property Contrasted,* chaps. 3, 6.

[34] "Peace, Law, and Order," 6.

Note that Hodgskin had better stick to something like an invested labor, rather than an occupancy and use, basis for property rights. For there will be no way for really productive people continuously *to occupy or use* all their earned and rightfully held automobiles, airplanes, and vacation homes. Also, and nicely in accord with his view that rightful possession is naturally occurring possession, Hodgskin maintains that those who are more capable of productive labor are also more capable of defending their resulting more extensive possessions.[35] Hence, the less industrious and skillful will still be naturally motivated to seek their happiness through their own productive efforts rather than by attempting to seize the heaps and heaps earned by the rich.

Hodgskin was clearly taken with the Smithian notion of highly artic-ulated and beneficial economic order arising *naturally* out of the actions of individuals who aim not at that order but rather at the satisfaction of their own interests. However, specifying what it means for an order—a harmony—to arise naturally is not a totally straightforward matter. Say-ing as Hodgskin does that such order is not dependent upon legisla-tive design does not yet identify the factors that do give rise to nondesigned, nonlegislated, order. What are those factors? According to Hodgskin, admirable harmony arises out of the combination of peo-ple's desires to feed and clothe themselves and the diversity of peo-ple's faculties and circumstances.

> [A]s individuals have different powers and capacities [and live in different circumstances], so they are adapted to different employ-ments, and contribute, by devoting themselves to them, to provide for the subsistence of the whole."[36]

"[T]he pursuit of individual happiness" in combination with these diver-sities among men and nations leads to a division of labor which tends to procure "subsistence for all, and tends to make society happy" even though these ends are "not contemplated by the individual." The greater the number of people who enter "this system of natural social order,"[37] the more pronounced is the harmonizing role of the division of labor. "As mouths, which mean wants, are multiplied, so are hands, talents, and powers, and exactly in that proportion facilities for extending division of labor and easily supplying the wants of all."[38] Hodgskin's culminating claim is that,

> All these various labourers, producers, buyers, and sellers work together, moreover, with admirable harmony, each producing what

---

[35] *The Natural and Artificial Right of Property Contrasted*, chaps. 2, 6.
[36] "Peace, Law, and Order," 9.
[37] Ibid., 10.
[38] Ibid., 9.

satisfies the demands of the other, though they know not even of the existence of one another.... This great scheme of social order is palpably and plainly not the will and work of man, but the will and work of that over-ruling Providence of which we trace the order and wisdom through every part of the visible world.[39]

Unfortunately, Hodgskin's invocation of an over-ruling Providence which operates through "decrees of nature" that possess "an irresistible power which man can neither change nor influence,"[40] suggests that factual truths about human conduct, e.g., that people seek food and shelter, combined with factual truths about how people attain what they desire, e.g., they work to attain food and shelter, themselves fully explain the existence of the "natural social order" that Hodgskin so prizes.

However, if the "natural social order" is entirely the product of factual regularities in human action and factual truths about means and ends, then the existence of that order does not at all depend upon recognizing and abiding by people's moral rights; and, so, there is no point in proclaiming that there are such rights and urging their recognition. If all natural principles are nonmoral factual regularities, then there is no room or need for a doctrine of natural moral rights—however precisely those rights are conceived. This problem for Hodgskin is what I had in mind earlier when I said that he has difficulty distinguishing between descriptive regularities and prescriptive norms and, hence, difficulty in assigning to each a distinct necessary role in the explanation of natural social order.

An instructive contrasting account of the conditions for admirable harmony is F. A. Hayek's discussion of the need for both "natural" and "conventional" rules, that is, factual regularities and prescriptive rules that proscribe theft and prescribe the fulfillment of contracts. The second category of rules—which Hayek labels "conventional"—are prescriptive in that they are "rules which do not simply follow from [persons'] desires and their insight into relations of cause and effect, but which are normative and tell them what they ought to or ought not to do."[41]

For Hayek, these "conventional" norms and general compliance with them combine with factual regularities about human conduct, for example, that people will work more if they expect to earn more, to engender the sort of complex coordination to mutual benefit that Hodgskin calls "admirable harmony." Due to their role in fostering cooperative interaction, Hayek takes these norms to be the true law. Legislation, which *is* a willful creation and which, according to Hayek, characteristically stymies the development and inhibits the operation of this true law, cannot itself be true law. In contrast, precisely because Hodgskin tends to leave

---

[39] Ibid., 11.

[40] *The Natural and Artificial Right of Property Contrasted*, chaps. 3, 10.

[41] F. A. Hayek, *Law, Legislation, and Liberty*, vol. 1, (Chicago: University of Chicago Press, 1973), 45.

no room for independent prescriptive rules as crucial factors in the emergence of admirable harmony, there is no room in Hodgskin's philosophy for a body of true law that stands in sharp contrast to legislation. Hence, as we are about to see, Hodgskin's powerful attack on legislation is taken by him to be an attack on law as such.

In fact, due of his identification of law with willful legislation, Hodgskin must assert—very mistakenly—that anti-authoritarian movements in British history never really appealed to *law*. The "reformers in the olden time" who seem to have appealed to common law against assertions of monarchical authority actually "struggled only for liberties and rights, and struggled avowedly against the law." In the English civil wars, "Our ancestors contended not for but against the law." And the Revolution of 1688 was fought on behalf of the rights of the people and "against the authority of the sovereign and the law." [42] What then is *this* law which all proponents of natural liberties and property must reject?

> What is the law?—Who are the law makers? The law is a great scheme of rules intended to preserve the power of government, secure the wealth of the landowner, the priest, and the capitalist, but never to secure his produce to the labourer. The law-maker is never a labourer, and has no natural right to any wealth. [43]

Law begins with the warrior who conquers and enslaves the honest and productive farmer and all current forms of the transfer of wealth from the productive to the parasitic grow out of this enslavement and are supported and directed by legislation. Law, that is to say, legislation began as the work of those "who followed no trade but war, and knew no handicraft but robbery and plunder." Legislation is now created and enforced by the descendents of these predators. [44]

> Laws being made by others than the labourer, and being always intended to preserve the power of those who make them, their great and chief aim for many ages, was, and still is, to enable those who are not labourers to appropriate wealth to themselves. In other words, the great object of law and of government has been and is, to establish and protect a violation of that natural right of property they are described in theory as being intended to guarantee. This chief purpose and principle of legislation is the parent crime, from which continually flow all the theft and fraud, all the vanity and chicanery, which torment mankind worse than pestilence and famine. [45]

[42] "Peace, Law, and Order," 16.
[43] *The Natural and Artificial Right of Property Contrasted,* chaps. 2, 3.
[44] Ibid., chaps. 2, 7.
[45] Ibid., chaps. 3, 4.

Every interference by "the law of politicians" with the great natural social order that grows up from man's pursuit of happiness deranges the social order and causes "great mischief." [46] Law itself is the enemy of peace and order. "If peace and order be good things, law cannot be a good thing." [47] "Law" and "order" should never to be used except "to signify totally opposite conditions of society." [48]

Given the factual naturalness of individuals retaining the fruits of their labor or those fruits that they get in voluntary exchange for their products, one cannot help being surprised that predation and legislation have taken hold in the world. If the peaceful and harmonious order that Hodgskin describes is a product of "decrees of nature" that possess "an irresistible power which man can neither change nor influence," [49] then how could that order ever be displaced? The answer would seem to be that provided by Hayek; this order also depends on prescriptive norms, compliance with which is hardly irresistible.

Hodgskin presents himself as a mainstream Lockean with respect to the rights of self-ownership and rights to the fruits of one's labor; and in his reformulations of Lockean doctrine he seems to follow Locke in subscription to a supervenient conception of basic rights. Nevertheless, his emphasis on the naturalness of the social order that he favors carries him toward the view that this order is irresistibly programmed into the factual regularities of the human condition. However, if such a social order is programmed into these factual regularities, we should never observe the artificial economic relationships and institutions that Hodgskin himself observes and condemns. In addition, we have noted that Hodgskin identifies law with (artificial) legislation; hence, he sees condemnation of legislation as a condemnation of law. As we shall see, in this respect he stands in stark contrast to Spooner who draws a sharp line between law—that is, the natural law—and legislation.

III. Herbert Spencer on Natural Rights as Norms of True Expedience

From the 1860s into the 1880s, Herbert Spencer was among the most prominent philosophic figures in the English speaking world. Although his first major work, *Social Statics* (1851)[50] was in political philosophy, he subsequently sought to present a systematic philosophical doctrine that incorporated and explained the truths of biology, ethics, political philosophy, psychology, and sociology. Aside from *Social Statics* (which was radically revised in the decades following 1851), his major works

---

[46] "Peace, Law, and Order," 14.
[47] Ibid., 13.
[48] Ibid., 15.
[49] *The Natural and Artificial Right of Property Contrasted*, chaps. 3, 10.
[50] Herbert Spencer, *Social Statics*, (New York: Robert Schalenbach Foundation, 1970).

included *The Principles of Psychology* (1855), *The Principles of Biology* (1864–1867), *First Principles* (1867), *The Principles of Sociology* (1876–1896), *The Principles of Ethics* (1879–1897), and *The Man versus the State* (1884). Within political philosophy, Spencer began as a radical libertarian who invoked the language of natural rights or justice or the law of equal freedom on behalf of individual freedom and strict limitations on governmental authority. Nevertheless, he always sought to trace the justification of these rights or principles of justice or freedom back to a correctly deployed principle of general utility. He also sought to integrate his contentions in political philosophy with an illuminating account of the evolution of mankind and of social order. It is a true bromide of Spencer scholarship that through his adult life Spencer's political position became less radical and more conservative. Most notably, he abandoned two striking positions taken in *Social Statics*. The first radical—albeit not necessarily *libertarian*—position was the social ownership of the earth. The second radical—and libertarian—position was the right of each individual to ignore the state.[51]

For the context-setting purposes of this essay, we need to consider the views of the early Herbert Spencer. I mean the *really* early, most Lockean-sounding Spencer who authored the rarely read *The Proper Sphere of Government* (1842–1843),[52] and the not-quite-so-early and less Lockean-sounding Spencer who authored *Social Statics*. In *The Proper Sphere of Government*, Spencer invokes the "natural rights of man" and natural rights appear as the measure of justice and legitimate legislation. "[N]o body of men can pretend that 'justice' requires the enactment of any law, unless they can show that their natural rights would otherwise be infringed." Corn laws are unacceptable because free trade violates no one's natural rights and an established church is unacceptable because freedom of religion violates no one's natural rights.[53]

Nevertheless, the story that Spencer tells leading up to the affirmation of "natural rights" is decidedly non-Lockean. We are asked to imagine,

> . . . a number of men living together without any recognized laws—without any checks upon their actions, save those imposed by their own fears of consequences—obeying nothing but the impulses of their own passions. . .[54]

---

[51] Spencer has been the object of a great deal of inaccurate interpretation and unfair criticism. Two noteworthy exceptions to this pattern are Michael Taylor, *Men versus the State: Herbert Spencer and Late Victorian Individualism* (Oxford: Oxford University Press, 1992) and David Weinstein, *Equal Freedom and Utility: Herbert Spencer's Liberal Utilitarianism* (Cambridge: Cambridge University Press, 1998).

[52] *The Proper Sphere of Government*, reprinted in Herbert Spencer, *Man versus the State and Other Essays*, ed. Eric Mack (Indianapolis: Liberty Classics, 1981), 181–263.

[53] *The Proper Sphere of Government*, 187–90.

[54] Ibid., 185.

In this state of nature, contrary to Locke, there is no governing law of nature. Largely because of this fact, every one of these men soon comes to the conclusion that,

> . . . his individual interest as well as that of the community at large, will best be served by entering into some common bond of protection: all agree to become amenable to the decisions of their fellows, and to obey certain general arrangements.[55]

Some individuals are then deputized to settle disputes among these men; hence, ". . . we have a government springing naturally out of the requirements of the community." The crucial question, however, is ". . . what are those requirements" that all have agreed to obey?[56]

According to Spencer, the requirements of the community do not include the state's direct provision of the substantive elements of a good social order—e.g., trade, religious life, charitable activities, and systems of communication and locomotion. These components of a desirable social order need not be "designed and constructed" for members of the community by "a supreme power." In a passage similar to Hodgskin's invocation of over-ruling Providence, Spencer says that people would only want such a designing and constructing government if they thought that "the Almighty" had been so negligent in designing social mechanisms that continuous intervention by government was necessary to keep beneficial social processes on track. However, people are not so foolish. They know or ought to know that thanks to the Almighty's design

> . . . the laws of society are of such a character, that natural evils will rectify themselves; that there is in society, as in every other part of creation, that beautiful self-adjusting principle, which will keep all its elements in equilibrium; . . . so the attempt to regulate all the actions of a community by legislation, will entail little else but misery and confusion.[57]

Spencer quickly moves to the conclusion that governments are created

> . . . to defend the natural rights of man—to protect person and property—to prevent aggressions of the powerful upon the weak—in a word, to administer justice. This is the natural, the original, office of government. It was not intended to do less; it ought not to be allowed to do more.[58]

---

[55] Ibid., 185.
[56] Ibid., 185.
[57] Ibid., 186–87.
[58] Ibid., 187.

Notice, though, that these "natural" rights are not rights superveniently conceived. They are not rights that adhere to individuals in virtue of some bedrock feature (or set of features) that individuals possess as individuals. If they were such rights, then there would not be a stage of human existence in which men live without checks on their action and are subject only to the direction of their impulses. Even in the Lockean-sounding *The Proper Sphere of Government*, rights are the implications of the basic norms that rational individuals would agree to in order to escape from a condition in which each may blamelessly prey upon others.[59] The directive force of the norms derives from the benefits of general compliance with them; and it is in virtue of these norms requiring that individuals be treated with certain circumspection that we ascribe rights to individuals to be treated with the necessary circumspection. We have here what I have called the beneficial norm conception of natural rights.

For example, a natural right of property is to be affirmed because general respect for the producer's possession of the fruits of his labor is beneficial.

> Man's happiness greatly depends upon the satisfaction of his temporal wants. The fruits of the earth are a necessary means of satisfying those wants. Those fruits can never be produced in abundance without cultivation. That cultivation will never prevail without the stimulus of certain possession. No man will sow when others may reap.[60]

Here are two factual regularities: One will sow only what one expects others will not reap; and others will reap what one sows unless they are subject to a normative rule that establishes one's "certain possession" of the fruits of one's sowing. These two factual regularities will yield the natural evil of a shortage of cultivated products unless a further and prescriptive law of society comes into play, namely, the law that forbids one's seizing what another has produced. The "laws of society" that, according to Spencer, give society its self-adjusting character must be understood to include both factual regularities of human action and patterns of rule compliance.

The problem with legislation is not that it disrupts the underlying factual regularities of human action; legislation *cannot* do this.[61] Rather, the problem is that it directly violates or undermines compliance with the norms—Hayek's "conventional" rules—that must also be abided by if the

---

[59] Ibid., 185.

[60] Ibid., 207.

[61] It is the false expectation that legislation will override the underlying factual regularities of human action that explains much of the unintended negative consequences of legislation.

system of natural liberty is to operate. It is because these norms are crucial to man's happiness that they are the crucial nodes of expediency. "[P]roperty greatly promotes the mental and bodily happiness of mankind; that is, it is expedient." [62] However, Spencer favors calling "natural" the norm that requires respect for the producer's possession and the right that this norm prescribes because ". . . there is implanted in every man, a desire to possess, which desire, by the accumulation of property, may be gratified without injury to his fellow-creatures." And in a manner highly reminiscent of Hodgskin, Spencer adds that ". . . this fact is in itself ample proof, that individual possession is in accordance with the will of the Creator." [63]

However, Spencer insists here, as he does throughout his political writings, that this appeal to expediency at large is radically different from empowering the legislature to design and construct the society so as to maximize the "general good"; this is because to authorize the government to aim directly at the "general good" is to authorize government to do whatever it chooses to do. For, ". . . the expression "general good," is of such uncertain character, a thing so entirely a matter of opinion, that there is not an action that a government could perform, which might not be contended to be a fulfillment of its duties." [64]

Like Hodgkin, the Spencer of *The Proper Sphere of Government* is concerned about the "land question." Yet Spencer is strikingly evasive about rights to portions of the earth. He tells us that, "Man *has* a claim to a subsistence derived from the soil." [65] This is a claim to the opportunity to engage in labor and, through that labor, to attain rights to *the fruits of that labor.* Spencer's primary concern here is to insist that each individual's sound claim to any created good is *conditional* upon that individual's laboring to produce that good—or, presumably, his laboring to produce whatever he traded away for the created good he now possesses. Spencer insists that this right of each to the fruits of his labor is incompatible with anyone having an *unconditional* right to the fruits of labor—which would mean an unconditional right to the fruits of *others'* labor.

> We cannot say to a man, "So much of the substance you have acquired by your labour is your own, and so much belongs to your fellow-creatures." We cannot divide the right. Either it is a right or it is not. There is no medium.

The right of each to the fruits of his labor is incompatible with any alleged "poor-law right." [66]

[62] *The Proper Sphere of Government,* 208.
[63] Ibid., 208.
[64] Ibid., 187.
[65] Ibid., 201.
[66] Ibid., 208–9. But if ultimately the issue is one of general expediency, why not hold (as Bentham did) that small losses in sowing due to a general policy of transferring some small

Spencer believed that the rights of many individuals to an opportunity
to labor were being infringed by the institutions of his day. But he is very
vague about which institutions are responsible for this widespread "want
of a field for labor." Spencer's language suggests that the problem is due
to unconditional private property rights *in land*. Moreover, there seems to
be room for him to draw this conclusion because in *The Proper Sphere of
Government* he never offers an argument on behalf of individual rights to
portions of the earth. His argument for property rights focuses entirely on
the cultivator's *crop* and not at all on the *field* that the cultivator has
readied for cultivation. In addition, Spencer offers nothing like a Lockean
labor-mixing account of property rights that could be applied as readily
to cleared fields as to raised crops. In support of rights to parcels of land
that have been readied for cultivation, Spencer *could* have argued that
clearers of land need to be able to count on reaping the benefits of their
productive activity just as much as do planters and harvesters of crops. If
the beneficial protection of the latter requires property rights in the crops,
the beneficial protection of the former requires property rights in readied
fields. But Spencer never makes this argument.

So we are left without any clear endorsement of property rights in
portions of the earth and without any indictment of such rights as the
cause of people being "prevented from earning their bread by the sweat
of their brow." [67] Spencer only tells us that people are blocked from exercising their productive capacities by "iniquitous laws" or "oppressive
taxation." It is crucial that "the laws that have induced this disorderly
state" be destroyed. [68] Once these "barriers to productive industry, which
selfish legislators have set up" are eliminated, society will be restored to
"its natural state." [69]

In his much better known, but still early and radical work, *Social Statics*,
Spencer continues to employ the language of rights—though "natural"
rights disappear. Even more explicitly than in *The Proper Sphere of* Government, Spencer endorses the greatest happiness principle as the ultimate normative standard. Yet, again, he rejects any direct appeal to this
standard in our deliberations about how we should act or what powers
political institutions ought to be granted. "It is one thing, however, to
hold that greatest happiness is the creative purpose, and quite another
thing to hold that greatest happiness should be the *immediate* aim of
man." [70] We have a basic concept of happiness, namely, "a gratified state

---

percentage of their product from the sowers to those in dire straits will be worth the gain
in utility bestowed on those in dire straits? If general expediency ultimately does the work,
the purported right of the producer will have no independent moral force against the
argument that such a policy of modest transfers would be just—precisely because of the
policy's (purported) general expediency.

[67] *The Proper Sphere of Government*, 202.
[68] Ibid., 202.
[69] Ibid., 209.
[70] *Social Statics*, 66.

of all the faculties."[71] However, people's faculties differ both in their character and in their degree of development; and for this reason different people have radically divergent conceptions of happiness. Hence, no single formula or (manageable) set of formulae for the achievement of happiness will be an apt guide to everyone's happiness. Moreover, even if we had such a well-defined measure of general happiness, we would not be able in practice to identify the trade-offs among persons' possible gratifications that would best satisfy that measure of happiness.

Fortunately, however, there are deep and persistent facts about human life—certain "fundamental necessities of our position"[72]—in light of which we can see that strict compliance with certain basic norms will most advance happiness in society. The most crucial of these rules are the law of equal freedom and the requirement of negative justice that each is to enjoy or suffer the consequences of his own chosen actions. Spencer, then, appears to be an early advocate of a type of indirect utilitarianism. Nevertheless, this is a bit misleading because Spencer's view was that a necessary condition of the attainment of the greatest general happiness is that everyone's happiness is (maximally?) advanced. So what recommends a basic norm is our recognition—in light of the fundamental necessities of our position—that strict compliance with this norm will advance everyone's happiness.

Indeed, at times general happiness seems to slip very much into the background and the core of Spencer's argument appears to be a move from the propriety of each individual pursuing his own happiness to a claim that each individual has a right to pursue his own happiness. Since each man's pursuit of happiness accords with the "creative purpose," each individual ought to advance his happiness (in ways that do not diminish the happiness of others). Since each individual's happiness derives from his exercise of his faculties, each ought to exercise his faculties; and since each individual's exercise of his faculties requires that he be free to do so, each has a right to the free use his faculties.

> Man's happiness can only be produced by the exercise of his faculties. Then God wills that he should exercise his faculties. But to exercise his faculties he must have liberty to do all that his faculties naturally impel him to do. Then God intends he should have that liberty. Therefore he has *a right* to that liberty.[73]

Since this right to liberty is a right possessed by all, the rightful freedom of each must "be bounded by the similar freedom of all."[74] The funda-

---

[71] *Social Statics*, 6.
[72] Ibid., 62.
[73] Ibid., 68–69.
[74] Ibid., 69.

mental social norm is, then, "*Every man has freedom to do all that he wills, provided he infringes not the equal freedom of any other man.*"[75]

A similar case for a basic right to freedom reappears, without the theological coloration and without any explicit reference to the *general* happiness, in Spencer's later essay, "The Great Political Superstition." (1884)[76]

> Those who hold that life is valuable, hold, by implication, that men ought not to be prevented from carrying on life-sustaining activities. In other words, if it is said to be "right" that they should carry them on, then, by permutation, we get the assertion that they "have a right" to carry them on.

Spencer adds that,

> Clearly the conception of "natural rights" originates in recognition of the truth that if life is justifiable, there must be a justification for the performance of acts essential to its preservation; and therefore, a justification for those liberties and claims which make such acts possible.[77]

But these "natural rights"—the scare quotes are provided by Spencer— lack "ethical character" because, according to Spencer, there is not yet a distinction between those life-sustaining acts that may be performed and those that may not be performed. Spencer seems to hold that this distinction only comes into play when we discover or observe the evolution of constraints on life-sustaining actions, the mutual regard for which is beneficial to each constrained agent. The idea seems to be that the "the conditions produced by social aggregation"[78] guide or nudge us toward these mutually advantageous restraints.

In *Social Statics*, the test for whether any more specific right, such as a right to free speech, is to be accepted or rejected is the consistency of that right with the basic right to equal freedom. Applying this test, Spencer judges that there can be no private right to parcels of the earth because private ownership of the earth infringes upon the equal liberty of the non-owners. For "... if the landowners have a valid right to [the earth's] surface, all who are not landowners, have no right at all to its surface. Hence, such can exist on the earth by sufferance only."[79] Thus, Spencer quite quickly concludes, the surface of the earth is naturally owned by

---

[75] Ibid., 100.

[76] Herbert Spencer, "The Great Political Superstition" reprinted in *The Man Versus the State and Other Essays*, 123–66.

[77] "The Great Political Superstition," 150.

[78] Ibid., 153.

[79] *Social Statics*, 104.

"the human race."[80] Or, within any society, "the lawful owner" of the land is "Society."[81] Society will then lease segments of the land to its individual members. Except for the rental payments due to society, society's tenants will have full private property rights over the fruits of their labor—although is not clear whether an individual tenant will have a private right to his "surplus produce" simply because it is the *product* of his permissible labor[82] or because the tenant's *contract with society* confers "the exclusive use of the remainder of that produce" upon him.[83]

As previously mentioned, Spencer later abandons the social ownership of land although he claimed that he continued to accede to the substance of this doctrine by affirming that the "ultimate proprietorship" of all land "vests in the community"[84] and that, if anything, the taxes actually paid by private landholders exceed the rental payments they would be making to land-leasing society.[85] However, with the abandonment of the social ownership and societal leasing doctrines, Spencer needs an alternative account of the basis for private property rights in land. Yet he seems never even to realize that he needs such a substitute account.

For our purposes, the key conclusions to be drawn from this examination of Spencer on rights is that even when Spencer sounded most Lockean, namely, in his very early *The Proper Sphere of Government*, he operated with a non-Lockean, beneficial norm understanding of rights and, indeed, he quickly abandoned the language of natural rights. Unlike Hodgskin, Spencer never offered anything like a Lockean labor-investment theory of private property rights. In fact, at his most radical vis-à-vis the ownership of land, Spencer opted for social ownership (whatever that exactly would amount to). When in later years he retreated from the social ownership doctrine he seems to have felt no need to provide an alternative account of the rights to land that he wished to affirm.

IV. SPOONER ON NATURAL LAW, NATURAL JUSTICE, AND NATURAL RIGHTS

In the United States during the nineteenth century, rights-based, radical libertarianism was most forcefully represented by the individualist anarchists who flourished from the 1830s into the 1890s. The founder of this school was Josiah Warren (1798–1874) author of *Equitable Commerce* (1846) and founder of the individualist utopian community of New Harmony, Indiana. Warren combined a Lockean affirmation of "the sovereignty of

---

[80] Ibid., 107.
[81] Ibid., 107.
[82] Ibid., 117.
[83] Ibid., 116.
[84] Herbert Spencer, *The Principles of Ethics* (1897), ed. T. R. Machan, (Indianapolis: Liberty Classics, 1981), 107.
[85] Ibid., 459.

the individual" and of the individual's right to the fruits of his labor with the conviction—which we have also seen in Hodgskin—that only income from labor is legitimate.[86] During the last couple of decades in which this individualist anarchist movement flourished, its flagship publication was the journal *Liberty* which was edited by Benjamin Tucker.[87] It should be noted that by the late 1880s Tucker himself abandoned the notion of natural rights for the sake of an (allegedly) more hardheaded philosophical egoism.

Beginning with his anti-slavery treatises and culminating in his essays on natural law and natural rights, Spooner staked out his position as the most philosophically engaging, forceful, and Lockean voice among the individual anarchists. Spooner's central message was that unchanging and universal principles of natural justice disclose the criminality of state action and legislation. And at the core of natural justice and law is the very Lockean-sounding affirmation of "a man's ownership of himself and the products of his labor."[88] Even had Spooner lived to see some of his fellow anarchists turn to philosophical egoism, it is most unlikely that Spooner would ever have abandoned his natural rights approach.

Spooner's most sustained treatments of natural law, natural justice, and natural rights appear in his 1882 pamphlet, *Natural Law* and his lengthy 1886 open letter, *A Letter to Grover Cleveland.*[89] One gets two immediate impressions upon reading the former essay. The first is that Spooner is quite unclear about the relationship among natural law, the science of justice, and natural rights—e.g., about whether natural rights are the deliverances of some independently recognized natural law, or whether the natural law is simply the body of proscriptions and prescriptions required by independently identified natural rights. The second impression is that Spooner is committed to some sort of moral intuitionism; the natural law or people's natural rights are detected by some special faculty or moral sense. With respect to the first impression, I want to offer a reading of Spooner that gives priority to natural rights; natural justice and natural law are best understood as expressions of the constraints required by those rights. With respect to the second impression, I want to suggest that there is more to Spooner's account of natural rights than this simple invocation of moral intuition.

Spooner's *Natural Law* opens with three claims about the science of justice. First, it is the science of "mine and thine;" it is the science of "all

---

[86] For an excellent overall survey of this school of thought including the views of Warren, see Martin's *Men Against the State.*

[87] *Liberty* was published in Boston from 1881–1908 albeit less and less regularly. It is available online at the very useful website *Travelling in Liberty,* http://travellinginliberty. blogspot.com/.

[88] Lysander Spooner, *No Treason, No. 1,* (1867) in *The Collected Works of Lysander Spooner,* vol. I, iii–iv.

[89] *Natural Law* and *A Letter to Grover Cleveland* in *The Collected Works of Lysander Spooner,* vol. I.

human rights; of all a man's rights of person and property." Second, it is the science "which alone can tell any man what he can, and cannot do . . . without infringing upon the rights of any other person." Third, it is the science—indeed, the only science—of peace; it "alone can tell us on what conditions mankind can live in peace, or ought to live in peace, with each other."[90] I conjecture that the order of these three claims is significant. The science of justice starts with an identification of man's rights which are (or are presumed to be) rights "of person and property."[91] This identification of rights enables us to go on to specify what human conduct is permissible or even morally protected and what human conduct is impermissible. And, it is our understanding of what conduct is permissible or even morally protected and what conduct is impermissible that enables us to articulate the conditions under which persons can live in peace with one another or *"ought* to live in peace, with one another."[92]

The conjecture that, for Spooner, the conditions for (morally acceptable[93]) peace among persons are to be spelled out in terms of normative propositions about how individuals should or should not behave toward others is supported by his further claims about the conditions for (morally acceptable) peace. For Spooner immediately tells us that there are two basic categories of conditions for that peace. There are the positive conditions, namely, "that each man shall do, toward every other, all that justice requires him to do," e.g., that "he shall pay his debts, that he shall return borrowed or stolen property to its owner. . ." And there are the negative conditions, namely, "that each man shall abstain from doing to another, anything which justice forbids him to do," e.g., that "he shall abstain from committing theft, robbery. . ." and so on. Whenever men have sought to live in peace with one another they have affirmed one "universal obligation: *viz., that each should live honestly towards every other.*"[94] And this honesty consists in abiding by the dictates of justice which themselves are expressions of the rights of person and property.

So it is crucial to understand what these bedrock rights are—or what principles of justice manifest these rights. Fortunately, according to Spooner, although the science of justice has to be learned, "it is very easily learned." It is "made up of a few simple elementary principles, of the truth and justice of which every ordinary mind has an almost intuitive percep-

---

[90] *Natural Law*, 5–6.

[91] Ibid., 5. See also *A Letter to Grover Cleveland*, 4. "This science of justice, or natural law, is the only science that tells us what are, and what are not, each man's natural, inherent, inalienable, *individual* rights, as against any and all other men."

[92] *Natural Law*, 5.

[93] I take Spooner's claim that the science of justice identifies the conditions under which "mankind can live in peace, or *ought to* live in peace" [emphasis added] to indicate that for Spooner the term "peace" is normatively loaded. It is not simply any old peace that we ought to live in. We ought not to live in the peace of a tyrannical regime even if it is so well entrenched that it never has to carry out violent acts against its subjects. It is not simply any old peace that counts as the peace the conditions of which Spooner seeks to elucidate.

[94] *Natural Law*, 6.

tion."[95] "Honesty, justice, natural law, is usually a very plain and simple matter, easily understood by common minds." Indeed, in a passage reminiscent of Hodgskin and indicative of a supervenient conception of rights, Spooner declares that children

> ... very early understand that one child must not, without just cause, strike or otherwise hurt, another; that one child must not assume any arbitrary control or domination over another; that one child must not, either by force, deceit, or stealth, obtain the possession of anything that belongs to another, that if one child commits any of these wrongs against another, it is not only the right of the injured child to resist, and, if need be, punish the wrongdoer, and compel him to make reparation, but that it is also the right, and the moral duty, of all other children, and all other persons, to assist the injured party in defending his rights, and redressing his wrongs.[96]

Similarly, in "Vices are not Crimes" (1875) Spooner asserts that *"Crimes are few, and easily distinguished from all other acts; and mankind are generally agreed as to what acts are crimes."*[97] In his *A Letter to Grover Cleveland* (1886) he asserts that man's rights are "easily ascertained."[98] These passages suggest a belief on the part of Spooner in a faculty of moral intuition that reveals to us an array of natural rights. Through the operation of this faculty every sensible person recognizes the criminality of the killing, maiming, enslaving, robbing, and deceiving of one's fellow man and the noncriminality of other actions, even those other actions which manifest various vices.

However, Spooner warns his reader against this reading of rights, as ascertainable by simple moral intuition when he says that natural rights are known through an "almost intuitive perception."[99] And, indeed, I believe that he offers a rather more complicated two-phase argument on behalf of certain natural rights. The first phase asserts that there are *some* principles of natural justice—reflective of *some,* as yet unspecified, natural rights. Within this phase, Spooner offers something like a "best explanation" argument for the existence of natural justice. The second phase proceeds to spell out what is the sensible specification of these natural rights. This project of sensible specification is governed by two ideas. The first idea is that the underlying rationale for rights is that they morally protect each individual's pursuit of happiness against the interfering actions of others. The second governing idea is that the rights that are ascribed to

[95] Ibid., 8.
[96] Ibid., 9. Recall Hodgskin's claim that such rights are known to "children long before they ever hear of law [i.e., legislation]." *The Natural and Artificial Right of Property Contrasted,* chaps. 2, 8.
[97] "Vices are not Crimes," 33.
[98] *A Letter to Grover Cleveland,* 22.
[99] *Natural Law,* 8.

any individual as moral protection for his pursuit of happiness must be "always consistent and harmonious with each and every other man's rights."[100] Despite some variation in their expression, the rights that emerge from this process of sensible specification turn out to be the standard Lockean rights to life, liberty, legitimately acquired property, and the fulfillment of contracts.

According to the first phase of his argument, ". . . from time immemorial," men have spoken and written about justice; they have identified various acts as criminal and contrasted criminal with noncriminal acts. If people have not been totally deluded when they have engaged in this practice and if men's claims that legitimate governments are those that act justly have not been "the mere gibberish of fools," it must be because there is such a thing as natural justice.

> If justice be not a natural principle, then there is no such thing as injustice; and all the crimes of which the world has been the scene, have been no crimes at all; but only simple events, like the falling of the rain, or the setting of the sun; events of which the victims had no more reason to complain than they had to complain of the running of the streams, or the growth of vegetation.[101]

If there are no moral rights, if there are no truths of justice, than all of the moral expressions which men have used in their judgments and contentions "should be struck out of all human language as having no meanings."[102] Moreover, if there were no natural rights, that is, if we come into the world "utterly destitute of rights,"[103] nothing we could do could generate any of the moral rights or principles of justice that are embedded in our moral discourse. So if even some of the assertions that men make about justice or injustice are not "the mere gibberish of fools," there must be some natural rights; there must be some principles of natural justice.

> [I]f there be no such natural principle as justice, there can be no such thing as dishonesty; and no possible act of either force or fraud, committed by one man against the person or property of another, can be said to be unjust or dishonest; or be complained of, or prohibited, or punished as such.[104]

The deep presumption of the many centuries of moral discourse and of attempts to condemn or to vindicate governments is that there is, in fact, a line—wherever precisely it is located—between just and unjust action,

---

[100] *A Letter to Grover Cleveland,* 21.
[101] *Natural Law,* 11.
[102] Ibid., 14.
[103] Ibid., 13.
[104] Ibid., 13.

between innocent (noncriminal) and criminal action. The best explanation of the soundness of this presumption is the existence of natural justice. Moreover, this natural justice will be a permanent feature of our human existence because the rights that constitute it derive from human nature. Hence, those rights "are incapable of being blotted out, extinguished, annihilated, or separated or eliminated from [any man's] nature as a human being. . ." [105] Those rights must endure as long as human nature endures.

It cannot be denied that even within what I have called the first phase of his argument Spooner strongly—and, strictly speaking, illicitly— anticipates a particular specification of man's natural rights, namely, rights of person and property that bestow upon each individual claims against being subjected to force or fraud. He proceeds as though his making a case that there are some principles of natural justice also amounts to his making a case for his specific understanding of natural justice. Part of my purpose in introducing the idea of a two-phase argument is to explore whether we can acquit Spooner of this illicit move by finding a genuinely second-phase argument in support of the specific natural rights that he wishes to affirm.

A beginning of such an argument can be found in a passage from *Natural Law* in which Spooner seeks to explain why men who are inter- acting with one another "*cannot avoid* learning the natural law, to a very great extent, even if they would." Or at least we get an explanation of why human interaction is the school in which the natural law is readily learned.

> The dealings of men with men, their separate possessions and their individual wants, and the disposition of every man to demand, and insist upon, whatever he believes to be his due, and to resent and resist all invasions of what he believes to be his rights, are continually forcing upon their minds, the questions, "Is this act just? or is it unjust? Is this thing mine? or is it his?" And these are questions of natural law; questions which, in regard to the great mass of cases, are answered alike by the human mind everywhere.[106]

Presumably for the sake of the satisfaction of his individual wants, each person makes certain claims against other men and takes the satisfaction of these claims as his due. He forms certain initial beliefs about what his rights are. But these claims are constantly met with counterclaims that others make on behalf of themselves. The adjustment of claims that pro- ceeds from one's advancing certain initial claims and confronting coun- terclaims is not understood by Spooner as a matter of bargaining among the parties to settle upon some set of claims that each perceives to be an

[105] Ibid., 12.
[106] Ibid., 9.

acceptable *modus vivendi*.[107] Rather, I believe that the adjustment of claims by each party in response to counterclaims by others is understood by Spooner to be a matter of these parties seeking to ascribe to each individual a set of rights that is identical to and harmonious with the set of rights that is ascribed to every other individual.[108] I assert a certain right on my own behalf, such as a right to be provided with a nice house. You counter with an assertion of a like right for yourself. These rights are in conflict because my respecting your asserted right may require that I forego the satisfaction of my asserted right. But I cannot dismiss your right to be provided with a nice house while still asserting my right to a nice house. So I have to adjust downward my claims about what is my due (as do others)—to, for instance, a right not to be deprived of a peacefully acquired nice house—so as to arrive at claimed rights such that the ascription of those rights to everyone yields a consistent and harmonious body of rights.

The natural strategy for such an adjustment is the affirmation that "one thing is one man's property and that another thing is another man's property."[109] And perhaps it is not so unreasonable for Spooner to assume that, when it comes to specifying what is mine and what is thine, the plausible view is that my person and my peacefully acquired possessions are mine and your person and your peacefully acquired possessions are yours. If natural rights exist and "each man's 'rights' are always consistent and harmonious with each and every other man's 'rights',"[110] it is plausible that—absent modification through contractual agreement—each person's rights will be rights to dispose of his person and (peacefully acquired) possessions as he sees fit.

Still, nothing yet has been said about why each individual has a rational concern for his rights being respected, that is, has a rational concern for being accorded the freedom of disposing as he sees fit of his person and property. Spooner's view is that each individual's freedom to dispose of his person and possessions as he sees fit

> ... is a right indispensable to every man's highest happiness: and to every man's power of judging and determining for himself what will, and what will not, promote his happiness. Any restriction upon the exercise of this right is a restriction upon his rightful power of providing for, and accomplishing, his own well-being.[111]

---

[107] For one thing, Spooner insists that this process yields an affirmation of *equal* rights; however, a contractarian adjustment of claims need not result in the various parties being assigned *equal* rights.

[108] If any man asserts the moral necessity of his possession of a certain right, he must acknowledge that everyone else's like right is "equally necessary" because "every other man's rights are as good as his own." "No Treason, No. 1," 11.

[109] *Natural Law*, 14.

[110] *A Letter to Grover Cleveland*, 21.

[111] Ibid., 7.

Such a restriction violates "the right of each and every individual to judge of, and provide for, his own well-being, according to the dictates of his own judgment, and by the free exercise of his own powers of body and mind..."[112] Each individual's concern for his own happiness (or well-being) is what makes it rational for him to claim rights against all other individuals. However, a crucial lesson is taught to all by "[t]he dealings of men with men, their separate possessions and their individual wants, and the disposition of every man to demand, and insist upon, whatever he believes to be his due, and to resent and resist all invasions of what he believes to be his rights..."[113] That lesson is that the whole set of rights possessed by individuals must be consistent and harmonious. If we add the natural and Lockean premise that all individuals are equal in their possession of natural rights, we get the conclusion that each person's natural rights must be equal to and consistent and harmonious with each other person's rights. For Spooner the rights that fit that bill and are protective of each person's pursuit of happiness are the rights of self-ownership, the rights to the fruits of one's labor, and the rights to contract for goods and services. (Note the parallel here with Spencer's argument from the propriety of each seeking his happiness to each having an *equal and constrained* right to pursue happiness.)

Indeed, it seems that the underlying rationale for a system of equal, consistent, and harmonious rights is that it provides to each individual what he needs and can reasonably demand from others as a condition of his attainment of his own happiness (or well-being).

> [T]he great "public good" of which any coercive power . . . is capable, is the protection of each and every individual in the quiet and peaceful enjoyment of all his own natural, inherent, inalienable, individual "rights." . . . It is a universal and impartial "good" of the highest importance to each and every human being . . . Let but this "equal and exact justice" be secured "to all men," and they will then be abundantly able to take care of themselves and secure their own highest "good."[114]

The enjoyment of his own rights constitutes that individual's enjoyment of "the widest possible field, that he honestly can have, for such industry as he may choose to follow. . . . With the possession of these rights, he must be content."[115]

---

[112] Ibid., 24.

[113] *Natural Law*, 9.

[114] *A Letter to Grover Cleveland*, 8. Spooner adds, "Or if any one should ever chance to need anything more than this, he may safely trust to the voluntary kindness of his fellow men to supply it."

[115] Ibid., 15.

A similar appeal to the reasonableness of each person's pursuit of happiness and a consequent natural right to pursue happiness appears in Spooner's 1875 essay "Vices are not Crimes." For each individual, virtuous actions are those noncriminal actions "on which his physical, mental, and emotional health and well-being depend." They are the actions that promote the agent's happiness.[116] Indeed, for each individual, his happiness is "the great purpose and duty of his life."[117] Furthermore, individuals differ from one another in their circumstances and physical, emotional, and mental powers and propensities and, therefore, they differ from one another in what sorts of (noncriminal) actions will enhance or damage their respective well-being. Moreover, each individual is both most able and most concerned to determine in his own case which actions are enhancing or damaging. These are questions that "no one can really and truly determine for anybody but himself."

On the basis of these claims about the reasonableness of each person's pursuit of happiness and each person's need to judge for himself how best to advance his happiness Spooner draws the conclusion that "the highest of all of [an individual's] rights as a human being . . . is his right to inquire, investigate, reason, try experiments, judge, and ascertain for himself, what is *to him,* virtue, and what is *to him,* vice. . ."[118] The affirmation of this basic right to freedom or to the pursuit of happiness is not in conflict with Spooner's affirmation of self-ownership and rights over the fruits of one's labor. As in Locke, the identification of "the right of one man to the control of his own person and property, and the *corresponding and coequal* rights of another man to the control of his own person and property"[119] delineates the scope of, and renders harmonious, our respective rightful freedoms.

Finally, in a discussion of conscription in "A Letter to Grover Cleveland," Spooner suggests a yet more Kantian-sounding argument on behalf of natural rights against deprivations of life and liberty. When government sends a conscript off to war to be blown to bits "as if he were a mere senseless thing" it treats him as if he were "a shell, a canister, or a torpedo;" it "does not recognize him at all as a human being, having any rights of his own. . ." The conscripting government ". . . denies [the conscript's] right to any will, any judgment, or any conscience of his own, as a moral being. . . [I]t takes his own life, as unceremoniously as if he were but a dog."[120]

---

[116] "Vices and Not Crimes," 25–26.

[117] Ibid., 28.

[118] Ibid., 27. The epistemic dimension of Spooner's argument will bring to mind Mill's argument in *On Liberty.* However, Spooner's argument actually more closely tracks Locke's argument in *A Letter Concerning Toleration.*

[119] "Vices are Not Crimes," 25.

[120] *A Letter to Grover Cleveland,* 31–32.

Despite initial appearances, Spooner offers a nuanced set of arguments on behalf of natural rights. Among the central contentions within these arguments are the strikingly Lockean claims that rational individuals seek their own happiness, that individuals must determine their own course to happiness, that the recognition of others as rational seekers of happiness on a moral par with oneself requires one to acknowledge every-one's equal right to seek happiness and, hence, a moral requirement upon oneself not to infringe upon this right of others, and that a significant component of each individual's constrained right to seek happiness is the right to discretionary control over his own person.

V. SPOONER ON PROPERTY RIGHTS, LEGISLATION, AND THE COMMON INTEREST

Natural rights of self-ownership suffice to condemn slavery and the coercive suppression of vice and imprudence; but they do not as such enable us to assess the justice of people's holdings of extra-personal objects, e.g., in parcels of land, in crops, in manufactured goods. As a basis for such assessment Spooner needs a theory of property rights; and he offers such a theory in the opening sections of his work on intellectual property rights, *The Law of Intellectual Property* (1855).[121] As we shall see, Spooner's doctrine cleaves more closely to Locke's position on property rights than does that of Hodgskin, Spencer, or Spooner's fellow individualist anarchists.

Spooner begins with an apparent divergence from Locke. For he asserts that there are two distinct procedures through which an individual can establish an initial property right in some extra-personal object. Spooner first says that an initial right to a parcel of land is established simply through taking first possession of that parcel whereas initial rights to chattel are established through Lockean labor investment.[122] However, although Spooner says that one's right in a parcel land arises "solely in consequence of one's taking possession of it,"[123] taking possession of a parcel of land turns out to consist in "bestow[ing] some valuable labor upon it."[124]

Thus, the apparently distinct first mode of just acquisition—acquisition by first possession—merges into the second, standard Lockean, labor-investment mode of just acquisition. A man's right to a labor-transformed parcel of land has the same sort of basis as his right to any other fruit of his labor; if he is deprived of the transformed object without his consent, he is deprived of his rightfully owned labor without his consent. The

[121] *The Law of Intellectual Property, The Collected Works of Lysander Spooner*, vol. III.
[122] Ibid., 21–3.
[123] Ibid., 21.
[124] Ibid., 22.

labor he has bestowed on *any* natural material "will be lost to him, if he is deprived of the commodity he has taken possession of." [125]

> [H]e holds the land in order to hold the labor which he has put into it, or upon it. And the land is his, so long as the labor he has expended upon it remains in a condition to be valuable for uses for which it was expended; because it is not to be supposed that a man has abandoned the fruits of his labor so long as they remain in a state practically useful to him. [126]

Note the contrast here with Hodgkin's view that a labor-investment account of rights to land will get one no more than occupancy and use rights because the effects of one's labor on land will dissipate as soon as one's occupancy and use ends.

Furthermore, according to Spooner,

> The principle of property is, that the owner of a thing has absolute dominion over it, *whether he have it in actual possession or not, and whether he himself wish to use it or not;* . . . and that he has a perfect right to withhold both the possession and use of it from others, from no other motive than to induce them, or make it necessary for them, to buy it, or rent it. . .[127]

Having broken with his fellow individualist anarchists—including Tucker—who held to the occupancy and use standard for just holdings in land,[128] Spooner naturally went on to disagree with them about the legitimacy of rent—even rent on land. Moreover, the fact that one can continue to be the owner of a resource even when another is using it enables one to employ someone else to bestow additional labor upon that resource and still remain the owner of the resultant product.[129]

In numerous other ways Spooner follows Locke closely on the question of initial rights to extra-personal objects. The "wealth of nature . . . was provided for the use of mankind." But man can effectively make use of this wealth of nature only by "making it private property." [130] The life of man, and his happiness and well-being depend upon his being able to make things his own. Hence, his natural rights to do as he sees fit in the promotion of his happiness requires that he have the right to engage in initial appropriation from nature.

[125] Ibid., 23.
[126] Ibid., 22.
[127] Ibid., 80.
[128] See, e.g., "Property under Anarchism," in Benjamin Tucker, *Individual Liberty* (New York: Vanguard, 1926).
[129] *The Law of Intellectual Property,* 25.
[130] Ibid., 22.

> The right of property [i.e., the right to make things one's own] has its
> foundation, first, in the natural right of each man to provide for his
> own subsistence; and secondly, in his right to provide for his general
> happiness and well-being. . . These rights, then, to live, and to obtain
> happiness, are the foundations of the right of property.[131]

Spooner argues that the "first comer" cannot be morally bound not to
appropriate. Indeed, as Locke argued, to deny individuals the natural
right to engage in such appropriation is to hold that people are born with
an obligation to starve in the midst of plentiful resources. As Spooner
puts it,

> The doctrine . . . that the first comer has no natural right to take
> possession of the wealth of nature, make it his property, and apply to
> his uses, is a doctrine that would doom the entire race to starvation,
> while all the wealth of nature remained unused, and unenjoyed around
> them.[132]

In a very nice reversal of Spencer's *Social Statics* argument for the societal
ownership of land, Spooner argues that,

> In asserting its right of arbitrary dominion over that natural wealth
> that is indispensable to the support of human life, [government or
> Spencerian "society"] asserts its right to withhold that wealth from
> those whose lives are dependent upon it. In this way it denies the
> natural right of human beings to live on the planet. It asserts that
> government owns the planet, and that men have no right to live on
> it, except by first getting a permit from the government.[133]

In addition, Spooner maintains that the first comer's acquisition can hardly
be said to disadvantage the later comer. Rather, the first comer's transformation of natural materials sets the stage for there being more and
better ways for later comers to gain through their own investment of
labor. "The first man is a hungry, shivering savage, with all the wealth of
nature around him. The last man revels in all the luxuries, which art,
science, and nature, working in concert, can furnish him." [134]

Like Locke, Spooner presumes that the difficult task in an account of
property rights concerns the explanation of initial rights over extra-
personal objects.[135] Once such objects become the rightful possessions

[131] Ibid., 28. Compare this with sections 86–88 of Locke's *First Treatise of Government*.
[132] Ibid., 25. Compare this with section 28 of Locke's *Second Treatise of Government*.
[133] *A Letter to Grover Cleveland*, 34.
[134] *The Law of Intellectual Property*, 24.
[135] Ibid., 29.

of individuals, any mutually voluntary transfer of the objects also transfers those rights. So, in principle, any set of holdings among members of society that results from individuals' engagement in peaceful labor investment and voluntary trade (and people's extraction of compensation for infringements upon their just holdings) is just. Unjust wealth and unjust poverty arise only through rights infringing interference with peaceful acquisition and trade. Spooner, along with his fellow individualist anarchists, held that a crucial instance of unjust and poverty-generating interference was governmental prohibitions on the issuance of credit; this restriction was taken to create an artificial scarcity of credit that greatly skewed the distribution of wealth on behalf of those already in possession of capital and against innocent and honest laborers. We can, however, slide past any discussion of the merits of Spooner's analysis of this issue because even if he were to give up this particular aspect of his condemnation of governmental interference, he could easily retain his basic representation of the role of governmental action and the function of legislation.

The representation that Spooner offers is remarkably like Hodgskin's critique of legislation—with the crucial difference that Spooner is in position to distinguish sharply between law, i.e., natural law, and legislation. For Spooner, the natural law is "applicable and adequate to the rightful settlement of every possible controversy that can arise among men." It is "the only standard by which any controversy whatever between man and man, can be rightfully settled." Legislation can have no purpose except to stand athwart of and interfere unjustly with the functioning of natural law. Legislation is, therefore, "self-evidently superfluous, false, absurd, and atrocious." [136] For Spooner, this natural law is a set of prescriptions, not merely a set of factual regularities of human conduct. Thus, there is nothing puzzling about people acting contrary to the natural law. And sometimes people will act contrary to these norms of natural justice when they perceive such action to be personally advantageous.

Some people will perceive opportunities for advantageous injustice when those around them become productive enough to be attractive targets for plunder. At that point some men

> ... associated and organized themselves as robbers, to plunder and enslave all others, who have either accumulated any property that could be seized, or had shown by their labor, that they could be made to contribute to the support or pleasure of those who should enslave them. [137]

---

[136] *Natural Law*, 16. For Spooner this is an overstatement. For surely there are controversies about virtue and vice, about what he calls "moral" duties, that are beyond the ambit of the science of *justice*.

[137] Ibid., 16–17.

These "bands of robbers" have become specialists in predation, "inventing warlike weapons, disciplining themselves, and perfecting their organizations as military forces."[138] They establish what they call "governments" and what they call "laws." The latter are

> ... only such agreements as they have found it necessary to enter into, in order to maintain their organization, and act together in plundering and enslaving others, and in securing to each [of the predators] his agreed share of the spoils.[139]

Presently existing non-slave societies are the result of the robber class having discovered that its interests are better yet served by giving their (now former) slaves "so much liberty as would throw upon themselves ... the responsibility of their own subsistence, and yet compel them to sell their labor to the land-holding class."[140] This compulsion is accomplished by illicit governmental action which maintains for the robber class "a monopoly of all lands, and, as far as possible, of all other means of creating wealth."[141] All these illicit, rights-violating, monopolies are sustained through legislation—the point of which is always to contravene and overturn the simple and easily perceived natural law. While most acts of legislation are "the impudent, fraudulent, and criminal usurpations of tyrants, robbers, and murderers," some legislation merely commands men to do justice and, thus, rises to the level of superfluous "idle wind."[142]

Spooner considers and rejects two purported vindications for legislation. It is within the natural rights of individuals to form connections with governments for the purpose of better securing their respective rights; and through such voluntary connections individuals may become bound to pay for governmental services and to cooperate in certain ways with permissible governmental endeavors. However, any degree of deference to governmental authority requires genuine voluntary consent to that authority. And in *No Treason, No. 6* Spooner constructs a powerful systematic attack on attempts to identify actual acts of consent that can plausibly be thought to ground either legislative or constitutional authority. I pass by the details of that attack here because it takes Spooner's natural rights framework as given and simply argues that people have not in fact exercised their rights in any of the ways that would create constitutional or legislative authority.[143]

---

[138] Ibid., 17.
[139] Ibid., 17.
[140] Ibid., 18.
[141] Ibid., 19.
[142] *A Letter to Grover Cleveland*, 4.
[143] Thus, according to Spooner, individuals have exercised one of the salient rights affirmed by Spencer in the early editions of *Social Statics*—the right to ignore the state.

In *A Letter to Grover Cleveland,* Spooner confronts a direct challenge to that rights framework. The challenge is that a fundamentally different morality exists to guide and vindicate governmental actions, namely, the morality of promoting the public good. Spooner might have challenged this alternative morality on two different high theoretical grounds. First, he might have reiterated his stance in "Vices Are Not Crimes" that each individual's happiness is "the great purpose and duty of his life" so that individuals have no duty to submit themselves to personal losses for the sake of greater gains for others. Second, he might have exploited another idea from that same essay: the idea that what constitutes well-being for any given person is likely to differ radically from what constitutes well-being for other persons. Spooner could then have argued, as we have seen Spencer argue from a similar premise, that effects of proposed public policies on the happiness of the diverse individuals who will be impacted by them cannot possibly be known, compared, or aggregated.

Spooner, however, seems to attack the public good proposal on a more practical level—with a quite well-worked out proto-public choice argument. Cleveland's inaugural address proclaims "a government pledged to do equal and exact justice to all men." But Cleveland envisions this equal and exact justice arising from legislators serving as advocates for various worthy interests and arriving at wise and considered collective judgments about which of these interests should really be advanced, which should be put on hold, and which should be sacrificed. Spooner's argument is that this is hardly a recipe for anything that could be described as the public good; rather, it is a recipe for the selection of legislators for their skill at serving the special interests of their (vocal and well-organized) constituents by means of making nimble deals with other skillfully predatory legislators. Recall here Spencer's claim that to assign government the task of directly promoting the general good is to sanction whatever actions the government chooses to perform. Indeed, according to Spooner, the promotion of the public good is in reality a formula for

> the boldest, the strongest, the most fraudulent, the most rapacious, and the most corrupt, men [gaining and exercising] control of the government, and mak[ing] it a mere instrument for plundering the great body of the people. . . .[144]

Spooner provides a wonderfully vitriolic account of the reality of the state's provision of equal and exact justice to all. It is difficult to select just one further passage from Spooner's analysis of how the invocation of "the general welfare" or "the common interest" calls forth the predatory hounds. But here is one passage that has a nice further twist:

[144] *A Letter to Grover Cleveland,* 17.

[U]nder such a system, every senator and representative—probably without an exception—will come to congress as the champion of the dominant scoundrelism of his own State or district; ... he will be elected solely to serve those "interests" as you call them; ... in offering himself as a candidate, he will announce the robbery or robberies, to which all his efforts will be directed; ... he will call these robberies his "policy"; or, if he be lost to all decency, he will call them his "principles." [145]

I have described Spooner's critique of guidance by the general welfare or the common good as a practical or proto-public choice criticism. Still Spooner has a theoretical explanation for the radical difference that he perceives between a legal order guided by respect for rights and a state order guided by interests or welfare.

The difference, he holds, is that men's true *rights* are consistent and harmonious; so, no one's rights have to be sacrificed in order for others' rights to be respected. But, because persons' *interests* or *welfare considerations* are open-ended, i.e., because interests or welfare considerations can always be better served, the desired degree of satisfaction of some of those interests or welfare considerations will always compete with the desired degree of satisfaction of other interests or welfare satisfactions. If political decisions are to be made on the basis of competing interests or considerations of welfare, even the most genuinely impartial legislator will have to be in the business of deciding whose interests or welfare is going to be sacrificed to who else's interests or welfare. Then political success will go to the boldest and most rapacious.

VI. CONCLUSION

I want to conclude by bringing together several strands that are present in my comparative exposition of the radical libertarianism of Hodgskin, the early Spencer, and Spooner. To begin, let us return to a contrast that I drew between the supervenient and the beneficial norm conceptions of rights. According to the supervenient conception, rights are correctly ascribed to individuals in virtue of some bedrock feature (or set of features) that individuals possess as individuals. Individuals are to abide by certain norms because certain patterns of action or constraint are required by those ascribed rights. Reciprocal compliance with these rights may be mutually beneficial; but that mutual benefit is a welcome unintended consequence rather than a basis for those rights. In contrast, according to the beneficial norm conception, certain patterns of action or constraint are morally required because reciprocal compliance with these patterns is mutually advantageous. Norms requiring those patterns of action or con-

[145] Ibid., 18–19.

straint qualify as principles of justice because of the mutual advantage of reciprocal compliance with them. The rights that are correctly ascribed to individuals are simply the claims they can advance on the basis of these principles of justice. I attributed the supervenient conception to Hodgskin and the beneficial norm conception to Spencer. Which conception ought to be attributed to Spooner?

I raise this question in part because in an excellent paper that focuses mostly on Spooner's constitutional thought Roderick Long attributes the beneficial norm conception to Spooner.[146] Long points to Spooner's repeated insistence that our compliance with the norms of justice is "indispensable to the peace of mankind everywhere" and Spooner's bolder yet claim that this compliance is "vital to the safety and welfare of every human being." [147] Spooner's belief in the timeless validity of the natural law is interpreted as his recognition that no social order can be sustained without some significant degree of compliance—among the members of that society—with the principles of what Spooner calls "natural law."

I believe, however, that my account of Spooner's case for natural rights puts Spooner firmly in the supervenient conception camp. I especially have in mind Spooner's focus on natural rights as the equal, consistent, and harmonious claims that each individual can reasonably advance against all others on the basis that he is a rational pursuer of his own happiness and well-being. There is a process of reasoning about which claimed rights will satisfy the requirement that they be part of a set of equal, consistent, and harmonious rights. But that reasoning process is not a bit of social scientific calculation aiming to identify the norms general compliance with which will produce peace (and even safety and welfare for everyone).

As I have argued at the outset of Section IV, Spooner is really interested in the conditions of *morally acceptable* peace; and the crucial condition of that *sort of peace* is the absence of violations of rights. So, one first has to identify those rights. Only then can one specify the peace that compliance with those rights will insure and explain why *that peace* should be promoted. Similarly, when Spooner says that compliance with natural law is "vital to the safety and welfare of every human being," he cannot mean vital to every *sort* of safety and welfare. For in the very next paragraphs of *Natural Law* he goes on to describe the gains in safety and (more clearly) welfare that some individuals attain through *robbery*—especially through the more organized, state-like, forms of robbery. If the suppression of such predation in the name of natural law and natural justice does not count as depriving some people of safety and welfare, it must be because the safety and welfare that Spooner has in mind is *morally acceptable* safety and welfare, i.e., the safety and welfare that emerges when

---

[146] Long, "Inside and Outside Spooner's Natural Law Jurisprudence."
[147] *Natural Law*, 16.

rights—which have been independently identified—are respected. Once again, first one must identify those rights. Only then can one specify the safety and welfare that compliance with rights will insure and explain why *that safety and welfare* should be promoted. The project of working out the beneficial norm conception of rights would require beginning with morally neutral notions of peace, safety, and welfare and then arguing that certain reciprocated patterns of conduct are vital to everyone attaining this peace, safety, and welfare. This clearly is not Spooner's project.

In seeking to ground natural rights on certain deeper yet and morally fertile features of human nature, namely, the fact that persons are rational pursuers of their happiness and are moral equals with respect to natural rights, Spooner shows his subscription to the supervenience conception of rights. And this is just one manifestation of how closely he cleaves to Locke.[148] Despite his extensive initial citation of Locke, Hodgskin neither grasps nor produces anything like Locke's arguments for natural rights. Moreover, his theory of rights to extra-personal objects depends heavily on the elusive idea that the producer naturally possesses whatever he creates (and does not trade away). Hodgskin matches Spooner in his denunciation of legislation; but unlike Locke and Spooner he is in no position to describe the measures that he opposes as in any sense *unlaw-ful*. Despite his very early apparent invocation of Lockean natural rights, Spencer is from the start a non-Lockean, beneficial norm, theorist. He offers beneficial norm arguments for recognizing the claims of individuals to the fruits of their labor but fails to affirm private property rights in land in *The Proper Sphere of Government* and denies such rights in *Social Statics*. The only fundamental philosophical stance all these authors share— which may in fact explain their common anti-authoritarianism—is their belief that each individual properly pursues his own happiness or well-being—within the constraints imposed by others' rights or others' claims to equal freedom.

In contrast to Hodgskin and Spencer, I have argued that Spooner has a reasonably well-worked out and strikingly Lockean doctrine of natural law and natural rights and acquired rights over extra-personal objects. The only fundamental component of Locke's political philosophy that Spooner rejects is the manifestly weakest component: Locke's belief that governments have attained legitimate authority through the consent of the governed.

Philosophy, Tulane University

---

[148] For a basic account of Locke on natural rights and on rights to extra-personal objects, see chapters 2 and 3 of Mack, *John Locke*.

PROGRESSIVISM AND THE DOCTRINE
OF NATURAL RIGHTS

By James W. Ceaser

I. Introduction

Progressive thinkers were revolutionary in their ends, not in their means. They generally condemned what John Dewey (1859–1952) called "radicalism," meaning efforts to overthrow the government by action beyond established law, let alone through violence. Progressivism, wrote Dewey, "both by its theory and by its own nature is committed to democratic methods of effecting social change."[1] At the same time, Progressives made clear their plans to attempt to change the basic character of the political and economic system and to discard the theoretical foundation of natural rights philosophy that underlay it.

The immediate target was the Constitution. Progressives saw it as an instrument that thwarted the democratic will and prevented the enactment of policies needed to meet the challenges of the new Industrial Age. (It was virtually an article of faith among Progressives that the people wished for, or could be persuaded to support, the programs that Progressives favored.) An effective system of modern policy-making, Progressives argued, required above all a capacity for planning and experimentation without the imposition of artificial limits on discretion. The Constitution, however, had as one of its primary aims the protection of liberty, understood in large part as individual rights. This objective was built into the structure of the government, with its fragmentation of authority among different institutions and its restrictions on governmental power; and it was further promoted by the listing of different rights in the original Constitution and in the Bill of Rights. The Constitution, as Woodrow Wilson (1856–1924) explained, was based on a "Newtonian" model, whereas what the nation needed was a system that rested on "Darwinian" principles: "There can be no successful government without leadership or without the intimate, almost instinctive, coordination of the organs of life and action. . . Living political constitutions must be Darwinian in structure and in practice."[2]

---

[1] John Dewey, "The Future of Liberalism," *Philosophy of Education* (Ames Iowa: Littlefield, Adams, & Co, 1956), 132.
[2] Woodrow Wilson, *Constitutional Government* (New Brunswick: Transaction Publisher, 2002, orig. 1908), 57.

doi:10.1017/S0265052511000239

For many Progressives the mere mention of "economic individualism" was enough to condemn the system. Walter Weyl (1873-1919), a well-known writer, was content to describe individualism as "self-confident, short-sighted, lawless, [and] doomed in the end to defeat itself."[3] But deeper thinkers like Dewey and historian Carl Becker (1873-1945) understood that opposition to individualism implicated the general doctrine of natural rights; that doctrine too, therefore, had to be exposed and rejected. No matter how much these thinkers praised the democratic "spirit" of Thomas Jefferson (1743-1826)—Dewey celebrated him as "the first modern to state in human terms the principles of democracy"[4]—they could not support the letter of Jefferson's goals. For Jefferson "nothing ... is unchangeable but the inherent and unalienable rights of man," whereas for the Progressives nothing was unchangeable, including therefore the idea of natural rights. Jefferson's fondest hope was that "all eyes are ... opening to the rights of man," whereas the Progressives urged our gaze to be turned elsewhere, to the Great Society in the future. For the Progressives, as Dewey made clear, the doctrine of natural rights was the foundation on which the old American system had rested. It was an idea, he wrote, "located in the clouds," whose "falsity may easily be demonstrated both philosophically and historically."[5] It would need to be swept away before the new system could come into being.

Progressives were not, of course, critical of the Enlightenment scientific project that Jefferson had helped introduce into America. On the contrary, they insisted that they were its modern champions. A new and expanded form of social science—what Dewey referred to famously as a "reconstruction" of the Enlightenment project—was their goal. It was just that economic and social conditions had reached a new stage in which old forms had to be set aside. Liberty in our time was to be achieved not by the recognition of rights, but by collective social action that supplied powers or capacities to individuals.

Political communities gravitate to a central principle of right. If, as Progressives asserted, the doctrine of natural rights was the reigning idea among the public, its elimination would create a vacuum. It is important therefore to ask what Progressives thought would take its place, and whether their answer (if they had one) has proven to be viable. An inquiry into this question is of more than merely historical interest. Adherents to contemporary liberalism have reclaimed the old label of "Progressives" and sometimes consider themselves—or are considered by others—as the heirs of that older movement. Some of the issues and problems that Progressives confronted in seeking to establish a new foundation in their time may shed light on challenges that liberals face today.

---

[3] Walter E. Weyl, *The New Democracy* (New Brunswick: Transaction Publishers, 2005 orig. 1912), 36.

[4] John Dewey, *Freedom and Culture* (New York: Capricorn Books, 1939), 156.

[5] Dewey, *Freedom and Culture*, 156. Dewey, *Reconstruction in Philosophy* (Boston: Beacon, 1957, orig. 1920), 44.

II. Progressive Interpretations of Natural Rights
in the American Founding

Progressive historiography has been clear on one point. Progressives never doubted the primacy or ascendancy of the natural rights doctrine for the American Founders. Carl Becker, in his famous study on the Declaration of Independence, noted: "The doctrine of natural rights was, I found to be, in the eighteenth century, so commonly accepted as the foundation of all social philosophy that Jefferson could defend his formulation of it by saying that he was only expressing 'the common sense of the matter.'"[6] Much historical writing since the Progressive era has called this claim into question, arguing that the importance of general philosophical speculation in the Revolution has been greatly exaggerated. The historian John Reid provocatively summed up this line of argument by referring to "the irrelevancy of natural rights."[7]

There appears on first glance to be a refreshing frankness in the Progressives' treatment of the Founders. As much as Progressives opposed the doctrine of natural rights, they never sought to read their opposition to it *into* the Founders' thought; they eschewed a reliance on "useable history," the practice of finding one's general position inside a privileged historical moment. (Consider how many strands of thought today, from a left-wing communitarianism to a conservative traditionalism, have discovered interpretations of the Founding that correlate with their own public philosophy.) Yet before crediting the Progressives with too much probity, one should ask whether their interpretive account might not also have derived from strategic considerations of their own. Progressives delighted in sharpening their conflict with the Founders, which was a stance consistent with their "revolutionary" project. If the plan was to replace the Founding, it was necessary to diminish the Founders' stature. The Founders' support of an erroneous or outmoded doctrine is of a piece with this approach. The Progressives also thought that they had a winning rhetorical strategy, one that fit with a powerful modern prejudice against custom or history. As John Dewey commented in *Reconstruction in Philosophy*: "The future rather than the past dominates the imagination. The Golden Age lies ahead of us not behind us."[8]

Setting aside further speculations about motives, were the Progressives correct in their assessment of the primacy of nature and natural rights at the time of the founding? One thing that even the modern doubters do not question is that the natural rights doctrine was important to a large

---

[6] Carl Becker, *The Declaration of Independence* (New York: Knopf 1951; orig. 1922), x.

[7] John Phillip Reid, *Constitutional History of the American Revolution: The Authority of Rights* (Madison: University of Wisconsin Press, 1993), 90.

[8] John Dewey, *Reconstruction in Philosophy* (Boston: Beacon Press, 1920), 48–49. Woodrow Wilson expressed a similar view in public during the 1912 presidential campaign: "We think of the future, not the past, as the more glorious time in comparison with which the present is nothing... The modern idea is to leave the past and press onward to something new." Woodrow Wilson, *The New Freedom* (New York: Doubleday, Page, 1913), 42.

segment of America's leaders, who regarded the introduction of a philosophical foundation into the political world as one of the great intellectual revolutions in human affairs. Nor did these leaders embark on this change casually. As John Adams (1735–1826) noted in recounting a key debate in the Continental Congress in 1774: "We very deliberately considered and debated . . . whether we should recur to the law of nature" along with the historical foundations of the tradition, such as the "common law" and "the charters" or "the rights of British subjects."[9] Here and elsewhere the Founders aired fundamental issues about natural law doctrine, including whether natural law *could* be a comprehensible political foundation, and, if so, whether it *should* be introduced. Many of the Founders were aware of philosopher David Hume's (1711–1776) warnings that a recurrence to the standard of nature might prove destabilizing to political society by providing a source of right beyond the positive law.[10]

If the importance of the doctrine of natural right to a segment of the leadership class is indisputable, determining its significance for the mass public is, and will likely remain, a difficult challenge. It may well be, as modern historians claim, that few went into battle during the Revolutionary war singing hymns to nature or nature's God. Yet this fact, if it is one, carries nowhere near the theoretical import that some have tried to ascribe to it. For even if the doctrine of natural rights was not, as Jefferson asserted a half-century later to Henry Lee (1756–1818), an "expression of the American mind" in 1776, it certainly became so sometime thereafter.[11] At some point in the late eighteenth or early nineteenth century Americans acknowledged, at least ritually, its primacy. As John Quincy Adams (1767–1848) observed in his July 4 Oration in 1821: "America, with the same voice which spoke herself into existence as a nation, proclaimed to mankind the inextinguishable rights of human nature, and the only lawful foundations of government."[12] Further proof of the importance of natural rights theory, if it is needed, is supplied, ironically, by its opponents. In the 1840s, defenders of slavery began a widespread public campaign to denounce the doctrine for being (in John Calhoun's (1782–1850) words) "the most false and dangerous of all political errors."[13] If the theory had been "irrelevant," there would have been no need to attack it.

---

[9] *The Works of John Adams,* (Boston: Charles C. Little and James Brown, 1850), 2: 371.

[10] See David Hume, "The Original Contract," in *Essays,* ed. Eugene F. Miller, (Indianapolis: Liberty Classics, 1985, orig. 1777), 465–88.

[11] Thomas Jefferson to Henry Lee, May 8, 1825. Available online at http://www.let.rug.nl/usa/P/tj3/writings/brf/jeflxx.htm#1825.

[12] John Quincy Adams, "An Address delivered at the Anniversary of Independence" July 4, 1821 (Cambridge: University press, 1821).

[13] John C. Calhoun, "Speech in the Senate on the Oregon Bill" June 27, 1848, *Union and Liberty: The Political Philosophy of John C. Calhoun,* ed. Ross M. Lence (Indianapolis: Liberty Classics, 1992), 565.

In the end, then, setting aside the quarrels about the timing of the popular acceptance of natural rights doctrine, Progressive historians seem to have gotten right the importance of natural rights philosophy to the American experiment. Can the same be said of the way in which they characterized natural rights doctrine? Most Progressives, in line with Carl Becker's analysis, interpreted the Founders to have understood the doctrine of natural rights as a discovery full of Enlightenment thought. Natural rights doctrine borrowed from the general spirit of modern science (with Newton in the background) and especially from the works of John Locke (1632–1704). The concept of nature referred to what man could grasp by the use of his reason about the permanent arrangement of the world. Nature, to the Founders, designated both the essential character of empirical phenomena, as in the constitution of man (human nature), and the necessary relations that exist among things. These relations were "laws of nature"; they could provide the intellectual understanding for the construction of models—not necessarily of things that currently existed but of things that could be brought into existence, in the way that an engineer builds something according to a plan. To construct government according to the laws of nature became the great aim of the Founders' doctrine of natural right. The science they followed began by distilling certain premises about psychology or human nature relating to man's strongest passions or needs; it then proceeded to construct a model of political organization that met or satisfied these needs, at least as they were relevant to political life, in a way that allowed for the establishment of just, decent, and enduring (legitimate) governments.

Subsequent historical scholarship has questioned this view of the Founders' understanding of natural rights, with some denying that they conceived of nature exclusively in terms of this Enlightenment rationalist framework. Instead, these scholars argue, many of the Founders worked from a view of nature influenced by deist Protestant thought or by older notions of natural law, both classical and Christian. Indeed, it has been pointed out that Jefferson himself, the Founder who was arguably most indebted to Enlightenment ideas, wrote in the same letter to Lee that the prevailing understanding of the doctrine was expressed "in the elementary books of public right, as Aristotle, Cicero, Locke, Sidney, etc."[14] Edwin Corwin, the famous constitutional scholar, initiated this general line of criticism of the Progressive view in 1928, in his revealingly entitled work, *The "Higher Law" Background of American Constitutional Law.*[15] Those Founders holding to a "higher law" understanding of nature had different views of human nature and, in some cases, slightly different notions of the purposes of government than those who followed thought.

---

[14] Thomas Jefferson to Henry Lee, May 8, 1825.
[15] Edwin S. Corwin, *The "Higher Law" Background of American Constitutional Law* (Ithaca: Cornell University Press 1928).

Much can be said in favor of this correction of the Progressive view. The Founders were probably less "Lockean" than the Progressives portrayed them. Or at any rate, they interpreted Locke in a less materialist or calculative sense than the Progressives make out. The question of the Founders' full understanding of the concept of nature—or different Founders' understanding—remains a topic for further research.

Yet even if we follow the Progressives on this point, and restrict the inquiry here to the natural rights doctrine as it derived from Enlightenment thought, it is important to note (as few Progressives did) that there were different interpretations of the character of rights within this tradition. One view emphasized the rights of individuals, while another put more weight on collective rights. The individualist view, which is the form Progressives stressed, identified the object of society as the protection of individual rights, whether untouched in their natural form or maximized in their practical realization by civil or municipal law. These rights needed protection not just from tyrants, but also (in James Madison's (1751–1836) words) from "the superior force of an interested and overbearing majority" within republics.[16] Property rights were an important element needing this protection, and courts in early America sometimes intervened on their behalf.[17]

The idea of collective rights, deriving from the Declaration's statement of "the right of the people to alter or abolish it [a form of government], and institute new government," was favored in the early nineteenth century by many Jeffersonians, especially in the South, and later by Jacksonians. For many Americans, as the historian Daniel Rodgers has explained, "the hard core meaning of Natural Rights was a collective right: the revolutionary right to begin society over again."[18] This idea of collective rights was extended almost to the point of identifying natural right with the wishes of the majority, or popular sovereignty. On the state level, the application of natural rights in this sense was often at odds with claims of property rights. Fearing the radical implications of this understanding of natural rights, some defenders of property therefore grew leery altogether of appeals to natural law, which they regarded as radical, and preferred instead to rely on the protections of positive law.

A final—and what became a highly contentious—Enlightenment understanding of natural law sought to anchor rights not just in the psychology of human beings (human nature) but in a much broader understanding of

---

[16] James Madison, *Federalist No. 10* in *The Federalist*, ed. George W. Carey and James McClellan (Indianapolis: Liberty Classics, 2001), 42.

[17] Mention of natural rights or natural justice in this sense was also introduced as a supplementary argument in legal reasoning in court cases. See for example, Justice Story's decision in *Terrett v. Taylor*, 9 Cranch 43, 52 (1815), where he speaks of "the principles of natural justice" in reference to certain vested property rights.

[18] Daniel Rodgers, *Contested Truths* (Cambridge: Harvard University Press 1987), 71.

the relations among all things. This view, to which Progressive historians sometimes alluded, derived from the new science of political economy. It identified the natural with harmony or spontaneous order. George Logan (1753–1821), the American political economist whom Jefferson tasked to criticize Alexander Hamilton's economic plan, expressed the natural law as follows: "The same Great Being who created man for the purposes of his own glory has also appointed an order of conduct calculated to conciliate the interests of men united in society." [19] This law was said to apply not just to economic exchanges, but to all political and social affairs as well—indeed, it seemed to pertain to the whole cosmic order. From this law derived the general inclination of Jeffersonians for noninterference.

Many strongly rejected this general understanding of nature, especially as it applied to political affairs. The intent of those with this understanding was to try to limit the exercise of government discretion beyond anything the Constitution had in mind. The Constitution, it should be remembered, envisaged a government endowed with many important powers. Some members of the Federalist Party in particular regarded the notion of spontaneous order as an unwarranted expansion of the concept of nature that unjustifiably brought principles of economics and physical science into political science. To them, it marked the beginning of a transformation of the political science of natural right into what one might call an "ideology." It may be asked whether Progressives were attacking this "ideology" of laissez faireism more than the Founders' view of nature itself, just as it may be asked if they were assailing a Jeffersonian interpretation of the Constitution rather than the Constitution itself.

III. Natural Rights Doctrine in the Nineteenth Century

Progressive thinkers were so vocal and insistent in criticizing the doctrine of natural rights that many of their readers may be excused for thinking that the Progressives were the first, other than some of the defenders of slavery, to have seriously challenged this foundation. But this is not the case. It is a curious fact about our "natural rights republic" that the idea of natural rights was subjected to early and widespread questioning, not only within intellectual circles, but in broad public discussions as well.[20]

The earliest critiques of natural rights doctrine grew out of opposition to the French Revolution, especially as expressed by Edmund Burke (1729–1797). The primary concern was that natural law discourse would encourage a turn, as it had in France, to radical or utopian politics. Proponents

[19] George Logan, *Letters Addressed to the Yeomanary of the United States* (Philadelphia: Oswald, 1791), 12.
[20] The Phrase "natural rights republic" is taken from the title of a work by Michael Zuckert, *The Natural Rights Republic* (Notre Dame, Indiana: University of Notre Dame Press 1996).

of this position were not hostile to individualism or property rights—usually just the contrary. What they now feared, however, was that property rights and social stability would be endangered by public recourse to "radical" natural rights philosophy.

This sentiment grew and went in a new direction in the 1830s under the influence of Romanticism, which turned a critical eye on the "materialist" philosophy of John Locke.[21] Without directly implicating the Founding or questioning property rights, many now argued that Locke's ideas were dismissive of higher and nobler virtues and inadequate for building social cohesion. The nation could not be held together by a foundation of natural rights. To create and sustain a strong and deep culture, America needed more than the thin gruel of abstract principles; it required powerful and moving accounts of Americans' common heritage (tradition) or a common civil religion. The nation needed a foundation that appealed to the heart as well as the head.

Accompanying this approach was a different understanding of the meaning of "natural." Nature, at least as it applied in human affairs, was no longer conceived of as a pattern or set of relations that man could grasp in the abstract; it consisted instead of the actual laws of historical development in each particular context. Nature was the organic development of traditions. This understanding drew on new ideas from philosophy of science, although these had yet to be credited with the status of a genuine science. As events turned out, this account of nature found some of its strongest advocates in the South, among those who were preparing the ground for breaking up the union rather than for building a thicker nationalism. If nature was the organic growth of a community, then the community was where the heart felt at home. Southerners like John Calhoun began to insist that community, for them, was the South, not the artificial construction of the United States of America. As Carl Becker rightly observed, "Calhoun identified natural law with the positive law of particular states, the state of nature with the state of political society as history actually gave it rather than as it might be rationally conceived and reconstructed."[22]

Another challenge to the doctrine of natural rights came from philosophy of history. Its adherents claimed that the most important kind of knowledge about political life derived from an understanding of the movement of history (which included the future), rather than from an understanding of the relations among permanent factors understood as models. History supplied an understanding of right, on the view that history's course was onward and upward. Right consists in moving forward, in the direction toward which history is already tending; wrong is what seeks to maintain tradition.

[21] For a highly instructive account of the views of John Locke in this period, see Merle Curti, *Probing Our Past* (Gloucester, MA: Peter Smith, 1962), 69–118.

[22] Becker, *Declaration of Independence*, 254–55.

Philosophy of history entered America in the 1790s under the influence of the thought of Nicolas de Condorcet (1743–1794), Jefferson's friend, who wrote the first full-scale universal history based on the idea of progress.[23] It achieved a greater following after 1830 in the form of a version of German Idealism, as introduced and modified here by the historian George Bancroft (1800–1891). Bancroft's central premise was that the next and likely the last phase of human history was the advent of democracy. America had been given the commission, so to speak, to bring democracy to the world. This theme became the central principle of late-Jacksonianism and found expression in such doctrines as Manifest Destiny. The influence of this view, insofar as it replaced the doctrine of natural rights, can be seen in the thought of Stephen Douglas (1813–1861), one of the main figures in this intellectual movement. Douglas ended in the 1850s by openly abandoning the doctrine of natural rights. This fateful step did not derive from a fondness to slavery but from his belief in philosophy of history. Diverting American energy from spreading democracy, which Douglas feared would be the effect of Lincoln's natural rights thought, thwarted progress.

Following the Civil War, a different version of philosophy of history — actually a return of the version that Condorcet had inaugurated — was imported into America. It was taken from Condorcet's chief adherent, French philosopher Auguste Comte (1798–1857), and was introduced into America by Lester Ward (1841–1913). This version was less poetic, less dialectical, and less attached to the notion of a commission given to America. It claimed the mantle of strict science. It was Comte who coined both the words "positivism" and "sociology," the latter designating the newest and latest scientific discipline that understood the laws of history. Lester Ward was the father of American sociology and the individual most responsible for shaping Progressivism, although he came too early — and wrote too abstrusely — to be counted as one of its main leaders. For Ward, sociology "stands at the summit of the scale of great sciences arranged in the ascending order of specialty and complexity according to the law of evolutionary progress."[24] Its ultimate purpose was not just to describe how things worked, but, in line with Comte, to enable men to direct society. Sociology would emerge as a true and full science when "social phenomena shall be contemplated as capable of intelligent control by society itself in its own interest."[25]

A third critique of the Founder's doctrine of natural rights individualism grew out of the science of ethnology (or natural history), which was

---

[23] Marie Jean Antoine Nicolas de Caritat, Marquis de Condorcet, *Sketch for a Historical Picture of the Progress of the Human Mind* (1795) in Liberty Classics Online, http://oll. libertyfund.org/index.php?option=com_staticxt&staticfile=show.php%3Ftitle=1669&Itemid =29.

[24] Lester Ward, "The Establishment of Sociology," Address of the President of the American Sociological Society at its First Annual Meeting, Providence, RI, December 27, 1906 at http://www.asanet.org/governance/presadd1906.html.

[25] Lester Ward, *Dynamic Sociology*, (New York: D. Appleton and Co., 1897), vol. 1, xxvi.

the most important of the empirical social sciences of the first half of the nineteenth century. Its key finding was that mankind was divided into different varieties or types corresponding to the different races. The varieties have distinct characteristics, not only in physical appearance, but also in such general endowments as reason, imagination, and artistic talent. Ethnology sat uncomfortably with the science of natural rights, even though there is nothing in theory incompatible between the alleged fact that different groups have different natural capacities and the fact that all individuals possess natural rights. The two sciences came into tension or conflict at the point where some ethnologists added further claims about nature. Jefferson, who introduced this science into America, argued that where varieties were unequal, they should not intermix. His reason was that nature bid or permitted man to maintain a hierarchy.[26] He accordingly called for a physical separation of the white and black races, with each, if possible, establishing a natural rights republic.

Some Southerners in the 1850s took the radical step of arguing that differences in the endowments of the races were so great that they justified slavery. This position asserted the additional claim, supposedly derived from nature, that the inferior should serve the superior, for the good of both. The inferior presumably could not establish decent government. Alexander Stephens (1812–1883), vice president of the Confederacy, explicitly denied the natural rights doctrine. The American Founding, he claimed, "rested upon the assumption of the equality of the races. This was an error . . ." He went on: "Our new government is founded upon exactly the opposite idea; its corner stone rests upon the great truth that . . . slavery— subordination to the superior race—is his [the negro's] natural and normal condition."[27] The South, Stephens maintained, was the first political order to be based on natural law correctly understood.

The final nineteenth-century challenge to the doctrine of natural rights came from Darwinism. "Darwinism" in this context refers not strictly to thought that derived from Charles Darwin (1809–1882), but to approaches that grounded political and social thought in biological theories of evolution. These approaches proceeded either directly, by charting the evolution of man as a species in the context of natural history, or indirectly or analogically, by arguing that social phenomena (institutions, languages, cultures) were governed by evolutionary laws similar to those found among biological species. The common element in such accounts was that the units in question were in a situation of struggle for survival, often against each other, and that the unit that was selected was stronger or

[26] Thomas Jefferson, *Notes on the State of Virginia,* ed. Thomas Perkins Abernathy, (New York: Tourchbook, 1964) Jefferson writes: "Will not a lover of natural history then, one who views the gradations in all the races of animals with the eye of philosophy, excuse an effort to keep those in the department of man as distinct as nature has formed them?" (188).

[27] See Harry Cleveland, *Alexander H. Stephens* (Philadelphia: National Publishing, 1866), 721.

better. The new "law of nature" described this reality. In the words of one of America's best-known Darwinists, the Yale sociologist William Graham Sumner (1840–1910), "Competition is a law of nature. Nature is entirely neutral; she submits to him who most energetically and resolutely assails her."[28] This law was a genuine scientific account, in contrast to the laws of nature described in natural rights philosophy. Although some proponents of Darwinism supported natural rights theories for tactical reasons, as a political doctrine protecting property rights, very few of them considered it to be true.

Despite the harshness of Darwinian natural law, it supported in its own way an idea of progress. Advancement might be slow and painful, but it was progress nonetheless. Part of the enormous appeal of Darwinism derived from the fact that it covered the categories of both science and history, folding them together into the same field of inquiry. No other foundational principle could claim the same kind of explanatory power. And no other science, then or now, could claim the same degree of influence over the thought of the intellectual community.

Darwinism assumed very different forms, depending on the unit that was held to be most important for political life. (The theory itself gave no clue as to which unit that would be.) An important variant, known as the laissez-faire approach, placed the primary emphasis on struggle among *individual* human beings. This variant favored a capitalist system with a very limited role for government as the arrangement that is in accord with nature. Economic liberty enables individuals to engage in the contest according to the range and application of their abilities, with the most productive forces being selected. This school counted on a steady, but hard-won kind of progress. It would be possible, of course, for societies to promote equality by curtailing liberty—this was the program of socialists and other sentimental reformers—but only at the cost of moving forward. The ultimate penalty for not respecting the law of nature was stagnation and decline.

Another variant of Darwinism held that the relevant unit in struggle was not the individual, but the collectivity, the people, or the race, or the nation. These collective units were locked in a struggle or competition, and the fate and survival of each collectivity depended on the outcome of this struggle. For these Darwinists, the power of the unit often depended on subordination of the individual to the collectivity, and they were often the most severe critics of the individualist approach. Theodore Roosevelt was of this school, and he attacked the Spencerians as being "the same types" who "stood against the cause of national growth, of national greatness, at the end of the century as at the beginning."[29]

---

[28] William Graham Sumner, *The Challenge of Facts and Other Essays*, ed. Albert Keller (New Haven: Yale University Press, 1914), 25.

[29] Theodore Roosevelt, *The Winning of the West* (New York: G. P. Putnam's Sons, 1900), xii.

IV. THE PROGRESSIVE CRITIQUE OF THE DOCTRINE
OF NATURAL RIGHTS

These nineteenth-century critiques of the doctrine of natural rights, especially the challenge coming from Darwinism, were in the background when Progressives came on the scene. The doctrine of natural rights, at least within high intellectual circles, was already moribund, in large part because it could no longer draw on the prestige of science, as it had at the time of the Founding. The theory was now classified as an argument of philosophy or, worse, of "metaphysics," in an age in which top billing went to science, understood as "positivism" or empiricism. Where natural rights doctrine survived was within the public mind and among jurists, but only, at least as Progressives told the story, as an inheritance of the constitutional tradition. "It was one of those ancient political ideas," wrote Walter Weyl, "which still cumber our brains; [a] political heirloom of revered—but dead—ancestors." [30]

If the Progressives cannot therefore claim the honor of being the first in America to challenge the doctrine of natural rights, they can at least boast of taking the lead in discrediting it in the eyes of the educated populace. Their sustained critique was conducted on a broad range of issues by some of the nation's ablest thinkers, with the arguments here drawn mostly from the leading Progressive thinker, John Dewey.

First, their most frequent and effective line of analysis, Progressives criticized the doctrine of natural rights as part of a sweeping historical and political argument. The nation, according to the Progressives, was undergoing a fundamental transition from an agrarian order to an industrial age. The challenges were unprecedented and produced, in the words of economist Richard Ely (1854–1943), "the farthest and deepest reaching crisis known to human history." [31] America had lost control of the forces shaping modern life and had degenerated from a democracy into a plutocracy. "The power possessed by the few," according to John Dewey, had taken the place of the "liberty for all envisaged by the liberals of the nineteenth century." [32] The chief cause of this dire situation was a continuing adherence to the idea of the old individualism, and there was no remedy as long as the nation operated under this ideology. The Progressives' main goal was to supply a new theory of governance. A crisis is a terrible thing to waste.

The problems posed by industrialism had an additional dimension. Mankind as a species, they argued, stood at a critical juncture in its evolutionary development, poised to take a new step, yet also on the precipice of disaster. A failure to meet the challenges at hand seemed to implicate the whole race, or at any rate its progress. Two kinds of history—ordinary political or social history and natural or biological

---

[30] Weyl, *The New Democracy*, 108.

[31] Richard E. Lee, *Social Aspects of Christianity* (New York: Thomas Y. Crowell, 1889), 137.

[32] John Dewey, *Liberalism and Social Action*, (New York: Putnam, 1935), 36.

history—thus intersected at the turn of the century, making this period one of the most momentous of all time. Progressivism was a philosophy of emergency.

Progressivism, as the word denotes, took its bearings from the idea of Progress. This idea was derived initially from philosophy of history, but it increasingly drew its strength from Darwinism, which was considered to be the most powerful of the sciences. Progressivism is thus a theoretical brother of Spencerian laissez-faire thought, although the fraternal bond between them resembled nothing so much as the relationship of Cain to Abel. Led by John Dewey, Progressives interpreted Darwin in a new way; they turned his first premise (adaptation and survival) against his second (intraspecies competition). The key to man's advancement as a species from the present period forward lay not in competition, but in intelligent cooperation. Man as a species has in his arsenal the distinctive quality of "intelligence," which in its highest form consists in what Dewey called "the social conception of intelligence" or "intelligence as the method of directing social action."[33] Until now man was able to progress without need of much social planning. The invisible hand had been sufficient. But no longer. Collective planning was an evolutionary necessity.

The Progressives' support of the "social conception of intelligence," to be put into effect by public authority (the "state") informed by social scientists, helps account for why Progressives were so opposed to rights, whether natural or conventional. Rights function as an automatic impediment to broad and intelligent government action; they institutionalize limitations on planning and discretion. But intelligent planning and discretion unfettered by artificial limitations were the best way to promote the public good and to provide individuals with the powers needed to promote liberty in a higher sense.

But would mankind accept the challenge to adapt and be willing to jettison the outmoded doctrine of natural rights? There were good reasons, Progressives argued, to think so. Besides being impelled to seek new solutions by the seriousness of the immediate crisis of industrial society, man had now also begun to develop a new theoretical consciousness. Darwin arrived, if not providentially, then at any rate in the nick of time. Darwin's thought set the stage for the abandonment of a fixed idea of nature that had dominated Western thought since the dawn of philosophy. "The influence of Darwin upon philosophy," Dewey argued, was found in the fact that he "freed the new logic [of the scientific method] for application to mind and morals and life."[34] Darwinism liberated man from metaphysics, allowing him to investigate social and political matters in a new and genuinely scientific spirit. Progressivism was the social philosophy that took cognizance of this fact. It was the intellectual vanguard of a new stage of human development.

---

[33] John Dewey, *Liberalism and Social Action*, 45, 50.
[34] John Dewey, *The Influence of Darwin on Philosophy*, (New York: Holt, 1910), 8–9.

A second, important Progressive critique of the doctrine of natural rights rested on what Dewey called the idea of "historic relativity." [35] According to this idea, all theoretical concepts are said to be relative to the period in which they are developed. Thought is bounded by the context in which it emerges, down to the language in which ideas are expressed. The terms thinkers employ are not just a matter of their presentation or rhetoric; they embody a structure of thought and cannot transcend their age.

History had sent a message in the form of a change of language that now made the idea of natural rights meaningless. According to Carl Becker, "To ask whether the natural rights philosophy of the Declaration of Independence is true or false is essentially a meaningless question." [36] It is meaningless because modern thought no longer assumes the form of reasoning from nature. Charles Beard (1874–1948) remarked, with even more clarity, "[E]fforts have been made to give force to rights by calling them natural [but] that was an eighteenth century custom." [37] The custom of speaking in this manner had now waned.

In light of this "relativist" position about language, there would seem to be no further need to treat the concept of nature on its merits. For whatever one might think of the concept, it was impossible any longer to use the term. Natural rights doctrine is an idea whose time had passed. "With the founders of American democracy," Dewey wrote, "the claims of democracy were inherently one with demands of a just and equal morality. We cannot well use their vocabulary. Changes in knowledge have *outlawed* the significations of the words they used" (emphasis added).[38] Historical shifts by this account can criminalize past concepts. The philosopher's task is to play sheriff, deputize a posse of polemicists, and round up any stray rustlers who persist in using outmoded terms. As for the matter of why such disciplinary action remained necessary at all, Dewey explained that there is a lag time during which public thinking has not yet caught up to theoretical developments. This period has been prolonged in the case of natural rights, because the doctrine was widely "asserted to be absolute and eternal truth, good for all times and all places." [39] A public teaching of this kind unfortunately encouraged its ability to hang on as a vestige or relic.

The barrier imposed by changing languages is not so great, however, that today's thinkers cannot look *back* to understand what past thinkers had in mind. Dewey found certain things in the Declaration of Independence of which he seemed to approve, and he suggested that these

---

[35] John Dewey, "Future of Liberalism" in *Philosophy of Education,* vol. 1 (Ames, Iowa: Littlefield, Adams, 1956), 35.

[36] Carl Becker, *The Declaration of Independence,* 277.

[37] Charles Beard, *The Republic,* (New York: Viking Press, 1943), 39.

[38] John Dewey, *The Political Writings,* ed. Debra Morris and Ian Shapiro (Indianapolis: Hackett Publishing, 1993), 229.

[39] Dewey, "Future of Liberalism," 135.

might be revived by engaging in a process of translation: "To put ourselves in touch with Jefferson's position we have to translate the word 'natural' into *moral*. . . [Jefferson's] fundamental beliefs remained unchanged in substance if we forget all special associations with the word *Nature* and speak instead of ideal aims and values to be realized." These aims, of which a right to property is not mentioned, stem from "something deep and indestructible in the needs and demands of humankind."[40] This formulation sounds suspiciously like talk of a fixed human nature, rather than an ideal people create or a value they prefer. But the main direction of Dewey's thought lay, of course, in opposition to the idea of nature.

A third, critique of the doctrine of natural rights goes to the question of the reasons for which thinkers develop their political ideas. Progressives by and large conceived that the main explanation comes from "class interests." As Becker notes, "the middle-class man" in the eighteenth century "readily identified the laws of nature and nature's God with his class interests."[41] Class interest could be conceived broadly as the general character of the political order and narrowly as a system of property relations. Dewey, for example, explains the doctrine of individualism as a way to conceive persons free from the control of preexisting associations like the Church or the Feudal order.[42] It was a central tenet in preparing the way for the revolt against the old order. Charles Beard's *An Economic Interpretation of the Constitution* (1913), by contrast defined the Founders' class interest more narrowly as an effort to defend their property from the threats from the state legislatures. The class interest account of the character of ideas not only has the effect of deflating them—after all, they are not permanent truths—but also of explaining why they become obsolete. They serve a specific purpose for their time, after which they cease to be helpful.

This argument of historical relativity allowed for a shifting judgment of the worth of these ideas. The Progressives were often highly complimentary of natural rights doctrine *for its time*. It served in the eighteenth century to help push forward economic development. Its utility in some accounts even extended to a defense of the great captains of industry of the middle and late nineteenth century, who could be credited, albeit by using unscrupulous means, for building America's industrial infrastructure. (Franklin Roosevelt (1882–1945) echoed this position in his Commonwealth Club address during the 1932 campaign, when he noted that "the history of the last half century is accordingly in large measure a history of a group of financial Titans, whose methods were not scrutinized with too much care, and who were honored in proportion as they

---

[40] Dewey, *Freedom and Culture*, 156.
[41] Carl Becker, *New Liberties for Old* (New Haven: Yale University Press, 1941), 21.
[42] John Dewey, *The Public and Its Problems* (Athens, OH: Swallow Press; orig. 1927), 86–87.

produced the results, irrespective of the means they used."[43]) But what
was laudable or excusable in the past no longer could be justified. In the
modern economy, as Dewey wrote, "We are in for some kind of socialism,
call it whatever name we please."[44]

These last two critiques of the doctrine of natural rights raise a question
analogous to the age-old query that asks why what is good for the goose
is not also good for the gander. If Progressives assert that social thought
is limited or partial and designed to promote "class interests" (this is the
goose), then the same should apply to the Progressives (the gander). Yet
one looks almost in vain among Progressive thinkers for a frank discussion of the class basis of their own thought. Indeed, for the most part they
seem oblivious of the difficulty, criticizing without embarrassment the
mythical ideas of past thinkers while proclaiming the objectivity of their
own, and insisting on the class interests of previous philosophers while
assuming their own disinterestedness.

There is, thankfully, one explanation for this "oversight," which John
Dewey has offered. Progressives have a sound reason to be exempt from
treating themselves in the way they treat others. For the first time in
history, there is a movement in possession of what amounts to a truth.
This point, of course, must be formulated carefully, since past thinkers
regularly used terms like "truth," whereas the Progressives generally
eschewed language of this kind. But setting all linguistic quibbles aside,
the discovery of historical relativity itself is not something relative or
something that will pass with time; it is absolute and eternal. Possessed
of this new insight, the Progressives were in a privileged position and
were able to view things as no others had viewed them before. They were
able to free themselves from the partial and class interests of previous
philosophers and think in a different way. This same idea also allowed
certain Progressives to continue to embrace a view of progress, despite
the fact that the older philosophy of history might now might be seen as
merely the expression of thought of a certain period. The new basis of
progress was found precisely in the idea that we have freed ourselves
from the past and could now reconstruct society according to our own
making.

Whether or not one is inclined to accept Dewey's last argument, it is
perhaps still interesting to try to hold the Progressives to their own general standard. If they have a class interest, what is it? And how is it
revealed in their ideas? The Progressives, of course, claimed to be acting
on behalf of the many, not the few, and there is no reason not to take them

[43] Franklin Roosevelt, "Campaign Address on Progressive Government at the
Commonwealth Club in San Francisco, California" September 23, 1932 online at http://
www.heritage.org/about/mission/lfa/initiatives/first-principles/primary-sources/fdrs-
commonwealth-club-address.
[44] John Dewey, *Individualism Old and New* (New York: Capricorn Books, 1962; orig. 1929),
119.

at their word. They are self-described democrats, not aristocrats. But as democrats, they defined a special function in society for those who have developed "social intelligence," or for those who might be call experts; policy experts do not claim to rule outright, but to be privileged counselors of the many. Those in this position, along with those who educate and influence them, might be thought of as kind of group or class, having a class interest. Progressive ideas would seem best suited to promoting the interests of this class. This interest can only be realized, however, if the many are inclined to accept the special function of this group and to acknowledge the primacy of this kind of expert knowledge as the best title to rule. If people cling stubbornly to their beliefs, they cannot be helped. It is for this reason that the interests of Progressivism require a wholesale reeducation of society.

Fourth, Progressives criticize natural rights doctrine because of its standard of human nature, which is seen as too low and unseemly. Its individualism serves to reinforce man's sense of isolation, and its materialism to pull man down to a life of crude consumption. This argument is a restatement of the Romantic and Idealistic critiques of the nineteenth century, which had a powerful variant among conservatives, who lamented that natural rights individualism undermined virtue or nobility or deep faith, and a variant on the culture left, which charged that the old individualism stifled man's artistic and creative talents. The Progressives, especially Dewey and Herbert Croly (1869–1930), adopted the latter variant, giving it the name of "individuality" (or sometimes the "new individualism").

Although the description of individuality was often vague, sometimes painfully so, it offered an elevated ideal meant to transcend a preoccupation with the realm of the economic and the technical. Individuality presents a package that nicely combines cooperation, personal growth, and self-realization. According to Dewey, the old individualism with its emphasis on "private pecuniary profit" was "the chief obstacle to the creation of a type of individual whose pattern of thought and desire is enduringly marked by consensus with others, and in whom sociability is one with cooperation in all regular human associations."[45] The "genuine individual," according to Croly, is one "who possesses some special quality which distinguishes him from other people, which unifies the successive phases of his life and which results in personal moral freedom."[46] This higher standard is not to be judged by any kind of general standard. Individuality is above all, individual. Each me is distinct, growing and developing in its various encounters with the world. Nearly all of the analogies invoked to explain individuality are to art, the artist, and to life

---

[45] Dewey, *Individualism Old and New*, 44.
[46] Herbert Croly, *The Promise of American Life* (New Brunswick: Transaction Publishers, 1993; orig. 1909), 410.

as a series of artistic creations—except, that is, where communal participation is invoked, whereupon individuality becomes social.

Progressives are perhaps best known for their high praise of science and the scientific method and for their calls to expand the domain of scientific inquiry to the problems facing society. They are often praised (or blamed) for preparing the way for the rule, direct or indirect, of the technical expert. Yet science was not man's highest activity. Science is no more than the servant that helps bring into being the domain of individuality, which favors aesthetic sensibilities over more rationalist ones.[47] It has sometimes been asked, in the way of a witticism, whether it is possible to imagine the rather buttoned-up John Dewey at Woodstock, throbbing to the beat of rock music and the odor of cannabis. Although the parts of his thought may not cohere, there is little doubt that one strand of Progressive thought leads in this direction. At a minimum, it is fully consistent with the oft-quoted passage by Justice Anthony Kennedy that "At the heart of liberty is the right to define one's own concept of existence, of meaning, of the universe, and of the mystery of human life. . . . "[48]

Finally, John Dewey insisted that the concept of nature *in any form* was dangerous to democracy. Dewey had no trouble arguing this point in the case of the classical philosophers, whose view of nature he saw as upholding the interests of the few. But the argument is apt to sound strange in the case of modern natural rights, the core claim of which is that "all men are created equal." It is hard to think of an idea that is more democratic or that has had a more democratizing influence on the world. Dewey nevertheless argues that this position is undemocratic, and not just because of its supposed connection with property rights and their defense. It is undemocratic because any position that asserts the existence of nature claims "insight into supreme reality or ultimate truth [and] shows how thoroughly philosophy has been committed to a notion that inherently some realities are superior to others, are better than others. Now any such philosophy inevitably works on behalf of a regime of authority, for it is only right that the superior should lord it over the inferior."[49] Asserting a standard outside of our will or opinion, even if that standard is democratic, undermines full democracy.

Metaphysical positions are never politically neutral. If the character of a view of reality contains an idea of hierarchy, its effect will be to underwrite claims to hierarchy inside of the political world. To avoid this implication, the cosmos must be conceived in such a way that there can be no such principle. Only if the cosmos is understood such that everything in it is on the same plane of matter is democracy safe. Whether politics is

---

[47] In Dewey's words, "a new individualism can be achieved only through the controlled use of all of the resources of the science and technology that have mastered the physical forces of nature," *Individualism Old and New*, 93.

[48] *Planned Parenthood v. Casey*, 505 U.S. 833 (1992).

[49] Morris, *The Political Writings of John Dewey*, 45.

father to cosmology or cosmology is father to politics is never said, although Dewey was doubtless in accord with the prevailing scientific view of the world as matter in motion. It is clear, in any case, that the pure case for democracy entails a theological position. The Progressives' move toward secularism is not just an incidental preference, but a fundamental article of their political philosophy.

V. LIBERALISM AND FOUNDATIONS

When it comes to the question of foundations, liberalism is under challenge today from the outside and is troubled and conflicted from the inside. The challenge from the outside has come in the form of a revival within political philosophy of the idea of nature and thus of the possibility of natural right. Progressives and liberals were convinced that thought of this kind was dying, needing at most the slightest of intellectual "nudges" to put it into its grave. The unexpected return of thinking in terms of natural right, especially in America, has discomfited liberals and forced them to share power, both political and intellectual, with forces they never imagined would still retain vitality and legitimacy.

From the inside, meanwhile, all of the foundations that Progressives proposed have been found to have no defensible theoretical basis, even by liberals' own standards. Philosophy no longer credits the reality of the idea of Progress; and however much liberals today echo the sentiments of progress under such substitute terms as "change" and "development," they do not—they cannot—ascribe to it the status of a genuine foundation, for this would entail a concept of nature. What applies to philosophy of history applies also to Darwinism. While there are a few on the Left who would reintroduce the neo-Darwinian science as a new political foundation, most have recoiled from this idea with horror. What remains, and what some liberals occasionally claim, is the doctrine of political non-foundationalism (or "anti-essentialism"). This doctrine holds that democratic societies both do not need and function best when there is no political discussion of first principles or "metaphysical" or theological truths. There must be a wall of separation between politics and these realms of thought. And yet, liberal leaders have found that they cannot adhere to this doctrine consistently or even defend it publicly. The requirements of politics, at least the politics of a great power, demand every so often that a first principle be asserted. Liberals may cringe at the mention of natural rights, but they do not hesitate, when the situation demands, to invoke "universal values." These values have no explicit foundation, but represent whatever is taken now to be the enlightened position of a self-proclaimed democratic and humanitarian elite. Where these values come from and what they may be tomorrow, no one can say. It is a philosophical case of the policy of don't ask, don't tell.

Politics, University of Virginia

SOME SECOND THOUGHTS ON PROGRESSIVISM AND RIGHTS

By Eldon J. Eisenach

Twenty years ago I wrote my first paper on the Progressives, in which I argued that the Progressives did not take rights seriously.[1] Most of my research and writing on the Progressives since then has extended and deepened that initial argument. In this essay, I want to summarize the main reasons why I held that position and to introduce some second thoughts on those reasons. I conclude with some reflections on contemporary American discourse on constitutionalism and rights.

I. First Thoughts

The overriding reason that Progressives were so often dismissive of rights claims and arguments is that they wanted to create a *national* democracy and they saw a rigid adherence to the prevailing norms of the U.S. Constitution standing in the way. Political philosopher Herbert Croly (1869-1930) was the most forceful advocate of this tension and what might follow from it.

> Public opinion can no longer be hypnotized and scared into accepting the traditional constitutionalism, as the final word in politics. . . .
> The Law in the shape of the Federal Constitution really came to be a monarchy of the Word. . . . The Constitution was really king. Once the kingdom of the Word had been ordained, it was almost as seditious to question the Word as it was to plot against the kingdom. A monarch exists to be obeyed. In the United States, as in other monarchies, unquestioning obedience was erected into the highest of political virtues.[2]

Croly admits that, like European monarchy, American constitutionalism initially served educative political purposes. "The monarchy of the Constitution satisfied the current needs and the contemporary conscience of the American nation. . . . It instructed the American people during their collective childhood. It trained them during their collective youth. With

---

[1] Eldon J. Eisenach, "Why the Progressives Didn't Take Rights Seriously," Unpublished paper, Conference for the Study of Political Thought, Yale University, 1991.
[2] Herbert Croly, *Progressive Democracy* (New York: Macmillan, 1914), 25-26, 44, 131.

doi:10.1017/S0265052511000240

its assistance the American people have become a nation."[3] This age has now passed. Democracy and the monarchy of the Constitution are now in conflict, and the monarchy must give way.

> The ideal of individual justice is being supplemented by the ideal of social justice. . . . Now the tendency is to conceive the social welfare, not as an end which cannot be left to the happy harmonizing of individual interests, but as an end which must be consciously willed by society and efficiently realized. Society, that is, has become a moral ideal, not independent of the individual but supplementary to him, an ideal which must be pursued less by regulating individual excesses than by the active conscious encouragement of socializing tendencies and purposes.[4]

Standing behind this anti-constitutionalist argument was the growing prestige of the social sciences, especially sociology and political economy, shaped by American academics who studied in Germany after the Civil War.[5] These academics came to dominate the political and moral spirits of the rapidly growing research universities. And, as sons and daughters of evangelical Protestant republicans, they also helped inform a Social Gospel Christianity that was, like the social sciences, embedded in an evolutionary and historicist worldview. It was this heady mixture that came to dominate not only American universities and churches, but also "public intellectuals" in higher journalism, charity and charitable foundations, the Women's Movement, and the professions. Governmental bureaucracies and regulatory bodies, created and expanded by Progressive political reforms, later gave these values some measure of permanent coercive public power.

---

[3] Ibid., 145–46.

[4] Ibid., 148–49. Charles Beard's textbook that dominated collegiate instruction in American politics from its inception in 1910 through the 1930s made this same historical argument in the 1928 edition: "No longer do statesmen spend weary days over finely spun theories about strict and liberal interpretations of the Constitution, about the sovereignty and reserved rights of states. . . . It is true that there are still debates on such themes as federal encroachments on local liberties, and that admonitory volumes on 'federal' usurpation come from the press. It is true also that conservative judges, dismayed at the radical policies reflected in new statutes, federal and state, sometimes set them aside in the name of strict interpretation. But one has only to compare the social and economic legislation of the last decade with that of the closing years of the nineteenth century, for instance, to understand how deep is the change in the minds of those who have occasion to examine and interpret the Constitution bequeathed to them by the Fathers. Imagine Jefferson . . . reading Roosevelt's autobiography affirming the doctrine that the President of the United States can do anything for the welfare of the people which is not forbidden by the Constitution! Imagine Chief Justice Taney . . . called upon to uphold a state law fixing the hours of all factory labor. . . . Imagine James Monroe . . . called upon to sign bills appropriating federal money for roads, education, public health . . . and other social purposes! . . . Why multiply examples?" Charles Beard, *American Government and Politics* (New York: Macmillan, 1928), 100–101.

[5] Eldon J. Eisenach, *The Lost Promise of Progressivism* (Lawrence, KS: The University Press of Kansas, 1994), chaps. 1–3.

The leading ideas and political values behind Croly's argument about the conflict between democracy and constitutionalism are easily summarized. The new industrial economy of the United States and the leading countries of Europe has socialized and made interdependent most human activities; our individual fates are increasingly bound up with the actions of countless unseen others leading to consequences we experience but do not understand. Indeed, everyday activities, economic, social, and political, are increasingly undertaken within complex organizations, often national in scope, and whose leadership is often distant, autonomous, and self-perpetuating.

In Croly's analysis, we are under the control of "bosses" in industry, finance, labor, and politics. The clashes of interest, always a part of politics, now take place between these organizations on a national stage. In this hierarchical organizational environment, effective political and moral agency requires the construction of new national associations in order for the average person to be seen and heard. In the words of the Progressive Party Platform of 1912:

> Political parties exist to secure responsible government and to execute the will of the people.
>
> From these great tasks both of the old parties have turned aside. Instead of instruments to promote the general welfare, they have become the tools of corrupt interests which use them partially to serve their selfish purposes. Behind the ostensible government sits enthroned an invisible government owing no allegiance and acknowledging no responsibility to the people.
>
> To destroy this invisible government, to dissolve the unholy alliance between corrupt business and corrupt politics is the first task of the statesmanship of the day. . . .
>
> Unhampered by tradition, uncorrupted by power, undismayed by the magnitude of the task, the new party offers self as the instrument of the people to sweep away old abuses, to build a new and nobler commonwealth.[6]

While the Progressive Party did not achieve electoral victory, two decades of earlier activities by reform organizations and social movements had already forced the two major parties both to confront the issues it raised and to adopt many of its reform ideas. By 1912, Progressive insights and ideas (with the exception of the South) permeated national political culture.[7]

---

[6] Quoted from Eldon J. Eisenach, ed., *The Social and Political Thought of American Progressivism* (Indianapolis: Hackett, 2006), 274.

[7] Benjamin Parke De Witt, *The Progressive Movement* (New York: Macmillan, 1915); Walter Weyl, *The New Democracy* (New York, Macmillan, 1912); Walter Lippmann, *Drift and Mastery: An Attempt to Diagnose our Current Unrest* [1914] (Englewood Cliffs, NJ: Prentice-Hall, 1961); and Croly, *Progressive Democracy*, all assume this ideological victory.

Institutionally, the clearest way to express this transformation is to say that, at the turn of the last century, the American national regime of "courts and parties" was increasingly discredited and partially replaced by a new regime dominated by national interest groups, political executives, and an administrative apparatus.[8] Each in their own ways, courts and parties reinforced constitutional norms and constitutional ways of thinking. Courts and the common law removed many economic issues from state and national legislative purview; locality- and state-dominated parties and patronage systems reinforced states rights and local jurisdictions, preventing national reforms. The perverse result was that parties prevented national reforms for the public welfare while courts gutted state exercise of traditional "police powers" to address new economic conditions. This post-Civil War pincer movement of party machines and newly assertive courts left our effective governing ideas *more* liberal and laissez faire than before the war. The national government of the nineteenth century, except for the momentous exception of the Civil War, largely acted "out of sight"[9] and was, by default, limited and "liberal" because it so rarely interfered with or coerced, individuals. State governments, however, which had always governed individual lives thickly and intrusively,[10] were now forbidden to act to protect the general welfare through regulation of the new industrial economy. And, even if states were permitted to act, their jurisdictional reach and limited viewpoint often made such regulation counterproductive and even parasitic.

The Progressive response was to attack both courts and parties through appeals to "direct democracy." As an ideal and in its earliest manifestations, its first object of attack was political party machinery and practices. Mandated primary elections, legislative initiative and referenda, recall of elected officials, civil service rules, and regulation of campaign contributions, all hit party organization where it lived, in its domination over elections from the precinct upwards. Another measure, direct election of U.S. senators, attacked party dictation of the composition of the upper house that had so much power in foreign policy and in presidential executive and judicial appointments. Women's suffrage was also part of antiparty politics because women symbolized consensual, disinterested, and community caring values.

Hostility to political parties was part of a much larger critique of prevailing politics. Opposition to party became opposition to constitutional understandings of representative government that the party system so

---

[8] Stephen Skowronek, *Building a New American State: The Expansion of National Administrative Capacities, 1877–1920* (New York: Cambridge University Press, 1982).

[9] Brian Balogh, *A Government Out of Sight: The Mystery of National Authority in Nineteenth-Century America* (New York: Cambridge University Press, 2009); William J. Novak, "The Myth of the 'Weak' American State" *American Historical Review* 113 (2008): 752–72.

[10] William J. Novak, *The People's Welfare: Law and Regulation and Nineteenth Century America* (Chapel Hill: University of North Carolina Press, 1996).

strongly reinforced. The more populist elements in Progressivism supported not only the recall of state judges but the overturning, by legislative initiative and popular referenda, of state court decisions regarding social provision and industrial regulation. While Theodore Roosevelt (1858–1919) was a late convert to many of these ideas and proposals, direct democracy and the centrality of executive leadership became the leitmotif of the campaign. And such was the enthusiasm generated by these ideas, that the 1912 campaign launched a serious national debate about the Constitution, the modern presidency, centralized administration, and the role of political parties in elections and governance.[11]

Ideas of direct democracy have deep cultural and religious roots in America, making the Progressive Party something of a religious crusade.[12] An obvious source is the antinomian and millenarian strains in reformed Protestantism—from John Winthrop's (1587/8–1649) contrast of "mere justice" with the higher "law of the gospel" enforced by ties of brotherhood and love, and William Penn's (1644–1718) dismissal of governmental forms in his 1682 Pennsylvania "Frame of Government"—to prominent Social Gospel preachers such as Samuel Batten (1859–1925) and George Herron (1862–1925). Batten held that party organizations and court legalisms were barriers to righteousness because they encouraged selfishness and social division. The political party "stands between the people and the government and makes a fully democratic government impossible. . . . A good partisan cannot be a good citizen."[13] George Herron added that, until political life is emancipated "from merely individual theories of freedom, it cannot see the divine social kingdom."[14]

The link between partisanship, individualism, and selfishness received philosophical expression as well. In his college text book, *Ethics*, John Dewey (1859–1952) first outlined the requisites for responsible citizenship and then excoriated "the 'machines' of political parties, with their hierarchical gradation of bosses from national to ward rulers, bosses who are in close touch with great business interests at one extreme and with those who pander to the vices of the community . . . at the other."[15] In an 1888 essay, Dewey condemned a theory of democracy premised on isolated individuals and aggregate majorities:

> To define democracy simply as . . . sovereignty chopped up into mince meat, is to define it as an abrogation of society. . . . When so

[11] Sidney M. Milkis, *Theodore Roosevelt, the Progressive Party, and the Transformation of American Politics* (Lawrence, KS: University Press of Kansas, 2009).

[12] Robert M. Crunden, *Ministers of Reform: The Progressives' Achievement in American Civilization 1889–1920* (Urbana: University of Illinois Press, 1984), chap. 7.

[13] Samuel Zane Batten, *The Christian State: The State, Democracy and Christianity* (Philadelphia: Griffith and Rowland Press, 1909), 239–40.

[14] George Herron, *The Christian Society* (Chicago: Fleming H. Revell, 1894), 110.

[15] John Dewey and James Tufts, *Ethics* (New York: Henry Holt, 1908), 478.

defined, it may be easily shown to be instable to the last degree, and so difficult that a common will must be manufactured—if not by means of a contract, then by means of a combined action of the firm of Party and Corruption.[16]

The new social sciences gave these arguments scientific standing. Sociologist Charles Horton Cooly (1864–1929) condemned American constitutional and legal formalism as the primary source of our moral and political failings:

> Formalism goes very naturally with sensuality, avarice, [and] selfish ambition . . . because the merely formal institution does not enlist and discipline the soul of the individual, but takes hold of him by the outside. . . . In so far as it is true of our time that the larger interests of society are not impressed upon the individual, so that his private impulses cooperate with the public good, it is a time of moral disintegration.[17]

Cooley's social psychology was seconded by sociologists and political economists. All condemned merely individualistic and negative liberties and saw both legalism and partisanship as the cause of moral and political vices.[18] Social justice required a higher citizenship and higher citizenship required the destruction of party machinery and the weakening of the domination of our political life by lawyers and courts. In their stead, a morally uplifting "public opinion" would be able to emerge, calling citizens to opt for a non-aggregative and substantive national good.

This call was clearly heard with the incredibly rapid formation of the Progressive Party. Starting from a breakaway faction of the Republican Party, within less than a year it recruited candidates for many major state and federal offices and mounted a national campaign that outpolled the Republican Party. This was possible because a large complex of institutions and associations (earlier termed "the benevolent empire") *already existed* within which this type of citizenship was honored. Of particular importance were the magazines *Outlook* (Theodore Roosevelt served on its editorial board) and *Independent*, both of which began as liberal evangelical Protestant church publications. Similarly, *Survey*, the publication of

---

[16] John Dewey, "The Ethics of Democracy" (1888), *The Early Works, 1882–1898*, vol. 1 (Carbondale, IL: Southern Illinois University Press, 1969), 231.

[17] Charles Cooley, *Social Organization: A Study of the Larger Mind* (New York: Scribner, 1909), 349 and 351.

[18] See discussions of Albion Small and Simon Patten in Eldon J. Eisenach, "Progressivism as a National Narrative in Biblical-Hegelian Time," in Ellen Frankel Paul, Fred D. Miller, Jr., and Jeffrey Paul, eds. *Liberalism: Old and New* (New York: Cambridge University Press, 2007), 55–83.

the National Conference of Charities and Correction, an umbrella organization for settlement houses and social workers, was a major source of
Progressive Party mobilization.[19]

Public opinion—what Tocqueville had termed "the principle of the
sovereignty of the people"[20]—not parties and elections, not courts and
constitutions, was to be the primary source of legitimate political authority. Led by moral, intellectual, and professional vanguards, public opinion, unlike elections and law, is able to penetrate not only all major social
institutions, imbuing them with a common will, but to structure the very
identities and self-understandings of democratic citizens. In Dewey's
words,

> Society and the individual are really organic to each other . . . the
> individual is society concentrated. . . . The organism must have its
> spiritual organs; having a common will, it must express it. . . . In
> democracy . . . the governors and the governed are not two classes,
> but two aspects of the same fact—the fact of the possession by society
> of a unified and articulate will. It means that government is the organ
> of society, and *is as comprehensive as society.*[21]

Thirty years later, what was implicit in Dewey was made explicit by
Mary Follett (1868–1933) in *The New State:*

> The old idea of natural rights postulated the particularist individual;
> we know now that no such person exists. . . . As an understanding of
> the group process abolishes "individual rights," so it gives us a true
> definition of liberty. . . . We see that to obey the group which we have
> helped to make and of which we are an integral part is to be free
> because we are then obeying ourself. Ideally the state is such a group,
> actually it is not, but it depends upon us to make it more and more
> so. The state must be no external authority which restrains and reg-
> ulates me, *but it must be myself acting as the state in every smallest detail
> of life.*[22]

Supported by the matrix of institutions and associations carrying these
messages, the Progressive Party was to be the party to end parties, the

---

[19] Milkis, *Theodore Roosevelt, the Progressive Party, and the Transformation of American Politics;* Eisenach, *The Lost Promise of Progressivism,* 11–16. Simon Patten, a political economist at
the Wharton school, coined the term "social work" to mark out one of the central tasks of
modern government and administration. See Simon Patten, *The New Basis of Civilization*
(New York: Macmillan, 1907), 201–220.

[20] Alexis de Tocqueville, *Democracy in America,* trans. Harvey C. Mansfield and Delba
Winthrop (Chicago: University of Chicago Press, 2000), I, I, 4, p. 53.

[21] Dewey, "The Ethics of Democracy, 237–39, *passim.* Emphasis added.

[22] Mary Parker Follett, *The New American State: Group Organization in the Solution of Popular
Government* (New York: Longmans, Green, 1918), 137–38. Emphasis added.

expression of enlightened public opinion expressed through mechanisms of direct democracy. Although the Progressive Party failed in the election of 1912, Progressive ideas triumphed in the larger culture of national organizations and institutions, in higher education and mainstream Protestant churches, in higher journalism and philanthropy—soon to be joined by management of large publicly held national business corporations, in money-center financial institutions, and in labor unions. Thanks to President Wilson's post-election shift to moderately Progressive reforms, parts of the national bureaucracy and most of the regulatory apparatus institutionalized some Progressive values as well.

Here one might draw what seem to be unproblematic conclusions about Progressivism and rights. Thanks to German historicism/romanticism, liberal Christian theology, and theories of Progressive social and moral evolution encoded in the new social sciences, the era of big government dawned while the space of individual liberty fell into the shadows. The rule of law and the supremacy of legislatures were increasingly replaced by bureaucratic administrators writing the actual rules that govern us under cover of legislative delegation. The engine of big government was executive power and rule by experts responsive to an elite "consensus" embodied in themselves and in those who dominate large and powerful national institutions which, in turn, were recipients of governmental resources and prestige. Enlightenment ideals of natural rights and individual liberty were replaced by theories of social progress and social justice defined as the redistribution of material resources and security against joblessness, disease, and hunger. In the meantime, the "living" Constitution, rewritten by the victory of progressive ideals, became a flexible source of legitimacy for every act of an ever-expanding government.

II. Second Thoughts

These conclusions, if not commonplace, are prominent among today's conservative intellectuals and constitute the core narrative that helped power the rise of conservatism in American political life since the 1980s. Moreover, as if to confirm this narrative, as "liberal" became an increasingly discredited term, the political left in America reappropriated the earlier term "Progressive." This story, however, contains two flaws. First (and both left and right seem to accept this), it assumes an almost seamless transition from "progressivism" to "liberalism," both historically and ideologically.[23] Second, the proof of this transition is the claim that Progressives (1890s–1920s) and liberals (1930s–1980s) were equally advocates of "big government" both in terms of increasing governmental regulation and in an ever-larger appropriation of national wealth.

[23] See, for example, Edward A. Stettner, *Shaping Modern Liberalism: Herbert Croly and Progressive Thought* (Lawrence, KS: University Press of Kansas, 1993).

I want to challenge that argument on a series of fronts. The first begins with the Progressives' understanding of the distinction between a "government" and a "state." Although these terms are often used interchangeably (Americans, it seems, are incapable of grasping European "state theory"), Progressive academics and intellectuals had a much clearer (if not always clearly expressed) understanding of the difference. This is entirely understandable in the political context that they confronted. Given the almost mindless and party-driven *expansion* of municipal, state, and national governments in the Gilded Age (federal revenues increased 400 percent between 1878 and 1908; Civil War pensions came to absorb over 40 percent of the national budget),[24] the earliest critics, in both academia and in the new nonpartisan press, equated this rapid governmental expansion with dominance of government by party machines. Parties lived by buying voters through jobs, favors, franchises, subsidies, tariff protections, and pensions. Thus, aside from corruption, one of the strongest condemnations of party government was its gross inefficiencies and waste. It was difficult for Progressives (and earlier Mugwumps) to see *any* relationship between this governmental expansion and the larger public interest, between "big government" and "strong state." Their response was to locate ideas of public interest, common good, and virtuous citizenship within an enlarged conception of the state.

One way to sort out this government/state distinction is to reflect on the difference between the formal institutions of governments in America at all levels—their respective constitutional powers, resources, and policies—and the authority of the American "state" conceived as the combination of *all effectively governing institutions*—whether nominally "public" or "private"—that pursue common ends and purposes.[25] In this view, one can see that at some periods of American history we have had ostensibly small and presumptively weak "governments" but an authoritative and powerful "state." At other times our national government has been big and intrusive but unable to generate enough authority from the "state" to address commonly recognized problems and concerns. Gilded Age politics (1876–1896) is the outstanding example of the latter.[26] An obvious example of the former is the Northwest Ordinance of 1787, passed under the Articles of Confederation, that forbade slavery in the federally administered territories. Under one of

---

[24] For examples, see Eisenach, *Lost Promise of Progressivism*, 150–56.

[25] Karen Orren and Stephen Skowronek, *The Search for American Political Development* (New York: Cambridge University Press, 2004), 22–24, use the term "plenary authority" to argue that all sites of political change already possess such generalized authority, whatever its source. This is to counter the common misperception that the growth of government is the same as an increase in authority. Thus, "America in the nineteenth century was no less fully governed than America in the twentieth; more of some forms of authority indicates less of others" (23).

[26] Morton Keller, *Affairs of State: Public Life in Late Nineteenth Century America* (Cambridge: Harvard University Press, 1977).

the constitutionally weakest forms of national government imaginable, a whole sector of the continent was declared free of slavery. In the 1850s, under the aegis of the much more robust United States Constitution, the power to forbid slavery in the territories was so seriously contested that secession and civil war followed.

Thus, combinations of "big government/weak state" and "small government/strong state" require modes of explanation that lie quite outside political theory expressed as constitutional law and powers, bills of rights, and the whole universe of language embedded in individual rights and formal governing powers. Cryptically put, "not all political institutions are governmental," and yet they exercise governing power.[27] The rise of election-based, mass political parties in the 1830s is the most prominent example of a governing institution that was not governmental. The term "party government" did not mean government *of* party but government *by* party. A new vocabulary of governance was created and institutionalized with the rise of party, a vocabulary far removed from constitutional and other "theory" discourse. Its governing ideas and mobilizing ideologies crossed not only political jurisdictions decreed by constitutional federalism, but across the divide between public institutions and private associations and institutions, whether economic, religious, racial, or cultural. Partisan identity, like religious identity, was passed through the family over many generations. In short, parties became part of the effective, authoritative "state" without which no formal political institutions could have governed democratically. Part of the Progressive reform project was to displace party as a powerful part of the *state;* clearly they did not want to simply replace it with an ever-larger set of *governments.* Cryptically put, they did not want to weaken parties to strengthen or enlarge *governments,* but to strengthen the *state* grounded in popular sovereignty. In short, they wanted to reinstate an understanding of democracy first articulated by Alexis de Tocqueville (1805–1859):

> There are countries where a power in a way external to the social body acts on it and forces it to march on a certain track.
> There are others where force is divided, placed at once in society and outside it. Nothing like this is seen in the United States; there society acts *by itself and on itself.* Power exists only within its bosom; almost no one is encountered who dares to conceive and above all to express the idea of seeking it elsewhere. . . . [O]ne can say that they govern themselves, so weak and restricted is the part left to the administration, so much does the latter feel its popular origin and obey the power from which it emanates. The people reign over the American political world as God over the universe. They are the

[27] Orren and Skowronek, *Search for American Political Development,* 84.

cause and the end of things; everything comes out of them and every thing is absorbed into them.[28]

Thus, when Dewey held that "government" and society are coterminous, and Mary Follett maintained that one must act "as the state" in every aspect of life, neither were advocating that external and formal laws backed by public coercion regulate all social and personal actions. Indeed, they usually meant the exact opposite—they wanted public-regarding democratic values to inform the family, the neighborhood, schooling, social and business relationships, and, finally, politics. Democratic citizenship and a free society require no less. For them, democracy was a way of life, not a set of public institutions and procedures.

If the "state" lost its common grounding, becoming a scene of warring wills—if, in Dewey's terms, "the public" became eclipsed by powerful self-regarding institutions—then the state must be restored. And if the state thus conceived was not powerful enough to direct all of its various "governments/administrations," good citizens must try to achieve democratic purposes in what governments they can, as well as in other institutions and groups: in school boards, universities, charitable societies, churches, and families. This is what Jane Addams (1860–1935) meant when she called her (private, voluntary) settlement house, "an experiment in social democracy." In a 1901 lecture at Berkeley, Arthur Hadley (1856–1930), a political economist and President of Yale University, equated authentic public opinion with popular sovereignty and the state. Like Jean-Jacques Rousseau's concept of the general will (but keeping all representative institutions), public opinion constitutes individuals into one sovereign people,

> represented by a common public sentiment which includes all good men, minorities as well as majorities, who support the government not as a selfish means for promotion of their own interest, but as a common heritage which they accept as loyal members of a body politic, in a spirit which makes them ready to bear its burdens as well as to enjoy its benefits.[29]

---

[28] Tocqueville, *Democracy in America*, I, I, 4, p. 55. Emphasis added. And see Dana Villa, *Public Freedom* (Princeton: Princeton University Press, 2008), chap. 2, on Tocqueville's "decentered public sphere" in his conception of civil society. Like the argument here regarding the Progressives, Villa holds that, while Tocqueville (like Hegel), "saw individualism (or 'atomism') as premised on a faulty idea of freedom as independence . . . [they both] upheld individual rights as the basis of a distinctively 'modern' form of liberty. . . . [E]ach saw the right of 'subjective' freedom as central to . . . the 'rational' state and any morally defensible democracy" (50–51).

[29] Arthur Twining Hadley, *The Relations between Freedom and Responsibility in the Evolution of Democratic Government* (New Haven: Yale University Press, 1903), 139–40.

The re-founding of America by President Abraham Lincoln (1809–1865) and the Civil War was, for the Progressives, just such a reinstatement of popular sovereignty as the democratic "state." The northern victory, however, was not the product of "big government" (though the national government grew beyond all previous bounds) but of a new political party that *became, for a time, the "state"*—the people/nation—noncoercively embracing women and children, churches, schools, and social clubs, and generating new associations and new organs of public opinion. Only this reassertion of "the principle of the sovereignty of the people" made possible the abolition of slavery and the victory of democracy. Lincoln and the Republican party-as-state were, for the Progressives, the symbol of their hopes for the restoration of democracy and the renewal of the national covenant made in the Declaration of Independence.[30]

The events preceding American entry into the Great War in Europe presented just such an opportunity for a renaissance of popular will. When, in 1916–1917, calls for national "preparedness" were heard, the voices almost uniformly came from Progressives who heard the distinct echoes of their abolitionist forbearers. Much of this preparedness and political mobilization took place independently of the bureaucratic instruments of the national government, ranging from the draft (fewer than one thousand federal officials) to war finance (Liberty Bond sales), to food supply and rationing. This explosion of hypervoluntarism, this sudden "state" expansion, exceeded the Progressives' highest expectations.[31]

Once war was declared, however, it rapidly spilled over into forms of social coercion and popular vigilantism that frightened many Progressives and cast doubt on their democratic hopes. As these passions became expressed in official governmental repression and censorship, these same Progressives stood at the forefront in defense of individual rights. Progressive academics were the founding members in 1915 of the American Association of University Professors (AAUP) that quickly established a committee on academic freedom. Once the war had ended and Wilson-Palmer launched the "red scare," Progressives were prominent in the founding in 1920 of the American Civil Liberties Union (ACLU), just as, eleven years earlier in 1909, Progressive leaders were prominent founders of the National Association for the Advancement of Colored People (NAACP) in response to the lynching of Negroes. In short, despite their disparagement of "rights" talk and constitutionalist language in the areas

---

[30] For examples, see Eisenach, ed., *The Social and Political Thought of American Progressivism*, chap. 1.

[31] See John E. McClymer, *War and Welfare: Social Engineering in America, 1890–1925* (Westport, CT: Greenwood Press, 1980); Ronald Schaffer, *America in the Great War: The Rise of the War Welfare State* (New York: Oxford University Press, 1991); Stephen Vaughn, *Holding Fast the Inner Lines: Democracy, Nationalism, and the Committee on Public Information* (Chapel Hill: University of North Carolina Press, 1980); Neil A. Wynn, *From Progressivism to Prosperity: World War I and American Society* (New York: Holmes & Meier, 1986).

of economic regulation and social welfare, free speech and civil liberties were assumed to be prerequisites for the formation of democratic public opinion. In one of the first American textbooks in sociology, Franklin Giddings (1855–1931) maintained that, in a democratic society, public opinion (he termed it "the social mind") "can exist only where men are in continual communication, and where they are free to express their real minds, without fear or constraint."[32]

American legal culture was changed as well. While it is correct to be reminded that it was Progressive intellectuals and reformers who undermined prevailing legal and constitutional principles in the name of "sociological jurisprudence" we must also remember that, in the larger legal and judicial community, first amendment jurisprudence hardly existed. Wilson's Espionage (1917) and Sedition (1918) Acts were barely challenged in law schools, the upper bar, and the courts, while states either mandated or permitted egregious violations of political speech. Thus, far from *undermining* a previously strong commitment to First Amendment freedoms, Progressive law professors and judges often led the way in its twentieth-century development.[33] Moreover, as Roscoe Pound (1870–1964) noted in his earliest articles,[34] state governments had, from the 1880s onward, increasingly created administrative bodies that robbed both courts and the rule of law of their authority. Pound, Dean of Harvard Law School (1916–1936) and father of sociological jurisprudence, argued from the start that federal and state courts must *regain* their authority against administrative and "expert" rule that rested on ad hoc decisions. Pound had always been an opponent of administrative discretion (he called it "justice without law"), even as he admitted that when courts failed to rule in accordance with prevailing moral ideals—he cites the prerogative origins of equity law in England—legislators and executives will necessarily undermine judicial authority and, thus, the protections of liberty. He began his 1907 critique of "executive justice" by quoting Montesquieu (1689–1755) from *Federalist No. 78* on separation of powers. Contrary to the New Dealers vilification of Pound as a late apostate to Progressive principles, Pound's opposition to New Deal delegation of power to administrative rule was there from the start. In short, he was sacrificed on the myth that New Deal measures fulfilled Progressive intellectual and philosophical values, a necessary myth, perhaps, given the paucity of articulate intellectual/ideological foundations for New Deal reforms. This myth still prevails.

[32] Franklin H. Giddings, *Elements of Sociology* (New York: Macmillan, 1898), 156–57, and see 324–29 on equality and rights.

[33] David M. Rabban, *Free Speech in its Forgotten Years* (New York: Cambridge University Press, 1997), chaps. 6–7; on Dewey's changing position on civil liberties, see 335–41.

[34] Roscoe Pound, "Executive Justice," *American Law Register* 46 (1907): 137–46; *The Organization of the Courts* (Philadelphia: The Law Association of Philadelphia, 1913).

The second part of my second thoughts on Progressives and rights is related to the first, the charge that Progressives were centralizing "statists." As argued above, to equate "big government" with "statism," only makes sense if one rejects the Progressive understanding of "state," in the same way that one might [mistakenly] equate "nationalism" with "nationalization," and equate both with the appropriation of social and economic institutions by the central government.[35] While the acceptance of this Progressive understanding does not necessarily exonerate them from undermining principles of constitutionalism encoding ideals of federalism and limited government, there are many other indices of Progressive fears of large, centralized government. While they supported national laws of incorporation and regulation of large economic organizations (trusts, money center banks, national labor unions), they clearly differentiated themselves from the ideology of state socialism. One indirect indicator is their international associations and colleagues. In Europe generally, their primary affinities were with moderate social democrats,[36] those who later led the fight against the rise of fascism and revolutionary socialism/ syndicalism. In England, they tended to have stronger and more enduring relationships with "pluralists" who distrusted central planning and "statism" than with Fabian Socialists who trusted such reforms.[37]

But here, another form of "statism" is charged against the Progressives: that of a statist form of "corporatism," especially as it was first expressed in Mussolini's Italy.[38] While most Progressive political economists were favorably disposed toward American forms of "welfare capitalism" that developed in America in the 1920s, so was Herbert Hoover (1874–1964), one of its main proponents when he was Secretary of Commerce.[39] And, like English pluralists, they certainly favored privately held but nationally regulated corporations to state ownership. Indeed, when Woodrow Wilson, by decree, created the War Industries Board, a politically-coordinated triumvirate of business, labor, and finance for industrial war planning, Progressives assumed it was a temporary

[35] Thus, the Whig statement of principles reads: "We wish, fully and entirely, TO NATIONALIZE THE INSTITUTIONS OF OUR LAND AND TO IDENTIFY OURSELVES WITH OUR COUNTRY; to become a single great people, separate and distinct in national character, political interest, social and civil affinities from any and all other nations, kindred and people on earth" (*American Republican*, 7 November, 1844).

[36] James T. Kloppenberg, *Uncertain Victory: Social Democracy and Progressivism in European and American Thought* (New York: Oxford University Press, 1986).

[37] Marc Stears, *Progressives, Pluralists, and the Problems of the State: Ideologies of Reform in the United States and Britain, 1896–1926* (New York: Oxford University Press, 2004).

[38] John Diggins, *Mussolini and Fascism: the View from America* (Princeton: Princeton University Press, 1972); Jonah Goldberg, *Liberal Fascism: The Secret History of the American Left from Mussolini to the Politics of Meaning* (New York: Doubleday, 2008).

[39] Stuart D. Brandes, *American Welfare Capitalism, 1880–1940* (Chicago: University of Chicago Press, 1976); Alfred Chandler, *Scale and Scope: The Dynamics of Industrial Capitalism* (Cambridge: Harvard University Press, 1990); Olivier Zunz, *Making America Corporate, 1870–1920* (Chicago: University of Chicago Press, 1990).

war measure not unlike the federal takeover of the railroads. The dominant model that many Progressives helped to create and sustain was the National Civic Federation, a voluntary body of labor, business, and public (but not governmental) representatives to inform and mediate industrial conflicts and to propose moderate sets of regulatory reform. This American form of "corporatism"[40] was far removed from both European syndicalism and corporatist fascism. For Progressive political and social economists of the period, large national institutions must be held to the same high standards of citizenship as demanded of individual citizens: "private business is a public trust" whether it is in the form of simple property and small business ownership or large labor unions and semi-public corporations.[41]

While these ideological commitments do not settle the issue of Progressive adherence to "liberal statism," other contextual evidence tends to support the second thoughts voiced here. Foremost is a book, published in 1928, that has recently received renewed attention: *The Pragmatic Revolt in Politics; Syndicalism, Fascism, and the Constitutional State.* Written by William Yandell Elliott (1896–1979), a political theorist at Harvard, it meticulously explores the philosophical and intellectual sources of the attacks on the liberal-constitutional state by communist syndicalism and corporatist fascism. Aside from fairly extensive discussion of William James (a favorite of Mussolini but a minor influence on Progressivism and the Social Gospel) and John Dewey, Elliott leaves the entire moral, religious, and social scientific edifice of American Progressivism untouched.

And well he might. American political understanding is thoroughly grounded in *popular* sovereignty. Elliott's commitment to national constitutional sovereignty as the guarantor of rights puts him at one remove from that understanding, closer perhaps to Alexander Hamilton (1755/57–1804), or Francis Lieber (1798 or 1800–1872), or Samuel Huntington (1927–2008).[42] When Jefferson said that our "republicanism"—our commitment to liberty—is "not in our Constitution certainly, but merely in the spirit of our people,"[43] he voiced a principle of American political identity that

[40] R. Jeffrey Lustig, *Corporate Liberalism: the Origins of Modern American Political Theory* (Berkeley: University of California Press, 1982); James Weinstein, *The Corporate Ideal in the Liberal State: 1900–1918* (Boston: Beacon Press, 1968).

[41] For early expressions of these values, see Albion Small, "The State and Semi-Public Corporations," *American Journal of Sociology* 1 (1895): 398–410 and "Private Business Is a Public Trust," *American Journal of Sociology* 1 (1895): 276–89; and Henry Carter Adams, *Relation of the State to Industrial Action and Economics and Jurisprudence* [1887], ed. Joseph Dorfman (New York: Columbia University Press, 1954).

[42] Samuel Huntington, *American Politics: The Promise of Disharmony* (Cambridge: Harvard University Press, 1981). Also at Harvard, Huntington (1927–2008) warned of populist "creedal passions" grounded in democratic ideals that periodically sweep across American politics and threaten national constitutional sovereignty and the rule of law. Both Elliott and Huntington were active in shaping national security policy.

[43] Thomas Jefferson, *The Writings of Thomas Jefferson,* vol. 10, Paul Leicester Ford, ed. (New York: G. P. Putnam's Sons, 1899), 39.

is as foundational as Lincoln's government of, by, and for the people. Croly, Dewey, and, indeed, the entire "course of American democratic thought"[44] rest squarely on a democratic faith in the sovereignty of the people.

In the era after World War I, when Progressivism as an effective political movement had disintegrated, both Croly and Dewey explored new meanings of "the people" through categories of faith and briefly showed interest in the rise of antiliberal faiths that were empowering social and political movements in postwar Europe.[45] Neither Croly nor Dewey, however, could imagine a theory of politics for America that started with the premise of the sovereignty of the national government and its administrative apparatus. This was not because they were proto-syndicalists, corporatists, or soft fascists, but simply because they were American. In America, effective political argument that begins with national constitutional sovereignty is politically powerless unless grounded in a prior democratic faith in popular sovereignty. In Lincoln's words, "The Union is older than the constitution." In *Promise of American Life,* Croly explicitly recognized this profound difference from Europe, this American "exceptionalism."[46] His ideal was to *reconstitute* the proper relationship between the people and its constitutional frameworks. This required a revolution in thought and opinion and not a revolution in law and government. In Dewey's terms, the "public" must be reconstituted before its problems can be addressed. And, when the Progressive Party, in a national election, failed in this reconstitution, other sources in American life were explored to achieve and make effective a democratic "common faith."[47]

III. Contemporary Argument

In 1928, Charles Beard's (1874–1948) textbook on American politics stated: "No longer do statesmen spend weary days over finely spun theories about strict and liberal interpretations of the Constitution . . ."[48] Boy, has he been proved wrong! He, like so many Progressives and New Dealers, thought that political discourse would henceforth be dominated by talk about the best, most effective, policies to achieve substantive ends agreed upon, not about pre-political rights and constitutional jurisdictions. And, so long as the "liberal establishment" dominated the national government from World War II through the 1970s, Beard was right. After

---

[44] Ralph H. Gabriel, *Course of American Democratic Thought* (New York: Roland Press, 1956).

[45] Discussed in Kloppenberg, *Uncertain Victory,* 349–94.

[46] Herbert Croly, *The Promise of American Life* (New York: Macmillan, 1909), chaps. 8 and 9.

[47] John Dewey, *The Public and Its Problems* (1927), *The Later Works, 1925–1953,* vol. 2 (Carbondale: Southern Illinois University Press, 1990) and *A Common Faith* (New Haven: Yale University Press, 1934); and see Melvin L. Rogers, *The Undiscovered Dewey: Religion, Morality and the Ethos of Democracy* (New York: Columbia University Press, 2008).

[48] See note 3 above.

World War II, social scientists declared an "end of ideology," to be replaced by the mediation and conciliation of concrete group interests. To examine why the Progressives and New Dealers eventually proved to be so wrong and why we now experience an explosion of rights talk and constitution-alist argument, we must examine how and why the liberal establishment failed, both politically and ideologically, and how this failure gave rise to contemporary arguments about rights.

Contemporary political discourse originated in a critique of the ideol-ogy and practices of a bipartisan "liberal establishment," created by the New Deal electoral alignment (1932–36) and the older Republican-Progressive institutions and practices that had remained in power in the 1920s—especially with the onset of World War II and its Cold War after-math. This establishment rested on Democratic Party majorities in Con-gress and relatively nonpartisan executive and bipartisan congressional leadership regarding foreign and defense policy, macroeconomic and inter-national economic policy, and the major national institutions supportive of those policies.[49]

The liberal establishment increasingly justified its rule in "nonideolog-ical" terms by appealing to purportedly objective and "value-free" pro-cedures and practices. Stemming from the New Deal electoral coalition and the partial reinstatement of more traditional models of party gov-ernment, political scientists shaped what was termed an "empirical theory of democracy" that came to be called "interest group pluralism," a gen-eralization covering the whole regime that previously was meant to describe legislative politics under strong party rule. Within a commonly accepted set of "rules of the game" (the closest this theory came to Con-stitutional ideas and a concept of the people), interest group elites and governmental actors, using the many available points of access to poli-cymaking, asserted, defended, and bargained their interests. The "state" as a complex of coercive governing institutions was pictured as a "black box" in which proposed policy "inputs" were processed into official "out-puts" as decisions and laws.[50] The New Deal and its aftermath was described as "practical," "experimental," and result oriented because its policies were created in response to the real interests and needs of the people as expressed through interest groups and elections and not through ideological political parties or philosophical debate.[51]

The "Progressive" side of the regime ideology accepted this model of legitimacy, but added two elements to it. The first is that those who

---

[49] David Plotke, *Building a New Democratic Political Order: Reshaping American Liberalism in the 1930s and 1940s* (New York: Cambridge University Press, 1996), on how and why this alliance was necessary to effectively govern.

[50] David Ciepley, *Liberalism in the Shadow of Totalitarianism* (Cambridge: Harvard Univer-sity Press, 2007).

[51] Daniel J Boorstin, *The Genius of American Politics* (Chicago: University of Chicago Press, 1953); Arthur Meier Schlessinger, *The Vital Center: the Politics of Freedom* (Boston: Houghton Mifflin, 1949).

governed both their own institutions (labor, finance, industry, education, public bureaucracies, the national media, legislatures, and so on) and participated in national governance, necessarily internalized liberal democratic values and were their most articulate defenders against antidemocratic and proto-totalitarian "mass" movements—movements that had plunged Europe into chaos and war. Higher courts, needed to interpret laws and adjudicate conflicts, justified their own power in these same value-free terms. "Neutral procedures" became the mantra of the courts; and so long as they adhered to this principle, their decisions were both legitimate and just. Here, too, the Constitution was more a vague background condition than an explicit guide to adjudication, serving largely as a warrant for procedural neutrality.[52]

Needless to say, given the political turmoil and the social, political, and ideological movements beginning in the 1960s, this set of rationalizations soon came under vigorous attack. These attacks shaped the formation of alternative legitimating ideas by both left and right that now dominate our political and ideological discourse.

The democratic left charged that the liberal establishment excluded many important groups and interests in policymaking. As a party lacking any substantive ideas of public good (except re-election), the Democrats strengthened and rewarded the party's major voting blocs, blocs that systematically prevented new voices and interests from being heard, especially those of the poor, women, and African-Americans. The left saw Great Society programs as a promising way that the government could include these interests and, while doing so, act as a patronage party in the act of rebuilding its disintegrating New Deal coalition by adding new constituents and dependents. But the left's understanding of the extension/expansion of "rights" was that of group rights on the model of all interest groups. This was not a very deep critique of the liberal establishment. The Democratic Party quickly (if sometimes painfully) acceded to these demands, as did leadership in the dominant institutions of the liberal establishment: universities, business corporations, foundations, and, less enthusiastically, labor unions.

In sum, the establishment's response to the new left critique was capitulation to a new liberal ideology of *rights expansion as social, economic, and political inclusion.* Universities, charitable foundations, liberal churches, and much of the national media came to admit that they had been complicit in continuing racism and sexism, supportive of an illiberal foreign policy, tolerant of the national security state, and driven by self-serving motives of riches and power. And their new policy was gradually to replace the leadership of these institutions and to alter their rhetorical style (and some policies) with what later became known as "multiculturalism" and political correctness. But this ideological capitulation was more

---

[52] Ciepley, *Liberalism in the Shadow of Totalitarianism,* chaps. 15–16.

of a minor revision than a revolution in thought or deed: interest group pluralism was given a much broader warrant to include noneconomic and "tacit" interests and whose inclusion in the polity required more explicit democratic credentials under the rubric of "expansion of rights."[53] Commitment to this expansion was the test of regime legitimacy.[54]

The left critique could be accommodated without significantly restructuring major national institutional powers and their legitimating ideas, because, in the words of Richard Lind, multiculturalism in all of its forms required an "overclass" of standing leadership to define, guide and adjudicate the group inclusions.[55] And as the center of liberal policy initiatives shifted from the presidency and congress to the courts, philosophers quickly developed a "court" philosophy of egalitarian rights expansion to legitimate court initiatives and activism.[56] In all its dimensions, the ideology from the left that replaced that of the liberal establishment is best known as "rights talk." Lacking in this discourse was any coherent notion of "people" and any clear discussion of civic and constitutional values that might serve to justify (or to limit) an ever-expanding list of rights and entitlement claims in terms of a common good. And without the earlier political limits imposed by the Progressive/liberal Republicans and Southern Democrats required for governance, the Democratic Party, exemplified by Franklin Roosevelt's national-planning brain trust and Lyndon Johnson's Great Society programs, might have become an engine of almost unlimited central government expansion. Lacking constitutional limits, in theory at least the national government could create an ever-expanding set of dependents, including state and local governments, public education, agriculture, and social welfare. What first stood in the way were its allies in governance and then the inability of the Democratic Party, without the South, to win national elections. The ideological challenge from the new right was gaining ever-larger numbers of adherents.

---

[53] For a time, the term "entitlements" was used to distinguish welfare from civil and political rights. This term was, for obvious reasons, soon dropped.

[54] The federal courts contributed to this new set of legitimating ideas by seeing itself as the special guardian of voices and interests that lacked electoral power or lacked enough respect in the larger culture to be given a fair say in the larger polity. See Martin Shapiro, *Freedom of Speech: The Supreme Court and Judicial Review* (Englewood Cliffs, NJ: Prentice-Hall, 1966); and Ciepley, *Liberalism in the Shadow of Totalitarianism*, chap. 14.

[55] Michael Lind, *The Next American Nation: The New Nationalism and the Fourth American Revolution* (New York: Free Press, 1995). An excellent example of justifying "overclass" rule as the extension of rights is Amy Gutmann, *Identity in Democracy* (Princeton: Princeton University Press, 2003).

[56] John Rawls's *Political Liberalism* (New York: Columbia University Press, 1993) and Ronald Dworkin's *Taking Rights Seriously* (Cambridge: Harvard University Press, 1978) seem particularly designed for courts and for hierarchical administrative and bureaucratic bodies rather than for legislators or electorates. The intended audience for Gutmann, *Identity in Democracy,* is precisely these leaders. Following a liberal colonial model of indirect rule, only after the larger society and electorate are properly educated in the leaders' democratic values can they be entrusted with self-government.

The response of the liberal establishment to a critique from the right, beginning in the 1970s, was, if not simply dismissive, muted and defensive. Every critique from conservatives regarding crime, public order, family breakdown, demoralizing welfare policies, and other social issues, was met with a flurry of denials and rationalization, especially by the social sciences, and charges of racism and threats to civil liberties by liberal elites. But with every electoral defeat, and the fiscal crisis and inflation under President Carter, this response became less and less effective, while support for Great Society social programs and its justifying principles grew increasingly demoralized (this was the time when liberals began to call themselves Progressives). The conservative emphasis on what came to be called "social issues" also included court decisions, especially those on abortion rights and sexual practices. Together, the ground was laid for an ideologically conservative renaissance.

Before addressing how this critique from the right became productive of an alternative set of legitimating ideas—of authoritative ideals for national governance—two other elements of the dual attack on the liberal establishment must be considered. The first was an attack on the prevailing regulatory regime of the liberal establishment. Typically, regulatory policy was dominated by insiders—called "iron triangles"—consisting of Congressional Committees, the regulatory bureaucracy, and the interest regulated (e.g., airlines, railroads). Beginning in the 1970s, "deregulation" was pursued by both Democratic and Republican administrations. Deregulation appealed to the right both on libertarian grounds of market efficiency and on Constitutional grounds of limited government and the strengthening of the institutions of civil society. Its appeal to the left was that breaking up policy triangles provided an opening for more inclusive sets of interests, either through ordinary market mechanisms (especially consumer interests) or through new patterns of "public" regulation (e.g., workplace safety, environmental and consumer protection, fair employment practices) that extended more rights to those previously excluded. The conservatives came to benefit more from their justification of deregulation than did the liberals because it accorded so well with a renewed emphasis on Constitutional limitations to federal power.

The other common ground was a direct attack on the philosophical basis of "interest group pluralism" as the primary ideological justification of this governing regime. By the 1980s, interest group pluralism was thoroughly discredited both as a viable description of liberal democracy and as a fountain of legitimacy for American national politics. Both sets of critics insisted that an "empirical" theory of democracy contained no substantive norms for public life. Both sought to replace this product of "value-free" social science with more philosophically oriented theories of rights, however differently they came to view the sources and meanings of those rights. Consistent with a "black box" image of government, the assumption of interest group pluralism was that rights, however under-stood, are the *product* of policy—a series of changing "outputs," not a stable *foundation.*[57] Both left and right critics rejected this understanding.

An indicator of this common ground was the favorable reception accorded by both sets of critics to Theodore Lowi's *End of Liberalism* (1969). But what kind of rights theory is to succeed the end of the ruling ideas of the liberal establishment? Lowi suggested a vaguely constitu-tionalist ideal of "juridical democracy" that had surface appeal to both sides. This solution, however, depended upon how both constitutional-ism and the Constitution were to be understood. Here enters the contem-porary debate between advocates of the "living" versus the "original" Constitution and the reintroduction of natural rights.

IV. CONCLUSION

The contemporary debate over "living" and "original" constitutional-ism cannot be explored here[58] but some features of that debate should be pointed out—features that echo both my first and second thoughts on Progressivism and rights. Given the ways in which both "rights talk" and neoconstitutionalism privilege the courts, both politically and epistemo-logically, both left and right projects seem initially to favor courts more than more democratic political institutions. This implicit bias not only undermines more accessible and open institutions of political democracy, especially elections, it privileges more elite forms of discourse quite removed from the rhetoric by and through which civic agency is empow-ered and political mobilization takes place. This weakness is especially true of the left, not only because liberalism was more entrenched in the courts, but because the leading lights of rights talk are in law schools and university philosophy departments rather than in "think tanks" that addressed the larger public more directly. And even as elections changed the ideological makeup of the federal courts, robbing liberal intellectuals and law school professors of its natural constituency, this language of public discourse seems ill-adapted for a more popular audience.[59] And

[57] Except for a rough set of "rules of the game" to encourage bargaining and compromise, standard college textbooks in American government in this period put the discussion of rights at the *end* of the text, not at the start. The theoretical basis for this placement is found in Robert Dahl, *Preface to Democratic Theory* (Chicago: University of Chicago Press, 1956) and *Pluralist Democracy in the United States* (Chicago: Rand McNally, 1967); and David Truman, *The Governmental Process* (New York: Knopf, 1951).

[58] Ken I. Kersch, "Ecumenicalism Through Constitutionalism: The Discursive Develop-ment of Constitutional Conservatism in *National Review*, 1955–1980, *Studies in American Political Development* 25 (April, 2011) 86–116.

[59] Mary Ann Glendon, *Rights Talk: The Impoverishment of American Political Discourse* (New York: Free Press, 1991) and Michael Sandel, *Democracy's Discontent: America In Search of a Public Philosophy* (Cambridge: Harvard University Press, 1996).

while liberal rights talk seems open to invocations of gender, sexual, and racial identities, it seems especially hostile to strong religious and moral commitments—commitments that are shared across the multicultural landscape and evoke strong patriotic sentiments.

So, one might ask, what would John Dewey think? Given today's liberal commitment to a "living Constitution" as rights extensions, without a coherent electorate with common ends, Dewey might argue that this "living" Constitution lacks vitality and organic unity, sustained largely by judicial power and its decidedly elite constituencies. For all of Dewey's commitment to a pragmatic and experiential constitutionalism, he would reject this solution as lacking a "public." And surely, the Democratic Party as a coalition of disparate interests (African-Americans, public employees, teachers, trial lawyers) to be placated and rewarded, cannot serve as a living model of such a public in the way that the Republican Party did under Lincoln and the way the Progressive Party attempted, and partially succeeded, in doing in the early twentieth century. And what would Dewey make of John Rawls or Ronald Dworkin and their many followers? He might argue that their theories of public discourse productive of an "empire of law" exist on a plane outside and above the discourse through which American citizens integrate their personal experience and their public lives. Modern liberals, especially when they lose elections, reject much popular discourse as "false consciousness" (or what people in Kansas think) lacking the philosophical coherence of liberal rights talk even as that talk sacrifices political coherence and popular appeal. The more fundamental issue is how and by whom liberal rights talk and rights extensions might be *authorized*? The two most obvious answers, the "sovereign" power of the federal courts or a "sovereign" numerical political majority would clearly fail Dewey's test. So, too, would the truth claims of academic political philosophers.

But what about the legitimating ideas that emerged from the right-wing critique of the liberal establishment? The Republican Party has always been a more effective vehicle to create and sustain an ideologically coherent public if only because its core constituency has always been more homogeneous (as was the Whig Party before them). As ardent nationalists and patriots who have generally been suspicious of "big government," they have the potential to serve as the electoral source for restoring some sense of popular sovereignty and a democratic public. The first source of this restoration has been a renewed stress on the Constitution as the primary expression of the will of the whole people. But this possibility has been undermined by an ofttimes foolhardy commitment to "original intent" (as if the Constitution were a mere super-majoritarian contract) that not only robs the Constitution of Lincoln's covenantal understanding of the Constitution as future projects and unfulfilled promises, but tends to subordinate a larger political and theoretical discourse to wrangles among constitutional lawyers.[60] This neoformalism (like an inerrant and bibliocentric Protestantism) is a barrier to reading the Constitution in ways that speak to the lived experiences of a democratic citizenry. The greatest constitutional achievement of Lincoln and the Republican Party was the abolition of slavery and the guaranty of national citizenship through the Thirteenth and Fourteenth Amendments. In particular, to ignore the transformative effect of the Fourteenth Amendment and the enormous *moral* expansion of the "unwritten" Constitution through common-law court decisions robs conservative constitutional theory of an organic connection to America's most powerful documents in our narrative of freedom, second only to the Declaration of Independence and the Bill of Rights.

Originalism as a constitutional hermeneutic serves better as a critique of an entrenched judicial and congressional liberalism than as a guide to conservative governance. So, too, is a more recent corollary to this neoconstitutionalism, that of new theory of a "unitary executive." This strong Hamiltonian reading of exclusive presidential power over the entire executive branch was useful to *thwart* the remnants of entrenched liberalism in Congress and the national bureaucracy. Under its mantle, earlier Progressive (public opinion) and New Deal (electoral majority) justifications for expansions of executive and bureaucratic power were effectively challenged.[61] But to discredit these extraconstitutional justifications for executive/bureaucratic power expansion is not the same as giving presidential power a clear constitutional sanction for what looks suspiciously like something approaching a constitutional monarchy. Moreover, the theory of a unitary executive seems to suggest a theory of the sovereignty of the national Constitution, not the sovereignty of the American people. This theory of the presidency will prove especially troublesome if both Congress and the federal courts become under the sway of originalist constitutional values and anchor *their* authority in the constitution as well.

There is an additional feature of constitutional originalism that does, however, provide a source for a public philosophy of sufficient prestige and power to become a basis for a reconstituted public and the restoration of popular sovereignty. This feature is the connection of the Constitution to a philosophy of natural rights. At first blush (and for most contemporary intellectuals), such a connection would only further discredit an originalist understanding of the Constitution as authoritative

---

[60] Steven Teles, *The Rise of the Conservative Legal Movement: The Battle for Control of the Law* (Princeton: Princeton University Press, 2008). This might be forgiven in the 1980s when Republican/conservative presidents confronted both Congress and the courts dominated by liberals.

[61] Stephen Skowronek, "The Conservative Insurgency and Presidential Power: A Developmental Perspective on the Unitary Executive." *Harvard Law Review* 122 (2009): 2070–2103.

for today. Natural rights philosophy, a theory of man and society born of the revolutionary Enlightenment and shaped in opposition to prevailing orthodox Christian understandings of politics, should hardly appeal to contemporary American intellectual culture, whether left or right. Shouldn't post-modern left and libertarian right intellectuals join hands with evangelical Protestants and traditionalist Catholics in rejecting this naive product of Deism and natural religion? But they do not, and for good reason. Whatever its philosophical and (anti)religious origins, the ideal of pre-political and pre-constitutional natural rights has strong affinities across a wide range of contemporary values and common memories. To reject natural law is to undermine closely held *moral* values across today's political spectrum: to defend human rights and dignity without some conception of natural rights is morally incoherent. While these affinities might be undercut by an articulate and purely *philosophical* defense of natural rights, they are strengthened and reinforced by defending natural rights as part of an American *moral narrative* of freedom and equality.

As part of a moral narrative, but *not* as a foundational philosophy, the idea of natural rights connects the Declaration of Independence, the Articles of Confederation, the Constitution, the Bill of Rights and the Thirteenth and Fourteenth Amendments to popular sovereignty. This same moral narrative incorporates popular religion and the "sacred violence" and sacrifice of our wars, giving body, strength, and purpose to the thin and abstract "Creator" evoked in our public documents. Read in this way, natural rights are not so much a philosophical foundation for liberal individualism as the main items of a common faith binding together a national community of moral equals. While Progressives and New Dealers would never countenance natural rights as a *philosophy* (neither, for that matter, would David Hume (1711–1776), Adam Smith (1723–1790), or Tocqueville), they incorporated and depended upon the history and power of natural rights in their own self-understandings and in their understanding of America. Only insofar as the notion of natural rights achieves and maintains its place in a larger moral narrative—call it a "living" narrative if you will—can a commonly shared commitment to most of the original values of the Constitution be secured.

To turn George Washington Plunkitt (1842–1924) on his head, the inclusion of natural rights in a shared national narrative of popular sovereignty would make the Constitution a constituent element of civic friendship.

Political Science, University of Tulsa

FREEDOM, HISTORY, AND RACE IN
PROGRESSIVE THOUGHT

By Tiffany Jones Miller

I. Introduction

Commentators discussing America's turn of the twentieth century enthusiasm for eugenics—an umbrella term encompassing various policies discriminating against races believed to be inferior, as well as individuals of all races deemed to be "degenerate"—typically emphasize that support for such policies spanned the ideological spectrum. "For most white Americans," as James B. McKee observes, "both common sense and scientific evidence seemed so obvious that one had to accept the prevailing racial theories whether one's political leanings were conservative or liberal."[1] America's experiment in eugenics, it would thus seem, was as much characteristic of the political views of the Left as of the Right—of the principles of late-nineteenth-century Progressivism (or any other incipient form of socialism) as those inherited from the American Founding. While this characterization is perhaps understandable in view of the conflicting definitions given to the political labels of the day, it is nonetheless odd, as the eugenists generally, and the Progressives specifically, repeatedly advocate such policies as *correctives* for the principles inherited from the American Founding.

The purpose of this essay, accordingly, is to explain why the eugenics agenda is so natural an outgrowth of Progressivism. Part of the reason for this, as Thomas C. Leonard well suggests, stems from the Progressives' rejection of "the individualism of (classical) liberalism"—of, that is, the fundamental principles of the Founders' theory of government. The cornerstone of the Founders' social compact theory is the idea of natural human equality, the idea that all men at all times in all places are "created

---

[1] See Thomas C. Leonard, "Mistaking Eugenics for Social Darwinism: Why Eugenics is Missing from the History of American Economics," *History of Political Economy* 37 supplement (2005): 203: "Eugenic thought not only crossed national borders; it also crossed political ideologies, traversing an extraordinary range of political views." (But see also, Leonard, "American Economic Reform in the Progressive Era: Its Foundational Beliefs and Their Relation to Eugenics," *History of Political Economy* 41:1 (2009): 110, in which he clearly indicates that this characterization overstates the matter.) See too Peter Quinn, "Race Cleansing in America," *American Heritage* 54: 1 (February/March 2003), accessed online at http://americanheritage.com/articles/magazine/ah/2003/1/2003_1_34.shtml: "The spreading influence of eugenics not only drew on a conservative fear of lower class behavior, and on the enthusiasm of middle-class progressives seeking scientific answers to the dislocations inflicted by industrialization and urbanization, but also attracted support from those even more radically opposed to the status quo."

doi:10.1017/S0265052511000276

equal." Two other essential principles flow from this foundation: first, since they are by nature equal, all men have an equal, natural right to rule themselves; second, individuals consent to establish government for the express purpose of securing this right. As we shall see, the Progressives rejected the Founders' understanding of equality in favor of a new conception of freedom inspired by early nineteenth century German idealism. Following Hegel and his students, the Progressives redefined individual freedom in "positive" terms: "true" or genuine freedom does not consist in the mere legal right to make decisions for oneself, but, rather, as Progressive economist Richard T. Ely has it, in the development "in the most complete manner possible all faculties, physical, mental, moral, spiritual[.]"[2] When understood in this way, freedom, though inhering in all human beings as an "ethical ideal"—as, that is, unrealized potential or "capacities"—essentially becomes "something to be achieved," a goal to be earned or a prize to be won.[3] The goal of freedom, in turn, is only gradually achieved through a "long and arduous constructive process," through a cumulative or *progressive* process of historical development or "social evolution."[4] Because the Progressives were convinced that the different branches of the human family were becoming free at different or unequal rates, they dismissed the idea that all men, as men, have an equal right to rule themselves as hopelessly "abstract" or ahistorical.[5] In so denying the Founders' understanding of equality, the Progressives also denied their understanding of equal, natural rights and limited government—the very doctrines eugenists repeatedly blame for obstructing the implementation of their agenda.[6]

---

[2] Richard T. Ely, *An Introduction to Political Economy* (New York: Chautauqua Press, 1889), 101.

[3] John Dewey, *Liberalism and Social Action* (Amherst, NY: Prometheus Books, 2000), 34.

[4] Richard T. Ely, "Industrial Liberty," *Publications of the American Economic Association* 3, no. 1 (Feb. 1902), 63.

[5] The Progressives' criticism of the Founders' understanding of equality—and hence the state of nature—is the outgrowth of Jean-Jacques Rousseau's criticism of both John Locke and Thomas Hobbes's teachings on the state of nature. As Peter Myers, *Our Only Star and Compass: Locke and the Struggle for Political Rationality* (Lanham, MD: Rowman and Littlefield Publishers, 1998), 112, well notes, this criticism has "contributed substantially to the discrediting not only of Locke's thought in particular, but more generally of the rationalist, natural-rights constitutionalism that marked the culmination of the political thought and practice of early modernity."

[6] Eugenists repeatedly and pointedly deny the equality principle and its corollaries—e.g., equal, natural rights and limited government. As Peter Quinn, "Race Cleansing in America," points out, Francis Galton, the very father of eugenics, declares, in his 1869 book *Hereditary Genius: An Inquiry Into Its Laws and Consequences*, that: "It is in the most unqualified manner that I object to pretensions of natural equality." As Quinn likewise notes, Harry Laughlin, the superintendent of the Eugenics Record Office (ERO), "hoped to bring about a new social order 'wherein selection for parenthood will not be held a natural right of every individual; but will be a prize highly sought and allotted to the best individuals of proven blood, and those individuals who are not deemed worthy and are by society denied the right to perpetrate their own traits . . . will be held in pity by their fellows.'" See also Donald K. Pickens, "The Sterilization Movement: The Search for Purity in Mind and State," *Phylon* 28, no. 1 (1960): 80, quoting A. B. Wolfe, "Eugenics and Social Attitudes," *Eugenics in Race and*

But Progressivism's affinity for eugenics goes well beyond a mere *rejection* of the Founders' conception of equality, natural rights, and limited government. In redefining freedom in "positive" terms, the Progressives also pronounced a new moral framework, a new conception of who is entitled (and obliged) to what and why, to replace the Founders' understanding. From the reformers' standpoint, although history or human development does not commence with the conscious promotion of "positive" freedom, individuals, over the course of a society's evolution, become increasingly conscious of their moral obligation to promote it in every aspect of their social relations, including government. In an advanced stage of development, accordingly, the promotion of "positive" freedom—and hence "improvement"—becomes the watchword of public policy. These characteristically idealistic ideas—that freedom is essentially a prize to be "achieved," that it is being won at different or unequal rates by the different branches of the human family, and that an advanced race understands its moral obligation to promote the freedom of all—inspired the Progressives' drive to raise or elevate the quality of the American (indeed the human) character generally. This aim, the raising of the American (and world) "average," was the lodestar of their reforms. It was the aim of their signature domestic policy reforms, e.g., wages and hours legislation, social insurance, public housing, etc., but it was no less the aim of a host of policies—including colonialism, disfranchisement, and segregation—designed to subjugate "backward," possibly "inferior," races, as well as other "degenerate classes."[7]

II. THE ORIGINS OF PROGRESSIVISM IN AMERICA

The Progressives' conception of "positive" freedom—and the derivative notions of history and the positive state—was principally inspired by early nineteenth century German idealism. These principles gained influence in America via two main paths. The first path was blazed by German-born and educated scholars like Francis Lieber. Lieber, who eventually ended up teaching at Columbia, emigrated to the United States in 1827 after attending the University of Berlin where he was influenced by Johann Fichte and Frederick Schleirmacher, among others. Lieber's efforts were bolstered by the energetic exertions of hundreds, perhaps thousands, of aspiring American social scientists who matriculated in German universities between 1820–1920, most of whom did so between 1870–1900.[8]

State: Scientific Papers at the Second International Congress of Eugenics Held at the American Museum of Natural History, Sept. 22–28, 1921 (Baltimore, 1923), vol. II, 413, 417: "'We are specifically the victim ... of a social inheritance of political and economic individualism carried over from the eighteenth century revolt when the emphasis was on individual right rather than where it must now be put, upon social function.'"

[7] Richard T. Ely, *Studies in the Evolution of Industrial Society,* 173, 180.

[8] John G. Gunnell, *The Descent of Political Theory,* (Chicago: University of Chicago Press, 1993), 28–30; Dorothy Ross, *The Origins of American Social Science* (New York, New York: Cambridge University Press, 1991), 55.

"Many of the new academic professionals of the 1870s and 1880s, and the young men who were responsible for defining and shaping political science as an integral discipline in this country's new universities," Sylvia Fries observes, "found intellectual nurture, not to mention relatively easy and inexpensive access to a doctoral degree, in the universities of Germany."[9] Those who received at least some measure of German training, and who returned home to become leading figures in the emerging disciplines of history, economics, political science, sociology, etc., include, among many others, Theodore D. Woolsey, John W. Burgess, William A. Dunning, Andrew D. White, Herbert B. Adams, Edmund J. James, Simon N. Patten, Richard T. Ely, Henry C. Adams, Charles R. Henderson, Albion Small, Edward A. Ross, E. R. A. Seligman, Charles E. Merriam, Frank J. Goodnow, Charles A. Beard, W. E. B. Dubois, and Walter Weyl.[10]

Following their return to the United States, most of these scholars eventually obtained positions in American colleges, which is where the import of their new thinking was initially most pronounced. "As early as the 1860s," Eldon Eisenach writes, "Americans who studied in German universities returned to launch powerful critiques of American colleges and universities and strongly urged adoption or adaptations of German models."[11] While several American universities soon became Progressive strongholds—e.g. Columbia, the University of Chicago, and the University of Wisconsin—arguably no American university produced as many influential Progressives as did The Johns Hopkins University. Founded in 1876, Hopkins was expressly modeled on the German university with its emphasis on research, scholarship, and graduate training. In its inaugural year, Austin Scott, a Ph.D. from the University of Leipzig, established a seminar on American historical and political studies. In 1883, Herbert Baxter Adams, a younger colleague who had earned a Ph.D. at the University of Heidelberg (where he had studied with Johann K. Bluntschli), took over Scott's course.[12] Adams, with the assistance of other German-trained faculty like Richard T. Ely, succeeded in producing a plethora of highly influential scholars.[13] "An

[9] Sylvia Fries, "Staatstheorie and the New American Science of Politics," *Journal of the History of Ideas* 34, no. 3 (1973): 392. See also Jurgen Herbst, *The German Historical School in American Scholarship: A Study in the Transfer of Culture* (Ithaca, NY: Cornell University Press, 1965), chap. 1; Daniel Rodgers, *Atlantic Crossings: Social Politics In a Progressive Age* (Cambridge, MA: The Belknap Press of Harvard University Press, 1998), chap. 3.

[10] Fries, "Staatstheorie and the New American Science of Politics," 392-95; Gunnell, *The Descent of Political Theory*, 35, 88; Jonah Goldberg, *Liberal Fascism: The Secret History of the American Left from Mussolini to the Politics of Meaning* (New York: Doubleday, 2007), 94; Axel R. Schaefer, "W. E. B. Du Bois, German Social Thought, and the Racial Divide in American Progressivism, 1892-1909," *Journal of American History*, 88 (Dec., 2001): 928.

[11] Eldon Eisenach, *Lost Promise of Progressivism* (University Press of Kansas, 1994), 93; Rodgers, *Atlantic Crossings*, 97-111.

[12] Fries, "Staatstheorie and the New American Science of Politics," 394-5. As Ross, *The Origins of American Social Science*, 68, notes, "Bluntschli . . . joined the idealist and historical branches of *Staatswissenschaft* into a single theory of the state."

[13] Ely is not particularly well known today, but he played a seminal role in transmitting German idealism to America. In addition to being a prominent member of the social gospel

impressive group was trained at Hopkins," John Gunnell notes, "and many did seminal research and institutional work in the emerging, yet often not clearly defined, social scientific disciplines at major graduate institutions."[14] John Dewey, Woodrow Wilson, Albert Shaw, John R. Commons, Westel W. Willoughby, Frederick Jackson Turner, and Frederic C. Howe were all among Hopkins' graduates.

In addition to founding new universities on the German model and reordering existing ones accordingly, these scholars also helped define the emerging disciplines of social science by founding a host of professional academic associations—e.g., the American Historical Association (1884), the American Economic Association (1885), the American Political Science Association (1903), and the American Sociological Society (1905). These institutions were patterned on German models, and, in some cases, at least, their founding was urged by the German professoriate.[15] The American Economic Association (AEA), for example, was consciously designed as an American version of the Verein für Sozialpolitik, the leading association of Historical School economists in Germany, which served as "an institutional nexus of professors and state officials, academic learning and practical policymaking."[16] Five of the AEA's six original officers, moreover, had studied in Germany, as had twenty of its first twenty-six presidents.[17] Like their German predecessors, these institutions were explicitly

movement, Ely played a pioneering role in the development of the German Historical School of political economy in America, and its offshoots in city-planning, agricultural economics, and conservation—all of which began to exert a significant impact upon public policy in the Progressive era and the New Deal. As a teacher, he helped cultivate a host of significant academics/reformers including Albert Shaw, Frederic Howe, John R. Commons, and Woodrow Wilson. He was the founding father of the American Economic Association (AEA), and played a prominent role in the governance of the highly influential advocacy organizations it spawned, e.g., the American Association of Labor Legislation (AALL), as well as the National Consumers' League (NCL). On Ely's accomplishments generally, see Benjamin G. Rader, *The Academic Mind and Reform: The Influence of Richard T. Ely in American Life* (University of Kentucky Press, 1966). Finally, during his long tenure at the University of Wisconsin, Ely, and especially his former students, like John R. Commons, played a central role in the development of Governor Robert LaFollette's "Wisconsin Idea," a mode of governance which sought to enhance the influence of the University of Wisconsin faculty over Wisconsin state policymaking. On this score, see Howe, *Wisconsin An Experiment in Democracy* (New York: Charles Scribner's Sons, 1912), chaps. 2–3.

[14] Gunnell, *The Descent of Political Theory*, 39.

[15] On the latter score, see Richard T. Ely, *Ground Under Our Feet: An Autobiography* (New York, New York: The MacMillan Co., 1938), 133.

[16] Daniel T. Rodgers, *Atlantic Crossings*, 94; see also, Richard T. Ely, *Ground Under Our Feet*, 132–49. For reasons that will be discussed later, the Progressives widely regarded Germany as their beau ideal of the state. "Germany," as Frederic C. Howe, *Wisconsin: An Experiment in Democracy* (New York: Charles Scribner's Sons, 1912), 38, writes, "has identified science with politics more closely than has any other nation. The state universities, technical and commercial colleges are consciously used for the advancement of the fatherland." Thanks especially to Robert La Follette's administration, he continues at p. 39, "Wisconsin is making the German idea her own." See also Axel Schafer, "W. E. B. Du Bois, German Social Thought, and the Racial Divide in American Progressivism, 1892–1909," *Journal of American History*, 88 (Dec., 2001): 930.

[17] Rodgers, *Atlantic Crossings*, 86, 101–2. Daniel M. Fox, "Introduction," Simon N. Patten, *The New Basis of Civilization* (Cambridge, MA: Belknap Press, 1968), xi–xii, notes that Patten,

reform-minded. The aim of combining scholarship and reform, as Jurgen Herbst notes, "marked the development of social science in late-nineteenth century America [e.g., in the formation of the American Historical Association (AHA)]. It was in evidence again when the political scientists and the sociologists separated themselves from the Social Science Association."[18] Through all these endeavors Progressive academics established an important beachhead for German idealism in America. "By the end of the first decade of the twentieth century," as Eisenach thus concludes, the Progressives'

> professional associations and journals were on a solid footing; their university departments and endowments were rapidly growing; their books and articles dominated intellectual and higher political discourse; their students and colleagues were actively sought by state and national political reform bodies; and reform journals and journalists were disseminating their ideas to ever growing audiences.[19]

III. REDEFINING INDIVIDUALISM: THE PROGRESSIVE EMBRACE OF THE IDEALISTIC CONCEPTION OF FREEDOM AND HISTORY

It is frequently suggested that the Progressives depreciated the importance of the individual and his rights in favor of the "social good" or "general welfare." In a 1903 survey of recent American political thinking, Charles Merriam seemingly confirms this view by describing the progressive redefinition of the end or aim of government as a movement away from "the individualistic . . . philosophy" of the Revolution:

> In the days of the Revolution, it was thought that the end of the political society is to protect the life, liberty, and property of its citizens and beyond this nothing more. The duty of the state was summed up in the protection of individual rights, in harmony with the individualistic character of the philosophy of that day. . . . In more recent times there has been in America a decided tendency to react against the early 'protection theory' of government . . . In the new view, the state . . . is not and cannot be limited to the protection of individual interests, but must be regarded as extending to acts for the advancement of the general welfare in all cases where it can safely act[.][20]

---

like the other founders of the AEA, e.g., Ely, Henry C. Adams, etc., "[was] deeply influenced by a group of economists called the Younger Historical School." These economists, including Gustav Schmoller, Adolf Wagner, and Johannes Conrad, were, in turn, "deeply influenced by Hegelian concepts of historical process . . . [.]"

[18] Jurgen Herbst, *The German Historical School in American Scholarship: A Study in the Transfer of Culture* (Ithaca, NY: Cornell University Press, 1965), 43–46. See also, Ely, *Ground Under Our Feet*, 142–3.

[19] Eisenach, *Lost Promise*, 70.

[20] Merriam, *A History of American Political Theories*, 315–16.

Whereas the Founders defined the end of government in terms of the individual and the natural rights to which he is entitled, the Progressives define it in terms of "the general welfare." In the Progressives' view, Merriam thus seems to suggest, the social good, that is, the "interests of the community as a whole," simply takes primacy over the individual and his rights.

While this formulation is, in the end, apt, it is nonetheless the source of much confusion, for it makes the Progressives sound as though they have no concern for the welfare of the individual, which is not the case. It is true, of course, that they were not concerned about individual rights in the *Founders'* sense. Despite occasional rhetorical obfuscations to the contrary, there is abundant evidence confirming that the Progressives rejected the Founders' understanding of individualism. "Across the range of Progressive writings, and throughout this entire period," as Eisenach concludes, "one finds a persistent attack on rights and individualism as worthy foundations for American national democracy . . . The rejection of natural rights as a foundation for moral or political reasoning was not even considered to require a defense."[21] By the turn of the twentieth century, in other words, intellectuals, if not the broader public, pervasively denied the Founders' understanding of equality and the natural rights doctrine which flows from it.

If we infer from this rejection that the Progressives were altogether unconcerned about the welfare of the individual in *any* sense, however, we shall be seriously misled, for the "social good" or "general welfare" itself cannot be understood apart from the welfare of the individuals comprising that society. Indeed, as Merriam's own subsequent discussion confirms, the Progressives' conception of the "general welfare" derives from a new conception of individualism—from, that is, a new conception of the welfare of the individual which not only differs in marked respects from the Founders' conception, but also grounds a new conception of moral right and obligation. Drawing on Theodore Woolsey's discussion of this question in his influential two volume treatise *Political Science*, among others, Merriam writes: "Woolsey took the position that the state cannot be limited to restraining individuals from injuring each other, but may justly act positively for the general welfare. 'The sphere of the state,' he said, '*may* reach as far as the nature and needs of man and of men reach,' " including, the "redress of wrongs," "prevention of wrongs," "care for the outward welfare of the community, as in respect to industry, roads, health," and "the cultivation of the spiritual nature."[22] For Woolsey, as

---

[21] Eisenach, *Lost Promise*, 187. Merriam, *A History of American Political Theories*, 308–9: "In the refusal to accept the contract theory as the basis for government, practically all the political scientists of note agree. The old explanation no longer seems sufficient, and is with practical unanimity discarded. The doctrines of natural law and natural rights have met a similar fate."

[22] Merriam, *A History of American Political Theories*, 316.

with the Progressives generally, the scope of the state is defined by the "general welfare," which is defined in turn by "the nature and the needs of man"—by the nature of the human being, as the Progressives, not the Founders, understand it. This nature, Woolsey clarifies, is comprehensive in the sense that it includes the whole of man's concerns—i.e., his "outward" (external, material, or physical) concerns, no less than his higher, "spiritual" concerns. The "general welfare" is promoted, accordingly, whenever policies seeking to promote the fullest possible development of this nature among Americans *generally* are adopted, howsoever such policies may violate what the Founders regarded as the natural rights of the individual: "It is not admitted that there are no limits to the action of the state," Merriam pointedly concludes, "but on the other hand it is fully conceded that there are no 'natural rights' which bar the way. The question is now one of expediency rather than of principle."[23] In stressing the primacy of the "social good" or the "general welfare" over individualism or individual rights, in short, the Progressives were, first and foremost, stressing the primacy of a new individualism over the old. The theory that society is "organic," and hence constitutes a whole which is ethically prior to the individual and his rights in the old sense, as John Dewey instructively notes, "can say not less, but more than any one else, that society exists for and by individuals," as it "is as much an account of the individual as it is of the whole."[24]

The Progressives thus discarded the Founders' conception of individual freedom as natural rights in favor of a new conception of freedom synonymous with the fullest possible development or "perfection" of human nature. For the Progressives, as Eisenach observes,

> [t]he alternative starting point ... was a conception of democratic citizenship informed by values of "positive" rather than "negative" liberty. [Progressive theologian Samuel Zane] Batten, while granting that the initial struggle for liberty "is almost wholly a story of negatives," insists that "true liberty is a positive thing, and to consider its negative aspects alone is to miss its high and divine significance."

The distinction between "negative" and "positive" liberty, and the rejection of the former for the latter, Eisenach continues, "was a litany in

---

[23] Ibid., 322.

[24] Dewey, "The Ethics of Democracy," 236. The Progressives were not only perfectly willing to subordinate the rights of the individual in the Founders' sense where it was believed to conflict with the "general welfare" as they understand it, but, as we shall see, they were also very willing to subordinate the welfare of the individual as they understand it, in a very severe measure, where it was believed to conflict with the wider "general welfare" (as defined in their own terms.) This is why, as suggested earlier, Merriam's formulation indicating that the Progressives elevated the social good or "general welfare" above the individual, is, in the end, apt.

Progressive writings, voiced in the languages of economics, ethics, sociology, and religion."[25] "Negative" freedom, as Dewey and Tufts explain,

> signifies freedom *from* subjection to the will and control of others;
> exemption from bondage; release from servitude; capacity to act with-
> out being exposed to direct obstructions or interferences from others.
> It means a clear road, cleared of impediments, for action. It contrasts
> with the limitations of prisoner, slave, and serf, who have to carry out
> the will of others.[26]

"Negative" freedom is "freedom from subjection to the will and control of
others." The Founders' conception of freedom is essentially "negative"
because government secures freedom to the individual primarily by
restraining (or holding back) others, as well as itself, from interfering
arbitrarily with his right to make decisions in his own life—to decide, that
is, how to pursue the lowest to the highest ends in life.

For the Progressives, however, "true" freedom is "positive" in character
because it consists in the actual development of one's full—and hence
highest—nature, not the mere legal right or opening to pursue such development. " 'When we speak of freedom as something to be highly prized,' "
Richard T. Ely, quoting the British neo-Hegelian T. H. Green, explains, we
" 'do not mean merely freedom from restraint or compulsion.' " On the
contrary, "true liberty means the expression of positive powers of the
individual" to "make the most and best of themselves."[27] It means, as he
clarifies elsewhere, the "most perfect development of all human faculties
in each individual, which can be attained," including that of "all the
higher faculties—faculties of love, of knowledge, of aesthetic perception,
and the like[.]"[28] Importantly, then, the Progressives neither abandoned
individualism per se, nor the idea that nature grounds freedom and morality. On the contrary, as progressive political scientist Westel W. Willoughby explains, "Hegel, Green, and their idealistic followers" (including
Willoughby himself), contend that

> man is by nature, potentially at least, a moral being, and the social
> state, though not the creator of the sense of ethical obligation, alone
> furnishes the means through which is presented the possibility of

---

[25] Eisenach, *Lost Promise*, 189.

[26] Dewey and Tufts, *Ethics*, 437.

[27] Ely, "Industrial Liberty," 63.

[28] Ely, "Ethics and Economics," in *Social Aspects of Christianity, and Other Essays* (New
York: Thomas Y. Crowell and Company, 1889), 123–4; see also Ely, *Ground Under Our Feet*,
66–67: "The end and purpose of all is the true growth of mankind; namely, the full and
harmonious development in each individual of all human faculties—the faculties of working, perceiving, knowing, loving—the development, in short, of whatever capabilities of
good there may be in us. And this development of human powers in the individual is not
to be entirely for self. . . It is for self and for others. . ."

concrete application; while the motive is self-realization, the attainment of that personal perfection, the possibility, as well as the desire for the attainment of which is innate in man, and is discoverable by a metaphysical inquiry into his spiritual and intellectual nature, and his relation to Divine or Absolute Reason.

According to the idealists, "metaphysical inquiry" into the "spiritual and intellectual nature" of man teaches us that human beings have a natural capacity or potential to achieve moral or "personal perfection." Both the "possibility" of achieving this end, as well as the "desire" to do so, are "innate in man." While the state is thus not the "creator of the sense of ethical obligation," it alone "furnishes the means" through which this human potential can be actualized or brought into "concrete application."[29]

---

[29] Westel Woodbury Willoughby, "The Right of the State to Be," *International Journal of Ethics* (Jul. 1899), 469. Willoughby, 470–71, stresses that recognition of man's spiritual nature as the foundation of right "does not carry with it the predication of the so-called 'natural rights'. . . It carries with it the declaration that there are eternal necessary principles of right and justice, but not that there are rights belonging to individuals in the sense that, apart from a state of society in which mutual restraints and obligations are recognized, there are certain spheres of action in which, under no circumstances, is it ethically justifiable that the individual should be restrained or constrained against his will. Right, apart from any social recognition or creation, exists, but not rights." On nature as the foundation of right, see also Theodore D. Woolsey's highly influential treatise, *Political Science or the State Theoretically and Practically Considered* (New York: Charles Scribner's Sons, 1886; first published in 1877), vol. I, 2: ". . . we admit that happiness is an end which the individual and the state may rightfully aim at, and an important one, although subordinate to the right and to the ends contained in the perfection of human nature." See also Dewey and Tufts, *Ethics* (New York: Henry Holt and Co., 1908), 6–7: "Man would not be here if self-preservation and self-assertion and sex instinct were not strongly rooted in his system. These may easily become dominant passions. But just as certainly, man cannot be all that he may be unless he controls these impulses and passions by other motives. He has first to create for himself a new world of ideal interests before he finds his best life. The appetites and instincts may be 'natural,' in the sense that they are the beginning; the mental and spiritual life is 'natural,' as Aristotle puts it, in the sense that man's full nature is developed only in such a life." That Dewey wrote this might strike some as odd. But, as Robert B. Westbrook, *John Dewey and American Democracy* (Ithaca: Cornell University Press, 1991), 37–38, demonstrates, Dewey, in the early decades of his career, was heavily influenced by T. H. Green, the English professor of philosophy who, in the 1870s, played a very important role in encouraging the study of Hegel in Britain. In the 1880s and 1890s, Dewey's understanding of morality "drew heavily on two fundamental concepts of British idealism: the neo-Hegelian understanding of society as a peculiar kind of moral organism and the related notion of individual freedom within this organic society as the positive freedom to make the best of oneself as a social being and not merely the negative freedom from external restraint or compulsion." Dewey's eventual "deconversion from absolute idealism," Westbrook subsequently notes, 104–5, "did not affect his identification of democracy with equal opportunity for all the members of a society to make the best of themselves as social beings, and thus he retained the link between self-realization and social service which was such an important aspect of the neo-Hegelian concept of positive freedom." In other words, Dewey's "deconversion" did not essentially alter the substantive content of moral or human excellence, and its implications for society, that he had advocated in his earlier period; it did, however, significantly, signal a waning confidence in the metaphysical foundations of these ideals and a desire to ground them in some other way.

For the Progressives, like Hegel, then, freedom does not consist in the individual's mere ability to govern himself absent the overt interference of others, but, rather, in his ability to actualize the potential inherent in his being becoming thereby "perfect" or complete. In other words, the Progressives redefined individual freedom in terms of an explicitly teleological conception of human nature, and, hence, in terms of the realization of a particular conception of virtue or human excellence. "True" freedom is thus "positive," not "negative," in character, and goes hand in hand with a particular understanding of history: When freedom is defined in "positive" terms, as Ely, quoting the British neo-Hegelian T. H. Green, emphasizes, it is the "result of a long and arduous constructive process."[30] This "long and arduous constructive process" is history or "social evolution" rightly understood. Importantly, then, while the Progressive conception of "social evolution" entails change, this change is no mere arbitrary or directionless flux. For "'amid all the . . . ebb and flow of social change,'" the Progressives nonetheless believed it was possible to discern certain "general" or "predominate" "tendencies" indicative of the Progressive "unfolding" (and hence actualization or fulfillment) of the human potential to be free.[31] For the Progressives, in short, freedom is inextricably tied to an evolutionary, or, more precisely, *Progressive,* conception of history, development, or growth in which each successive stage, like an infant maturing into adulthood, represents a fuller or more complete flowering of man's inherent nature than the previous one.

The Progressive conception of "social evolution" or "progress," accordingly, cannot be understood apart from the ideal of freedom which provides its basic engine, aim, and hence general trajectory. "History," as Richard Gamble, following progressive theologian Shailer Mathews, notes, "possessed a distinct and discernable tendency, a teleology. It moved from the physical to the spiritual, from perdition to redemption."[32] The Progressives were thus "evolutionists," but neither solely nor even primarily of the Darwinian variety, as is commonly suggested.[33] "The peculiar service of Darwin," Ely explains, "was the explanation of the method

---

[30] Ely, "Industrial Liberty," 62–3.

[31] For "'the ebb and flow of historical change,'" see Dewey and Tufts, *Ethics,* 428. Commentators typically emphasize the Progressives' empiricism, their reliance upon what Ely, *Ground Under Our Feet,* 154, 161, 185, called the "look and see" method. But progressive social science, in contrast to contemporary social science, did not draw a sharp distinction between what is empirical (or the "facts") and what is normative (or "values"). In their view the facts reveal the growth of the ideal. "As has been well pointed out by Professor [Franklin] Giddings," Ely, "Ethics and Economics," 119, thus writes, "what is includes what ought to be. The ideal exists, but not universally. The ethical aim of reformers is to render general that excellence which at the time is isolated. Past, present, and future are organically connected. The germs of a better future always exist in the present, but they require careful nursing."

[32] Gamble, *The War for Righteousness,* 36.

[33] See, for example, I. A. Newby, *Jim Crow's Defense: Anti-Negro Thought in America, 1900–1930* (Baton Rouge, LA: Louisiana State University Press, 1965), 52.

of biological development by means of the theory of natural selection . . . [S]o convincing was the evidence he submitted" in his 1859 essay, "The Origin of Species by Means of Natural Selection," "that the general acceptance of the idea of evolution dates from the publication of this book." But, while Darwin may have been the great popularizer of evolution, he was hardly the first to advance some concept of it: "[T]he idea of the evolution of industrial society," Ely continues,

> was clearly advanced more than fifty years ago [i.e., in the early 1850s and thus prior to the publication of "The Origin of Species"] . . . by the group of German economists who are now ordinarily designated as the German Historical School. Of these, the three most prominent were Bruno Hildebrand, Wilhelm Roscher, and Karl Knies[.]"[34]

As suggested previously, these scholars, the founders of the German Historical School of economics, were the teachers, and the teachers of the teachers, of many of the German-trained Progressive social scientists. The idea of evolution that they developed, in turn, reflected the influence of an even earlier exponent of evolution, for the German Historical School, as Daniel M. Fox notes, was "deeply influenced by Hegelian concepts of historical process[.]"[35] The Progressives' thought thus reflects the influence of a pre-Darwinian conception of evolution, a conception which, though not entirely at odds with a Darwinian-based explanation, was ultimately in considerable tension with it. "Attempts have been made," Ely observes, "to carry over the principle of natural selection from biology into the study of the social life of man." While natural selection might explain the mechanism of evolution in a merely "organic" sense, it cannot adequately explain human or "social evolution": "It has been well said that as organic evolution gives us man, so social evolution gives the ideal man." "This thought," Ely notes, "finds beautiful expression in the following language of the late Professor Joseph Le Conte":

> Organic evolution reached its term and completion in achieving man. But evolution did not stop there; for in achieving man it achieved also the possibility of another and higher kind of evolution, and was therefore transferred to a higher plane, and continued as social evolution or human progress. Now, as the highest end, the true significance, the *raison d'etre* of organic evolution, was the achievement of

---

[34] Ely, *Studies in the Evolution of Industrial Society*, 4–5, 21.

[35] Daniel M. Fox, "Introduction," in Simon N. Patten, *The New Basis of Civilization*, ed. Daniel M. Fox (Cambridge, MA: Harvard University Press, 1968), xi–xii. At the University of Heidelberg, Karl Knies was Ely's major professor. In his autobiography, *Ground Under Our Feet* (New York: The MacMillan Co., 1938), 43–44, Ely declares that "It is Knies . . . whom I am glad to acknowledge, more than any other man, as My Master."

man; so the highest and real meaning of society and social progress is the achievement of ideal man.[36]

From the Progressives' standpoint, the suggestion that society always evolves through the blind and unbridled pursuit or struggle for survival—i.e. unfettered selfishness or "competition"—flew in the face of the general or predominate "tendencies" (or trends) they widely regarded as the hallmarks of human development. Although the Progressives defined progress essentially in terms of the increasing actualization of various latent "capacities"—e.g., the "the religious nature, the moral sense, the taste, the intellect"—they put special stress on the actualization of man's social and intellectual capacities.[37] "The history of morals," as Dewey and Tufts explain,

> manifests a twofold movement. It reveals, on one side, constantly increasing stress on *individual* intelligence and affection.... [It] also reveals constantly growing emphasis upon the *social* nature of the objects and ends to which personal preferences are to be devoted.[38]

The first process, the "rationalizing or idealizing process," is the process through which man's reason develops initially as a blind or unconscious tool in the service of his most primitive or spontaneous (and hence physical) instincts—e.g., to eat, seek shelter, generate offspring, etc. The development of reason in this respect is manifest in the development of "skilled occupations, in industry and trade, in the utilizing of all resources to further man's power and happiness." Gradually, however, man's reason develops to the point where it begins to "introduce new ends." Man, Dewey and Tufts continue,

> does not live by bread only, but builds up gradually a life of reason. Psychologically this means that whereas at the beginning we want what our body calls for, we soon come to want things which our mind takes an interest in. As we form by memory, imagination, and reason a more continuous, permanent, highly-organized self, we require a far more permanent and ideal kind of good to satisfy us. This gives rise to the contrast between the material and ideal selves, or in another form, between 'the world' and 'the spirit.'[39]

[36] Ely, *Studies in the Evolution of Industrial Society*, 9, 148.
[37] Merriam, *A History of American Political Theories*, 316.
[38] Dewey and Tufts, *Ethics*, 427.
[39] Ibid., 10–11.

Like Hegel, the Progressives argue that the human mind advances from unconscious through increasingly conscious phases of development.[40] Over the course of this development reason begins to function not only as an increasingly powerful tool in the service of man's material desires, but also, though more gradually, as an increasingly self-aware faculty capable of distinguishing man's lower, material or physical existence from his higher "ideal" or spiritual nature, thereby elevating the latter, and its desires, over the former. In this respect, at least, Progressive historian John W. Burgess was hardly alone in believing, as John Gunnell notes, that history represents "the objective record of 'the progressive revelations of the human reason' and 'spirit' and 'its advance toward its own perfection.' "[41]

For the Progressives, accordingly, the development of the sciences generally, and the social sciences particularly, was both a manifestation of this developmental process, as well as its agent. Because reason develops historically in terms of its ability to grasp man's end, as well as its ability to devise means of attaining that end, as a race advances it grows increasingly able to understand, acquire control over, and thus reengineer the various "forces" shaping its existence. "We now have such scientific knowledge of social laws and forces, of economics, of history," as social gospel theologian Walter Rauschenbusch emphasizes,

> that we can intelligently mold and guide the evolution in which we take part. Our fathers cowered before lightning; we have subdued it to our will. Former generations were swept along more or less blindly toward a hidden destiny; we have reached the point where we can make history make us.[42]

Man, or, rather, advanced man, having acquired "scientific knowledge" of the various processes shaping his existence, and having become more fully aware of his previously "hidden destiny," could now consciously harness those processes to facilitate a wider and more efficient arrival at his proper end or "destiny." For the Progressives, then, the very devel-

---

[40] See, for example, Georg Wilhelm Friedrich Hegel, *The Philosophy of History* (New York: Dover Publications, Inc., 1956), 25: "The History of the World begins with its general aim— the realization of the Idea of Spirit—only in an *implicit* form (*an sich*) that is, as Nature; a hidden, most profoundly hidden, unconscious instinct; and the whole process of History (as already observed), is directed to rendering this unconscious impulse a conscious one."

[41] Gunnell, *Descent of Political Theory*, 55. On the flagrantly Hegelian aspect of Burgess's conception of history, see Ross, *The Origins of American Social Science*, 71.

[42] Walter Rauschenbusch, *Christianizing the Social Order* (New York: MacMillan Co., 1919), 40–41. See also Ely, *Studies in the Evolution of Industrial Society*, 484: "To an ever increasing extent . . . society is governed by the operation of self-conscious social forces. There is a dawning self-consciousness of society, and there is clear evidence of a determination on the part of society that the advantages of civilization shall be widely diffused. . ."

opment of the social sciences in America not only confirmed that a high
degree of rational development had already occurred, but also augured in
the sciences' anticipated development, as well as their integration into the
actual substance of public policy, a wider and more rapid realization of
this developmental process for everyone.

The other main line of moral or historical progress, the "socializing
process," is the process through which human beings develop "an increased
capacity to enter into relations with other human beings." "Like the growth
of reason," this building up of a "'social self,'" as Dewey and Tufts call
it, is "both a means and an end." [43] Just as the development of reason is
initially valuable merely as a means of attaining some other end, but
ultimately becomes an end in itself, so too are man's relations with others.
The social development of humanity, in other words, would culminate in
social relations of a particular kind. The "socializing process," as Dewey
and Tufts explain, "consists in the *extension* of the area or range of persons
whose common good is concerned, and in the deepening or *intensification*
in the individual of his social interest: 'the settled disposition on each
man's part to make the most and best of humanity in his own person and
the person of others.'" [44] As man advances, in other words, the locus of
his concern widens: his preoccupation with his own narrow and largely
material concerns increasingly gives way to concern for others, which
others, are understood in increasingly wider terms—e.g., family, nation,
and ultimately all humanity. At the same time, the kind or nature of
concern man takes in this growing circle of "others" also changes. Instead
of viewing others as mere tools in the service of his own gain, man would
increasingly view these others as beings to whom he owed an obligation,
an obligation which would ultimately be understood in terms of their
fullest possible growth or development. The Progressives thus not only
believed that history was moving individuals into increasingly wider and
more complex social groups—e.g., economic and political units—but that
this very process was accompanied, albeit more slowly, by a "deepening"
sense of moral obligation. "Day by day," Ely enthuses, "the phrase, 'All
men are brothers,' comes to mean more and more, and the time is surely
coming when it will ethically mean as much in the world at large as once
it did in the village community." [45] The "socializing process" of history, in

---

[43] Dewey and Tufts, *Ethics*, 11–12.

[44] Dewey and Tufts, *Ethics*, 429; see also 427: "The moral history of the race also reveals
constantly growing emphasis upon the *social* nature of the objects and ends to which personal preferences are to be devoted."

[45] Ely, *Studies in the Evolution of Industrial Society*, 429–31. For Ely, ibid., 431, this expectation was no mere ideal but increasingly an empirical reality: "The widening and deepening range of ethical obligation rests upon a basis of solid facts. One of the most characteristic
features of the latter half of the nineteenth century is the extension of international connections. Men of all nations are drawing nearer and nearer together in every department of
social life." On the increasingly social development of man economically, see Ely, *An Introduction to Political Economy*, chaps. 2–3.

short, would culminate in the formation of men dedicated to the fullest possible development of all humanity.

For the Progressives, then, the "rationalizing" and "socializing" processes of history were gradually effecting a reconstitution of the objects of human desire: "as man advances," says Ely, "material wants give way to higher social, mental, and spiritual wants."[46] Individuals were not only increasingly taking greater interest in their "mental" development, but were also growing increasingly self-forgetting or "service"-oriented in the sense of being willing to subordinate their own concerns to promote the moral growth of others. Men are, Ely insists, increasingly bringing "ethical tests to bear upon all relations of life . . . rejecting as unsound all practices and customs inconsistent with genuine brotherhood."[47] In America, as elsewhere, these historical forces were forming a new and improved citizen, a "new patriot," or, more precisely, a super patriot, whose relative willingness to sacrifice his personal affairs for the sake of others would be like that of a soldier in wartime: "In the days of '61 to '65," as Charles Van Hise, a leading Progressive conservationist, economist and, president of the University of Wisconsin, writes,

> a million men laid aside their personal desires, and surrendered their individualism for the good of the nation. Now it is demanded that every citizen shall surrender his individualism not for four years, but for life,—that he shall think not only of himself and his family, but of his neighbors, and especially of the unnumbered generations that are to follow.[48]

The extraordinary degree of self-sacrifice once characteristic of Americans only in exceptional, short-lived periods of wartime, the reformers believed, not only should but actually *was* increasingly becoming the norm in all areas of life. From their standpoint, moreover, such self-sacrifice cannot even properly be described as *self*-sacrificial: for the individual, in the very act of subordinating his own "personal desires" for the sake of promoting others' welfare, was actually achieving his highest level of growth. "This view," Ely assures, "does not imply a conflict between the development of the individual and the development of society. Self development for the sake of others is the aim of

---

[46] Ely, *Introduction to Political Economy*, 70.

[47] Ely, *Studies in the Evolution of Industrial Society*, 430–31. The socializing process of man, which culminates in an awareness of one's obligation to promote the fullest development of others, is an end which cannot be transcended. In *Introduction to Political Economy*, 101, Ely pointedly declares that this end is one which "[h]uman progress can never pass . . . for it satisfies the highest aspirations of which we are capable."

[48] Charles R. Van Hise, *The Conservation of Natural Resources in the United States* (New York: The MacMillan Co., 1913), 377.

social ethics. Self and others, the individual and society, are thus united in one purpose." [49]

The Progressives were thus confident that humanity generally—and the most advanced or progressive races particularly—was developing an increasingly broader conception of duty to an ever-enlarging circle of men, including, ultimately, all humanity. As mentioned previously, however, their understanding in this regard was in tension with those Darwinian-minded scholars who sought to explain "social evolution" solely in terms of natural selection. In a review essay of Benjamin Kidd's 1894 book, *Social Evolution*, for example, Theodore Roosevelt criticizes Kidd on precisely this point. Roosevelt, David Burton explains,

> centered his disagreement with Kidd's espousal of social Darwinism on the ground that it was faulty scientific method, reflecting a dangerously narrow orientation, for anyone to argue that the single postulate of natural selection could alone explain social progress. There were other factors, along with a notable body of contrary evidence, to be taken into account.

Roosevelt insisted that "[s]ide by side with the selfish development in life, there has been almost from the beginning a certain amount of unselfish development too; and in the evolution of humanity the unselfish side has, on the whole, tended steadily to increase at the expense of the selfish, notably in the progressive communities." [50] "Competition," Ely likewise agrees, "begun far below man with the very beginnings of life, persists as one of the most fundamental laws of animate existence, but evolution carries it to higher and ever higher planes." [51] From the Progressives' standpoint, as Wilson Carey McWilliams rightly notes, "evolution—pace Darwinian individualism—rewarded the capacity for cooperative action." [52] The idea that natural selection, understood as

[49] Richard T. Ely, *Social Aspects of Christianity, and Other Essays* (New York: Thomas Y. Crowell & Company, 1889), 129–30.

[50] David H. Burton, "Theodore Roosevelt's Social Darwinism and Views on Imperialism," 106–7. Burton is quoting Theodore Roosevelt, "Social Evolution," *The Works of Theodore Roosevelt*, Memorial Edition (New York, 1923–1926), XIV, 114.

[51] Ely, *Studies in the Evolution of Industrial Society*, 134. See also Ross, *The Origins of American Social Science*, 198, and Eisenach, "Progressive Internationalism," 233–4: "The social evolutionary perspective," articulated by Progressive political economists, "posited both increasing integration of economic units and their increasing interdependence—all pointing to a coming era where individualist competition is increasingly supplanted by cooperation and mutual responsibility."

[52] McWilliams, "Standing at Armageddon," 114. Gamble, *The War for Righteousness*, 34, makes much the same point in relation to the Social Gospel Movement: "[A] teleological, pre-Darwinian evolutionary cast of mind certainly characterized the progressive clergy's interpretation of the world." By "pre-Darwinian," however, Gamble means that the Progressives were Neo-Lamarckians, evolutionists, who, following the early nineteenth-century French biologist Jean-Baptiste Lamarck, believed that behavior acquired over the course of an organism's life could be inherited by its offspring. But, other aspects of Gamble's analysis

the unbridled pursuit of survival, was the sole—or even ultimately the chief mechanism of progress—was simply not supported by the facts.

For the Progressives, in sum, "true" freedom is "positive" in nature because it consists in the individual's actual ability to develop and exercise properly the different capacities of his entire nature. To link the progressive conception of freedom, and hence morality, to the fulfillment of human nature, is, of course, to depart in an important respect from the conventional view, for the Progressives are widely regarded as thoroughgoing moral relativists. As Axel Schafer contends, for example, the professors constituting the German Historical School of economics "exhorted their students to study and understand economic life in the context of social customs, values, and institutions. They urged them to look at culture, rather than nature; at the environment, not genetics; at historical differences, not universal laws; and at ethical change, not moral absolutes." Gustav Schmoller, arguably the most influential member of this school, Schafer continues, "maintained that ethics were embedded in historically developed institutions, and were neither based on fixed ideas intuited *a priori,* nor determined by nature."[53] The problem with characterizing the Progressives as moral relativists is that this is only partially correct, and proceeds from an emphasis upon one aspect of the progressive conception of history to the virtual exclusion of—or, at least, a confusion about—its ultimate implication. Specifically, the Progressives, like the German Historical School, did deny the existence of "moral absolutes" both in the sense of moral principles which are accessible or capable of being understood at all times and in all places, as well as in the sense of motives (or principles of action) which govern human behavior at all times and in all places, e.g., the "iron law" of self-interest or natural selection. This denial follows from the development of human reason from unconscious through increasingly conscious stages of awareness, on the one hand, and the development of an increasingly social will, on the other.[54] As has been previously suggested, however, this developmental process does not represent the abandonment of nature in *any* sense as the source of human morality. Indeed, as Schafer himself somewhat concedes, for all their relativism, Schmoller (and the German Historical School

---

suggest that German idealism played an important role in forming the Progressives' evolutionary thinking. At p. 32, for example, he notes that Washington Gladden, one of the leading clergymen of the Social Gospel Movement (and founding lay member of the AEA), attributed "the historical sense" that so dominated the thought of his day "to the German thinkers Kant, Fichte, and Hegel[.]"

[53] Schafer, *American Progressives and German Social Reform, 1875–1920,* 17, 47. Much the same confusion characterizes Rader's analysis of Ely in *The Academic Mind and Reform,* 41–53.

[54] One implication of this view, as Ely, *Studies in the Evolution of Industrial Society,* 48, presents it, is that slavery is not simply unjust, i.e., unjust at all times and in all places: In an "early stage of industrial development, labor, it is generally maintained, had to be forced if there was to be any steady labor at all, and thus slavery may be looked upon as a necessary stage in the evolution of industrial society."

more generally) also embraced a teleological conception of history and ethics:

> In spite of this historical relativism, however, Schmoller embraced a concept of ethics that was linked to a teleological theory of progress derived from romanticism and Hegelian idealism. Ethical development was part of a cultural and civilizational process, which Schmoller defined, quite traditionally, as an advance in rationality.[55]

To put the point more baldly, the Historical School, like its members' American progeny, believed that history is teleological precisely because they believed in a teleological conception of human nature. History is teleological because it is a developmental process ordered toward the realization of a definite end—i.e., man's highest nature which is innate in the form of unrealized or latent potential, capacities, or faculties. This process is progressive, moreover, because the specific capacities constituting this human potential are *increasingly* actualized, a process the Historical School believed was proceeding at different rates among the different races of the human family. For the Historical School the various races (and their civilizations) were not simply different, as a consistent relativist would maintain, but could be ranked *hierarchically* in terms of their relative development of reason, as well as their relative development of a social will. The reformers' confidence in the basic aim, content and hence direction of history, in short, provided a standard by which they evaluated and ranked the different branches of the human family—which is why, as Rodgers observes, "it was the mark of those who shaped the Atlantic progressive connection to see the world as a long line of runners pumping down *a common track of progress,* some in advance, others straggling in the rear."[56]

IV. THE PROGRESSIVE CONCEPTION OF FREEDOM, HISTORY AND THE TRANSFORMATION OF PUBLIC POLICY

The Progressives' redefinition of freedom in idealistic or "positive" terms literally transformed the Founders' theory of government, and, thereby, the principles informing the formulation of public policy in America. As the Progressives themselves were very well aware, this change implied two significant changes in the substance of public policy.

First, despite superficial appearances to the contrary, the reformers' embrace of the idealistic conception of freedom transformed the object or purpose of government and hence its legitimate scope. "More than any-

---

[55] Schafer, *American Progressives and German Social Reform, 1875–1920,* 47.

[56] Rodgers, *Atlantic Crossings,* 368. My emphasis. See also E. A. Ross's, *The Old World in the New: The Significance of Past and Present Immigration to the American People* (New York: The Century Co., 1914), for an excellent example in this regard.

thing else," as Michael McGerr rightly notes, "progressivism, 'the great
work of reconstruction,' was the attempt to reconstruct the individual
human being."[57] As we have seen, the reformers' disposition in this
regard follows from their embrace of the idealistic conception of freedom
and history. It follows, more precisely, from the Progressives' belief that as
a race advances its members become increasingly conscious of the full
scope of the duty they owe to others, including, ultimately, the duty to
promote the moral growth of all humanity. The more "progressive" a race
becomes, in other words, the more its members would recognize that all
men have an "innate" or "natural" right to actualize their full potential,
which government, no less than every other social institution, is obliged
to promote.[58] Although the Progressives continued to define the end of
government in terms of individual freedom, then, their redefinition of its
content—from negative to positive—prompted them to deny the natural
rights doctrine of the Founding, and thus the idea that the power of
government is limited, in principle, to securing such rights. In their view
all of the decisions previously reserved to the individual by virtue of the
Founders' natural rights doctrine were now subject to public disposal in
whatever degree those in government believed was necessary: "It is not
admitted that there are no limits to the action of the state," as Charles
Merriam concludes in his 1903 survey of progressive thinking,

> but on the other hand it is fully conceded that there are no "natural
> rights" which bar the way. The question is now one of expediency
> rather than of principle. In general it is believed that the state should
> not do for the individual what he can do as well for himself, but each
> specific question must be decided on its own merits, and each action
> of the state justified, *if at all*, by the relative advantages of the pro-
> posed line of conduct.[59]

"[I]n general," as Ely likewise writes, "there is no limit to the right of the
State, the sovereign power, save its ability to do good."[60] In redefining

---

[57] McGerr, *Fierce Discontent*, 80.

[58] Although generally reluctant to use the language of natural rights to describe rights,
largely because of the concept's identification with the older and hence "outdated" rights
doctrine, more than a few leading Progressives explicitly acknowledged the prepolitical
origin of what Dewey and Tufts, 447, refer to as the individual's "right ... to spiritual
self-development and self-possession." See, for example, Theodore Woolsey, *Political Science*,
vol. I, 10–11: "[E]very one has a right to be what he was meant to be; that he has a right to
develop himself, to maintain and carry out his true nature." See too W. W. Willoughby, *The
Ethical Basis of Political Authority*, (New York: the MacMillan Co., 1930), 245: "[T]he only
rights which may be claimed as natural, in the sense of being innate or essential are those
which are necessary for the realization of one's highest ethical self ... 'that arise out of, and
are necessary for the fulfilment of, a moral capacity without which a man would not be a
man.'"

[59] Merriam, *A History of American Political Theories*, 322. My emphasis.

[60] Ely, *Introduction to Political Economy*, 92. See also Ely, *Studies in the Evolution of Industrial
Society*, 61: "In many ways, too, our habits of thought have to be changed as we pass from

freedom, accordingly, the Progressives not only denied that securing the natural rights of the individual, as the Founders' understood these rights, was a proper object of public policy, but also affirmed that the power of government could rightfully expand in whatever degree promotion of a wider and deeper realization of the "ethical ideal" was believed to require. As the agent of progress, in other words, government could now rightfully determine to what extent, if any, individuals should be allowed to make decisions in their own lives. This momentous change not only paved the way for an unprecedented level of public control, but in so doing, as Merriam suggests, rendered the time-honored American practice of questioning whether government could rightfully intrude upon any specific aspect of individual decision-making virtually obsolete.

Second, the Progressives' redefinition of freedom not only stripped government of its obligation to secure the natural right of individuals to govern themselves, but also put an end to the idea that men, as men, are entitled to the same or equal legal rights. For although the Progressives believed men had an equal right to develop, and were actually treading a common path of development, they were no less convinced that the different races (and classes therein) were advancing at markedly different rates. "The last few years have witnessed a great change of mind," as Progressive political scientist Paul Reinsch observes in a 1905 article entitled "The Negro Race and European Civilization":

> the ... idea of the practical equality of human individuals wherever they may be found, has been quite generally abandoned.... [I]t is clear that conditions of environment and historical forces have combined in producing certain great types of humanity which are essentially different in their characteristics. To treat these as if they were alike, to subject them to the same methods of government, to force them into the same institutions, was a mistake of the nineteenth century which has not been carried over into our own.[61]

The process of "social evolution" has produced "certain great types of humanity" so "essentially different in their characteristics," Reinsch con-

---

one stage to another. This is irksome, and we resist it for a time. The idea that a business is a man's own and ought not to be interfered with by the public is one that belongs to this early part of the industrial stage, and it has been only with extreme slowness and obstinacy that it is coming to be recognized by business men that such an attitude is an anachronism."

[61] Paul S. Reinsch, "The Negro Race and European Civilization," *The American Journal of Sociology* (Sept. 1905): 148. Rader, *The Academic Mind and Reform*, 128, 173, reports that Ely hired Reinsch as an assistant professor of political science at the University of Wisconsin, and that he appears to have played an important role in the elaboration of the "Wisconsin idea." "The "Wisconsin idea" refers to the progressive transformation of Wisconsin state governance initiated by the election of Robert M. La Follette, a graduate of the University of Wisconsin, as governor in 1900. The integration of the University of Wisconsin professoriate into policy-making at various points, as well as the implementation of "social and industrial legislation," were among the leading features of the "idea."

tends, that government cannot treat them "as if they were alike"—as if, that is, they possess the same or equal rights. In the "Declaration of Independence," Ely likewise pointedly observes, "liberty is associated with equality. Natural equality is held to be a fundamental fact, and not by any means a goal to be reached slowly and painfully." "[W]e," in contrast,

> have discovered human nature to be a more complex thing than it was thought to be in the last quarter of the eighteenth century. Instead of a very simple psychology, we have a very complex psychology underlying our twentieth century thought. Inequalities among men we now know are natural... Men are what they are as a result of heredity, as well as environment. Moreover, we have heredity of environment itself, which is felicitously termed social heredity."

For reasons not only of heredity, but also environment, the different races of the human family were developing at different or unequal rates. Thus, whereas the Founders "were inclined to regard men as substantially equal, and to suppose that all could live under the same economic and political institutions," Ely concludes, "[i]t now becomes plain that this is a theory which works disaster, and is, indeed, cruel to those who are in the lower stages, resulting in their exploitation and degradation." [62] To treat the different races equally by securing to their individual members the same legal rights, in short, was simply to foster the "degradation and exploitation" of those still in the "lower stages" of development.

Whereas the Founders emphasized the equal natural and legal rights of man, the Progressives, though recognizing a common, equal natural right to develop, nonetheless emphasized that the rights granted at law must vary in relation to the relative development of the group in question. [63] The particular legal rights granted to any group—e.g., to what extent they should be allowed to make decisions in their own private matters, participate in public decision-making, or receive positive resources—should be determined, in part, in relation to how relatively developed the group

[62] Ely, "Industrial Liberty," 60, 64; *Studies in the Evolution of Industrial Society*, 62. John R. Commons, *Races and Immigrants in America* (New York: The MacMillan Co., 1907), 3–4, makes substantially the same point.

[63] As John Marini, "Progressivism, Immigration and Citizenship," in *The Founders on Citizenship and Immigration: Principles and Challenges in America*, ed. Edward J. Erler, Thomas G. West, and John Marini (Lanham, MD: Rowman and Littlefield Publishers, Inc. 2007), 145, points out, the Progressives advanced the very same view of rights advocated by the leading defenders of slavery prior to the Civil War. Some of the reformers acknowledged this parallel: "[F]rom the standpoint of modern political science," Merriam, *A History of American Political Theories*, 250–51, writes, "the slave holders were right in declaring that liberty can be given only to those who have political capacity enough to use it, and they were also right in maintaining that two greatly unequal races cannot exist side by side on terms of perfect equality." On this point, see also C. Vann Woodward, *The Strange Career of Jim Crow* (New York: Oxford University Press, 2002; orig. published 1955), 95: "Southern sentiment in 1904 suggested to Carl Schurz 'a striking resemblance to the pro-slavery arguments ... heard before the Civil War[.]' "

was perceived to be—and why. "Race improvement," Ely contends, "is a result of selection on the one hand, and of environment on the other."[64] By "selection," of course, Ely meant the transmission of qualities—e.g. physical size, susceptibility to disease, extent of psychological abilities, etc.—from one generation to the next via sexual reproduction or "the blood." "Race differences," Progressive economist John R. Commons explains,

> are established in the very blood and physical constitution. They are most difficult to eradicate, and they yield only to the slow processes of the centuries. Races may change their religions, their forms of government, their modes of industry, and their languages, but underneath all these changes they may continue the physical, mental and moral capacities and incapacities which determine the real character of their religion, government, industry and literature.[65]

Although the Progressives widely believed humanity was endowed with the same basic capacities, and was, as a consequence, treading a common path of development, they did not typically believe nature had been equally generous to each race. In terms of the magnitude of their native "endowments," in other words, the Progressives believed there were "superior" and "inferior" races, just as there were also superior and inferior individuals.[66] "Society," as Progressive sociologist (and feminist) Char-

---

[64] Ely, *Studies in the Evolution of Industrial Society*, 168. Or, as Commons, *Races and Immigrants*, 209, puts it, "amalgamation" must be distinguished from "assimilation." "The term amalgamation may be used for that mixture of blood which unites races in a common stock, while assimilation is that union of their minds and wills which enables them to think and act together. Amalgamation is a process of centuries, but assimilation is a process of individual training. Amalgamation is a blending of races, assimilation a blending of civilizations."

[65] Commons, *Races and Immigrants in America*, 7. Along with Ely, Commons was one of the single most important architects of the positive state in America. Commons earned his Ph.D. under Ely's direction during the early part of his career at Johns Hopkins. After moving to the University of Wisconsin, Ely hired Commons to teach economics. Among other things, Commons played a key role in the elaboration of the "Wisconsin idea," as well as in the founding and governance of the American Association for Labor Legislation (AALL). Kenneth Boulding, "Institutional Economics—A New Look at Institutionalism," *American Economic Review* 7, supp. 1 (May 1957): 7, sums up his influence by declaring that "through his students," including the AALL's long-time executive director, John B. Andrews, as well as Edwin Witte (the "father of the Social Security Act") and Wilbur Cohen ("the man who built Medicare"), Commons "was the intellectual origin of the New Deal, of labor legislation, of social security, of the whole movement in this country towards a welfare state." On Commons's connections to Ely, and his involvement with the AALL, see David A. Moss, *Socializing Security: Progressive-Era Economists and the Origins of American Social Policy* (Cambridge, MA: Harvard University Press, 1996), chaps. 1–2.

[66] Did the Progressives believe that some individuals and/or races were so far inferior as to fall effectively outside of humanity—outside, that is, the group of those who have a right to develop? They certainly believed that the developmental potential of some in a physical, mental, and/or moral respect was so relatively small, that such groups could rightfully be subjugated, even killed, lest their existence magnify problems that would frustrate (or worse) the moral growth of others. Here, as elsewhere, the "general welfare" takes precedence over the right of the individual. As Merriam, *American Political Theories*,

lotte Perkins Gilman explains, "is an organic relation, it is not composed of constituents all alike and equally developed, but most diverse and unequal. It is quite possible to have in a society members far inferior to other members, but yet essential to the life of the whole."[67] For the Progressives, then, neither racial equality in the sense of an equal potential to develop, nor even racial equality at law, was an essential feature of a just or well-ordered society. Michael McGerr, thus, overstates only slightly in observing that "progressives, North as well as South, did not believe in any sort of equality between the races at the turn of the century."[68]

While the Progressives believed that a race's "original endowment" functioned like a developmental ceiling, they also stressed the influence of various environmental factors. Those who seek to understand the "processes of racial disintegration," Progressive economist Simon N. Patten writes, have begun to recognize "the force of Social Heredity, which has wrought from past conditions a psychological environment that exercises power side by side with its twin force, the material environment of to-day's soil, food and climate."[69] On the one side, then, the Progressives emphasized how a race's prospect for development depended, in part, upon its

---

314, following John W. Burgess harshly notes, "... the Teutonic races must civilize the politically uncivilized... Barbaric races, *if incapable,* may be swept away; and such action 'violates no rights of these populations which are not petty and trifling in comparison with its transcendent right and duty to establish political and legal order everywhere.' " See also Roosevelt's stunning indifference to the methods by which the Indians in the American West were overcome in Dyer, *Theodore Roosevelt and the Idea of Race* (Baton Rouge, LA: Louisiana State UP, 1980), 76, 79. Many Progressives also favored weeding "defective classes" out of the larger population, which is why they widely supported "negative eugenics." As Rudolph J. Vecoli, "Sterilization: A Progressive Measure?" *Wisconsin Magazine of History* (Spring, 1960): 194, explains: "Negative eugenics, i.e., the restriction of procreation among the 'unfit,' rested on three policies: segregation, restrictive marriage laws, and sterilization." The purpose of these policies was to reduce the presence in the population of various classes regarded as "defective," including, among others, the insane, criminals, paupers, the feeble-minded, and epileptics. In 1907, under a progressive legislature and governor, Vecoli, 195, notes, the Wisconsin state legislature approved a measure which "not only prohibited the marriage of epileptic, feeble-minded and insane persons, but declared it a misdemeanor for such defectives to have sexual intercourse as well as to marry and for anyone to unite such persons in marriage." Between 1907 and 1913, moreover, there was a determined campaign to authorize the forced sterilization of idiotic, imbecile, and epileptic inmates in state and county institutions. This campaign was heartily endorsed by the University of Wisconsin professoriate, including sociologist E. A. Ross—who looked forward to expanding the reach of the project—and President Charles Van Hise. (Ely, *Studies in the Evolution of Industrial Society,* 163–88, also enthusiastically advocates segregating the "degenerate classes," that "sad human rubbish heap," through institutionalization, as well as denying them the right to marry and procreate by virtue of compulsory sterilization.) As Vecoli, 195–201, concludes: "Thus the State University, which was a powerful force in directing Wisconsin Progressivism, cast its weight on the side of eugenic reform." In 1913, under a progressive legislature and governor, Wisconsin joined eleven other states which had already approved compulsory sterilization.

[67] Charlotte Perkins Gilman, "A Suggestion on the Negro Problem," *American Journal of Sociology* 14, 1 (July, 1908): 79–80.

[68] Michael McGerr, *A Fierce Discontent: The Rise and Fall of the Progressive Movement in America, 1870–1920* (New York: Oxford University Press, 2003), 191–92.

[69] Simon N. Patten, *The New Basis of Civilization,* 32.

"material environment," upon, that is, the relative lack of food, harshness of its climate, etc. To the extent to which its material environment frustrated mere subsistence, the potential for growth was significantly retarded: "The sharp and unjustifiable antithesis of spiritual and material in the current conception of moral action," Dewey and Tufts write, "leads many-well-intentioned people to be callous and indifferent to the moral issues involved in physical and economic progress. Long hours of excessive physical labor, joined with unwholesome conditions of residence and work, restrict the growth of mental activity[.]" [70] In order to release the poor from the "material" constraints upon their growth, accordingly, the Progressives advocated a host of economic reforms including factory legislation, minimum wage laws, maximum hours laws, public housing, and a comprehensive package of social insurance. Once such reforms were implemented, the reformers had high hopes concerning how the poor would respond: "When sanitation, good housing, and shorter hours of work have generated enough energy to release starving faculties," Patten predicts, "poverty men will adjust themselves as capably as normal men and will also appreciate culture and morality." [71]

But the character of its material environment was not the only environmental factor that determined a race's prospect for development. No less important was a race's "social heredity." By "social heredity," the Progressives meant the transmission, from one generation to the next, of the acquired "customs, manners, and habits of thoughts" characterizing a particular civilization.[72] When discussing the low quality of a race, Commons cautions, we must be precise about the particular cause or character of its lowliness:

> We speak of superior and inferior races, and this is well enough, but care should be taken to distinguish between inferiority and backwardness—between that superiority which is the original endowment of race and that which results from the education and training we call civilization. While there are superior and inferior races, there are primitive, mediaeval, and modern civilizations, and there are certain mental qualities required for and produced by these different grades of civilization. A superior race may have a primitive or mediaeval civilization, and therefore its individuals may never have exhibited the superior mental qualities with which they are actually endowed, and what a modern civilization would have called into action.

[70] Dewey and Tufts, *Ethics*, 445; see also the section entitled "Restrictions from Inadequate Economic Conditions," 447. See also Tiffany Jones Miller, "Transforming Formal Freedom into Effective Freedom: John Dewey, the New Deal and the Great Society," *Modern America and the Legacy of the Founding*, ed. R. J. Pestritto and Thomas G. West (Lexington Books, 2006).
[71] Patten, *The New Basis of Civilization*, 208.
[72] Ibid., 33.

While Commons plainly believes there are inferior stocks, he nonetheless stresses that a race's lowliness may be mere "backwardness." A race's apparent inferiority, in other words, might be due merely to the poor quality of its inherited culture or civilization rather than a scant "original endowment." The "Chinaman," he clarifies,

> comes from a mediaeval civilization—he shows little of those qual-ities which are the product of Western civilization, and with his imitativeness, routine and traditions, he has earned the reputation of being entirely non-assimilable. But the children of Chinamen, born and reared in this country, entirely disprove this charge, for they are as apt in absorbing the spirit and method of American institutions as any Caucasian. The race is superior but backward.[73]

To the extent to which a race's low grade of development was believed to be attributable to the inheritance of a less developed civilization, of course, it was particularly open to social melioration or reform. Such reforms, importantly, could not seek merely to release the race from the material or poverty-related constraints upon its development. "The reasons why the Southern negro has not established an agricultural civilization," Patten thus notes, "are psychological and in no sense economic."[74] In order to reform a backward "Social Heredity," accordingly, policies designed to educate or inculcate the views and practices of a higher grade of civili-zation into more primitive peoples—policies seeking to effect a veritable "transfusion of civilization," as Charlotte Perkins Gilman characterizes it—would be essential.[75]

V. "Transfusing Civilization": Colonialism, Disfranchisement and Segregation

Just how dramatically the Progressives' embrace of the idealistic con-ception of freedom reconstituted the character of the relationship between the individual and his government can most clearly be seen in the specific

---

[73] Commons, *Races and Immigrants in America*, 211 and 97 (in relation to the "French Canadians"). See also Edward Alsworth Ross, *The Old World in the New*, 232-33: "As this country fills up with the densely ignorant, there will be more of this sort of thing [thousands of people gathering at a shrine in Ohio "reputed to possess miraculous healing virtue"]. The characteristic features of the Middle Ages may be expected to appear among us to the degree that our population comes to be composed of persons at the medieval level of culture." From the Progressives' standpoint, importantly, Americans who continued to advo-cate the relevance of the Founding principles to American governance were also effectively clinging to the "Social Heredity" of an earlier period. See, for example, Ely, *Studies in the Evolution of Industrial Society*, 61.

[74] Patten, *The New Basis of Civilization*, 33.

[75] See Charlotte Perkins Gilman, "A Suggestion on the Negro Problem," 78: "Transfusion of blood is a simple matter compared with the transfusion of civilization; yet that is precisely what is going on between us and the negro race."

policies the Progressives advocated—in many cases successfully—for those races and individuals they deemed least developed. Why is this? It is true, on the one hand, that the principles informing the Progressives' approach to the governance of these groups are the same as those informing their approach to the governance of all Americans. For the Progressives, as we have seen, government, as the agent of progress, is obliged to promote the fullest possible development of all. On the other hand, however, the Progressives also clearly believed that some groups were more advanced than others. Whereas those deemed more advanced could be allowed to exercise a higher measure of control over their own most immediate concerns, as well as public decision-making, those groups lagging furthest behind could not. Such groups faced a particularly steep developmental ascent, and were thus especially in need of the government's control and "tutelage." While the Progressives' approach to the governance of the least developed groups thus differs only in degree, and not in kind, from their approach to the governance of all Americans, their treatment of the former casts the paternal character of their conception of government in an especially stark or clear light.

In foreign policy, the Progressives' embrace of the idealistic conception of freedom, and the conception of right and duty following from it, necessitated a frankly "colonial" or "imperialistic" policy. America, Merriam stresses, "must have a colonial policy."

> Liberty is not a right equally enjoyed by all. It is dependent upon the degree of civilization reached by the given people, and increases as this advances. The idea that liberty is a natural right is abandoned, and the inseparable connection between political liberty and political capacity is strongly emphasized. After an examination of the principle of nationality, and the characteristic qualities of various nations or races, the conclusion is drawn that the Teutonic nations are particularly endowed with political capacity. Their mission in the world is the political civilization of mankind.

As a predominately Anglo-Saxon nation, the United States was part of the most advanced branch of humanity, the Germanic or "Teutonic" race. As such, it not only had a "right and privilege" to promote "the political civilization of mankind," this was its special "mission and duty, the very highest obligation incumbent on the Teutonic races[.]" In carrying this duty out, moreover, the United States was wholly justified in interfering in the affairs of other nations, regardless of whether they posed a threat to America. "[I]nterference with the affairs of states not wholly barbaric, but nevertheless incapable of effecting political organization for themselves," Merriam continues," is fully justified. Jurisdiction may be assumed over such a state, and political civilization worked out for those who are unable to accomplish this unaided."[76]

These principles, as Merriam himself observes, found no mere academic expression but were shared and expressed by leading Progressive politicians, including Theodore Roosevelt, Albert Beveridge, and Henry Cabot Lodge, in the aftermath of the Spanish-American war.[77] In a speech delivered in the Senate in 1900, for example, Senator Beveridge—the future keynote speaker at the Progressive Party Convention of 1912— argued that American withdrawal from the Philippines, a Spanish colony ceded to American control by the Treaty of Paris, would be to "renounce our part in the mission of our race, trustee under God, of the civilization of the world." Americans, he urged, should not be squeamish about ruling the Filipinos without their consent, about forcing them, that is, to live as the United States directs:

> Let men beware how they employ the term "self-government" . . . Self-government is a method of liberty—the highest, simplest, best—but it is acquired only after centuries of study and struggle and experiment and instruction and all the elements of the progress of man. Self-government is no base and common thing to be bestowed on the merely audacious. It is the degree which crowns the graduate of liberty, not the name of liberty's infant class, who have not yet mastered the alphabet of freedom. Savage blood, Oriental blood, Malay blood, Spanish example—are these the elements of self-government?[78]

"Self-government," the right, that is, to consent to one's government, is not the right of men as men, but, rather, the fruit of long development— "the degree which crowns the graduate of liberty[.]" As such, the U.S. cannot bestow it upon "liberty's infant class," upon races like the Filipinos who, by virtue of "blood" and culture (e.g., "Spanish example"), have yet to master even the mere "alphabet of freedom."

President Roosevelt shared Beveridge's position in this regard. In Roosevelt's view, as David Burton explains, "[h]uman progress required the more politically sophisticated race to rule people unable to govern themselves until they had sufficiently matured." In the case of the Philippines, then, "[t]he best interests of the Filipinos required a period of preparation for self-government under American tutelage." "In the Philippine Islands," as Roosevelt explained in a letter to Andrew Carnegie, "we are training a people in the difficult art of self-government . . . We are

---

[76] Merriam, *A History of American Political Theories*, 313–14.

[77] See ibid., 315, note 1.

[78] Albert J. Beveridge, "In Support of an American Empire," *Record*, 56 Cong., I Sess., pp. 704–12, accessed online at: http://www.mtholyoke.edu/acad/intrel/ajb72.htm.

doing this because we have acted in a spirit of genuine disinterestedness, of genuine and single-minded purpose to the benefit of the islanders."[79] Just as parents must rule their children for their own good until they mature, so the United States must rule the Filipinos, though the period of its minority would be far less definite: "We ourselves," Roosevelt wrote in a letter to Joseph G. Cannon, "must be the judges as to when they become 'fit' and when it would be 'prudent' to approve of independence."[80]

In subjecting the Filipinos, the United States was simply implementing the moral obligation, and explicitly paternal means, it had already begun implementing at home, particularly in the South. In assuming "the White Man's Burden" in the Philippines, as C. Vann Woodward thus observes, American foreign policy came to embody "many Southern attitudes on the subject of race."

> The doctrines of Anglo-Saxon superiority by which Professor John W. Burgess of Columbia University, Captain Alfred T. Mahan of the United States Navy, and Senator Albert Beveridge of Indiana justified and rationalized American imperialism in the Philippines, Hawaii, and Cuba differed in no essentials from the race theories by which Senator Benjamin R. Tillman of South Carolina and Senator James K. Vardaman of Mississippi justified white supremacy in the South. The *Boston Evening Transcript* of 14 January 1899, admitted that Southern race policy was 'now the policy of the Administration of the very party which carried the country into and through a civil war to free the slave.'[81]

As the *Boston Evening Transcript* implies, the Republican Party's embrace of "the White Man's Burden," and hence "Southern race policy," marked an important reversal in the party's principles. In the aftermath of the Civil War, the party of Lincoln had taken important steps toward implementing "the most perfect civil and political equality," as Frederick Douglass put it, by adding the Thirteenth, Fourteenth, and Fifteenth Amendments to the Constitution, thereby respectively outlawing "slavery or involuntary servitude," promising the "equal protection of the

---

[79] David H. Burton, "Theodore Roosevelt: Confident Imperialist," *The Review of Politics* 23 no. 3 (July, 1961); 363, 366.

[80] As quoted in ibid., 370, note 42. See also Thomas G. Dyer, *Theodore Roosevelt and the Idea of Race* 140–41: "Roosevelt regarded both Filipinos and Latin Americans as occupants of low rungs of the civilization ladder. . . . As 'backward peoples' these individuals occupied positions of inferiority in Roosevelt's scheme of things and thus were fair game for American imperialistic desires. . . . Like the American black, Filipinos and Latin Americans would have to proceed through the slow process of racial evolution before acquiring the skills necessary to manage their own affairs. And like the blacks, Latin Americans and Filipinos could count upon the supervision of white 'stewards' as guardians of civilization."

[81] C. Vann Woodward, *The Strange Career of Jim Crow* (New York: Oxford University Press, 2002; orig. pub. 1955), 72–73.

laws" to all "person[s]," and barring the states from denying or abridging the "right of citizens . . . to vote . . . on account of race, color, or previous condition of servitude."[82] These substantial legal gains to blacks proved, of course, to be short-lived, but not as short-lived as is commonly thought. "The impression often left by cursory histories of the subject," Woodward complains, "is that Negro disfranchisement followed quickly if not immediately upon the overthrow of Reconstruction," upon, that is, the withdrawal of the federal government from southern governance in 1877. Although "Negroes were often coerced, defrauded, or intimidated" in this period, he allows, they nonetheless "continued to vote in large numbers in most parts of the South for more than two decades after Reconstruction." "Not only did Negroes continue to vote after Reconstruction," he adds, "they continued to hold office as well."[83]

Between 1890 and the beginning of World War I, however, state law became sharply more racial in character, actually rolling back previous gains and elaborating a host of new restrictions. "The political nadir of American Negroes," as I.A. Newby likewise observes,

> lasted roughly from 1890 to 1920 . . . In 1890 Mississippi commenced the long, dreary process of constitutional amendments and statutory enactments which disfranchised the Negro and made his segregation virtually complete. Before 1900 South Carolina and Louisiana followed suit, and by 1910 Oklahoma and the remaining states of the old Confederacy had done likewise.[84]

The imposition of property qualifications, literacy tests, and/or poll taxes ultimately prevented most blacks and, no less deliberately, more than a few poor whites from voting.[85] "The effectiveness of disfranchisement,"

---

[82] On Douglass's advocacy of "the most perfect civil and political equality," see Peter C. Myers, "Frederick Douglass's America: Race, Justice and the Promise of the American Founding," accessed online at http://www.heritage.org/Research/Reports/2011/01/Frederick-Douglass-s-America-Race-Justice-and-the-Promise-of-the-Founding.

[83] Woodward, *The Strange Career*, 53–54.

[84] Newby, 143.

[85] On the exclusion of whites, see Woodward, *The Strange Career*, 84. See also Eileen L. McDonagh, "Race, Class and Gender in the Progressive Era," in *Progressivism and the New Democracy*, eds. Sidney M. Milkis and Jerome M. Mileur (Amherst: University of Massachusetts Press, 1999), 157. Newby, *Jim Crow's Defense*, 151, suggests that the exclusion of lower class whites was no less deliberate than that of blacks: "'The restriction of suffrage in Mississippi was the wisest statesmanship ever exhibited in that proud Commonwealth, and its results have been . . . beneficent and far-reaching,' said Congressman Eaton J. Bowers in 1904. 'We have disfranchised not only the ignorant and vicious black, but the ignorant and vicious white as well, and the electorate in Mississippi is now confined to those, and to those alone, who are qualified by intelligence and character for the proper and patriotic exercise of this great franchise.'" See also Edgar Gardner Murphy, *Problems of the Present South: A Discussion of Certain of the Educational, Industrial and Political Issues in the Southern States* (New York: Negro Universities Press, 1969; originally published in 1904), 192–93: "But there were two defective classes—the unqualified negroes of voting age and the unqualified white

Woodward writes, "is suggested by a comparison of the number of registered Negro voters in Louisiana in 1896, when there were 130,334 and in 1904, when there were 1,342."[86] The disfranchisement of blacks was accompanied, he adds, by *"the mushroom growth* of discriminatory and segregation laws," intrusively dictating a thoroughgoing separation of the races in transportation, the workplace, hospitals, mental and penal institutions, recreational facilities, voluntary associations, etc. Two states even went so far as to forbid the members of fraternal societies from addressing fellow members of another race as brother.[87]

The disfranchisement of blacks and growth of segregation was no mere resurgence of indigenous prejudice. Although it is the case, as was suggested earlier, that the "anti-Negro attitudes in the late nineteenth and early twentieth centuries" had their root in "the refurbished ideas of antebellum slavocrats," Newby notes, "after 1875 were added the ideas and myths of European science and race theory, and the natural and social sciences which blossomed between 1875 and 1925 provided the framework within which a new 'science of race' matured."[88] The rise of Jim Crow, in other words, was not only catalyzed, in important part, by Progressive academics, but was also explicitly championed by Southern Progressives. "The omission of the South from the annals of the progressive movement," Woodward observes,

> has been one of the glaring oversights of American historians. Not only were all phases and aspects of the movement acted out below the Mason and Dixon line, but in some particulars the Southern progressives anticipated and exceeded the performance of their counterparts in the West and East.

Southern Progressives racked up "spectacular gains" against bosses and their machines, corporations and railroads, as well as in "humanitarian legislation for miners, factory workers, child labor, and the consumer." These successes, Woodward continues, "coincided paradoxically with the crest of the wave of racism." But this was no real coincidence, as Woodward subsequently concedes, for the leaders of both movements "were often identical." "In fact," he declares, "the typical progressive reformer rode to power in the South on a disfranchising or white-supremacy movement."[89]

Progressive politicians, like Progressive academics (many of whom played a leading role in the drive for labor legislation and social insurance

---

men. Both could not be dropped at once. . . . The unqualified white men of voting age might be eliminated by gradual process, but they must first be included in the partnership of reorganization. Such a decision was a political necessity."

[86] Woodward, 85.
[87] Ibid., 97–100. My emphasis.
[88] Newby, *Jim Crow's Defense*, 7–8.
[89] Woodward, 90–91.

on the national level), widely believed the enactment of the Fifteenth Amendment had been a serious mistake. One implication of the fact that America, though a predominately Anglo-Saxon nation, was nonetheless a nation of mixed races, Merriam explains in his 1903 survey of progressive thinking, was that "the Teutonic race can never regard the exercise of political power as a right of man, but it must always be their policy to condition the exercise of political rights on the possession of political capacity." [90] And yet this was precisely what the Fifteenth Amendment failed to do. "[B]y the cataclysm of a war in which [the "Negro" race] took no part," Commons complains,

> this race, after many thousand years of savagery and two centuries of slavery, was suddenly let loose into the liberty of citizenship and the electoral suffrage. The world never before had seen such a triumph of dogmatism and partisanship. It was dogmatism, because a theory of abstract equality and inalienable rights of man took the place of education and the slow evolution of moral character.

The problem with the Fifteenth Amendment was that it was based on "a theory of abstract equality and [the] inalienable rights of man." To confer rights upon men as men, rather than conditioning them upon the proven capacity to engage in self-government, the fruit of long development, was mere "dogmatism." The Fifteenth Amendment failed

> because [it was] based on a wrong theory of the ballot. Suffrage means self-government. Self-government means intelligence, self-control, and capacity for cooperation. If these are lacking, the ballot only makes way for the 'boss,' the corruptionist, or the oligarchy. The suffrage must be earned, not merely conferred . . .

The legal right to vote, Commons concludes, should not be extended to blacks until such time as they, as individuals, develop sufficient "intelligence, self-control, and capacity for cooperation," which fitness could best be determined through "an honest educational test," that is, a literacy test.[91]

[90] Merriam, *A History of American Political Theories*, 313.

[91] John R. Commons, *Races and Immigrants in America* (New York: The MacMillan Co., 1907), 42–43, 51–52. On the pervasiveness of Commons's view among the Progressive historians, including John W. Burgess and William A. Dunning, see Newby, *Jim Crow's Defense: Anti-Negro Thought in America, 1900–1930*, 64–67. (Dunning was one of Charles Merriam's teachers and the man to whom Merriam dedicated *A History of American Political Theories*.) As Dyer, *Theodore Roosevelt and the Idea of Race*, 92, 97, explains, this was also Theodore Roosevelt's view: Roosevelt "harbored no conviction that the mass of blacks were ready for active involvement in political matters, constitutional amendments notwithstanding. Even the 'white' races had to pass through developmental stages before they became fit for self-government. . . . 'Such fitness,' Roosevelt explained in Lamarckian terms, 'is not a God-

From the Progressives' standpoint, though blacks and other "back-ward" races might not yet merit the right to consent, they must nonetheless be ruled with a view to preparing them for such participation. "The great lesson already learned," Commons continues, "is that we must 'begin over again' the preparation of the negro for citizenship. This time the work will begin at the bottom by educating the negro for the ballot, instead of beginning at the top by giving him the ballot before he knows what it should do for him."[92] The Progressives thus advocated various reforms designed, in important part, to educate blacks, including segregation. "Perhaps the best known [southern] reformer," McGerr writes, was "Edgar Gardner Murphy."[93] In his 1904 book, *Problems of the Present South*, Murphy—whom Newby characterizes as "one of the most conscientious and sincere friends of the Negro in the South"—argues that in the years following the Civil War "the South was right" to conclude

> that white supremacy, at that stage in the development of the South, was necessary to the supremacy of intelligence, administrative capacity and public order, and involved even the existence of those economic and civic conditions upon which the progress of the negro was itself dependent.

The "policy of the South in reference to the negro," he emphasizes, represents no abdication of moral responsibility, but, rather, a "deeper acceptance of obligation," the outgrowth of that "spirit of . . . tender and generous paternalism" which had developed under slavery. "There is a distinct assumption of the negro's inferiority," Murphy concedes, "but there is also a distinct assumption of the negro's improvability. It is upon the basis of this double assumption that the South finds its obligation."[94] From this point of view, segregation would not only better protect blacks—that "child-race"—from white violence, but would also throw blacks back upon their own resources to provide for themselves, thereby forcing them to develop economically. "The very process which may have seemed to some like a policy of oppression," Murphy concludes, "has in fact resulted in a process of development."[95]

---

given natural right, but comes to a race only through the slow growth of centuries, and then only to those races which possess an immense reserve fund of strength, common sense, and morality.' For blacks, self-government would be a 'slowly learned and difficult art which our people have taught themselves by the labor of a thousand years.' "

[92] Commons, *Races and Immigrants*, 45; see also Newby, *Jim Crow's Defense*, 158: ". . . [A]nti-Negro spokesmen were frequent advocates of the educational, economic, and social improvement of Negroes."

[93] McGerr, *Fierce Discontent*, 192–3.

[94] Newby, *Jim Crow's Defense*, 48. Murphy, *Problems of the Present South*, 3–8, 21, 190.

[95] Murphy, *Problems of the Present South*, 176; Murphy, as quoted in McGerr, *Fierce Discontent*, 192–3. McGerr, ibid., 196, also notes that there were a "few progressives," like Jane Addams, who disputed segregation on the ground that it discouraged, rather than promoted, the improvement of blacks.

Segregation, as implemented, was relatively mild compared to what some Progressives advocated. In a 1908 article entitled "A Suggestion on the Negro Problem," for example, Progressive sociologist (and feminist) Charlotte Perkins Gilman proposes forcing certain blacks to live and work in quasi-military labor camps. "The problem," she explains, "is this:"

> Given: in the same country, Race A, progressed in social evolution, say, to Status 10; and Race B [the "negro race"] progressed in social evolution, say, to Status 4. . . . Given: that Race B, in its present condition, does not develop fast enough to suit Race A. Question: How can Race A best and most quickly promote the development of Race B?[96]

Gilman's solution to the problem of "transfusi[ng] . . . civilization," was to compel all blacks beneath "a certain grade of citizenship," i.e., all those who were not "decent, self-supporting, [and] progressive," to live and work in labor camps until such time that they proved themselves worthy of acting under their own direction. In these camps, blacks, whose very presence "in many ways retards the progress of Race A," would be separated from whites but also forced to labor productively for themselves. In so doing they would be taught how best to provide for themselves, thereby developing economically, and their children would be educated in a progressive manner. "This proposed organization," Gilman feels obliged to clarify, "is not enslavement, but enlistment."

> It is no dishonor but an honorable employment from the first, and the rapid means of advancement. Men, women, children, all should belong to it—all, that is, below the grade of efficiency which needs no care. For the children—this is the vital base of the matter—a system of education, the best we have, should guarantee the fullest development possible to each; from the carefully appointed nursery and kindergarten up to the trade school fitting the boy or girl for life; or, if special capacity be shown, for higher education.[97]

[96] Charlotte Perkins Gilman, "A Suggestion on the Negro Problem," 79.

[97] Ibid., 79, 81. As David A. Moss, *Socializing Security: Progressive Era Economists and the Origins of American Social Policy*, 51, notes, many AALL members "supported the idea of industrial colonies," like those Gilman proposes for blacks, for "the habitually unemployed." Moss quotes Elizabeth S. Kite, of the New Jersey Department of Charities and Corrections: "'The remedy [for "the habitually unemployed"] seems to be segregation. . . Colonized upon waste land, this class can be made to contribute largely to its own support. Once recognized to be only children in mind, responsibilities beyond their power will no longer be placed upon these dependents or permitted to them. Being children they can easily be made happy and their comfort assured at a cost not exceeding what is at present so ineffectually expanded upon them by charity organizations, while the benefit to society at large and to the labor problem in particular will be immeasurable.'"

VI. Conclusion

"The high tide of progressive reform," Schafer observes, "coincided with some of the darkest moments of segregation, discrimination and racial violence." Although the foregoing suggests that this was no coincidence, Schafer contends that it was a coincidence of a peculiar sort. Although he concedes the Progressives' racism, and also recognizes how profoundly their exposure to German idealism shaped their thinking, he nonetheless denies that their idealism was the source of their racial policies: "Although the ideas of the German historical school made Americans doubt the received dogmas of economic thought," he contends, "they did next to nothing to equally dissolve the accepted dogmas of racial thought." The reformers' racial policies, their concern for "[t]he so-called 'Negro problem,'" in other words, was the one aspect of their inherited thought which went undisturbed by their exposure to idealism. The reformers' approach to the issue of race was, accordingly, "the major blind spot of progressivism."[98]

While Schafer deserves credit for acknowledging and treating the Progressives' racial views more thematically than most, the truth about the Progressives' support for these policies is exactly the reverse. In embracing the idealists' conception of positive freedom, and the process of historical development or "social evolution" through which the ideal of freedom progressively unfolds, the Progressives also accepted the idea that the different races of the human family are advancing at dramatically different rates. This understanding prompted them to repudiate the Founders' understanding of equality as encompassing all men at all times and in all places, and the idea, in turn, that government is obliged to secure the equal rights of all. As the agent of progress, government must mete out legal rights to groups in accord, in part, with their perceived grade of rational and moral development. The more advanced a group was perceived to be, the greater its control over both private and public concerns should be; the less advanced, the less control. Even in the most basic aspects of life, in short, the right to make decisions for oneself had to be earned.

Politics, University of Dallas

---

[98] Schafer, *American Progressives and German Social Reform, 1875–1920*, 69–70.

THE PROGRESSIVE ERA ASSAULT ON INDIVIDUALISM AND PROPERTY RIGHTS*

By James W. Ely, Jr.

I. Introduction

The Progressive Era of the early twentieth century witnessed sustained condemnation of individualism and individual rights. "The idea of the liberty of the individual," Washington Gladden (1836–1918) declared in 1905, "is not a sound basis for a democratic government."[1] Gladden, a Progressive and leader of the Social Gospel movement, was hardly alone in expressing such sentiments. A few years later Herbert Croly (1869–1930), a prominent Progressive theorist, attributed economic ills to "the peculiar freedom which the American tradition and organization have granted to the individual."[2] Indeed, most Progressives viewed skeptically claims of individual rights, which they associated with property rights. Progressives, in short, moved dramatically away from the classical liberalism of John Locke (1632–1704), which stressed the primacy of the individual over the state. Instead, Progressives invoked concepts such as "public welfare," "social justice," and "common good" to justify greater statist control of society.

This essay examines the widespread criticism of individualism and property rights which flourished in the late nineteenth and early twentieth centuries, and which would eventually have a profound influence on the polity. The intellectual currents of the Progressive era called into question the individualist values of classical liberalism, and paved the way for the political triumph of the New Deal. The Progressive agenda amounted to a fundamental challenge to the prevailing view of the proper role of government. To this end, Progressives virtually revamped the traditional understanding of the Constitution, rejecting the notion of limited government. "They saw in constitutional interpretation," legal scholar Richard A. Epstein aptly pointed out, "the opportunity to rewrite a Constitution that showed at every turn the influence of John Locke and James

* I wish to thank David E. Bernstein, Mark Brandon, and David N. Mayer for their insightful comments on earlier versions of this essay.
[1] Washington Gladden, *The New Idolatry and Other Discussions* (New York: McClure, Phillips & Co., 1905), 171.
[2] Herbert Croly, *The Promise of American Life* (Boston: Northeastern University, 1909; reprint, Cosimo, Inc., 2005), 23.

doi:10.1017/S0265052511000252

Madison into a different Constitution, which reflected the wisdom of the
leading intellectual reformers of their own time."[3]

One must of course, tackle the Progressive Movement with caution.
There is a vast literature on the subject.[4] Historians are by no means in
agreement about the nature, goals, or achievements of Progressivism. Nor
did all the participants in the movement share the same priorities. Progressivism flourished among members of both the Republican and Democratic parties, and found its most expansive expression in the Progressive
Party of 1912 under Theodore Roosevelt (1858–1919). "The Progressive
movement," one historian has emphasized, "sheltered uneasy alliances in
a big tent."[5] Progressives, then, were not always cohesive or consistent.
At root, Progressivism was a response to the sweeping economic changes
which transformed American society at the end of the nineteenth century.
Alarmed by the consolidation of large-scale businesses, labor conflict, and
an increase in urban poverty, Progressives had confidence that governmental action could reshape society and eliminate social problems. "Among
the most durable and controversial characteristics of Progressive legal
thought," legal scholar Herbert Hovenkamp has cogently observed, "were
its distrust of the market and its faith that the government agency, whose
salaried officials did not profit from their decisions, could regulate the
economy better."[6]

An outpouring of legislation, such as workplace safety laws, food and
drug regulations, conservation programs, child labor laws, and strengthened antitrust provisions, attest to the regulatory zeal of the Progressives.
The Sixteenth Amendment, promoted by the Progressives, authorized
Congress to levy an income tax. This new source of revenue facilitated the
growth of national power, undercutting state autonomy. With their stress
on governmental intervention in the economy, the Progressives laid the
groundwork for the growth of the modern welfare state.

Yet to gain a full appreciation of Progressivism one must avoid
an overly sanitized view. It bears emphasis that Progressives were
generally hostile to claims of individual rights, which might complicate
the achievement of their vision of the common good. Thus, they displayed little interest in free speech,[7] were indifferent to racial segrega-

---

[3] Richard A. Epstein, *How Progressives Rewrote the Constitution* (Washington, D.C.: Cato
Institute, 2006), 135.
[4] See, e.g., Richard Hofstadter, *The Age of Reform From Bryan to F.D.R.* (New York: Alfred
A. Knopf, 1955), 131–269; John D. Buenker, *Urban Liberalism and Progressive Reform* (New
York: Scribner, 1973); John Morton Blum, *The Republican Roosevelt*, 2d ed. (Cambridge, MA:
Harvard University Press, 1977); Michael McGerr, *A Fierce Discontent: The Rise and Fall of the
Progressive Movement in America* (New York: Oxford University Press, 2003).
[5] Jackson Lears, *Rebirth of A Nation: The Making of Modern America, 1877–1920* (New York:
HarperCollins Publishers, 2009).
[6] Herbert Hovenkamp, "The Mind and Heart of Progressive Legal Thought," *Iowa Law
Review*, 81 (1995): 157.
[7] Mark A. Graber, *Transforming Free Speech: The Ambiguous Legacy of Civil Libertarianism*
(Berkeley: University of California Press, 1991), 78–79 ("Most prominent early twentieth-

tion,[8] promoted eugenics and immigration restriction,[9] pursued quixotic campaigns against vice,[10] and supported prohibition.[11] The Progressive Party Platform of 1912 made no mention of rights. As Daniel T. Rogers has pointed out, "a striking phenomenon of the late nineteenth and early twentieth centuries was the abandonment of rights talk by Americans who aligned themselves with the progressive movements of the day."[12] In this regard, Progressives were entirely unlike post-World War liberals, who were preoccupied with an eruption of rights claims.

---

century proponents of federal and state economic regulations also supported federal and state speech regulations."); David M. Rabban, *Free Speech in Its Forgotten Years* (New York: Cambridge University Press, 1997), 212 (noting that Progressives had a limited conception of free speech).

[8] McGerr, *A Fierce Discontent*, supra note 4, at 182–218 ("Progressives seldom contested the increasing division of Americans into separate enclaves."); David E. Bernstein, *Rehabilitating Lochner: Defending Individual Rights Against Progressive Reform* (Chicago: University of Chicago Press, 2011), 78 ("Most Progressive political and intellectual leaders shared the racism of the day and did not support equal rights for African Americans.").

[9] Donald K. Pickens, *Eugenics and the Progressives* (Nashville: Vanderbilt University Press, 1968), 102–30; Michael Willrich, "The Two Percent Solution: Eugenic Jurisprudence and the Socialization of American Law, 1900–1930," *Law and History Review*, 16 (1998): 63, 64 (". . . eugenicists in the Progressive Era were eager to use the full range of state police powers to prevent the reproduction of criminality, deviancy, and dependency."); Vincent J. Cannato, *American Passage: The History of Ellis Island* (New York: Harper-Collins, 2009) (discussing the affinity between Progressives and immigration control).

[10] David J. Langum, *Crossing Over the Line: Legislating Morality and the Mann Act* (Chicago: University of Chicago Press, 1994), 6. (Progressives believed that by "the proper use of social engineering, often employing the coercion of the federal government, individual behavior could be controlled and changed through legislation."); McGerr, *A Fierce Discontent*, supra note 4, at 81–94 (discussing Progressive campaigns against prostitution and divorce); Susan M. Schweik, *The Ugly Laws: Disability in Public* (New York: New York University Press, 2009) (discussing municipal ordinances in the Progressive era which banned the appearance of maimed or deformed persons on the streets); Mark Thomas Connelly, *The Response to Prostitution in the Progressive Era* (Chapel Hill, N.C.: University of North Carolina Press, 1980), 7 (treating efforts to eliminate prostitution during the Progressive era, and concluding that "in one sense anti-prostitution was a progressive reform and, like much of the progressive reform impulse, had its optimistic and confident, not to mention self-righteous, strains"); Steven Schlossman and Stephanie Wallach, "The Crime of Precocious Sexuality: Female Juvenile Delinquency ant the Progressive Era," in D. Kelly Weisberg, ed., *Women and the Law: A Social Historical Perspective* (Cambridge, MA: Schenkman Publishing Company, 1982, 2 vols.), vol. II, (detailing Progressive campaign against prostitution and female delinquency).

[11] James H. Timberlake, *Prohibition and the Progressive Movement, 1900–1920* (Cambridge: Harvard University Press, 1963), 2 (". . . prohibition was actually written into the Constitution as a progressive reform. As an integral part of the Progressive movement, prohibition drew on the same moral idealism and sought to deal with the same basic problems."). In fact, many conservatives opposed prohibition on grounds that it infringed property rights and enlarged the power of the federal government. Ibid., 176–77. See also, Ken I. Kersch, *Constructing Civil Liberties: Discontinuities in the Development of American Constitutional Law* (Cambridge: Cambridge University Press, 2004), 74 ("Prohibition, moreover, like the assertion of regulatory power over other aspects of economic life at the time, was understood as a progressive measure and a full part of the progressive political program.").

[12] Daniel T. Rodgers, "Rights Consciousness in American History," in David J. Bodenhamer and James W. Ely, Jr., eds., *The Bill of Rights in Modern America*, rev. ed. (Bloomington: Indiana University Press, 2008), 18.

In addition, much of the economic legislation sponsored by the Progressives was harmful. Stringent railroad regulations did a great deal to hurt the economic health of the industry.[13] Protective legislation for working women proceeded on paternalistic assumptions and often handicapped women in the job market by pigeonholing them in certain occupations.[14]

My purpose is not to dismiss wholesale the Progressive legislative program, but to emphasize that the legacy of the movement was decidedly mixed and defies easy categorization. Despite its somewhat ambiguous character, I submit that Progressive thought was characterized by several central features:

1. Rejection of individualism in favor of statist ideology
2. Antipathy to the central place of property rights in American society and constitutional thought
3. Confidence in regulatory agencies, staffed by nonpolitical experts, to carry out legislative policy
4. Intense suspicion of the judiciary as unduly protective of individual and property rights, and therefore as an obstacle to the Progressive program

These points mark a sharp break from the classical legal tradition.

II. Locke and Classical Liberalism

Most historians agree that John Locke had an enormous influence on the Founding generation. "By the late eighteenth century," Pauline Maier observed, "'Lockean' ideas on government and revolution were accepted everywhere in America: they seemed, in fact, a statement of principles built into the English constitutional tradition."[15] Among these Lockean precepts was a belief in natural law that embodied certain individual rights which existed before the formation of political authority. Important among these was the right of private property ownership. Locke viewed private property as a necessary component of individual liberty. He fur-

[13] James W. Ely, Jr., *Railroads and American Law* (Lawrence: University Press of Kansas, 2001), 225–39; Albro Martin, *Enterprise Denied: Origins of the Decline of American Railroads, 1897–1917* (New York: Columbia University Press, 1971).

[14] Nancy S. Erickson, "Historical Background of 'Protective' Labor Legislation: *Muller v. Oregon*," in D. Kelly Weisberg, ed., *Women and the Law: The Social Historical Perspective* (Cambridge, Mass: Schenkman, 2 vols., 1982), vol. 1, 155–86 (stressing that Progressives favored paternalistic legislation that limited employment opportunities for women); Joan Hoff, *Law, Gender, and Injustice: A Legal History of U.S. Women* (New York: New York University Press, 1991) 193–203. For an expression of the typical Progressive attitude, see Richard T. Ely, *Socialism and Social Reform* (New York: Thomas Y. Crowell & Co., 1894), 322 ("Night work should be prohibited for women and persons under eighteen years of age; and, in particular, all work injurious to the female organism should be forbidden to women.").

[15] Pauline Maier, *American Scripture: Making the Declaration of Independence* (New York: Knopf, 1997), 87.

ther articulated the social contract theory under which legitimate government was grounded on an implicit compact between the people and their rulers. According to Locke, government was primarily instituted to safeguard the natural rights of individuals. Both the natural law and social contract doctrines stressed protection of individuals by limiting governmental power, which was seen as the greatest threat to individual liberty.[16] Locke's classical liberalism, with its focus on natural law and the rights of individuals, was reflected in the Declaration of Independence as well as the constitution-drafting experience at both the state and federal level in the years following the American Revolution.[17] The Bill of Rights also manifested a Lockean spirit, providing additional safeguards for individual liberty and private property.

Building upon Locke's philosophy, Anglo-American constitutional thought had long emphasized individual liberty and the close tie between liberty and private property. For example, the 1776 Virginia Declaration of Rights proclaimed: "All men . . . have certain inherent rights, namely, the enjoyment of life and liberty, with the means of acquiring and possessing property, and pursuing and obtaining happiness and safety." [18] Members of the 1787 Constitutional Convention repeatedly stressed the tie between liberty and property.[19] The close association between liberty and property prevailed throughout the nineteenth century.[20] As John Dewey (1859–1952) noted: "The concern for liberty and for the individual, which was the basis of Lockean liberalism, persisted." [21] A New York judge provided a thoughtful analysis of the values which characterized American society during the nineteenth century:

> The 19th century was a period of individualism. In politics a minimum of government was best; in economics free competition was essential; and in law the preservation of the rights of persons and property, including freedom of contract, was fundamental.[22]

[16] John Dewey, *Liberalism and Social Action* (New York: C. P. Putnam's Sons, 1935): 16 ("The whole temper of [Locke's] philosophy is individualistic in the sense in which individualism is opposed to organized social action.")

[17] Ellen Frankel Paul, "Freedom of Contract and the 'Political Economy' of *Lochner v. New York*," *NYU Journal of Law & Liberty* 1 (2005): 528–37 (pointing out that Lockean principles are evident in the Declaration of Independence and the state constitutions of the Revolutionary period).

[18] Virginia Constitution of 1776, sec.1.

[19] Walter Dellinger, "The Indivisibility of Economic Rights and Personal Liberty," *Cato Supreme Court Review* 2003-2004: 19 ("Economic rights, property rights, and personal rights have been joined appropriately, since the time of the founding.").

[20] In 1890, Justice Stephen J. Field declared: "It should never be forgotten that protection to property and to persons cannot be separated. Where property is insecure, the rights of persons are unsafe. Protection to one goes with protection to the other; and there can be neither prosperity nor progress where either is uncertain." "Centenary of the Supreme Court," 134 U.S. 729, 745 (1890).

[21] John Dewey, *Liberalism and Social Action,* supra note 16, at 18.

[22] Leonard C. Crouch, "Judicial Tendencies of the Court of Appeals During the Incumbency of Chief Judge Hiscock," *Cornell Law Quarterly* 12 (1927): 142.

Not until the end of the nineteenth century did a political and constitutional order based on individual rights come under prolonged attack.
The transformation of the economy and the rise of large-scale business
enterprise caused some to reconsider Locke's assumptions about liberty.
Howard Gillman has argued: ". . . the last quarter of the nineteenth century witnessed changes that crushed the Lockean state of nature that
inspired many of America's founders. . . ."[23] Moreover, with the rise of
social science and new schools of jurisprudence, natural law theory fell
out of favor. Oliver Wendell Holmes (1841–1935), for instance, famously
ridiculed the concept.[24] The doctrine of natural rights, Charles A. Beard
(1874–1948) declared in 1908, "really furnishes no guide to the problems
of our time."[25] Beard approvingly noted that there were decreasing references to natural law in political writings and suggested that at best
natural rights were merely moral aspirations. By 1900 classical liberalism
found itself on the defensive.

III. THE INITIAL ASSAULT

Attacks on individualism and private property can be traced to
eighteenth-century France and such writers as Jean-Jacques Rousseau
(1712–1778), with his insistence that the general will must triumph over
individuals. Under the notion of the general will the collective spirit of
the community must prevail over all claims of individual rights.[26]

Perhaps a better starting place for this inquiry, however, would be the
publication of Edward Bellamy's *Looking Backward 2000–1887* in 1888.[27] In
this futuristic novel Bellamy pictures a socialist utopia set in the then far
away year of 2000. The government is the sole landowner and employer,
providing a guaranteed maintenance for all citizens by means of an annual
credit card. There is no money, and no private property beyond personal
belongings. Competition is dismissed as wasteful. This utopia is a highly
regimented society in which both young men and women must serve in
an industrial army until the age of forty-five. Additionally, Bellamy sketches

[23] Howard Gillman, *The Constitution Besieged: The Rise and Demise of Lochner Era Police
Powers Jurisprudence* (Durham: Duke University Press, 1993), 63.

[24] Albert W. Alschuler, *Law Without Values: The Life, Work, and Legacy of Justice Holmes*
(Chicago: University of Chicago Press, 2000), 9, 26.

[25] Charles A. Beard, *Politics* (New York: Columbia University Press, 1908), 31.

[26] Under Rousseau's theory of the social contract individuals must surrender all rights to
the community and abandon ideas of natural liberty. The community acts "under the supreme
direction of the general will" for purposes of "the common good." Rousseau did not scruple
to embrace authoritarian means to achieve his goals. "In order, therefore," he wrote, "that
the social compact may not be a meaningless formality, it includes the tacit agreement,
which alone can give force to the rest, that anyone who refuses to obey the general will shall
be forced to do so by the whole body; which means nothing more or less than that he will
be forced to be free." Frederick Watkins, ed., *Rousseau—Political Writings* (New York: Thomas Nelson and Sons, 1953).

[27] Edward Bellamy, *Looking Backward 2000–1887* (Boston: Tichnor & Co., 1888; reprinted,
Matthew Beaumont, ed., New York: Oxford University Press, 2007).

a centralized society. The individual states are abolished and decisions are made by shadowy councils and bureaus. There is only a limited degree of popular control over the government. Most striking for our purposes is that Bellamy repeatedly criticizes individualism, which he contrasts unfavorably with the cooperative society of the future. Moreover, he decries "the imbecility of the system of private enterprise."[28]

There was a long tradition of utopian literature but *Looking Backward* stands out because it was a huge success. The book sold thousands of copies, was compared in its influence to *Uncle Tom's Cabin*, and stimulated the formation of clubs to promote Bellamy's socialist vision.[29] As might be expected, the volume had its share of critics, and it appears neither realistic nor appealing to modern eyes. Nonetheless, Bellamy's critique of individualism and his utopian fable attracted a host of readers in the Gilded Age (1875-1900). Clearly there were people receptive to Bellamy's call for a different type of society. Many followers of Bellamy were attracted to the Populist movement of the 1890s. By the same token, other citizens were alarmed. Protesting a New York scheme to regulate grain elevator prices, Justice David J. Brewer warned that a state might seek to control prices for all services and uses of property. "And if so," he lamented, "'Looking Backward' is nearer than a dream."[30]

IV. Sources of Progressive Thought

The rapid changes in American society at the end of the nineteenth century stimulated the Progressive movement. Still, the economic and social conditions did not dictate the particular direction of reform efforts. To understand the Progressive mentality one must probe the formative influences which guided the movement. One wellspring of Progressivism was an unlikely source: Imperial Germany. A number of individuals who were later leaders of the Progressive movement, notably Richard T. Ely (1854-1943), pursued graduate study in Germany.[31] They were impressed with the steps taken by Chancellor Otto von Bismarck (1815-1898) to deal with social problems arising from industrialization. Bismarck not only centralized the German nation, but introduced social welfare measures,

---

[28] Ibid. at 141.

[29] Elizabeth Sadler, "One Book's Influence: Edward Bellamy's 'Looking Backward'," *New England Quarterly* 17 (1944): 530–55.

[30] *Budd v. New York*, 143 U.S. 517, 551 (1892) (Brewer, J., dissenting).

[31] Eldon J. Eisenach, *The Lost Promise of Progressivism* (Lawrence: University Press of Kansas, 1994), 92–94 ("By the first decade of the twentieth century the connection between study in Germany and reform in America had become clear."); Daniel T. Rodgers, *Atlantic Crossings: Social Politics in a Progressive Age* (Cambridge: Belknap Press of Harvard University Press, 1998), 76–89 (discussing impact of study in German universities on young Progressive intellectuals); Lears, *Rebirth of A Nation*, supra note 5, at 198 ("Some Progressive Intellectuals were also profoundly impressed by the welfare-state policies emerging in Berlin and other European centers of social-democratic thought."). See also Epstein, *How Progressives Rewrote the Constitution*, supra note 3, at 3 (noting that "Progressives were influenced in part by Bismarckian social initiatives in nineteenth-century Germany").

such as pensions and laws protecting industrial workers. He was able to effectively impose this social legislation and tolerated little dissent. Bismarck's purpose, of course, was to forestall greater socialism by undercutting the political Left within Germany through governmental largess. He had little interest in nurturing either democracy or individual liberty. Nonetheless, Bismarck's legacy significantly influenced American Progressivism to look favorably upon the construction of a powerful welfare state.

Another admirer of Bismarck was Herbert Croly, who helped to formulate Theodore Roosevelt's New Nationalism policy and was a founder of the *New Republic*. Although Croly never studied in Germany, he was an enthusiast for Bismarck's program. Among the leaders of the modern German nation, Croly wrote in *The Promise of American Life* (1909), "The man who planned most effectively and accomplished the greatest results was Otto von Bismarck." Croly pointedly observed that Bismarck rejected the nation-building path of allowing "the individual every possible liberty."[32] Instead, Croly explained at length:

> Bismarck's whole scheme of national industrial organization looked in a very different direction. He believed that the nation itself, as represented by its official leaders, should actively assist in preparing an adequate domestic policy, and organizing the machinery for its efficient execution. He clearly saw that the logic and purpose of the national type of political organization was entirely different from that of a so-called free democracy ... and he successfully transformed his theory of responsible administrative activity into a comprehensive national policy.[33]

Note Croly's emphasis on organization, planning, and a strong executive, as well as his dismissal of democratic individualism. As we shall see, these themes figure prominently in Croly's Progressive creed. For many Progressives, Bismarck's Germany became the model for a reformed United States. Amusingly, with the outbreak of World War I many Progressives found it convenient to forget the German inspiration for their social policies.

In addition to faith in planning and scientific government, Progressive thought was shaped by the emergence of the Social Gospel theology. The Social Gospel movement had a significant impact on Protestant Christianity in the early twentieth century. Moving away from a focus on individualistic pietism, Social Gospel adherents sought to adjust Christianity to the insights of evolutionary science. Emphasizing the need for a changed social and economic environment rather than personal regeneration, they advocated action by government to alleviate

[32] Croly, *The Promise of American Life*, supra note 2, at 249–50.
[33] Ibid.

social problems. They were especially concerned about the conditions of industrial workers and urban housing, and were generally hostile to laissez-faire economics. Indeed, some Social Gospel theologians, notably Walter Rauschenbusch (1861–1918), advocated a form of Christian socialism.[34] Broadly speaking, Social Gospel leaders rejected economic competition and the market in favor of a cooperative society. In order to transform the political and social environment, Social Gospel advocates called for governmental action. "Since the Christianizing of the social order was a central component of social Christianity," one scholar stated, "it was essential for the movement to find some way to relate to the political life of the nation."[35]

One consequence of the Social Gospel theology was a blending of Christianity with the Progressive political agenda.[36] Not surprisingly, a number of prominent Social Gospel figures spoke in favor of a variety of social causes and became involved in Progressive era political life. The Social Gospel outlook left a deep mark on Progressivism by imparting a moralistic tone to the movement.[37] Calls for regulatory intervention in the economy were cloaked in a Christian message. Recall that the two presidents most closely associated with the Progressive movement, Theodore Roosevelt and Woodrow Wilson (1856–1924), often employed messianic rhetoric and depicted their programs in religious terms.[38] Wilson apparently viewed himself as an instrument of God. This moralistic dimension of the Progressive movement is another marked difference between Progressives and post-World War II liberals, who largely jettisoned explicit religious appeals.[39]

[34] In a series of writings Walter Rauschenbusch assailed capitalist society, urged a more egalitarian distribution of wealth, attacked economic competition, and called for public ownership of the means of production. See, e.g., *Christianity and the Social Crisis* (New York: Macmillan, 1907; reprint Louisville, KY: Westminster/John Knox Press, 1991) Rauschenbusch complained: "Our industrial individualism neutralizes the social consciousness created by Christianity." Ibid. at 388.

[35] Donald K. Gorrell, *The Age of Social Responsibility: The Social Gospel in the Progressive Era, 1900–1920* (Macon, GA: Mercer University Press, 1988), 191.

[36] Walter Rauschenbusch, "The Ideals of Social Reformers," *American Journal of Sociology* 2 (1892): 202 ("One of the special tasks of our generation is the work of wedding Christianity and the social movement").

[37] Lears, *Rebirth of A Nation*, supra note 5, at 196–97 ("In fact it was the religious dimension of reform that underwrote its intensity and its virtually limitless scope."). See Walter Rauschenbusch, *Christianizing the Social Order* (New York: Macmillan Company 1912) (urging "socializing property").

[38] Gerald Gunther, *Learned Hand: The Man and the Judge* (New York: Albert A. Knopf, 1994), 230 (commenting that 1912 Progressive Party convention, which nominated Theodore Roosevelt for president, "had more the air of a religious crusade than a political gathering"); Gorrell, *The Age of Social Responsibility*, supra note 35, at 182–89 (discussing the number of Social Gospel advocates who actively supported the Progressive Party in 1912).

[39] Lears, *Rebirth of A Nation*, supra note 5, at 352–53 (pointing out that when Progressive ideas reappeared in the 1930s they were presented in secular terms and characterized as "liberal" rather than Progressive). See also Ronald D. Rotunda, *The Politics of Language: Liberalism as Word and Symbol* (Iowa City: University of Iowa Press, 1986), 14–17, 38–51 (discussing how the term "liberal" replaced the older term "progressive" in the 1930s).

The most important aspect of the Social Gospel movement for our purpose was its repeated denunciation of individualism as a basis for society. In 1889 Gladden declared: "It begins to be clear that Christianity is not individualism. The Christian religion has encountered no deadlier foe during the last century than that individualistic philosophy which underlies the competitive system."[40] In the same vein, Rauschenbusch proclaimed in 1896 that under current economic conditions "individualism means tyranny."[41] Returning to the same theme a decade later, Gladden insisted: "I do not believe that political society or industrial society or any other society will endure on a purely individualistic basis."[42] In 1914, as Social Gospel thinking approached the height of its influence, one organization affiliated with the movement boldly proclaimed: "We believe that the age of sheer individualism is past and the age of social responsibility has arrived."[43]

V. The Apotheosis of Government

While hardly alone, Croly was among the most influential intellectuals to tackle Progressivism. In two revealing books, *The Promise of American Life* (1909) and *Progressive Democracy* (1914), he explored the meaning and purpose of the movement. Croly called for a new social order to redress the imbalances in economic and political power that he attributed to the emergence of large-scale business organizations. His remedy was to strengthen governmental authority, a step which would allow Americans to realize the "national purpose" and "the idea of social justice." Advocates of Progressivism, Croly explained, "are committed to a drastic reorganization of the American political and economic system, to the substitution of a frank social policy for the individualism of the past, and to the realization of this policy, if necessary, by the use of efficient governmental instruments."[44] Whereas the framers of the Constitution were suspicious of government as a potential threat to liberty, Croly welcomed expanded government. He made clear his impatience with constitutional doctrines that restrained the role of the national government.

Several aspects of Croly's thought warrant further attention. He was an unstinting cheerleader for vigorous executive power modeled after Theodore Roosevelt. "Progressive democracy needs executive leadership," Croly insisted, because "it organizes and vitalizes the rule of the

---

[40] William Gladden, "Christian Socialism," Minutes of the National Council of the Congregational Churches of the United States, October 9–14, 1889 (Boston: Congregational Sunday School and Publishing Company, 1889), 338.

[41] Walter Rauschenbusch, "The Ideals of Social Reformers," supra note 36, at 211.

[42] Gladden, *The New Idolatry*, supra note 1, at 130.

[43] "Declaration of Principles," *Religious Education* 9 (April 1914): 98.

[44] Croly, *Progressive Democracy* (New York: Macmillan Company, 1914), 15.

majority."[45] He added: "As a consequence of bestowing the leadership of the state upon one man who represents the dominant phase of public opinion, it develops and consolidates majority rule as it has never yet been developed and consolidated in the history of democracy."[46]

Croly was also a proponent of centralized government, and saw a diminished role for the individual states. "The state governments, either individually or by any practicable methods of cooperation," he observed, "are not competent to deal effectively in the national interest and spirit with the grave problems created by the aggrandizement of corporate and individual wealth and the increasing classification of the American people."[47] Croly maintained that changes in the economy had rendered obsolete the distinction between interstate and intrastate commerce, and that consequently all commerce should be under national control. He even questioned whether marriage should remain a state responsibility.

In fashioning his proposed economic policy, Croly lost no opportunity to denounce competition. He regarded big business as efficient and a major contributor to economic growth. He believed that such organizations should be accepted as part of modern life. Croly therefore argued that it was both foolish and futile to attempt to break up large business enterprises. He called for repeal of the Sherman Anti-Trust Act, and urged instead a regime of regulation by commissions. Consistent with his preference for collective rather than individual action, Croly declared that "it should be the effort of all civilized societies to substitute cooperative for competitive methods."[48]

To effectuate his vision of good government, Croly stressed the need for increased administrative authority. He lovingly described the independent and efficient agencies that would, in theory, carry out the policies of a progressive democracy. Croly positively gushed in picturing the qualities of his imagined administrative officials. Such an official must be an expert who follows scientific methods, must be reasonable and flexible, must be indifferent to shifts in political opinion, and must generally function as an agent of democracy.[49] Borrowing from the military and perhaps Bismark, Croly suggested that expert administrators "must provide a general staff for a modern progressive state."[50] Croly was perhaps naively optimistic about the future of the modern administrative state. Funda-

---

[45] Ibid., at 304.

[46] Ibid. See Charles Forcey, *The Crossroads of Liberalism: Croly, Weyl, Lippmann, and the Progressive Era, 1900–1925* (New York: Oxford University Press, 1961), 40–41 (stressing Croly's virtual obsession with executive power to effectuate reform).

[47] Croly, *The Promise of American Life,* supra note 2, at 275.

[48] Ibid., at 359.

[49] Croly, *Progressive Democracy,* supra note 44, at 347–77. Croly revealingly contrasted the administrative process and traditional courts: "The administrative court represents a social policy based on a collective social ideal. The common-law judge represents a social policy founded on the protection of individual rights." Ibid., at 368.

[50] Ibid. at 370.

mental economic problems involved disputes over policy, and could not be removed from the political realm by resort to supposed experts.[51] Nonetheless, Croly championed a trained bureaucracy which relied on scientific expertise to solve problems. Like many Progressives, he had great faith in the ability of an educated elite to manage the economy.

Croly's confidence in disinterested experts to effectuate his program highlights an unresolved tension within Progressive thought. Progressives were fond of claiming to represent "the people" and to speak for the popular voice. They sponsored political reforms, such as the direct election of senators, the initiative, and the referendum, in order to promote democratic government. "Progressives often spoke of their commitment to democracy," Michael McGerr has observed. "But many reformers, so critical of individualism and individual rights, were not very democratic at all."[52] Hovenkamp reached a similar conclusion: "Progressive Era social sciences were much more paternalistic than democratic. . . . Almost from the beginning, social scientists were committed to the view that important decisions should be made by experts."[53] At root, many Progressives favored governance by educated elites (like themselves) who would lead the nation and guide the political process.[54] This attitude had profound consequences for the polity. Voter participation dropped in the 1912 presidential election, a sign of lack of public interest at the height of the Progressive movement. At least part of the explanation for this decline was the growth of the new administrative state, which removed much decision-making from the political arena. "People saw less reason," one political historian concluded, "to take part in elections that often produced meaningless results."[55]

Conspicuously absent from Croly's theory of government was any emphasis on individual rights. He tended to associate claims of rights with judicial support for the rights of property owners. For example, Croly gave virtually no attention to racial or gender issues,[56] or to the role of expressive freedom. As we have seen, there was a pervasive hostility to individual rights among leaders of Progressivism. In their view, rights

[51] Robert Higgs, *Crisis and Leviathan: Critical Episodes in the Growth of American Government* (New York: Oxford University Press, 1987), 112. ("Certainly the Progressive Faith in the efficacy of placing 'experts' in positions of authority—social engineers to solve social problems—was naïve at best".)
[52] McGerr, *A Fierce Discontent*, supra note 4, at 217.
[53] Herbert Hovenkamp, *Enterprise and American Law, 1836–1937* (Cambridge: Harvard University Press, 1991), 77.
[54] Forcey, *The Crossroads of Liberalism*, supra note 46, at 38–40, 43. (". . . Croly had an abiding faith in the powerful few.")
[55] Lewis L. Gould, *Four Hats In The Ring: The 1912 Election and the Birth of Modern American Politics* (Lawrence, Kan. University Press of Kansas, 2008), 182. See also Mark Lawrence Kornbluh, *Why America Stopped Voting: The Decline of Participatory Democracy and the Emergence of Modern American Politics* (New York: New York University Press, 2000), 138–60 (discussing impact of administrative governance on participation in politics).
[56] Edward A. Stettner, *Shaping Modern Liberalism: Herbert Croly and Progressive Thought* (Lawrence, KS: University Press of Kansas, 1993), 166.

were grounded in natural law, which most Progressives rejected. Further, rights claims could well stand in the way of realizing their conception of a good society. Individual rights, therefore, must be curtailed for the benefit of the nation. This helps to explain the Progressive strictures against individualism, because that concept denoted a society focused on individual rights.[57]

Croly did not overtly attack private property ownership, but his statist philosophy entailed diminished respect for property rights. He complained that the legal system in practice "is tantamount to automatic operation in the interests of existing property owners."[58] He vaguely urged "the radical transformation" of the institution of property, but made clear that he favored its modification not elimination.[59] Croly also called for a more equal distribution of wealth, a proposal that would threaten existing ownership rights to some extent.[60] It is fair to conclude that Croly never systematically addressed the issue of property rights in his notion of progressive democracy, but he certainly intimated that property, like other individual rights, was subordinate to the public will.

Obviously Croly has wandered intellectually from the fear of arbitrary government which animated classical liberalism. Indeed, in the 1920s Croly, like a number of Progressives, found much to admire in the Italian fascism of Benito Mussolini (1883–1945). Croly saw in fascism an exciting experiment under the guidance of a strong leader. To his mind, fascism offered a seemingly rational scheme of economic planning, known as corporatism, which promised a middle path between Marxism and individualistic capitalism. In addition, it appeared to bridge the gap between social classes. While recognizing the warts of the fascist movement, Croly nonetheless reacted positively to the fascist attempt to remake Italian society.[61]

Another important figure in shaping Progressive thought was Richard T. Ely. Educated in Germany and affiliated with the Social Gospel movement, Ely was an influential economist at Johns Hopkins and the University of Wisconsin as well as a founder of the American Economic Association.[62] His numerous writings blended scientific inquiry with eth-

---

[57] Ibid. at 59–60 (stressing Croly's confidence in a trained bureaucracy).

[58] Croly, *Progressive Democracy,* supra note 44, at 314.

[59] Croly, *The Promise of American Life,* supra note 2, at 209.

[60] Ibid. at 209–10. Croly declared that "under a legal system which holds private property sacred there may be equal rights, but there cannot possibly be any equal opportunities for exercising such rights." Ibid. at 181.

[61] John P. Diggins, *Mussolini and Fascism: The View from America* (Princeton: Princeton University Press, 1972), 204–5, 228–31. Croly, of course, was not the only Progressive intellectual to initially look with favor upon Italian fascism. But see Stettner, *Shaping Modern Liberalism,* supra note 56, at 155–57 (disputing contention that Croly was sympathetic to fascism).

[62] Benjamin G. Rader, *The Academic Mind and Reform: The Influence of Richard T. Ely in American Life* (Lexington, KY: University of Kentucky Press, 1966), 1–66.

ical and Christian preachments.[63] Ely consistently advocated a statist approach to social problems. Indeed, he tended to exalt the state as a means to reform the society. As one scholar stressed:

> In Ely's eyes, government was the God-given instrument through which we had to work. Its preeminence as a divine instrument was based on the post-Reformation abolition of the division between the sacred and the secular and on the State's power to implement ethical solutions to public problems. The same identification of sacred and secular which took place among liberal clergy enabled Ely to both divinize the state and socialize Christianity: he thought of government as God's main instrument of redemption.[64]

Drawing upon Darwinian theory, Ely rejected the Lockean concept of natural rights and denied the existence of natural law. In Ely's estimation, private economic power, not the state, was the primary threat to individual liberty. Contrary to Locke, Ely maintained that property and contract were products of society created for "social purposes."[65] It followed that society could regulate or even abolish private property and contracts. Ely, in the words of one commentator, "had little loyalty or nostalgia for the older individualistic America of the early nineteenth century."[66]

As might be expected, Ely regularly lambasted economic competition and what he perceived as laissez-faire capitalism in the United States. Sympathetic to socialism, he urged public ownership of railroads and "natural monopolies." Still, Ely stopped short of a full endorsement of socialism and seemed to be searching for some middle path between socialism and capitalism.[67] Like Croly, he favored regulation rather than an antitrust programs to break up large enterprises.[68] Again like Croly, he gave little attention to the plight of racial minorities,[69] and at times was openly hostile to civil liberties claims.

Woodrow Wilson's relationship to the Progressive movement has long perplexed historians, and they have failed to achieve any consensus. Until about 1908 Wilson appears to have been a conservative Demo-

---

[63] Jean B. Quandt, "Religion and Social Thought: The Secularization of Postmillennialism," *American Quarterly* 25 (1973): 402–3; Hovenkamp, *Enterprise and American Law,* supra note 53, at 101. ("the economics of Progressives such as Ely contained a good deal of religious moralizing that proved unacceptable to more positivist economists in the 1930s and after.")

[64] Quandt, "Religion and Social Thought," supra note 63, at 403.

[65] Richard T. Ely, *Property and Contract in Their Relations to the Distribution of Wealth* (New York: Macmillan Company, 1914, 2 vols.), vol. I at 165–90 (property), II at 615–18 (contract).

[66] Rader, *The Academic Mind and Reform,* supra note 62, at 103.

[67] Richard T. Ely, *Socialism and Social Reform* (New York: Thomas Y. Crowell & Co., 1894), 253–54; Rader, *The Academic Mind and Reform,* supra note 62, at 102–3.

[68] Rader, *The Academic Mind and Reform,* supra note 62, at 104–5.

[69] Ibid., at 235.

crat, supportive of states' rights and free markets, and suspicious of expanding governmental power. As he became more active in the political arena, however, Wilson gravitated gradually toward Progressive ideology. Whether this shift was motivated by political expediency or by principled conviction remains a matter of debate.[70] Certainly Croly and other Progressive intellectuals, who had given their hearts to Roosevelt, were initially skeptical about Wilson and his New Freedom program. Although as president Wilson successfully promoted such Progressive measures as a reduced tariff and the Federal Reserve System to oversee banking, leading Progressives continued to bemoan his reluctance to endorse more pervasive governmental intervention in the economy.[71]

In contrast to Croly and Ely, Wilson often spoke in terms of individual rights. At the center of his New Freedom program in 1912 was a pledge to destroy monopolies and restore competition. He championed "the liberating light of individual initiative, of individual liberty, of individual freedom, the light of untrammeled enterprise."[72]

Yet, for all the rhetoric about individual liberty, much of Wilson's emerging philosophy cut in the statist direction. Early in his academic career Wilson dismissed the Lockean contract theory of the origins of government, rejecting the idea of natural law. He pictured the role of government in a broad light. "Government does not stop with the protection of life, liberty, and property, as some have supposed," he declared in 1889, "it goes on to serve every convenience of society."[73] Wilson added: "It is of the nature of government to regulate property rights: it is of the policy of the state to regulate them *more* or *less*."[74] Brushing aside laissez-faire theory, he maintained that government was essential and potentially beneficial, not just a necessary evil. Americans, Wilson maintained, should act "as believers in the wholesomeness and beneficence of the body politic."[75] Moreover, he asserted that "modern individualism has much about it that is hateful, too hateful to last."[76]

As we have seen, Progressives sought to break the traditional tie between individual liberty and the minimal state. Wilson helped to advance this program of so-called positive liberty. He stated that Thomas Jefferson's philosophy that the best government consisted in governing as little as

---

[70] Clifford F. Thies and Gary M. Pecquet, "The Shaping of a Future President's Economic Thought: Richard T. Ely and Woodrow Wilson at 'The Hopkins'," *The Independent Review* 15 (2010): 267–75.

[71] Forcey, *The Crossroads of Liberalism*, supra note 46, at 169, 185–86.

[72] Woodrow Wilson, *The New Freedom* (New York: Doubleday, Page & Co., 1913, reprint 1919), 286.

[73] Woodrow Wilson, *The State* (Boston: D.C. Heath, 1889, rev. ed. Boston: D.C. Heath, 1901), 621.

[74] Ibid., at 623.

[75] Ibid., at 631.

[76] Ibid., at 632.

possible was obsolete in modern circumstances, and that government must assist individuals. "Freedom to-day," Wilson famously observed, "is something more than being let alone. The program of a government of freedom must in these days be positive, not negative merely."[77] Such sentiments opened the door for the Progressive legislative and redistributive agenda to gain legitimacy in the polity.

Wilson's view of the Constitution is also revealing as to the Progressive mindset. As early as 1893 Wilson denied that the Constitution expressed fixed norms. "It seems to me impossible to treat a written Constitution as you would any other document," he declared. "A Constitution must hold (contain) *the prevalent opinion,* and its content must change with national purpose."[78] During the 1912 presidential campaign he dismissed the constitutional system of checks and balances as outmoded and a barrier to good government. Wilson asserted "Government is not a machine, but a living thing. It falls, not under the theory of the universe, but under the theory of organic life. It is accountable to Darwin, not to Newton."[79] He continued: "Living political constitutions must be Darwinian in structure and in practice. . . . All that progressives ask or desire is permission—in an era when 'development,' 'evolution,' is the scientific word—to interpret the Constitution according to the Darwinian principles."[80] The evolutionary lessons of Darwin made clear to Wilson that constitutional norms must adapt to changed economic and social conditions and that Americans should abandon devotion to the views of the Framers. Indeed, Wilson even suggested that the Constitution was not the true basis of political life. "Justly revered as our great Constitution is," he wrote, "it could be stripped off and thrown aside like a garment, and the nation would still stand forth clothed in the living vestment of flesh and sinew, warm with the heartblood of one people, ready to recreate constitution and laws."[81] As this indicates, Wilson was an early champion of what would later be described as a "living Constitution" cut free from any original understanding of the document.

In sum, Wilson's constitutional vision regarded the growth of governmental power as part of an inevitable evolutionary process, treated provisions limiting governmental authority as outdated impediments to efficient governance, and gave little heed to the constitutional rights of individuals. It is true that, as president, Wilson sometimes pursued a more conservative course than some ardent Progressives would have

[77] Wilson, *The New Freedom,* supra note 72, at 284.
[78] Woodrow Wilson to Hermann Eduard von Holst, June 29, 1893, in Arthur S. Link, ed. *The Papers of Woodrow Wilson,* vol. 8 (Princeton: Princeton University Press, 1970), 271.
[79] Wilson, *The New Freedom,* supra note 72, at 47.
[80] Ibid., at 39.
[81] Link, ed., *The Papers of Woodrow Wilson,* vol. 5, supra note 78, at 69. See also George Thomas, *The Madisonian Constitution* (Baltimore: Johns Hopkins Press, 2008), 65–69 (examining Wilson's dislike of the separation of powers doctrine, and desire to reconstruct constitutional authority to effectuate popular will).

preferred. This, however, represented a policy decision, not a recognition of constitutional restraints on the reach of government.

Of course, Croly, Ely, and Wilson were not the only voices in the dialogue over the meaning of Progressivism. But they were key figures, and were united by a commitment to activist government, and by hostility to traditional notions of individualism, laissez-faire economics, and concepts of limited government. Together they underscore the profound ideological shift in the early twentieth century toward a more extensive role for government at all levels.

VI. PROGRESSIVE JURISPRUDENCE

It remains to consider the impact of Progressivism upon constitutional jurisprudence. Although Progressives demonstrated considerable political strength and were able to enact a host of laws which intervened in the economy to an unprecedented extent, they remained apprehensive about the judicial reaction to their program. Both federal and state courts generally adhered to a constitutional philosophy grounded on limited government and respect for the rights of property owners. Progressives, as we have seen, displayed little patience with constitutional doctrines which constrained the reach of government. Despite their preference for governance by experts, Progressives saw themselves as champions of greater democratic rule. They soon viewed the judiciary as a barrier to their reform ideas. In 1912 Senator Robert M. LaFollette of Wisconsin forcefully articulated this sentiment: "Gradually the judiciary began to loom up as the one formidable obstacle which must be overcome before anything substantial could be accomplished to free the public from the exactions of oppressive monopolies and from the domination of the property interests."[82] In the same year, Theodore Roosevelt charged that the New York courts and the Supreme Court "have placed well-nigh or altogether insurmountable obstacles in the path of needed social reforms."[83]

Such complaints were in fact considerably exaggerated. It is simply a myth that the federal or state courts invalidated wholesale legislation of the Progressive Era, much less that they sought to impose a laissez-faire legal regime. Attacking the notion of laissez-faire constitutionalism as an invention by supporters of the Progressive movement, David N. Mayer has insisted "judges did not read Herbert Spencer's Social Statics or any other laissez-faire writing into the Constitution."[84] The United States has never had a period of strict laissez-faire, and courts could not have imple-

---

[82] Robert M. LaFollette, Introduction to Gilbert E. Roe, *Our Judicial Oligarchy* (New York: Huebsch, 1912), v.

[83] Theodore Roosevelt, "Judges and Progress," *Outlook* 100 (January 6, 1912): 42.

[84] David N. Mayer, *Liberty of Contract: Rediscovering a Lost Constitutional Right* (Washington, DC: Cato Institute, 2011) 6.

mented one if they tried.[85] In reality, courts were surprisingly receptive to Progressive legislation, and the regulatory state grew steadily in the first decades of the twentieth century.[86]

Nonetheless, legal writers associated with the Progressive movement seized upon a handful of atypical decisions, such as *Lochner v. New York* (1905),[87] to launch a far-ranging attack on judicial review, constitutionalized property, and the individualistic ethos. Employing moralistic rhetoric common to the movement, Progressives pictured the Supreme Court as the last bulwark of property rights, and a one-sided defender of the wealthy and big business against the interests of workers.[88] This demoniac tale had only a slight relation to reality, but it served the needs of Progressive political leaders.

The Progressive era produced numerous proposals to curb the courts. Some historians reopened the question of whether the framers of the Constitution had ever envisioned judicial review of legislation.[89] Many Progressives went a step further in their desire to reign in the judiciary, calling for enactment of provisions for the recall of state judges. They reasoned that the availability of the recall remedy would keep judges in sync with prevailing public opinion.[90] Joining this debate, Roosevelt particularly championed the recall of state judicial decisions. He reasoned that "when a judge decides a constitutional question, when he decides what the people as a whole can and cannot do, the people should have the right to recall the decision if they think it wrong."[91] This radical idea aroused fury among conservatives and even upset many of Roosevelt's Progressive allies. Critics feared that recall of either judges or judicial decisions would erode judicial independence. Yet such proposals dramatized the deep discontent of many Progressives with the judiciary. Ultimately the Progressive recall campaign faded with little result.

---

[85] Ibid. at 115 (pointing out that judicial invocation of laissez-faire principles "would have resulted in the overturning of literally hundreds of laws that the Court upheld as valid exercises of the police power").

[86] James W. Ely, Jr., *The Guardian of Every Other Right: A Constitutional History of Property Rights*, 3d ed. (New York: Oxford University Press, 2008), 108–9.

[87] 198 U.S. 45 (1905). For assessments of this important case, see David E. Bernstein, *Rehabilitating Lochner*, supra note 8 ; David A. Strauss," Why Was *Lochner* Wrong?, *University of Chicago Law Review* 70 (2003): 373; David N. Mayer, *Liberty of Contract*, supra note 84, at 70–76.

[88] David E. Bernstein, "*Lochner* Era Revisionism, Revised: *Lochner* and the Origins of Fundamental Rights Constitutionalism," *Georgetown Law Journal* 92 (2003): 2–9 (criticizing historians of the Progressive and New Deal eras for tailoring constitutional history to serve political objectives).

[89] William G. Ross, *A Muted Fury: Populists, Progressives, and Labor Unions Confront the Supreme Court, 1890–1937* (Princeton: Princeton University Press, 1994), 49–69 (discussing Progressive denunciation of judicial review as a usurpation of power).

[90] Ibid., at 110–29.

[91] Theodore Roosevelt, "Judges and Progress," supra note 83, at 46; *New York Times*, February 22, 1912; "A Charter of Democracy", in Theodore Roosevelt, *Social Justice and Popular Rule* (New York: Charles Scribner's Sons, 1926), 119: Ross, *A Muted Fury*, supra note 89, at 130–54. See also, William Draper Lewis, "The Recall of Judicial Decisions," *Proceedings of the Academy of Political Science* 37 (1913): 37.

While debates continued over the appropriate role of the courts in American political life, Progressive historians began to ask fundamental questions about the Constitution itself.[92] They emphasized that the Constitution was essentially an undemocratic document. Some even contended that the Constitution was not sacrosanct, and argued that the United States in the early twentieth century could not be successfully governed by eighteenth-century principles. In this context Charles A. Beard published his landmark book, *An Economic Interpretation of the Constitution* (1913). This volume has long been a topic of controversy and cannot be treated in detail here. Beard saw the Constitution as the product of political conflict, and stressed that the Framers were skeptical about majority rule. He maintained that most of the framers anticipated economic benefits to themselves from the new constitutional order. Beard concluded: "The Constitution was essentially an economic document based on the concept that the fundamental private rights of property are anterior to government and morally beyond the reach of popular majorities"[93] Such a conclusion was uncongenial to the Progressive mind. Yet by urging people to view the Constitution with less awe Beard may have hoped to encourage constitutional change. This may explain the appeal of the book to the Progressive generation. "It first took root in the Progressive era," Richard Hofstadter commented, "because it was suited to the spirit of protest and the hope for reform."[94]

Even at the zenith of the Progressive movement, however, it was difficult to bring about formal changes in the judiciary itself. Progressives enjoyed more success in pioneering a supposed new outlook toward the nature of law. Roscoe Pound (1870–1964) was instrumental in promoting the development of "sociological jurisprudence."[95] A student of biology as well as law, Pound was readily inclined to see law from an evolutionary perspective. He repudiated natural law and natural rights as anachronisms which encouraged thinking of law in terms of abstract legal doctrines. Instead, he urged courts to utilize data provided by social science.

In advancing his call for "sociological jurisprudence" Pound fashioned myths which have long plagued the history of constitutional law in the late nineteenth century. He was primarily responsible for crafting an image of courts adhering to so-called "mechanical jurisprudence". Pound asserted that courts followed a closed method of making deductions from

---

[92] Richard Hofstadter, *The Progressive Historians: Turner, Beard, Parrington* (Chicago: University of Chicago Press, 1968), 182–206.

[93] Charles A. Beard, *An Economic Interpretation of the Constitution of the United States* (New York: Macmillan Company, 1913), 324.

[94] Hofstadter, *The Progressive Historians*, supra note 92, at 218.

[95] Paul L. Murphy, "Holmes, Brandeis, and Pound: Sociological Jurisprudence as a Response to Economic Laissez-Faire," in Ellen Frankel Paul and Howard Dickman, eds., *Liberty, Property, and Government: Constitutional Interpretation Before the New Deal* (Albany, NY: State University of New York Press, 1989), 56–60; Bernstein, *Rehabilitating Lochner*, supra note 8, at 42–47.

predetermined conceptions without regard to underlying facts or social consequences. He took special aim at the liberty of contract doctrine under the Fourteenth Amendment, particularly as exemplified in *Lochner*.[96] Discussing the Fourteenth Amendment, Pound made this extraordinary comment: "Starting with the conception that it was intended to incorporate Spencer's Social Statics in the fundamental law of the United States, rules have been deduced that obstruct the way of social progress."[97] On its face this statement is overly broad and requires qualification. First, the only authority cited by Pound for such a sweeping contention is the dissent by Justice Oliver Wendell Holmes (1841–1935) in *Lochner*,[98] which he apparently accepts as gospel. But the Holmes dissent is a slender reed indeed, because Holmes in turn makes dubious generalizations with no evident support. Second, whether judicial decisions "obstruct the way of social progress" is a value-laden matter of opinion. Third, as I have argued elsewhere, there is ample evidence that courts in the late nineteenth century were neither mechanical in their approach to issues nor inclined to block all Progressive reform measures.[99] Indeed, the Supreme Court under Chief Justice Melville W. Fuller (1888–1910) pursued instrumental goals of protecting investment capital and safeguarding the national market.[100] In short, Pound has created a "mechanical jurisprudence" straw man.

According to Pound, the remedy for alleged "mechanical jurisprudence" lay in the adoption of "sociological jurisprudence." Pound elaborated his thinking about "the new juristic theory" in a series of articles. One is struck with the extent to which he relied upon European schools of jurisprudential thought as a basis for his conclusions, and how little attention he paid to American law. The danger was that Pound would draw lessons from civil code systems and apply them uncritically to common law courts, thus reaching erroneous conclusions about judicial behavior in the United States. In discussing the purpose of "sociological jurisprudence," Pound insisted that "the conception of law as a means

---

[96] Pound's vigorous assault on the liberty of contract doctrine is quite curious. In fact, the doctrine was rarely invoked by the Supreme Court. Gregory S. Alexander, "The Limits of Freedom of Contract in the Age of Laissez-Faire Constitutionalism," in Francis H. Buckley, ed., *The Fall and Rise of Freedom of Contract* (Durham, N.C.: Duke University, 1999) (". . . even during the period between 1885 and 1930, the supposed height of laissez-faire constitutionalism, the courts, federal and state, did not uniformly sustain the liberty of contract principle."); Kermit L. Hall and Peter Karsten, *The Magic Mirror: Law in American History*, 2d ed. (New York: Oxford University Press, 2009), 264 ("The Lochner decision was in many ways an aberration with limited impact."). This raises a serious question of whether Pound was simply tilting at windmills.

[97] Roscoe Pound, "Mechanical Jurisprudence," *Columbia Law Review* 8 (1908): 616.

[98] 198 U.S. at 75–76.

[99] Consider the jurisprudence of Justice Rufus W. Peckham, the author the majority opinion in *Lochner*. See James W. Ely, Jr, "Rufus W. Peckham and Economic Liberty," *Vanderbilt Law Review* 62 (2009): 637 ("Even a glance at Peckham's opinions makes it evident that he was not engaged in abstract deduction from legal principles and precedents. Instead, Peckham championed what he regarded as socially desirable outcomes in defense of property rights and contractual freedom. Peckham cannot fairly be described as a legal formalist.").

[100] James W. Ely, Jr., *The Chief Justiceship of Melville W. Fuller, 1888–1910* (Columbia, SC: University of South Carolina Press, 1995), 73–74, 83–149.

toward social ends" would require judges "to keep in touch with life."[101] He explained: "The main problem to which sociological jurists are addressing themselves today is to enable and to compel law-making, and also interpretation and application of legal rules, to take more account, and more intelligent account of the social facts upon which law must proceed and to which it is to be applied."[102] Pound added that "sociological jurists" favor "equitable application of law" in which rules are treated as "a general guide to the judge", who remains free "within wide limits" to dispense justice in individual cases.[103]

As Pound saw it, courts were ill-equipped to ascertain the necessary "social facts." "Judicial law-making cannot serve us," he bluntly declared.[104] Instead, Pound reasoned that only legislative bodies were in a position to conduct hearings, assess expert opinions, and then determine "social facts." It followed that judges under a regime of "sociological jurisprudence" should defer to legislative findings. In a revealing comment in 1908 Pound hailed the Holmes dissent in *Lochner* as "the best exposition" of "sociological jurisprudence."[105] But Holmes mentioned no facts, "social" or otherwise, in his *Lochner* opinion.[106] Holmes simply made a series of pronouncements that he apparently regarded as self-evident and concluded that the Supreme Court should affirm "the right of a majority to embody their opinions in law." Pound's endorsement of this opinion indicates that he was less interested in "social facts" than in a policy of judicial deference to legislation. Indeed, for all his professed devotion to facts, Pound offered virtually no empirical evidence to support his claims.

The emerging "sociological jurisprudence" was in harmony with the political aims of Progressives, who saw claims of individual right as inconsistent with their dedication to activist government. Pound and other elite legal figures associated with Progressivism shared these attitudes. For example, Pound complained about "[t]he currency in juristic thought of an individualistic conception of justice, which exaggerates the importance of property and of contract, exaggerates private right at the expense of public right, and is hostile to legislation. . . ."[107] Rights do not figure prominently in his thinking. Similarly, Learned Hand, a supporter of Roosevelt in the 1912 presidential campaign, assailed the notion that the due process norm "embalms individualistic doctrines of a hundred years ago."[108] Taking a somewhat different tack, Beard in 1908 enthused that

---

[101] Roscoe Pound, "The Scope and Purpose of Sociological Jurisprudence," *Harvard Law Review* 25 (1911): 146–47.

[102] Pound, "Sociological Jurisprudence" supra note 100, part III, (1913): 512–13.

[103] Ibid. at 515.

[104] Pound, "Mechanical Jurisprudence," supra note 97, at 621.

[105] Roscoe Pound, "Liberty of Contract," *Yale Law Journal* 18 (1909): 464.

[106] See William E. Leuchtenburg, *The Supreme Court Reborn: Constitutional Revolution in the Age of Roosevelt* (New York: Oxford University Press, 1995), 19 (calling attention to Holmes's "disdain for facts").

[107] Pound, "Liberty of Contract," supra note 105, at 457,

[108] Learned Hand to Van Vechten Veeder, December 11, 1913, as quoted in Gerald Gunther, *Learned Hand: The Man and the Judge* (New York: Alfred A. Knopf, 1994), 211.

"the stress once laid on individual liberty in the juristic sense is being diminished."[109]

Pound's invectives against "mechanical jurisprudence" rested upon deeply flawed history and a heavy dose of German legal science. Recently Brian Z. Tamanaha has charged that Pound simply created an imaginary account of how cases were actually decided at the turn of the twentieth century.[110] Nonetheless, by virtue of frequent repetition and Pound's prestigious position as Dean of Harvard Law School, his views gradually gained widespread acceptance in the academy.

Pound helped to advance the Progressive political agenda in several ways.[111] He stigmatized a period of judicial history in which courts defended economic rights, an era that Progressives particularly disliked. This would ultimately degenerate into a morality tale about how "good" Progressives battled reactionary Supreme Court justices to uphold salutary laws.[112] Yet such an account is very wide of the mark. There never was a brief period in which judges suddenly began to reason in the mechanical and deductive manner depicted by Pound. As Morton J. Horwitz has pointed out: ". . . by seeking to stigmatize the *Lochner* era, Progressives lost sight of the basic continuity in American constitutional history before 1937."[113] Nonetheless, the historical fiction created by Pound formed the basis for a new orthodoxy.

Pound was influential in other respects as well. He popularized the view that law could be a vehicle for social change, a position congenial to Progressives. Further, his appeal for judicial deference marked a sharp break from the past and became a centerpiece of Progressive jurisprudence. The ominous implications of judicial deference for individual rights are obvious, but, as we have seen, rights did not bulk large in Progressive thought.

Themes developed by Pound found ready acceptance among legal intellectuals. Charging that "legal science" had become static, Louis D. Brandeis (1856–1941) pictured an obtuse judiciary mechanically invoking legal rules without regard to their actual consequences. He complained: "Courts

[109] Beard, *Politics,* supra note 25, at 29.

[110] Brian Z. Tamanaha, *Beyond the Formalist-Realist Divide: The Role of Politics in Judging* (Princeton: Princeton University Press, 2010, 24–43 (". . . contrary to what Pound and others have asserted, lawyers, academics, and judges at the time did not widely believe that judging was an exercise in mechanical deduction"). See also Alschuler, *Law Without Values,* supra note 24, at 91–100 (rejecting notion that judges in the nineteenth century adhered to mechanical jurisprudence, and insisting that judges adapted law to meet changing circumstances).

[111] Bernstein, *Rehabilitating Lochner,* supra note 8, at 41 (". . . the Progressive legal elites' support for 'sociological jurisprudence' often masked a political agenda that favored a significant increase in government involvement in American economic and social life").

[112] Morton J. Horwitz, *The Transformation of American Law, 1870–1960: The Crisis of Legal Orthodoxy* (New York: Oxford University Press, 1992), 7: ("Although in every other field of American history, Progressive historiography, premised on a conflict between the "people" and the "interests" has been overthrown as simplistic, in the constitutional history of the *Lochner* era it has continued to be the standard mode of explanation.")

[113] Ibid.

continued to ignore newly arisen social needs. They applied compla-
cently 18th century conceptions of the liberty of the individual and of the
sacredness of private property. . . . Where statutes giving expression to
the new social spirit were clearly constitutional, judges, imbued with the
relentless spirit of individualism, often construed them away." [114] To support this broad caricature of judicial behavior, Brandeis took aim at *Lochner*
and a handful of other state and federal decisions dealing with workplace
regulations, the usual suspects rounded up by Progressives.[115] The remedy for this perceived problem, in Brandeis's mind, was the "living law"
which harmonized "law with life." This result could best be achieved by
integrating economics and sociology into legal education and legal arguments. Implicit in Brandeis's thinking was the view that legislatures were
more in tune with the "living law" than courts, and that judges should
move slowly in overturning statutes as violations of liberty or property.

In the same vein, Edwin R. Keedy, a University of Pennsylvania law
professor, extolled Pound and "sociological jurists" for their pragmatism.
He was pleased to find that the trend of legal thought "is away from
reverence for fixed principles toward consideration of the economic, industrial and social merits of the particular controversy, away from artificiality
towards simplicity, and from an individualistic towards a collective attitude." [116] Accepting without question Pound's treatment of a supposed
earlier school of "mechanical jurisprudence" based on deductive reasoning, Keedy posited that under "sociological jurisprudence" courts "should
take into consideration the social and economic conditions underlying the
cases that come before them and should not base their decisions entirely
upon abstract rules." Like Pound, he gave no attention to the thought that
this point was not a novel insight. Keedy linked individualism with private property, contractual freedom, and economic competition. Happily,
he concluded, individualism was in decline. Cooperation had replaced
competition in business affairs, and property was regulated "for the public benefit." Keedy broke no new ground, but helped to perpetuate Pound's
message of a retrograde judiciary and the need for a more collectivist
approach to legal issues. Not surprisingly, he made no mention of individual rights or of the Constitution as a restraint on governmental authority.

VII. Militant Progressivism

The new constitutional thinking stirred up by the Progressive movement found expression in a number of utopian novels. Among the most

---

[114] Louis D. Brandeis, "The Living Law," *Illinois Law Review* 10 (1916): 464.

[115] In addition to *Lochner*, Brandeis singled out *Ives v. South Buffalo Railway Co.*, 201 N.Y.
271 (1911) (invalidating New York's workers' compensation law) and *Adair v. United States*,
208 U.S. 161 (1908) (striking down on liberty of contract doctrine a congressional measure
outlawing so-called yellow dog contacts). These were favorite targets of the Progressives.

[116] Edwin R. Keedy, "The Decline of Traditionalism and Individualism," *University of
Pennsylvania Law Review* 65 (1916): 772.

revealing of such works was *Philip Dru Administrator: A Story of Tomorrow 1920–1935*, published anonymously in 1912 as the Progressive movement gained ascendancy in American life.[117] Four years later it was discovered that the author was the influential Edward Mandell House (1858–1938). Better known as Colonel House, although he never held a military commission, the author was a close friend and confident of President Wilson.[118] *Philip Dru*, which incorporates Progressive values into a dramatic and disturbing tale, lays open both the promise and perils of Progressivism. It warrants careful investigation.

Philip Dru, the title character, is a graduate of West Point who resigns from the army after suffering an eye injury. A career as a journalist and social worker in New York City exposes Dru to the plight of the urban poor and the sordid state of politics. Anxious to seek reforms to assist the unfortunate, Dru finds both political parties controlled by wealth. Plutocrats form a league for the "nefarious plan" of electing a president favorable to their interests. Orchestrated by a corrupt but powerful senator, this plan succeeds. When the scheme comes to light, the president uses force to prevent free elections. As the nation veers toward civil war, the impending conflict pits the rich and very poor against the middle class. Recall that Progressives were fond of picturing themselves as champions of the middle class. Dru takes command of an insurgent force and defeats the regular army. The president flees and Dru assumes dictatorial powers. He proclaims himself Administrator of the Republic, but promises to eventually restore democratic government.

For several years Dru is busy reconstructing American political institutions along Progressive lines. His first target is the legal system. Dru reduces the number of courts and eliminates judicial review. Dru limits the power of courts "to the extent that they could no longer pass upon the constitutionality of laws, their function being merely to decide, as between litigants, what the law was, as was the practice of all other civilized nations." Nor were private lawsuits exempt from Dru's reformist zeal. Because the United States had "the most complicated, expensive and inadequate legal machinery of any civilized nation," Dru takes steps to prevent lawyers from bringing frivolous lawsuits "of doubtful character, and without facts and merit to sustain them." Moreover, he names an expert commission to revise and prune down both federal and state laws. To assist in this endeavor Dru selects as advisors "eminent lawyers" from England, France and Germany. He directs that states should simplify land

---

[117] Edward Mandell House, *Philip Dru Administrator: A Story of Tomorrow 1920–1935* (New York: B. W. Huebach, 1912, reprinted Memphis, Tenn.: General Books, 2010). *Philip Dru* has received surprisingly little attention from scholars. For exceptions, see Lears, Rebirth of A Nation, supra note 5, at 330–31; Maxwell Bloomfield, "Constitutional Ideology and Progressive Fiction," *Journal of American Culture* 18 (1995): 3–4. See also a review of this work by Walter Lippman, "America's Future," *New York Times*, December 8, 1912.

[118] For the close relationship between Wilson and House, see Arthur S. Link, *Woodrow Wilson and the Progressive Era, 1910–1917* (New York: Harper & Row, 1954), 26.

titles to facilitate real estate transfers and should adopt uniform divorce laws.

Dru also mandates many changes on the economic front. He imposes a graduated income tax and abolishes protective tariffs. Dru realizes that improvements in communication and travel "were, for all practical purposes, obliterating State lines and molding the country into a homogeneous nation." Thus, he feels that the national government should assume certain functions that have previously been under state control. Dru proposes a Federal Incorporation Act, which included the requirement that government and "Labor" should have representatives on corporate boards. Railroads and public service corporations are to function under the supervision of regulatory commissions. Significantly, Dru does not directly attack private property and declares that investors should have reasonable profits as well as protection against unfair state interference. Only the telephone and telegraph companies are to be taken over by the government, and that upon payment "for their properties at a fair valuation."

Dru's ideas regarding the labor force are noteworthy. In exchange for profit sharing, strikes are forbidden. All grievances must be submitted to arbitration. Dru further directs that work shall be limited to eight hours a day, six days a week. The government would become the employer of last resort for those who cannot find work. Dru then makes plans for old-age pensions and a disability insurance law.

Some of Dru's most radical moves are in the area of constitutional law. Sympathetic to the women's movement for greater equality with men, Dru grants universal suffrage. He then turns to overhauling the Constitution. Dru proceeds on the premise that "America is the most undemocratic of democratic countries." "Our Government," he charges," is, perhaps, less responsive to the will of the people than that of almost any of the civilized nations." Therefore Dru set out to fashion a more responsive government. Like many Progressive leaders, he has little time for the system of checks and balances. We have already seen how Dru drastically curtailed the power of the judiciary. In contrast to Croly, Dru expresses the view that the office of president is too powerful. Under the new constitution the executive is chosen by the House of Representatives and serves at the pleasure of the House. The executive may select a cabinet, but has no veto power and appears to function as a sort of parliamentary leader in the British manner. The president occupies a purely ceremonial post. The weakening of the executive branch is palpably ironic given the fact that this change is made by a dictator. Senators are to be elected directly by popular vote, but the place of the Senate in the new legislative process is secondary to the House. There is no mention of a Bill of Rights, reflecting the general Progressive lack of interest in individual right. Nor is there any provision for amendment.

Amid his prodigious efforts to overhaul the political system of the United States, Dru remains keenly interested in international affairs. He pursues a highly aggressive policy to promote United States interests abroad, a reminder that many prominent Progressives, such as Roosevelt and Senator Albert J. Beveridge of Indians, were ardent imperialists.[119] For example, Dru engineers an Anglo-American alliance to secure commercial freedom. Much of the world is divided into spheres of influence among the United States and European powers. England relinquishes control of Canada, and that nation moves closer to the orbit of the United States. More striking, Dru invades Mexico to check political chaos in that country. Again victorious, Dru imposes a sort of protectorate over Mexico to maintain order, and directs that Mexican officials prepare a new form of government. This portion of the novel may well have been inspired by actual events, for in 1912 Mexico was engulfed in civil conflict. Indeed, Dru's actions with respect to Mexico seem to have prefigured Wilson's military interventions to safeguard democracy there. However, the fictional Dru was far more successful than Wilson's ill-fated "missionary diplomacy."[120]

There is a strong note of coercion throughout the novel. Dru comes to power as part of a military overthrow of the established government, a troublesome development for modern readers who recall the rise of totalitarian dictators by means of military coup. Although a benevolent despot, Dru nonetheless imposes his reforms by decree. There is nothing democratic about his period of rule. Dru talks in terms of government for "the people," but he in fact relies on expert boards, not popular input to devise his new laws. Evidently Dru and his experts know best what the people need. Paternalism and efficiency guide his lawmaking, not democratic accountability. Another pronounced theme is increased national authority over the states, a view congruent with that of many Progressives. Dru even incorporates some elements of Social Gospel thinking in his planning. Picturing his program as an application of Christian morality, Dru proclaims: "And from the blood and travail of an enlightened people, there will be born a spirit of love and brotherhood which will transform the world; and the Star of Bethlehem, seen but darkly for two thousand years, will shine again with a steady and effulgent glow."

More a political tract than a novel, *Philip Dru* is largely forgotten today. Still, the work affords troublesome insight into the Progressive mindset. Colonel House comes close to suggesting that the Progressive goals of social and economic transformation can best be achieved by a military putsch, repudiation of the Constitution, and a temporary dictatorship.

---

[119] William E. Leuchtenburg, "Progressivism and Imperialism: The Progressive Movement and American Foreign Policy, 1898–1916," *Mississippi Valley Historical Review* 39 (1952): 483–504.

[120] Link, *Woodrow Wilson and the Progressive Era*, supra note 118, at 81–114 (discussing Wilson's extensive interventions in Caribbean nations and Mexico, and noting that Wilson was "dedicated to the democratic ideal, at least theoretically, and obsessed with the concept of America's mission in the world.").

One can only guess what impact House had on President Wilson, who described House as his "alter ego." Certainly House fashioned a mythical great leader who would dominate the nation. Croly would have approved. Others may detect a whiff of totalitarianism, anticipating the enormous expansion of the coercive power of government by the Wilson administration during World War I.

VIII. CONCLUSION

Individualism and economic rights continued to have strong defenders during the Progressive era. In 1913 Elihu Root (1845–1937), a prominent conservative, challenged the premises that lay at the heart of Progressive ideology. In contrast to the Progressive writers, he asserted: "I assume an agreement that the right of individual liberty and the inseparable right of private property which lie at the foundation of our modern civilization ought to be maintained." [121] Root argued that the essential features of our constitutional system "all aim to preserve rights by limiting power." Pointing to the natural law tradition, he maintained that government was not the source of individual rights but was an instrument for preserving them. Root saw the separation of powers among the three branches of government as a "security for liberty." He took issue with the Progressive view that courts should defer to legislative decisions, reasoning that "the effect of this would be that the legislature would not be limited at all except by its own will." Indeed, he expressed concern that legislatures "frequently try to evade constitutional provisions." [122] But Root was speaking against the day. The Progressive assault on individualism and property proved highly influential and left a lasting legacy.

It is perhaps surprising that this should be the case. After all, most historians agree that Progressivism as a political force collapsed in the aftermath of World War I.[123] Nonetheless, the Progressives succeeded in bringing about a profound shift in the dialogue about constitutionalism in the United States. Lockean liberalism, premised on a theory of natural rights, was largely abandoned in favor of a statist ideology. Despite setbacks and disappointments, Progressives achieved greater social control by means of an expanded government. This development necessarily entailed a diminished regard for individualism and claims of right against the state. Moreover, Progressives laid the intellectual groundwork for a jurisprudence which substantially stripped property of constitutional protection, an agenda brought to fruition by the New Deal Supreme Court after 1937.

---

[121] Elihu Root, *Experiments in Government and the Essentials of the Constitution* (Princeton: Princeton University Press, (1913), 3.

[122] Ibid. at 43, 44, 53, 62–63, 75.

[123] Hofstadter, *The Age of Reform,* supra note 4, at 273 ("Participation in the war put an end to the Progressive movement."); McGerr, *A Fierce Discontent,* supra note 4, at 299–313.

To be sure, there has been sharp criticism of the Progressive movement, and revisionist scholars have called into question many aspects of Progressive jurisprudence. Yet the classical liberal position remains on the sidelines in the academy and the courts. So perhaps the last word should go to the cantankerous H. L. Mencken (1880–1956) who defined a Progressive as "one who is in favor of more taxes instead of less, more bureaus and jobholders, more paternalism and meddling, more regulation of private affairs and less liberty."[124]

Law and History, Vanderbilt University

[124] H. L. Mencken, *Baltimore Sun,* January 19, 1926.

SAVING LOCKE FROM MARX: THE LABOR THEORY OF VALUE IN INTELLECTUAL PROPERTY THEORY*

By Adam Mossoff

I. Introduction

John Locke's labor theory of value is a significant part of his argument for property in his *Two Treatises of Government* (1690),[1] and legal scholars and philosophers widely agree that it fails to justify intellectual property rights. The consensus is that his argument is weak or backwards in its claim that property rights secure preexisting values created through labor.[2] Law professors in particular deride the "fallacies in the fundamental assumptions . . . [in] this 'if value, then right' theory," and, as a prudential matter, they express concern that this theory "lacks a coherent limit" in defining the scope of legal protection of intellectual property rights.[3] Since the early twentieth century, American legal scholars have assumed that Locke's labor theory of value is incoherent, viciously circular, and indeterminate,[4] and this judgment prevails in intellectual property theory as much as it does in traditional property theory.

* For comments on earlier drafts, thank you to the participants at a workshop at Cardozo Law School, the 2011 Annual Meeting of the Association for Law, Property and Society, the Property Colloquium at George Mason University School of Law, and the other contributors to this volume. For their thoroughgoing feedback and constructive criticism of earlier drafts, a special thank you to Eric R. Claeys, James E. Penner, C. Bradley Thompson, and the editors of *Social Philosophy and Policy*.

[1] References to Locke's writings will be made in the main text using the following convention: "*TT* II.28" refers to John Locke, *Two Treatises of Government*, Peter Laslett ed. (Cambridge: Cambridge University Press, student ed. 1988), Second Treatise, section 28. "*ECHU* II.28.6" refers to John Locke, *An Essay Concerning Human Understanding*, ed. Peter H. Nidditch (Oxford: Clarendon Press, 1979), book 2, chapter 2, section 6. "*STCE* 185–86" refers to John Locke, *Some Thoughts Concerning Education*, Ruth W. Grant and Nathan Tarcov eds. (Indiana: Hackett Publishing Co., 1996), sections 185–86. "*QCLN* 153" refers to John Locke, *Questions Concerning the Law of Nature*, trans. and ed. Robert Horwitz, Jenny Straus Clay, & Diskin Clay (Ithaca: Cornell University Press, 1990), 153.

[2] See Richard A. Epstein, "Liberty versus Property: Cracks in the Foundation," *San Diego Law Review* 42, no. 1 (2005): 14–15; Lloyd Weinreb, "Custom, Law and Public Policy: The INS Case as an Example of Intellectual Property," *Virginia Law Review* 78, no. 1 (1992): 144.

[3] Rochelle Cooper Dreyfuss, "Expressive Genericity: Trademarks as Language in the Pepsi Generation," *Notre Dame Law Review* 65, no. 3 (1990): 405. Given this problem with defining limits, Larry Lessig writes that "the 'if value, then right' theory of creative property has never been America's theory of creative property. It has never taken hold within our law." Lawrence Lessig, *Free Culture* (New York: The Penguin Press, 2004): 19.

[4] I discuss this critique among realist legal scholars in Adam Mossoff, "The Use and Abuse of Intellectual Property at the Birth of the Administrative State," *University of Pennsylvania Law Review* 157, no. 6 (2009): 2015–18.

doi:10.1017/S0265052511000288

These scholars have found ample support in many assessments of Locke's labor theory of value by contemporary philosophers. Interestingly, while philosophers have spilt much ink on how Locke's "mixing labor" argument applies to intellectual property rights, there has been comparatively very little attention paid to his labor theory of value.[5] Even within general philosophical commentary on Locke's property theory—such as the canonical texts by James Tully, Robert Nozick, C. B. Macpherson, and Richard Ashcraft—it has been observed that Locke's labor theory of value has been "relatively neglected."[6] One exception is Edwin Hettinger, who devotes a substantial portion of a philosophy journal article to argue that Locke's labor theory of value fails to justify intellectual property rights;[7] but more often than not one finds expressions of disapproval in at best very brief passages or at worst in off-hand references.

These critiques, however, have been misdirected. In their assault on Locke's labor theory of value, philosophers construe Locke's concept of labor in purely *physical* terms and they construe his concept of value in purely *economic* terms, but these are not Locke's concepts of labor or value. His concept of labor refers to production, which has intellectual as well as physical characteristics, and his concept of value serves his moral ideal of human flourishing, which is a conception of the good that is more robust than merely physical status or economic wealth. This is hardly surprising given that his property theory is firmly rooted in his natural law ethical theory, which is imbued with the classical natural law theorists' concern with the flourishing life of a rational being. Although legal scholars might be forgiven for conceptual or analytical mistakes in their philosophical arguments, one finds the same mistaken conceptual assumptions—and, as a result, the same mistaken critique—in the work of political and legal philosophers.

[5] Some examples of recent philosophical scholarship addressing how Locke's property theory applies to intellectual property rights includes Jonathan Peterson, "Lockean Property and Literary Works," *Legal Theory* 14, no. 1 (2008): 257–80; Seana Valentine Shiffrin, "Lockean Arguments for Private Intellectual Property," in Stephen R. Munzer, ed., *New Essays in the Legal and Political Theory of Property* (Cambridge: Cambridge University Press, 2001): 138–67; Adam Moore, "A Lockean Theory of Intellectual Property," *Hamline Law Review*, 21, no. 1 (1997): 65–108.

[6] Andrew Williams, "Cohen on Locke, Land and Labour," *Political Studies* 40, no. 1 (1992): 51. In Stephen Munzer's *A Theory of Property*, for instance, the labor theory of value receives no attention at all in his chapter on "Labor and desert." Stephen R. Munzer, *A Theory of Property* (Cambridge: Cambridge University Press, 1990): 254–91. Munzer writes that his argument for property "has little in common with Locke's views about gaining property rights by mixing one's labor with unowned things. . . . It is, however, somewhat related to his overall thought that since no one would labor without expecting some benefit, it would be unfair to let the idle take the benefit of the laborer's pains." (Ibid., 256, footnote 1). If these benefits are the values created by a laborer, then it would seem that some type of labor theory of value remains a crucial premise of his property theory.

[7] Edwin C. Hettinger, "Justifying Intellectual Property," *Philosophy & Public Affairs* 18, no. 1 (1989): 36–40.

If Locke's property theory justifies intellectual property rights—and Locke himself believes that it does[8]—the principle of interpretative charity demands reconsideration of his labor theory of value on its own terms and in its proper intellectual context. This is particularly important given the significance of intellectual property rights today, as legal scholars and policy activists have increasingly relied on the mistaken philosophical critiques of Locke's labor theory of value in making their own arguments in the raging policy debates. Hettinger's wide-ranging critique of a Lockean theory of intellectual property rights, for instance, has been cited in at least one hundred twenty-two law review articles.[9] It is now imperative to return to both the text and the philosophical context of Locke's property theory in order to better understand what he means in his labor theory of value.

The scope of my thesis about Locke's labor theory of value bears emphasizing at the outset. This essay describes Locke's argument for his labor theory of value in order to expose the strawman attack on his property theory by contemporary philosophers, especially within intellectual property theory, but it does not purport to justify his labor theory of value. This justification, which raises difficult questions about the foundations of value theory, such as whether values are objective, subjective, or intrinsic, must be left for another day.[10] The focus here is solely on explicating the labor theory of value within Locke's property theory, which reveals why Locke thought his property theory applied to writings and inventions.

This essay thus makes a small, but important, contribution to philosophical scholarship on Locke's labor theory of value and its application to intellectual property rights: it distinguishes between the *natural law* and *economic* concepts of value, as philosophers today equivocate between these two concepts in their critiques of Locke's property theory. Here, the economic concept of value, whether referred to as "market value," "exchange value," "wealth," or some other economic term, encompasses the mistaken assumption that Locke is arguing in his labor theory of value that there is a quantifiable (and thus measurable) relationship between physical exertion and money that justifies property rights. For purposes of shorthand, I refer to this as a distinction between Locke (natural law value) and Marx (economic value).

Identifying how the conventional wisdom equivocates between Locke and Marx is important for philosophers or legal scholars who are inter-

---

[8] Mossoff, "Use and Abuse of Intellectual Property at the Birth of Administrative State," 2048.

[9] This is based on a search, performed on October 10, 2011, of all of the law journals in the Westlaw legal database.

[10] For some examples of this debate among contemporary philosophers, see Darryl F. Wright, "Evaluative Concepts and Objective Values: Rand on Moral Objectivity," *Social Philosophy & Policy* 25, no. 1 (2008): 149–81; David Gauthier, *Morals by Agreement* (Oxford: Clarendon Press, 1986): 21–59; J. L. Mackie, *Ethics: Inventing Right and Wrong* (New York: Penguin Books, 1977): 15–63.

ested in either critiquing or resuscitating a labor theory of value in intellectual property theory. Before one can assess the validity of Locke's
property theory and its purchase for intellectual property rights, it is
necessary to identify why so many philosophers conflate two different
concepts of value, resulting in a strawman attack and hasty dismissal of
significant elements of Locke's property theory. Without explaining why
Locke is not Marx, one is unable to get past the widespread belief that
Locke's labor theory of value has been rightly relegated to the dustbin of
the history of philosophy.

In explicating why Locke is not Marx, at least in the limited context of
their respective labor theories of value, this essay proceeds in four parts.
First, it will briefly review the various critiques of Locke's labor theory of
value, focusing mostly on Hettinger's well-known argument against a
Lockean justification for intellectual property rights, but also on equally
influential and more general critiques of Locke's labor theory of property
by Robert Nozick, G. A. Cohen, and others. Second, it will explicate
Locke's labor theory of value through a careful textual analysis of the
actual argument he presents in the *Two Treatises of Government*. Since the
Two Treatises is only a work in political theory, it is necessary to further
discuss his natural law ethical theory, which defines and informs the basic
normative concepts, such as value, that he employs in his arguments in
the property theory he presents in the *Second Treatise*. Accordingly, this
part will incorporate his arguments about the meaning of labor and value
from his other works, such as *An Essay Concerning Human Understanding*.
Third, once Locke's labor theory of value has been properly described, it
is possible to discuss his approval of property rights in inventions and
books; in fact, Locke explicitly endorses copyright in an essay he wrote in
1695. Lastly, the essay will conclude by discussing Marx's labor theory of
value, identifying the ways in which it is substantively different from
Locke's superficially similar-sounding labor theory of value, but identifying how these superficial aspects of Locke's arguments have been used
improperly to equivocate between Locke and Marx.

II. The Critics of Locke's Labor Theory of Value in Intellectual Property Theory and Beyond

There is widespread misunderstanding today about Locke's property
theory, which is something I have addressed in my own scholarship on
how natural rights philosophy influenced the historical development of
Anglo-American patent law.[11] In a previously published essay, I explained

---

[11] Mossoff, "The Use and Abuse of Intellectual Property at the Birth of the Administrative
State," 2001–2050; Adam Mossoff, "Who Cares What Thomas Jefferson Thought About
Patents? Revaluating the Patent 'Privilege' in its Historical Context," *Cornell Law Review* 92
(2007): 953–1012; Adam Mossoff, "Patents as Constitutional Private Property: The Historical
Protection of Patents under the Takings Clause," *Boston University Law Review* 87, no. 3

how Robert Nozick, Jeremy Waldron, and other philosophers have mis-interpreted Locke's "mixing labor" argument,[12] but I have not yet addressed their misunderstanding of Locke's labor theory of value. Although I have addressed how *legal scholars* have misunderstood Locke's labor theory of value as a normative argument for a property right in economic value,[13] the shibboleth of economic value within critiques of Locke's labor theory of value by *philosophers* needs to be addressed on its own terms.

With respect to Locke's labor theory of value, prominent contemporary philosophers have assumed that "labor" means only physical exertion, that "value" means only socially-defined economic value, and that the fulcrum in Locke's normative argument is that physical exertion inputs and economic outputs are necessarily measurable in quantifiable propor-tions. The critiques of his labor theory of value proceed on these often unstated assumptions, and thus it is necessary to review the arguments to reveal how philosophers are equivocating conceptually between Locke and Marx. Accordingly, this section will first discuss Hettinger's analysis of Locke's labor theory of value, as this represents the most extensive critique by a contemporary philosopher of a Lockean theory of intellec-tual property rights. It will then discuss some of the more prominent critiques of Locke's labor theory of value by other philosophers, such as Nozick and Cohen, who are writing outside the context of intellectual property theory, but whose arguments support or are identical to the conclusions reached by Hettinger.

In *Justifying Intellectual Property*, Hettinger maintains that "justifying intellectual property rights is a formidable task," and that attempts to do so on the basis of the "[n]atural rights to the fruits of one's labor are not by themselves sufficient." Although a Lockean theory of intellectual prop-erty rights captures a "power intuition," it has two "significant shortcom-ings" that are revealed under closer analytical scrutiny.[14] First, it cannot separate out the proportional contributions of intellectual labor by past and present creators in the market value of an invention or book, and, second, it ignores the necessary social context that defines economic value as such. In sum, Hettinger argues that Locke's labor theory of value fails to justify a property right to the economic value in an invention or book given the inherent social nature of the creative process on the front end and the inherent social nature of economic value on the back end of a theory of intellectual property rights.

(2007): 689–724; Adam Mossoff, "Rethinking the Development of Patents: An Intellectual History," *Hastings Law Journal* 52, no. 6 (2001): 1255–1322.

[12] Adam Mossoff, "Locke's Labor Lost," *The University of Chicago Law School Roundtable* 9, no. 1 (2002): 155–64.

[13] Mossoff, "The Use and Abuse of Intellectual Property at the Birth of the Administrative State," 2001–2050.

[14] Hettinger, "Justifying Intellectual Property," 36, 51.

Although Hettinger believes that there is some validity in the labor
theory of value in situations in which someone makes improvements to
fallow land or to other unimproved objects, the same cannot be said of
intellectual creations. Contrary to a laborer's improvement of completely
barren wasteland into a bountiful farm, Hettinger observes that

> Invention, writing, and thought in general do not operate in a vac-
> uum: intellectual creation is not creation *ex nihilio*. Given this vital
> dependence of a person's thoughts on the ideas of those who came
> before her, intellectual products are fundamentally social products.
> Thus even if one assumes that the value of these products is entirely
> the result of human labor, this value is not entirely attributable to *any
> particular laborer* (or small group of laborers).[15]

Hettinger's basic point here is not new; as Isaac Newton poignantly
observed, "If I have seen further it is only by standing on the shoulders
of giants."

But Hettinger is not making merely a descriptive observation about
sequential and complementary innovation; rather, this observation leads
him to conclude that, according to the labor theory of value, there is no
morally justified property claim to the total "market value" in an invention or book. This economic value arises from untold contributions of
many intellectual laborers in the distant past and in the present, and
according to Hettinger, the labor theory of value demands that this *"market value* should be shared by all those whose ideas contributed to the
origin of the product."[16] The absurdity of this idea, or at least that it is an
untenable if not an impossible task, is left unstated. His ultimate conclusion, though, is clear: the labor theory of value does not morally justify a
creator's intellectual property rights.

In addition to the problem in identifying the proportional contributions
to the total economic value of a new invention or book, Hettinger also
argues that Locke's labor theory of value fails to account for the fact that
"[m]arket value is a socially created phenomenon." It is an economic
truism that market value—price—is determined by the aggregate supply
of and demand for a product, which is itself defined by such variables as
the existence of market substitutes, the "opportunity costs" incurred by
firms and consumers, the transaction costs in selling and purchasing
goods, the economies of scale achieved by firms, and so on. These are all
factors that are exogenous to the specific efforts by the inventor or author
in creating intellectual property, which thus explains why the "market
value of the same fruits of labor will differ greatly with variations in these
social factors." In sum, there is no correlation between the proportional

[15] Ibid., 38.
[16] Ibid. (emphasis added).

contribution of an inventor or author in one's efforts in creating a new product of intellectual property and the market price for that product. Hettinger bluntly concludes: "The notion that a laborer is naturally entitled as a matter of right to receive the market value of her product is a myth."[17]

The careful reader will note a subtle conceptual shift in Hettinger's analysis of how Locke's labor theory of value fails to justify intellectual property rights. With no explanation, Hettinger replaces Locke's normative concept of "value" with the economic concept of "market value." Moreover, Hettinger assumes that Locke's labor theory of value justifies a property right in this "market value" given a quantifiable ratio of measurable physical labor to economic value. He does not explain why he thinks Locke's concept of value refers solely to economic value or why his labor theory of value requires a proportional relationship between physical labor inputs and dollar outputs. Hettinger simply assumes that this is what Locke means by "labor" and "value"—an assumption that drives his critique of how the labor theory of value fails to justify intellectual property rights.

It is neither surprising nor inexplicable why Hettinger makes these assumptions about Locke's labor theory of value, because he explicitly bases his argument on Nozick's famous criticism of Locke's labor theory of property in *Anarchy, State and Utopia*.[18] There Nozick advances a broadside against Locke's property theory. In addition to his criticism of Locke's "mixing labor" argument, in which he construes "labor" in a literal sense of referring only to physical actions,[19] Nozick also rejects Locke's labor theory of value on the exact same grounds asserted by Hettinger. In a single, brief paragraph, Nozick rejects Locke's labor theory of value wholesale by pointing out that it cannot justify an entitlement to "the whole object rather than just to the *added value* one's labor has produced." Nozick simply assumes that a labor theory of value mandates that there is an identifiable, proportional relationship between physical labor inputs and value outputs, and Hettinger adopts this assumption without question.

Moreover, Nozick thinks that identifying or measuring a proportional relationship between one's contribution of physical labor and the value produced thereby is impossible, although he does not explain why he thinks so. He merely jumps to his conclusion that "No workable or coherent value-added property scheme has yet been devised. At least, no labor theory of value has been worked out since the demise of "the theory of Henry George."[20] Nozick's reference to Henry George is telling. George was a nineteenth-century economist who is viewed today as a fellow

---

[17] Ibid., 38–39.
[18] Robert Nozick, *Anarchy, State and Utopia* (New York: Basic Books, Inc., 1974): 175.
[19] I have criticized this egregious strawman attack on Locke's "mixing labor" argument in Mossoff, "Locke's Labor Lost."
[20] Nozick, *Anarchy, State, and Utopia*, 175.

traveler of Marx because he argued that the labor theory of economic value proves that land could not be the subject of private property.[21] By conflating Locke with George, Nozick reveals that he makes the same assumption as does Hettinger about Locke's concept of value: value means economic value. As with his criticism of Locke's concept of labor, Nozick does not explain his equivocation between Locke and Marx.[22]

Not all philosophers assume that Locke employs a concept of *economic value* in his labor theory of value; in fact, G. A. Cohen recognizes that Locke and Marx are talking about two different concepts of value in their respective labor theories of value.[23] But Cohen still agrees with Nozick and Hettinger that *labor*—the other central concept in Locke's labor theory of value—refers only to physical actions. For instance, he expresses agreement with Marx's criticism of Locke's labor theory of value because such value is comprised only of "concrete labour," such as the "labour considered in its concrete form of ploughing, sowing and so forth." Moreover, for this "concrete labour" to justify a property right to the value it produces, according to Cohen, it must be capable of quantifiable measurement relative to the total value produced. Of course, like Nozick, Cohen thinks this proposition is nonsensical: "In short, Locke goes from (i) facts about marginal contributions, to (ii) claims about comparative physical contributions, to (iii) conclusions about rewards." Given the logical infirmities in an argument that results in moral claims to *total* products based only on *relative* physical contributions, Cohen thus concludes that Locke's version of the labor theory of value is "indefensible" and "meaningless."[24]

Jeremy Waldron agrees with Cohen that Locke's labor theory of value is concerned with "use-value," not the "exchange-value" of market prices,[25] and he also seems to agree with Cohen that the problem with Locke's

[21] See Henry George, *Progress and Poverty* (New York: D. Appleton & Co., 1886). The book was first published in 1879.

[22] If there was any doubt about this assumption, Nozick later confirms it when he refers to "the crumbling of the labor theory of value" in his discussion of the failure of Marxist labor-exploitation economics. Nozick, *Anarchy, State, and Utopia*, 253–60.

[23] Cohen writes that the Marxist labor theory of value is a theory about economic value—what Marx and economists call "exchange-value"—but not so for Locke's labor theory of value, which claims only that "labour is responsible for virtually all of the use-value." See G. A. Cohen, *Self-Ownership, Freedom and Equality* (Cambridge: Cambridge University Press, 1995), 178. He further explains:

> Locke's premiss is often described as a rough statement of what, since Marx, has been known as the labour theory of value. That is misleading, since the value which Locke says is (nearly all) due to labour is not the value Marx says labour created. Locke's topic is use-value, not exchange-value.

Cohen, *Self-Ownership, Freedom and Equality*, 178. For Marx's discussion of the distinction between use-value and exchange-value, see Karl Marx, *Das Kapital*, vol. 1, in Robert C. Tucker, ed., *The Marx-Engels Reader*, 2d ed. (New York: W.W. Norton & Co., 1978): 302–29.

[24] Cohen, *Self-Ownership, Freedom and Equality*, 182–88.

[25] Jeremy Waldron, *The Right to Private Property* (Oxford: Clarendon Press, 1988): 192.

labor theory of value is with his concept of *labor*. Following in the foot-steps of Nozick and Cohen, he implicitly frames Locke's concept of labor as solely a physical process. Thus, for instance, he contends that Locke's labor theory of value is "most plausible in the case of [improved] land" and with "manufactured artifacts," but he believes that it is "implausible in regard to food and other items that have been merely gathered from their natural state."[26] The implicit premise is that the relative contribu-tion of physical labor to the use value in the final product is much greater for a manufactured article than for preexisting goods, and thus the moral claim to ownership in the former has greater force. Furthermore, his assumption that Lockean labor must refer only to physical actions is brought to the foreground in his statement that "Locke attempts to show that it is labour which is responsible for the wealth and prosperity of modern societies, and that explains why it is legitimate to take labour as a basis for property entitlements. But we know that if, indeed, it is labour which creates modern prosperity, it is the unpleasant and alienated drudg-ery of the proletariat, not the autonomous and self-possessed activity of Lockean farmers."[27]

Interestingly, Waldron does not say whether he thinks *ideas* are goods that are either manufactured or merely gathered through physical drudg-ery. Nonetheless, a substantial contingent of legal scholars and philoso-phers would have no truck with this distinction because they have long argued that patents and copyrights are appropriated by intellectual prop-erty owners from a preexisting intellectual or cultural commons.[28] More-over, in his writings on intellectual property rights, Waldron accepts as given (for the purpose of criticism) the dominant theory today that intel-lectual property rights, such as copyrights, are justified given their *eco-nomic value* and overall contribution to social welfare.[29]

These criticisms of Locke's labor theory of value seem to have traction—and the traction of one criticism is so obvious to Nozick that he does not even feel it necessary to explain it—but only because they make funda-mental assumptions about what Locke means by *labor* and *value*. The

---

[26] Ibid., 193.

[27] Ibid., 321.

[28] See, for example, James Boyle, *The Public Domain: Enclosing the Commons of the Mind* (New Haven: Yale University Press, 2008). Boyle's reference to the mind as a "commons" is deliberate; for, as Locke argues, in the beginning "God . . . hath given the World to Men in common . . . . and no body has originally a private Dominion exclusive of the rest of Man-kind." (II.26) Justin Hughes similarly writes, "It requires some leap of faith to say that ideas come from a 'common' in the Lockean sense of the word. Yet it does not take an unrehabilitated Platonist to think that the 'field of ideas' bears a great similarity to a common." Justin Hughes, "The Philosophy of Intellectual Property," *Georgetown Law Journal* 77 (1988): 315. Among philosophers, see, for example, Herman T. Tavani, "Locke, Intellectual Property Rights, and the Information Commons," *Ethics and Information Technology* 7, no. 2 (2005): 87–97.

[29] Jeremy Waldron, "From Authors to Copiers: Individual Rights and Social Values in Intellectual Property," Chicago-Kent Law Review 68 (1992): 841–87.

conventional wisdom among philosophers is that Locke's labor theory of value justifies property rights in economic values based on proportional contributions of physical labor in the creation of these economic values. Even when philosophers such as Cohen and Waldron recognize that Locke does not define value solely in terms of economic value, they still assume that labor means some form of quantifiable physical effort that should be directly correlated with the resulting value in a produced object. Absent some kind of proof of this direct correlation—and the category mistake in shifting between proportional physical effort and total value in a completed object is palpable—Locke's labor theory of value collapses into a non sequitur. This perhaps explains why it has been given such short shrift by contemporary philosophers across the ideological spectrum— from libertarians (Nozick) to socialists (Cohen).

Nonetheless, these philosophical critiques now constitute the baseline assumptions within contemporary intellectual property theory, particularly among many legal scholars in the Law and Economics Movement. In *The Economic Structure of Intellectual Property Law* (2003), for instance, William Landes and Richard Posner merely assert as a foundational truism that "making intellectual property excludable creates value."[30] Of course, as leaders of the Law and Economics Movement, they mean *economic value* when they speak of value, and they do not feel it necessary to even consider the proposition that value is created, not by the legal definition of property rights under the law, but by the labor of a creator. If pressed, they would not need to point any further than to Nozick or Hettinger to confirm that value—economic value—is a socially created phenomenon and that Locke's labor theory of value makes a nonsensical claim to a quantifiable correlation between proportional physical labor and total economic value.

Beyond the economic theory of intellectual property rights, legal scholars generally assume that Locke's property theory rests on a basic claim about a relationship between *physical labor* and the *value* in a work of intellectual property. This is best evidenced by the reaction of legal scholars to the 1990 Supreme Court decision in *Feist Publications v. Rural Telephone Services*. In this copyright case, the Supreme Court overruled the "sweat of the brow" doctrine, which represented the theory in copyright law that legal protection of a copyright work is justified by the physical effort involved in creating the work.[31] Following this decision, scores of intellectual property scholars have asserted that "the Supreme Court in *Feist Publications* clearly and unequivocally disposed of the pure labor theory as justification for copyright."[32] In sum, they have assumed—just

[30] William Landes and Richard Posner, *The Economic Structure of Intellectual Property Law* (Cambridge: Harvard Univ. Press, 2003): 379.

[31] *Feist Publications v. Rural Telephone Services*, 499 U.S. 340, 352–54 (1991).

[32] Kenneth L. Port, "The 'Unnatural' Expansion of Trademark Rights: Is a Federal Dilution Statute Necessary?" *Seton Hall Legislative Journal* 18 (1994): 485. For other references to

as Nozick, Hettinger, Cohen and Waldron—that rejecting a theory of property rights that justifies protection of valuable creative works given the *physical labor* employed to produce these works is tantamount to rejecting Locke's labor theory of property.

But *Feist* is even more significant, because it also exposes the conceptual blinders that have been created by the equivocation today between Marx and Locke. Although intellectual property scholars widely believe that *Feist* represents an unequivocal rejection of Locke's labor theory of property in copyright law, they have all failed to read the *Feist* Court's explicit approval of the nineteenth-century justification for copyright as securing the "fruits of intellectual labor."[33] Of course, it is just as widely accepted that the ubiquitous references within Anglo-American property law to "securing the fruits of one's labors" is an explicit invocation of Lockean property theory, particularly of the labor theory of value that functions as a central premise within Locke's justification for property rights.

How could intellectual property scholars miss such an overt invocation of Locke's labor theory of value in the very decision in which they claim the Supreme Court rejects Locke's labor theory of value? The obvious answer is that they failed to see this because they have misconstrued Locke's labor theory of value, relying on the conventional wisdom among philosophers that Locke's concept of labor refers only to *physical* labor, that his concept of value refers only to *economic* value, and that he is asserting that a proportional contribution of physical labor in the creation of a creative work justifies claiming a property right in the total value therein. In other words, what Nozick, Cohen, Hettinger and Waldron all ascribe to Locke is exactly the "sweat of the brow" doctrine rejected by the *Feist* Court. It is time to set the record straight and establish the proper textual and philosophical context that gives meaning to Locke's labor theory of value. This context was well understood by early American jurists, which is why they believed that intellectual property rights secure the "fruits of intellectual labor." In fact, as I have explained elsewhere, such natural rights justifications for intellectual property rights are ubiq-

---

Feist as representing a rejection of Locke's labor theory or to the "sweat of brow" doctrine as representing (Lockean) labor theory, see John William Nelson, "The Virtual Property Problem: What Property Rights in Virtual Resources Might Look Like, How They Might Work, and Why They Are a Bad Idea," *McGeorge Law Review* 41 (2010): 292; Robert Brauneis, "The Transformation of Originality in the Progressive-Era Debate Over Copyright in News," *Cardozo Arts & Entertainment Law Journal* 27 (2009): 328–29; Shubha Ghosh, "Copyright as Privatization: The Case of Model Codes," *Tulane Law Review* 78 (2004): 722–23; Wendy J. Gordon, "A Property Right in Self-Expression: Equality and Individualism in the Natural Law of Intellectual Property, *Yale Law Journal* 102 (1993): 1540, footnote 37. For an example of a legal scholar claiming that focusing on intellectual labor and creativity allegedly *conflicts* with the historical uses of labor theory in copyright, see Jane Ginsburg, "Creation and Commercial Value: Copyright Protection of Works of Information," *Columbia Law Review* 90 (1990): 1875–81.

[33] *Feist Publications*, 499 U.S. at 346 (quoting *The Trade-Mark Cases*, 100 U.S. 82, 94 (1879)).

uitous in patent law cases and commentaries in the early American Republic.[34] The next section will proceed to make clear why this is so.

III. LOCKE'S PROPERTY THEORY: THE NATURAL LAW OF LIFE, PRODUCTION, AND VALUE

Since many legal scholars and philosophers spend so much of their
time discussing the two provisos in Locke's property theory—the waste
proviso and the "enough and as good" proviso—it is easy to forget that
these are merely corollaries of his two primary arguments for the right to
property. The first premise is the "mixing labor" argument and the second
is his labor theory of value. Waldron believes that one can and should
separate the mixing labor argument from the labor theory of value,[35] but
Locke would reject this attempt at analytically dicing up his property
theory. As his property theory unfolds in Chapter Five of the *Second
Treatise*, it is clear that he thinks these two premises are necessary and
sufficient in explaining "how Men might come to have a *property* in several parts of that which God gave to Mankind in common." (*TT* II.25)

Given the interrelated nature of Locke's two central premises in his
property theory—his "mixing labor" argument and his labor theory of
value—it is necessary to discuss in some detail both of the premises
constituting his property theory. Specifically, it is necessary to identify the
textual and *philosophical* context in which Locke claims that "mixing labor"
creates value in things that one can claim as one's property. Rediscovering
this all-important context in defining the basic terms in Locke's property
theory, such as labor and value, exposes the misrepresentations and anachronisms in the widespread critiques, particularly of his labor theory of
value. To wit, it belies the conventional wisdom today that Locke and
Marx are of one mind when it comes to the labor theory of value. Moreover, this is essential to understand why Locke believes his property
theory justifies intellectual property rights in inventions and writings.

A. "Mixing labor" as productive labor

The first premise in Locke's property theory is his widely known and
equally widely misunderstood "mixing labor" argument. As I and others
have explained, "mixing labor" is Locke's metaphor for the *productive
activities* that man must engage in so that he can create the objects necessary for maintaining his life—transforming wheat into bread, animals

---

[34] See Adam Mossoff, "Who Cares What Thomas Jefferson Thought About Patents? Reeval-
uating the Patent 'Privilege' in Historical Context," *Cornell Law Review* 92 (2007): 953–1012.

[35] Waldron believes that the "mixing labor" argument is nonsensical and thus he thinks
that the labor theory of value should be conceptually separated from it. See Waldron, *The
Right to Private Property*, 193. As I noted earlier, this is based on Waldron's misunderstanding
of the "mixing labor" argument, see Mossoff, "Locke's Labor Lost."

into livestock and steaks, and timber and rocks into houses.[36] Thus, I will call it the *productive labor* argument to avoid the misinterpretations of the "mixing labor" metaphor.

First, as a matter of textual analysis, Locke is absolutely clear in the *Second Treatise* that he defines his poetic phrase of "mixing labor" as referring to productive activities. The many examples of "mixing labor" that he employs throughout Chapter Five are all examples of production, such as husbandry, preparation of food, manufacture of clothes, and the creation of other basic commodities, including even wine. All of these examples illustrate his argument that "subduing or cultivating the Earth, and having Dominion, we see are joined together. The one gave Title to the other." (*TT* II.35) In addition to his consistent references to productive activities, such as cultivation, as examples of "mixing labor," Locke also repeatedly uses "industry" as a synonym for "labor" (see, for example, *TT* II.31, II.34, II.36–38, II.42–43, II.45–46). And beyond the book covers of the *Second Treatise*, Locke continues to refer to productive activities by the term, "labor"; this is perhaps best evidenced by his aptly titled essay, *Labour*.[37] Labor means production—the creation of valuable things for use by men—and mixing labor is merely his poetic metaphor in making this basic point. Thus, he writes, "God gave the World . . . to the use of the Industrious and Rational, (and *Labour* was to be *his Title* to it;) not to the Fancy or Covetousness of the Quarrelsom and Contentious." (*TT* II.34)

But this textual identification does not explain *why* Locke believes that production is a moral activity that justifies the laborer claiming a property right in his created works. We should first be clear as to what Locke is not saying in his productive labor argument, as confusions abound in philosophical and legal literature. First, it is not because Locke merely asserts as an axiom that man owns his self. The idea that self-ownership is the axiomatic foundation of Locke's justification for property rights, adopted by Nozick and many others who have misunderstood both the productive labor argument and the labor theory of value, results from reading the *Second Treatise* as a political treatise without reference to the ethical concepts and principles that inform Locke's arguments therein.[38] For Locke, the reason why "every Man has a *Property* in his own *Person*" (*TT* II.27)

[36] Mossoff, "Locke's Labor Lost," 159–61. The same arguments are made by Stephen Buckle, *Natural Law and the Theory of Property: Grotius to Hume* (Oxford: Clarendon Press, 1991), 151; A. John Simmons, "Maker's Rights," *Journal of Ethics* 2, no. 3 (1998): 210; Daniel Russell, "Locke on Land and Labor," *Philosophical Studies* 117 (2004): 318.

[37] See Mark Goldie, ed., *John Locke: Political Essays* (Cambridge: Cambridge University Press, 1997): 326–28. Here, for instance, Locke writes that "if the labour of the world were rightly directed and distributed there would be more knowledge, peace, health and plenty in it than now there is. And mankind be much more happy than now it is." Ibid., 328.

[38] See, for example, Nozick, *Anarchy, State, and Utopia*, 174–78; J. W. Harris, "Who Owns My Body?" *Oxford Journal of Legal Studies* 16, no. 1 (1996): 68–69. Tibor R. Machan, "Self-Ownership and the Lockean Proviso," *Philosophy and the Social Sciences* 39, no. 1 (2009): 93–98. While criticizing Nozick's use of the idea of self-ownership, which Nozick claims to take from Locke, Cohen maintains that "those who stand to the left of Nozick . . . might relax

is because, as he explains in the *First Treatise* and in *An Essay Concerning Human Understanding*, man is a rational animal who chooses to direct his actions in order with the natural law obligation to preserve his life (more on this below).[39]

Second, it is not because human labor merely replicates God's workmanship in making the universe (including humanity itself), as argued by Tully and other philosophers.[40] God does reign supreme in Locke's ethical and political philosophy, which is why the "workmanship model" has *prima facie* appeal as an explanatory theory, but God's role is not merely to serve as a role model whose actions man must imitate as a categorical imperative. Rather, God is important in Locke's ethical theory because he is the ultimate source of both the divine law and man's rational nature—the latter serving as the basis of the natural law (*ECHU* II.28.6-8). Natural law and divine law, according to Locke, are complementary sources of moral obligation, and each instructs man in his basic moral duty: "Every one . . . is *bound to preserve himself* and not to quit his Station willfully." (*TT* II.6) In the *First Treatise*, Locke writes that

> God having made Man, and planted in him, as in all other Animals, a strong desire of Self-preservation, ... and Being having been Planted in him, as a Principle of Action by God himself, Reason, *which was the Voice of God in him*, could not but teach him and assure him, that pursuing that natural Inclination he had to preserve his Being, he followed the Will of his Maker, and therefore had a right to make use of those Creatures, which by his Reason or Senses he could discover would be serviceable thereunto. (*TT* I.86)[41]

In his property theory, Locke applies this basic moral duty—the preservation of life—to both explain and justify why productive labor is both the descriptive source and moral justification for property rights. In fact, Locke could not be clearer about this moral standard: the first sentence in Chapter Five ("Of Property") informs readers that "natural *Reason* . . . tells us, that Men, being once born, have a right to their Preservation,"

---

their opposition to the idea of self-ownership. . . ." Cohen, *Self-Ownership, Freedom and Equality*, 71.

[39] See James Tully, *A Discourse on Property: John Locke and his Adversaries* (Cambridge: Cambridge University Press, 1980), 62-63, 105-17.

[40] John Simmons rightly criticizes the "workmanship model," first developed by Tully in *A Discourse on Property*, as lacking support in either the text or the analytical content of Locke's property theory. See Simmons, "Maker's Rights," 197-218.

[41] Earlier in the *First Treatise*, Locke writes that it is "the Priviledge of Man alone to act more contrary to Nature than the Wild and Untamed part of the Creation . . . . and seem to forget that general Rule which Nature teaches all things of self Preservation, and the Preservation of their Young." (*TT* I.56; see also I.92) In the *Second Treatise*, Locke repeatedly refers to self-preservation as the primary moral duty, see, for example, *TT* II.6, II.19, II.35 and II.129, which should always be understood as a duty within his natural law ethical theory.

which Locke also points out is equally confirmed by *"Revelation."* (*TT* II.25) In sum, the divine law and the natural law both direct man to preserve himself, and thus he has the right to take the actions necessary to preserve himself, such as laboring to create the products necessary to maintain his life. "God and his Reason commanded him to subdue the Earth, *i.e.*, improve it for the benefit of Life, and therein lay out something upon it that was his own, his labour." (*TT* II.32)[42]

Ultimately, this is Locke's solution to the problem in the consent-based property theories of Hugo Grotius (1583–1645) and Samuel Pufendorf (1632–1694). (*TT* II.25) It is not consent that justifies property, it is self-preservation, and productive labor is the means by which man sustains his life. An individual thus has "a Property in all that he could affect with his Labour: all that his *Industry could extend to, to alter* from the State Nature had put it in, was his." (*TT* II.46; emphasis added) But the productive labor argument does more than merely serve as an end-run around the problems faced by consent-based property theories; rather, Locke derives it directly from his natural law ethical theory, which establishes as its foundational principle that self-preservation is man's primary moral duty. Accordingly, the actions that serve this moral duty, such as producing the values required for the life of a rational animal, are morally justified. In sum, since man must preserve his life, he has a moral right to produce the values that fulfill this moral obligation, such as creating food, clothing, ships, factories, and all of the other examples of productive labor that Locke uses to illustrate this point. Thus, Locke glorifies the "Industrious and Rational" as a moral ideal (*TT* II.34), and this logically brings him to the second premise in his property theory—the labor theory of value.

B. *The labor theory of value: producing values for human flourishing*

Once we have established the moral import and function of productive labor within Locke's property theory, we can now profitably discuss his second argument for property rights: the labor theory of value. Productive labor, according to Locke, is a moral activity because it creates the goods that sustain human life, and thus, by definition, productive labor must be a *value-creating activity*. As Stephen Buckle writes, "labour is the improving, value-adding activity required by the duty to preserve oneself

---

[42] These two sources of obligation—God (divine law) and Reason (human nature and natural law)—are ubiquitous in Locke's productive labor argument in his property theory. In section 35, for example, Locke writes that "The Law Man was under, was rather for *appropriating*. God commanded, and his Wants forced him to *labour*. . . . And hence subduing or cultivating the Earth, and having Dominion, we see are joyned together. The one gave Title to the other. So that god, by commanding to subdue, gave Authority so far to *appropriate*. And the Condition of Human Life, which requires Labour and Materials to work on, necessarily introduces *private Possessions*." (*TT* II.35)

and others."[43] Although Locke does not always explicitly define his terms, he does not hide the ball concerning the meaning of value: "the intrinsick value of things . . . depends only on their usefulness to the Life of Man." (*TT* II.37) In sum, the moral standard that justifies productive labor is also what justifies the labor theory of value—productive labor is a moral activity because it sustains human life and the goods that result from productive labor are a value because they sustain human life.

In what *sense* of value are the goods created through productive labor? If one hews closely to Locke's text and always remembers the overarching framework of his natural law ethical theory, it is evident that he has a thicker concept of value than merely money (or some social variant thereof). As always, we begin with his actual text and then we will situate this text within the context of his broader philosophical framework.

Locke first introduces the labor theory of value in section 36, a pivotal paragraph in Chapter Five of the *Second Treatise*, because it summarizes the preceding discussion of productive labor and it introduces the ensuing analysis of the labor theory of value. At a minimum, section 36 is a reminder that, in Locke's mind, the productive labor argument and the labor theory of value are necessarily linked together in his justification for property rights—contra Waldron's assertion that it is necessary to separate these two arguments. Here, Locke restates the main thrust of his productive labor argument that "the measure of Property, Nature has well set, by the extent of Mens *Labour, and the Conveniency of Life.*" He then asserts for the first time his labor theory of value by inferring a corollary from his definition of labor as production: "*Ground* is of so little value, *without labour.*" He thus transitions from a productive labor argument to his labor theory of value by first asserting the *conclusion* of the labor theory of value; for the rest of the chapter, Locke fills out the details of his labor theory of value to prove his bald-faced assertion in section 36.

Before addressing the substance of his labor theory of value, it is important to recognize that Locke sometimes illustrates how values are created through productive labor by using money or by making quantitative comparisons of value from productive labor and from other materials (see, for example, *TT* II.37 and II.43). These examples are entirely consistent with his natural law concept of value—something that serves the self-preservation of man as a rational animal—but they have nonetheless given superficial plausibility to the conventional wisdom today that Locke is Marx. But this confusion is easily dispelled when one focuses on the substance of his argument for the labor theory of value, as apart from out-of-context examples. For instance, Locke begins his argument for the labor theory of value in section 37 by first distinguishing between (1) the consent-based value in "*a little piece of yellow Metal*" (money) and (2) the "intrinsick value" that necessarily serves "the Life of Man." Of

[43] Buckle, *Natural Law and the Theory of Property*, 151.

course, his labor theory of value explains how men claim property rights in the latter, not the former, and it is this context that must be remembered when interpreting his examples of value-creating, productive labor that use monetary values or quantified proportions of relative contributions of value.

This also reconfirms the importance of construing his labor theory of property within the context of his prior argument for the moral justification for property rights arising from productive labor. The reason Locke distinguishes between money and "intrinsick value" is precisely because he has already explained why man must produce the goods necessary to support his life—this is a morally justified activity given that it serves the duty of self-preservation—and thus man has a moral claim to these produced values.[44] (*TT* I.92) Although money can serve this function, which is one reason why Locke uses it approvingly in his examples, the act of producing values to sustain one's life is more fundamental than market exchanges in complex commercial societies. The underlying normative claim is self-preservation of man as a rational animal—and the right to create, use, and dispose of those things that serve this fundamental moral duty is the focus of Locke's argument for the labor theory of value. Hopefully, by Chapter Five, the reader has not forgotten Locke's injunction at the start of the *Second Treatise* that "To understanding Political Power right," we must "derive it from its Original." (II.4)

1. Locke's moral ideal of human flourishing. What does Locke mean by the duty of self-preservation? More precisely, what is the nature of the values that man has a right to produce and to use in order to meet this fundamental moral obligation? The key is to recognize that Locke does not refer merely to "life" when he discusses the moral justification both for productive labor and for the property right to the values created thereby. Throughout the *Second Treatise*, Locke consistently explains that value-creating, productive labor serves "Life, and convenience" or the "Conveniences of Life" (*TT* II.26, II.34, II.36–37, II.48).

The "conveniences of life" is Locke's term for the flourishing life of a rational animal that is preserved through productive labor. The duty of self-preservation is not a duty to maintain one's life as a brute, physical animal, and thus productive labor is not the purely *physical effort* employed by lower animals in sustaining their lives. Working within the classical natural law tradition, Locke recognizes that man is a *rational* animal. In fact, Locke begins *An Essay Concerning Human Understanding* with this

---

[44] This explains the spoilage and "enough and as good" provisos, which delimit in the state of nature the scope of the initial acquisition of a property right through productive labor. (TT II.27 and II.31) Unlike the labor theory of value, the nature and function of these two provisos are heavily debated in the literature today. This debate is beyond the scope of this essay, which focuses solely on the labor theory of value. Yet it is important to acknowledge these two additional premises within Locke's property theory, and it is my belief that they are consistent with the construction here of both productive labor and the labor theory of value, although this argument must be presented in another essay.

poignant observation: "Since it is the *Understanding* that sets Man above the rest of sensible Beings, . . . it is certainly a Subject, even for its Nobleness, worth our *Labour* to enquire into." (*ECHU* 1.1.1; "Labour" emphasis added) It is unsurprising here that Locke recognizes that the intellectual exercise of man's rational faculty in understanding his nature and the world at large is an act of "labour," i.e., it produces the requisite values necessary for sustaining the conveniences of life. In this case, it is the "Information of Vertue" (*ECHU* I.1.5; see also I.3.6) that is required for man to live a life in accord with his nature as a rational animal—a flourishing human life.

Locke's oeuvre—the works in which he develops the larger philosophical framework that he presupposes in the political tract of the *Two Treatises*—reveals his commitment to a thick notion of human flourishing as a moral ideal. Locke vividly demonstrates this in his early work as a professor of moral philosophy at Christ Church, Oxford,[45] as well as in his more mature philosophical work completed later in his life. In his treatise on education, for instance, he reconfirms his knowledge of and commitment to ideals of natural law ethical theory. Thus, for instance, in his recommendation of study on moral and political philosophy, he identifies works by Grotius and Pufendorf as necessary for a student to be "instructed in the natural rights of men, and the original and foundations of society." Yet he maintains that Grotius and Pufendorf should be read only after the student "has pretty well digested Tully's *Offices*," referring to Cicero's monograph on ethical theory, *de Officiis* (*On Duties*). (*STCE* 185-86)[46] As Locke explains in the introduction to his treatise on educa-

---

[45] See John Locke, *Questions Concerning the Law of Nature*, trans. and ed. Robert Horwitz, Jenny Straus Clay & Diskin Clay (Ithaca: Cornell University Press, 1990). This posthumously published monograph comprises Locke's lecture notes as a professor of moral philosophy, and it is rife with citations, quotations and paraphrases of classical sources. Although there are differences here from Locke's more mature thought, the similarities are evident:

> the law of nature is knowable by the light of nature. Since, in truth, the light of nature is the sole thing that directs us as we are about to enter the path of this life and that guides us . . . . it is fitting, not only to use this light as do animals for the necessities of life and to employ it to direct our steps, but to investigate also by a deeper inquiry what this light is and [to discover] its nature and its principle. Now inasmuch as this light of nature is not tradition (as has been shown elsewhere), nor any inner principle of action inscribed in our minds by nature, there remains nothing that can be called the light of nature except reason and sense. (Ibid., 153)

The essays by the translators and editors in this edition also do much to establish the classical influences, both explicit and implicit, in this work. For an excellent analysis of how Locke and the other modern natural rights philosophers were generally influenced by classical virtue ethics theory, see Eric R. Claeys, "Virtue and Rights in American Property Law," *Cornell Law Review* 94, no. 4 (2009): 889–934. The natural rights philosophers generally embraced the classical philosophical ideal of the good as human flourishing. See Adam Mossoff, "What is Property? Putting the Pieces Back Together," *Arizona Law Review* 45, no. 2 (2003): 371, footnote 166.

[46] Although Cicero self-identified as a skeptic, *de Officiis* is based explicitly on the moral teachings of stoicism. See Miriam Griffin, "Introduction," *On Duties* (Cambridge: Cam-

tion, dedicating a child's education to the moral ideal of human flourishing is essential in creating a "sound mind in a sound body," which "is a
short but full description of a happy state in the world." (*STCE* 1)

Although Locke does not explicitly cite or quote from Cicero or other
classical philosophers in the *Second Treatise*, revealing that he intended
this work for popular as well as scholarly consumption, his argument for
property is rife with evidence of his intellectual debt to natural law ethical
theory. To take but one example: In *de Officiis*, Cicero explains that "it is
clear that without the labour of men's hands we could not in any way
have acquired the fruits and benefits that are culled from inanimate
objects," [47] and Cicero makes clear that labor is not just physical effort, as
he defines this concept in terms of "the application of craft and manip-
ulative skills" and "human organization." [48] In other words, "labor," according to Cicero, refers to value-creating, productive labor. And this is a
moral activity precisely because it serves a flourishing human life:

> Why do I need to enumerate the multitude of arts without which
> there could be no life at all? What assistance would be given to the
> sick, what delights would there be for the healthy, what sustenance
> or comfort, if there were not so many arts to minister to us? It is
> because of these that the civilized life of men differs so greatly from
> the sustenance and the comforts that animals have.[49]

This is essential to Cicero's thesis that "nothing more pernicious can be
introduced into human life" than "separating virtue from expediency." [50]
In strikingly similar terms, Locke concludes his argument for the right to
property in the *Second Treatise* by observing that his property theory shows
how "Right and conveniency went together." (*TT* II.51)

As made clear by Locke's commitment to natural law ethical theory, a
proper life is one lived in accord with man's nature—a rational animal
capable of understanding and guiding his actions by the moral law, both
divine and natural. As I noted in the previous section, Locke argues in the
First Treatise for psychological egoism: all men have "a strong desire for
Self-preservation" that is achieved through the proper use of the "Senses

---

bridge University Press, 1991): xix–xx. In Locke's shorter and lesser known essay, *Some
Thoughts Concerning Reading and Study for a Gentleman*, he again identifies only two books in
his discussion of the "study of morality": the New Testament and Cicero's *de Officiis*. See
Mark Goldie, ed., *John Locke: Political Essays* (Cambridge: Cambridge University Press, 1997),
351.

[47] Cicero, *On Duties*, 67.

[48] Ibid., 67.

[49] Ibid., 68.

[50] Pufendorf approvingly quotes this line from Cicero in *On the Law of Nature and Nations*.
See Samuel Pufendorf, *De Jure Naturae et Gentium*, C. H. Oldfather and W. A. Oldfather,
trans. (Oxford: Clarendon Press, 1934), 195. As I noted, Locke recommends Pufendorf's
treatise as necessary for a proper education in political theory.

and Reason" that are given to him by God. (*TT* I.86) In the *Essay*, Locke affirms that "all Men's desires tend to Happiness," and here he employs a metaphor of bees and beetles to distinguish between two types of happiness pursued by two different types of men (revealing that his preference for the literary device of metaphors goes beyond the "mixing labor" metaphor in the *Second Treatise*).[51] The bees, according to Locke, pursue higher values ("Flowers, and their sweetness"), but beetles pursue only crude and limited physical values ("Viands; which having enjoyed for a season, they should cease to be, and exist no more"). (*ECHN* II.21.55) Although Locke does not explicitly draw out his moral evaluation, the nature of the comparison makes it clear as to which of the two animals represent the pursuit of values through productive labor. In their pursuit of the higher-value of sweetness, the bees seek true happiness—a flourishing life.

Accordingly, Locke criticizes the "Philosophers of old" who attempted to reduce value to a single source, whether "Riches, or bodily Delights, or Virtue, or Contemplation." Such reductionism is absurd, according to Locke, as they "might have as reasonably disputed, whether the best Relish were to be found in Apples, Plumbs, or Nuts; and have divided themselves into Sects upon it." (*ECHU* II.21.55) To cross the metaphors between the *Essay* and the *Second Treatise*, the bees seek the happiness in accord with a flourishing human life through "mixing their labor" and creating all of the sweet values that comprise the "conveniences of life."

That Locke believes that the self-preservation pursued by rational men is that of a flourishing life served by the many physical and intellectual values that are produced through value-creating labor is not merely something that must be inferred from mixing his poetic metaphors of bees and labor. In the *Essay*, he writes that "the highest perfection of intellectual nature, lies in a careful and constant pursuit of true and solid happiness" (*ECHU* II.21.51), and to prevent people from concluding that happiness comprises purely intellectual contemplation, Locke explains in the *Two Treatises* that man is "an intellectual Creature" and thus he is "capable of *Dominion*." (*TT* I.30)[52] Man's intellectual nature—his rational faculty—is the ultimate source of labor that produces both intellectual values, such as the principles of virtue, and physical values, such as clothing, shelter and

---

[51] Thank you to Eric Claeys for bringing this metaphor in the *Essay* to my attention. Locke's use of metaphors in the *Second Treatise* is not unusual, as he uses many metaphors throughout his philosophical writings. See Tom West, "The Ground of Locke's Law of Nature," *Social Philosophy & Policy*, vol. 29, no. 2 (2012): Section IV.

[52] The full sentence in the *First Treatise* is: "God makes [man] *in his own Image after his own Likeness,* makes him an intellectual Creature, and so capable of *Dominion*." This is important, because it also shows again how the "workmanship model" misconstrues the role of God in Locke's argument for property. Locke thinks that God is essential for property, not as a role model by which man mimics his own actions, but because God made man a rational animal capable of learning both the divine law and the natural law, and which oblige him respectively to engage in value-creating, productive labor to sustain a flourishing human life.

food. In sum, Locke's property theory, especially his labor theory of value, must be construed within the context of his natural law ethical theory. It is only within this intellectual context that one can recognize the two premises of Locke's argument that value-creating, productive labor is the fountainhead of property because it is only such labor that serves the happiness of a flourishing human life.

Toward the end of Chapter Five of the *Second Treatise*, Locke summarizes his argument for property

> that though the things of Nature are given in common, yet Man (by being Master of himself, and *Proprietor of his own Person,* and the Actions or *Labour* of it) had still in himself *the great Foundation of Property;* and that which made up the great part of what he applyed to the Support or Comfort of his being, when Invention and Arts had improved the conveniences of Life, was perfectly his own, and did not belong in common to others. (*TT* II.44)

This single sentence captures the entire context of Locke's moral argument for property rights—both in tangible goods and in inventions and books. Since man is a rational animal he is "Proprietor of his own Person," and this is why he has "in himself the great Foundation of Property," because it is his rational mind that guides his productive labor. This productive "labour" is a moral activity because it is what secures his "support or comfort of his being," and this does not mean just support of his physical or animal nature; rather, it is support of "the conveniences of life"—the flourishing life of a rational being. Thus, value-creating, productive labor is a moral activity that creates in the laborer a moral claim to the products of his labor—such things are "his own," meaning he has a right to the use, enjoyment, and disposal of them. Moreover, that labor includes "invention and arts," which "improved the conveniences of life," reveals Locke's moral approval of inventive activity and property rights therein. I'll say more on this shortly, but first we must directly confront the conventional wisdom that Locke defines value in terms of physical labor, money, or both.

2. Value and money in Locke's labor theory of value. Contrary to the claims of Nozick, Cohen, Hettinger and others, when Locke writes that " 'tis *Labour* indeed that *puts the difference of value* on everything," (*TT* II.40) he is not referring to money or to the products of merely physical effort. Textually and substantively, Locke's argument for the labor theory of value is clear that the values created through productive labor comprise all things that serve a flourishing human life, intellectual as well as physical. In a letter Locke wrote in 1698, for instance, to his friend, William Molyneux:

> If I could think that discourses and arguments to the understanding were like the several sorts of cates [i.e., food] to different palates and

stomachs, some nauseous and destructive to one, which are pleasant and restorative to another; I should no more think of books and study, and should think my time better imploy'd at push-pin than in reading or writing. But I am convinc'd of the contrary: I know there is truth opposite to falsehood, that it may be found if people will, and is worth the seeking, and is not only the most valuable, but the pleasantest thing in the world.[53]

Locke believes that truth is "valuable" and "the pleasantest thing in the world" because, like Cicero and other ancient natural law philosophers, he believes that one cannot separate virtue from expediency. (*TT* II.51) Thus, truth is as necessary for the productive labor in the intellectual realm as the Earth is as necessary for productive labor in the physical realm; it is the combination of the intellectual and the physical that makes possible a flourishing life. (*ECHU* 1.1.1; 2.21.51) As applied in his property theory, his labor theory of value further recognizes that if individuals are to have such a life, then they must engage in value-creating, productive labor to create these values in both the intellectual and physical spheres of human life.

One does not need to read Locke's personal letters or the *Essay* to understand that he does not define value solely in terms of economic value, because he explicitly makes this point within the bounds of the *Second Treatise*. In Chapter Five, Locke explains that money is not necessarily a moral value, because it "has its *value* only from the consent of Man." (*TT* II.50) In other words, it is neither man's nature nor the nature of values that man must produce in order to live a flourishing life that makes money valuable; economic value is based entirely in social agreement, i.e., consent among participants in the marketplace. This is a particularly striking passage given that Locke's labor-based property theory responds to the failings in the consent-based theories of property of Grotius and Pufendorf. For Locke, then, to claim that economic value is based in consent means that it is fundamentally distinct from the labor and values that comprise the foundation of his property theory, including his labor theory of value.

But economic value is not necessarily arbitrary nor does it necessarily contradict Locke's labor-based property theory; quite the contrary, economic value can be a proper value that is justified by his natural law principles and his property theory so long as "Labour yet makes, in great part, *the measure*" of this economic value. (*TT* II.50) The symmetry of this proposition with his earlier statement that productive labor is the *measure* of property is not accidental. (*TT* II.36) Given the core argument of Locke's property theory—it is value-creating, produc-

---

[53] E. S. de Beer, ed., *The Correspondence of John Locke*, vol. 6 (Oxford: Clarendon Press, 1976), 294–95.

tive labor that creates property—the development of money has moral import if and only if it serves as a storehouse of these produced values. Accordingly, Locke acknowledges that money is invented solely to serve as a medium of exchange for produced goods, and that the consent to this development is morally justified only insofar as it is consistent with the principles that validate the property arising from value-creating, productive labor. To extend Locke's point about the role of human decision-making in the state of nature: "though this be a *State of Liberty,* yet it is *not a State of License.*" (*TT* II.6)

The moral status of economic value—money—within Locke's ethical and political theory is that it is a *derivative* concept of a broader normative concept of value that is both logically and temporally antecedent to economic value. Textually, this is evident from the noneconomic uses of "value" that one finds throughout Locke's oeuvre (see, for example, *ECHU* II.21.46 and *ECHU* II.28.14), which reveal that this concept has a moral sense for Locke that is not restricted solely to quantities of money. Moreover, it is evident in the analytical structure of Locke's justification for money as the natural consequence of value-creating, productive labor. Locke writes that the "different degrees in Industry were apt to give Men Possessions in different Proportions, so this *Invention of Money* gave them the opportunity to continue and enlarge them." (*TT* II.48) Money, according to Locke, develops from and refers to the values created, used and possessed by men after they engage in different degrees of value-creating, productive labor ("Industry"). If it were otherwise, then such a statement would be nonsensical. How else could money "continue and enlarge" the "Possessions" previously produced through "Industry"? Locke is clear that it is these possessions—the products of value-creating, productive labor—that men "agreed, that a little piece of yellow Metal" would represent in their commercial transactions. (*TT* II.37) To wit, value-creating, productive labor is the progenitor of economic value if only because there cannot be consent to the use of money without goods being created in the first place. Since the concept of value encompasses economic value, just as the human good encompasses all values that serve the "conveniences of life," Locke argues that the moral justification for men to consent to the use of money is rooted in the same value-creating, productive labor that produces all values in a flourishing human life.

Admittedly, Locke uses quantitative ratios and monetary sums in his favored farming examples of how "'tis *Labour* indeed that *puts the difference of value* on everything" (*TT* II.40). In discussing farming and its resulting products, he initially posits that labor accounts for 90 percent of the value in improved land and its products, but he quickly increases the labor-created value in a farm to 99 percent. (*TT* II.37) A few sections later, he repeats the claim that productive labor is responsible for between 90 percent and 99 percent of the value in improved land and its products (*TT* II.40), and in his final reference to his beloved farming example, he claims that productive labor is responsible for 99.9 percent of the value of improved land and its products. (*TT* II.43) In his final farming example, he even frames the 99.9 percent marginal contribution of value-creating, productive labor in monetary terms. (*TT* II.43)

What to make of these references to quantitative proportions of value and to money in Locke's explication of his labor theory of value? First and foremost, there is nothing in the text of the farming examples that indicates that he intends the proportional contributions of value to be construed literally; that is, it is arguable that his references to the numeric ratios of value contributions, even in terms of economic value, reflects his literary preference for metaphors, such as his "mixing labor" and bees and beetles metaphors. These are expressions that Locke employs with artistic license to emphasize the substantial degree to which productive labor is the source of values in a flourishing human life.

Furthermore, at this late juncture in Chapter Five, it makes some sense for Locke to speak in terms of money in his examples because it is in these sections that Locke transitions to his final analysis of the consent-based institutions of civil society and money. (*TT* II.45–50) As he writes in the penultimate section of Chapter Five: "But since Gold and Silver, being of litte useful to the Life of Man in proportion to Food, Rayment, and Carriage, has its *value* only from the consent of Men, whereof Labour yet makes, in great part, *the measure,* it is plain." (*TT* II.50) The labor theory of value, based in nonconsensual productive labor (*TT* II.28–29), precedes and informs Locke's discussion of the "Invention of Money," as it arises through "mutual consent" (*TT* II.47–48) or "tacit and voluntary consent" (*TT* II.50).

Interestingly, when contemporary philosophers have reframed and criticized Locke's labor theory of value, they have all missed the fact that Locke never says that the respective value contributions between pre-existing materials and productive labor is a quantifiable economic relationship that can or should be measured in justifying property rights. In fact, in the first two farming examples that Locke uses in his discussion of the labor theory of value, he expressly states that he is making only loose assessments; i.e., he explains that he must "speak much within compasse" (*TT* II.37) and that "we will rightly estimate" (*TT* II.40) the values arising from productive labor. Making an estimate is hardly something a philosopher would do if he intends to claim that there is a necessarily quantifiable relationship between productive labor and value, and that identifying this proportional relationship is the analytical fulcrum for his normative justification for property rights in such values. In sum, the farming examples do not support the claim that Locke defines his concept of labor in solely *physical* terms or that he defines his concept of value in solely *economic* terms.

Similarly, Locke's contemporary critics have all missed the logical structure of his argument for the labor theory of value and its final conclusions—

the development of money, civil institutions, and advanced commercial transactions. Locke's acknowledgment that money is a derivative concept of value that arises logically and temporally from value-creating, productive labor that serves a flourishing human life is hardly a concession to the allegation that his labor theory of value justifies only economic values. It is true that he concludes his genetic argument for property rights in the values produced through productive labor—the values that serve a flourishing human life—with a discussion of money and a commercial economy, but this does not justify the interpretative claim that he defines the antecedent concept of value solely in terms of the consequent of economic value. Locke argues for a temporal and logical hypothetical proposition, P (value) → Q (economic value), and Nozick, Hettinger, and other contemporary philosophers have thus concluded that Locke asserts an identity proposition, P = Q. This is a non sequitur and, when used to criticize his labor theory of value, it is a strawman attack as well.

Lastly, Locke's loose references to quantitative, monetary ratios in his farming examples must be metaphorical if we are to interpret him as being consistent in using the same concept of value in both his ethical theory and in his political theory—values are those things that serve a flourishing human life. Otherwise, Locke would be explicitly embracing a flagrant contradiction between his ethical theory and political theory, because he stridently rejects as absurd the reductionist theories of value by "ancient Philosophers" and yet he would be committing the exact same reductionism if he was Marx—arguing for a labor theory of economic value. In response to this contradiction imposed on him by his contemporary critics, Locke might write today: "Hence it was, I think, that the [Philosophers of new] did in vain enquire, whether *Summun bonum* consisted in Riches" in my theory of how property rights arise from value-creating, productive labor. (*ECHU* II.21.55) Since this problem arises only from the *interpretation* of Locke's labor theory of value by contemporary philosophers and scholars who have paid no heed to the principle of interpretative charity, it has been necessary to reconsider Locke's labor theory of value within its proper framework of his natural law ethical theory. Now that we have done this, we can profitably assess why Locke approves of intellectual property rights as rightly securing what early American judges often referred to as "the fruits of intellectual labor."

IV. LOCKE'S JUSTIFICATION FOR INTELLECTUAL PROPERTY RIGHTS

In considering what Locke would think of intellectual property rights, it bears observing that one must be careful to avoid anachronisms in construing what a philosopher in the seventeenth and early eighteenth centuries might think about legal concepts like patents and copyrights. Patents, copyrights and the other legal concepts within the category of *intellectual property rights* began to take shape in the eighteenth century and did not really come to full fruition until the nineteenth century,[54] just as with other legal concepts that we now take for granted, such as contracts and corporations. In fact, the first time an American judge uses the phrase, "intellectual property," is in a patent decision in 1845.[55] The early American court cases and commentaries reveal that judges and scholars explicitly invoked Lockean property theory to justify their creation and protection of property rights in inventions (patents) and creative works (copyrights),[56] but this does little to establish whether Locke himself would approve of such property rights.

But we do not need to merely infer from Locke's property theory that he would approve of intellectual property rights, because he recognizes their moral validity as property rights. In fact, he states such approval explicitly about copyright, and he also expressly praises the value-creating, productive labor in *inventive activity* within his exegesis of this property theory in the *Second Treatise*. Each of these points will be addressed in turn, but it is important to reassert the normative framework of the ethical theory at work in his property theory—value-creating, productive labor is a moral activity because it is the means by which man meets his fundamental moral obligation to live a flourishing life. This is what gives Locke's particular arguments about property rights in literary works and inventions their normative import.

As before, it is best to begin with the text, as Locke's express endorsement of an author's property right in a literary work is the easiest way to disabuse the conventional wisdom among many law professors today that intellectual property rights contradict Locke's property theory.[57] In 1695, Locke pens an essay that criticizes a proposed law in Parliament that would extend the monopoly originally granted to the Stationers'

---

[54] See generally Mossoff, "Rethinking the Development of Patents," 1255–1322; Stuart Banner, *American Property: A History of How, Why, and What We Own* (Cambridge: Harvard University Press, 2011), 23–44.

[55] See *Davoll v. Brown*, 7 F. Cas. 197, 199 (C.C.D. Mass. 1845) (No. 3,662).

[56] In *Davoll v. Brown*, Circuit Justice Levi Woodbury explicitly invokes Locke's value-creating, productive labor justification for property rights in inventions, writing that "we protect intellectual property, the labors of the mind, productions and interests as much a man's own, and as much the fruit of his honest industry, as the wheat he cultivates, or the flocks he rears." *Davoll*, 7 F. Cas. at 199. Moreover, Chancellor James Kent, a famous antebellum jurist and legal scholar, classified both copyrights and patents in his 1826 treatise, *Commentaries on American Law*, in a section entitled, "Original Acquisition by Intellectual Labor." There, he argued for the Lockean principle that "It is just that [authors and inventors] should enjoy the pecuniary profits resulting from mental as well as bodily labor." James Kent, *Commentaries on American Law*, vol. 2 (Little, Brown & Co., 12th edition, 1873): 474. For further discussion of the ubiquitous Lockean justifications for intellectual property rights, especially patents, in the early American Republic, see Mossoff, "The Use and Abuse of Intellectual Property at the Birth of the Administrative State," 2022–24; Mossoff, "Who Cares What Thomas Jefferson Thought About Patents?," 990–98; Mossoff, "Patents as Constitutional Private Property," 705–7 & 718–19.

[57] I discuss this conventional wisdom in Mossoff, "The Use and Abuse of IP at the Birth of the Administrative State," 2047.

Company by the Licensing Act of 1662 as the sole printer of literary works in the English Realm.[58] By this law, Locke argues, "the Company of Stationers have a monopoly of all the classic authors and scholars," such as Cicero, whose works figure prominently in his argument that there is no "reason in nature why I might not print them as well as the Company of Stationers if I thought fit." (Of course, as I discussed earlier in Section III, it is hardly surprising that Locke would be so interested in the dissemination of Cicero's works given his own admiration for the ethical theory of this Roman philosopher.) Locke laments that "By this Act scholars are subjected to the power of these dull wretches who do not so much as understand Latin," and that ultimately, this printing monopoly "is very unreasonable and injurious to learning." Thus, he concludes that "'tis very absurd and ridiculous that anyone now living should pretend to have a property in or a power to dispose of the property of any copies or writings of authors who lived before printing was known or used in Europe."[59]

Moreover, the printing monopoly in literary works runs counter to what contemporaneous "authors" can rightly claim as "their property," which should be secured to them, their heirs, or assignees for their lifetimes plus "50 or 70 years." And just to be clear that Locke believes that it is authors who have a property right in their literary works, not printers, he proposes an amendment to the 1695 bill in which the precatory clause states "To secure the author's property in his copy, or to his whom he has transferred it, ..."[60] In sum, Locke believes firmly in an "author's property in his copy"—what we now call *copyright*.

Substantively, Locke's commitment to what was then a nascent concept of copyright makes sense, given that his property theory is grounded in his natural law ethical theory in which he recognizes that man is a rational animal for whom productive labor of both intellectual as well as physical values is the means by which man lives a flourishing life. In this respect, it is significant that he criticizes the Stationers' Company's printing monopoly as "injurious to learning," a breach of a fundamental virtue, according to Locke. (*ECHU* 1.1.1) As he explains in his writings on education, the labor of learning produces the "Information of Vertue" (*ECHU* 1.1.5), which is fundamental to right action and to achieving the "conveniences of life"—a flourishing life.

Locke's commitment to copyright thus reflects his belief that all manifestations of value-creating, productive labor, whether philosophical or

---

[58] This 1695 memorandum was recently brought to light by Justin Hughes, "Copyright and Incomplete Historiographies: Of Piracy, Propertization, and Thomas Jefferson," *Southern California Law Review*, vol. 79 (2006): 1012. In his earlier work, though, Hughes embraces the conventional wisdom that Locke's labor theory of value refers to only physical labor and "social value" (i.e., money). See Hughes, "The Philosophy of Intellectual Property," 299–310.

[59] Mark Goldie, ed., *John Locke: Political Essays* (Cambridge: Cambridge University Press, 1997), 330–38.

[60] Goldie, *John Locke: Political Essays*, 338.

physical, are rooted in man's nature as a rational animal. In the *First Treatise*, for instance, he explains that it is man's nature as "an intellectual Creature" that makes him "capable of *Dominion*." (*TT* I.30). Previously, in Section III, I highlighted this sentence to show that Locke understands that a flourishing human life consists of both intellectual and physical labor—the production of the intellectual and physical values that serve the "conveniences of life" through the uniquely human capacity for rationally guided action. Here, this sentence serves a different function, as it reveals that Locke grasps that it is man's intellectual nature—his rational mind—that is the ultimate source of the labor that produces physical values, such as clothing, shelter, and food. He does not explicitly explain this point, but the implication is that physical values are made possible only through the exercise of man's rational mind in learning how to produce these goods. When a rational man engages in this value-producing labor, he creates property—*dominion* in the Latin of the Roman Law and of modern political philosophy.[61]

This foundational principle from his ethical theory explains why many of his examples of value-creating labor in the *Second Treatise* consist of the "Industry" of technological inventions, such as the bread that is made by the "Mill [and] Oven," the "Plough" that tills the soil, "all the Materials made use in the Ship," and so on. (*TT* II.43) And we must not forget the conceptual skills of artisans that made possible "the Labour of those who broke the Oxen, who digged and wrought the Iron and Stones, who felled and framed the Timber." (*TT* II.43) This is what Locke means that "the ordinary Provisions of Life, through their several progresses, before they come to our use, . . . receive of their *value from Human Industry*." (*TT* II.42) His examples of his labor theory of value reflect his moral approval and admiration for how technological inventions secure for man "the conveniences of life"—a flourishing human life. This shows the degree to which Locke's farming examples, which are highlighted by legal scholars and philosophers to show that his property theory is allegedly restricted to only parcels of Earth or tangible chattels, have been widely misconstrued. His repeated references to farming as illustrations of value-creating, productive labor are replete with conspicuous references to the technological inventions that make farming an example of value-creating, productive labor.

Ultimately, this is why Locke approvingly includes "Inventions and arts" in his seminal summation of his theory of how value-creating, pro-

---

[61] There is an ambiguity in the Latin *dominion*, which also refers to political authority (see, for example, *TT* II.4, II.90 II.120), but Locke's usage of this term in the context of discussing property rights is consistent with other modern natural law philosophers who also referred to property as *dominion*. (*TT* I.29, I.39, II.26, II.35) This explains William Blackstone's reference to "the rights of dominion, or property," in discussing the views of "writers on natural law." It also explains his famous definition of "the right of property; or the sole and despotic dominion which one man claims and exercises over the external things of the world, in total exclusion of the right of any other individual in the universe." William Blackstone, *Commentaries on the Laws of England*, vol. 2 (Chicago: The University of Chicago Press, 1979): 1–2.

ductive labor creates property rights—property rights that are morally justified because they serve the "conveniences of life." (*TT* II.44) Although the legal concept of patents—property rights in inventions—did not exist yet in 1690,[62] there could hardly be a more explicit indication of his willingness to include what would later become patents within his property theory. If anything, Locke's explicit approval of copyright—an author's property right in copies of a literary work—reaffirms the validity of this inference, as copyright and patents are both intellectual property rights. And the ease by which early American judges and commentators embraced a Lockean justification for patents reveals the extent to which these intellectual property rights conformed to Locke's justification for property rights as arising from the intellectually-based value creation in productive labor.

The natural law ethical theory that informs Locke's argument for property rights explains why he thinks his property theory applies to inventions and books. In section 34 of the *Second Treatise*, Locke explains that God gave the world "to the use of the Industrious and Rational" who obtain the "greatest Conveniences of Life they were capable to draw from it" by the "*Labour* [that] was to be *his Title* to it." It is man's rational nature as an "intellectual Creature" (*TT* I.30) that is the source of both the moral ideal—the virtues that guide one toward a flourishing life of happiness— and the means to that end—value-creating, productive labor. It is not wolves, lions, or other "dangerous and noxious Creatures" (*TT* II.16) who have invented the plough, the mill, and ships. Such inventions represent the achievements of the value-creating, productive labor that serves the flourishing life, and this is why Locke highlights them as exemplars of his property theory generally and of his labor theory of value specifically.

V. Locke's Labor Lost: Why Locke Became Marx

Locke's labor theory of value has suffered much at the hands of contemporary philosophers. In critiquing his property theory and its application to intellectual property rights, Hettinger, Nozick, Cohen and others have redefined Locke's fundamental concept of labor in purely *physical* terms, they have redefined his concept of value in purely *economic* terms, or they have made such conceptual assumptions in imposing on Locke's argument for the labor theory of value a methodology of quantifying physical inputs relative to economic value outputs. But as I made clear in the previous sections, these are not Locke's concepts of labor or value. His concept of labor refers to production, which has intellectual as well as physical characteristics, and his concept of value serves his moral ideal of human flourishing, which is a conception of the good that is more robust than merely physical status or economic wealth. Even more importantly,

---

[62] See Adam Mossoff, "Rethinking the Development of Patents," 1255–1322.

he never says that property rights in the values created through productive value are justified by a measurable or quantifiable relationship between labor inputs and value outputs.

How has such a widespread misunderstanding of Locke's labor theory of value come to pass? There is probably no single answer to this question, and Locke would agree. To insist on a single answer would commit the same reductionist error of the "Philosophers of old" that Locke chastises in *An Essay Concerning Human Understanding.* (*ECHU* II.21.55) Just as there are myriad intellectual and physical values that serve a flourishing life, there are many reasons for why a mistaken conventional wisdom comes about; they all have at least some explanatory force, and thus a single essay cannot delve into all of them or fully engage with the historian about which are the most fundamental or causal factors. In this concluding section, I will briefly identify one possible source for the misunderstanding of Locke's labor theory of value today, and I must leave it to philosophers and intellectual historians to explore in greater depth the issues that I can only briefly touch on in this section.

Locke, unfortunately, has himself to blame for this misunderstanding of his theory. Admittedly, he disagrees with Marx's labor theory of economic value (what Marx and economists call "exchange-value"), as he does not think that the purpose of his labor theory of value is solely to explain how and why economic value arises in commodities in the marketplace. As the previous sections made clear, Locke does not define value solely in terms of economic value, and, even more important, he believes that the ethical concept of value is broader and more fundamental than the derivative concept of economic value. However, Locke endorses some ideas in his labor theory of value that are shared by Marx, and thus there is an undeniable historical link between the two theories. Locke's arguments for the labor theory of value in the *Second Treatise,* or more specifically, his use of the now-famous farming examples to illustrate the labor theory of value, made it plausible for follow-on philosophers to link Locke and Marx more closely than merely as a matter of family resemblance.

As a preliminary matter, it is unfortunate that Locke does not have an explicitly developed theory of value, or at least there is no standalone analysis of the normative concept of value in his extant writings. Thus, philosophers and scholars have been forced to make inferences from what he does say about value throughout his philosophical writings generally, such as in his ethical theory presented in *An Essay Concerning Human Understanding* and in his property theory presented in the *Second Treatise.* When one considers the full context of these works, it is clear that Locke believes that a value is something that serves a flourishing human life—it is something that provides intellectual and material support for the life of a rational animal. Thus, for instance, his observation that when men quit "the Common Law of Reason," they become "dangerous and noxious Creatures" (*TT* II.16), because they then take actions that threaten everything that makes a flourishing human life possible to other men who are living according to their rational nature and engaging in value-creating, productive labor.

But just as it is necessary to explain how Locke identifies the ultimate source of property in value-creating, productive labor, it is equally necessary to ask what is the ultimate source and meaning of Locke's concept of value. He never explicitly identifies this beyond noting that value serves human life: "the intrinsick value of things, which depends only on their usefulness to the Life of Man." (*TT* II.37) In his property theory, he argues that it is productive labor that leads to this value, and in his labor theory of value, he uses a recurring farming example to support his claim that "'tis *Labour* indeed that *puts the difference of value* on everything" (*TT* II.40). The farming examples are as ubiquitous in his property theory as they are important (*TT* II.36–38, II.40, II.42–43, II.46, II.48), especially when it comes to his arguments for his labor theory of value. They are important because they reveal that Locke believes that there is some value in the raw materials of the world that *preexists* any value-creating, productive labor, and this becomes the conceptual linchpin for the equivocation between Locke and Marx.

The refrain in Locke's farming examples is that there is *proportional* value contribution between productive labor and the preexisting material of the land, ore, or other natural products in the world. He claims that the relative contribution of productive labor to the total value in a finished thing of usefulness ranges between 90 percent to as much as 99.9 percent. (II.40) Locke thus assumes that there is some value, however negligible, that preexists the rational thought and action that produces a value—whether a farm, a mill, or a ship, to use his own examples from the *Second Treatise*. Locke's concept of "intrinsic value" means that productive labor is not the *sole* source of creating value in the world. In fact, he readily acknowledges this point in one of his farming examples in his discussion of his labor theory of value: "the improvement of *labour makes* the far greater part of the *value*." (*TT* II.43) Thus, Locke's farming examples confirm that he does believe, as he states, that there is "natural, intrinsick Value" that exists separately from any productive labor by men. (*TT* II.43) Again, he intends his concept of value to be limited to neither physical conditions nor economic relationships—this "natural, intrinsick Value" is defined in terms of the happiness of a rational man seeking a flourishing human life. But, unfortunately, his argument does not equal his intention.[63]

---

[63] Ayn Rand also identifies this as the concept of "intrinsic value," using the same terminology that Locke uses in referring to his own concept of value (*TT* II.37, II.43), but she differentiates Locke's concept of value from her "objective" concept of value, which she defines as "that which one acts to gain and/or keep." See Ayn Rand, "The Objectivist Ethics," *Virtue of Selfishness* (1964), 15. In other words, for Rand, values arise *solely* from the goal-directed actions that a living organism must engage in to preserve its life. There is no value until a living being takes the actions necessary to sustain itself, and then *one-hundred percent of the value* is directly attributable to the action of the living organism pursuing a specific purpose. See Tara Smith, "The Importance of the Subject to Objective Morality: Distinguishing Objective from Intrinsic Value," *Social Philosophy & Policy* 25, no. 1 (2008)

The concession to proportional contributions of value naturally led to the questions about the *source* of value, such as whether it is created by quantifiable physical labor, and the *meaning* of value, such as whether it is the economic value (the pound and pence). At this level of conceptual analysis in metaethics, Locke simply asserts that value-creating, productive labor creates 90–99.9 percent of the total value in a final product that is "useful to the Life of Man" (*TT* II.37). Why this is so, and, even more important, how this justifies a moral claim—a right to property—to 100 percent of the final product is an argument Locke does not make.

Unsurprisingly, this represents the critique—the unanswered rhetorical questions, to be precise—raised by Hettinger, Nozick, Cohen and others. Apparently, when these philosophers thought about these questions, which were legitimate given the nature of Locke's belief in a preexisting, intrinsic value in the world, Locke's references to money in his labor theory of value pointed the way to an answer, at least this is what can be garnered from the nature of their brusque criticisms. That is, Hettinger and Nozick assume that Locke is speaking of economic value, which is measurable and quantifiable in terms of its inputs and outputs. Moreover, defining labor solely in terms of physical action, which is measurable and quantifiable, seemed like another plausible way to make sense of Locke's argument for marginal contributions to the value of things used by men. This of course is the alternative interpretive move made by Cohen and others. In sum, to make sense of Locke's labor theory of value, as it is presented only in the *Second Treatise*, contemporary philosophers filled in the conceptual gap—Locke's ethical concept of value—and assumed that Locke defines labor in terms of physical actions, that he defines value in terms of economic value, or both.

In making these assumptions, this is why it seems like Marx is channeling Locke when Marx develops his own labor theory of economic value. In language that appears to mirror Locke's farming examples, Marx writes in *Das Kapital* "that labour is not the only source of material wealth, of use-values produced by labour. As William Petty puts it, labour is its father and the earth its mother." [64] Of course, the substantive content of their respective concepts of value are different—Locke is speaking about the myriad things that serve the flourishing life of a rational animal and Marx is speaking about measurable physical and economic data. Yet, they both agree that there are two independent *sources* of value—that value which exists in the world and that value which arises from productive labor.

126–48. For instance, many people believe that a parcel of fecund soil in the American Midwest is valuable and a parcel of desert in the American Southwest is not, but this is only because they assume an unstated premise that the purpose for the use of the two parcels is farming. If one changes the purpose, such as building semi-conducting silicon chips for computers, then the sand in the desert is extremely valuable and the fecund soil is not. The value is defined by the specific goal and then created by the specific action undertaken by a living organism in pursuing this goal in sustaining its life, such as the flourishing life of rational individual.

[64] Marx, *Das Kapital*, vol. 1, 309.

One must be careful not to carry this point too far, though. Although Locke embraces the concept of intrinsic value, this does not mean that either his concept of value or its application in his labor theory of value is the same as Marx's. Locke and Marx may have shared the belief in preexisting intrinsic values in the world to which there is added a contribution by productive labor, but unlike Locke, Marx believes that value means economic value or at least some other socially determined form of wealth. As Marx explains in *Das Kapital:* "Use-values become a reality only by use or consumption; they also constitute the substance of all wealth, whatever may be the social form of that wealth." Thus, Marx ultimately believes that "exchange-value is the only form in which the value of commodities can manifest itself or be expressed." [65] For Marx, identifying use-values in things is only a premise in explaining the complete meaning of such values in society: "An increase in the quantity of use-values is an increase of material wealth." [66] At the end of the day, for Marx, value means economic value—no more, no less. [67]

Marx's labor theory of economic value reflects his underlying belief in the inherently social nature of ethical and political concepts. As Marx argues, "to stamp an object of utility as a value, is just as much a *social product* as language." [68] (This is why, Cohen argues, Marxists believe that the labor theory of value is essential to their critical political theory of the ideology of capitalist exploitation.[69]) Such a fundamental communitarianism in Marx's ethical theory stands in sharp contrast to the ethical theory of Locke, which is individualistic insofar as it posits an individual's productive labor as the progenitor of the values that serve that individual's flourishing life. In this metaethical sense, Locke and Marx stand on opposite sides of a deep conceptual divide about the meaning of value, and thus their respective labor theories of value reflect this fact.

But even if one can successfully drive a conceptual wedge between Locke's and Marx's labor theories of value, despite their mutual embrace of an intrinsicist concept of value, Locke's farming examples made it seem reasonable for follow-on commentators to conclude that he believes that there are specific proportional contributions of value, whether they are measurable in physical labor, economic value, or both. Locke admits that some "natural, intrinsick Value" exists in the world apart from productive labor (*TT* II.43), regardless of whether it is quantifiable or even

[65] Ibid., 303–05.
[66] Ibid., 312.
[67] Ronald L. Meek, *Studies in the Labor Theory of Value,* 2d ed. (New York: Monthly Review Press, 1956): 157–200. David Ramsay Steele writes that "The Marxian labor theory of value (LTV) is intended to explain the determination of prices under commodity production (this is occasionally denied, but see Steele 1986). In Marxian terminology, there can be no 'value' in post-capitalist society." David Ramsay Steele, *From Marx to Mises: Post-Capitalist Society and the Challenge of Economic Calculation* (La Salle: Open Court Publishing Co., 1992), 127.
[68] Marx, *Das Kapital,* vol. 1, 303–05, 322 (emphasis added). Marx explicitly and repeatedly argues that value is purely relational or social. See pp. 315–17, 321–23, 328.
[69] Cohen, *Self-Ownership, Freedom and Equality,* 172–73.

measurable, and this has been the fulcrum by which philosophers today have equated Locke with Marx.

The influence of this equivocation between Locke and Marx on contemporary intellectual property theory is beyond doubt. Today, legal scholars are wont to assert that "Intellectual property rights are justifiable only to the extent that excludability does in fact create value."[70] As two of the founders of the American Law and Economics movement proclaim: "making intellectual property excludable creates value."[71] On their face, such pronouncements sound vaguely Lockean, as they imply that the justification for intellectual property rights is the value creation that follows from their protection under the law—the legal definition and enforcement of these rights as "excludable" from others. But on closer inspection, this is deeply mistaken. The assumption in such statements is that value *follows* from the legal enforcement of exclusion; in other words, intellectual property rights cannot be commodified and valued on the market until the law secures them exclusively to their owners, who then can contract with them in commercial transactions once people are legally forbidden from copying the invention or book. Such an economic argument, though, turns Locke's property theory on its head. For Locke, productive labor creates values that preexist civil society, civil government, or the market. According to Locke's theory of natural property rights, the legal enforcement of exclusion in property and intellectual property rights *follows* from the creation of value.

In short, Locke is not Marx, despite the terminological similarity in their respective labor theories of value. It is time to rediscover the original meaning of Locke's property theory, as presented in his own words and in the context of his own natural law ethical theory. As evidenced by his heavy debt to such classical natural law ethicists as Cicero, Locke argues that value-creating, productive labor is morally justified insofar as it contributes to a flourishing human life—serving all of the "conveniences of life." This is why Locke believes that the products of such labor, whether in land, technological inventions, or books, are the producer's property, and thus deserving of protection under the law.

VI. Conclusion

Locke's labor theory of value is widely misunderstood today, and this is especially true in intellectual property theory, in which it is accused of being incoherent, weak, backwards in its logic, or simply wrong. These attacks, however, are based on a deeply mistaken conceptual assumption

[70] Mark Lemley, "Property, Intellectual Property, and Free Riding," *Texas Law Review* 83 (2005): 1057. Lemley is describing the conventional wisdom here, as he disagrees with this statement, but only because he disputes the assumption that intellectual property rights are justifiable on grounds of economic value.

[71] Landes and Posner, *The Economic Structure of Intellectual Property Law*, 379.

that Locke defines labor solely as physical action, value solely as economic value, or that his labor theory of value utilizes a methodology of quantifying proportional contributions of physical labor inputs to economic value outputs. Although these critics claim to be targeting Locke, they are in fact thrashing Karl Marx and his labor theory of economic value, in which exchange-value does arise from proportional contributions of materials and physical actions. It is time to save Locke from Marx, identifying his labor theory of value on its own terms and in its philosophical context, such that we can better understand how and why Locke applies it to intellectual property rights in inventions and books.

When Locke's labor theory of value is understood within its proper context—it is an application in political theory of his natural law ethical principles—it is anything but incoherent or Marxist. Although Locke does not advance an explicit theory of value, his writings on this fundamental ethical concept throughout his mature philosophical works reveal that he defines it in terms of those things that serve a flourishing life of a rational individual. In the *Second Treatise*, written for consumption by public intellectuals and the like, he repeatedly refers to this moral standard by his ubiquitous turn of phrase, "conveniences of life."

The products of value-creating, productive labor comprise both intellectual and physical values—and thus they represent the *dominion* that follows from man's nature as an "intellectual creature." This is why Locke recognizes the moral validity of an author's property right in controlling copies of books. In his full-throated defense of property rights in the *Second Treatise*, he identifies "Inventions and Arts," as exemplars of his theory of how property arises from the value-creating, productive labor of the "Rational and Industrious." His approval of what we now call intellectual property rights is no more tenuous than it is oblique. It is for this reason that many early American judges and commentators looked to Locke's natural rights philosophy for the moral justification in securing the rights of inventors, authors, and other creators of intellectual property in the nineteenth century.

Law, George Mason University School of Law

ROOSEVELT, WILSON, AND THE DEMOCRATIC
THEORY OF NATIONAL PROGRESSIVISM

By Ronald J. Pestritto

I. INTRODUCTION

America's original Progressives, rising to prominence at the turn of the twentieth century, sounded the theme of democratic reform. The American Constitution, they contended, placed too much distance between the people and their government, due to an inordinate fear by the Constitution's Framers of the factious tendencies of unfiltered public opinion. Because of this indirect and representative form of popular government, Progressives complained that popular majorities of their own day were unable to direct the government to act effectively in response to the pressing social and economic crises of the nation.[1] Instead, a small but powerful minority, Progressives argued, was taking advantage of the Constitution's limits on popular rule to benefit itself at the expense of the great mass of people.[2] It is for this reason that many of the reforms advocated by Progressives involved reducing or eliminating the distance between majority opinion and governing at the federal, state, and local level. Progressives, regardless of certain important differences among them, universally supported movements toward more direct forms of democracy: the ballot initiative, recall, referendum, and direct primaries for elections. Democratization was, arguably, the most important theme of the Progressive Movement, as it sought to place more governing power in the hands of popular majorities.

The Progressive push for democratization, however, is complicated by the fact that the Movement was also the launching point for the modern administrative state.[3] It helped put into place a system whereby significant portions of government decisionmaking are exercised not by the

---

[1] Progressives lamented, for example, the gap between rich and poor (see Jane Addams, "Subjective Necessity for Social Settlements," in Ronald J. Pestritto and William J. Atto, eds., *American Progressivism* [Lanham, MD: Lexington Books, 2008], 105), the effects on urban life of immigration (see Theodore Roosevelt, "State of the Union Message," December 3, 1901, in *State of the Union Addresses of Theodore Roosevelt* [Echo Library, 2007], 4–38), and the state of working conditions (see Theodore Roosevelt, "State of the Union Message," December 3, 1907, in *State of the Union Addresses*, 201–48).

[2] For a representative example of this argument, see Theodore Roosevelt, "The Right of the People to Rule," in Pestritto and Atto, eds., *American Progressivism*, 251–52.

[3] For an elaboration on the founding of the administrative state in the Progressive Era, and its connection to contemporary governance, see Ronald J. Pestritto, "The Progressive Origins of the Administrative State: Wilson, Goodnow, and Landis," *Social Philosophy and Policy* 24, no. 1 (Winter 2007): 16–54.

doi:10.1017/S026505251100029X

traditional branches of government that are accountable to the people through elections, but by unelected, bureaucratic agencies that regulate with substantial independence from political control. While Progressives, on the one hand, sought to make the nation's traditional political institutions much more accountable to majority opinion, on the other hand they also believed that those institutions were not capable of managing all of the new activities in which Progressives wanted the national government to become involved.[4] Under the Progressive model, political institutions were to become both more democratic and less important. How democratic, then, was national Progressivism? In what ways does its reliance upon expert governance complicate its democratic theory?

The relevance of these questions comes from the influence that this dual character of Progressivism has had on contemporary American government. American politics today maintains a near obsession with public opinion; even minute movements in benchmarks such as the presidential approval rating are watched as intently as heart monitors on critical patients. And yet while public opinion occupies a place of tremendous importance, its authority is also deflected in ways that reflect Progressive governing principles. In spite of the intense focus on national political debates, most real governing today is done by bureaucratic agencies. Often, these agencies govern in ways that defy public opinion. Most of the critical activity in the second half of President Barack Obama's first term, for instance, will take place in regulatory agencies rather than the national legislature.

The Environmental Protection Agency (EPA) is presently in the process of issuing final rules regulating greenhouse gas emissions. Due mostly to concerns over the impact of such rules on the economy, a similar scheme of regulation garnered strong, bipartisan opposition in the 111th Congress and failed to pass. (One Democratic Senate candidate, Joe Manchin, won election from West Virginia in 2010 due in part to a television commercial which featured him shooting a copy of the proposed legislation with a high-powered rifle). In spite of the legislative failure, these rules are now in the process of becoming law. Such a maneuver is possible because when Congress enacted the Clean Air Act and its subsequent amendments, it defined the EPA's power in such broad and vague terms that it amounted to a delegation of near plenary legislative power.[5] In a similar example, Congress in 2008 considered, and voted against, a taxpayer-

---

[4] For an enumeration of these aims, see "Progressive Party Platform of 1912," in Pestritto and Atto, eds., *American Progressivism*, 273–87.

[5] In *Massachusetts v. Environmental Protection Agency*, 549 U.S. 497 (2007), the U.S. Supreme Court ruled that the Clean Air Act not only granted the EPA the authority to regulate greenhouse gas emissions, but in fact obligated it to do so. Specifically, the Court held that, since such emissions fall under the Act's very broad definition of air pollutant, the EPA was obligated to regulate the emissions unless it 1) found that the emissions did not contribute to global climate change, or 2) had a reasonable explanation for its unwillingness or inability to determine if the emissions contributed to global climate change.

funded bailout of major American automobile manufacturers. Nonethe-less, the national government proceeded to bailout both General Motors and Chrysler. It was able to do so because the previously enacted Trou-bled Asset Relief Program (TARP)[6]—enacted for the purpose of bailing out banks and other financial service entities—had been written vaguely enough that the Treasury Department had ample discretion to divert funds to a wide array of entities having little to do with the financial services industry. Many such examples could be drawn from a variety of policy areas, the point of which would be to demonstrate that much governing today is done by expert agencies—sometimes with political support and sometimes without it.

The tension within today's administrative state—between democratic governance and governance by unelected experts—reflects a similar ten-sion in the democratic theory of America's original Progressives. This essay is a preliminary effort to explore this tension in Progressive dem-ocratic theory by looking to Theodore Roosevelt (1858-1919) and Woodrow Wilson (1856-1924), the two most prominent Progressives on the national political stage.[7] This is an admittedly limited scope (among others, the Progressive writer Herbert Croly (1869-1930) would deserve attention in a fuller treatment of this question), necessitated by the confines of space; it focuses largely on national Progressivism as opposed to the very impor-tant state and local elements of the Movement, and it speaks more to the political issues as opposed to the many social and cultural facets of Pro-gressivism. Yet in the thought of Roosevelt and Wilson we find an impor-tant contrast which helps to illuminate the nature of Progressive democratic theory. Roosevelt offered the typical Progressive critique of the republican constitutionalism of the Federalists, and insisted upon very direct popu-lar control over national government. Almost implausibly, Roosevelt sees little or no tension between his strong democratic impulse and his call for the employment of expert commissions in the national regulation of busi-ness and property. Wilson, on the other hand, while equally convinced about the necessity of pushing democratic reforms, more readily acknowl-edged the uneasiness of the coexistence he envisioned between an increas-

---

[6] For the language on the Treasury Department's authority, see 12 USCS § 5211 (a)(1). On the extension of TARP authority beyond banks and ordinary financial institutions, see: *The Troubled Asset Relief Program: Report on Transactions through June 17, 2009,* http://www.cbo.gov/ftpdocs/100xx/doc10056/MainText.4.1.shtml#1094296, accessed February 5, 2011. See also *United States Department of the Treasury Section 105(a) Troubled Asset Relief Program Report to Congress for the Period December 1, 2008 to December 31, 2008,* http://www.treasury.gov/press-center/press-releases/Documents/0010508105_a_report.pdf, accessed February 5, 2011.

[7] In its discussion of Wilson, this essay will reflect research conducted for my book-length treatment of his political thought: *Woodrow Wilson and the Roots of Modern Liberalism* (Lanham, MD: Rowman & Littlefield, 2005). That research pointed to the tension in Wilson between democratization and expert governance. The present essay is an attempt to take the analysis a step further—to think about how the competing elements within this tension might have been reconciled by Wilson, and to introduce Roosevelt's view of the matter as a means of more fully understanding the uniqueness of Wilson's position.

ingly democratized politics and an increasingly expert and powerful administrative apparatus. The result would be, as the essay argues, a more nuanced and realistic democratic theory which has, as a consequence, a greater relevance for contemporary American government.

II. Roosevelt and the People's Right to Rule

For Theodore Roosevelt, the Constitution's Federalist Framers had obsessed about majority tyranny and thus erected a system which enshrined minority tyranny.[8] Worried that the many in a democracy would use their legislative power to vote in such ways that they themselves would benefit from the wealth of the few, the Framers had given a pride of place to individual property rights which had turned, in Roosevelt's time, into a system of concentrated wealth and power. The courts—both state and federal—had become to Roosevelt the institutional enablers of this form of minority tyranny.[9] Roosevelt crusaded against antimajoritarian judicial decisions, contending that majority tyranny was no longer a problem in America: "I have scant patience with this talk of the tyranny of the majority. . . . We are today suffering from the tyranny of minorities. . . . The only tyrannies from which men, women, and children are suffering in real life are the tyrannies of minorities."[10] The Founders had limited the power of popular majorities on the basis of an abstract theory of individual, natural rights; fundamentally, Roosevelt believed any system that deliberately thwarted majority opinion in this way—or in any way—could not call itself popular. Such was the thrust of his crusade against the courts and his push for mechanisms of direct democracy. "How can the prevailing morality or a preponderant opinion," Roosevelt asked, "be better and more exactly ascertained than by a vote of the people?"[11]

Roosevelt believed that if the real will of the people was allowed to prevail, a fundamental recasting of the scope of national government would be in order. The existing concentrations of wealth, upheld by a

---

[8] For an example of the kind of thinking that Roosevelt complained about, see James Madison, *Federalist No. 10*, in *The Federalist*, ed. George W. Carey and James McClellan (Indianapolis, IN: Liberty Fund, 2001), 42: "Complaints are every where heard from our most considerate and virtuous citizens, equally the friends of public and private faith, and of public and personal liberty . . . that measures are too often decided, not according to the rules of justice, and the rights of the minor party; but by the superior force of an interested and overbearing majority."

[9] See, for example, *Lochner v. New York*, 198 U.S. 45 (1905), where the U.S. Supreme Court overturned a state law limiting the number of hours bakers could agree to work, *Hammer v. Dagenhart*, 247 U.S. 251 (1918), where the U.S. Supreme Court upheld a lower court's ruling that a law preventing interstate commerce in products produced by child labor was unconstitutional, and *Ives v. South Buffalo Railroad*, 201 N.Y. 271 (1911), where the New York Court of Appeals overturned the state's Workmen's Compensation Act of 1910.

[10] Roosevelt, "Right of the People to Rule," 251–52.

[11] Ibid., 256.

theory of abstract equality, would have to give way to a system that
regulated business and property in order to effect an actual or real "equality of opportunity" for the average man. Roosevelt's speech on the "New
Nationalism," which he gave in 1910 and which became the foundation
for his subsequent attempt to recapture the presidency, laid out a vision
of national power that would spark progress toward real equality. The
speech identifies the enemy as "special privilege," or "special interests,"
"who twist the methods of free government into machinery for defeating
the popular will." [12] The way to defeat the special interests, Roosevelt
argued, was to employ "a policy of far more active governmental interference with social and economic conditions in this country than we have
yet had." Combinations of wealth could not be undone, Roosevelt reasoned, as they were "the result of an imperative economic law which
cannot be repealed by political legislation." But their effects could be
controlled, and could be transformed for the benefit of all men. "The way
out lies," Roosevelt concluded, "not in attempting to prevent such combinations, but in completely controlling them in the interest of the public
welfare." [13]

How could such "complete control" be accomplished? Through the use
of expert agencies. Among other tactics, Roosevelt emphasized in the
New Nationalism the role of the Federal Bureau of Corporations and the
Interstate Commerce Commission, the powers of which "should be largely
increased." [14] When launching his run for the presidency in 1912, Roosevelt elaborated that the key to investing such agencies with regulatory
power was their expert and nonpartisan character. The problem had been
that regulatory policy, to the extent it had been practiced at the national
level, was overly subject to the influence of politics. Such influence led to
unscientific policy. In order to remedy this problem, Roosevelt called for
"administrative control of great corporations. . . . A national industrial
commission," he contended, "should be created which should have complete power to regulate and control all the great industrial concerns engaged
in interstate business." [15] Tariff policy, too, had suffered by having itself
subject to the political process. Special interests were too influential in
that process, leading again to "unscientific" regulatory policy. The remedy was to empower a "permanent commission of nonpartisan experts." [16]

In calling both for increased popular control over national government
and for removing economic policy from the political process and granting
it to expert commissions, Roosevelt did not see a tension between the two
aims, nor did he seem to think that it called into any question "the right

---

[12] Theodore Roosevelt, "The New Nationalism," in Pestritto and Atto, eds., *American Progressivism*, 214.

[13] Ibid., 216.

[14] Ibid., 217.

[15] Theodore Roosevelt, *Theodore Roosevelt's Confession of Faith before the Progressive National Convention, August 6, 1912* (Roosevelt Memorial Association, 1943), 19.

[16] Ibid., 23.

of the people to rule." The problem was not that democratic politics itself was corrupt and unscientific, but rather that *decentralized* politics—particularly as practiced by the national legislature—was corrupt. Thus the way to ensure objective and scientific regulation was not, as Wilson was arguing, through separating administration from politics altogether; it was instead to place ultimate accountability for expert regulating in the hands of the popular executive—the one political entity that could claim to embody the broad national will. Experts and commissions were to govern—this was the only way, Roosevelt acknowledged, for the national government to handle the many new tasks that Progressives had in mind for it—but constantly with the understanding that they answered to the people. He explained in 1912 that "we, the people, rule ourselves, and what we really want from our representatives is that they shall manage the government for us along the lines we lay down. . . . We welcome leadership and advice, of course, and we are content to let experts do the expert business to which we assign them without fussy interference from us. But the expert must understand that he is carrying out our general purpose."[17] Policy could be managed by experts, Roosevelt later explained, but "it is for the people themselves finally to decide all questions of public policy and to have their decision made effective."[18]

Roosevelt did not see any significant tension between policymaking by commission and rule by the people. Expert commissions could be given great power, could be shielded from the influence of special interests by insulating them from the legislature, all while being held strictly accountable to democratic opinion. The key, Roosevelt explained, was centralization. In his 1908 State of the Union message, he argued that

> the danger to American democracy lies not in the least in the concentration of administrative power in responsible and accountable hands. It lies in having the power insufficiently concentrated, so that no one can be held responsible to the people for its use. Concentrated power is palpable, visible, responsible, easily reached, quickly held to account. Power scattered through many administrators, many legislators, many men who work behind and through legislators and administrators is impalpable, is unseen, is irresponsible, cannot be reached, cannot be held to account.[19]

Roosevelt clearly meant that the national government's new powers of economic control could be made democratic by concentrating ultimate responsibility for them in the president—that is to say, in himself. In

[17] Theodore Roosevelt, "The Meaning of Free Government," in Theodore Roosevelt, *Social Justice and Popular Rule* (New York: Charles Scribner's Sons, 1925), 236–37.

[18] Theodore Roosevelt, "The Purpose of the Progressive Party," in *Social Justice and Popular Rule*, 460.

[19] Theodore Roosevelt, "State of the Union Message," December 8, 1908, in *State of the Union Messages*, 6–7.

looking to the presidential leader as the key to balancing democracy and expert governance, Roosevelt would have something in common with Woodrow Wilson.

III. WILSON AND MODERN DEMOCRACY

Like Roosevelt, Wilson believed that the American system of government was too undemocratic and, also like Roosevelt, he pinned blame on the Framers' obsession with a highly individualized and abstract notion of liberty. Fear of majority tyranny, or faction, had led the Framers to restrict too severely the powers of the national government by means of mechanistic checks and balances, thereby impeding the people from using the government as an instrument of their will. While Roosevelt frequently railed against the courts for their antimajoritarian decisions, Wilson criticized the separation of powers system as a whole. He was an Anglophile, and had from his earliest years of thinking seriously about government been an admirer of the British parliamentary model. The parliamentary model stood for democracy and efficiency, providing for the smooth translation of democratic will into public policy through the overlapping of and cooperation between legislative and executive functions. The American separation of powers system, by contrast, with its intentional antagonism between the legislative and executive branches, was designed to protect the people from themselves, purposely throwing up as many obstacles as possible to the people getting their way.

While Roosevelt's favored remedy for the undemocratic character of America's original system of government was to advocate direct popular means of circumventing institutions altogether (the ballot initiative, referendum, etc.), Wilson preferred to reform the institutions themselves. He suggested new ways of conceiving of American political institutions that would facilitate the functional, if not formal, demise of the separation of powers system.[20] The point of these reforms was to make the system responsible. Wilson explained the challenge in his book *Congressional Government:*

> It is ... manifestly a radical defect in our federal system that it parcels out power and confuses responsibility as it does. The main purpose of the Convention of 1787 seems to have been to accomplish this grievous mistake. The 'literary theory' of checks and balances is simply a consistent account of what our constitution-makers tried to do; and those checks and balances have proved mischievous just to the extent which they have succeeded in establishing themselves as realities. It is quite safe to say that were it possible to call together again the members of that wonderful Convention to view the work of their hands in the light of the century that has tested it, they would

---

[20] See Pestritto, *Wilson and the Roots of Modern Liberalism*, 123–27.

be the first to admit that the only fruit of dividing power had been to make it irresponsible.[21]

The criticism of separation of powers from the perspective of responsibility is a consistent feature of Wilson's writings, from the earliest to the most mature. He called repeatedly for America to be made more democratic by instituting some form of cabinet or parliamentary government — where the national legislature depends closely upon majority public opinion and the executive branch exists by virtue of sustained support in the legislature. The only means of bringing genuine democracy to American government, Wilson made clear, were "certainly none other than those rejected by the Constitutional Convention."[22]

Wilson's criticism of the Constitution for its undemocratic institutional arrangements was grounded in a democratic theory sharply distinct from that of the Founding generation. The political theory of the Founding is the subject of much debate, and I have addressed it elsewhere at greater length.[23] For the sake of understanding how Wilson's democratic theory departs from it, I will say here only that it was based on the idea of social compact: the end of government is understood in light of certain rights which all human beings possess by virtue of their human nature. The Declaration of Independence thus speaks of "the Laws of Nature and of Nature's God," and man's fundamental rights come neither from government nor from some particular set of historical conditions. They are not contingent upon the current sentiment of a popular majority or whatever a particular society deems expedient at a given time. Government is consented to and constituted by men for the purpose of securing these rights. Wilson and other Progressives identified this social compact principle as the heart of the American Founding, and it was the point of departure for their own very different democratic theory.

Wilson criticized natural rights theory as contrary to the reality of historical development. It relied upon a fixed and speculative picture of man which, Wilson argued in his 1889 book *The State*, "simply has no historical foundation."[24] Instead, rights ought to be viewed through the lens of history, where their nature and extent depend upon social circumstance. Wilson offered his evolving understanding of human liberty as "destructive dissolvent" to the social compact principles of political philosopher John Locke (1632–1704) and others who had influenced the American Founding generation. Locke and other social compact thinkers, Wilson

---

[21] Woodrow Wilson, *Congressional Government* (1885; reprint, New York: Meridian Books, 1956), 187.

[22] Woodrow Wilson, "Cabinet Government in the United States, August, 1879," in *The Papers of Woodrow Wilson*, 69 vols., ed. Arthur S. Link (Princeton, NJ: Princeton University Press,1966–1993), 1: 497.

[23] Ronald J. Pestritto, "Founding Liberalism, Progressive Liberalism, and the Rights of Property," *Social Philosophy and Policy* 28, no. 2 (Summer 2011): 57–60.

[24] Woodrow Wilson, *The State* (Boston, D.C. Heath, 1889), 13–14.

claimed, put forth an unrealistic and static account of nature that served as the foundation for keeping government permanently limited and unresponsive to the evolving historical spirit. The true foundation of government, Wilson countered, could only be uncovered by looking to the actual history of its development, where one would see that the individual never had any primary or special existence that preceded or transcended society.[25]

Wilson took his democratic theory not from a conception of the autonomous individual, but from what he said was the true historical origin of government: the patriarchal family or tribe. Yet if such a rejection of the pre-political, abstract individual sounds certain Aristotelian themes, we should not mistake Wilson's democratic theory for a call to return to the classical model. Wilson rejected classical democratic theory just as thoroughly as he rejected the modern social compact. The classical conception of democracy, Wilson proclaimed, "exaggerates the part played by human choice."[26] He rejected the classical notion of prudence, where statesmen possess wisdom with respect to what is good universally and employ it as best they can in particular historical situations.[27] Such a conception gives too much credit to the ability of human choice to affect the course of history. Great individuals, Wilson countered, cannot transcend their environments but are instead the products of great historical forces.[28]

Wilson rejected classical democratic theory not only because it falsely exalted the prudence of great men over the power of history, but also because it adhered to a "cycle" of regimes.[29] The problem with the Aristotelian cycle was that it failed to conceive of democracy as a permanent condition of man. While Aristotle had suggested a continuous cycle of regime change based both upon fortune and the wise or imprudent choices made by individuals, Wilson countered that history leads to the *permanent* victory of the modern democratic state. History is not cyclical, but linear; and the historical conditions were such, or were in the process of becoming such, that democracy was here to stay. Earlier periods of democratic activity were fleeting, Wilson reasoned, because history had not then adequately prepared a permanent home. He explained that "the cardinal difference between all the ancient forms of government and all the modern" is that "the *democratic idea* has penetrated more or less deeply all the advanced systems of government."[30] In an 1885 essay on "The Modern Democratic State," Wilson

---

[25] Ibid., 11.

[26] Ibid., 14.

[27] Aristotle, *Nicomachean Ethics*, trans. Terence Irwin (Hackett Publishing Co., 1985), 1134a23–1135a5, 1141b10–1145a10.

[28] For more on the differences between classical and modern democracy, see Wilson, "The Real Idea of Democracy, August 31, 1901," in *The Papers of Woodrow Wilson*, 12: 177–78.

[29] See Aristotle, *The Politics*, trans. Carnes Lord (University of Chicago Press, 1984), Book V, esp. 1301a20–1301b30.

[30] Wilson, *The State*, 600, 603–5. Emphasis in original; hereafter all emphasis is in the original unless stated otherwise.

argued that modern democracy (as contradistinguished from both classical democracy and Founding-era, rights-based democracy) is the permanent and most advanced form of government. "Democracy is the fullest form of state life: it is the completest possible realization of corporate, cooperative state life for a whole people."[31] The classical world had not been ready for genuine democracy. Neither had America been ready for it during the Founding era. This is why the Framers were fearful of popular majorities and had structured the Constitution so as to limit their influence. "Democracy is poison to the infant," Wilson wrote, "but tonic to the man." It "is a form of state life which is possible for a nation only in the adult stage of its political development."[32] The nation, Wilson argued, had matured to adulthood, but strict adherence to the Constitution would keep it bound to a form of government suited for infancy.

The critical ingredient for modern democracy—the historical condition that had been missing from earlier attempts—was unity in the mind of the public. The old fear of faction, which James Madison had surmised was a permanent condition "sown in the nature of man,"[33] no longer applied. That the many might abuse their democratic power and rule only for their own advantage at the expense of the few was one of the "childish fears" about democracy that "have been outgrown." The difference was that "this democracy—this modern democracy—is not the rule of the many, but the rule of the *whole*."[34]

With the people thus unified in mind, the power of popular sentiment could be unleashed without fear of tyranny, in spite of the fact, Wilson argued, that "many theoretical politicians the world over confidently expect modern democracies to throw themselves at the feet of some Caesar."[35] The course of America's own history, as Wilson understood it, demonstrated the advance of the permanent democratic idea. In spite of the rigid and mechanistic structure of the Constitution, America had overcome its decentralized and individualistic origins to evolve into a true nation. Wilson brought up the presidency of Andrew Jackson to make his point. Jackson had tried to turn the clock back on national progress through his autocratic attack on the national bank. Jackson's "childish arrogance and ignorant arbitrariness" in seeking to retard the growth of national power proved futile; history was on the side of national growth and America had marched steadily from primitive to modern democracy.[36]

While Wilson's work reveals several intellectual influences—from that of English political writer Walter Bagehot on Wilson's love for the British

---

[31] Woodrow Wilson, "The Modern Democratic State, December, 1885," in *The Papers of Woodrow Wilson*, 5: 92.

[32] Ibid., 5: 71.

[33] Madison, *Federalist No. 10*, 43.

[34] Wilson, "Modern Democratic State," in *The Papers of Woodrow Wilson*, 5: 76, 79.

[35] Ibid., 5: 81.

[36] Ibid.

constitution to that of social Darwinism on Wilson's concept of the American constitution as "living" organism—his idea of modern democracy as the permanent endpoint of history shows his profound debt to the German philosopher Georg Hegel.[37] Wilson believed that the modern democratic state was the preordained end of history, and that the history of regimes had not been mere random adaptation, as a Darwinian analysis might suggest, but had instead been leading up to the permanent victory of modern democratic ideas. In early essays such as "The Art of Governing," Wilson commented that history points to the development of a single kind of human government.[38] And in later works such as *The New Freedom*, Wilson put forth a vision of modern democracy as the end-state of historical progress. Given the campaign context of his New Freedom speeches, he used a parable about building a house to explain his vision:

> What we have to undertake is to systematize the foundations of the house, then to thread all the old parts of the structure with the steel which will be laced together in modern fashion, accommodated to all the modern knowledge of structural strength and elasticity, and then slowly change the partitions, relay the walls, let in the light through new apertures, improve the ventilation; until finally, a generation or two from now, the scaffolding will be taken away, and there will be the family in a great building whose noble architecture will at last be disclosed, where men can live as a single community, co-operative as in a perfected, coordinated beehive, not afraid of any storm of nature.[39]

Wilson went on to reassure his audience that the triumph of democracy at the end of history was guaranteed and irreversible—that it would not be subject to any cycle of degeneration: "Nor need any lover of liberty be anxious concerning the outcome of the struggle upon which we are now embarked. The victory is certain."[40]

With history having thus prepared the ground, Wilson described his New Freedom as "A Call for the Emancipation of the Generous Energies of a People." He spoke on the campaign trail of the Founding-era antipathy toward democracy and contrasted it to the Progressive embrace of democracy. He spoke of these as "two theories of government," and identified the Founding-era plan with the Federalist thought of Alexander Hamilton—"a great man," claimed Wilson, "but, in my judgment, not

---

[37] For more on the influence of Hegel on Wilson, see Pestritto, *Wilson and the Roots of Modern Liberalism*, 14–19, 34–40, 213–16. See also Scot J. Zentner, "President and Party in the Thought of Woodrow Wilson," *Presidential Studies Quarterly* 26, no. 3 (Summer 1996): 666–77; Zentner, "Liberalism and Executive Power: Woodrow Wilson and the American Founders," *Polity* 26, no. 4 (Summer 1994): 579–99.

[38] Woodrow Wilson, "The Art of Governing, November 15, 1885," in *The Papers of Woodrow Wilson*, 5: 53.

[39] Woodrow Wilson, *The New Freedom* (New York: Doubleday, Page, 1913), 51–52.

[40] Ibid., 245.

a great American." Hamilton and his fellow Federalists had constructed the Constitution on the principle of "guardianship"—a fear of what the people would do if they were given the freedom to govern themselves.[41] "I believe," Wilson countered, "in the average integrity and the average intelligence of the American people." He employed this argument to attack Roosevelt, connecting the old, Hamiltonian, guardianship theory with Roosevelt's plan to grant regulatory power to expert commissions. "I do not believe," he explained, "that the intelligence of America can be put into commission anywhere. I do not believe that there is any group of men of any kind to whom we can afford to give that kind of trusteeship. I will not live under trustees if I can help it." He proclaimed in the same speech that "I don't want a smug lot of experts to sit down behind closed doors in Washington and play Providence to me."[42]

Wilson used this kind of democratic, anti-expert rhetoric effectively against Roosevelt on the campaign trail. Yet when he won and assumed office, most of Wilson's major domestic initiatives involved the very kind of regulation by commission that Roosevelt had advocated in the New Nationalism.[43] In fact, Wilson's agenda looked so much like that on which Roosevelt had campaigned that one Roosevelt scholar has remarked that it was "exceedingly embarrassing to the Progressive Party. Wilson had stolen its thunder and much of its excuse for being."[44] As much as Wilson's domestic agenda as president was a sharp departure from the attacks on commission government he had made while campaigning, President Wilson was not actually setting off in a new direction. Instead, he was reverting to an embrace of expert administration which he had developed and endorsed throughout his voluminous writings on government, and from which his presidential campaign had been a convenient and temporary diversion.

IV. Wilson and Modern Administration

For as long as Wilson had been writing about the theory and practice of government, he anticipated, as has been shown, that the increasing unity of the public mind would facilitate a final and permanent democratic state. And as intense as his democratic rhetoric could get, he did not think that democratic politics would be of the greatest importance in the modern democratic state. Since, instead, the people were already in agreement—at least implicitly—on what they wanted, once their will was emancipated the real task of modern government would be administration. Once history had overcome factiousness and established the "rule of

---

[41] Ibid., 55–56.

[42] Ibid., 60, 64.

[43] Among other key pieces of regulatory legislation, Wilson signed the Federal Trade Commission Act and the Clayton Antitrust Act in 1914.

[44] George E. Mowry, *Theodore Roosevelt and the Progressive Movement* (New York: Hill and Wang, 1960), 287.

the whole," the vital question became one of means, not of ends. In the "Study of Administration," Wilson wrote: "The trouble in early times was almost altogether about the constitution of government; and consequently that was what engrossed men's thought. . . . The weightier debates of constitutional principle are even yet by no means concluded; but they are no longer of more immediate practical moment than questions of administration. It is getting harder to *run* a constitution than to frame one."[45] In spite of his attacks on Roosevelt's regulatory proposals in the 1912 campaign, Wilson had been saying since the mid-1880s that the wide scope of governmental responsibility that progressives advocated would require a system in which the particulars of policymaking were delegated to expert administrators. In attacking commissions as undemocratic in 1912, Wilson was actually attacking proposals that were largely consistent with his own, long-stated views. That he almost immediately turned to expert agencies upon assuming the presidency should surprise no one who read just about anything he wrote prior to coming on the national political stage.

Since the mid-1880s, Wilson's writings reflect a strong apprehension about the influence of politics on administration. He insisted that if Progressives wanted to entrust the national government with significantly increased supervision of private business and property, they could not do so until they had found a way for expert administrators to make decisions on the basis of objectivity and science as opposed to political considerations. In an 1887 essay "Socialism and Democracy," Wilson embraced socialism in principle, explaining that it is perfectly consistent with genuine democratic theory. Genuine democracy, like socialism, will not allow individual rights to be a barrier to unfettered state action. But, Wilson explained, democrats could not quite accept the socialist agenda in practice, because socialists wanted the government to act in areas where it was not then capable of doing so competently.[46] In order to remedy this practical obstacle to the adoption of the socialist agenda by progressive democrats, a new science of administration first had to be developed.[47] Administration had always been a part of American national government, of course, but it had been administration within the confines of the republican executive, and thus subject to political control. In order to move forward with modern democracy, administrative entities would, Wilson concluded, have to be shielded, to some considerable degree at least, from traditional political accountability.

It was in his landmark essay "The Study of Administration," written just around the same time (1886), that Wilson directed his most sustained

---

[45] Woodrow Wilson, "The Study of Administration," in Pestritto and Atto, eds., *American Progressivism*, 193–4.

[46] See, for example, the Socialist Party Platform of 1912, http://www.academicamerican. com/progressive/docs/SocialistPlat1912.htm, accessed February 5, 2011.

[47] Woodrow Wilson, "Socialism and Democracy," in Ronald J. Pestritto, ed., *Woodrow Wilson: The Essential Political Writings* (Lanham, MD: Lexington Books, 2005), 77–79.

thoughts to this new kind of administration, and where he advocated—at least to some degree—the separation of administrative governance from politics. As such, it was an essay that would come to have a profound influence on the birth and development of the public administration discipline in the United States. Administration, Wilson wrote in the essay, could be freed from the control of politics because it differed from politics in fundamental ways. "Administration," he argued, "lies outside the proper sphere of *politics*. Administrative questions are not political questions." Understood in this way, it was questionable if administration could even be subject to constitutional definition. "The field of administration is a field of business," Wilson argued. "It is removed from the hurry and strife of politics; it at most points stands apart even from the debatable ground of constitutional study." [48] In making this argument, Wilson was extending the line of reasoning from an even earlier essay—"Government By Debate" (written in 1882)—where he had contended that large parts of the national administration could be immunized from political control because the nature of the policies it made were matters of science as opposed to matters of political contention. The administrative departments, wrote Wilson, "should be organized in strict accordance with recognized business principles. The greater part of their affairs is altogether outside of politics." [49]

Civil Service Reform had been a start to the neutral science of administration that Wilson sought to develop. Wilson believed that continuing down that path would allow the increasingly complex "business" of national government to be handled by a professional class of experts. The most important achievement of the Civil Service Reform movement had been the establishment of the principle that it was desirable, at least in some cases, for politics to be kept out of administration. Wilson explained that "civil service reform is thus but a moral preparation for what is to follow. It is clearing the moral atmosphere of official life by establishing the sanctity of public office as public trust, and, by making the service unpartisan, it is opening the way for making it businesslike." [50] Perhaps most important, a Civil Service appointment, with its secure tenure and independence from politics, would allow an expert to disregard special interests and act on behalf of the general interest. For Wilson, the importance of this calling can be traced back to his earliest works, where as a young man he frequently expressed disgust with the dominance of politics by narrow, special interests. He said repeatedly that a career in politics was no longer a respectable or worthy goal for an educated young man who was interested in public service. He envisioned that the young and educated could, instead, form the foundation of a new, apolitical class of expert policymakers, trained in the emerging social sciences for

[48] Wilson, "Study of Administration," 5: 370–71.
[49] Woodrow Wilson, "Government By Debate, December, 1882," in *The Papers of Woodrow Wilson*, 2: 224.
[50] Wilson, "Study of Administration," 5: 370.

service in a national government with greatly expanded responsibilities. "An intelligent nation cannot be led or ruled save by thoroughly-trained and completely-educated men," Wilson explained. "Only comprehensive information and entire mastery of principles and details can qualify for command." He championed the power of expertise—of "special knowledge, and its importance to those who would lead."[51]

V. RECONCILING DEMOCRACY AND ADMINISTRATION?

In championing the importance of educated experts, of their independence from political influence, and of their being given, at least to some degree, a role in governing, the obvious question is how one squares this with Wilson's fervently stated democratic principles. While Roosevelt seems not to have acknowledged this conundrum, Wilson understood that he needed to deal with the question of public opinion. "The problem," Wilson explained, "is to make public opinion efficient without suffering it to be meddlesome." Public opinion is a "clumsy nuisance" when it comes to the "oversight of the daily details and in the choice of the daily means of government." While Wilson called for introducing public opinion more directly into politics, politics must confine itself to general superintendence—to the role of setting the broad goals of the nation.[52] In conceiving of the separation of politics and administration, Wilson sought to maintain the veneer of popular government while giving fairly wide berth to unelected administrators. The greatest obstacle to the necessary growth of apolitical administration, Wilson candidly acknowledged, is what Roosevelt would call the "right of the people to rule." "What then," Wilson asked, "is there to prevent" this "much-to-be-desired science of administration"? And he answered: "Well, principally, popular sovereignty."[53]

If Progressive governance was to involve the exercise of at least some authority over policymaking by unelected experts, then, as Wilson acknowledged, expert governance would somehow have to be reconciled with progressive democratic theory. This was true for Roosevelt as well, even if he did not quite see the difficulty in the way that Wilson did. For both men, the key to this reconciliation seems to have come from their notions of leadership. Roosevelt's was much more populist in tone and in its actual character than Wilson's. It was also, arguably, more simplistic and self-serving. As explained above, Roosevelt believed that expert governance could be reconciled with democracy by centralizing power. While the legislative process had become corrupted due to the influence of special interests, the president represented the unified whole of public

[51] Woodrow Wilson, "What Can Be Done for Constitutional Liberty: Letters from a Southern Young Man to Southern Young Men, March 21, 1881," in *The Papers of Woodrow Wilson*, 2: 34–36.

[52] Wilson "Study of Administration," 5: 374–75.

[53] Wilson, "Study of Administration," 5: 368.

opinion. Expert administration, held accountable to the people through their popular president, could thus be unleashed to make policy on behalf of the general interest over and against special interests.

Wilson, too, spoke to the necessity of a popular leader embodying the unified public mind.[54] Yet he had reflected much more thoroughly on the question, and his conception of democratic leadership included not only the president as a popular focal point, but an entire class of administrators as discerners of the public's objective will. It was because, in Wilson's mind, history had overcome the problem of faction and had brought about a unified public mind that the focus of modern government would be on expert administration. Having come together on the broad questions of political justice, the people could now entrust administrators to manage the complex details involved in regulating a modern economy. Empirically, of course, such a claim of political unity may seem to fly in the face of the fierce contention of interests that characterized the Progressive Era as much as any other era of American history. But beneath such contentiousness on the surface of American politics, Wilson argued, was a deeper, implicit will of the people as a whole. This implicit, objective will was one of which the people themselves might be unaware; hence the task of leadership was to see through the superficial clash of subjective interests and to discern the true popular mind. Such a task requires a leader to distinguish between mere majority opinion and the implicit, objective will of society as a whole. Wilson could reconcile expert or elite governance with democratic theory because, for him, elites are able to discern the public's objective mind better than the public itself. The key to the democratic legitimacy of elite governance is the elites' ability to discern what Wilson called the "general" or "objective" will: it is "an assumption, still more curious when subjected to analysis," that "the will of majorities,—or rather, the concurrence of a majority in a vote,—is the same as the *general* will." He argued further that

the will of majorities is *not* the same as the general will: that a nation is an *organic* thing, and that its will dwells with those who do the *practical* thinking and organize *the best concert of action:* those who hit upon opinions *fit to be made prevalent,* and have *the capacity to make them so.*[55]

[54] See Pestritto, *Wilson and the Roots of Modern Liberalism,* 167–72, 206–16. See also Paul Eidelberg, *A Discourse on Statesmanship: The Design and Transformation of the American Polity* (Urbana: University of Illinois Press, 1974), 4, 279, 286; Henry A. Turner, "Woodrow Wilson: Exponent of Executive Leadership," *The Western Political Quarterly* 4 (1951): 97–115; James W. Ceaser, Glen E. Thurow, Jeffrey K. Tulis, Joseph M. Bessette, "The Rise of the Rhetorical Presidency," *Presidential Studies Quarterly* 11 (Spring 1981): 159, 161, 163, 166; Robert Eden, "Opinion Leadership and the Problem of Executive Power: Woodrow Wilson's Original Position," *Review of Politics* 57 (Summer 1995): 483–503.
[55] Woodrow Wilson, "Democracy, December 5, 1891," in *The Papers of Woodrow Wilson,* 7: 355.

Under this construction, democratic rule is cast in terms of expert or elite governance. The example Wilson used to illustrate his vision of democratic rule confirms the point: the Civil Service. While administrative agencies might not comport with traditional notions of democracy (their agents are unelected and are drawn from the educated classes), Wilson believed administration was democratic in a much deeper sense: Civil Service experts would not be distracted by special interest contentions in ordinary politics, and would be free instead to discern the true and implicit will of the public as a whole. Administrators would be in the best position to adjust governmental policy to the general will.

In thinking about administration in this way—as a means of reconciling democratization with expert governance—Wilson thought in terms that have proved to be more relevant to contemporary American government than Roosevelt did. Popular presidential leadership, championed by both Wilson and Roosevelt, has proved to be a central feature of American politics. But the delegation of significant policymaking authority to expert administrative agencies, which has also become a staple of American government, was thought through much more comprehensively by Wilson. This is not to suggest that today's administrative governance is fully or even mostly Wilsonian (legislators are far too involved in agency decisionmaking, and politics is still far too dominant, to have satisfied Wilson's model), but that contemporary American governance seems to reflect the dilemma between the democratic impulse and the deference to expertise that Wilson identified and thought it necessary to confront.

Politics, Hillsdale College

ON THE SEPARATION OF POWERS: LIBERAL AND PROGRESSIVE CONSTITUTIONALISM

By Michael Zuckert

I. Introduction

We live in an age when *Pride and Prejudice and Zombies* is a best seller, when *The Zombie Survival Guide* draws 617 customer reviews on Amazon, when we can celebrate the holidays with *The Zombie Night Before Christmas*, and, if all of this seems too low brow, when we can read *Zombie: A Novel* by Joyce Carol Oates, one of our most high-brow authors. The early years of the twenty-first century are clearly "The Age of the Living Dead." It is little wonder then that our politics now seem to be oriented around a political movement itself among the living dead. On both sides of the political spectrum, partisans are more and more orienting themselves around the Progressives, a political movement that had its good times on earth in the late nineteenth and early twentieth centuries, but now, a century later, has crawled out of its grave to walk the earth and, it might appear, ravage (or whatever Zombies do) our politics. Those more or less on the left have increasingly come to call themselves Progressives, at least in part because the term "liberal" had became something of a political liability. It has now come to designate more specifically those on the further left segment of the Democratic Left. It has the advantage of eschewing the dreaded "L" word and of distinguishing those who carry this insignia into political battle from an older Left, which was Marxist or Marxist tinged.

Those on the right half of the political spectrum, of course, do not call themselves "Progressives." They are "conservatives," although, ironically, most of them more firmly believe in progress, i.e., in the benignity of the direction that more or less unfettered economic and technological development are taking us, than do the so-called "Progressives," who fear the direction of technological change and economic development. Consider the respective positions of our Progressives and our conservatives on issues like climate change. In any case, Progressives are increasingly important for the non-Progressives, for it is they against whom the conservatives are more frequently defining themselves. A case in point is Glenn Beck, surely the hottest conservative figure of the day. He obsesses about the Progressives, and speaks often of how much he "hates them," and especially how much he hates that arch-Progressive, Woodrow Wilson.

Indeed, while the Left has revived the term "Progressive" it is the Right that has resurrected the Progressives themselves and which thus contrib-

doi:10.1017/S0265052511000331
335

utes more deeply to the Zombieness of the twenty-first century. The conservatives are not doing battle against the dead they have summoned from their graves merely as a historical matter. They see the Progressives as the source of contemporary liberalism, New Deal and beyond, and apparently see Progressivism as a deeper, more philosophical, and more dangerous movement. The conservatives see the Progressives along the line of the title of one recent text, that is, as *Texas Biker Zombie(s) from Outer Space*. American conservativism is, of course, a variegated thing and not all sorts of conservatives are equally concerned about the Progressives. Those who are more concerned seem to be those who are most attached to some form of past-liberalism—classical liberals, admirers of the American Founding, and such-like conservatives. The Progressives are important to these conservatives because the Progressives were the ones who mounted an attack on classical liberalism and on the political principles and political work of the American Founders. Their heirs, the liberals of the post-New Deal era, took for granted and as accomplished the Progressive critique of the earlier liberalism. Conservatives, many of whom are would-be liberals of a different stripe from George McGovern or Barack Obama, return to the Progressives because they wish to refight the old fight our contemporary liberals believe was won long ago by the Progressives.

This essay shares something of that aspiration. I wish to explore an aspect of the Progressive critique of liberal constitutionalism, the focused Progressive attack on the separation of powers as the essential feature of constitutionalism as embodied in the American Constitution and endorsed by the American Founders, and by their intellectual authorities John Locke and Charles de Secondat, Baron de Montesquieu. This paper is inspired by the suspicion that the Progressives' critique of the separation of powers was based primarily on a deficient understanding of that doctrine and secondarily on a misplaced analysis of potential substitutes for the separation of powers. I wish to mount, in other words, a tentative defense of the separation of powers against its past and present critics.

My defense is "tentative" for a number of different reasons, but most immediately for its limited scope. In order to achieve some depth of understanding I am limiting myself to the chief Progressive critic of the separation of powers, Woodrow Wilson. He was both President of the American Political Science Association, testifying to his credentials as a political analyst as judged by his fellow political scientists, and President of the United States, testifying to his credentials as a political leader as judged by his fellow citizens.

I will hold up to this critic of liberal constitutionalism its originator, John Locke. In Locke's *Second Treatise* we find the first theoretical statement of the separation of powers idea as it comes to define liberal constitutionalism. My focus on Locke is not meant to deny the significance of other contributors to the theory of separation of powers—Montesquieu,

Blackstone, de Lolme, and the American Founders chief among them. Locke's is not the final or even most sophisticated form of the separation of powers theory, but his is crucial for bringing out the connection of the doctrine to the foundational ideas of natural rights and modern natural law, which were so formative for liberal constitutionalism.

II. The Progressive Critique: Woodrow Wilson

There is perhaps no better ingress to our problem than the observation, now becoming commonplace, that for the Progressives, and especially for Wilson, the distinction between politics and administration was intended to supplant the old and traditional notion of the separation of powers.[1] Wilson's critique of the separation of powers begins with his account of what that institutional structure was intended to accomplish, accompanied by an account of its failure to accomplish its end. That is, he began with a critique of the separation of powers as a means or instrument of governance. He moves on, however, to a critique of the ends sought in the system of separation as well. The critique is completed with Wilson's theory of the end that ought to be sought and his presentation of why the politics-administration distinction and institutional embodiments thereof is a superior system of governance.

Like other Progressive critics—Charles Beard comes to mind—Wilson was bold and open in announcing his desire to challenge the political science and the political achievement of the American Founding generation. He was struck by the fact that although the Constitution was intensely controversial when first proposed, that changed almost immediately upon ratification. Political debate from then on was between what Wilson called "two rival sects of Pharisees, professing a more perfect conformity and affecting greater 'ceremonial cleanliness' than the other."[2] All criticism of the Constitution ceased and was replaced by an "almost blind worship of its principles," with the result that "the general scheme of the Constitution went unchallenged."[3] A further result was the growth of the insular "conviction that our institutions were the best in the world, nay more, the model to which all civilized states must sooner or later conform."[4]

---

[1] The first scholar that I know of who made this important observation was Herbert Storing in his 1964 essay on "Political Parties and the Bureaucracy" in Joseph Bessette, ed., *Toward a More Perfect Union: Writings of Herbert Storing* (Washington, DC: The AEI Press, 1995), 319. A similar point about the Progressives was made by M. J. C. Vile, *Constitutionalism and the Separation of Powers* (Indianapolis, IN: Liberty Fund, 1998, 2d. ed.), 304–5, 308–9; Dennis Mahoney, "The Separation of Powers," in Sarah B. Thurow, ed., *E Pluribus Unum: Constitutional Principles and the Institutions of Government* (Lanham, MD: University Press of America, 1988), 25; Ronald J. Pestritto, *Woodrow Wilson and the Roots of Modern Liberalism* (Lanham, MD: Rowman and Littlefield, 2005), Kindle edition, loc. 3503.

[2] Woodrow Wilson, *Congressional Government*, (Cleveland, OH: Meridian Books, 1956 [1885]), 26.

[3] Ibid., 27.

[4] Ibid.

Wilson, well read in European history and political science, particularly in British history and German political science, felt he had freed himself from this Americentric view of the world. Understating his own break from the American consensus on American political superiority, Wilson claims to speak as but one voice among many in his generation: "we of the present generation are in the first season of free, outspoken, unrestrained constitutional criticism. We are the first Americans to hear our own countrymen ask whether the Constitution is still adapted to serve the purposes for which it was intended; the first to entertain any serious doubts about the superiority of our own institutions as compared with the systems of Europe."[5] As M. J. C. Vile points out, one of the very first voices of his generation to engage in this "outspoken, unrestrained constitutional criticism" was Wilson himself, for "only fourteen years after the end of the civil war the young Woodrow Wilson wrote his essay proposing the adoption of cabinet government in America" in place of the separation of powers.[6] Wilson may have been one of the first, but he was soon joined by many others, who, as American political scientist Dwight Waldo put it, had "almost complete lack of sympathy" for the constitutional system of separated powers.[7]

Americans were not only "Pharisaical" in their attachment to the fundamental law of the Constitution, but they were "still reading *The Federalist* as an authoritative constitutional manual."[8] One of the reasons Americans were so attached to the Constitution is that they thought it operated as *The Federalist* prescribed it. But *The Federalist*, Wilson claimed, presented only the "literary theory" of the Constitution. Wilson sought to give a realistic portrait of the actual workings of American government. Americans had to first understand that the constitutional system did not operate as it was intended and as they persisted in believing that it did.

Wilson shared much with his fellow Progressives, but on the question at hand he had a subtler and more nuanced view than many. For example, "J. Allen Smith and Charles A. Beard both believed that the doctrine of separated powers was a part of a coherent scheme of wealthy conservatives to build into the American constitutional structure devices to frustrate the popular majorities that would otherwise use the national government to the disadvantage of the wealthy in general (Smith) or of

[5] Ibid.

[6] Vile, *Constitutionalism*, 291. Vile is referring to Wilson's essay "Cabinet Government in the United States," *International Review*, Aug. 1879. Vile sees the Civil War as the "turning point." It ushered in a long intense period of criticism and attack upon the established constitutional theory, of an unprecedented ferocity conducted alike by practical politicians, journalists, and academics." Vile, *Constitutionalism*, 290.

[7] Dwight Waldo, *The Administrative State* (New York: Ronald Press Co., 1948) 105; quoted in Vile, *Constitutionalism*, 294.

[8] Woodrow Wilson to Ellen Axson as quoted in Walter Lippmann's "Introduction" to Wilson's *Congressional Government*, 11.

the class of speculators in government bonds (Beard)."[9] They thought the separation of powers was part of an antidemocratic, countermajoritarian plan, whereas Wilson saw the separation of powers as part of a set of "checks and balances" meant to prevent the concentration of power in any one set of hands or institution. Thus, he saw federalism—a device for dividing power between the central government and the states—and the separation of powers—a device for dividing powers within the central government—as simply parallel and inspired by a fear of concentrated power.[10] By and large, Wilson endorsed the conclusion of one of his literary heroes, the English political analyst Walter Bagehot: "They [the American Founders] shrank from placing sovereign power anywhere. They feared it would generate tyranny."[11] The Founders, Wilson concluded, "would conquer, by dividing, the power they so much feared in a single hand."[12]

More specifically, Wilson saw the separation of powers as a device adapted from British Whig attempts to clip the wings of the irresponsible monarchy by setting a checking Parliament alongside the king. In the eighteenth century, when the Americans were setting off on their constitution-making enterprise, many Whigs in both England and American were distressed at the way the British constitution was operating in practice. The Parliament was supposed to be an independent checking agency, but the monarch had instruments in hand with which he could overcome parliamentary independence and exercise the kind of concentrated power that Whigs feared. The king could appoint ministers and give position and place to members of Parliament or their connections, and thereby make Parliament nominally independent but factually subservient. "It was something more than natural that the Convention of 1787 should desire to erect a Congress which would not be subservient and an executive which would not be despotic. And it was equally to have been expected that they should regard an absolute separation of these two great branches of the system as the only effectual means for the accomplishment of that much desired end."[13]

Wilson, inimical as he was to the separation of powers, was nonetheless happy to concede that the American Founders made a great advance on the English Constitution as it was in their day. But, as we will see, this concession did not prevent him from affirming that "the English Consti-

---

[9] Mahoney, "Separation of Powers," 27. Mahoney is referring to J. Allen Smith, a University of Washington political scientist, who published *The Spirit of American Government* in 1907 and Charles A. Beard, Columbia University historian, who published *An Economic Interpretation of the Constitution of the United States* in 1913.

[10] Wilson, *Congressional Government*, 31–34; Woodrow Wilson, *Constitutional Government in the United States* in Pestritto, ed., *Essential Political Writings*, 202.

[11] Wilson, *Congressional Government*, 202, quoting Bagehot, *The English Constitution*.

[12] Ibid.

[13] Ibid., 201.

tution . . . is now superior" to the American.[14] Haven't we had enough, Wilson asked rhetorically, "of the literal translation of Whig theory into practice, into Constitutions?"[15]

Wilson considered the system of separation of powers a failure in the first instance because it failed so completely to accomplish its intended aims. In his first and still most programmatic book, *Congressional Government*, Wilson set out to show that the Founders aimed at a system of checks and balances through dividing and separating the institutions of power in the federal system and in the separated powers of the central government. Instead, they had created a system of consolidated government. The Founders failed at their own game and produced not quite the monstrosity they feared—it was a different monstrosity—but it was definitely not the order they had aimed at. Wilson saw his task to be to awaken his fellow citizens from their conceptual slumbers, slumbers in which, because of the veneration in which the Constitution and the Founders were held, Americans persisted in believing that *The Federalist*, the "literary theory of the Constitutions," adequately described their political arrangements.

Whether he quite believed it himself or not, one way in which Wilson hoped to awaken his readers was by attempting to convince them that they were misunderstanding the Founders. The authors of *The Federalist*, for example, wrote "to influence *only* the voters of 1787," not to lay out an eternally valid plan of government.[16] The Constitution the authors of *The Federalist* were defending was itself "a thing of action rather than of theory, *suited to meet an exigency*."[17] The American of the nineteenth century, said Wilson, needs to turn away from misplaced piety, "to escape from theories and attach himself to facts, not allowing himself to be confused by a knowledge of what that government was intended to be."[18] In order to understand the "reality" of his system of government, the American needed to seek out "the real depositary and the essential machinery of power."[19]

Americans believed that they had a decentralized, dispersed system of power, but in reality "there is always a centre of power."[20] "The balances of the Constitution are for the most part only ideal. For all practical purposes the national government is supreme over the state govern-

---

[14] Ibid., 202.

[15] Wilson, *Constitutional Government*, 221. Wilson does not, then, accuse the Founders of designing a system in which "government would act slowly and inefficiently." Pestritto, *Wilson*, loc. 3494–3495.

[16] Wilson, *Congressional Government*, 30. Emphasis added.

[17] Woodrow Wilson, "Fourth of July Address on the Declaration of Independence." (1907), reprinted in Scott Hammond, Kevin Hardwick, and Howard J. Lubert, eds., *Classics of American Political and Constitutional Thought* (Indianapolis, IN: Hackett Publishing Co., 2007), vol. II, p. 318.

[18] Wilson, *Congressional Government*, 30; Vile, *Separation of Powers*, 295.

[19] Wilson, ibid.

[20] Ibid.

ments, and Congress predominant over its so-called co-ordinate branches." The separation of powers along with federalism is the target of Wilson's attack, in the first instance, not because it disperses power, as many of the other Progressives, like Herbert Croly or Theodore Roosevelt argued, but because it fails to disperse power as it was intended to do. The "checks and balances which once obtained are no longer effective. . . . [T]he actual form of our present government is simply a scheme of congressional supremacy." [21]

Wilson devotes a fair amount of his text to probing the reasons for this concentration of power in Congress, so contrary to the original intentions of the Founders. The chief causes seem to be three in number. First, the "natural, the inevitable tendency of every system of self-government like our own and the British is to exalt the representative body, the people's parliament, to a position of absolute supremacy." [22] Although he does not do it, he could have quoted James Madison on the "legislative vortex." This "political law . . . written in our hearts," overrides the merely written parchment law of the Constitution. The power to make laws and the power to control taxing and spending overwhelms all other powers; it "practically sets [the popular legislative] assembly to rule the nation as supreme overlord." [23] Although Wilson does not explicitly draw the conclusion, his point is that experience has shown that the Constitution's Framers did not adequately understand the dynamics of democratic politics. They established a representative popular democracy with huge powers centered in the branch closest to the people. The result—congressional supremacy—was inevitable, or nearly so.

But quite another set of factors at work in the world pushed in the same directions. "The times seem to favor a centralization of governmental functions such as could not have suggested itself as a possibility to the framers of the Constitution." [24] Wilson has in mind technological changes that on the one hand make possible a degree of centralization that would have been completely impossible in the eighteenth century, and on the other hand generate a set of problems that would not have existed in the eighteenth century, and that now call for centralized address. He refers explicitly, on the one side, to technologically inspired changes in transportation and communication that make central action possible. Like James Madison before him, Wilson sees that these various technological advances in effect make the nation smaller, and make it ever more possible for the center and the periphery to become better integrated. [25] At the same time,

[21] Ibid., 53.
[22] Ibid., 203.
[23] Ibid.
[24] Ibid., 54.
[25] See, for example, James Madison to _____ (1833), reprinted in Marvin Myers, *The Mind of the Founder* (Waltham, MA: Brandeis University Press, 1981), 411.

"questions of policy which manifestly demand uniformity of treatment and power of administration such as cannot be realized by separate, unconcerted actions of the states" become ever more prevalent as transportation, communication, and commerce create thicker ties and connections across state lines.[26]

Finally, Congress has adapted itself so as to be the unchallenged beneficiary of these centralizing forces. "Congress was very quick and apt in learning what it could do and in getting into thoroughly good trim to do it."[27] In particular it developed a system of standing committees, possessing "very comprehensive and thorough-going privileges of legislative initiative and control."[28] Through its very effective internal organization, Congress was able to extend its power into the executive branch and has proven able to counter the power of the presidency through its superior means of action.[29] Because Congress has attained preeminence in the system, the presidency is not able to attract to it the caliber of man who could make that office strong. Weakness begets further weakness.[30]

The Courts, Wilson concedes, retain some power, but it is largely to control the presidency, not Congress. The courts too "are for the most part in the power of Congress."[31] He takes very seriously congressional power to control the size of the Supreme Court, the very existence of a lower federal court system, and the jurisdiction of the federal courts. It is worth recalling that these are all powers Congress had exercised in the recent past when Wilson was formulating his thoughts on congressional supremacy.[32]

Despite his belief that constitutional regimes like America's tend inevitably toward legislative supremacy, Wilson finds the pattern of congressional government in America to be troubling. He has a long list of complaints against the system. First, so far as there is value in a system of checks and balances, of which, we shall see, he has some doubts, this arrangement does not produce these goods.[33] Receiving more emphasis, however, is, secondly, his concern that congressional government actually consists in "government by standing committees of Congress."[34] The centralization of power in Congress is not matched by centralization of power within Congress. The results of the diffusion of power to the

---

[26] Wilson, *Congressional Government*, 54–55.

[27] Ibid., 49.

[28] Ibid.

[29] Ibid., 48–49.

[30] Ibid., 48.

[31] Ibid., 45.

[32] Ibid., 45–46. With the admission of new states, Congress regularly changed the shape of the lower federal court system. Congress had increased the size of the Supreme Court to ten in 1863 and lowered it again to nine in 1866. In 1868 Congress had stripped the Supreme Court of its jurisdiction to hear appeals in habeas corpus cases, a law upheld in *Ex Parte McCardle* 74 U.S. 506 (1869).

[33] Ibid. 49–50.

[34] Ibid., 56.

committees in turn produces a number of now familiar complaints about the way Congress does its job, ranging from the toehold this arrangement provides to special interests to legislation by logrolling and aggregating compromise.[35] The result is that "legislation is without consistency. Leg islation is conglomerate. The absence of any concert of action amongst the committees leaves legislation with scarcely any trace of determinate party course."[36] The system lacks "intelligent cooperation;" it also lacks "intelligent differences and divisions." In a word, the system of congressional government in the United States produces a Congress that "has no common mind."[37] Wilson takes it for granted that rational, consistent, and coherent policy is preferable to irrational, inconsistent, and incoherent policy. It is hard to see that the Founders would disagree.

Incoherent policy is bad enough, but the system of government by standing committee falls short in yet another way that Wilson seems to find even more distressing. Incoherent legislation is matched or preceded by incoherent debate. Incoherent debate, in turn, leads to failure in one of the chief functions of the representatives of the people—public political education and enlightenment. Wilson took this aspect of governmental responsibility very seriously: "The informing function of Congress should be preferred even to its legislative function."[38] Government should not merely reflect public opinion but should help to shape it.

Some critics take this to be an example of Wilson's elitism and undemocratic commitments. As Ronald J. Pestritto puts it, "the rhetoric is intensely popular and democratic, yet the reality of the argument is to put political power into the hands of governing elites."[39] That political leaders should take the lead in informing and shaping public opinion in the way Wilson commends, through free discussion among partisans with different points of view, is not undemocratic. It is certainly not contrary to the spirit of American representative democracy as voiced by the American Founders. A conception of leadership by the representatives of the people may strike some as undemocratic, but we must recall that even Jean-Jacques Rousseau, the patron saint of radical democracy, conceded the role of political leadership. Wilson is quite clear: "thought and opinion, like conscience, should be free."[40]

As Wilson saw it, coherent, principled debate within Congress could help educate public opinion and enable it to exercise better its ultimate role as "sovereign" in the system of democratic governance. He did not have in mind a single-voiced government controlling opinions, but a number, preferably two, of organized and coherent parties formulating

[35] Ibid., 208–11.
[36] Ibid., 211.
[37] Ibid. Vile, *Separation of Powers*, 292.
[38] Wilson, *Congressional Government*, 198.
[39] Pestritto, *Woodrow Wilson*, loc. 3059 (ch. 6).
[40] Woodrow Wilson, *The State* (Boston: D.C. Health and Co., 1900), 637–38.

analyses of problems and bringing proposals before the country for its judgment.[41] There are other possible theories of what democracy requires, but Wilson's is well within the pale of American theory and practice.

According to Wilson, then, the separation of powers scheme failed as a means to the Founders' own aim of limiting government by means of checking and balancing powers. But it is significant that, unlike the seventeenth and eighteenth century Whigs who saw the failure of separated powers to check the king, Wilson did not call for a revitalization of separated powers. Instead, in his younger days, he called for the institution of cabinet government on the model of the late nineteenth century Parliamentary system, and in his later years, he looked to the presidency, together with a purified party system, to provide the unity and leadership in the American context that the cabinet system supplied in Britain.[42]

Wilson did not seek a "new and improved" version of the separation of powers because he did not believe that the ends the Founders were seeking were any longer the appropriate ends in the industrial age. As Wilson put it in *Congressional Government*:

> The government of a country so vast and various must be strong, prompt, wieldy, and efficient. Its strength must consist in the certainty and uniformity of its purposes, in its accord with national sentiment, in its unhesitating actions, and in its honest aims. It must be steadied and approved by open administration diligently obedient to the more permanent judgments of public opinion.[43]

It should be evident that a system of separated powers functioning as the Founders wished would not operate to accomplish the political needs of the day. As Pestritto comments, "Wilson saw the separation of powers as a key obstacle to America's progress as a nation."[44] It should be just as evident that the system of "government by Congressional Committee" that was the actual consequence of the Founders Constitution would not suffice either.

[41] Consider, for example, Pestritto's own account of Wilson on political parties and party competition: *Woodrow Wilson*, locs. 2720–2910.

[42] As Walter Lipmann points out in his Introduction to *Congressional Government*, Wilson did not quite come out for cabinet government in that book, but he surely hinted at it in the concluding chapter. For Lippmann's claim, see *Congressional Government*, 13. Wilson was much more explicit in seminal essays he published prior to *Congressional Government*. See "Cabinet Government in the United States" (1879) in Woodrow Wilson, *Papers of Woodrow Wilson*, vol. I (Princeton: Princeton University Press), 493–510; and "Committee or Cabinet Government" (1884), in *Papers of Woodrow Wilson*, vol. 2, 614–40. For his later position, the locus classicus is his *Constitutional Government*.

[43] Wilson, *Congressional Government*, 206.

[44] Pestritto, *Woodrow Wilson*, loc. 2053.

Although some important scholars argue that Wilson was hostile to the political vision of the American Founders, the evidence better supports the conclusion that he was ambivalent.[45] For example, Pestritto says that "Wilson attacked those who were devoted to the principles of the Declaration of Independence" in his book *The New Freedom*.[46] Wilson indeed spoke of citizens who "never get beyond the Declaration of Independence," but his point is not to urge Americans to forget or reject the Declaration, but rather to urge them to ask how it applies to the problems of their own day, how it translates into policies for the early twentieth century. "[I]t means nothing unless one can translate its terms into examples of the present day and substitute these" for the particulars with which the Declaration deals.[47] "The Declaration of Independence, so far as I recollect, did not mention any of the issues of 1911," said Wilson in 1911.[48] Wilson was consistent in his view that many of the specific political maxims endorsed by the Founding generation were no longer of beneficial use to America, but at the same time, he insisted, "the business of every true Jeffersonian is to translate the terms of those abstract portions of the Declaration of Independence into the language and problem of his own day." The task is "to realize the conceptions of the author of the Declaration of Independence in our own day."[49] Or, as he said on another occasion: "We return to Jefferson not to borrow policies but to renew ideals."[50]

But how does Wilson understand these "ideals"; how does he understand the "principles" and "abstract portions of the Declaration" that he does commend to the nation? Wilson did not understand the Declaration in the way many contemporary readers do, or at least he did not mean to affirm the reading that these scholars give it. The leading view of the Declaration sees it as an expression of Lockean social contract philosophy, affirming the familiar ideas of natural rights as the foundation, basis, and purpose of government, the social contact operating via consent of the governed as the rightful origin of government, and the right of revolution

[45] Pestritto is most forceful in making the case for hostility. Ibid., passim. But he is joined by Kesler: Charles Kesler, "Separation of Powers and the Administrative State," in *The Imperial Congress*, ed., Gordon S. Jones and John A. Marini (New York: Pharos Books, 1988), 20–40; Charles Kesler, "The Public Philosophy of the New Freedom and the New Deal" in *The New Deal and Its Legacy*, ed. Robert Eden (New York: Greenwood Press, 1989), 155–66; and Charles Kesler, "Woodrow Wilson and the Statesmanship of Progress," in *Natural Right and Political Right*, ed. Thomas B. Silver and Peter W. Schramm (Durham, N.C.: Carolina Academic Press, 1984), 103–27. And of course there is Glenn Beck.

[46] Pestritto, *Woodrow Wilson*, loc. 1884.

[47] Woodrow Wilson, *The New Freedom* in Ronald J. Pestritto, ed., *Woodrow Wilson: The Essential Political Writings* (Lanham, MD: Lexington Books, 2005), 122.

[48] Woodrow Wilson, "Address to the Jefferson Club of Los Angeles" (1911), reprinted in Scott Hammond, Kevin R. Hardwick, and Howard J. Lubert, eds., *Classics of American Political Thought*, (Indianapolis, IN: Hackett Publishing Co., 2007) vol. 2, p. 323.

[49] Ibid.

[50] Wilson, "Address to Jefferson Club," 93.

as a corollary of those starting points. In his most theoretical work, *The State*, Wilson made it clear that he had no sympathy with Lockean social contract theory, even though it was "once of almost universal vogue."[51]

Wilson understands the social contract theory to be, literally, a history of political society, and thus readily falsifiable by "modern research into the early history of mankind."[52]

> The defects of the social compact theory are too plain to need more than a brief mention. That theory simply has no historical foundation. The family was the original, and *status* the fixed basis of primitive society. The individual counted for nothing; society—the family, the tribe—counted for everything. Government came, so to say, before the individual and was coeval with his first human instincts. There was no place for contract.[53]

Wilson then finds the social contact theory of the Declaration unacceptable as a descriptive matter; he also finds it unacceptable as a normative matter. In an essay on one of his political and intellectual heroes, Edmund Burke, Wilson endorsed Burke's vehement rejection of the "French revolutionary philosophy," which was the same philosophy that found expression in the Declaration. "That philosophy," Wilson said "is in fact radically evil and corrupting. That is, it is not only incorrect as a matter of fact; it is morally repugnant as well, "evil."[54] "No state," Wilson went on,

> can ever be conducted on its principles. For it holds that government is a matter of contract and deliberate arrangement whereas in fact it is an institute of habit, bound together by innumerable threads of association, scarcely one of which has been deliberately placed.[55]

Wilson has a more historical or even sociological view of the origin and ongoing basis of government. The contract theory is not only false in fact, but is pernicious in effect for it encourages men to believe that deliberate action can accomplish more than it does; it encourages men to step outside the web of "habit" and "threads of association" that truly hold society together and substitute a contractual perspective, that is, an approach that emphasizes the quid pro quo character of common life and governance. Citizens who approach common life in that way always ask, "What's

---

[51] Wilson, *The State*, 9.
[52] Ibid., 11.
[53] Ibid., 12.
[54] Woodrow Wilson, "Edmund Burke: The Man and his Times," in Mario DiNunzio, *Woodrow Wilson: Essential Writings and Speeches of the Scholar-President* (New York, NYU Press, 2006), 89.
[55] Ibid.

in it for me." They do not, as a matter of course, see themselves as members of an ongoing organic whole.

Although Wilson seldom spoke of the natural law or natural rights affirmed in the "abstract portions of the Declaration," it is evident that his historical critique implies deep skepticism about them as well. Natural rights are said to be the possessions of individuals in the pre-political state antedating the social contract. But, as Wilson has it, there is no antecedent pre-political state, and there are no individuals prior to government. Individuals and individualism are the result, not the cause, of government.

The idea of a contractual basis for government coheres well with another aspect of the Founders' political theory of which Wilson was also regularly critical. The contract view implies that political life is consciously constructed. It misses or denies what Wilson sees as the truth—that society is mostly "grown" not "made." He frequently spoke of both government and society as "organic," as responding to the laws of life as articulated by Darwin, rather than the laws of Newtonian mechanics, as embodied in the theories of Montesquieu and the authors of *The Federalist* and intended to be the law of operation of the Constitution and its scheme of separation of powers.[56] The "mechanics" of the Constitution was the system of "checks"—one element in the system "checking" another through a collision of forces. As a goal, checking fits well with the individual rights-oriented social contract theory. It led to the view that "good government just had a policeman role" in society, with the "ideal . . . to let every man alone and not interfere." Wilson associates the American Founding theory with the formula "that government is best which governs least," a formula he thinks no longer descriptive of the kind of government needed for America.[57]

Wilson rejects the theory in the "abstract portions of the Declaration," the Newtonian principles of political construction the American Founders used to make their Constitution, the Constitution's system of separation of powers, and the overall conception of governmental function on which the Founders acted. Are not Pestritto and the others correct to see Wilson as hostile to American Founding principles and practices? Not quite. When Wilson spoke of the need to "return to [Jefferson's] ideals," he had something real in mind. Jefferson, as Wilson put it, had two principles: "the right of the individual to opportunity and the right of the people to a free development." Jefferson's "creed" was one of "individualism not socialism."[58] The Jeffersonian—and Wilsonian—principle was hostile not to the individual but to the "socialist" principle. Adopt socialism and

---

[56] See Wilson, *The New Freedom,* 120–21; *Constitutional Government,* in Pestritto, ed., *Essential Political Writings,* 176; "The Study of Administration," in Pestritto, ed., *Essential Political Writings,* 242.

[57] Wilson, *The New Freedom,* 112.

[58] Wilson, "Address on Jefferson," 92.

"you would enslave the individual by making him subject to the organization. You would make the biggest, most dangerous, corruptible organization that you could possibly conceive." A collectivist future would turn each man into a "fraction" of the state, not allowing him to be a "whole man."[59]

In Wilson's view, Jefferson endorsed very limited government in order to "vitalize individuals." The threats to individuals in Jefferson's day came from too intrusive government and the project of restraining government made sense in that context. But in Wilson's day the threat to the individual comes from elsewhere also. The modern corporation and the modern system of production expose the individual to dwarfing forces of which the Founding generation knew nothing. The specifics of their constitutional and political intentions no longer speak to public needs, and so Wilson favors political reform and a more positive role for government. But the Founders' principle, the commitment to individualism as both end and means of government, still stands.

Wilson may reject the Founders' understanding in some very important ways, but he still plausibly sees himself as carrying on their work. Thus, Herbert Storing could say that "Woodrow Wilson ... saw himself as building upon and to some extent restoring the work of the Founders."[60] Wilson's emphasis on the individual, on free competition, and restoring markets, while not expressed in the specific terms of the Declaration nonetheless can claim descent from those doctrines. Accordingly, for Wilson, individual liberty was the end of government: he took as the slogan that captured his political aims "the new freedom." Well before his entry into politics he provided his most general statement on the proper "objects [aims] of government":

> Government ... is the organ of society ... its objects must be the objects of society. What then are the objects of society? What *is* society? It is an organic association of individuals for mutual aid. Mutual aid to what? To self-development. The hope of society lies in an infinite individual variety, in the freest possible play of individual forces.[61]

Although Wilson believed that government had to be more active and less limited in the twentieth century than in the eighteenth, he nonetheless strongly affirmed "natural and imperative limits to state action."[62] Contrary to the claims of some of his recent detractors, he took his bear-

[59] Ibid., 93.

[60] Herbert J. Storing, "American Statesmanship: Old and New," in Joseph Bessette, ed., *Toward a More Perfect Union: Writings of Herbert J. Storing* (Washington, DC: The AEI Press, 1995), 411.

[61] Wilson, *The State*, 633.

[62] Ibid., 636.

ings by the liberty and self-development of the individual and recognized specific areas where the state should not go. "The state, for instance, ought not to supervise private morals because they belong to the sphere of separate individual responsibility, not to the sphere of mutual dependence. Thought and conscience are private. Opinion is optional [i.e., voluntary]. The state may intervene only where common action, uniform law are indispensible. Whatever is merely convenient is optional, and therefore not an affair of the state." [63]

Wilson's ambivalence toward the political philosophy and constitutional theory of the Founding should now be clear. He had a nested set of disagreements with the Founders, as applied to his day, if not to theirs. He disagreed with their commitment to a constitution organized around the separation of powers, for that constitution proved neither to achieve what it set out to achieve—limited government through dispersed power—nor did it seek the aim needed for the present day—active and responsible government. The Founders sought the end they did in their constitutionalism because they accepted the political theory of the social contract, along with its accompanying doctrines of natural rights and the state of nature. Wilson could not accept this version of political philosophy. He saw this philosophy however, as an attempt to articulate a yet more general and higher-level goal: individual liberty for the sake of individual development as harmonized with the social whole as the only context in which such liberty could be realized. It is in this respect that Wilson believed his understanding of the aims of political life converged with that of the Founders. In fact, he and the Founders had a common ultimate goal; for both, this goal required a highlighting and safeguarding of the individual; for both, this goal required limits on the state. But for Wilson, as opposed to the Founders, at least as he understood them, this goal meant more positive government, more tasks to be done, and a government better fitted to do them.

As we have already seen, Wilson held the view that "we must think less of checks and balances and more of coordinated power, less of separation of functions and more of synthesis of action." [64] Wilson frequently urged that America would do well to look to Europe for guidance on how to achieve the "coordinated power" and "synthesis of action" he sought. In his seminal essay on "The Study of Administration" Wilson explained much of what he meant by urging his fellow citizens to look to Europe. The Europeans, particularly the French and Germans, had developed both a "science" of administration and an administrative apparatus that Wilson believed were worthy of imitation and cultivation in America. Both the science and the apparatus were developed within political con-

[63] Ibid., 637–38.
[64] Wilson, *Constitutional Government*, 202.

texts very different from the American context; but, Wilson argued, the distinction between politics and administration made it possible to transplant both to America, with some necessary adaptation to the new world context. The politics-administration distinction was to be fundamental for Wilson's thinking about politics and central to his hopes for institutional transformation of the American system. That distinction, and not that of the separation of powers—between legislative, executive, and judicial—was to be fundamental.

Hardly anything Wilson ever said has been more controversial than the conceptual distinction he drew between politics or policy and administration. A century of political scientists have challenged it as conceptually unworkable and descriptively false in the American context. Despite their importance, I leave such questions aside. My interest is in Wilson's interest in advocating this new political schema. Some critics of Wilson's have urged that his point was to take power from the people and turn it over to a group of elite experts, who could discern the people's good and fashion policies to achieve it. That is, these critics see the distinction as part of an allegedly elitist, antidemocratic, antiliberty Wilsonian agenda. This view misses Wilson's aims.

The distinction between politics and administration arises for Wilson in the first place because he wishes to borrow administrative techniques and practices from political systems decidedly unlike ours. German administration began under the Kaisers; French under the Napoleonic regime. These practices and techniques are not thereby disqualified from being adapted to American democracy because administration is a matter of means, which in many essentials is neutral between political regimes. "Administrative questions are not political questions." As Wilson said in one of his more picturesque metaphors: "If I see a murderous fellow sharpening a knife cleverly, I can borrow his way of sharpening the knife without borrowing his probable intention to commit murder with it; and so, if I see a monarchist dyed in the wool managing a public bureau well, I can learn his business methods without changing one of my republican spots." [65] In what I believe even he sees as an overstatement, Wilson goes so far as to claim that there is "but one rule of good administration for all governments alike." [66]

Wilson's adumbration of the politics-administration dichotomy is a direct result of his analysis of the tasks facing modern democratic states. These tasks can be stated as two: first, the efficient accomplishment of the tasks of positive governance, and second, democratic responsibility. As we have seen, Wilson believed that America fell short on both tasks. The system of government by standing committee of Congress led to both ineffective administration and irresponsible politics. The politics-

[65] Wilson, "The Study of Administration," 240, 247.
[66] Ibid., 245.

administration dichotomy responds directly to those two tasks. Administration, depoliticized, staffed by individuals with relevant expertise, and generally rationalized, can provide efficiency in meeting the tasks facing government. But government can only be responsible if the political side, the side responsible directly to the people, both is able to translate popular mandates into policy, which it can then pass on to administration, and is able at the same time to oversee, supervise and hold the administration responsible. The existing system, as Wilson saw it, fell short on all these tasks because the institutional structure led to political meddling in, but not control of, the administration. It led to fragmented policy that neither spoke to the needs of the nation nor responded well to the preferences of the people.

Wilson's political thought attempted to coordinate three entities—the genuine needs of the nation, public opinion, and policy output. In a well-working system the three are connected. Public opinion focuses on the genuine needs of the nation and formulates relatively clear-cut policy responses to these needs. The policy responses are then administered to properly produce policy effectively responsive to the needs. The political side of the politics-administration dichotomy is essential to the proper working of this projected system. In the kind of political debate Wilson believed occurred within the British Parliamentary system, public opinion was focused on the problems and given a menu of policy options from which the ruling democratic populace could choose by electing a government. The government, not separated from but merged at the top with the administration, could formulate policy which the nonpolitical expert administration could implement, always under the watchful eye of the political authorities. The administrators, as experts, could of course be given a certain amount of discretion in implementing the policies with which they were charged. Many matters of modern policy are, after all, technical matters. That there should be a policy for testing new drugs before they are brought to market is an appropriate decision for the political branches, but how to design tests for drug safety is a matter for experts. There are of course gray areas which Wilson admitted would always need to be worked out. For example, what level of risk would be acceptable for a new drug—is this a policy or an administrative matter? Clearly it partakes of both, but an alert and effective political directorate should be able to work this problem through.

It must be remembered, as some of the generations of political scientists who have criticized Wilson's scheme have sometimes not done, that the whole idea depended on reforms of various sorts on the political side of the dichotomy. Thus, he first looked to a cabinet system and later to a presidential system operating through a much-reformed responsible party system. It must also be remembered that as Wilson sought to liberate administrative expertise from political meddling (but not political control), so he sought to focus responsibility in order that the people could better exercise the democratic control to which they had a right, and in order that the whole could better serve the purposes of securing the liberty of the individual.

III. Lockean Liberalism and Separation of Powers

Wilson makes a powerful case for rethinking the separation of powers. In brief, that case includes rejection of what we might call the infrastructure of the doctrine in the liberal theory of natural rights, state of nature, and social contract. These are rejected as "unhistorical." Wilson implicitly connects the theoretical infrastructure with the constitutional doctrines of separation of powers through the notion that the chief or even sole end of the scheme of separated powers is to limit government by checking power; the political task of checking power is set by the notion that the point of government is, as Jefferson's Declaration of Independence puts it, "to secure" the preexisting rights through the Whiggish devices of restraining and restricting governmental threats to rights.

In the modern age, if not always, this negative understanding of the chief aim of constitutional design is too narrow, avers Wilson. The need in an age of commerce and industry, of huge conglomerates of private power, which themselves threaten liberty, is not weak and checked government, but strong, active, national government. That kind of government has not been achieved, Wilson believed, by the American system as it came from the hands of its Framers, nor as it developed over time. Indeed, by the late nineteenth century Wilson saw that American government had developed so as to produce the worst of all possible worlds. It did not achieve the nicely limited government of the Founders' hopes because power was not divided and checked, but concentrated in Congress. This did not, however, produce the potent, coordinated and national governance Wilson looked to, but a different sort of fragmentation from what the Founders sought and a government more often than not captured by the interests that needed to be controlled in the interests of the democratic majority; those who should be controlled were instead controlling, using government to reinforce their "natural" advantages.

Wilson's solution was to advocate a political structure more capable of the kind of rational, democratic action he thought was needed; the separation of powers as understood by the Founders was no part of his plan for the future of the American constitutional order. Wilson's guiding idea reached academic expression in the "two pyramids" model of governance as developed by Frank Goodnow, an American political scientist and pioneer of the study of public administration that Wilson had called for.[67] The first pyramid of Goodnow's model was a disciplined party system, in which visions and policy goals could be formulated and brought before

---

[67] Frank J. Goodnow, *Politics and Administration* (Charleston, SC: Nabu Press, 2007).

the public for deliberation, consideration, and choice. The public choice would be carried up the pyramid via the party system into government, where policy goals achieve concrete formulations as policies. The second pyramid is the administration side, to which formulated policies are passed on via an executive head, who is also, on the Goodnow's model, legislative-party head. That is, the system depends not on a separation of legislative and executive, but a combination of the two at the apex of both pyramids. An administrative structure responsible to the legislative-party leadership then implements policy, exercising much discretion as it brings to bear the particular kinds of expertise the administrators possess. In theory at least, that discretion and expertise are in service to, ministerial to, the democratically selected policies as formulated up the steps of the first pyramid. Thus, the distinction and partial separation of politics and administration is to replace the classical liberal theory of separation of powers.

I propose to examine Wilson's critique of classical liberal constitutionalism in two phases: first, to consider his (and other Progressives') rejection of the infrastructure of liberal theory, and then to consider the superstructure of the separation of powers scheme. To begin then: can the Lockean theory—can the ideas of a state of nature, social contract, and all the rest—be salvaged from the potent critique by Wilson and the other Progressives. I believe the answer is yes.

We must begin by asking: Does Locke mean his narrative about the state of nature to be historical—i.e., descriptive of what actually happened at some point in human history? Locke goes out of his way in many places to suggest that the answer is yes. He defines the state of nature as a condition of "men living together ... without a common superior on Earth, with authority to judge between them" (sec. 19).[68] It is a very common experience that there are men in such a state. Locke gives the example of "all Princes and rulers of independent governments all over the world" as in a state of nature (sec. 14). Or two otherwise unconnected men who meet on a desert island, or "Swiss and an Indian in the woods of America"—these are all men in a state of nature. If he had been around in the twenty-first century Locke might have added the survivors of the plane crash on the television program *Lost*—but then John Locke was among those survivors and knew their situation well. From these examples, Locke concludes that "the world never was, nor ever will be, without a number of men in that state" (sec. 14). So, Locke's state of nature is meant as a real historical situation—no doubt about that.

However, the examples Locke gives are not the sort that proves the historicity of his main narative—of all men starting out in a state of nature and making a social contract, and so on. The examples he gives are clearly

---

[68] John Locke, *Two Treatises of Government*, ed. Peter Laslett (Cambridge: Cambridge University Press, 1988). References to Locke's book will be in the text by section number. All references are to the *Second Treatise*. All emphasis is in the original text.

exceptions to the way the normal run of men live and the examples all take for granted as a background condition the existence of political communities such as those the rulers of independent governments rule. The Progressive critiques of state of nature thinking that I mentioned earlier could be correct and still Locke would be right to say that heads of state, men on a desert island, and so on are in a state of nature. But this of course says nothing about the main issue.

Another way to understand the state of nature doctrine is to see it as purely hypothetical, not at all historical.[69] As one recent book on Locke put it—the state of nature is like a thought experiment: imagine away the state and see what happens as a way of coming to understand what difference government and the state make in human life. This understanding of the state of nature is not sufficient either, for it misses out on the main thing Locke uses his state of nature/social contract narrative to establish—the outlines of the legitimate state. His is a normative, almost a legislative project. He seeks to discover the good or rightful state and not a merely descriptive account of the state. So while the theory that the state of nature is a merely hypothetical construct saves Locke from the criticisms of the idea of a historical state of nature, it does not capture his main use of the doctrine.

Let me put forward a third idea then, an idea that I think both absolves Locke from the criticisms and fits his own agenda better. For want of a better term I call this a "conceptual account," in contrast to both the historical and the hypothetical accounts I have mentioned.

To understand the conceptual account, we must step back a bit and remind ourselves of Locke's chief affirmations about the state of nature. It is, first of all, a state of equality and freedom, by which Locke means a state of no authority, a state where nobody has the right to rule or command another. This is actually merely another way to say what Locke says when he defines the state of nature as the situation where there is no common superior. There is no common superior because there is no superior whatsoever. When Locke refers to the situation in which there is no superior as the natural state, he is saying that authority, the right to rule or govern, is not natural. His notion of the state of nature is thus a thoroughly normative idea, by which I mean it is not meant to describe how men live. It does not say anything about whether men live in society or not, or whether men live under others who command or rule them. He is saying that neither nature nor God produces authority, i.e., the right to rule. There are no natural or divine right rulers.

Now, why does Locke say that? To answer that question we must notice the other main feature of the state of nature. It is a state in which human beings possess rights. There is no rule by nature, but there are rights by nature. And what are these rights? The famous triad: life, liberty, and

---

[69] Eric Mack, *John Locke* (New York: Continuum Publishing, 2009).

property. Men have a right to these three things, which Jefferson in the Declaration of Independence sums up as the "right to pursuit of happiness": That is to say, men have a right to give a shape to their own lives such as they believe might lead them to happiness, the thing that all men seek. I think most of us, even in our post-Progressive age, can accept the idea of human rights such as Locke affirms here.

My claim is that for Locke the state of nature follows necessarily from the affirmation of these natural rights. We can understand the relation between the rights and the state of nature in two different but completely complementary ways. Let us think for a moment of what a right in the full sense is. Let us take something more concrete than Locke's rights—my right to my car. My right to my car has two aspects: first, I have a right—a morally valid power—to control my car, to do with it what I will, subject of course to any limitations that the rights of others may impose. Thus, I may drive it or leave it in my garage. I may sell it, or I may even take a sledgehammer to it and smash it up. Just as I have these rights of control, so others are excluded from these same rights. That is, there is something exclusive about rights. So—without my permission *you* do not have a right to drive my car, to say nothing of your lacking a right to bash my car with a sledgehammer.

Now let us transfer this idea to the rights Locke affirms. I have a right to life and liberty. This does not mean that you are obliged to give me life, or even to give me the means to living, but you are obliged not to interfere with my life. If you kill me, you have committed a wrong by interfering with my right. More generally, we note that life depends on the body. My right to life must translate into a right of bodily integrity, a part of which is an immunity against others interfering with my body or, related to my right to liberty, with my actions. My basic rights translate into an immunity against others using violence or coercion against me. But as Locke points out in the early pages of his *Second Treatise,* political power or authority is *precisely* the right to command and apply coercion. If we all possess these natural rights and thus a natural immunity from the application of coercion, then it cannot be that there is natural authority, for natural authority would be a negation of our natural rights, of our natural immunity from coercion.

We can look at the relationship between rights and the state of nature in yet another way also. Taking Jefferson as a good interpreter of Locke, we can say that the basic rights sum up to a right of pursuit of happiness. Such a comprehensive right means that I have a comprehensive right to give shape to my own life, as I have already mentioned. If I have such a right by nature, then that is incompatible with someone having a natural authority over me, for if someone has a right to rule me by nature, then I do not have the right to give my own life its own comprehensive shape. Thus, starting with the idea of rights as including immunities from interference and coercion or simply with the right to pursue happiness as a comprehensive right of self-direction, we end up at the same place—the claim that nature does not supply authority, or that no one has a natural right to command and coerce others; and all have a right to command themselves. In other words, if we have natural rights, we are created equal, i.e., in a state of nature.

This is a conceptual beginning point, derived from a reflection on the moral situation of human beings as possessors of natural or human rights. Note that this is not a historical account, nor is it a mere hypothesis. It is a description of basic moral reality. The nature of moral reality is such that political power, government, and the state must be seen to be artificial— made things, which Locke will go on to show can be made only via consent of the governed. Locke shows that human beings can therefore rightfully consent to only *certain* sorts of political authority. Authority cannot be absolutist; it cannot be indifferent to the basic rights of its citizens. Indeed it must be devoted first and foremost to "securing these rights." It must be government devoted to liberty and embodying the consent of the governed. In its developed form, the Lockean doctrine of the state of nature and rights points to the sole legitimacy of the kind of regime we have come to call liberal democracy. The American Founders were the first in the world to follow out the implications in the Lockean philosophy and create an almost fully legitimate government. They fell short in at least one very crucial way—the institution of slavery was a violation of rights and an exercise of authority that could not be legitimate on Lockean grounds.

Please note that this conceptual account of the state of nature does not require that we think of human beings in the state of nature understood as a literally historical condition of asociality. Locke knows that human beings qua human are and always have been social beings. He knows that men have almost always lived under institutions vested with political power. Thus Locke does not have to deny Wilson's "historical" knowledge that government began in the family and first evolved into monarchy. Indeed, Locke presents a version of that very theory as his account of the actual historical origins of government (secs. 107–112). But he also knows that men have often misunderstood their true natural condition, or their true moral claims, and have most often lived under and accepted false claims to rule and have constructed or accepted the wrong sorts of governments. Once we understand the moral situation of human beings better we can establish public and political institutions that correspond better to that moral situation. That is what the American Founders believed they were doing when they took Locke as their guide in making what James Madison called "a revolution which has no parallel in the annals of human society" and then went on to "rear fabrics of government which have no model on the face of the globe." [70]

[70] *Federalist No. 14* (J. Madison), in Clinton Rossiter, ed. *The Federalist Papers* (New York: New American Library, Mentor Books, 1961).

Neither Locke nor the American Founders thus fall to the Wilsonian critique of social contract theory as patently false, once one understands the claims actually being made.

The constitutional structure the Americans built on this foundation was indeed the separation of powers scheme that Wilson and the Progressives criticized. It is a striking fact about the Founding era that all sides in the debates over the Constitution—Federalists and Antifederalists alike— favored the separation of powers. They often disagreed about the best way to effectuate the scheme and Antifederalists often claimed that the proposed Constitution did not go far enough in separating the powers. But the near universal agreement on the separation of powers belies one major strand of Progressive critique of the Founding, the strand that identifies the complicated institutional structure as a device whereby wealthy-creditor-sponsors of the Constitution attempted to get an advantage over the poorer-debtor-opponents of the Constitution.

Without question, the intellectual authority to whom Federalists and Antifederalists both looked for insight on the separation of powers was the French philosopher Montesquieu, who had presented the classic version of the doctrine in the account of the British Constitution in his *The Spirit of the Laws*. Montesquieu did not, however, invent the doctrine. There is a fair amount of debate over who did invent it, but it is not necessary to settle that debate for the purposes of this essay. It is fairly clear that the doctrine emerged in the seventeenth century in England, perhaps under pressure of the need to rethink the nature of the English Constitution after the regicide of 1649. Previous to that the English Constitution was most often conceived in terms of the theory of the mixed regime, that is, the description of the constitution as a mix of classical regime elements—monarchy, aristocracy, and democracy—with the three main institutions of government corresponding nicely to the three regimes. With no king, and soon no aristocratic House of Lords, it was necessary to conceptualize the constitution in some others terms. At the same time, the surge in republican or at least antimonarchic sentiment led to an effort to develop nonmonarchical constitutional designs. The English republicans like John Milton, and the levelers like John Lilburne and Richard Overton, were prominent among those who did this. Some scholars believe that genuine separation of powers systems emerged or were proposed at this time.[71]

I propose to set these candidates for the original version of separation of powers aside and instead concentrate attention on John Locke. There are two reasons that suggest that strategy in this context. First, it remains debatable whether these earlier candidates do indeed qualify as genuine separation of powers proponents; there is no such debate about Locke. Moreover, in Locke, the separation of powers is linked to, indeed derived

---

[71] I am following the account of Vile, *Constitutionalism*. 58–82.

from, what we have called the infrastructure of liberal theory. Wilson and other Progressives criticize the entire package, i.e., the constitutional arrangement of separated powers and the theoretical construct of natural rights and social contract. To look at Locke rather than, say, the Levelers, gives us an account at the same level of comprehensiveness as the Progressive critique.

Locke's most revealing reflections on the separation of powers come not in the section of the *Second Treatise* where he is delineating the legislative, executive, and what he calls the "federative power" (chaps. 11–14), but rather in his chapter on "The Ends of Political Society and Government" (chap. 9). Separation of powers seems not to be only a means to, but also to be closely associated with, the ends of political life. Locke begins that chapter with a recapitulation of the first half of the *Treatise*, the half that in effect deals with the pre-political aspects of political life. He begins with a question that readers who have been struck by the very non-Hobbesean character of Locke's description of the state of nature must have been asking: "If man in the State of Nature be so free, as has been said; if he be absolute Lord of his own Person and Possessions, equal to the greatest, and subject to no Body, why will he part with his Freedom? Why will he give up this Empire, and subject himself to the Dominion and Control of any other Power?" (sec. 123). Locke's answer, contrary to the impression he sometimes gives us (cf. sec. 19 esp.), is that the state of nature is not in fact such an idyllic place. "For all being Kings as much as he, every Man his Equal, and the greater part no strict Observers of Equity and Justice, the enjoyment of the property [i.e., life, liberty, and estate] he has in this state is very unsafe, very unsecure." Men have the right of complete self-command in the state of nature, "yet the Enjoyment of it is very uncertain, and constantly exposed to the Invasion of others" (sec. 123). Given that uncertainty and insecurity men rationally opt to give up the independence and equality of the state of nature in exchange for the promise of rights and property protection under government.

Life in the state of nature is not conducive to the enjoyment of property in Locke's extended sense, because "in the state of nature there are many things wanting." Locke proceeds to list the chief things lacking in the state of nature; this is the moment when the conceptual foundations of his doctrine of separation of powers comes to light. "First, there wants an *establish'd*, settled, known *Law*, received and allowed by common consent to be the standard of Right and Wrong, and the common measure to decide all controversies between them." (sec. 124; emphasis in the original). "Secondly, in the state of nature there wants a *known and indifferent Judge*, with Authority to determine all differences according to the established law" (sec. 125; emphasis in original). "Thirdly, in the state of nature there often wants Power to back and support the sentence when right, and to *give* it due *Execution*" (sec. 126; emphasis in original). What are lacking in the state of nature are the three powers, lawmaking, law-adjudicating, and law-executing. It is the lack of those three that make the state of nature a condition where rights are thoroughly insecure.

The first and surely the most important point to notice in Locke's identification of the three powers as the *sine qua non* of securing rights is how differently he conceptualizes the point of the powers from the way Wilson and the Progressives do. Wilson, it will be recalled, saw the separation of powers scheme as identical to, its point exhausted by, the related idea of checks and balances in the service of the aim of limiting governmental power. Locke will later speak of "well-order'd Commonwealths" where the legislative power is put in hands separate and different from those into which the executive power is placed (secs. 143–144, and esp. 159).[72] For Locke, checking and balancing may have a part, but the primary point is first the identification of the different powers as functions and then the placement of these in suitable political bodies. According to Wilson's conception of separation of powers, how powers are divided and separated matters hardly or not at all; what matters is merely that they are separated and can check each other.

This initial difference suggests that Locke and Wilson have two quite different things in mind under what has come to be one label. If we say that Locke has divided powers as functions, we need to ask: functions of what? The answer is clear from his initial statement: these are functional aspects of the effective rule of the law of nature. In the state of nature, these functions are not performed, and therefore the law of nature is not an effective guardian of the rights of men in that state. Government must supply the content, the execution, and the adjudication of law that is lacking in the state of nature. That is to say, the separation of powers is, in the first instance, an identification of the separate and essential aspects of the rule of law. It is in service to the rule of law, for it is the rule of law that can accomplish the end of civil society, the security of human rights.

Lockean separation of powers does not take its bearings from limiting government but from accomplishing the positive tasks government must accomplish to justify its existence. Locke, despite affirming natural rights and despite his deep concern that government not threaten or infringe on those rights, emphasizes governmental tasks and governmental powers. The most striking example occurs at the end of his famous chapter on

[72] It is a well-known fact that Locke's version of separation of powers falls short of the theory as Montesquieu, the American Founders, and American government textbooks expound it in that he does not have a fully developed conception of the independence of the judiciary. He explicitly calls for the separation of legislative and executive powers but he more or less takes for granted that the judicial power is part of the executive (Cf. Grant, *Locke's Liberalism*, 75). Montesquieu not only made the case for the separation of the judicial power, but gave special prominence to the independent judicial power. This must be considered an important advance in liberal constitutional theory (see Montesquieu, *Spirit of the Laws*, Bk. XI, ch. 6). Nonetheless, Locke indicates in various places that the judiciary should be independent of the executive head, without, however, specifying an institutional means to effectuate that independence. (See Locke, *Second Treatise*, secs. 125, 131, 136.)

property. Having gone to great lengths to establish the naturalness of property and a natural right to property, he nonetheless concludes his chapter with the affirmation that "in Governments the Laws regulate the right of property, and the possession of land is determined by positive constitutions." (sec. 50) Neither property nor the other rights are untouchable by government. The chief point of constructing government is not to immunize rights from government but to empower government to regulate them. The "Laws of the Society in many things confine the liberty he had by the Law of Nature" (sec. 129).

This is not to say that natural rights and natural law have no lingering effect, no point in civil society, as opposed to their formative effect in the state of nature. As Locke summarily puts it: "But though Men when they enter into Society, give up the Equality, Liberty, and Executive Power they had in the state of nature, into the hands of the Society, to be so far disposed of by the Legislative, as the good of the Society shall require; yet it being only with an intention in everyone the better to preserve himself his Liberty and Property; ... the power of the Society, or Legislative constituted by them, *can never be suppos'd to extend farther than the common good;* but is obliged to secure every ones Property by providing against those defects above mentioned, that made the State of Nature so unsafe and uneasie." (sec. 131; emphasis in the original, cf. sec. 135); "The Obligations of the Law of Nature, cease not in Society, but only in many Cases are drawn closer" (sec. 135). As Locke makes clear throughout, government is to secure not threaten rights; but it must, in the first instance, do so through acting to effect "the Publick Good" (sec. 3). Rather than the single agenda Wilson believes the classical liberal constitution is to serve—protecting rights from government oppression through a system of separated powers checking and balancing each other—the Lockean constitution faces a much more difficult task: being strong enough to act to serve rights and the public good without, at the same time, being a greater threat to these rights than continued life in the state of nature would be.

The history of constitutional theory since Locke is the history of successive attempts to achieve that dual aim. In Locke that achievement requires building institutions around the theoretically identified aspects of the rule of law. The first element in the constitution is the legislative power. It makes the laws that regulate behaviors and property and normally makes levies on the property of citizens in the form of taxes. Locke does not set out limitation on the legislative power in the form of enumerated powers, or of explicit limitations in the form of reserved rights, devices one find in the American Constitution. Instead Locke insists on a number of structural and institutional features that are intended to produce the rule of law. He is most insistent on one thing: "the *Legislature,* or Supreme Authority, cannot assume to itself a power to rule by extemporary Arbitrary Decrees, but *is bound to dispense Justice,* and decide the

Rights of the Subject *by promulgated standing* Laws" (sec. 136). "Absolute Arbitrary Power, or Governing without *settled standing Laws,* can neither of them consist with the ends of society and government" (sec. 137). These *"promulgated establish'd Laws"* are to apply equally to all; they are "not to be varied in particular cases, but to have one Rule for Rich and Poor, for the Favourite at Court, and the Country Man at Plough" (sec. 142). In particular, the laws must also apply to the legislators themselves and to their near and dear as well (sec. 138).

Locke combines his emphasis on the character of legislative output with strictures on the proper structure of the legislative. The ideal legislature appears to be one where "the *legislative* consists, wholly or in part, in Assemblies which are variable, whose Members upon the Dissolution of the Assembly, are Subjects under the common Laws of their Country, equally with the rest."(sec. 138) He puts a lot of weight on the combination of the structural features of the legislature with the mandate to govern by general, neutral, settled, standing, promulgated law. That combination maximizes the chances that the legislature will seek the common good and minimize the risk that it will be oppressive to the rights of the governed. It will also satisfy the requirement that the government, when taking, rather than just regulating, the property or rights of the citizens operates via the consent of those whose property is being taken in the form of taxation or the consent of their representatives. The property owners themselves are to be the ones to make the judgment whether the sacrifice of some part of their property is worth the amount of public good the government can supply in return.

Another way Locke describes the legislative power is to say that it "has a right *to direct* how the *Force of the Commonwealth* shall be imploy'd for preserving the Community and the Members of it" (sec. 143). It is very undesirable, however, "for the same Persons who have the Power of Making Laws, to have also in their hands the power to execute them." (sec. 143). He has several reasons for insisting on separate institutions for these two functions. The first and most important relates to the central purpose of the separation of powers scheme. If the same persons both direct the use of community force (i.e., make the laws), and exercise that force, "they may exempt themselves from Obedience to the Laws" (sec. 143). Exempting themselves means in the first instance that the society is no longer marked by the rule of law, for some are not bound by law. In the second instance, it inevitably affects the character and quality of the laws, producing law that does not serve the public good but rather the good of the leaders.

There is another set of reasons for the separation of power as well. As we have seen, the legislative is best composed of many individuals, selected as representatives from the society, who periodically return to the society and feel directly and personally the impact of the laws they adopt. The legislative need not and should not be "always in being" (secs. 151, 153), "but absolutely necessary that the *Executive Power* should, because there is not always need of new Laws to be made, but always need of Execution of the Laws that are made" (sec. 153). Locke speaks regularly of the executive as a "Prince" and as "him." This does not commit Locke to a hereditary executive, for he nowhere sets that as a feature of the executive, but it does seem to commit him to "unity in the executive." In so far as that is so, the executive must be structured differently from the legislative, or, put otherwise, the legislative structure is not fit to exercise the executive power. The main business of the legislative is making law, which requires deliberation and information, best provided by many heads. The main business of the executive is action—deployment of the force of the community; unity of command better conduces to effective enforcement of law than does multiplicity. The considerations pointing to executive unity are accentuated when we take account of two powers Locke associates with the executive head. First is the so-called "federative power," the power to employ the force of the community in relation to foreign states and entities. Although the source of this power is different, says Locke, nonetheless, it, like the executive power proper, involves the forces of the community and so this power must reside in the same hands as the executive power. The executive also has a wide-ranging discretionary power, called prerogative, to act without or even against the law in certain kinds of extraordinary situations. The federative power and the prerogative share the quality that they are the places where the government faces emergencies. They put a premium on the kind of quick, decisive, and disciplined action a unified office with power of command over its subordinates can effect.

The legislative and the executive should be separate and should be constructed quite differently in order to accomplish their respective tasks. The separation and the difference are not, I must emphasize again, for the sake of limiting government, the task that Wilson thought exhausted the point of the separation of powers. As much as anything the separation and the difference of powers are for the sake of effective action.

Given the emphasis on separation and difference, given the fact that lawmaking was appropriately a task only for a body not possessing in its own hands coercive authority, and only for a body constructed as Locke said the legislature was to be constructed, it followed for Locke that the legislature could not transfer or delegate its legislative power to any other body. In particular, the executive was on both counts not to wield legislative power. So Locke propounded on multiple occasions the nondelegation of legislative power principle that became an integral part of separation of powers doctrine—until the Progressive Era. Although Wilson's politics (or policy)-administration dichotomy bears a family resemblance to the distinction between legislative and executive powers in Locke, one place where there is a great difference is on the issue of lawmaking or rule-making administrative power. As Wilson makes clear, he anticipates that administration will exercise far more discretion and rulemaking authority than the orthodox doctrine of separation of powers would allow. At the extremes, this could amount to the massive delegation the Natural Industrial Recovery Act provided for, a delegation that the Supreme Court invalidated in *Schechter Poultry Co. v. U.S.* This act probably went beyond anything Wilson contemplated as acceptable, but his rejection of the separation of powers certainly opened the door to it. And, it must be noted, although the Court, in a gesture to orthodox doctrine, rejected that delegation, Courts and Congresses since have accepted great amounts of delegation.[73]

IV. Conclusion

We might now summarize some of the differences between Lockean, or classical liberal, and Wilsonian, or Progressive Liberal, constitutionalism. Wilson blurs and even tends to obliterate both the conceptual and the institutional aspects of the separation of powers. In the latter's constitutionalism there is no clear line between legislature and administration. One result in the post-Progressive era has been much more delegation, or administrative exercise of rulemaking, or legislative authority, which, contrary to Wilson's intentions, has diminished responsibility in government by producing politically irresponsible rulemaking power in the administration and the shirking of its proper legislative role by Congress. Wilson's blurring of the lines is related to his inadequate understanding of liberal constitutionalism, although he can be partially excused by the fact that much thinking about governmental power had hardened in the post-Civil War era into a rigid notion of limited government in service of a laissez-faire theory of the proper handling of the economy.

Wilson's various shortcomings regarding the separation of powers derive in large part from his having a less clear notion of the business of government than Locke, for example, had. As argued above, Wilson was not the socialist, communist, collectivist many contemporary conservative critics accuse him of being. He stands as an heir—though a much modified one—of the liberal tradition: he seeks to protect and foster individual freedom in new and unprecedented circumstances, but his notion of the end and the means to that are much vaguer and less capable of disciplined thought and action than Locke's. In order to free the nation from the strictures of laissez-faire orthodoxies and to empower needed governmental action, he goes so far as to reject or at least ignore the doctrine of natural rights, and thus gives up the guidance these rights supply.

---

[73] For a reaction against this trend from within contemporary political science, see Theodore J. Lowi, *The End of Liberalism* (New York: Norton, 1969).

From this comparison of the traditional constitutionalism that affirmed separation of powers and the Progressive constitutionalism that rejected it, it has become apparent that the Wilsonian critique, which has had tremendous impact in political life as well as in political science, does not merit the sway it has held in public and professional minds. Based on an inadequate understanding of what it opposed, lacking an appreciation of the real goods and aims of the separation of powers, it fell—and falls—far short of its alleged achievements.

Political Science, University of Notre Dame

INDEX

Absentee ownership, 147
Absolute monarchy, 16, 21
Achilles, 19, 38
Acquisition (just), 168–69
Adam (biblical figure), 16, 22
Adams, John, 98–99, 105, 107; and philosophical method, 110; and private property, 132; on American Revolution, 104; on liberty, 131; on natural law, 180; on reason, 108–9; on rights as inherent, 125; on the meaning of the Declaration of Independence, 138
Adams, John Quincy, 180
Adams, Samuel, 92, 105, 134; on the conformity of positive law with natural law, 107
Addams, Jane, 206
Administration: and expertise, 329
Air, value of, 28
Alexander the Great, 39
Allen, Ethan, 11, 115
American Association of University Professors (AAUP), 207
American Board of Customs Commissioners, 92
American Civil Liberties Union (ACLU), 207
American Economic Association, 224
American Historical Association, 224
American Law and Economics movement, 316
American Political Science Association, 224
American Revolution, 104; justification of, 118
An Inquiry into the Rights of the British Colonies (Bland), 89
Anarchism, 159–60
Anarchy, State, and Utopia (Nozick), 289
Anti-statism, 140
Antifederalists, 75, 77, 80, 357
Appropriation, 146
Arbitrary power, 360; in Locke, 9
Aristocracy, 63–64, 104
Aristotle, 181; and nature as an end, 37; and the desire to produce offspring, 18; as elitist, 9; on three kinds of human being, 36; on virtue, 39
Articles of Confederation (1781), 102
Atheism, 10
Austin, John, 141
Authority, 84, 332, 354; to govern, 91

Ballot initiative, 324
Bancroft, George, 185
Batten, Samuel, 200
Beard, Charles, 190–191, 273, 337
Beccaria, Cesare, 75
Becker, Carl, 22, 178, 184, 190; on natural rights as common sense, 179
Belief: *versus* knowledge of natural law, 7
Bellamy, Edward, 260
Bentham, Jeremy, 141; and the dismissal of natural rights, 142
Beveridge, Albert, 247
Bible, the, 16, 135
Bill of Rights, 103, 259
Bismarck, Chancellor Otto von, 261–62
Blackstone, William, 74, 84
Bland, Richard, 87, 111, 118
Board of Customs Commissioners, 94
Boston Tea Party, 94
Boycott, 92
Brandeis, Louis D., 276–77
Brewer, David J., 261
British Constitution of Government, 87
British Parliament, 339
Buckle, Stephen, 297
Bureaucracy, 266
Burke, Edmund, 74, 183
Burlamaqui, Jean-Jacques, 107

Calhoun, John, 180, 184
Cannibalism, 19–20
Cannon, Joseph C., 248
Capitalism, 267
Carter, Jimmy, 215
Cause and effect: governing moral law, 114
Centralization, of government power, 79, 323, 340
Change: implications of for political systems, 178
Charles I, 59, 70
Checks and balances, 52, 270, 339
Child sacrifice, 21
Children: as the workmanship of parents, 10; obligations to, 17; parental love for, 18; rational capacity of, 6
Christianity, 67; as opposed to individualism, 264; reasonableness of, 45
Church, the, 191
Cicero, Marcus Tullius 181, 301, 309

Economic value, 288, 304–305

Education, 23, 34; of gentlemen, 35; toward philosophic reason, 36

Eisenach, Eldon, 223

Elitism, 343; in Locke's political theory, 9

Elliot, William Yandell, 210

Ely, Richard T., 188, 221, 223, 228, 267

Emancipation Proclamation, 133

Endowments, natural, 27, 243

English Bill of Rights, 129

Enlightenment, 24, 105, 108, 178, 181

Environment: and development, 244

Environmental Protection Agency, 319

Epstein, Richard A., 255

Equal treatment (under the law), 53

Equality, 10, 95, 220–21, 251, 322; as dependent on law of nature, 12; contractual, 65; in Locke's natural rights theory, 3–4, 11; in the state of nature, 60; Progressive denial of, 241

Error, 43–44

Essay Concerning Human Understanding (Locke), 5, 10, 30, 110

Ethnology, 185–86

Eugenics, 220, 257

Europe, 76

Evil concupiscence, 19

Evolution: and Progressivism, 230

Exchange value, 285

Expediency, 155

Expertise, 322

Faith, 16; *versus* reason, 11

Farmer Refuted, The (Hamilton), 114

Federal Bureau of Corporations, 322

Federalism, 52, 72, 77, 79, 93–94, 96, 209, 328–29, 341, 357

Federalist No. 78, 208

Federalist Party, 183

Feist Publications v. Rural Telephone Services (1990), 292–93

Ferguson, Adam, 74

Feudal order, 191

Fifteenth Amendment, 51, 248

Filmer, Robert, 14, 15, 19

First Continental Congress, 107

First Treatise, from *Two Treatises of Government* (Locke), 4, 15–16, 33

Flourishing, 284; and rights, 127

Follett, Mary, 202, 206

Force: and problematic transfers of products, 146; physical, 124

Fortune, 28–29

Founders, American, 80, 104, 325; and individualism, 227; and Lockeanism, 182; and the framing of the Constitution, 75, 78–80, 318; and workmanship

argument, 12; conception of rights, 82; moral theory of, 105

Founding, American, 82, 336, 357

Fourteenth Amendment, 218, 248

Fox, Daniel M., 231

Franklin, Benjamin, 76, 111

Free speech, 256

Freedom, 95, 221, 237; "positive," 222; and reason, 26, 73; basic right to, 158; natural right to, 4

French Revolution, 183

Fuller, Melville W., 274

Gage, Thomas, 94

Galloway, Joseph, 97

General Court, 87

General Motors, 320

General welfare, 225–26

General will, 333–34

George III, 118

George, Henry, 289–90

Georgetown Republicans, 117

German Historical School, 237

German Idealism, 185

Gibbon, Edward, 74

Giddings, Franklin, 208

Gilded Age, 204

Gillman, Howard, 260

Gilman, Charlotte Perkins, 253

Gladden, Washington, 255

Glorious Revolution (1688–1689), 66, 70

God: and human need, 25; and rule by the rational and wise, 9; as a first cause of nature, 116; as a lawgiver, 44–45, 47; as a principle of nature, 10; as equivalent in meaning to nature in Locke, 16; as the source of unalienable rights, 135; as the owner of human beings, 10; belief in, 13; law of, 87; nature of, 11; role of in Locke's natural rights theory, 3, 5 n. 19, 296; role of in moral law, 114

Godkin, E. L., 51, 53, 80

Golden Age, 179

Golden Rule, 116

Good: and nature, 24; common, 38, 41, 255; intrinsic, 37; social, 225–26

Goodnow, Frank, 352

Goodrich, Elizur, 113

Government, 57–58, 105, 238; and self-correction, 69; "big" 203–4; forms of, 78; function to protect rights of man in Spencer, 154; limited, 183

Great Britain, 73, 89

Great Society, 81, 178

Great War, 207

Green, T. H., 228

Grotius, Hugo, 115, 297

Guardianship, 329